The Criminal Justice System

Second Edition

The Criminal Justice System

Volume 3:
Corrections
Special Issues

Edited by
Michael K. Hooper, Ph.D
Sonoma State University
Department of Criminology and Criminal Justice Studies

Ruth E. Masters, Ed.D
California State University, Fresno
Department of Criminology

SALEM PRESS
A Division of EBSCO Information Services, Inc.
Ipswich, Massachusetts

GREY HOUSE PUBLISHING

Copyright © 2017 by Salem Press, A Division of EBSCO Information Services, Inc., and Grey House Publishing, Inc.

All rights reserved. No part of this work may be used or reproduced in any manner whatsoever or transmitted in any form or by any means, electronic or mechanical, including photocopy, recording, or any information storage and retrieval system, without written permission from the copyright owner. For information contact Grey House Publishing/Salem Press, 4919 Route 22, PO Box 56, Amenia, NY 12501.

∞ *The paper used in these volumes conforms to the American National Standard for Permanence of Paper for Printed Library Materials, Z39.48 1992 (R2009).*

Publisher's Cataloging-In-Publication Data
(Prepared by the Donahue Group, Inc.)

Names: Hooper, Michael (Michael K.), editor. | Masters, Ruth, editor.
Title: The criminal justice system / edited by Michael K. Hooper, Ph.D, Sonoma State University, Department of Criminology and Criminal Justice Studies [and] Ruth E. Masters, Ed.D, California State University, Fresno, Department of Criminology.
Other Titles: Criminal justice. 2017.
Description: Second edition. | Ipswich, Massachusetts : Salem Press, a division of EBSCO Information Services, Inc. ; Amenia, NY : Grey House Publishing, [2017] | Originally published as: Criminal justice / edited by Phyllis B. Gerstenfeld. ©2006. | Includes bibliographical references and indexes. | Contents: Volume 1. Crime, criminal law — Volume 2. Law enforcement, courts — Volume 3. Corrections, special issues.
Identifiers: ISBN 978-1-68217-310-7 (set) | ISBN 978-1-68217-312-1 (v. 1) | ISBN 978-1-68217-313-8 (v. 2) | ISBN 978-1-68217-314-5 (v. 3)
Subjects: LCSH: Criminal justice, Administration of—United States—Encyclopedias. | Criminal procedure—United States—Encyclopedias. | Crime—United States—Encyclopedias. | Criminal law—United States—Encyclopedias. | LCGFT: Reference works.
Classification: LCC KF9217 .C75 2017 | DDC 345.73/05—dc23

PRINTED IN THE UNITED STATES OF AMERICA

Contents

Complete List of Contents vii

Corrections
Addiction 737
AIDS 740
Ashker v. Brown (2015) 741
Auburn system 743
Battered child and battered wife syndromes 744
Boot camps 746
Chain gangs 748
Community-based corrections 749
Community service 750
Conjugal visitation in prison 751
Crime victimization: primary and secondary 752
"Dark figure of crime" 754
Elderly prisoners 755
Forestry camps 756
Good time 757
Halfway houses 758
History of incarceration 759
Homeless women and victimization 761
House arrest 763
Incapacitation 764
LGBTQ prisoners 765
Medical model of offender treatment 766
National Crime Victimization Survey 767
National Organization for Victim Assistance 768
"Not-in-my-backyard" attitudes 769
Opioid treatment breakthroughs 770
Palmer raids 773
Parole 773
Parole boards 777
Parole Commission, U.S. 779
Parole officers 780
Pennsylvania system of corrections 781
Prison and jail systems 783
Prison escapes 787
Prison guards 789
Prison health care 790
Prison industries 792
Prison inmate subculture 793
Prison overcrowding 794
Prison/prisoner classification systems 797
Prison Rape Elimination Act (PREA) of 2003 798
Prison violence 800
Prisoner rights 802
Prisons, Federal Bureau of 804
Privatization of institutional and community
   corrections, including faith-based programs 805
Probation, adult 806
Probation, juvenile 809
Realignment (PSR) policy 811
Recidivism 813
Rehabilitation 815
Scandinavia's prison experience 818
Security threat groups (STGs)/prison gangs 819
Smith Act 819
Solitary confinement 820
Supermax prisons 822
Victim and Witness Protection Act 824
Victim assistance programs 824
Victim impact statements 825
Victim-offender mediation 827
Victim recovery stages 827
Victimization theories 829
Victimless crimes 832
Victimology 833
Victims of Crime Act 834
Victims of Trafficking Act of 2015 835
Victims services 836
Walnut Street Jail 838
Work camps 838
Work-release programs 840
Youth authorities 841

Special Issues
Adam Walsh Child Protection and
   Safety Act (2006) 845
Antiterrorism and Effective Death Penalty Act 846
Bloodstains 848
Boston Marathon Bombing (2013) 848
Bounty hunters 850
Bureau of Justice Statistics 851
Civil disobedience 851
Clear and present danger test 855
Computer crime 855
Computer forensics 859
Computer information systems 861
Contributing to delinquency of minors 863
Coroners 864
Crime labs 866
Criminal history record information 867
Criminal justice education 868
Criminal records 869

Cybercrime investigation	871
DNA testing	875
Document analysis	878
Electronic surveillance	879
Espionage	881
Fingerprint identification	884
Forensic accounting	886
Forensics	887
Freedom of assembly and association	890
Fusion Centers	891
Gault, In re	893
Geographic information systems	894
Identity theft	895
Juvenile courts	899
Juvenile delinquency	900
Juvenile Justice and Delinquency Prevention Act	904
Juvenile Justice and Delinquency Prevention, Office of	905
Juvenile justice system	905
Juvenile waivers to adult courts	908
Katz v. United States	909
Latent evidence	910
Lone wolf	911
Medical examiners	913
National Crime Information Center	914
National Institute of Justice	915
Nonviolent resistance	915
Olmstead v. United States	917
Parens patriae	918
Paris terrorist attacks (2015)	918
Patriot Act	920
Pedophilia	921
People v. Nidal Hasan (2013)	923
Polygraph testing	924
Pornography, child	926
Post-traumatic stress disorder	929
President's Commission on Law Enforcement and Administration of Justice	931
Print media	931
Privacy rights	934
Psychological profiling	936
Religious sects and cults	938
Roper v. Simmons (2005)	941
San Bernardino terrorist attack (2015)	942
Schall v. Martin	944
School violence	944
September 11, 2001, attacks	946
Sex discrimination	948
Shoe prints and tire-tracks	952
Social media	952
Status offenses	954
Surveillance cameras	954
Technology's transformative effect	956
Terrorism	957
Toxicology	963
Trace evidence	964
Uniform Juvenile Court Act	965
USA FREEDOM Act (2015)	966
Victims of Child Abuse Act Reauthorization Act (2013)	968
Wiretaps and criminal justice	970
Youth gangs	971
Bibliography of Basic Works on Criminal Justice	977
Glossary	963
Crime Rates and Definitions	1003
Crime Trends	1007
Supreme Court Rulings on Criminal Justice	1009
Famous American Trials	1019
Time Line	1031
Topics by Subject Category	1047
Index to Court Cases	1065
Index to Laws and Acts	1069
Personages Index	1073
Subject Index	1077

Complete List of Contents

Volume I

Publisher's Note ix
Contributors xi
Complete List of Contents xvii
Introduction xxv

Crime

Abortion 3
Adultery 5
Alcohol use and abuse 6
Animal abuse 9
Anti-Racketeering Act of 1934 12
Arson 12
Assault and battery 15
Attempt to commit a crime 18
Autopsies 19
Bigamy and polygamy 20
Blackmail and extortion 21
Breach of the peace 24
Bribery 25
Bullying 27
Burglary 29
Carjacking 31
Child abduction by parents 32
Child abuse and molestation 33
Commercialized vice 38
Comprehensive Addiction and Recovery
    Act of 2016 (CARA) 41
Comprehensive Drug Abuse Prevention
    and Control Act 42
Comstock law 43
Conspiracy 44
Constitution, U.S. 46
Consumer fraud 49
Corporate scandals 51
Counterfeiting 55
Crime 59
Crime index 64
Crimes of passion 64
Criminal justice in U.S. history 65
Criminal justice system 70
Criminals 75
Criminology 78
Date rape 83
Designer and date rape drugs 84
Disorderly conduct 85
Domestic violence and criminal justice 86
Drive-by shootings 91
Drug legalization 92
Drug testing 95
Drunk driving 97
Embezzlement 100
Environmental crimes 103
Female offenders 104
Feminist criminology 106
Forensic psychology 107
Forgery 109
Fraud 110
Gambling 113
Graffiti 116
Hate crime 117
Hit-and-run accidents 120
Hobbs Act 121
Hoover, J. Edgar 121
Human trafficking 122
Illegal aliens and criminal justice 124
Inchoate crimes 126
Indecent exposure 127
Insider trading 128
Insurance fraud 129
Jaycee Lee Dugard case (2009) 131
Jaywalking 133
Justice 134
Kidnapping 136
Ku Klux Klan 139
Loitering 140
Lynching 141
Mafia 143
Mann Act 143
Manslaughter 144
Mass and serial murders 145
Mental illness and crime 150
Missing persons 152
Money laundering 154
Mothers Against Drunk Driving 155
Motor vehicle theft 156
Murder and homicide 160
National Commission on the Causes
    and Prevention of Violence 166

National Narcotics Act	167
National Stolen Property Act	168
Omnibus Crime Control and Safe Streets Act of 1968	168
Opium Exclusion Act	169
Organized crime	170
Organized Crime Control Act	173
Pandering	174
Peacemaking criminology	174
Perjury	176
Pickpocketing	177
Political corruption	177
Pornography and obscenity	181
Principals (criminal)	185
Prohibition	186
Psychopathy	187
Public-order offenses	189
R.A.V. v. City of St. Paul	190
Racketeer Influenced and Corrupt Organizations Act	191
Rape and sex offenses	193
Reckless endangerment	199
Recreational and medical marijuana movements	200
Regulatory crime	201
Right to bear arms	202
Robbery	204
Schools of criminology	208
Seditious libel	210
Sexual harassment and criminal justice	211
Sherman Antitrust Act	213
Shoplifting	214
Skyjacking	217
Sobriety testing	219
Sports and crime	221
Stalking	225
Suicide and euthanasia	226
Suspects	229
Tax evasion	230
Telephone fraud	233
Television news	235
Texas v. Johnson	237
Theft	238
Treason	241
Treasury Department, U.S.	244
Trespass	246
Unabomber	249
Uniform Crime Reports	251
Vandalism	252
Vigilantism	254
Violent Criminal Apprehension Program	256
Virginia v. Black	257
Voting fraud	258
War crimes	259
White-collar crime	261
Wisconsin v. Mitchell	266

Criminal Law

Accomplices and accessories	271
Aggravating circumstances	271
Amicus curiae briefs	272
Annotated codes	273
Antitrust law	273
Arizona v. Fulminante	277
Arrest	278
Arrest warrants	282
Asset forfeiture	283
Atwater v. City of Lago Vista	285
Automobile searches	285
Bill of Rights, U.S.	287
Bivens v. Six Unknown Named Agents	290
Brown v. Mississippi	291
Burden of proof	292
California v. Greenwood	293
Chimel v. California	294
Circumstantial evidence	295
Citizen's arrests	296
Color of law	297
Common law	299
Comprehensive Crime Control Act	300
Confessions	301
Consent searches	303
Criminal intent	304
Criminal law	305
Criminal liability	309
Criminal procedure	310
Cultural defense	314
Decriminalization	314
Defenses to crime	315
Diminished capacity	319
Diplomatic immunity	319
Double jeopardy	320
Due process of law	321
Duress	324
Entrapment	325
Equal protection under the law	326
Escobedo v. Illinois	327
Ex post facto laws	328
Exclusionary rule	329
Excuses and justifications	331
Extradition	331

Federal Crimes Act	334
Felon disfranchisement	334
Felonies	335
Gun laws	336
Harris v. United States	340
Hearsay	340
Hurtado v. California	341
Ignorance of the law	342
Illinois v. Gates	343
Illinois v. Krull	343
Illinois v. McArthur	344
Illinois v. Wardlow	345
Incorporation doctrine	346
Information (written accusation)	347
Insanity defense	347
International law	350
Jim Crow laws	354
Knowles v. Iowa	357
Lesser-included offenses	358
Lindbergh law	358
Magna Carta	359
Mala in se and *mala prohibita*	359
Malice	361
Manhattan Bail Project	361
Mapp v. Ohio	362
Martial law	363
Maryland v. Buie	363
Maryland v. Craig	364
Massachusetts v. Sheppard	365
Mens rea	366
Military justice	367
Miranda rights	369
Miranda v. Arizona	372
Misdemeanors	372
Mitigating circumstances	374
Model Penal Code	374
Moral turpitude	375
Motives	375
Multiple jurisdiction offenses	376
New Jersey v. T.L.O.	377
No-knock warrants	378
Payne v. Tennessee	378
Plain view doctrine	379
Presumption of innocence	380
Preventive detention	381
Privileged communications	382
Probable cause	383
Proximate cause	385
Punitive damages	386
Reasonable doubt	387
Reasonable suspicion	387
Rules of evidence	388
Search and seizure	391
Search warrants	393
Self-defense	395
Sex offender registries	396
Sexually Violent Predator Acts	398
Statutes	400
Statutes of limitations	401
Stop and frisk	401
Strict liability offenses	403
Terry v. Ohio	404
Traffic law	404
United States Code	407
United States Statutes at Large	407
United States v. Alvarez-Machain	408
United States v. Leon	409
United States v. Lopez	409
Vagrancy laws	410
Vicarious liability	411
Violent Crime Control and Law Enforcement Act	412
Weeks v. United States	413
Whren v. United States	414
Wilson v. Arkansas	415

Volume II

Law Enforcement

Alcohol, Tobacco, Firearms and Explosives, U.S. Bureau of	419
Black Lives Matter Movement/ Blue Lives Matter Movement	421
Body-worn cameras	422
Booking	424
Border patrols	425
Boston police strike	427
Broken windows theory	427
Campus police	429
Civilian review boards	431
Cold cases	432
Community-oriented policing	434

Crime analysis 436
Crime scene investigation...................438
Dallas and Baton Rouge police officer
   attacks (2016) 439
DARE programs 440
Deadly force 441
Discretion 443
Drug Enforcement Administration, U.S. (DEA) ...444
Drugs and law enforcement 445
Evidence-based policing....................448
Federal Bureau of Investigation, U.S............450
Frankpledge and watch system................454
Graham v. Connor (1989) 455
High-speed chases.........................457
Highway patrols 459
Homeland Security, U.S. Department of 459
Intelligence-led policing 462
Internal affairs 463
Internal Revenue Service, U.S..................465
Interpol 466
Justice Department, U.S. 467
King beating case 472
Knapp Commission........................474
Kyllo v. United States 475
Law enforcement..........................475
Law Enforcement Assistance Administration 479
Marshals Service, U.S. 480
MOVE bombing 481
National Guard...........................482
Neighborhood watch programs.................484
Noble cause corruption......................485
Peace Officer Standards and Training 487
Police..................................488
Police academies 491
Police brutality 493
Police chiefs.............................498
Police civil liability 498
Police corruption..........................500
Police detectives 504
Police dogs..............................506
Police ethics.............................507
Police lineups...........................509
Police militarization.......................510
Police powers............................511
Police psychologists........................514
Police subculture..........................514
Posse comitatus 516
Predictive policing..........................517
Preventive patrol..........................518
Private police and guards 519

Problem-oriented policing 521
Procedural justice 522
Racial profiling and criminal justice.............523
Reasonable force 526
Resisting arrest 527
Secret Service, U.S.........................527
Sheriffs.................................529
Slave patrols 530
Special weapons and tactics teams (SWAT) 531
Stakeouts..............................533
State police 534
Sting operations 536
Strategic policing..........................537
Tennessee v. Garner 538
Treasury Department, U.S....................539
Use of force 541
Vehicle checkpoints 542
Warrior versus guardian mentality 544
Wickersham Commission 545
Women in law enforcement and corrections 546

Courts
Acquittal...............................553
Amnesty...............................553
Appellate process 554
Argersinger v. Hamlin....................556
Arraignment 557
Attorney ethics 557
Attorney General, U.S. 559
Attorneys general, state 561
Australia's "Reintegrative Shaming" approach 562
Bail system.............................564
Bailiffs 567
Barker v. Wingo 568
Batson v. Kentucky 569
Bench warrants 570
Bifurcated trials..........................570
Bill of particulars 571
Blended sentences.........................571
Brady v. United States....................572
Capital punishment........................573
Case law 578
Cease-and-desist orders 579
Certiorari 579
Chain of custody..........................580
Change of venue 581
Citations 581
Civil commitment.........................582
Clemency..............................584
Clerks of the court 584

Coker v. Georgia	585
Competency to stand trial	585
Concurrent sentences	587
Contempt of court	587
Convictions	588
Corporal punishment	589
Counsel, right to	591
Court reporters	592
Court types	593
Criminal prosecution	595
Cross-examination	598
Cruel and unusual punishment	599
Death qualification	603
Defendant self-representation	604
Defendants	606
Defense attorneys	607
Deportation	608
Depositions	610
Deterrence	611
Discovery	612
Dismissals	613
District attorneys	614
Diversion	616
Drug courts	617
Effective counsel	619
Execution, forms of	622
Execution of judgment	624
Expert witnesses	625
Eyewitness testimony	626
False convictions	629
Faretta v. California	631
Fines	632
Ford v. Wainwright	633
Furman v. Georgia	634
Gag orders	635
Gideon v. Wainwright	635
Grand juries	636
Gregg v. Georgia	638
Habeas corpus	639
Harmelin v. Michigan	641
Harmless error	642
Hearings	642
Hung juries	643
Immunity from prosecution	644
Impeachment of judges	645
In forma pauperis	645
Indeterminate sentencing	646
Indictment	647
Inquests	648
Jessica's Law/Jessica Lunsford Act (2005)	648
Judges	650
Judicial review	652
Judicial system, U.S.	652
Jurisdiction of courts	655
Jury nullification	657
Jury sequestration	658
Jury system	659
Just deserts	663
Mandamus	664
Mandatory sentencing	664
Massiah v. United States	666
McCleskey v. Kemp	667
Minnick v. Mississippi	668
Miscarriage of justice	669
Night courts	670
Nolle prosequi	670
Nolo contendere	670
Objections	671
Obstruction of justice	671
Opinions	672
Palko v. Connecticut	672
Pardons	673
People v. George Zimmerman (2013)	675
Plea bargaining	676
Pleas	677
Powell v. Alabama	678
Precedent	679
Preliminary hearings	680
Presentence investigations	681
Prosecutorial abuse	681
Public defenders	683
Public prosecutors	686
Punishment	688
Restitution	692
Restorative justice	693
Restraining orders	695
Reversible error	695
Robinson v. California	696
Rummel v. Estelle	697
Santobello v. New York	698
Scottsboro cases	699
Self-incrimination, privilege against	701
Sentencing	703
Sentencing guidelines, U.S.	705
Solem v. Helm	706
Speedy trial right	707
Standards of proof	707
Stanford v. Kentucky	708
Stare decisis	709
Subpoena power	710

Summonses	711
Supreme Court, U.S., and criminal rights	711
Suspended sentences	714
Testimony	715
Three-strikes laws	716
Tison v. Arizona	717
Traffic courts	718
Traffic fines	719
Trial publicity	720
Trials	721
United States Sentencing Commission	725
Verdicts	726
Voir dire	727
Witherspoon v. Illinois	727
Witness protection programs	728
Witnesses	730
World Court	733

Volume III

Corrections

Addiction	737
AIDS	740
Ashker v. Brown (2015)	741
Auburn system	743
Battered child and battered wife syndromes	744
Boot camps	746
Chain gangs	748
Community-based corrections	749
Community service	750
Conjugal visitation in prison	751
Crime victimization: primary and secondary	752
"Dark figure of crime"	754
Elderly prisoners	755
Forestry camps	756
Good time	757
Halfway houses	758
History of incarceration	759
Homeless women and victimization	761
House arrest	763
Incapacitation	764
LGBTQ prisoners	765
Medical model of offender treatment	766
National Crime Victimization Survey	767
National Organization for Victim Assistance	768
"Not-in-my-backyard" attitudes	769
Opioid treatment breakthroughs	770
Palmer raids	773
Parole	773
Parole boards	777
Parole Commission, U.S.	779
Parole officers	780
Pennsylvania system of corrections	781
Prison and jail systems	783
Prison escapes	787
Prison guards	789
Prison health care	790
Prison industries	792
Prison inmate subculture	793
Prison overcrowding	794
Prison/prisoner classification systems	797
Prison Rape Elimination Act (PREA) of 2003	798
Prison violence	800
Prisoner rights	802
Prisons, Federal Bureau of	804
Privatization of institutional and community corrections, including faith-based programs	805
Probation, adult	806
Probation, juvenile	809
Realignment (PSR) policy	811
Recidivism	813
Rehabilitation	815
Scandinavia's prison experience	818
Security threat groups (STGs)/prison gangs	819
Smith Act	819
Solitary confinement	820
Supermax prisons	822
Victim and Witness Protection Act	824
Victim assistance programs	824
Victim impact statements	825
Victim-offender mediation	827
Victim recovery stages	827
Victimization theories	829
Victimless crimes	832
Victimology	833
Victims of Crime Act	834
Victims of Trafficking Act of 2015	835
Victims services	836
Walnut Street Jail	838
Work camps	838
Work-release programs	840
Youth authorities	841

Special Issues

Adam Walsh Child Protection and
  Safety Act (2006)........................845
Antiterrorism and Effective Death Penalty Act....846
Bloodstains................................848
Boston Marathon Bombing (2013)..............848
Bounty hunters.............................850
Bureau of Justice Statistics..................851
Civil disobedience..........................851
Clear and present danger test................855
Computer crime............................855
Computer forensics.........................859
Computer information systems................861
Contributing to delinquency of minors.........863
Coroners..................................864
Crime labs................................866
Criminal history record information..........867
Criminal justice education...................868
Criminal records...........................869
Cybercrime investigation....................871
DNA testing...............................875
Document analysis.........................878
Electronic surveillance......................879
Espionage.................................881
Fingerprint identification...................884
Forensic accounting........................886
Forensics..................................887
Freedom of assembly and association..........890
Fusion Centers.............................891
Gault, In re...............................893
Geographic information systems..............894
Identity theft..............................895
Juvenile courts.............................899
Juvenile delinquency.......................900
Juvenile Justice and Delinquency Prevention
  Act....................................904
Juvenile Justice and Delinquency Prevention,
  Office of................................905
Juvenile justice system.....................905
Juvenile waivers to adult courts..............908
Katz v. United States......................909
Latent evidence............................910
Lone wolf.................................911
Medical examiners.........................913
National Crime Information Center...........914
National Institute of Justice..................915
Nonviolent resistance......................915
Olmstead v. United States..................917
Parens patriae............................918

Paris terrorist attacks (2015)................918
Patriot Act................................920
Pedophilia................................921
People v. Nidal Hasan (2013)...............923
Polygraph testing..........................924
Pornography, child.........................926
Post-traumatic stress disorder................929
President's Commission on Law Enforcement
  and Administration of Justice.............931
Print media...............................931
Privacy rights.............................934
Psychological profiling.....................936
Religious sects and cults....................938
Roper v. Simmons (2005)...................941
San Bernardino terrorist attack (2015).........942
Schall v. Martin..........................944
School violence............................944
September 11, 2001, attacks.................946
Sex discrimination.........................948
Shoe prints and tire-tracks..................952
Social media..............................952
Status offenses............................954
Surveillance cameras.......................954
Technology's transformative effect............956
Terrorism.................................957
Toxicology................................963
Trace evidence............................964
Uniform Juvenile Court Act.................965
USA FREEDOM Act (2015)...................966
Victims of Child Abuse Act Reauthorization
  Act (2013)..............................968
Wiretaps and criminal justice................970
Youth gangs...............................971

Bibliography of Basic Works on Criminal Justice...977
Glossary..................................963
Crime Rates and Definitions................1003
Crime Trends.............................1007
Supreme Court Rulings on Criminal Justice....1009
Famous American Trials....................1019
Time Line................................1031

Topics by Subject Category.................1047
Index to Court Cases......................1065
Index to Laws and Acts....................1069

Personages Index.........................1075
Subject Index............................1079

Corrections

Addiction

Definition: A chronic disease of the brain that is related to the use of substances affecting the mind and consequently affecting thought processes, feelings, and behaviors. The most severe form of substance-use disorder is referred to as an addiction.

Criminal justice issues: Medical and health issues; mental disorders; rehabilitation; substance abuse; and crime prevention

Significance: Addiction and crime are strongly linked. There is high prevalence of concomitant substance abuse and other mental disorders in populations involved in the criminal justice system.

Addiction is a significant public health challenge. This fact was recently acknowledged in the U.S. Surgeon General's report on *Facing Addiction in America* published in November 2016 and the discussion centered on alcohol, drugs, and health. Addiction is related to other substance disorders and specific, clear definitions based on the report will assist in the understanding of this chronic disease. Although there are different types of addiction such as substance-related addictions and behavioral addictions (e.g., eating, gambling, shopping, use of the Internet), this article will focus on addiction to substances.

Definitions

Substances include alcohol, illicit drugs, prescribed medications, and over-the-counter (OTC) items used for unintended purposes. Illicit drugs as a group include a broad category of substances such as marijuana, heroin, crack/cocaine, methamphetamines, hallucinogens (e.g., lysergic acid diethylamide [LSD], phencycline [PCP], ecstasy) and others; of note, some states allow legal recreational and medical use of marijuana in their jurisdictions. Prescribed medications include pain relievers (e.g., opioids and narcotics), stimulants (e.g., methylphenidate), tranquilizers (e.g., benzodiazepines), and sedatives (e.g., benzodiazepines). Over-the-counter examples include gasoline, spray paint, and cough and cold medicine.

Substance misuse is the behavior when individuals use substances that can harm themselves and others.

Substance-use disorder is the prolonged, repeated, and uncontrolled substance misuse. This is a medical illness that affects a person's health and others around them. This single diagnosis, according to the fifth edition of the Diagnostic and Statistical Manual of Mental Disorders (DSM-5), replaced the DSM-fourth edition diagnoses of substance abuse and substance dependence.

Addiction is a chronic disease of the brain that is related to the use of substances affecting the mind and consequently affecting thought processes, feelings, and behaviors. It is further characterized by uncontrolled craving, compulsive, and continued use of substances despite harm to self and others. The most severe form of substance-use disorder is referred to as an addiction.

Diagnosis of Substance-Related Disorders

Diagnosis of an addiction is complex, requiring a distinction between substance-use disorders and substance-induced disorders. Examples of substance-induced disorders include intoxication, withdrawal, and medication-induced mental disorders including mood disorders, anxiety disorders, and psychotic disorders. According to the *DSM-5*, a diagnosis of substance-related disorders is based on a pathological pattern of behaviors that are related to the use of a substance. The pathological pattern includes such behaviors as impaired control, social impairment, risky use, and specific pharmacological criteria (i.e., tolerance). Severity and course specifiers (i.e., remission or use in a controlled environment) are also assessed. A thorough clinical interview, incorporation of collateral information (i.e., from medical records and/or family or friends), and laboratory work/diagnostic evaluation is a good approach for diagnosis. Although all drugs involve use of the brain's reward system circuit to develop a type of addiction, proper diagnosis usually involves a mental health professional who is experienced in substance-related disorders, addictive disorders, and dual diagnosis.

Drug-Related Criminal Justice System Issues

The link between crime and drug use is well-known. According to the National Institute on Drug Abuse (NIDA), there are at least five types of drug-related offenses. As noted from the NIDA, these include: drug possession or sales; crimes related to obtaining drugs (e.g., stealing money for drugs); a lifestyle associated with other offenders or with illicit markets; abusive and violent behaviors such as domestic violence and sexual assault; and driving under the influence (DUI) or driving while intoxicated (DWI) with bad outcomes, including property damage, accidents, injuries, and fatalities.

Epidemiology, Statistics, and Economics

According to the 2015 data from the National Survey on Drug Use and Health (NSDUH), for the U.S. population aged twelve and older, over 175 million individuals (65.7 percent of this population) reported alcohol use and over 66 million (24.9 percent of this population) reported binge drinking. Once again, definitions are also important in learning about drinking behaviors. The Substance Abuse and Mental Health Services Administration (SAMHSA) defines binge use of alcohol for males and females as "drinking five (for males)/four (for females) or more standard alcoholic drinks on the same occasion (i.e., at the same time or within a couple of hours of each other) on at least one day in the past 30 days" and heavy use of alcohol for both males and females as "binge drinking on each of 5 or more days in the past 30 days." Figure 1 shows what a standard alcoholic drink measurement is in the United States. One "standard" alcoholic drink contains about fourteen grams of pure alcohol.

The NSDUH also reported the use of other substances in 2015 for the U.S. population aged twelve and older including 36 million who used marijuana, 12.5 million misused pain relievers, and greater than 300,000 used heroin in the past year; of note, some states have legalized marijuana for medical and recreational purposes within their jurisdiction. About 8 percent of this population met the diagnostic criteria for a substance-use disorder for alcohol or illicit drugs, and 1 percent of this population met dual diagnostic criteria for an alcohol and illicit drug use disorder. Based on the NSDUH data of 2015, there is suboptimal use of treatments available for individuals with substance-use disorder; only 10.4 percent of the 20.8 million individuals who met the diagnostic criteria for a substance-use disorder received any type of treatment. Unfortunately, more individuals end up in the criminal justice system instead of being treated in the healthcare system.

The National Institutes of Health (NIH) reported facts and statistics about individuals involved in the criminal justice system. These facts directly reproduced from the NIH fact sheet include: (1) the rate of substance abuse and dependence in criminal offenders are more than four times that of the general population; (2) approximately half of state and federal prisoners meet the criteria for substance abuse and dependence, however, less than 20 percent of these individuals receive treatment; (3) similar to the general population, substance use and other mental disorders both occur in about 45 percent of local jail and state prisoners; and (4) an estimated 75 percent of prisoners with mental illness meet the diagnostic criteria for substance abuse and vice-versa. These facts from the NIH reflect the need for screening criminal offenders for both substance-abuse disorder and mental illnesses and for providing an integrated multidisciplinary intervention in treating dual medical conditions.

In economic terms, according to the U.S. Surgeon General's report, substance-use disorders and related problems cost the country over $400 billion expenses in healthcare, motor vehicle accidents, law enforcement, involvement in the criminal justice system, and lost productivity in the workplace (including the factor of premature mortality).

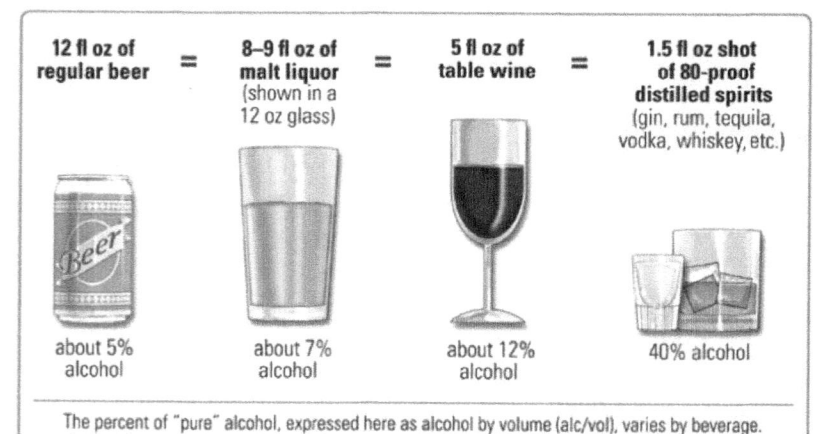

Biological Basis of Addiction

It has been established that addiction has a neurobiological basis affecting the brain function and, as such, there are some effective treatments that allow recovery from this chronic disease. As researchers learn more about the relationships between addiction and the brain function, more opportunities on how to improve treatment and control of this chronic disease is on the horizon. According to the U.S. Surgeon General's report, there are three stages of the addiction cycle in major parts of the brain. The normal functioning of the brain and its circuits of communication in the reward

An illustration of what a standard alcoholic drink measurement as considered in the United States. One "standard" alcoholic drink contains approximately fourteen grams of pure alcohol. (Source: https://www.niaaa.nih.gov/alcohol-health/overview-alcoholconsumption/what-standard-drink)

system is referred to as "hijacked" by the addictive substances in the chronic disease of addiction.

This cycle is related to four major behaviors: (1) impulsivity—the impulse to use substance; (2) positive reinforcement or a "reward" obtained from using the substance; (3) negative reinforcement—bad feelings or emotions increase the urge to take the substance for a "reward"; and compulsivity—repetitive behavior of substance use despite bad outcomes.

Management of Substance-Abuse Disorder and Addiction

A comprehensive multidisciplinary approach in the management of these medical conditions both in the healthcare and criminal justice systems is a vital part of addressing this public health problem. An increased awareness of the risk factors would help healthcare professionals and others in the family/school/community/criminal justice system in helping at-risk individuals. The U.S. Surgeon General's report discussed risk factors as well as protective factors related to addiction. There are early life stressors as risk factors; these include different types of abuse (physical, emotional, and sexual), neglect, poverty, and household problems (such as parental substance use, conflicts, mental illnesses, or incarceration of household members). The adolescent stage in life is a high-risk time period for substance use and experimentation; the risk factors for this stage include negative influences of the individual/peer interactions, family, school, and community. However, there are protective factors as well and these include an individual's self-efficacy, spirituality, resiliency, positive social involvement, strong family/social support systems, healthy beliefs, and proper behavior.

Substance-Use Disorder Treatment

Treatment for substance-related disorders exist in different formats, including group-led with a mental-health professional; peer-led groups; individual therapy; and inpatient and outpatient settings. Evidenced-based interventions, such as Miller and Rollnick's Motivational Enhancement Therapy, incorporate the Prochaska, DiClemente, and Norcross' Transtheoretical Model to tailor therapy to a person's stage for change en route to reaching treatment goals.

The National Institute on Drug Abuse (NIDA) established research-based guiding principles of drug abuse treatment for criminal justice populations; further details of these principles can be found on their website. The principles directly reproduced from the NIDA publication include:

- ✓ 1. Drug addiction is a brain disease that affects behavior.
- ✓ 2. Recovery from drug addiction requires effective treatment, followed by management of the problem over time.
- ✓ 3. Treatment must last long enough to produce stable behavioral changes.
- ✓ 4. Assessment is the first step in treatment.
- ✓ 5. Tailoring services to fit the needs of the individual is an important part of effective drug abuse treatment for criminal justice populations.
- ✓ 6. Drug use during treatment should be carefully monitored.
- ✓ 7. Treatment should target factors that are associated with criminal behavior.
- ✓ 8. Criminal justice supervision should incorporate treatment planning for drug abusing offenders, and treatment providers should be aware of correctional supervision requirements.
- ✓ 9. Continuity of care is essential for drug abusers reentering the community.
- ✓ 10. A balance of rewards and sanctions encourages pro-social behavior and treatment participation.
- ✓ 11. Offenders with co-occurring drug abuse and mental health problems often require an integrated treatment approach.
- ✓ 12. Medications are an important part of treatment for many drug abusing offenders.
- ✓ 13. Treatment planning for drug abusing offenders who are living in or reentering the community should include strategies to prevent and treat serious, chronic medical conditions, such as human immunodeficiency virus (HIV)/acquired immunodeficiency syndrome (AIDS), hepatitis B and C, and tuberculosis.

In summary, drug addiction is a mental illness with a neurobiological basis and there is treatment for such a chronic disease. There is a significant link between addiction and criminal offenses. A comprehensive patient-centered multidisciplinary approach in the treatment of this chronic disease is effective not just for the individual's welfare and for society but also in economic terms. The NIH reported that between two to six dollars are saved for every dollar spent on treatment for addiction; this in part represents a decrease in criminal behavior, reduction in reincarceration, and less involvement with the criminal justice system. Management of addiction will depend on the patient's preferences, type of substance(s) abused, severity of the addiction, and other concomitant diseases. Management options include medications, counseling, and support from community recovery groups, family members, circle of friends and other social networks. Thus, effective treatment of addiction is possible and this will ultimately benefit the individuals with addiction, the people around them, and the society at large.

Miriam E. Schwartz
Sandra Martinez

Further Reading

American Psychiatric Association. *Diagnostic and Statistical Manual of Mental Disorders*, Fifth Edition (DSM-5). Arlington, Va.: American Psychiatric Association, 2013. The authoritative guide on diagnosis and classification of mental disorders.

Center for Behavioral Health Statistics and Quality. *Results from the 2015 National Survey on Drug Use and Health: Detailed Tables*. Rockville, Md.: Substance Abuse and Mental Health Services Administration, 2016. A government resource focusing on helping and increasing awareness of mental and/or substance use disorders in our society.

Miller, W. R. "Motivational Enhancement Therapy: Description of Counseling Approach." In *Approaches to Drug Abuse Counseling*, J. J. Boren, L. S. Onken, and K. M. Carroll, eds. NIH Publication No. 00-4151. Washington, D. C.: U.S. Department of Health and Human Services, 2000. This is a comprehensive resource on enhancing motivation for change in patients or clients.

National Institute on Drug Abuse. *Principles of Drug Abuse Treatment for Criminal Justice Populations: A Research-Based Guide*. NIH publication No. 11-5316. Bethesda, Md.: National Institutes of Health, National Institute on Drug Abuse, 2012. http://www.drugabuse.gov/publications/principles-drug-abuse-treatment-criminal-justice-populations. A comprehensive resource on treatment of individuals involved in the criminal justice system.

National Institute on Drug Abuse. *Research Reports: Comorbidity: Addiction and Other Mental Illnesses*. Bethesda, Md.: National Institutes of Health, National Institute on Drug Abuse, 2010. https://www.drugabuse.gov/publications/research-reports/comorbidity-addiction-other-mental-illnesses/letter-director. A detailed analysis and discussion of the co-occurrence of substance use disorders and mental illnesses.

National Institutes of Health. *Fact Sheet: Addiction and the Criminal Justice System*. Bethesda, Md.: National Institutes of Health, 2010. https://report.nih.gov/nihfactsheets/ViewFactSheet.aspx?csid=22. One of the fact sheets published by the NIH for public awareness of the link between addiction and the criminal justice system in our country.

Office of the Surgeon General. *Facing Addiction in America: The Surgeon General's Report on Alcohol, Drugs, and Health*. Washington, DC: U.S. Department of Health and Human Services, 2016. The first comprehensive, historic, and up-to-date government report that acknowledges addiction as a major public health challenge in the country. The report also includes state-of-the art treatments, preventive measures, and research for this chronic disease.

Prochaska, J. O., C. C. DiClemente, and J. C. Norcross. "In Search of How People Change: Applications to the Addictive Behaviors." *American Psychologist* 47 (1992): 1102-14. PMID: 1329589. This reference discusses the assessment of readiness for change in patients.

Sussman, S., N. Lisha, and M. Mark Griffiths. "Prevalence of the Addictions: A Problem of the Majority or the Minority?" *Evaluation & the Health Professions* 34, no. 1 (March, 2011): 33-56. https://www.ncbi.nlm.nih.gov/pmc/articles/PMC3134413/. This article discusses a wide range of process and substance addictions that are related to problems of lifestyle as well as to person-level factors.

See also Alcohol use and abuse; Domestic violence; Drug courts; Mental illness.

AIDS

Definition: Acquired immunodeficiency syndrome, a sexually transmitted disease that is conveyed by the human immunodeficiency virus, better known as HIV

Criminal justice issues: Homicide; medical and health issues; morality and public order; sex offenses

Significance: Punishing those who knowingly expose others to HIV infection without their consent poses many legal and social challenges.

Criminalizing the act of intentionally exposing others to HIV infections without their consent involves complex legal issues. AIDS is caused by the human immunodeficiency virus, which is transmitted through blood-to-blood contact or body fluids. It destroys the body's defense mechanism (T-cells) and shortens life spans. The term HIV/AIDS is used to encompass the entire spectrum of the disease, from a patient's testing positive for HIV, without symptoms, to contracting the full-blown disease, AIDS. Persons infected with HIV can infect others, even if they do not have AIDS themselves.

Intentionally transmitting or exposing other persons to HIV without their knowledge and consent can result in criminal charges ranging from reckless endangerment to homicidal intent. Prosecution and sentencing for such offenses vary among the U.S. states. Among the points of difference are such questions as whether knowledge of one's HIV infection is enough to constitute "intent," what transmission modes of the virus can be considered criminal, and whether condom use in sexual intercourse reduces the culpability of carriers. Among the modes of HIV transmission that have been the bases of prosecution are sexual relations with partners; donating infected body fluids, tissues, or organs; rape; child abuse; prostitu-

> ### An HIV "Predator"
>
> In one well-known case that began in 1997, a HIV-carrier named Nushawn Williams infected at least thirteen young women and teenagers with the virus after he was told that he was HIV positive and was counseled. He denied believing that he was HIV-positive or having harmful intentions. Since HIV has a lengthy disease course, none of the women he infected died, and he thus could not be charged with murder or manslaughter.
>
> When disregard for the serious risks that a behavior poses to other people can be shown, reckless endangerment charges can be made. That was the charge to which Williams eventually pled guilty, along with statutory rape. He was sentenced to four to eighteen years in prison. His full story is told in Thomas C. Shevory's *Notorious H.I.V.: The Media Spectacle of Nushawn Williams* (Minneapolis: University of Minnesota Press, 2004).

tion; sharing hypodermic needles used for drugs; spitting; biting; and throwing infected fluids.

If purposefulness of conduct to expose other people to HIV can be shown, levels of prosecution can be elevated to assault. HIV assault may be considered either aggravated—an interpretation that would classify HIV as a deadly weapon—or even attempted murder, if it can be shown that offenders use their bodies as weapons intentionally to expose others to HIV.

The early twenty-first century has seen an ongoing debate over question surrounding whether HIV exposure should be criminalized because it victimizes other persons or because it poses a serious public health threat. The latter argument is especially controversial, and there has been virtually no public support for it. Extending prosecution into drug and sex subcultures generally has raised complex issues. Because drug and sex subcultures by their very nature entail the participants' awareness of certain risks, consent may be considered implicit.

Harm reduction and public health proponents argue that extending prosecution into these subcultures would serve only to drive the illicit behaviors farther underground and thereby increase the spread of HIV. Harm-reduction proponents support a strategy of promoting education, treatment, testing and counseling, and sterile-needle exchange for drug users. There is additional concern that prosecution at this level would further stigmatize, and promote discrimination against, HIV carriers.

Debra L. Murphy

Further Reading

Baldwin, Peter. *Disease and Democracy: The State Faces AIDS in the Industrialized World.* Berkeley: University of California Press, 2005.

Jackson, M. H. "The Criminalization of HIV." In *AIDS Agenda: Emerging Issues in Civil Rights*, edited by N. D. Hunter and W. B. Rubenstein. New York: New Press, 1992.

Orcutt, James D., and David R. Rudy, eds. *Drugs, Alcohol, and Social Problems.* Lanham, Md.: Rowman & Littlefield, 2003.

See also Commercialized vice; Prison health care; Prison violence; Rape and sex offenses.

Ashker v. Brown (2015)

Definition: A class-action lawsuit brought by inmates in California's Pelican Bay prison asserting solitary confinement for indeterminate periods is cruel and unusual punishment

Criminal justice issues: Constitutional protections; prisons; punishment

Significance: The September 2015 settlement of this lawsuit fundamentally altered California's use of solitary confinement. It required definite solitary confinement sentences for rule-breaking, rather than just gang status; provided for judicial review of sentences; and created alternatives to using solitary at all. These changes are illustrative of a trend in recent years to move away from solitary confinement.

Ashker v. Brown (Governor of California) is a federal class-action lawsuit brought by inmates at California's Pelican Bay State Prison. The plaintiff prisoners have spent ten years or more in solitary confinement in the Security Housing Unit (SHU). The suit charges long-term solitary confinement constitutes cruel and unusual punishment as defined by the Eighth Amendment. In addition, it alleges that solitary confinement at Pelican Bay is instituted without proper due process in violation of Fourteenth Amendment protections.

The suit was initially filed in 2009 as a pro se action by two SHU inmates, Todd Ashker and Danny Troxell. Both men had been in solitary confinement for over ten years. In September 2012, The Center for Constitutional Rights took up the case and refiled it as a classaction. The lawsuit included eight additional inmates who had each spent more than ten years in solitary. At that time, California had more people held in solitary confinement than any other state.

Eighth Amendment Claim

The Eighth Amendment to the U.S. Constitution prohibits the federal government from imposing "cruel and unusual punishment" on federal prisoners. The classaction alleged that the conditions in the SHU units were so harsh that they were cruel and unusual, causing significant physical and psychological damage. The effects were so severe for some that they did not heal, even after being released from solitary.

Inmates in SHU live in a small cell, approximately eleven by seven feet, without any windows for twenty-two to twenty-four hours a day. They have limited access to telephone calls, no-contact visits, and programs for vocational training and recreation. They are also prevented from interacting or communicating with other prisoners. All the members of the suit had lived in these conditions for ten years; some of them had been in solitary for over twenty continuous years.

In both 2011 and 2013, thousands of SHU prisoners participated in hunger strikes protesting the long-term solitary confinements. Both Ashker and Troxell were involved in orchestrating the hunger strikes.

The prisoners were not alone in their concerns about the cruelty of long-term solitary confinement. Researchers have found that solitary confinement can cause a variety of ailments, including increased anxiety, insomnia, nightmares, and heart palpitations. It can affect thought processes, create irrational anger and mood swings, depression, and suicidal thoughts. U.S. Supreme Court Justice Anthony Kennedy, in his concurrence in *Davis v. Ayala* (135 S.Ct. 2187), outlined evidence from a variety of cases as far back as 1890 criticizing the use of solitary confinement in prisons. He stated: "Research still confirms what this Court suggested over a century ago: Years on end of near-total isolation exacts a terrible price." Juan Mendez, the United Nations Special Rapporteur on torture and other cruel, inhuman or degrading treatment or punishment, stated that as few as fifteen days in solitary confinement constitutes torture and may cause permanent psychological damage.

Fourteenth Amendment Claim

In addition to the Eighth Amendment claim, the suit asserted that the California Department of Corrections and Rehabilitation's (CDCR) procedures for assigning inmates to the SHU violate the Fourteenth Amendment's guarantee of due process. Prisoners could be assigned to solitary confinement simply for being associated with a gang—they did not need to break any prison rules. California is the only state that used a process called " gang validation," which relied on confidential informants and various other indicators, such as tattoos, certain types of literature, and even passing acquaintances. A large percentage of inmates serving indeterminate length SHU terms were not gang members, but gang "associates." One could be designated a gang associate just by talking to another inmate who is a gang member. Once a prisoner had been gang validated, he could be sent to solitary confinement for an indefinite period.

Once placed in solitary, an inmate would have a review every six months to determine release back into the general population. However, in order to secure release from solitary, the inmate was required to "debrief" or renounce their gang membership and provide information on the gang to prison officials. This put the prisoner and his family in danger of retaliation from other prisoners, and was an infrequent occurrence.

Gang-validation status was reviewed every six years, and like the six-month reviews, the inmate was required to debrief. The suit alleged that this left prisoners in the SHU no real means to return to the general population without putting themselves or their families in harm's way. Their complaint asserted that they were "entitled to meaningful notice of how they may alter their behavior to rejoin general population, as well as meaningful and timely periodic reviews to determine whether they still warrant[ed] detention in the SHU."

September 2015 Settlement

The class-action suit was settled on September 1, 2015. The settlement made sweeping changes to the use of solitary confinement within California's federal prisons.

The settlement changed the basis of solitary confinement from gang status-based to a behavior-based system. Now, inmates can only be placed in solitary for breaking an "SHU-eligible" rule. For instance, defined violations include such actions as murder, threats, or escape.

Previously, gang-validated inmates could be kept in solitary for an indefinite period, as reviews to return them to the general population only occurred every six years and release depended upon the inmate debriefing. After the settlement, gang-validated inmates who commit a SHU-eligible offense will enter a two-year step-down program after they serve a defined solitary confinement sentence. Indeterminate solitary sentences cannot be imposed. The step-down program allows for more phone calls, additional privileges, and more programming outside the cell.

A new alternative to solitary confinement, Restricted Custody General Population (RCGP) Unit was created by the settlement. This option is for those who refuse to participate in step-down programming or who engage in conduct that is not an SHU-eligible offense. RCGP is a high-security, but nonsolitary, unit where inmates work to earn release back into the general population.

California has agreed to review all currently gang-validated SHU prisoners within one year to determine if they can be released from solitary. It is estimated that most of the inmates held in solitary confinement will return to the general population after this review. That means anyone not guilty of an SHU-eligible offense, and those inmates who have spent over ten years in solitary, will be immediately placed in RCGP. The only exception would be if it can be shown that the move would create an unreasonable security risk by a preponderance of the evidence.

Long-term solitary confinement will be limited, and those serving SHU sentences will receive more out-of-cell time. When there is overwhelming evidence that a prisoner presents an immediate threat that precludes placement in the general population, he will be placed in "administrative SHU." In this status, he will receive twenty hours a week of out-of-cell time for recreation and programming, which is double the out-of-cell time of other SHU prisoners. The confinement is reviewed by a prison board every 180 days, a judge may be called in to review the sentence, and prison officials must describe the efforts being made to transition the inmate out of SHU. No prisoner may be held involuntarily in SHU for more than five years.

Noelle Sinclair

Further Reading

The Center for Constitutional Rights (Interviewer) & *Ashker* suit plaintiffs (Interviewees). Depositions [Transcripts and video]. The Center for Constitutional Rights website. https://vimeopro.com/ccrmedia/pelican-bay.

Ford, Matt. "The Beginning of the End for Solitary Confinement? California's Settlement with Prisoners Will Massively Reduce the State's Use of Isolation—And Is the Latest Win for the Movement against the Practice." *The Atlantic*. September 2, 2015. http://www.theatlantic.com/politics/archive/2015/09/scaling-back-solitary/403441/.

Joyce, Katie Lynn. "Stars, Dragons, and the Letter 'M': Consequential Symbols in California Prison Gang Policy." *California Law Review* 104 (2016): 733. Examines the evolution of California's gang validation policy, including regulations before 2012, after 2012, and the 2015 *Ashker* settlement.

Reiter, Keramet. *23/7: Pelican Bay Prison and the Rise of Long-Term Solitary Confinement*. New Haven, Conn.: Yale University Press, 2016. This book describes how Pelican Bay was created, how easily prisoners can be sentenced to solitary, and the psychological and social costs of years in isolation.

Shalev, Sharon. *Supermax: Controlling Risk Through Solitary Confinement*. Portland: Willan Publishing, 2009. This book examines the rise since the late 1980's of "Supermaxes," which are large prisons dedicated to holding inmates in long-term solitary confinement.

Skarbek, David. *The Social Order of the Underworld: How Prison Gangs Govern the American Penal System*. New York: Oxford University Press, 2014. The author uses economics to explore how gangs form alternative governance institutions to facilitate illegal activity, and why they have influence outside prison walls.

See also History of incarceration; Prison/Prisoner classification systems; Security Threat Groups (STGs)/Prison gangs; Realignment (PSR) policy; Prisoner rights; Prison inmate subculture; Prison Rape Elimination Act (PREA) (2003); Supermax prisons; Solitary confinement; Prison violence; Prison overcrowding; Prison and jail systems.

Auburn system

Identification: Prison-design plan developed and implemented during the penitentiary movement of the early nineteenth century
Date: Begun in 1822
Place: Auburn, New York
Significance: The Auburn system of prison design was the architectural plan for the first large-scale prison built to maximize the rehabilitation and the labor potential of incarcerated offenders, while reducing construction and operating costs. Even though this model of incarceration was the key mechanism implemented to reform offenders during the penitentiary movement, it has been noted, even since its inception, for pervasive offender abuse and prison overcrowding.

At the turn of the nineteenth century, Americans pushing for prison reform embraced the ideals and promises of the penitentiary. In essence, the penitentiary's purpose was to rehabilitate the offender through silent reflection and penance. Initially, penitentiary design followed the model of the Pennsylvania system plan, wherein individual offenders were housed in solitary cells at all times. However, that prison and jail system was too expensive to build and manage, as considerable land was needed to erect the large structures, and exceptional numbers of qualified staff were required for inmate surveillance and control. The Auburn system was thus developed and implemented to counter the negative reality of the Pennsylvania system design.

The Auburn Correctional Facility, where the Auburn System originated. (Public domain, via Wikimedia Commons)

The Auburn system penitentiary called for offenders to sleep in small, individual cells, yet dine and work silently in common areas. Hence, this design and its inherent regimes were often referred to as the congregate system. The first two penitentiaries built according to this plan were New York's Auburn and Sing Sing prisons, both which opened during the 1820s.

Cells in Auburn-style facilities were positioned back-to-back and stacked in tiers within hollow buildings. The ideal of the Auburn-style prison was maximization of the rehabilitation and labor potential of offenders. This ideal of the Auburn design was so widely embraced, it influenced prison construction throughout the United States during the remainder of the nineteenth and the early twentieth centuries. In fact, Sing Sing prison remains in use today.

Auburn-style facilities were often built to be large, foreboding structures, in the hope that the very essence of the prisons would serve as a deterrent to potential offenders. Nevertheless, penologists have questioned the rehabilitative and deterrent value of the Auburn system design, as offender recidivism, unsanitary conditions, and corporal punishment have been the reality in many facilities built according to the design plan of the Auburn system.

Courtney A. Waid

Further Reading

Blomberg, Thomas G., and Karol Lucken. *American Penology*. New York: Aldine de Gruyter, 2000. Print.

Johnston, Norman. *The Human Cage: A Brief History of Prison Architecture*. New York: Walker, 1973. Print.

Pollock, Joycelyn M. *Prisons and Prison Life: Costs and Consequences*. New York: Oxford UP, 2013. Print.

Waid, Courtney A., and Carl B. Clements. "Correctional Facility Design: Past, Present and Future." *Corrections Compendium* 26.11 (2001). Print.

See also Prisons, Federal Bureau of; Corporal punishment; Criminal justice system; Incapacitation; Prison and jail systems; Prison industries; Prison overcrowding; Punishment; Rehabilitation; Solitary confinement; Pennsylvania system of corrections.

Battered child and battered wife syndromes

Definition: Condition of sufferers of family violence who have undergone physical abuse that leaves them with both physical and psychological trauma

Criminal justice issues: Women's Issues; Medical and health issues; Violent crime

Significance: The terms battered child syndrome and battered wife syndrome have brought to public attention the prevalence of family violence and the need to enact new laws to protect children and women. In addition, the terms are important in the criminal prosecution and defense of child abuse and domestic violence cases.

Although family violence is not a new problem in the United States, the criminal prosecution of family members who physically or sexually abuse relatives is a relatively recent development. Medical and social science research during the 1960s and 1970s documented the unique kinds of injuries, both physical and psychological, that are suffered when family members are the abusers. The researchers who identified and brought to public attention battered child syndrome and battered wife syndrome helped increase public awareness of family violence and helped change criminal justice policy concerning prosecution of such cases. In addition, recognition of the psychological trauma associated with such victimization, led to the development of controversial criminal defenses that attempt to utilize battered child syndrome and battered wife syndrome as justifications for victims killing their abusers.

Battered Child Syndrome

Battered child syndrome is the condition suffered by children who have undergone physical abuse that has left them with both physical and psychological trauma. Dr. Henry C. Kempe and his associates coined the term in a landmark article published in the *Journal of the American Medical Association* in 1962. Kempe presented the group's findings in a nationwide survey of hospitals that documented 302 cases of battered child syndrome during one year in which thirty-three battered children had died and eighty-five had suffered permanent brain injury.

In analyzing the data from the study, Kempe found that the studied cases shared certain characteristics. First, battered child syndrome usually occurred to children younger than the age of three. Second, noticeable discrepancies usually appeared between the medical findings and the parents' explanations of how their children's injuries occurred. Third, histories of previous injuries in many children revealed various stages of healing that indicated that people were intentionally injuring the children. Kempe's research received a great deal of public attention and was the impetus for drafting a federal child-abuse reporting statute.

All U.S. states now have child abuse laws mandating that certain caretakers such as physicians, nurses, and teachers report cases of suspected child abuse. While Kempe focused on using physiological data to identify battered child syndrome, later researchers have tended to focus on examining psychological data to identify emotional effects suffered by children with the syndrome. These data include hyper-vigilance, helplessness, and posttraumatic stress disorder.

Courts have recognized the importance of battered child syndrome in prosecuting cases of child abuse. Prosecutors use battered child syndrome particularly in cases in which a child's death results from abuse and in which very young children sustain serious injuries. In the latter cases, the children are not able to testify about their abuse, so prosecutors must rely upon expert witnesses. The experts testify about previous injuries suffered by the children, even though there may be no direct proof that their battered children's parents have caused their injuries. In its 1991 *Estelle v. McGuire* ruling, the U.S. Supreme Court evaluated the use of evidence of battered child syndrome and held that in battered child cases it was constitutional for courts to admit as evidence prior injuries of children, even without proof that the defendants caused the prior injuries.

Although courts frequently use battered child syndrome to prove the intent to commit child abuse, they rarely permit its use in situations in which children kill their parents and then try to use battered child syndrome as their defense. Such cases typically involve adolescent children or adults who make claims about the long-term psychological effects of past parental abuse on them. While experts may be able to testify about the psychological effects of battered child syndrome, most courts reject it as a defense because it departs too much from traditional self-defense theory.

Battered Wife Syndrome

Battered wife, or battered woman, syndrome is a set of psychological and behavioral symptoms exhibited by victims of severe, long-term domestic violence. The term is associated with the pioneer research of Dr. Lenore Walker who introduced the term in her 1979 book, *The Battered Woman*. While Walker's definition of the syndrome encompasses any woman who has been the victim of physical, sexual, or psychological abuse by her partner, not all battered women develop battered woman syndrome. The syndrome applies only to a woman who has been the victim at least twice of physical, sexual, or serious psychological abuse by a man with whom she has an intimate relationship. Walker's research advances a psychological theory of the process of victimization of battered women. Her theory explains why even after prolonged spousal abuse, battered women lack the psychological ability to leave their abusive relationships.

Walker defined battered woman syndrome as comprising two distinct components: a cycle of violence and learned helplessness. The term cycle of violence refers to a three-part repetitive pattern of interaction between batterers and their victim that consists of gradual periods of tension building—expressed in verbal and psychological abuse—followed by acute battering incidents, and concluding with calm, loving respites, during which the batterers apologize for their behavior. Walker identified this third phase as the one that most victimizes women psychologically because the cycles of violence almost inevitably recur. Battered women become increasingly demoralized as they realize that their abusive partners have again fooled them into believing that they will change.

The second component of Walker's theory, learned helplessness, explains the psychological paralysis that prevents some women from leaving their abusers. Walker argued that learned helplessness occurs in domestic violence situations when the battered women cannot ensure their own safety because—regardless of their own behavior—they face their partners' unpredictable abusive behavior. Believing that there is no way for them to prevent the violence, battered women simply give up and accept the abuse. In some cases, battered women resort to violence themselves and kill their partners to free themselves from further abuse.

Criminal courts in all fifty U.S. states permit the introduction of expert testimony on battered woman syndrome. Often this occurs in the context of murder trials in which women homicide defendants claim to have been battered women and argue that they have acted in self-defense. In many cases, objective evidence is lacking that meets traditional standards for self-defense, namely fear of imminent death or serious injury at the time of the homicide. Therefore, the mental states or beliefs of the battered women are considered in evaluating self-defense claims. Expert witnesses testify about battered woman syndrome and the psychological states of the defendants at the time of their homicides to assist juries in determining whether the defendants have acted out of reasonable beliefs that they were in imminent danger of death or great bodily harm.

Patricia E. Erickson

Further Reading

Crosson-Tower, Cynthia. *Understanding Child Abuse and Neglect.* 9th ed. Boston: Allyn, 2014. Print.

Giardino, Angelo P., and Eileen Giardino. *Recognition of Child Abuse for the Mandated Reporter.* 4th ed. St. Louis: STM Learning, 2015. Print.

Monteleone, James A. *A Parent's and Teacher's Handbook on Identifying and Preventing Child Abuse.* St. Louis: G. W. Medical, 1998. Print.

Raphael, Jody. *Saving Bernice: Battered Women, Welfare and Poverty.* Boston: Northeastern UP, 2000. Print.

Wallace, Harvey, and Cliff Roberson. *Family Violence: Legal, Medical and Social Perspectives.* 7th ed. New York: Routledge, 2016. Print.

See also Arrest warrants; Child abuse and molestation; Criminal intent; Criminals; Cultural defense; Defenses to crime; Domestic violence; Excuses and justifications; Pornography, child; Self-defense; Victimology; Post-traumatic stress disorder; Victims services; Victim recovery stages; Victimization theories; Victims of Child Abuse Act Reauthorization (2013).

Boot camps

Definition: Alternative form of incarceration using rigid discipline modeled on military training camps

Criminal justice issues: Juvenile justice; Punishment; Prisons

Significance: The United States incarcerates a higher proportion of juveniles and young adults than most of the nations of the world. The resulting high costs and overcrowding, with few positive rehabilitation benefits, have created a need for more cost-effective programs that reduce recidivism rates. It was initially hoped that boot camps would meet these goals; however, they have failed to fulfill their promise.

Boot camps—or, as they are also known, shock incarceration programs—were first established during the 1980s in response to rising crime rates, overcrowding in prisons, and high recidivism rates. The camps were intended to be an intermediate sanction between long-term institutionalization and immediate supervised release. While boot camp programs were originally designed for adults, the juvenile justice system has also adopted them. Some boot camps are financed and run by state governments, while others are privately owned and operated. Private boot camps often operate with little regulation. The great majority of boot camps are for male prisoners only, but a few have included female prisoners, and some have been designed exclusively for female prisoners.

Shock Incarceration

The types of programs known as "boot camps" vary considerably. The military "basic training" aspect of boot camps is what distinguishes them from other correction programs. These camps are referred as "shock incarceration" because they offer short, stressful experiences that are intended to encourage reform by the offenders. The first-generation boot camps emphasized military discipline, physical training, and hard physical work. Second-generation camps placed more emphasis on rehabilitation by adding such components as alcohol and drug treatment and social skills counseling. By the early twentieth century, some boot camps—particularly those for juveniles—were placing greater emphasis on educational and vocational skills than on military components, while still providing similar structure and discipline.

Adult boot camp programs are generally designed for younger, nonviolent offenders with first felony convictions. However, some camps have age limits as high as forty years. Juvenile boot camps are also generally restricted to nonviolent, first-time offenders. Lengths of stay are generally from three to six months in adult boot camps and from one to three months in juvenile camps. Adults are placed in boot camps though criminal courts.

Riverina Juvenile Justice Centre. (By Bidgee, via Wikimedia Commons)

State courts also send juveniles to state-run boot camps, but juveniles are also sent to private boot camps by other courts and parents.

Oklahoma and Georgia were the first states to implement boot camp programs during the early 1980s. Other states followed in rapidly increasing numbers during the late 1980s and early 1990s. However, during the mid-1990s, both the numbers and daily populations of boot camps started decreasing, and that trend has continued through the first half decade of the twenty-first century. The state of Texas, formerly a leading state in boot camps, provides one example. By August, 2004, officials in Texas had shut down or converted six of the state's seven boot camps that had been created during the 1990s. Georgia, Colorado, North Dakota, and Arizona have all ended their programs, and Florida and California have both scaled back their programs.

Decline of Boot Camp Programs

The two most prominent reasons for the decline of boot camps are research findings indicating that the camps have failed to achieve their goals and widespread reports of abuses, deaths, and lawsuits. In 2003, the National Institute of Justice concluded a summary of research done on boot camps over a ten-year period. That study analysis found that while boot camps did have positive effects on the attitudes, perceptions, behaviors, and skills of inmates in the programs, the programs did not result in reduced recidivism, with limited exceptions. Subsequent meta-analyses in 2009 and 2013 produced similar results. The National Institute of Justice study, as well as other research, indicates that boot camps cost somewhat less than prison or juvenile training schools, resulting in modest reductions in correctional costs. They can also contribute to small reductions in prison and training school populations.

Numerous reports of abuses, deaths, and suicides at both juvenile and adult boot camps across the country have also contributed to their decline, both because they have outraged people and because they have resulted in expensive lawsuits. Notorious examples include a 2000 case involving a fourteen-year-old girl who died from heat exhaustion in a South Dakota boot camp, where she was placed for shoplifting, after her drill instructors decided that her complaints were merely malingering. In 2001, a sixteen-year-old in Arizona died after being punished for discipline violations. By 2003, at least thirty-six juveniles had died in boot camps. A 2005 investigation by the Government Accountability Office found 1,619 instances of abuse in juvenile boot camps throughout the country.

Financial risks may have as much to do with the reduction in use of boot camps as abuses and deaths. Courts have ordered many states and private corrections corporations to pay large amounts in punitive damages. For example, a class-action suit in Maryland led to a court order for the state to pay four million dollars to juveniles abused at its boot camps from 1996 to 1999. The largest such award was in Texas in 2003, when a Tarrant County jury ordered the Correctional Services Corporation to pay the parents of a juvenile named Bryan Alexander $5.1 million in punitive damages and $35 million in actual damages for their son's death and suffering and their mental anguish. The boy had died at the Mansfield boot camp run by the Correctional Services Corporation, which is based in Florida.

Due to their dangers and lack of demonstrable effect, boot camps have declined in popularity. By 2009, only eleven states operated juvenile boot camps, down from thirty in 1995.

The Future of Boot Camps

It is generally believed that if boot camps are to have a future in either the adult or juvenile justice system, they must be better regulated and be more successful in reducing recidivism. Moreover, the study conducted by the National Institute of Justice and other smaller research studies indicate that if boot camps are to be more successful in the future there should be a standard boot camp model that includes therapeutic programs as well as discipline, with more emphasis on re-entry into the community and post-release supervision and assistance.

Jerome L. Neapolitan

Further Reading

Allen, Harry E., Clifford E. Simonsen, and Edward J. Latessa. *Corrections in America: An Introduction*. 10th ed. Upper Saddle River: Pearson Education, 2004. Print.

Champion, Dean John. *The Juvenile Justice System: Delinquency, Processing, and the Law*. 4th ed. Upper Saddle River: Prentice-Hall, 2003. Print.

Kempinen, C., and M. Kurlychek. "An Outcome Evaluation of Pennsylvania's Boot Camp: Does Rehabilitative Programming Within a Disciplinary Setting Reduce Recidivism?" *Crime and Delinquency* 49 (2003): 581-602. Print.

MacKenzie, D. L., and G. S. Armstrong. *Correctional Boot Camps: Military Basic Training or a Model for Corrections?* Thousand Oaks: Sage, 2004. Print.

Nellis, Ashley. *A Return to Justice: Rethinking Our Approach to Juveniles in the System*. Lanham: Rowman, 2016. Print.

Parent, D. *Correctional Boot Camps: Lessons from a Decade of Research*. Washington, D.C.: U.S. Dept. of Justice, Natl. Inst. of Justice, 2003. Print.

Sanchez, Matheson, and Gang Lee. "Race, Gender, and Program Type as Predictive Risk Factors of Recidivism for Juvenile Offenders in Georgia." *Journal of Public and Professional Sociology* 7.2 (2015): 1+. PDF file.

Whitehead, John T., and Steven P. Lab. *Juvenile Justice: An Introduction*. 8th ed. New York: Routledge, 2015. Print.

See also Chain gangs; Forestry camps; Juvenile justice system; Prison and jail systems; Prison overcrowding; Recidivism; Rehabilitation; Sentencing; Work camps.

Chain gangs

Definition: Definition: Groups of prisoners who are chained together while performing manual labor outside prisons.

Criminal justice issues: Punishment; Civil Rights and Liberties; Prisons

Significance: Although commonly perceived to be an invention of states in the Southern United States, compulsory penal labor was popularized in the Northern U.S. in the 1820s, beginning with the Auburn system in New York State. The leasing of prisoners to private industry quickly became popular in the Northern U.S. and spread to the Western U.S. by the middle of the 1800s. The Southern U.S. also used penal servitude during this time period, but it consisted mostly of white male prisoners due to their reliance of slavery as a source of labor.

After the Civil War, the Southern states struggled to replace slave labor and they relied heavily on prison labor in an attempt to fill some of the gap. This new penal servitude focused more heavily on the use of African American prisoners and it evolved into what is now known as the traditional "chain gang." Specifically, chaining prisoners together became a correctional strategy used when transporting inmates out of a prison, often to plantations, for the purpose of performing manual labor. Members were chained together in groups while wearing distinct uniforms identifying them as prisoners.

While the chaining of prisoners provided extra safeguards against prisoner escapes, traditional chain gangs became criticized as outdated and cruel and eventually began to fall out of favor in the 1940's. The lease system had been abolished in all states by 1951, but use of prisoners for manual labor in the South continued for many years afterward until it was finally discontinued. During the mid-1990's, however, chain gangs began to make a small comeback in a few southern and western states. Although the original purpose of chain gangs was largely economic, their renewed use was influenced by a number of other rationales. Included in these justifications were an increased desire to get tough on prisoners, the revival of shaming as a correctional strategy, and a desire to keep prisoners active and avoid the problems associated with idle time.

In 1996 the U.S. Supreme Court found that many types of chain gangs violated the 8th Amendment's protection against cruel and unusual punishment. Thus, modern chain gangs largely consist of volunteer prisoners who are not chained together and who prefer to work outside of the prison. Nevertheless, much national and international attention still follows chain gangs. Critics claim that chain gangs are inefficient and that their use lacks deterrence value and violates prisoners' protections from cruel and unusual punishment.

Brion Sever

Further Reading

Burley, L. "History Repeats Itself in the Resurrection of Prisoner Chain Gangs." *Law and Inequality* 15 (1997): 129-130.

Colvin, M. *Penitentiaries, Reformatories, and Chain Gangs: Social Theory and the History of Punishment in the Nineteenth Century*. New York: St. Martin's Press, 1997.

Larson, D. "Slaves of the State: Black Incarceration from Chain Gang to the Penitentiary." *Law and Society Review* 50 (2015): 521-524.

Reinert, A. "Reconceptualizing the Eighth Amendment: Slaves, Prisoners, and 'Cruel and Unusual' Punishment." *North Carolina Law Review* 94 (2016): 817-860.

See also Boot Camps: Community Service; Cruel and unusual punishment; Prison and jail systems; Prison escapes; Work camps.

Community-based corrections

Definition: Sentence, or post-sentence arrangement, in which offenders are allowed to remain in their own communities, with supervision and sometimes assistance with rehabilitation and reintegration into their communities

Criminal justice issues: Probation and pretrial release; Punishment; Rehabilitation

Significance: Community-based corrections are alternatives to incarceration and are increasingly and innovatively being used by judges and corrections administrators to alleviate prison and jail overcrowding.

An array of community-based correctional strategies is in use, but this was not always the case. Around the time of the American Revolutionary War, offenders were routinely punished in their local communities, with public humiliation as the goal. Criminals, for example, were placed in stocks and forced to endure thrown garbage and insults while they were, literally, on display in the town square. Such punishments aimed to deter would-be offenders and provided obvious retribution for wrongdoing. These early humiliating punishments, however, did not aim to reintegrate the offender.

Over time, penal reformers argued that rehabilitation should also be an objective of punishment and that offenders could be corrected within their communities. By the mid-nineteenth century, some offenders were placed on probation and parole, the earliest attempts at their correction outside an institution. Until the late 1950s, these were the only widely employed community-corrections strategies. During the 1960s and 1970s, increased interest and support for the idea of correction in the community led to the proliferation of work-release programs, halfway houses, substance-abuse centers, and other community-based corrections. By the 1980s, support for rehabilitation and community-based corrections had decreased; the number of offenders removed from society via incarceration grew. Prison and jail populations skyrocketed. Consequently, alternatives to incarceration are now sought, if only to alleviate prison overcrowding.

Probation and Parole

Probation and parole began to be used in the United States during the nineteenth century. Adult probation originated in Boston in 1841, through the work of John Augustus, an influential business owner. As a sentence, probation allows convicted offenders to remain in their communities, under supervision and with specified conditions. Liberty is, therefore, conditional. The conditions of probation quite often focus on an offender's rehabilitative needs. For example, an offender with substance-abuse problems will likely be required to attend Narcotics Anonymous or other appropriate meetings.

Unlike probation, parole is not a sentence. A parole board, rather than a judge, decides whether an offender may soon rejoin society. If the decision is favorable, an inmate is granted early release from the prison system. Therefore, all parolees have recently been incarcerated. New York, through its adoption of an indeterminate sentencing law in 1876, was the first state to allow prisoners to be released on parole.

The aim of parole, like that of all community-based corrections, is to assist with an offender's reintegration. Like a probationer, a parolee is supervised while in the outside community and must abide by conditions of release. For both probationers and parolees, failure to abide by the conditions specified for release may result in reimprisonment.

The Mid-Twentieth Century

From the late-1950s to the late-1970s, the scope of community-based corrections expanded beyond probation and parole. Penal reformers argued that released inmates faced many problems as they made the transition from imprisonment to life back in the community. To combat the challenges former inmates faced, organizations such as the International Halfway House Association (now known as the International Association of Residential and Community Alternatives) and the American Correctional Association were instrumental in increasing the resources available for community-based corrections, and some were secured through legislation. For example, the Federal Prisoner Rehabilitation Act of 1965 authorized the establishment of halfway houses for both juveniles and adults. Largely because of these efforts, from 1966 to 1982 the number of halfway houses operating in the United States and Canada increased from fewer than fifty to more than fifteen hundred. The aim of halfway houses, both then and now, is to assist with an offender's successful reintegration back into society. Some halfway houses also provide in-house rehabilitation, which may include job skills training, substance-abuse treatment, or mental health counseling.

The number of inmates granted temporary release from prisons and jails also grew notably. In 1957, for example, North Carolina became the first state to permit selected convicted felons to leave prisons during the day to work in the local community. Other states followed suit. The U.S. Congress, in 1965, allowed work release for prisoners in federal institutions. Authorization for other temporary-release programs, such as furlough release and study release, also became more widespread. The aim of all temporary-release programs is to promote offenders' positive ties to society by allowing them to maintain regular societal interaction.

The 1980s and Beyond

Belief in the value of rehabilitation waned in the 1980s. Critics argued that high recidivism rates were indicative of a correctional system that was not working, suggesting that "correction" was not possible. Consequently, deterrence, retribution, and incapacitation became the primary justifications for punishment. With this came an increased likelihood of incarceration for an offender.

By 2010, the rate of incarceration was at an all-time high, having increased 700 percent since 1970. Prisons and jails in many jurisdictions across the United States remained severely overcrowded. One method of reducing overcrowding is to sentence offenders to something other than incarceration. Intermediate sanctions, which are simply punishments that are more severe than probation but less severe than incarceration, provide an alternative.

Use of most intermediate sanctions originated in the 1980s or 1990s. For example, Georgia became the first state to implement intensive supervised probation (ISP), in 1982, and widely to use correctional boot camps, in 1983. Both were done, in part, to avoid a federal takeover of its overcrowded prison system. New Jersey and Massachusetts also began utilizing ISP during the early 1980s.

The use of house arrest, with or without electronic monitoring, has also spread rapidly. In 1984, Florida was the first state extensively to use the sanction of home confinement. For many offenders, this punishment is the last chance to avoid incarceration in jail or prison. As technology has advanced, more and more jurisdictions have added electronic monitoring into their repertoire of punishment options.

Day-reporting centers are among the newest of intermediate sanctions. In 1990 only thirteen day-reporting centers existed in the United States. By the early 2000s, most major jurisdictions had at least one center to which offenders are sentenced to report on a daily basis. At the center, where offenders may spend up to eight hours of their days, focus is placed on an offender's rehabilitation needs. Over time, expectations are that intermediate sanctions will increasingly be used.

Pauline K. Brennan

Further Reading

Abadinsky, Howard. *Probation and Parole*. 12th ed. Boston: Pearson, 2015. Print.

Allen, Harry E., Clifford E. Simonsen, and Edward J. Latessa. *Corrections in America: An Introduction*. 14th ed. Boston: Pearson, 2016. Print.

Clear, Todd R., and Harry R. Dammer. *The Offender in the Community*. 2nd ed. Belmont: Wadsworth, 2003. Print.

Haas, Kenneth C., and Geoffrey P. Alpert. *The Dilemmas of Corrections*. 4th ed. Prospect Heights: Waveland, 1999. Print.

Stohr, Mary K., and Craig Hemmens. *The Inmate Prison Experience*. Upper Saddle River: Pearson, 2004. Print.

Vera Institute of Justice. *The Potential of Community Corrections: To Improve Communities and Reduce Incarceration*. New York: Vera Inst. of Justice, 2013. PDF file.

See also Community service; Criminology; Deterrence; Drug courts; Electronic surveillance; Forestry camps; Halfway houses; House arrest; Incapacitation; "Not-in-my-backyard" attitudes; Parole; Prison overcrowding; Probation, adult; Recidivism; Rehabilitation; Restorative justice; Sentencing; Work camps; Work-release programs; Australia's "Reintegrative Shaming" approach; Probation, juvenile; Peacemaking criminology; Privatization of institutional and community corrections, including faith-based programs; Realignment (PSR) policy.

Community service

Definition: Form of punishment that as an alternative to incarceration requires offenders to do work that improves the community or restores the damage their actions have caused

Criminal justice issues: Punishment; Restorative justice

Significance: Community service has proven to be a cost-effective alternative to incarceration and offers other benefits to communities. At the same time, it requires a measure of accountability and responsibility on the part of the offenders.

Offenders who are sentenced to perform community service are typically required to do set amounts of unpaid labor for some project or operation that benefits the community in which they have been convicted. The logic behind this practice follows a principle of restorative justice holding that reparations to victims or communities as a whole create a better end than simply punishing offenders through incarceration. While part of restoration may include imposition of fines, the amounts of the fines

Community service work detail. (By Dwight Burdette, via Wikimedia Commons)

may be influenced by the offenders' ability to pay and thus have unequal impact on the communities. Restitution to the community as a whole through tangible service can be a more even-handed way of achieving restorative justice, as the sentences imposed on the rich and the poor are more likely to be the same.

Community service offers many benefits. While still holding offenders accountable for their actions, the communities can receive tangible forms of compensation. Moreover, monitoring completion of community service is nearly always less expensive than incarceration, allowing the limited incarceration resources to be directed to offenders who pose greater risks to the community. Another benefit is the offering of positive, structured activities for the offenders' free-time. However, although offenders themselves may benefit from performing their service, being forced to give up leisure time or opportunities to earn money clearly has a punitive aspect.

The quality of community service is often dependent on the relationships between the court officers overseeing the work and the organizations for which the offenders perform services. An important aspect of community service is that the work performed serves genuine needs in the community, and that it is actually done. Assignments may be client-specific, to take advantage of individual offenders' special skills, or offense specific, such as assigning someone charged with animal cruelty to work in an animal shelter.

Most offenders reside in their homes while completing their service, but some states have created centers in which the offenders are required to reside while performing their service. Residents of such centers are supervised twenty-four hours a day, but the centers create opportunities for the residents to work in programs that help the community. Upon release, the residents are generally better prepared to be reintegrated into their communities, and they may have developed new marketable job skills, along with positive feelings of involvement in the community.

While research findings on the effectiveness of community-service programs have been mixed, most studies find that offenders sentenced to community service are, at the least, no more likely to become repeat offenders afterward than offenders who go into the prison and jail system. On the other hand, if community service is overused for repeat offenders and jail is not an alternative, incentives for offenders to provide quality service may be diminished. One thing is clear, however: The cost savings and general benefit of the offenders' work to the community makes the programs attractive alternatives to traditional sentences of incarceration for many offender populations.

John C. Kilburn, Jr.

Further Reading
Clear, Todd R., and Harry R. Dammer. *The Offender in the Community.* 2nd ed. Belmont: Wadsworth, 2003. Print.
Karp, David R., and Todd R. Clear. *What Is Community Justice? Case Studies of Restorative Justice and Community Supervision.* Thousand Oaks: Sage, 2002. Print.
McDonald, Douglas. *Punishment without Walls: Community Service Sentences in New York City.* New Brunswick: Rutgers UP, 1986. Print.

See also Animal abuse; Chain gangs; Community-based corrections; Punishment; Restitution; Restorative justice; Sentencing; Sentencing guidelines, U.S.; Australia's "Reintegrative Shaming" approach; Peacemaking criminology.

Conjugal visitation in prison

Definition: Simply put, a conjugal visit is a visit for a prisoner who is permitted to spend time in private in which sex is permitted. The visit may be several hours or even days. It is allowed in only four states (California, New York, Connecticut, and Washington) and is not allowed in any federal prisons in the United States. Into the 1990's, seventeen states had allowed such visits.

Criminal justice issues: Medical and health issues; rehabilitation; prisons

Significance: The purpose of extended family visits, the current term for conjugal visits, is to preserve family life. Additionally, these visits are a humanitarian effort seeking to counter recidivism. They also provide a means for encouraging good behavior with the visits serving as a reward. The reason for the name change is to provide the inclusion of all family members on the visits.

Some Facts about the Visits

Although specifics may vary, states that have extended family visits provide certain amenities. These may include special-type housing, apartments, or trailers, for example. Toiletries may be available as may condoms and lubes. Even DVD players and TVs or games may be provided. Some states allow visitors to bring food.

Generally, prisoners must have good health and behavior to be allowed family visits. Moreover, only prisoners in minimum- and medium-security facilities are eligible. As one would expect, spouses are checked before being allowed to visit as are other visitors.

A few other facts are of interest. The first conjugal visits took place in Mississippi in 1918 at the Mississippi State Penitentiary. The visits were not with the prisoners' wives but with paid prostitutes because the warden, James Parchman, thought that would encourage his African-American prisoners in their work. Each Sunday the warden would have prostitutes brought in to encourage the men to work harder. Other male prisoners had to wait until the 1930's to become part of the program.

As expected, other countries have their own laws governing conjugal visits. India, for example, has ruled that prisoners have a legal right to have children. In Arabia men have a right to have sex with each of their wives for one night per wife. These are only a few examples of such programs.

Conclusion

The purpose for conjugal visits, extended family visits, is to lessen some of the problems that plague prisons. These problems include male rape, psychological problems of prisoners' families and of prisoners, and basic respect for prisoners. The visits are also granted in the hope of lowering the risk of recidivism. Research has demonstrated the value of extended family visits and its role in achieving these goals. However, those advocates of making punishment the primary goal of the criminal justice system argue that such visits show a softness on crime and coddle those who should be punished. The great reduction in these programs indicates that those who are "tough on crime" seem to be winning the argument.

Frank A. Salamone

Further Reading

Peterson, Bryce, Lindsey Cramer, Emma Kurs, and Jocelyn Fontaine. Toolkit for Developing Family-Focused Jail Programs Children of Incarcerated Parents Project. http://www.urban.org/sites/default/files/alfresco/publication-pdfs/2000255-Toolkit-for-Developing-Family-Focused-Jail-Programs.pdf.

Burstein, Jules. Conjugal Visits in Prison: Psychological and Social Consequences. Lanham, Md.: Lexington Books 1977.

Hopper, Columbus B. "The Conjugal Visit at Mississippi State Penitentiary." The Journal of Criminal Law, Criminology, and Police Science. 53, no. 3 (September, 1962): 340-43.

Reid-Pharr, Robert. Conjugal Union: The Body, the House, and the Black American. New York and Oxford: Oxford University Press, 1999.

Vacheret, Marion. "Private Family Visits in Canada, Between Rehabilitation and Stricter Control: Portrait of a System." Champ pénal/Penal field [En ligne], Vol. II | 2005, mis en ligne le 21 septembre 2007, consulté le 05 janvier 2017. http://champ penal.revues.org/2322.doi:10.4000/champpenal.2322.

Wyatt, Rachel. "Male Rape in U.S. Prisons: Are Conjugal Visits the Answer?" Case Western Reserve Journal of International Law 37 (2006): 579.

See also History of incarceration; LGBTQ prisoners; Privatization of intuitional and community corrections, including faith-based prisons; Prisoner rights; Prison Rape Elimination Act (PREA) (2003); Pennsylvania system of corrections; Rehabilitation; Prison violence; Prison overcrowding; Prison health care; Prison and jail systems; Medical model of offender treatment.

Crime victimization: primary and secondary

Definition: Primary victimization occurs when someone suffers as a direct or indirect result of the commission of a crime. Secondary victimization arises as an adverse consequence of crime victims' negative interactions with people and institutions in the aftermath of a crime.

Criminal justice issues: Civil rights and liberties; domestic violence; restorative justice; victims; women's issues

Significance: Victimization studies inform criminal justice processes, allow the system to respond better to the needs of victims, and promote judicial efficacy by sustaining victim involvement in the prosecution process.

Victimization occurs when a person suffers adverse consequences as a result of a criminal act perpetrated by an individual or an institution. A person can be victimized physically, financially, psychologically, mentally, and socially. According to Jennifer Truman and Rachel Morgan, in 2015, 0.98 percent of the U.S. population (approximately 2.7 million people) aged twelve and older suffered a violent victimization, and there were five million total violent victimizations that year. In that same year, 7.6 percent of all households suffered one or more property victimizations, and there were 14.6 million total property victimizations. Rates of victimization have been decreasing steadily since 1993, but there was an uptick in rape, sexual assault, intimate partner, and domestic violence in 2015. Data on victimization derive from several national, state, and local sources. The federal government relies primarily on the National Crime Victimization Survey (NCVS), which interviews a nationally representative sample of households. Not all victimizations are reported to police, so the NCVS describes a broader scope of victimizations that data from police departments or from the Federal Bureau of Investigation's Uniform Crime Report UCR).

Historically, men have been victimized at higher rates than women. However, in 2015 Truman and Morgan noted that trend reversed, with a victimization rate of 21.1 percent among women and 15.7 percent among men. Adolescents suffer victimization more often than other age groups; people sixty-five and older have the lowest rates of victimization. There appears to be an inverse relationship between poverty and victimization. The lower the household income, the higher the victimization rate. Persons who identify their race as Other have the highest victimization rates, followed by Black, White, and Hispanic. Finally, persons who are married or widowed have the lowest victimization rates. People who are separated or divorced have the highest victimization rates.

Victimization is one component of victimology, which is the study of the relationships among victims, offenders, the criminal justice system, and society. Victimization focuses on the experience of the people impacted by the crime. Victimization studies emerged in Europe after World War II and gained traction in the United States in the 1970's. Since then, legal and social services professionals consistently and increasingly have succeeded in implementing reforms to respond to victimization and its consequences. There is now a federally recognized Crime Victim Bill of Rights, and victims have the constitutionally protected right to provide victim impact statements during trial and at sentencing (*Payne v. Tennessee*).

Secondary victimization arises when crime victims experience negative impacts from their contact with social services, criminal justice systems, and others with whom they interact in relation to investigation and prosecution of the underlying crime. Secondary victimization is not a product of the initial injury or crime. Instead, it is a product of institutions' and individuals' reactions to crime victims. Examples include victim blaming, medical personnels' indifference to pain and shame associated with certain forensic tests, stigmatization, and insensitivity of medical and mental health professionals who work with persons suffering from post-traumatic stress. Victims and family members also may suffer secondary victimization through the cumbersome criminal justice process. These alienating experiences take many forms: Lengthy legal proceedings protract victims' suffering and delay recovery. Victims and witnesses lose income and time when they must testify. Justice professionals fail to acknowledge the impact of the crime upon family members. Police, investigators, and medical personnel behave callously to friends and family of injured victims. Schools ignore or miss signs of child abuse. Doctors overlook signs of spousal abuse. Coroners delay or deny access to victims' bodies. Therapists, social workers, or clergy attempt to facilitate reconciliation before the victim is ready. Secondary victimization can arise procedurally, as well. Victims and witnesses report that lack of notice of hearing dates, unexplained delays in proceedings, and poor communication about the substance and meaning of legal terms all contribute to secondary victimization. It can occur with any crime, and secondary victimization entails critical implications for individuals' well-being as well as the institutional integrity of the criminal justice system.

Scientific understandings of secondary victimization first gained prominence in relation to the experiences of victims of sexual assault and domestic violence. Research originating in the 1970's and continuing through today reveals that certain investigative practices and rules of evidence exacerbate rape victims' suffering by subjecting them to police who historically discounted their reports; cross examinations that made them justify whether they "resisted enough" and social stigmatization if they dressed or acted in a way that allegedly could have provoked the assaults. Secondary victimization with all crimes, but particularly with those involving sexual assault, frequently manifests when the victim and defendant abused substances contemporaneous with the original assault and when the offender and victim had a prior relationship.

The problem of secondary victimization related to sexual assault captured national attention when a woman who was raped by a Stanford University swimmer released her poignant victim impact statement describing the indignities and mistreatment she suffered during the investigation and prosecution of the crime perpetrated against her. In the wake of that letter, and through the efforts of another rape victim, Congress passed the Sexual Assault Victims' Bill of Rights in 2016 to address some practices that exacerbate secondary victimization.

Research also documents that secondary victimization can cause greater injury than the original crime. Problems with procedural due process and fairness erode victims' and witnesses' faith in the justice system. Secondary victimization causes individual as well as institutional injury. Victims and witnesses who lose faith in the system are less likely to participate in legal proceedings in the future. They are less willing to report crime or to provide evidence, and they display increased apathy towards crime and prosecution.

The term secondary victimization often is confused with the distinct phenomenon of revictimization, which refers to the statistically documented likelihood that crime victims have an increased risk of being victims of crime again, either contemporaneous with the first victimization or in years later. Revictimization most often occurs with domestic violence and survivors of child abuse who later experience violent relationships. Revictimization also may arise in relation to community factors, such as living in high crime communities or participating in high risk activities.

Anne S. Douds

Further Reading
Englebrecht, C., D. T. Mason, and M. J. Adams. "The Experiences of Homicide Victims' Families with the Criminal Justice System: An Exploratory Study." *Violence and* 29, no. 3 (2014): 407-21.
Groenhuijsen, M. S., and R. M. Letschert. "Secondary Victimization and the Media: An International and Comparative Perspective." In *Establishing Victimology*, 205-12. Germany: Hochschule Niederrheim, 2014.
National Institutes of Justice. Victims and Victimization. http://www.nij.gov/topics/victims-victimization/pages/welcome.aspx. Sickmund, M., and C. Puzzanchera. *Juvenile Offenders and Victims: 2014 National Report*. Pittsburgh: National Center for Juvenile Justice, 2014.
Truman, Jennifer L, and Rachel E. Morgan. Criminal Victimization 2014. Bureau of Justice Statistics. www.bjs.gov/content/pub/pdf/cv15.pdf.

See also National Crime Victimization Survey; Uniform Crime Reports; Victim impact statements; Victimization theories; Victimology; Victims services.

"Dark figure of crime"

Definition: This term refers to the crimes that are unknown to the police, usually because they were not reported by the victim or a witness to the crime.
Criminal justice issues: Crime statistics; criminology; technology
Significance: The dark figure of crime represents a threat to the validity of reported crime data; data that are commonly relied upon by crime analysts, criminologists and the media.

It is unknown how many crimes occur each year in an area or jurisdiction, but there are crime statistics that are used to provide criminal justice officials with estimates of the crime problem. Crime reported to the police is the most relied-upon crime statistic to date in the United States. This measure is generally considered a superior estimate of crime to arrest data because very small percentages of some crimes (burglary, theft, etc.) end in arrest, and because changes in arrests in an area can be highly influenced by the arrest polices or strategies in an area. For instance, if a police department creates a drug task force with a protocol to remove drug dealers from an area, drug dealing arrests will likely increase, but, the actual amount of drug dealing may have remained the same or even decreased.

Crimes reported to the police are the favored crime statistic by most crime analysts and criminologists because a higher percentage of crimes are reported to the police than end in arrest, and because they are less influenced by police policies. But, there are also drawbacks in relying on crimes that are reported to police as an estimate of crime. Crimes not reported to police, that is, the dark figure of crime, are perhaps the most significant threat to the validity of this crime measure. The National Crime Victimization Survey polls household occupants about their crime victimization in the past year and includes questions about whether respondents reported their crime to the police. This survey has found that the majority of crimes are not reported to the police.

The suspected size of the dark figure of crime raises concerns about the reliance in criminal justice on reported crime data. Indeed, crime analysts who find that burglary reports have increased in a given section of town have to be wary that other factors might be present that might have increased reports of burglaries rather than the actual volume of burglary.

Similarly, comparing reported crimes across cities assumes that each city reports a similar percentage of crime, so that if one city reports 35 percent of burglaries that occur within its city, other cities report a similar percentage. If cities report substantially different percentages of crimes, reported crime data lose validity as a tool used to compare crime across cities. This problem exists for any comparison made across aggregate units.

There are a number of suspected reasons for the dark figure of crime. For instance, some victims of crime may fear retaliation should they report crime. Victims who are on the fringe of criminal activity themselves may not want to involve law enforcement in their lives despite the damage caused by their victimization. Other victims may have low confidence in the police in their area and believe that they are simply wasting their time by reporting their victimization to the police. Moreover, witnesses to crime may be indifferent to their community and may not want to get involved to aid the crime problem in an area in which they have no desire to live in the future. If all or some of these factors are different from one city to the next, then it is likely that each city reports a different percentage of the crime that occurs within its jurisdiction.

Criminal justice personnel and criminal justice analysts have not ignored the dark figure of crime and have made some attempts to counteract this problem. In fact, the National Crime Victimization Survey was created in part as a way to measure crime without the restraints of the dark figure of crime. Its critics, however, believe that the shortcomings of this crime statistic outweigh its avoidance of the dark figure of crime. Law enforcement has also attempted to reduce the dark figure of crime through community policing efforts that seek to increase community participation and their reporting of crime. The effectiveness of these efforts in improving crime reporting is still under examination.

Brion Sever

Further Reading
Gove, Walter, Michael Hughes, and Michael Geerken. "Are Uniform Crime Reports a Valid Indicator of the Index Crimes? An Affirmative Answer with Minor Qualifications." *Criminology* 23 (1985): 451-502.
Levitt, Steven. "The Relationship between Crime Reporting and Police Implications for the Use of Uniform Crime Reports." *Journal of Quantitative Criminology* 14 (1998): 61-81.
Murphy, K., and J. Barkworth. *Victim Willingness to Report Crime to the Police, 1992-2000.* Washington, D.C.: U.S. Department of Justice, Office of Justice Programs, 2003. NCJ 195710. http://www.bjs.gov/index.cfm?ty=pbdetail&iid=1142.
Nicksa, S. "Bystander's Willingness to Report Theft, Physical Assault and Sexual Assault: The Impact of Gender, Anonymity, and the Relationship with the Offender." *Journal of Interpersonal Violence* 29 (2014): 217-36.
Ranapurwala, Shabbar, Mark Berg, and Carri Casteel. "Reporting Crime Victimizations to the Police and the Incidence of Future Victimizations: A Longitudinal Study." *PloS ONE* 11, no. 7 (2016): e0160072. doi:10.1371/journal.pone.0160072.
Turner, Ken, and Klaus Von Heusinger. "The Dark Figure of Sexual Offending: New Evidence from Federal Sex Offenders." *Journal of Clinical Psychology* 6 (2011): 3-15.

See also Crime; Crime index; Criminology; National Crime Victimization Survey; Uniform Crime Reports.

Elderly prisoners

Definition: Prison inmates who require special attention because of their advanced ages
Criminal justice issues: Medical and health issues; Prisons; Rehabilitation
Significance: Aging prison inmates present challenges to corrections administrators that go beyond the normal issues of custody and control in confinement settings.

With the advent of public policy encouraging longer sentences and the aging of the baby boomer population born shortly after World War II, the number and percentage of elderly inmates confined in American prisons and local jails has increased dramatically. The special challenges presented by elderly inmates reflect similar experience in the mainstream of American life. Those who are confined at older ages or those who grow old in confinement require different health care systems, different recreational and rehabilitation programs, special housing, different hygiene care, and different diets. They even have different preferences for the items sold in prison commissaries. Although free society is attuned to the interests of senior citizens outside prisons, most correctional institutions are struggling to meet the needs of elderly incarcerated persons.

One of the greatest challenges to corrections officials is providing adequate health care to aging inmates. Deteriorating health is a natural function of aging and elderly inmates face the same debilitating illnesses as those on the outside. Moreover, inmate health is typically worsened by prisoners' use of drugs, alcohol, tobacco, and other manifestations of unhealthy lifestyles. Correctional

An elderly convict. (Library of Congress)

administrators are required by law to provide the same standards of health care to inmates that free members of society expect, but they often lack sufficient resources to deal with serious and lingering diseases, such as heart conditions, AIDS, cancer, and dementia.

Debilitating long-term medical conditions frequently require concerted and expensive medical care to preserve life or provide an acceptable quality of life. Some prison systems have developed hospice care inside their facilities to care for terminally ill inmates. Their goal is to keep such patients comfortable and allow them to come to terms with their coming deaths. In some prison systems, administrators seek compassionate releases from incarceration for terminally ill inmates.

Inmate-classification systems, which assign housing, programs, and privileges to inmates, make the safety of inmates a priority. Such systems face unique challenges in classifying aging inmates. On one hand, most elderly inmates are physically weaker than younger inmates; however, some possess criminal sophistication that allows them to continue to present serious dangers to other inmates, staff, and prison guards. Older and more sophisticated inmates are often respected and renowned prison gang members who control the activities of fellow inmates. Because of the danger such inmates can present, they may be confined in the most secure settings that the prisons have. On the other hand, elderly inmates who are serving time for their first offenses may need to be protected from younger inmates who prey on the weak. Thus, no single formula exists for classifying aging inmates.

Older inmates often have special dietary and recreational needs. They may not be capable of playing common recreational games and need alternative exercise programs to maintain health and fitness. Human metabolism slows down as people age, so elderly inmates may require smaller meals with different food values. Even the range of items sold at inmate commissaries may need to be expanded to offer snacks and hygiene items preferred by aging inmates.

Michael Hackett

Further Reading
Allen, H. E., C. E. Simonsen, and E. J. Latessa. *Corrections in America*. 10th ed. Upper Saddle River: Pearson/Prentice-Hall, 2004.
California Department of Corrections. *Older Inmates: The Impact of an Aging Inmate Population on the Correctional System: An Internal Planning Document for the California Department of Corrections*. Sacramento: California Department of Corrections, 1999.
Hackett, Michael. *The Impact of an Aging Inmate Population in Local Detention Facilities by the Year 2003*. Sacramento: California Commission on Peace Officer's Standards and Training Library, 1999.
Johnson, R. *Hard Time: Understanding and Reforming the Prison*. 3d ed. Belmont: Wadsworth, 2002.
Leigey, Margaret E. "Growing Old in Prison" *The Forgotten Men*. New Brunswick: Rutgers UP, 2015. 131-159. Critical Issues in Crime and Society.

See also Prison and jail systems; Prison health care; Prison industries; Prison overcrowding; Prison violence; Work camps; Prison inmate subculture; Prison/prisoner classification systems; Prisoner rights.

Forestry camps

Definition: Minimum-security facilities in which low-risk adult and juvenile offenders work with local, state, and federal forestry departments to maintain public forests

Criminal justice issues: Prisons; punishment; rehabilitation

Significance: Forestry camps have become an attractive alternative to prison incarceration for both adult and juvenile low-risk offenders. Not only are they less costly to operate than prisons, they also provide valuable services to states and the nation as a whole and are often effective in providing rehabilitative training for inmates.

Forestry camps are therapeutic alternative correctional facilities and programs in which inmates work as members of fire squads, create fire breaks, thin forests, participate in reforestation projects, assist local communities with forestry beautification projects, and work in such support positions as food preparation and housekeeping.

Forestry camp programs began during the Depression years of the 1930's with the implementation of the medical model of rehabilitation in an effort to alleviate prison overcrowding. Usually located in state and federal forests, the camps provided cheap labor to forestry departments experiencing budget shortages due to the depressed economy. By the 1940's, the camps were becoming popular sites for placement of offenders convicted of evading the military draft. At that time, camp inmates were required to perform hard labor, while paying their states fees for the privilege of working in camps instead of being sent to prisons. The rehabilitative characteristics of most forestry camps included behavior-modification programs based on individual counseling and group therapy.

Inmates of forestry camps have always been mostly low-risk adult and juvenile offenders. In the beginning, adults convicted of lesser property crimes or nearing the ends of prison sentences after proving themselves trustworthy were the most likely candidates for forestry camps. By the 1950's, some states were beginning to experiment with forestry camps for juvenile offenders. However, it was not until 1974 that forestry camps were recognized nationally as alternative punishments for low-risk juveniles. This change was a direct result of the Juvenile Justice and Delinquency Prevention Act of that same year.

Forestry camps are now so diverse that it is difficult to describe them in general terms. For example, some camps have military-type boot camp facilities, while others reflect the more relaxed therapeutic medical model. In some facilities, inmates engage in hard labor, while in others they participate in activities such as gardening classes taught by members of gardening clubs.

Forestry camps were originally designed only for adult men. Camps for juveniles opened later, and now forestry camps exist for female offenders. One such program is located in the Federal Bureau of Prisons' facility for women at Bryan, Texas. Based on the boot camp model, that program began during the early 1990's. Women in the program are a mixture of volunteers from the general prison population and women who enter the program through plea agreements.

Some of the positive accomplishments of forestry camps include the protection of habitats for an endangered woodpecker species in the Sam Houston National Forest, clearing brush for the public park at the George Bush Presidential Library, and maintenance of public parks at Lake Summerville in Bryan, Texas.

Elizabeth H. McConnell

Further Reading

Rojek, J. E., and G. G. Jensen. *Exploring Delinquency: Causes and Control.* Los Angeles: Roxbury Publishing, 1996.

Selke, W. A. *Prisons in Crisis.* Bloomington: Indiana University Press, 1993.

See also Boot camps; Prisons, Federal Bureau of; Community-based corrections; Pleas; Prison escapes; Rehabilitation; Work camps.

Good time

Definition: Reduction of prison sentences based on good behavior or participation in some kind of program by inmates

Criminal justice issues: Legal terms and principles; prisons; rehabilitation

Significance: Inmates may reduce the lengths of time they serve in prison based on their good behavior. This policy has the additional effect of freeing up needed space in penal institutions.

Good time allows correctional officials to reduce days, months, and years from inmates' sentences if the inmates behave well in prison. Correctional officials utilize the policy of good time to maintain institutional order and to reduce crowding. The first such statute was passed in New York in 1817, implementing good time at Newgate prison in Greenwich Village. The statute permitted a sentence reduction of up to 25 percent for first-time offenders.

There are different forms of good time. Statutory good time is given automatically when inmates serve their time without incident. Meritorious good time is given to inmates who perform exceptional acts. Earned good time allows inmates to receive time off their sentence for participation in some kind of work, education, or rehabilitation program. The amount of good time varies by state. Usually, five to ten days can be accrued for behaving well for one month. In some states, when an inmate earns a certain amount of good time, say ninety days, the time can be vested. Then the days cannot be taken away for poor behavior. In some states, good time is subtracted from the minimum sentence. As a result of good time, some inmates are eligible for parole before the minimum sentence is served.

Good time is not a right of all inmates. The policy must be state-created, and some states eliminated good time during the "get-tough-on-crime" era. Wisconsin has adopted "bad time" to allow time to be added, delaying an inmate's release date. There has been controversy about good time. The pressures in favor of increasing the amount of good time a prisoner can earn come from overcrowded prison populations and court decrees ordering states to place limits on prisoners. It is relatively straightforward for a legislature to shave days off prison sentences by increasing good-time credits that can be earned. This type of reform avoids the negative publicity that can accompany a parole release. When good-time credits lead to very early releases, however, the policy receives criticism as being "soft" on crime, and some believe it creates the possibility of placing the community in danger.

Harry R. Dammer

Further Reading

Abadinsky, Howard. *Probation and Parole*. 7th ed. Upper Saddle River, N.J.: Prentice-Hall, 2000.

Glaze, Lauren, and Seri Pella. *Probation and Parole in the United States, 2003*. Washington, D.C.: Bureau of Justice Statistics, 2004.

Petersilia, Joan, ed. *Community Corrections: Probation, Parole, and Intermediate Sanctions*. New York: Oxford University Press, 1998.

Travis, Jeremy, and Sarah Lawrence. *Beyond the Prison Gates: The State of Parole in America*. Washington, D.C.: Urban Institute, 2002.

See also Indeterminate sentencing; Pardons; Prison escapes; Prison overcrowding; Rehabilitation.

Halfway houses

Definition: Use of supervised living arrangements, usually in urban areas, as an alternative to prisons
Criminal justice issues: Probation and pretrial release; punishment; rehabilitation
Significance: The use of halfway houses as an alternative to incarceration is on the rise.

Halfway houses have many different forms and treatment philosophies and serve different populations. Offenders on probation and those facing potential prison sentences are referred to as "halfway in," while offenders planning to be released into the community soon after serving prison time are referred to as "halfway out."

A structured living environment is provided to halfway-in offenders in the attempt to remove bad influences that may lead to more criminal behavior. Residents are held accountable for their time. Frequently, they are required to work or at least look for a job, be drug free, obey curfew hours, and perform duties around the halfway house. Offenders create a life for themselves in a community, but they are also held accountable for their activities and are supervised under specific house rules. In addition to room and board, they are frequently given vocational training, treatment for substance abuse, anger management therapy, and other assistance.

Leaving prison may lead to the so-called revolving door of recidivism because former convicts often lack social support and ties to conventional society. For the halfway out, halfway houses are successful at offering support for individuals lacking family and friends willing to support and sponsor them as they return from prison.

Halfway house programs are frequently criticized for coddling inmates and for punishing them too lightly for their crimes. Observers frequently criticize the nature of room and board, which is less institutional than that of a jail, and the benefits offenders receive of free education, vocational training, and health care.

Most often, halfway houses are located in urban settings where there are increased access to public transportation, flexible job opportunities, social services, and health care facilities. In order to keep costs down, the homes are usually located in lower-income neighborhoods. Residents of neighboring communities are frequently concerned that the residents of halfway houses are criminal offenders living in neighborhoods already facing significant crime and declining property values. The phrase "not in my backyard" has been popularized to describe a situation in which citizens see the overall benefit of specific programs such as halfway houses but claim that those programs should exist in some other community.

Zoning boards and town councils frequently attempt to stifle the growth of local halfway houses by refusing accommodations for building changes or creating rules that limit the number of unrelated individuals residing in one residence. This leads to communities getting several smaller operations housing five to eight people instead of a larger operation with many people under one roof.

It is difficult to assess the success or failure of halfway houses as a general concept because there is a great deal of variability among the services offered, types of staffing, rules, location of the building, and general community support for the house residents. This variability results in ample support for and against the development of these facilities. However, the number of halfway houses is expected to increase because of a number of factors including substantial overcrowding in prisons and jails, cost savings of halfway houses over traditional incarceration, the popular acceptance of alternative sanctions for nonviolent offenders, and the promise of greater reintegration into the community.

John C. Kilburn, Jr.

Further Reading
Clear, Todd, and Harry Dammer. *The Offender and the Community.* Belmont, Calif.: Wadsworth, 1999.
Petersilia, Joan, ed. *Community Corrections: Probation, Parole, and Intermediate Sanctions.* New York: Oxford University Press, 1998.

See also Community-based corrections; Criminal justice system; House arrest; "Not-in-my-backyard" attitudes; Prison escapes; Prison industries; Prison overcrowding; Recidivism; Rehabilitation; Work camps; Work-release programs.

History of incarceration

Definition: Events over time in the historical evolution of U.S. incarceration
Criminal justice issues: Criminal justice issues: Prisons; punishment; rehabilitation; women's issues
Significance: Watershed incidents in the development of incarceration as punishment in contrast to incarceration for punishment in the United States.

In ancient times, confinement was used to hold offenders until trial or until a sentence (usually some form of corporal punishment) was delivered. The beginning of modern prison incarceration can be found in sixteenth-century Britain. Although corporal punishment or banishment was the preferred method of punishment, houses of correction were built in which offenders charged with minor crimes lived and had to work under guard supervision to repay the debt. Workhouses were similar but were used to house the poor, who also had to work under guard supervision. In addition, jails were developed to detain suspects until trial.

Criminal justice reformers in Britain incited the movement toward the use of prisons for punishment as alternatives to the brutality of corporal punishment. These reformers argued that the punishment should be proportional to the offense, or in other words, the punishment must fit the crime. Also, the reformers protested the appalling conditions in the jails and workhouses, as well as on prison ships, where prisoners awaiting banishment to Australia were forced to live in the hulks of ships that never left the dock. The demise of the use of corporal punishment was set in motion by the reformers, and prisons were built. However, the conditions in the early prisons were still deplorable because of rampant disease, filth, and overcrowding.

Prisons did not exist in Britain's American colonies originally. Jails primarily were used to hold debtors or confine offenders until the trial or sentence of punishment. The early jails in the colonies were similar to their British counterparts as overcrowded depositories for disease. Replacing corporal punishment with confinement was an idea first postulated by William Penn, a Quaker. The founder of Pennsylvania argued that offenders should be punished by using confinement. Penn passed the Great Law of 1692, which abolished corporal punishment, except in the case of murder, and mandated the building of prisons. A visionary, Penn established prisons nearly a century earlier than Britain and the other U.S. colonies. However, the Great Law was repealed one day after his death in 1718.

Corporal punishment continued to be the primary method of punishment through the American Revolution. The Constitution and the Bill of Rights, developed as a guide for the newly independent states, included many protections for individuals suspected of crimes. The emphasis on protection from the abuses of government was influenced by the abuses the colonists had suffered under Britain's rule. The concept of the penitentiary, based on the work of William Penn, was developed and implemented by the Quakers in Pennsylvania. These penitentiaries would allow the offenders the time and solitude to repent for the crimes, to pay penance through manual labor, and to reform. The first prison under this new system was the Walnut Street Jail, opened in Philadelphia in 1790. The Walnut Street Jail served as a model for the prisons built in Pennsylvania in the 1820's.

By 1830, Western Penitentiary was opened in Pittsburgh and Eastern Penitentiary in Philadelphia. These prisons followed the philosophy of the Quakers' penitentiary and were referred to as the Pennsylvania system or the separate system. A similar system, minus the complete isolation of the inmates, was employed in the Auburn Prison opened in New York in 1817. The slightly different system became known as the Auburn system, the New York system, or the congregate system. Both types of systems operated under the assumption that crime was a result of problems in the external environment.

Eventually, the Pennsylvania system was abandoned because of multiple factors, including the financial burden of operating a prison in which inmates were individually celled. The Auburn system became the model for the American penitentiary until after the Civil War. A large prison reform movement protesting the squalid prison conditions gained momentum after the war. In part because of the prison reform movement, a prison emphasizing rehabilitation was opened in Elmira, New York, during the late 1870's. The Elmira [Elmira system] Reformatory adopted indeterminate sentencing practices whereby prison officials could determine how much of a sentence the inmate served by using reward systems for good behavior and work or educational achievements.

The Elmira model, or reformatory model, gained popularity, and by the 1920's nearly every state had adopted the system. The focus on rehabilitation continued, and new treatment programs continued to be implemented in American prisons until after World War II. By the 1950's, the number of prisoners was increasing, and the prison system experienced a wave of riots, thought to be caused by deplorable prison conditions. During the 1960's and 1970's, several landmark Supreme Court and federal court cases passed legislation that allowed certain prisoner rights and mandated improved prison conditions.

The 1970's sparked a shift in penal philosophy from an emphasis on rehabilitation to one of deterrence and incapacitation. Indeterminate sentencing was replaced with determinate sentencing systems in which the parole boards could no longer release an inmate before the sentence expired. The shift in philosophy was influenced by published research studies claiming that not one of the rehabilitation programs in place in U.S. prisons actually reduced recidivism or crime rates.

The shift from rehabilitation to deterrence and incapacitation marked the "get tough on crime" era that began during the 1970's and continued through the end of the twentieth century. The increase in availability of crack cocaine in the 1980's ensured that a continual supply of drug offenders filtered into the prison system through sentencing reforms resulting from the so-called war on drugs. These reforms included mandatory minimums for possession of certain amounts of drugs, "truth-in-sentencing" laws that forced offenders to serve the full sentence, and "three-strikes" laws that gave life sentences to inmates receiving convictions for a third felony. The impact on the prison system was profound, resulting in overcrowded conditions and millions of dollars toward new prison construction as more prisoners were incarcerated and for longer periods of time.

Women's Prisons

Until the reformatory era of the 1870's, prisons were not segregated by gender, and abuses were common. During the late nineteenth century, three states (Indiana, New York, and Massachusetts) opened separate prison facilities for women, which were also staffed by women. By 1975, thirty-four states had opened separate facilities for women. In the states that did not have a separate facility, women and men were segregated, or the state contracted with private companies or other states to house its women inmates. In 1925, the first federal prison for women opened in Alderson, West Virginia.

The early prisons for women followed the cottage system design, which embodied the rehabilitation philosophy of the late nineteenth century. The facilities were operated by women staff, and the inmates' time of incarceration was spent learning domestic skills. When the popularity of reformatory prisons waned, a college campus design replaced the cottage system. Although these prisons offered vocational training programs, the programs were gender-specific. For example, the inmates learned job skills that would translate into secretarial positions upon release. One controversial experiment was New York's operation of a shock incarceration camp for female prisoners in the boot camp style.

Historically, women made up a small percentage of the incarcerated population. However, this number continues to rise, mainly due to the overall increase in incarceration—even for nonviolent offenders—due to the War on Drugs. Many states have only one facility for women, which houses inmates from every classification. In the modern prison, the vocational skill training often includes training considered to be traditionally male-oriented, such as firefighting. An administrative and medical issue in prisons for women is that of inmate pregnancies. Some women enter prison pregnant, and the institution must provide specialized care for these inmates. Some prisons have allowed infants to remain with the incarcerated mother for a brief period of time after the delivery.

Tammy L. Castle

Further Reading

Allen, H. E., C. E. Simonsen, and E. J. Latessa. *Corrections in America*. 10th ed. Upper Saddle River, N.J.: Pearson/Prentice-Hall, 2004.

Gido, R. L., and T. Alleman, eds. *Turnstile Justice: Issues in American Corrections*. 2nd ed. Upper Saddle River, N.J.: Pearson/Prentice-Hall, 2002.

Herivel, T., and P. Wright, eds. *Prison Nation: The Warehousing of America's Poor*. New York: Routledge, 2003.

Johnson, Robert. *Hard Time: Understanding and Reforming the Prison*. 3rd ed. Belmont, Calif.: Wadsworth, 2002.

Mays, L. G., and T. L. Winfree. *Contemporary Corrections*. 2nd ed. Belmont, Calif.: Wadsworth, 2002.

Owen, B. *In the Mix: Struggle and Survival in a Women's Prison*. Albany: State University of New York Press, 1998.

"The Prison Crisis." *American Civil Liberties Union*. ACLU, 2015. Web. 7 Dec. 2015.

Santos, M. G. *About Prison*. Belmont, Calif.: Wadsworth, 2004.

Schmalleger, Frank. *Criminal Justice: A Brief Introduction*. Boston: Pearson, 2014.

Scott, David Gordon. *Why Prison?* Cambridge: Cambridge UP, 2015.

See also Auburn system; Boot camps; Bureau of prisons; Chain gangs; Elderly prisoners; Preventive detention; Prison escapes; Prison guards; Prison industries; Prison overcrowding; Prison violence; Supermax prisons; Walnut Street Jail; *Ashker v. Brown* (2016); Conjugal Visitation; Pennsylvania system of corrections; Female offenders; Medical model of offender treatment; Parole boards; Prison Rape Elimination Act (PREA) (2003); Prison inmate subculture; Prisoner rights; Privatization of institutional and community corrections, including faith-based prisons; Realignment (PSR) policy; *Roper v. Simmons* (2005); Scandinavia's prison experience; Security Threat Groups (STGs)/Prison gangs; Technology's transformative effect; LGBTQ prisoners; History of incarceration; Prisoner classification systems.

Homeless women and victimization

Definition: A homeless person is an individual without permanent housing who may live on the streets; stay in a shelter, mission, single room occupancy facilities, abandoned building or vehicle; or in any other unstable or nonpermanent situation. Victimization due to domestic violence is an asymmetrical interpersonal relationship that is abusive, painful, destructive, parasitical, and unfair. While a crime is in progress, offenders temporarily force their victims to play roles (almost as if following a script) that mimic the dynamics between predator and prey; winner and looser; victor and vanquished; and even master and slave.

Criminal justice issues: Domestic violence; victims, medical and health issues; mental disorders; women's issues

Significance: Homeless women report a higher rate of victimization than both non-homeless women and homeless men. Homeless women's "routine" day-to-day activities expose them to potential offenders and victimization risks such as physical and sexual violence and exploitation which, cyclically, are the main precipitating riskfactors for homelessness among women. This paper will elucidate a connection between early-age victimization, that is, domestic violence and adulthomelessness through the unique experiences of two homeless women. These women suffered victimization and witnessed domestic violence as children and then suffered negative consequences of victimization, self-victimization, experiencing domestic violence, adult medical and health issues, mental disorders, and ultimately homelessness.

Research indicates women who are victimized early in life establish a pattern of behavior that contributes to adult vulnerability of risky experiences including committing criminal offenses, victimization, self-victimization, and becoming homeless. Those types of behaviors are apparent in the behaviors that youth exhibit during adolescence. Women that witness domestic violence in their own home, as youth, have an increased risk to become victims and self-victimizing. In order to escape abusive home environment, young girls or women may run away from or move out at a young age. This behavior of running away or moving out before reaching eighteen years of age amplifies an increased women's rate to become victims or victimized. Women who run away from home are at an increased risk for victimization due to seeking shelter with any available person. This starts the pattern for women to become involved in unhealthy romantic relationships. The pattern once again repeats itself for these women to become victimized and even experience domestic violence, either from their romantic partners or on the streets.

Though an ultimate assertion cannot be reached about the connection between childhood abuse and engaging in risky behaviors, homeless women who experienced abuse, due to domestic violence, when younger are prone to substance abuse, exploitation, mental illness (depression), and medical and health issues, which exacerbate their homeless state. This connection between the early age of witnessing domestic violence and its subsequent effects and adult homelessness can be exemplified through the unique experiences of many women who suffered victimization as children and then suffered negative consequences of becoming domestic violence victims, self-victimization, that is alcohol and drug dependency, medical and health issues, mental disorders (depression), and ultimately homelessness later in life.

This strong association between homelessness, domestic violence, victimization, self-victimization, and committing offenses is illustrated in the following two different cases of women's lives at the agency St. Vincent de Paul/Ozanam Manor located in Phoenix, Arizona. Indicated in these narratives is that women show a greater incidence of substance abuse, and past physical and sexual abuse appears to be a strong correlation between such experiences that contribute to homelessness, criminal offending, victimization, and self-victimization. Both women and their experiences reveal that a violent, dysfunctional household creates an early sense of homelessness that is nurtured by witnessing domestic violence, absent family members, drinking, dropping out of school, forming relationships with abusers, out-of-wedlock children, working at menial jobs, and physical and mental illness.

Jennifer became a victim early in life. Raised in a blue-collar household, her father was a miner, whom she described as being funny and kind. Jennifer suffered abuse at the hands of her mother and uncle. Her father complicated the situation by knowing abuse was occurring, but minimized it, at times avoiding it by not coming home and thus failing to intercede. Jennifer's mother, possibly mentally ill, both verbally and physically abused her and Jennifer's father as well; she would hear fights in the night, and at times flee to her grandmother's house. The haven of her grandmother's house was then destroyed when her uncle sexually abused her there. Jennifer's teenage years were marked by her father's unemployment in the advent of a strike, which finally caused him to leave to find work. Her parents separated, and Jennifer dropped out of school and left home at sixteen, at which time she began to self-victimize. Though she hoped to support herself, and help her siblings back home, she started abusing drugs. Her siblings began to show signs of their own problems; one brother would eventually commit suicide, one died of acquired immunodeficiency syndrome (AIDS), and another went to prison for dealing drugs. Jennifer, at this time employed, had a romantic relationship with a man who also abused her. By this man she had a baby, whom she raised on her own, while working three jobs. Her daughter revealed signs of mental illness and had violent tendencies. Added to this history was a violent event: She was carjacked, drugged, and raped. At the time she was interviewed she was facing further medical and health issues. Jennifer had become disabled from torn ligaments in her foot, and had entered a domestic violence shelter after being unable to pay rent. She suffered homelessness at one point, while, living in her car for five weeks and cleaning up at the Quick Trip gas station. At the time of the interview, she was living in Ozanam Manor, and working as a cab driver.

Alisa's story is similar, being victimized due to domestic violence when a child, both physically and sexually, and not having family members to help or provide sufficient help. Alisa was verbally and physically abused by her father, for which she in some ways takes the blame in that her mother passed away six months after she was born. Her sexual abuse was not by a family member, but a friend's father who interrupted her and his son's playing together to throw them into the back of a truck, telling them to take their clothes off, and he sprayed them with a hose. Rather than reporting this incident, she remained silent as she did not feel loved nor protected at home. Her father being unable to support them adequately further stressed Alisa's home life, and he verbally and physically abused his second wife and his stepdaughter. Alisa began to self-victimize when she turned to drinking and marijuana to deal with her stressful home situation, and at sixteen moved out. She was swiftly involved with an accident, and when her brother, a firefighter, attempted to take her home, her father would not accept her. Alisa moved in with a boyfriend and attempted to finish her education. The boyfriend also proved abusive behaviors and she moved back in with her father, bringing home a daughter from another relationship. Being with her father aggravated her depression. Her mental health was then complicated by medical and health issues as she has suffered several strokes. In Ozanam Manor she is confined to a wheelchair.

In studies conducted on large populations, and in these two particular cases, the links between being victimized in a dysfunctional family environment (usually complicated with sexual abuse), leads to engaging in systematic risky behaviors: leaving home before maturity is achieved, and subsequent experiences with abusive boyfriends, drug use, having children out of wedlock, domestic violence, victimization, self-victimization, medical and health disorders, and mental illness. Women who are caught in this cycle of emotional and physical violence due to domestic violence seem to have their futures destroyed by others, a conclusion to which they seem to helplessly contribute to by their own actions. Their own actions stem into this cycle by refusing to leave their abusers.

Danielle J. Covolo
Francisco J. Alatorre

Further Reading

Belknap J. *The Invisible Women.* 3rd ed. Wadsworth/Cengage Learning, 2007.

Cause A., M. Paradise, J. Ginzler, C. Embry, C. Morgan, Y. Lohr, and J. Theofelis. "The Characteristics and Mental Health of Homeless Adolescents. *Journal of Emotional and Behavioral Disorders* 8, no. 4 (2000): 230-39.

Charmaz, K. *Grounded Theory.* In *Contemporary Field Research*, edited by R.M. Emerson, 335-52. Long Grove, Ill.: Waveland Press, 2001.

Fischer, P. J. "Victimization and Homelessness: Cause and Effect." *New England Journal of Public Policy* 8, no. 1 (2007): 229.

Karmen, A. *Crime Victims: An Introduction of Criminology.* Wadsworth/Cengage Learning, 2013.

Taylor A. K., D. Hoyt, L. Whitbeck. "The Effects of Early Sexual Abuse on Later Sexual Victimization Among Female Homeless and Runaway Adolescents." *Journal of Interpersonal Violence* 15, no. 3 (2000): 235-50.

Xiaojin, C., K. A. Taylor, L. Whitbeck, and D. R. Hoyt. "Early Sexual Abuse, Street Adversity, and Drug Use among Female Homeless and Runaway Adolescents in the Midwest." *Journal of Drug Issues* 34, no. 1 (2004): 1-21.

See also Domestic violence; Mental illness; Victim Assistance Programs; Feminist criminology; Victimology; Crime victimization: Primary and secondary; Post-traumatic stress disorder; Victims services; Victim recovery stages; Victimization theories.

House arrest

House arrest can be used as a stand-alone sanction, however, it is commonly used in conjunction with adult probation and juvenile probation

Definition: Intermediate form of sanction that allows offenders to remain in their homes under specific restrictions

Criminal justice issues: Probation and pretrial release; Punishment; Sentencing

Significance: House arrests are an alternative to incarceration, one often used in order to help manage the strained resources of correctional facilities

House arrest is a punitive sanction that allows convicted offenders to remain in their homes instead of going to prison. There are three levels of house arrest: curfew, home detention, and home confinement. Specific restrictions are imposed at all three levels. Curfew, the mildest version of house arrest, is frequently used in the juvenile justice system and requires that the offender be home by a certain time each day. The next level, home detention, is more restrictive in that it limits the amount of time that offenders may be away from their homes and also dictates where they may go. For example, travel is usually prohibited except for that which involves work, medical treatment appointments, or church. The most restrictive level of house arrest is home incarceration, calling for offenders to remain at their homes the majority of the time, with allowances only to attend specific and limited appointments. For house arrest to be effective, there must be an organized and well-equipped system to monitor offenders. House arrest has been touted as an effective response to prison overcrowding by allowing nonviolent offenders and offenders convicted of minor offenses to serve their correctional time within their own community.

House arrest has also been considered an effective way to reduce the increasing costs of corrections. The average annual amount spent monitoring an offender on house arrest is typically significantly less than the cost to incarcerate an offender. In some court jurisdictions, certain expenses associated with house arrest are passed to the offender, making the financial aspect an attractive one to proponents of house arrest. Other benefits associated with house arrest extend beyond the offender and may positively affect the stability of the offender's family. Because the offender is allowed to maintain employment, that person is better able to contribute to the family's well-being.

Just as there are perceived benefits of using house arrest as an intermediate sanction, there are perceived problems. Although offenders may be ordered to be home daily by a prescribed time, opportunities exist for the offender to get around the mandate, particularly when telephone calls are used for tracking the offender's compliance. Also, offenders are often admonished to refrain from socializing with known felons, but this mandate is difficult to monitor and control when the offender is under house arrest. Difficulties also arise when the monitoring of offenders is contracted to outside vendors who use rotating staff who have little personal knowledge of the offender.

Tonya Y. Willingham

Further Reading

Del Carmen, A. *Corrections*. St. Paul: Coursewise, 2000. Print.

McShane, M., and W. Krause. *Community Corrections*. New York: Macmillan, 1993. Print.

Rackmill, S. J. "An Analysis of Home Confinement as a Sanction." *Federal Probation* 58.1 (1994): 45-53. Print.

Schenwar, Maya. "The Quiet Horrors of House Arrest, Electronic Monitoring, and Other Alternative Forms of Incarceration." *Mother Jones*. Mother Jones and the Foundation for Natl. Progress, 22 Jan. 2015. Web. 26 May 2016.

Tiberiu, Dutu. "House Arrest as a Preventive Measure." *Contemporary Readings in Law & Social Justice* 6.1 (2014): 558-62. Print.

See also Community-based corrections; Electronic surveillance; Halfway houses; Parole; Prison overcrowding; Probation, adult; Suspended sentences; Work camps; Prison and jail systems.

Incapacitation

Definition: Aim or rationale of punishment that seeks to control crime by rendering criminals unable, or less able, to commit crimes, such as by incarceration of the offenders

Criminal justice issues: Crime prevention; Legal terms and principles; Punishment

Significance: Incapacitation provides a justification for certain forms of punishment as well as a strategy for crime control.

"Incapacitation" refers to the idea that certain forms of punishment are effective means of reducing crime if they restrict the abilities and opportunities of criminals to commit crimes. For example, confining offenders in prison removes them from society and renders them unable to commit further crimes against the general public. Execution has the ultimate incapacitating effect. Even parole may help incapacitate criminals by limiting their movements and thus restricting their opportunities for committing crimes.

The nineteenth-century British utilitarian philosopher Jeremy Bentham discussed incapacitation in *An Introduction to the Principles and Morals of Legislation* (1789), a treatment of the ends of punishment. Bentham regarded the principal end of punishment as control of conduct, and he used the term "disablement" to refer to the effect of punishment on the offender's "physical power." This was contrasted with "reformation," which refers to the use of punishment to control conduct by influencing the offender's will, and with "example"—that is, deterrence—whereby punishment sets an example and thus controls the conduct of people besides the offender. Con-

Execution is the ultimate form of incapacitation. (Public domain, via Wikimedia Commons)

temporary discussions of the aims and effects of punishment follow Bentham, at least roughly, in distinguishing among reform or rehabilitation, incapacitation, and general deterrence by example or by threat of punishment.

Incapacitation is an expected, or at least hoped for, effect of punishment. Incapacitative effects, however, do not occur in two types of situations. The first is cases in which offenders would not have committed any additional crimes even if they had not been punished. The second is situations in which other individuals take the place of the incarcerated criminals, taking advantage of the opportunities that have opened. This often occurs in the case of criminal activity related to gangs, when the arrest and imprisonment of one member may not result in a decrease in crime. Other gang members or new recruits often fill the positions vacated by the arrest of fellow gang members.

Studies have not established that a strict incapacitation approach to crime control is likely to lead to a significant reduction in the rate of crime. Skeptics point to periods during which crime rates have risen despite increased use of imprisonment. Studies have yielded mixed estimates of any incapacitative effect, with some research projecting a slight increase in crime (4 or 5 percent) with a reduction in prison use. Other research has projected a substantial decrease in crime if the prison population were increased. There is some evidence that the effect of incapacitation varies with types of criminal behavior. Some criminologists have recommended a policy of selective incapacitation—for example, of "career criminals" or violent criminals. Some states have enacted laws imposing life sentences on persons convicted three times of violent or serious crimes; these are sometimes colloquially called "three strikes" laws.

Mario F. Morelli

Further Reading
Foucault, Michel. *Discipline and Punish: The Birth of the Prison.* Trans. Alan Sheridan. 1977. New York: Vintage, 1995. Print.
Garland, David. *Punishment and Modern Society: A Study in Social Theory.* Chicago: U of Chicago P, 1990. Print.
Honderich, Ted. *Punishment: The Supposed Justifications Revisited.* Rev. ed. Ann Arbor: Pluto, 2006. Print.
Zimring, Franklin E., and Gordon Hawkins. *Incapacitation: Penal Confinement and the Restraint of Crime.* New York: Oxford UP, 1995. Print.

See also Auburn system; Community-based corrections; Criminology; Deterrence; Just deserts; Mandatory sentencing; Psychological profiling; Punishment; Recidivism; Rehabilitation; Solitary confinement; Supermax prisons; Three-strikes laws; Pennsylvania system of corrections; Schools of criminology.

LGBTQ prisoners

Definition: Lesbian, Gay, Bisexual, Transgender, and Questioning (LGBTQ) prisoners are incarcerated individuals who do not identify as heterosexual. They are considered an at-risk group within the prison population.

Criminal justice issues: Civil rights and liberties; constitutional protections; federal law; medical and health issues; prisons

Significance: Lesbian, Gay, Bisexual, Transgender, and Questioning (LGBTQ) prisoners provide a unique challenge for the criminal justice system. Overall, prisoners who identify as LGBTQ are considered a vulnerable group, as they tend to encounter more harassment and mistreatment as compared to the non-LGBTQ prison population.

Because of issues of family rejection, homelessness, and overall discrimination, the LGBTQ population tends to have a higher rate of contact with the criminal justice system. According to a National Transgender Discrimination Survey, around 15 percent of those in juvenile detention facilities identify as LGBTQ, as compared to approximately 6 percent of the overall juvenile population. Almost 8 percent of adults in state or federal prisons identified as LGBTQ, which is double the percentage of nonincarcerated adults who identify as LGBTQ. Sixteen percent of adults who identify as transgender have served one or more prison terms.

Those who identify as LGBTQ and are incarcerated are a highly vulnerable population. They are at risk for abuse and maltreatment both by fellow prisoners as well as prison staff. A National Former Prisoner's Survey, published by the U.S. Department of Justice, reported that 39 percent of gay males reported being assaulted in prison. Almost 50 percent of transgender former inmates reported being assaulted or harassed during their time in prison. These percentages do not take into consideration the high number of LGBTQ inmates who have reported overall humiliation and poor treatment by prison staff and fellow inmates.

Housing and providing proper self-care items to LGBTQ inmates also serves as a challenge. Lesbian, gay, bisexual, transgender, and queer inmates have reported being denied gender appropriate clothing or grooming items. Also, many jails and prisons still house transgender inmates with other male or female inmates based upon their current genital anatomy. This leads to greater issues and a higher prevalence of abuse, especially in inmates who may not have yet surgically or medically completed their transition.

When vulnerability or mistreatment is recognized, prisons tend to respond by placing the LGBTQ inmate in solitary confinement, which leads to further isolation and withdrawal. Those in solitary confinement experience little human contact, and a very small amount of activity. Isolation tends to increase amounts of psychological distress, and may lead to psychological issues or relapse of an existing mental or emotional issue.

In response to the rising concern regarding the health and welfare of LGBTQ inmates, correctional facilities have attempted to create and initiate new policies focusing on LGBTQ rights and needs. Many of these policies stem from the federal Prison Rape Elimination Act (PREA) (passed in 2003), which led to federal legislation in 2012 published as *National Standards to Prevent, Detect, and Respond to Prison Rape* (NPREC). Many of these national standards specifically focus on those inmates who identify as LGBTQ, and are shaped by various court decisions, including decisions focusing on how the law has been violated by denying transition-related services (such as hormones and surgery) to transgendered prisoners.

Reforms included within the Prison Rape Elimination Act and *The National Standards to Prevent, Detect, and Respond to Prison Rape* include providing those who are transgender with housing and medical care appropriate to their preferred gender identity. The standards also include a focus on the recruitment and hiring of more

LGBTQ staff in correctional facilities, and increased existing staff training on LGBTQ issues. A section was also included on providing non-prison term-based measures and sanctions when appropriate to all those who enter the criminal justice system.

The roll out of these standards has been slow moving. As of late 2016, many standards are still being put into effect within correctional facilities. As a result, LGBTQ inmates are continuously experiencing prejudice, harassment, and unfair treatment due to their gender or sexual identity.

Gina Riley

Further Reading
Marksamer, Jody, and Harper Jean Tobin. *Standing with LGBT Prisoners: An Advocates Guide to Ending Abuse and Combating Imprisonment*. National Center for Transgender Equality. 2013. A tool kit for working with correctional facilities on LGBTQ inmate issues. Includes a summary of proper intake procedures, classification and placement assessments, inmate management, and a section on identification and reporting of sexual abuse.
National Institute of Corrections. *Lesbian, Gay, Bisexual, Transgender, and Intersex Offenders*. http://nicic.gov/lgbti. A website run by the U.S. Department of Justice. Provides general information regarding the rights of LGBTQ inmates and juvenile offenders, as well as additional information regarding addressing the medical and mental health needs of LGBTQ inmates.
U.S. Department of Justice. *National Standards to Prevent, Detect, and Respond to Prison Rape*. http://ojp.gov/programs/pdfs/prea_final_rule.pdf. A complete listing of the *National Standards*, based upon elements of the Prison Rape Elimination Act of 2003. Includes a summary of major provisions, an in depth explanation of the standards, and a government based cost/benefit analysis.

See also Prisons, Federal Bureau of; Equal Protection Under the Law; Prison and jail systems; Prison health care; Prison violence; Punishment; Victimology; Crime victimization: Primary and secondary; Prison Rape Elimination Act (PREA) (2003); Prison inmate subculture; Prisoner rights; Security Threat Groups (STGs)/Prison gangs; Prison/prisoner classification systems; *Ashker v. Brown* (2016).

Medical model of offender treatment

Definition: The medical model is a rehabilitative penology. It was most prominent from World War II into the 1970's. It was abandoned when it became fashionable and popular to launch a war on crime, drugs, and deviant behavior. Recent cases, especially *Brown v. Plata*, suggest the beginning of a return of the model. There is a growing concern about the incidence of mental and physical illness inside prisons and the constitutional issues involved in lack of humane punishment and treatment. There is a concern that prisoners are treated in a careless manner and subject to undue punishment and neglect. The Plata decision directed California to reduce the prison population greatly and to implement reforms in its health care delivery system.

Criminal justice issues: Crime prevention; medical and health issues; mental disorders

Significance: Mass incarceration has led to numerous problems and difficulties. There is a growing understanding not only that many mentally and physically ill people are incarcerated, but also that the type of incarceration that has become common in many states of the United States has exacerbated and caused mental and physical illnesses. The reason for mass incarceration was usually given as a need to protect society from criminals. It is obvious, however, that mass incarceration was not the best way to do so and had severe consequences for the imprisoned and society at large. The major issue is how to develop a humanitarian model of rehabilitation, one that protects society as well as inmates.

Medical Model

There is no single medical model; rather, there are various treatments from social worker casework to psychoanalytic approaches. Ideally, the work would be done one-on-one, which is often impossible. However, alternate approaches may be substituted successfully in the hands of skilled practitioners who have special training. Although changes have come into the model over the years, the basic idea that crime is somehow an illness because the criminal may have a defect, be maladjusted, or have a personal mental or physical disease, is common to these various approaches.

The medical model includes the idea of rehabilitation. This does not mean that the offender did not have "free will," but rather that there is some outside influence that restricted "free will," more accurately, free choice. These outside factors may be psychological, biological, or sociological. These outside factors are said to put people at risk to break the law. Perhaps, it is lack of appropriate parental love, or exposure to juvenile delinquents (the gang), or severe poverty or any of several other possible risk factors. The work of the medical rehabilitation model is to address these risk factors: to fix or change them.

Here is where the term medical model comes into play. The role of rehabilitation is to fix the "illness" of criminality. In common with medicine, rehabilitation addresses an individual situation and seeks to cure what is causing the "disease" of criminal behavior. The cure must be fitted to the individual. The treatment must be individualized to get the best results. The medical model requires experts who are scientifically prepared to treat their clients. They will know how to individualize treatment to fit the need. Until this professionalization is required and found in corrections, the model will not work.

Comparison of the Medical Model and Other Models

Of course, the medical model has rivals. It has similarities with two of these other models and major differences with a third. The first model is called retribution. Its goal does not have a means to an end. Rather, it is an end in itself. Its purpose is to punish the offender. It is payback in the purest sense. This perspective holds that all offenders have total free will to follow or break the law. By breaking the law, they deserve pain, the pain of punishment.

The second model, deterrence, is a utilitarian goal. Punishment will deter crime because punished criminals will learn that crime will not pay. The model assumes rationality in the offender. This will serve the purpose of specific and general deterrence. Specific deterrence is achieved when the criminal refrains from crime because of punishment. General deterrence results when others do not commit crime because they have seen how crime does not pay.

Incapacitation is the third model. This model notes that when a criminal is locked up or otherwise incapacitated, then that person can no longer commit a crime while out of general circulation.

The medical model can be used along with deterrence or incapacitation. It is incompatible with retribution because there is no attempt in retribution to change the conditions of criminality or the criminal. It is simply a version of retribution with no further aim.

Conclusion

The medical model seeks to rehabilitate offenders. It seeks to find causes for actions that are considered, rightly or wrongly, criminal. Like medical professionals its practitioners, who may be medical professionals, seek to fit their treatments to individuals and to prepare them to address situations that promote criminal behavior. The assumption is that free choice is not totally free. Social, cultural, psychological, and medical conditions may hinder free choices.

Frank A. Salamone

Further Reading
Banja, J. D. "The Disability Movement's Critique of Rehabilitation's Medical Model: A Rebuttal." AMA *Journal of Ethics* 17, no. 6 (June 1, 2015): 562-67. doi:10.1001/journalofethics.2015.17.6.msoc1-1506.
Blomberg, Thomas G., and Karol Lucken. *American Penology: A History of Control.* New York: Aldine de Gruyter, 2000.
Clear, Todd R. *Imprisoning Communities: How Mass Incarceration Makes Disadvantaged Neighborhoods Worse.* New York: Oxford University Press, 2007.
Cullen, Francis T. "The Twelve People Who Saved Rehabilitation: How the Science of Criminology Made a Difference." *Criminology* 43 (2005): 1-42.
Evans, Jeffrey E. "Why the Medical Model Needs Disability Studies (and Vice-Versa):
"A Perspective from Rehabilitation Psychology." *Disability Studies Quarterly* 24, no. 4 (Fall, 2004): _____.
Freud, S. *Civilization and Its Discontents.* Translated by Joan Riviere. New York: Jonathan Cape & Harrison Smith, 1930.
Goel, S. "An Introduction to Community Based Rehabilitation Continuing Medical Education." *The Internet Journal of Health* 6, no. 2 (2006): _____.
Phelps, M. S. "Rehabilitation in the Punitive Era: The Gap between Rhetoric and Reality in U.S. Prison Programs." *Law Soc Rev* 45, no. 1 (March, 2011): 33-68.
"What Is Rehabilitation?" http://law.jrank.org/pages/1933/Rehabilitation-What-rehabilitation.html.
Zimring, Franklin E., et al. *Punishment and Democracy: Three Strikes and You're Out in California.* Oxford: Oxford University Press, 2003.

See also Schools of criminology; Scandinavia's prison experience; Rehabilitation; Punishment; Prison health care; Mental illness; Criminology; History of incarceration; Prison and jail systems; Community-based corrections.

National Crime Victimization Survey

The Bureau of the Census collects the data under the direction of the Bureau of Justice Statistics
Definition: Biannual collection of data on crime conducted by the US Bureau of Justice Statistics
Date: Established in 1973
Significance: The statistics collected by the National Crime Victimization Survey are considered an outstanding source for understanding crime in the United States.

The National Crime Victimization Survey (NCVS) program was originally published as the National Crime Survey (NCS) in 1973. The federal program collects data through surveys of approximately 100,000 individuals, aged twelve and older, from about 50,000 households.

> **Crime Statistics on the Web**
>
> The findings of the National Crime Victimization Survey can be quickly found on the Website of the U.S. Department of Justice's Bureau of Justice Statistics at www.ojp.usdoj.gov/bjs/cvict.htm. To reach the site quickly, simply type "BJS home page" in a search engine such as Google. This well-organized site offers textual summaries, tables, and graphs of crime statistics. The site also offers links to other sites with crime statistics.

The survey methodology attempts to offer a sample that represents nearly all sociodemographic and geographical categories in the United States. The large sample size allows the NCVS to offer comprehensive pictures of reported and unreported crimes. This bureau's work allows researchers to address the primary flaw in the Uniform Crime Reports (UCR), run by the Federal Bureau of Investigation. Because data from the UCR include only crimes that are reported to police, many crimes go unrecorded. Recent reports suggest that more than two million violent crimes go unreported every year in the United States.

Because the survey is performed every six months, respondents' recollections of details are considered reasonably fresh in their minds. Also, publishing data from each year allows for an understanding of crime trends. The survey was updated and redesigned in 1992, but continued to measure specific annual crime rates in a consistent and reliable manner.

Data from this survey make it possible to study characteristics of crime victims and offenders and relationships among them and the consequences they face, as well as actual crime incidence rates, whether or not reported to the police. The data also make possible clearer understanding of crime trends by providing consistent crime definitions and measures over time and location.

Some professionals in the field of criminal justice have questioned the validity of the NCVS because self-reported data may be inaccurate and not subject to detailed scrutiny of respondents' reported validity. However, the survey methodology itself is widely respected as a legitimate source of understanding the nature of crime in the United States.

John C. Kilburn, Jr.

Further Reading

Doerner, William G. *Victimology*. Cincinnati: Anderson Publishing, 2002.

Mosher, Clayton J., Terance D. Miethe, and Dretha Phillips. *The Mismeasure of Crime*. Thousand Oaks: Sage, 2002. Print.

SEARCH, The National Consortium for Justice Information and Statistics. *Public Attitudes Toward Uses of Criminal History Information*. Washington, D.C.: Bureau of Justice Statistics, 2001.

See also Bureau of Justice Statistics; Crime index; Domestic violence; National Organization for Victim Assistance; Uniform Crime Reports; Victim and Witness Protection Act; Victim assistance programs; Victimology; Victims of Crime Act; "Dark Figure of Crime"; Victims services; Victimization theories.

National Organization for Victim Assistance

Identification: Oldest victim-assistance organization in existence, a private, nonprofit organization made up of practitioners, academics, criminal justice agents, victims, and survivors

Date: Founded in 1975

Criminal justice issues: Medical and health issues; Victims

Significance: In addition to advocating for victims' rights, the National Organization for Victim Assistance (NOVA) helps crime, trauma, and disaster victims by providing direct services and education.

The mission of the National Organization for Victim Assistance is to bring attention to victims' rights and services. NOVA has four main purposes: national advocacy for the purpose of implementing or promoting victims' rights; direct services to victims, including training staff, volunteers, and others to meet the needs of victims; assistance to professional colleagues, including aiding victim advocates and others through training and publications and identifying imminent issues; and services to member organizations and individuals, including monthly bulletins and up-to-date programs concerned with victim assistance. Significant contributions to victim assistance by NOVA include crime victim compensation programs in every state, the District of Columbia, and the U.S. Virgin Islands; establishing the practice of reading victim impact statements at sentencing and parole in most states; enactment of victims' bills of rights in almost every state; providing support to victims through personal contact; improvement of agency response to major incidents; providing training to all manner of personnel who work with victims, including criminal justice, mental health, clergy, and medical personnel; and identifying key issues in victim assistance that need attention.

Elizabeth Quinn DeValve

Further Reading

Office for Victims of Crime. *New Directions from the Field: Victims' Rights and Services for the Twenty-first Century*. Washington, D.C.: U.S. Department of Justice, 1998.

Young, Marlene A. *Victim Assistance: Frontiers and Fundamentals*. Dubuque, Iowa: Kendall/Hunt, 1993.

See also National Crime Victimization Survey; Victim and Witness Protection Act; Victim assistance programs; Victimology; Victims of Crime Act; Victims services; Victimization theories; Victims of Child Abuse Act Reauthorization (2013); Victims of Trafficking Act (2014).

"Not-in-my-backyard" attitudes

Definition: Supporting socially and environmentally valuable policies and projects while opposing the location of facilities to provide those policies or projects in the local neighborhoods of the supporters

Criminal justice issues: Medical and health issues; Morality and public order; Prisons; Substance abuse

Significance: Not-in-my-backyard (NIMBY) attitudes may lead to failures of social justice, prevent the construction of facilities in the most effective and efficient locations, and limit the availability of needed services to client populations.

The NIMBY syndrome develops when members of a community say they support a policy or project so long as it is located where others bear the social and economic costs of the project. They claim their neighborhood is not suited for the proposed project because of the size of the facility, the clients to be served, or some other issue.

The earliest reference to the term "NIMBY" appeared in a 1980 article referring to citizen opposition to locating landfills anywhere nearby. The term was originally associated with opposition to environmentally sensitive facilities but has been expanded to include the location of power lines, rental housing, public housing, homeless shelters, halfway houses for troubled teens or drug abusers, medical facilities for diseased patients, housing for those on parole, and any other facilities deemed undesirable. Opposition may be directed toward the nature of the facility, the administration and procedures of the facility, or the nature of the clients being served, including race, criminal background, or income status. The term

The City of San Francisco has installed coin-operated automatic self-cleaning public toilets. These toilets in many spots are used as private drug parlors/shooting galleries for junkies. (Public domain, via Wikimedia Commons)

"locally unwanted land use" (LULU) refers to all types of socially beneficial developments opposed by locals.

Three major concerns expressed by potential neighbors of unwanted facilities are reduction in local property values, decreased personal and neighborhood security, and increased social fragmentation and community disorganization. Related concerns include to the appearance and size of the facility, parking and traffic patterns, noise and odor, and lax operating procedures and supervision. Tactics used by neighborhood residents to actively oppose such projects include creating petitions, letter writing and media campaigns, lobbying public officials, staging demonstrations, forming opposition groups, and packing zoning hearings with opponents. These residents are generally supporters of no- or slow-growth policies, dwellers in rural or pleasant neighborhoods, and earners of middle or high income who are educated and professionally employed. They often show a strong social concern but are also motivated to protect what is theirs.

Social Justice and Inefficiency Issues

The NIMBY attitude, when successfully integrated into law or government decisions, forces people and communities without political or economic clout, or without the persistence and stamina to last the course of the battle, to bear the costs of social goods desired by those with political and economic clout. Social justice requires that all those who play a part in creating the problem or need, and in deciding the policy, must share in the subsequent burden. This includes paying the taxes, suffering the economic or commercial loss, and sharing in the siting of the facilities.

While Benjamin Chavis was executive director of the United Church of Christ Commission for Racism and

In the Washington, DC, neighborhood known as Tenleytown, this tower was not finished as residents considered it to be too ugly for such an upscale area. (By Kate Mereand, via Wikimedia Commons)

Justice, he created the term "environmental racism" to describe a correlation that he saw in the 1970s and 1980s between the racial composition of neighborhoods and the siting of unwanted facilities, especially ones for storing hazardous waste. Subsequent studies proved that 76 percent of landfills were located in predominantly nonwhite neighborhoods. Social and environmental facilities were located in areas where the geology, geography, low land values, zoning laws, and political climate allowed the siting. These factors were also correlated with low incomes, depressed communities, and the homes and businesses of racial and ethnic minorities.

NIMBY attitudes also can lead to siting social facilities where they are less efficient than they could be in meeting needs. For example, new, environmentally sound landfills are often sited on preexisting, already contaminated sites in depressed neighborhoods where their use is grandfathered into zoning, but the facility is bound to suffer the effects of the earlier abuse of the land. Some facilities are located in geographically remote locations where they cause problems related to traffic, fuel, and trucking or make access difficult for less mobile citizens.

Because the NIMBY attitude makes siting facilities so difficult, construction of needed facilities is delayed and sometimes abandoned. Communities go without hospitals, prisons, waste disposal facilities, or services for the most needy citizens.

Implications for Criminal Justice

Delayed or abandoned construction of prisons in particular has meant a continuation of prison overcrowding and early release of unrehabilitated offenders, denial of rehabilitation and education services to incarcerated youth and adults, delay in the introduction of new incarceration and alternative sentencing methods, and the continued housing of mentally ill, substance-addicted, or homeless persons in facilities intended for criminals.

Perceptions of social injustice that are a consequence of the NIMBY syndrome lead to social dissatisfaction, racial and social class animosities, and subsequent criminal behavior. The concentration of social facilities in already depressed areas leads to further economic and social depression of the neighborhood and to other social problems. On the positive side, some depressed communities have benefited from increased employment and the development of secondary service industries as a consequence of siting large-scale social projects like penitentiaries, secure hazardous or nuclear waste facilities, power plants, and mental hospitals.

Gordon Neal Diem

Further Reading
Davy, Benjamin. *Essential Injustice: When Legal Institutions Cannot Resolve Environmental and Land Use Disputes.* Wien, N.Y.: Springer, 1997. Print.
Dear, M. J. "Understanding and Overcoming the NIMBY Syndrome." *Journal of the American Planning Association* 59, no. 3 (1992): 288-300. Print.
Horah, Jan. *NIMBYs and LULUs.* Chicago: Council of Planning Librarians, 1993. Print.
Inhaber, Herbert. *Slaying the NIMBY Dragon.* New Brunswick, N.J.: Transaction, 1998. Print.
McAvoy, Gregory. *Controlling Technocracy: Citizen Rationality and the NIMBY Syndrome.* Washington, D.C.: Georgetown University Press, 1999. Print.
Munton, Don, ed. *Hazardous Waste Siting and Democratic Choice.* Washington, D.C.: Georgetown University Press, 1996. Print.
O'Looney, John. *Economic Development and Environmental Control: Balancing Business and Community in an Age of NIMBYs and LULUs.* Westport, Conn.: Quorum Books, 1995. Print.
Piller, Charles. *The Fail-safe Society: Community Defiance and the End of American Technological Optimism.* New York: Basic Books, 1991. Print.

See also Community-based corrections; Environmental crimes; Halfway houses; Neighborhood watch programs; Prison and jail systems; Prison escapes; Regulatory crime; Work camps; Homelessness; Privatization of institutional and community corrections, including faith-based programs.

Opioid treatment breakthroughs

Definition: New drugs have been proven effective in medication-assisted treatments (MATs) for opioid addiction, allowing many to end the cycle of misusing opioid drugs, rehabilitation, and further misuse. These drugs, in combination with advanced counseling techniques, help in the initial treatment, as well as being possibilities for maintenance programs.

Criminal justice issues: Crime prevention; medical and health issues; rehabilitation; substance abuse

Significance: With opioid misuse and addiction escalating since the 1990's, ways to end this legal and medical morass have been sought. Several drugs, or combinations of drugs, have been proven to help those seeking to transform their lives, from addiction to approaching "normalcy." While not effective for all individuals, this treatment has had a significant effect in ending not only the criminal activity and health risks of using the illegally obtained the drug, but also those related to obtaining the drug.

Opioid Addiction

With references to the use of the opium poppy in Sumerian texts from about 5,400 years ago, this is thought to be the oldest continuallyused intoxicant, other than alcohol. While the medicinal qualities of opium were known, the translation of the name given in antiquity, "the joy plant," indicates it was also used recreationally. During the era of the European colonization of Africa and Asia, the sale and use of opium was encouraged; the modern era of addiction had begun. The distillation of morphine from opium, for controlling pain, in the early nineteenth century, increased the number addicted. The 1895 development of heroin, as a more potent form of morphine with fewer side effects, ended up increasing drug addiction. The relatively recently developed semisynthetic opioids (a class of drugs based on opioid molecular structure) greatly increased the accessibility, and acceptability, of this type of drug, medically and "recreationally." Because of certain engineered qualities, such as delayed release, it was hoped this would diminish the chance of addiction. However, by early in the second decade of the twenty-first century the estimate is that at least twenty-six million people worldwide misuse these drugs and heroin. By 2013, in the United States, more than four and a half million people had experimented with non-heroin opioids with almost two million addicted, while about 700,000 had tried heroin with more than 500,000 of these addicted. Death due to the use of drugs has become the leading cause of accidental death in the United States.

Early Attempts at Treatment

When smoking, or ingesting, opium was the only manner in which this family of drugs was used, it was possible for many to use it only occasionally. However, for others the physical and mental effects of the drug caused them to seek it out on a regular basis. With the increased medical use of drugs derived from opium in the nineteenth century, as well as the invention of the hypodermic needle, addiction became more widespread, especially at that time, in injured war veterans and women. Throughout most of the time people have been using opium/opioids, the only possible treatment was to abruptly stop using the drug, as it was difficult to diminish doses in a controlled manner. Going "coldturkey" caused a great deal of physical, as well as mental, suffering for the person. In addition, the addictive qualities of this family of drugs meant that there was a very high rate of relapse. In that era, most medical professionals allowed those addicted to continue prescriptions, to maintain the habit. As pharmacology advanced, some sought an affordable and relatively "harmless" drug that could be given addicted individuals, allowing them to be gradually weaned from drugs, or as a substitute for the drug that was destroying their lives. By the beginning of the twentieth century, the two camps in the medical profession—advocates of drug maintenance versus total cessation— were in place and advocated for laws to be enacted to uphold their views. The cessation view held sway, with federal laws regulating narcotics (opioids) being

Recent Treatment Advances

Although a 1914 law prohibited the prescription of narcotics for the maintenance of a drug habit, the post-World War II increase in drug use in the United States caused medical professionals to seek ways of skirting this law. Even in the best setting, withdrawal from opioids, in the 1950's, had a success rate of no more than 30 percent, and in most programs the success rate was in the single digits. Thus various forms of MAT were sought, including finding a drug for which patients would not develop a tolerance, had fewer side effects than heroin, could be administered in clinical settings, and was relatively inexpensive. New York City experimented with methadone, and found it to be a successful drug replacement therapy, using one dose a day. This was used only for individuals who had tried cessation/detoxification programs and had continually relapsed into drug use. The federal government, in the early 1970's, because of the success of methadone in keeping people away from the dangers of acquiring and using street drugs (at that time virtually all illegal opioid use was heroin), put regulations in place for the use of methadone as a maintenance drug, rather than pretending it was being used only in long-term detoxification programs. In the following decades, the number in this type of drug maintenance program grew from a few thousand in New York to about half a million nationwide. While some doctors used this drug to wean people totally off opioids, this was not easy. Therefore, this MAT always had strong critics who saw methadone as only replacing one drug with another, although most had to admit that it did tend to decrease criminal activity related to drug use. It is an opioid, and tolerance and misuse is a possibility, and it has the highest mortality rate among all opioids.

Advances in psychiatry, and non-opioid drugs to relieve some symptoms of opioid withdrawal, have allowed twenty-first century non-opioid cessation programs to have greater success rates than previous ones. This is the preferred method for non-heroin opioid users. However, for some of these users, and for most heroin users, only a MAT seems to be successful in weaning them from opioids.

The growth in non-heroin users in MAT is seen in the statistic that in 2002 only 2 percent of the individuals entering substance abuse programs were non-heroin opioid users, but by 2012 it was 10 percent. During the same period the number of heroin users admitted continually hovered around 15 percent. For those entering substance abuse treatment programs, three relatively newly approved drugs (Levo-Alpha-Acetyl-Methadol (LAAM), 1993; buprenorphine, 2002; and naltrexone, 1984) were tried as part of the treatment, in addition to counseling and other behavior modification efforts.

Levo-Alpha-Acetyl-Methadol acts similarly to methadone (and is an opioid), with many of the same benefits and drawbacks. Only a small number of people, who had severe side effects from methadone, switched to LAAM. In 2001, LAAM was shown to cause certain cardiac problems, and domestic manufacturing of this drug was stopped in 2004. It is no longer an allowable method of treatment.

Naltrexone is not an opioid. Naltrexone reacts with the same receptors as opioids and even when both are present in the bloodstream, naltrexone binds with the receptors, blocking the effects of opioids. When tried in a manner similar to methadone, patients had a hard time sticking with the program and thus it was not widely used. However, early in the twenty-first century, it was discovered that when administering this drug to those experiencing opioid overdose can often revive them and save the patient's life. Belatedly in 2015, the Food and Drug Administration (FDA) approved this use of the drug by all first responders and widespread programs began to supply them with naltrexone.

The acceptance of buprenorphine, as another opioid derivative, in 2002, meant that this treatment carried many risks. However, the way it is structured, buprenorphine does not give a dramatic "high" even when taken in larger doses. Thus, its abuse is less likely. A positive aspect of this treatment is that rather than a daily dose (methadone), it can be taken every two or three days and achieve the same results. It also seems to be a better drug to use as part of a cessation program, than is methadone. At the time it was accepted by the FDA, a combination drug of buprenorphine and naltrexone was approved. The use of this combination makes it even more difficult to misuse the drug, because the naltrexone generally keeps any pleasurable opioid effects from occurring. This combination drug is useful in reducing the time needed for a successful cessation program. Although methadone is cheaper and has proven to be a suitable maintenance drug, buprenorphine is often preferred because it can be given to the patient to take outside a clinic setting, allowing a more normal life. As a result, in 2013, almost three times the number of prescriptions were written for buprenorphine than for methadone.

Donald A. Watt

Further Reading

Mattick, Richard P., et al. "Buprenorphine Maintenance versus Placebo or Methadone Maintenance for Opioid Dependence." *Cochrane Library*. New York: Wiley Online Library, 2014. A summary of various studies regarding the treatment of opioid addiction.

Seppala, Marvin D., with Mark E. Rose. *Prescription Painkillers: History, Pharmacology, and Treatment*. (The Library of Addictive Drugs). Hazelden Minn.: Hazelden, 2010. An examination of opioid use, including its abuse and treatments for dependence.

Slotts, Angela L., Carrie L. Dodrill, and Thomas R. Kosten. "Opioid Dependence Treatment: Options in Pharmacotherapy." *PubMed Central*. Bethesda, Md.: National Center for Biotechnology Information, U.S. National Library of Medicine, 2009. Discussion of the drugs and methods of using these drugs in treating opioid addiction.

Soyer, Richard, and Stefan Schumann, eds. *Treatment versus Punishment for Drug Addiction: Lessons from Austria, Poland, and Spain*. (SpringerBriefs in Criminology) New York: Springer, 2015. A study of three European countries' "bifurcated" approach to controlling illegal drug use during the past century.

Substance Abuse and Mental Health Services Administration. "Medication-Assisted Treatment (MAT)." *SAMHSA*. Washington, D.C.: Department of Health and Human Services, 2016. Government site with links to information about drugs used in treatment of opioid abuse and medication and counseling therapy.

Tetrault, Jeanetter M., and David A. Fiellin. "Current and Potential Pharmacological Treatment Options for Maintenance Therapy in Opioid-Dependent Individuals." *PubMed Central*. Bethesda, Md.: National Center for Biotechnology Information,

U.S. National Library of Medicine, 2013. Investigation and explanation of MAT treatment options in the United States.

Weiss, Roger D., et al. "Adjunctive Counseling during Brief and Extended Buprenorphine-Naloxone Treatment for Prescription Opioid Dependence." *PubMed Central*. Bethesda MD: National Center for Biotechnology Information, U.S. National Library of Medicine, 2011. The results of a study of treatment options, with major differences while treatment was occurring, but poor results for all methods in the longterm.

See also Alcohol use and abuse; Comprehensive Drug Abuse Prevention and Control Act; Drug Enforcement Administration, U.S.; Drug courts; Drug legalization debate; Drug testing; Drugs and law enforcement; Addiction; Designer and date rape drugs; Medical model of offender treatment; Recreational and medical marijuana movements.

Palmer raids

The Event: Federal government sweep through dozens of American cities to arrest alien residents suspected of being radicals
Date: January, 1920
   Place: Throughout the United States
Criminal justice issues: Espionage and sedition; government misconduct; political issues
Significance: The Palmer raids represented one of numerous aspects of post-World War I hysteria that resulted in the infringement of the civil liberties of both foreign residents and American citizens and helped to give rise to a period known as the "Red Scare."

After the United States entered World War I, a strong desire to eliminate political dissent arose throughout the country. That desire was intensified by the Bolshevik overthrow of the Russian government in 1917 and what was perceived as a developing communist threat to American institutions. Anticommunist fear continued into the post-World War I years. In 1918, Congress passed a Sedition Act that authorized the secretary of labor to deport aliens belonging to revolutionary organizations.

After that law was enacted, U.S. attorney general A. Mitchell Palmer became concerned that it was not being applied as rigorously as necessary. Without the knowledge of Secretary of Labor William Wilson, Palmer obtained arrest warrants from a Labor Department official with which he could deport aliens. On the evening of January 2, 1920, Palmer initiated a series of raids that led to arrest of more than three thousand suspected radicals in thirty-three cities. The raids continued on January 5 and rounded up many people who were only remotely con-

The Man Behind the Palmer Raids

Attorney General A. Mitchell Palmer was born in 1872 in Pennsylvania, where he was raised a Quaker. After training as a lawyer, he was active in Democratic Party politics and became a prominent supporter of Woodrow Wilson. After serving three terms in the House of Representatives, he lost a bid for the U.S. Senate and took a job as the federal government's alien property custodian during World War I. In 1919, President Wilson appointed him attorney general. Palmer used his two years in that office to wage vigorous campaigns against political radicals of all stripes. He is best known for deporting anarchist Emma Goldman and for his notorious "raids" in 1920. His blatant disregard for due process and civil liberties during those raids probably ruined his bid for the Democratic presidential nomination that same year. However, he remained an active supporter of Democratic leaders until his death in 1936.

nected with revolutionary organizations, including many innocent people visiting relatives in jails. Many of those arrested were held for long periods without being charged.

Outraged by Palmer's abuse of government power, Secretary Wilson took charge of the deportation hearings. Eventually, 556 of the arrested aliens were deported. The remainder were released.

Richard Adler

Further Reading
Feuerlicht, Roberta Strauss. *America's Reign of Terror: World War I, the Red Scare, and the Palmer Raids*. Foreword by Norman Dorsen. New York: Random House, 1971.
Hoyt, Edwin Palmer. *The Palmer Raids, 1919-1920: An Attempt to Suppress Dissent*. New York: Seabury Press, 1969.
Pfannestiel, Todd J. *Rethinking the Red Scare: The Lusk Committee and New York's Crusade Against Radicalism, 1919-1923*. New York: Routledge, 2003.

See also Federal Bureau of Investigation, U.S.; Illegal aliens; Presumption of innocence; Smith Act.

Parole

Definition: Conditional release of prisoners before the completion of their full sentences
Criminal justice issues: Convictions; pardons and parole; punishment; rehabilitation
Significance: In order to rehabilitate criminals and manage overcrowding in prisons, the state releases, or pa-

roles, prisoners before the end of their sentences on the promise that they will not break the law again or violate the conditions of parole.

The word "parole" comes from the French word *parol*, which means "word of honor." Originally, it referred to the practice of releasing prisoners of war who promised not to resume fighting. Modern parole is the conditional release of prisoners by a parole board before the expiration of their sentences. Parole does not mean that a felony offender is free from the legal custody and supervision of the state. Parole is a privilege granted by the state, which could just as easily keep the prisoner in jail.

Purpose of Parole

The mission of parole is to prepare, select, and assist offenders who, after a reasonable period of incarceration, could benefit from early release. At the same time, the state protects the public through the conditions of release and supervision. The state and the prisoner sign a contract under which the prisoner promises to abide by certain conditions in exchange for conditional freedom. The state justifies parole on the grounds that prisoners need supervision and help if they are to readjust to freedom successfully. Most parole failures occur relatively soon after release. In fact, approximately one-quarter of parole failures occur within the first six months.

Incarceration ensures the protection of society, acts as a deterrent to criminal activity, and functions as punishment for criminal acts. However, it is limited in its ability to prepare offenders for return to the free world. Parole is based on the belief that the majority of offenders can benefit from a period of transition back into the community. Conditional release affords a continuing measure of protection to the public while supporting parolees in their effort to become productive, law-abiding citizens. If parolees violate the conditions of their parole or commit crimes, parole can be revoked and the offenders returned to jail.

Not all offenders have the same potential and motivation to earn or to benefit from conditional release. Offenders must be judged on their own merits and in the light of their offenses, sentence lengths, and personal backgrounds. Parole authorities use risk assessment tools to evaluate the potential success of offenders if paroled. These studies help determine whether prisoners should be released and the conditions of parole.

Society benefits from a successful parole program. Most incarcerated offenders eventually complete their sentences and return to the community. Parole is viewed as a positive means of promoting successful reintegration. It also helps reduce unnecessary expenses at correctional institutions while, at the same time, maintaining an appropriate degree of supervision and control to ensure the protection of society. Parole also mitigates the harshness of criminal law, equalizes disparities in sentencing, and helps prison authorities maintain order and reduce crowding.

The purpose of parole is to improve public safety by reducing the incidence and impact of crime committed by parolees. Parole is not leniency or clemency but a logical extension of the sentence to provide the opportunity to return offenders to society after a reasonable period of incarceration and when they are assessed to have the capability and desire to succeed and live up to the responsibilities of their release.

Offenders who comply with the conditions of their parole and do not violate the law receive an absolute discharge at the end of their sentences. The parolee may be required to abstain from alcohol, keep away from undesirable associates, maintain good work habits, and not leave the community without permission. The revocation of parole occurs when the parolee commits a new crime or violates the conditions of parole. Half of all convicted felons are released on parole. Parole boards release approximately 99 percent of prisoners from prison to serve the remainder of their sentences outside prison walls. An estimated 35 to 40 percent of all parolees have their paroles revoked and are sent back to prison.

Legal Issues

The U.S. Constitution does not require states to maintain a parole system. There is no constitutionally protected right to parole or to due process in release hearings unless state statutes or regulations create a liberty interest in parole release. The parole board can do just about anything it pleases with respect to a prisoner's parole release. Whatever the board decides and does prevails, because it enjoys immense discretion in the parole decision process. Although parole boards are not constitutionally required to provide reasons for denying release, the use of state-mandated parole guidelines provides prisoners with such information.

Prisoners' federal constitutional rights with respect to parole are limited. For example, the U.S. Constitution places few limits on parole boards. Boards may rely on allegations of conduct of which the prisoner was found innocent or may even consider information from charges of which the prisoner was not convicted. The board can deny parole because of the severity of a prisoner's crime.

The parole board may not consider race or inaccurate information to make its decision. To obtain judicial relief, prisoners must show that their files contain errors and that the board relied on false information in denying or revoking parole or time off for good behavior. Prisoners must also show that they requested prison authorities to correct their files but that the latter refused to do so. Often state law and regulations provide prisoners with greater rights. Even when an offender has a federal constitutional claim, a prisoner must exhaust remedies available in state courts before a federal court will intervene.

History of Parole

America's parole system originated during the late 1870's. Well-behaved prisoners in the reformatory in Elmira, New York, had their prison sentences shortened. This system was based on programs developed in England and Ireland. The concept of parole was created by Alexander Maconochie, who was superintendent of the British penal colony on Norfolk Island, off the coast of Sydney, Australia, during the mid-nineteenth century. Sir Walter Crofton, director of the Irish prison system during the late nineteenth century, was influenced by Maconochie's work. A modified version of the Irish system, under which a prisoner could earn early release from prison, was adopted in England and then at Elmira. Other American prisons copied the Elmira system.

A feature of the Elmira system was the indeterminate sentence. Under this system a judge imposed a prison sentence with a minimum and a maximum length. The parole board determined the prisoner's release date. In most states inmates who followed prison rules were entitled to good time off-time deducted from a prisoner's maximum sentence. A prisoner could shorten his sentence by one-third under the good-time-off system. A side effect of indeterminate sentencing was that persons convicted of the same crime could receive different sentences.

Under determinate sentencing systems, a judge imposes a sentence of a specific length. This sentencing system provides for early release because of good behavior—often one day off a sentence for every day served. In theory, this system promotes prison discipline. Violation of prison rules could result in jail time being added to the sentence.

The idea of parole release spread slowly throughout the United States until the Great Depression of the 1930's. Pressing economic conditions—notably the cost of incarceration, not the press of prison reform—led to the rapid spread of parole release systems. Conditional release is the term used to describe prisoners released on good time.

Many efforts to abolish or change the parole system have been tried. For example, the Sentencing Reform Act of 1984 abolished parole eligibility for federal offenders who committed offenses after November 1, 1987. It also provided for the abolition of the U.S. Parole Commission on November 1, 1992. However, the Judicial Improvements Act of 1990, the Parole Commission Phaseout Act of 1996, and the Twenty-first Century Department of Justice Appropriations Authorization Act of 2002 extended the commission in five-year increments through November 1, 2005.

The history of prisons and parole in the United States shows that parole release has been used, and possibly misused, to maintain prison discipline and to reduce prison overcrowding. Parole boards evolved out of the power of governors to issue pardons to selected prisoners. Before the creation of parole boards, governors often used their pardoning powers to relieve overcrowding in state prisons. For example, during the mid-nineteenth century, pardons accounted for over 40 percent of prisoner releases.

The Parole Decision

The goal of all parole decisions is the protection of society. In the short term, the parole board examines whether there is a high degree of risk to society if it releases the prisoner. To meet the longer-term goal, the board considers whether parole would help the offender return to the community.

Parole may be discretionary or mandatory. Discretionary parole occurs when the parole board voluntarily grants parole before the offender completes a sentence. Mandatory parole is the automatic release of an offender upon completion of the sentence (less any good time credit). Under many state parole systems, the department of corrections determines when an offender is eligible for parole. The corrections department uses a formula that includes, but is not limited to, length of sentence, institutional adjustment, treatment or educational program involvement, and prior prison experience.

To guide its decision, the board conducts a risk assessment. The assessment has two parts—a preliminary risk assessment and a special factor evaluation. The first part includes gathering information about the offender. The information includes details of the offense, criminal history, social problems such as alcohol or drug use and family violence, mental status (especially if it affects the likelihood of future crime), performance on earlier releases, information about family relationships, and employment prospects. The board then consults statistical guidelines that assess the probability that the offender will commit another crime. The guidelines indicate how often a group of offenders with characteristics and histories similar to those of the prisoner under review commits new offenses. The second step focuses on a review of reports from psychologists, police, victims, and prison authorities.

After considering the evidence and holding a hearing with the prisoner, the board decides whether to grant parole. If denied, another parole review date may be set. The offender usually has the option to appeal the board's decision when errors in fact, unknowingly considered during the review process, are identified later. The board reconsiders cases when significant new information is presented that was unavailable when the case was originally examined. If parole is granted, the board determines the conditions of release. A parole board may be independent of the prison system or a division of the organization that administers correctional institutions. In most states, parole board members are appointed by the governor.

The core services of parole boards are to help offenders develop release plans and to supervise persons released on parole. Parole authorities may also provide employment and life skills counseling, halfway house accommodations, counseling, community work programs, and family services. Parole board members usually hold release hearings in the state prison. Prisoners usually do not have legal representation at such hearings.

During the 1990's, many states permitted victims or their next of kin to appear before the parole board. Some states permitted victims to introduce written statements at parole hearings. Such statements could include information concerning the crime, the extent and severity of the personal or family injury and economic loss, and the victim's attitude toward the offender's potential parole release. All parole boards consider opposition to an inmate's parole from the police and news media. The parole board determines the actual amount of time to be served based on the prisoner's institutional adjustments as measured by the prisoner's accomplishments, vocational education, academic achievement, work assignments, therapy, and interpersonal relationships with other inmates and prison authorities. Other factors include the prisoner's prospects for outside employment, education, training, eligibility for community services such as halfway house placements, and help with personal problems.

Overcrowded and underfinanced prisons pressure parole boards into accelerating the release of inmates. Unfortunately, there are too few parole officers to cope adequately with all the parolees.

During most of the twentieth century, parole boards decided when most prisoners would be released. With the advent of determinate sentencing and parole guidelines, releasing power has essentially been taken away from the parole boards in many states.

Parole Violations

If after a reasonable length of time parolees continue to show that they can obey all the rules of parole, they may be discharged from parole supervision. At that time, they receive a certificate stating that the current sentence and parole obligations have been met and discharged.

Every paroled prisoner signs an agreement to abide by certain regulations, including obeying the law and not possessing or using narcotics or carrying weapons. Parole violations are either technical violations or new offense violations. Technical violations occur when the conditions of parole are violated. New offense violations involve an arrest and criminal prosecution and conviction. Parolees alleged to have committed a violation are given a preliminary hearing to determine whether there is probable cause to believe the conditions of parole were violated. If probable cause is determined, the offender is held in custody pending a hearing to determine whether parole should be revoked. The purpose of the revocation hearing is to determine whether the violation is serious enough to revoke parole and return the parolee to prison. If probable cause is not determined, the prisoner is released. Prisoners are entitled to due process at parole revocation hearings.

Reinventing Parole

Parole boards are often criticized when a parolee commits a high-profile crime. Studies of intensive-supervision programs for high-risk parolees have found that the programs cut neither recidivism nor costs. Critics have favored some types of "three strikes and you're out" laws or a no-parole policy after three convictions for some categories of violent and repeat felons. In an effort to reinvent the parole system, some experts have advocated use of a voucher system. For a specific period, parolees can use the voucher to seek an education, job training, drug treatment, or other services from state-selected providers. If parolees want to help themselves, they can. If not, they are on their own. Parolees who commit new crimes are sent back to prison to do their time and are given additional time for the new violation.

Some experts have advocated privatizing the parole system and would have bail bond agencies manage the parole system. With their own money at risk, bondsmen would supervise their parolees closely. Privatizing the parole system would save taxpayers money. Prisoners eligible for parole would be required to post a financial bond against specified violations such as reporting regularly to their bail bond agents or submitting to drug testing. Persons violating parole would forfeit their bond, generating revenue for the state and victim compensation. Bond would be set by the courts or parole boards based on the criminal's history and prospects for a productive, law-abiding life.

Fred Buchstein
Updated by Frank Salamone

Further Reading

Abadinsky Howard Probation and Parole: Theory and Practice (10th Edition) 10th Edition Pearson; 10 edition ,
Boston, John, and Daniel E. Manville. *Prisoners' Self-Help Litigation Manual.* Dobbs Ferry, N.Y.: Oceana, 1995. Self-help guide for prisoners seeking parole. Offers other readers insights into prisoners' perspectives on parole.
Clear, Todd R., and George F. Cole. *American Corrections.* Belmont, Calif.: Wadsworth, 1997. Excellent overview of correctional system with a thorough discussion of how parole works and fits in the correctional system.
del Carmen, Rolando V.Civil Liabilities and Other Legal Issues for Probation/Parole @HG = Officers and Supervisors: 3rd Edition Paperback BiblioGov 2012
Glaze, Lauren, and Seri Pella. *Probation and Parole in the United States, 2003.* Washington, D.C.: Bureau of Justice Statistics, 2004. Federal government report on the workings of the parole system over the previous year.
Jacobson, Michael Downsizing Prisons: How to Reduce Crime and End Mass Incarceration New York: New York University Press :2005
Ogletree Jr., Charles J, Austin Sarat Life without Parole: America's New Death Penalty? New York :2012
Petersilia, Joan, ed. *Community Corrections: Probation, Parole, and Intermediate Sanctions.* New York: Oxford University Press, 1998. Broad survey of parole and other alternatives to incarceration.
Travis, Jeremy, and Sarah Lawrence. *Beyond the Prison Gates: The State of Parole in America.* Washington, D.C.: Urban Institute, 2002. Evaluation of the workings of the parole system at the turn of the twenty-first century.

See also Clemency; Community-based corrections; Discretion; Marshals Service, U.S.; Pardons; *Parens patriae*; Parole officers; Prison and jail systems; Probation, adult; Probation, juvenile; Suspended sentences; Parole Commission, U.S.; Work-release programs; Rehabilitation; Medical model of offender treatment; Parole boards; Realignment (PSR) policy; Jaycee Lee Dugard case (2009); Prisoner rights; Women in law enforcement and corrections; Halfway houses; Privatization of institutional and community corrections, including faith-based prisons.

Parole boards

Definition: A government agency that determines whether an offender will be released from prison after the minimum sentence is served, but prior to the maximum. The committee (parole board) members who make this decision are normally appointed by an official in the executive branch, with legislative confirmation, where required, varying in different jurisdictions.

Criminal justice issues: Crime prevention; pardons and parole; punishment; rehabilitation

Significance: Most individuals convicted of a crime, and sentenced to prison, receive a sentence that defines a minimum and maximum length for the time the offender can be incarcerated. The parole board is the organization that determines if an offender is released prior to serving the maximum sentence, normally basing its decision on the type of crime, how the person acted in prison, what threat the person seems to hold for society, and input from the victim, or representatives of the victim.

History

Alexander Maconochie, a British administrator, is generally credited with the first attempt to introduce the ideas of rehabilitation and treating prisoners as individuals with personal dignity into the penal system. This included setting goals for the imprisoned offender that would allow the individual to gain release from prison. In the United States, during the 1870's, a similar system was introduced by Zebulon Brockaway in Elmira, New York. Previously, the norm in the nineteenth century for any possible release prior to serving the full sentence was solely based upon good behavior in prison, as judged by the prison warden. The first federal system lessened the sentence by one month for each year of good behavior, with various revisions made throughout the next forty years. In 1902, a formal system of review for federal prisoners, by three officials at the prison, was instituted. In 1910, a formal federal parole system was created, still under control of local officials. It was not until 1930 that a national parole board was created for all federal prisoners. The first state system of parole was in New York in 1907. In 1942, the last state instituted such a system, making prisoners in all jurisdictions eligible for parole, if not prohibited by the sentence handed down by the judge. However, changes in how society has viewed parole resulted in the federal government and three states doing away with the possibility of parole by the end of the 1980's. In these locations, determinate sentences were mandated, with a reduction in the sentence if the incarcerated individual met certain goals related to behavior or completing courses, or activities, which are viewed as steps toward the rehabilitation of the individual.

Goals

Parole is different from a pardon or having one's sentence commuted. In these latter two cases, the individual is no longer under the jurisdiction of the judicial or correctional systems, it having been decided, by the appropriate official, that any debt to society has been fulfilled. When a parole board grants parole, specific conditions are given to the offender that must be met in order not to be reincarcerated for the remainder of the original sentence. The parole board attempts to balance the safety of the general public with the hope of assisting the individual to be successfully reintegrated into society. The use of a parole system assumes that it can contribute positively to the rehabilitation of the individual, lessening the chance of recidivism.

The beginning of formal parole systems in the early twentieth century was based on the desire by some to make the possibility of leaving prison the same for all individuals across the entire correctional system of a jurisdiction and the social reform movement of the Progressive Era. The power of the warden, in determining who would be granted some form of early release, was unacceptable to many. Thus, parole boards were created to work with prison officials regarding the length of time the person would be incarcerated. The idea was that this board would insure that those incarcerated in all the various prisons within the judicial system would be treated the same. In the changes that have occurred in recent decades, this goal was never challenged.

The incorporation of the beliefs and ideals of the social reform movement into the parole system has been greatly challenged by many in the last half of the twentieth century and beyond. In the early days of the parole systems within the United States, there were no concerns about prison overcrowding or the cost of the correctional system. The basic belief of the Progressive Era social reform movement was that each individual was of value and could live a life that contributed positively to society, which in the case of prisoners meant that they could be rehabilitated. The work of the parole board was to recognize steps in this process, which had been completed in prison and establish a setting where it could continue upon release. Essentially through the 1970's this positive view of human nature held sway in the parole system.

Changing Outlooks

However, since the 1980's the strong push for public safety over the possibility for rehabilitation through being granted parole has proportionately decreased the number of individuals being granted parole. In some fourteen jurisdictions, the category of parole was done away with completely, or the possibility greatly reduced. As of 2015, parole boards in only half the states have full authority to grant paroles. While the more conservative, safety first, approach to having, or granting, paroles has been the norm for decades, the ideal of the rehabilitation and reintegration into society of offenders is still the goal for any who are granted parole. Part of the mistrust of parole boards is that only ten states have completely open parole board records. Longer sentences and the decrease in paroles have both contributed to the massive growth in prison populations. While a few parolees make headlines by committing serious crimes, most complete their parole without major incident, although, during the first decade of this century, more than half were incarcerated within five years. The parole board mandates certain actions by those on parole to hopefully increase a positive outcome for society and the individual. Those who support the use of parole believe that offenders who receive this guidance have a better chance to do well upon completion of their terms, as opposed to those who serve the maximum sentence in jail, being released without any assistance. Because a 1984 federal law changed all sentences to determinate sentences, effective in 1987, the federal parole commission was to be phased out in five years. However, it now is authorized to continue until 2018 to handle pre-1987 cases and District of Columbia offenders.

Parole boards face public mistrust. The recent push to drastically limit the number of prisoners who do not serve their maximum sentence has placed many board members under public scrutiny. This has created greater turnover on the boards, for those who are more favorably inclined toward granting parole. In balancing the needs of the public versus that of the individual, the trend among parole boards is to weigh things heavily toward public safety. Although new technology is being used by many parole boards, assisting them in the reduction of recidivism among parolees, neither technology nor people can fully predict the actions of individuals upon their release from incarceration.

Donald A. Watt

Further Reading

Department of Justice. "United States Parole Commission." *The United States Department of Justice.* Washington, D.C.: Department of Justice, 2016. Official website of the U.S. Parole Commission.

Jannetta, Jesse, Justin Breaux, Helen Ho, and Jeremy Porter. "Examining Racial and Ethnic Disparities in Probation Revocation: Summary Findings and Implications from a Multisite Study." *Urban Institute.* Washington, D.C.: The Urban Institute, 2014. A study of four judicial areas in the United States regarding patterns in the way the parole boards deal with offenders of various backgrounds.

Markman, Joshua A., Mathew R. Durose, Ramona R. Rantala, and Andrew D. Tiedt. "Recidivism of Offenders Placed on Federal Community Supervision in 2005: Patterns from 2005 to 2010." *Bureau of Justice Statistics.* Washington, D.C.: U.S. Department of Justice, Office of Justice Programs, 2016. Although focusing on federal parolees, it does contain information comparing federal versus state parolees. Undertaken by the Department of Justice, this contains "official" statistics, in addition to an understandable interpretation.

Reamer, Frederic G. *On the Parole Board: Reflections on Crime, Punishment, Redemption, and Justice.* New York: Columbia University Press, 2016. Reflections of an individual, a professor of social work, who served on the Rhode Island parole board for twenty-four years.

Schwartzapfel, Beth. "Life Without Parole: Inside the Secretive World of Parole Boards, Where Your Freedom May Depend on Politics and Whim." *The Marshall Project.* New York: The Marshall Project, 2015.

See also Medical model of offender treatment; History of incarceration; Community-based corrections; Indeterminate sentencing; Parole; Parole officers; Parole Commission, U.S..

Parole Commission, U.S.

Identification: Agency within the U.S. Department of Justice

Date: Created as the United States Board of Parole in 1930; renamed United States Parole Commission in 1976

Criminal justice issues: Federal law; pardons and parole; punishment

Significance: The United States Parole Commission grants, alters, and revokes paroles to federal criminals and supervises parolees.

In May, 1976, the Parole Commission and Reorganization Act renamed the United States Board of Parole (which was formed in 1930) the United States Parole Commission (USPC) and made it an independent agency of the Justice Department. The major responsibility of the USPC was to make parole decisions for eligible federal offenders. In 1984, the Sentencing Reform Act ended parole eligibility for individuals who committed federal offenses after November 1, 1987. Since then, the USPC has made parole decisions only for offenders who committed offenses prior to November 1, 1987. The Anti-Drug Abuse Act of 1988 gave USPC authority to make release date determinations and set supervised release terms for transfer treaty prisoners who committed their foreign crimes on or after November 1, 1987.

In 1997, in passing the National Capital Revitalization and Self-Government Improvement Act of 1997, Congress extended the jurisdiction of the USPC to include the District of Columbia federal prisoners, a responsibility Congress had previously delegated to the District of Columbia Board of Parole. The USPC also has jurisdiction for conducting hearings and setting release dates for U.S. citizens who are returned to the United States to serve sentences imposed by foreign countries. The commission is also authorized to grant or deny parole to military prisoners who are serving sentences in facilities of the Federal Bureau of Prisons. In all of its decisions, the USPC applies the least restrictive sanctions that ensure justice and public safety.

Between 1992 and 2002, Congress enacted legislation on three different occasions to abolish the USPC. On each occasion, however, it was determined that no other federal agency was ready to assume the duties of the USPC, so it was maintained. In 2002, realizing that the parole functions regulated by the USPC were still necessary, the U.S. Congress extended the lifetime of the agency until November 2005, with the passage of the 21st Century Department of Justice Appropriations Authorization Act of 2002. Congress last reauthorized the USPC in 2013, since it still has offenders under its jurisdiction, including federal and D.C. offenders on or eligible for parole and D.C. offenders on supervised release or serving a prison sentence that includes supervised release

The current mission of the U.S. Parole Commission is to promote public safety and strive for justice and fairness in the exercise of its authority to release and revoke offenders under its jurisdiction. The vision of the U.S. Parole Commission is to build an organization that balances justice through fair and equal treatment with dignity and respect for offenders, staff, and the community we serve. Currently, the major functions of the USPC are to: 1) Manage the offender's risk in the community; 2) Prescribe, modify, and monitor compliance with the terms and conditions governing offenders' behavior while on parole or mandatory or supervised release; 3) Issue warrants for violation of supervision; 4) Determine probable cause for the revocation process; 5) Revoke parole, mandatory or supervised release; 5) Make parole release decisions; 6) Authorize methods of release and conditions under which release occurs; 7) Release from supervision those offenders who no longer pose a risk to public safety; and 8) Promulgate rules, regulations, and guidelines for the exercise of the USPC's authority and the implementation of a national parole policy.

J. Patricia Wilson Smoot was nominated to the United States Parole Commission by President Barack Obama. She was confirmed by the United States Senate on September 16, 2010. On January 29, 2015 Commissioner Smoot became Vice Chairman of the agency. She was designated as Chairman on May 29, 2015.

Alvin K. Benson
Updated by Christopher T. Anglim

Further Reading
United States Parole Commission. *History of the Federal Parole System*. Washington, D.C.: U.S. Department of Justice, 2003.
_____. *An Overview of the United States Parole Commission*. Washington, D.C.: U.S. Department of Justice, 1997.

See also Criminal justice in U.S. history; Criminal justice system; Criminals; Law enforcement; Marshals Service, U.S.; Military justice; Pardons; Parole; Prison and jail systems; Sentencing; United States Sentencing Commission; Parole boards; Realignment (PSR) policy.

Parole officers

Definition: Government employees charged with supervising parolees, convicted criminals who have been released, or exempted, from incarceration
Criminal justice issues: Pardons and parole; Probation and pretrial release; Punishment
Significance: Parole officers, or parole agents as they are called in some states, are responsible for ensuring that parolees, or criminals who have been allowed to serve the remainder of their sentences outside prison, abide by the conditions stipulated at the time of their release.

It is the duty of the parole officer to ensure that the parolee abide by the conditions of parole, as dictated by the parole board, until final discharge is granted. The requirements for employment as a parole officer vary considerably. Some states require that parole officers have graduate degrees in appropriate fields. Others expect that parole officers have only a high school diploma or a general equivalency diploma (GED) and limited training. Persons interested in becoming parole officers often study law enforcement, social work, or counseling. Parole officers must acquire expertise in all these areas of study, because they are responsible for supervising, assisting, and monitoring the persons assigned to them. In their role as counselors, parole officers assist convicted felons under their supervision who try to reenter society from prison.

Parole officers offer counseling and help parolees find employment and job training, if needed. Many persons released from the prison system, as well as their families, find the transition very difficult. Persons are often reluctant to accept ex-convicts into the community, and many employers will not hire convicted felons. The transition is sometimes made more difficult in some states by legislation requiring that communities be notified when a parolee moves into the area. Some states have special units and programs that focus on specific problem areas complicating the transition, such as alcoholism, drug addiction, and unemployment. Mentally ill and developmentally challenged offenders often require special programs as well.

It is the goal of the parole officer to smooth a former convict's transition from being a prisoner to being a productive member of society. Although assisting with the transition to life outside prison is a primary concern, parole officers are also required to police the activities of those under their supervision. Parole officers are recognized as armed law-enforcement officers in many states and are required to undergo the same training as other law-enforcement personnel. Such training is often necessary, as parolees tend to be dangerous offenders who have been imprisoned for long periods of time. In Delaware and South Carolina the responsibilities of the parole officer and probation officer are performed by the same individual. Other states, however, make a clear distinction between these two law-enforcement functions.

Donald C. Simmons, Jr.

Further Reading
Abadinsky, Howard. *Probation and Parole*. 12th ed. Boston: Pearson, 2015. Print.
Glaze, Lauren, and Seri Pella. *Probation and Parole in the United States, 2003*. Washington, DC: Bureau of Justice Statistics, 2004. Print.

Johnson, Ida. "Women Parolees' Perceptions of Parole Experiences and Parole Officers." *American Journal of Criminal Justice* Dec. 2015: 785-810. Print.

Petersilia, Joan, ed. *Community Corrections: Probation, Parole, and Intermediate Sanctions.* New York: Oxford UP, 1998. Print.

Travis, Jeremy, and Sarah Lawrence. *Beyond the Prison Gates: The State of Parole in America.* Washington, DC: Urban Inst., 2002. Print.

See also Community-based corrections; Criminal law; Pardons; *Parens patriae;* Parole; Probation, adult; Probation, juvenile; Parole Commission, U.S.; Work-release programs.

Pennsylvania system of corrections

Definition: An approach to incarceration originating in Pennsylvania in the early nineteenth century that used solitary confinement as a means to encourage reform and penitence in prisoners. Also known as the "separate system" in reference to the prisoners' isolation from each other.

Criminal justice issues: Prisons; punishment; rehabilitation

Significance: This separate system of corrections influenced prison construction and prison regimes throughout the world. However, serious concerns emerged regarding the impact of solitary confinement on prisoners' well-being.

It was not until the late eighteenth century that prison sentences began to emerge as a common response to a criminal conviction. Prior to then, prisons were typically used as places where convicted offenders awaited their actual sanction, including barbaric corporal punishment and execution often for minor offenses. By contrast, Age of Enlightenment thinkers such as Cesare Beccaria (1738-1794) in Italy and Jeremy Bentham (1747-1832) in England proposed that prisons sentences would be a more appropriate response to crime and would have the benefit of deterring further offending and encouraging offenders to reform. Their views are representative of the Classicist perspective that behavior is rational and crime the result of poor decision-making by offenders.

At the same time that intellectuals such as Beccaria and Bentham were developing their ideas about prisons, John Howard (1726-1790), an English prison reformer, was campaigning for improved conditions in prisons and jails (then often known as gaols). These facilities, often simply a collection of holding cells, housed prisoners in unsanitary and inhumane conditions, with men, women, and children commonly detained in the same large cell, sometimes shackled to walls with nothing but straw on the floor. "Prison fever," a form of typhus, spread rapidly in such conditions, and Howard expressed concern about alcohol consumption among prisoners. Howard argued that prisons should instead provide a place where men, women, and children could be held separately, and housed in an environment where there would be an opportunity to reflect on wrongdoing and find a new way forward in life. Howard believed that prisoners could find such a path through careful study of the Bible. The origin of the word penitentiary comes from this belief that prisoners might be encouraged through religious means to repent and express penitence, or remorse, for their crimes. Howard's views were greatly influenced by his Quaker faith, a Christian denomination that believes in the innate goodness of human beings. Those who stray from a moral path can be restored through divine guidance.

Early Years of Corrections in Pennsylvania

The Classicist perspective on crime and sentencing, as well John Howard's views on penal reform, spread throughout Europe and to the newly created United States. John Howard's beliefs had particularly strong influence in Pennsylvania, a state largely founded by Quakers who had fled religious persecution in England. In 1787 influential residents of Philadelphia including Dr. Benjamin Rush (1745-1813), a signer of the Declaration of Independence, established the Philadelphia Society for Alleviating the Miseries of Public Prisons. The Society sought to humanize and reform the city jails, and in 1790 reform of the Walnut Street Jail in Philadelphia led to this becoming the first penitentiary in the United States. Significantly, individual cells were constructed for the most serious offenders, laying the groundwork for Pennsylvania's "separate system" of incarceration. Although founded on high ideals, the Walnut Street Jail later suffered from overcrowding and corruption that by 1818 had undermined its original vision. However, Walnut Street Jail was superseded by Eastern State Penitentiary, a prison that likewise was founded on lofty principles and influenced by the Quaker tradition.

Eastern State Penitentiary and the Pennsylvania System

Located on what were then the outskirts of Philadelphia, Eastern State Penitentiary, also known as Cherry Hill State Prison, opened in 1829. The prison was designed by English architect, John Haviland. Haviland was a proponent of Jeremy Bentham's model prison, the panoptican, which allowed for complete observation of prisoners. Bentham proposed that prisoners could be reformed through constant surveillance; prisoners would have no reason to misbehave because any wrongdoing would be detected and punished and would therefore not be to their benefit. Drawing on this influence, Eastern State was built on a radial design, with wings of the prison extending out from a central hub like spokes from a wheel. Guards situated in the central hub would have a clear view of all of the wings. Cells lined each wing on both sides.

Still to this day, the outside of the prison consists of an imposing stone façade resembling a medieval castle. The prison construction's incorporated the most advanced technology in plumbing in use at that time and was even more sophisticated than the White House in this regard.

However, the most significant innovation at Eastern State was the nature of its regime. Based on the belief that prisoners could be reformed through quiet religious reflection and introspection, an extreme system of solitary confinement was imposed. The regime came to be known as the Pennsylvania system of corrections, and alternatively as the "separate system" of corrections, in reference to the solitary nature of the prisoners' existence. Upon arrival, a new prisoner would be led to an individual cell from which they would ideally not emerge until the completion of their sentence. Cells included a bed, a Bible, and tools and equipment needed to engage in work such as shoemaking and weaving. Most cells had their own exterior area, a small enclosure surrounded with walls of a height that prevented seeing out, where prisoners could take their exercise and breathe fresh air. The solitary nature of the regime was taken so seriously that when prisoners were first led to their cells they were hooded to prevent them seeing others within the prison. Human contact was extremely limited, typically restricted to guards, prison chaplains, and the occasional high-profile visitor to the prison. Communication with family and friends was prohibited. The prison founders hoped that the removal of potentially negative influences was the best way for the prisoners to regain their moral bearings. While other prisons in Pennsylvania also adopted a separate system, Eastern State became the model prison for this approach that spread throughout the world.

Competing Systems of Corrections

The Pennsylvania system stood in contrast to New York State's Auburn system of corrections. Opened in 1817, Auburn Prison developed a "silent or congregate system." Silence was rigidly imposed under the threat of severe punishment, but prisoners were allowed to assemble. This enabled prisoners to work on production lines in rudimentary factories housed within the prison. The comparative virtues and weaknesses of each of the systems formed a subject of public discussion.

Eastern State itself became a tourist attraction, with members of the public visiting the prison to view the building and witness the nature of the regime. By the 1850's up to 10,000 visitors toured the prison per year. One high-profile visitor was the English writer Charles Dickens, who stated in an 1842 account of his visit that he believed solitary confinement to be exceptionally damaging to the mental and emotional well-being of prisoners, even if the prison administrators acted with good intentions. Although the authorities vigorously defended the value of their regime for moral reform, evidence suggests that the nature of this incarceration was having a profoundly detrimental effect on the mental health of at least some of the prisoners. Dickens considered the Auburn system to be far more satisfactory in this respect.

Collapse of the Pennsylvania System

Following the Civil War, the National Prison Congress in 1870 debated the dueling models of incarceration. The Auburn system found greater favor in the United States, a position influenced largely by financial imperatives. The Auburn system proved cheaper to replicate because such prisons did not require construction of individual cells with their own outside extensions. Additionally, goods produced in the factories at Auburn were more lucrative for the prison than what could be produced individually at Eastern State. But by this time the solitary system itself was already beginning to break down at Eastern State in large part through overcrowding. Prisoners were increasingly housed two to a cell, or appointed to work together on additional construction at the site. Female prisoners, a very small percentage of the overall population, had already been housed together. Complaints had also surfaced of prison staff and administrators engaging in licentious parties at the prison at which prohibited alcohol flowed. Like Walnut Creek Jail before it, the original intentions that informed the prison began to slip away. The Pennsylvania system officially ended at Eastern State in 1913. However, its belief in the potential for prisoners to change their lives endures in the rehabilitation approach to imprisonment that emerged in the twentieth century.

Eastern State Penitentiary continued to operate as a prison until its closure in 1971. Today it is open again as a prison museum run by a nonprofit organization. Visitors can tour restored sections of the prison and learn and imagine what the nineteenth century system of solitary confinement would have been like. Given the continued and extended use of solitary confinement in the twenty-first century United States, the Eastern State experience has particular relevance today. However, it must be remembered that the Pennsylvania system of corrections imposed solitary confinement with the intended goal of personal growth and reform, rather than to impose maximum punishment, incapacitation, and deterrence in prison in spite of potential personal costs.

Emma Hughes

Further Reading

Barnes, H. E. "The Historical Origin of the Prison System in America." *Journal of the American Institute of Criminal Law & Criminology* 12, no. 1 (1921): 35-60. A lively and historic account of the development of the Pennsylvania and Auburn systems of corrections.

Eastern State Penitentiary. *General Overview.* 2016. http://www.easternstate.org/learn/research-library/history. The website of the Eastern State Penitentiary includes a historical overview, photographs, and information about visiting the prison museum.

Kahan, P. *Seminary of Virtue: The Ideology and Practice of Inmate Reform at Eastern State Penitentiary, 1829-1971.* New York: Peter Lang, Inc., 2012. This book focuses on education programs at Eastern State, but also offers insight into how the prison's culture and regime changed over time.

Manion, J. Liberty's Prisoners: Carceral Culture in Early America. Philadelphia: University of Pennsylvania Press, 2015. A scholarly examination of the experiences of incarcerated women in early penitentiaries.

See also Auburn system; Prisons and jail systems; Prison overcrowding; Prison violence; Punishment; Solitary confinement; Walnut Street Jail; *Asker v. Brown* (2016); Female offenders; Medical model of offender treatment; History of incarceration; Prison/Prisoner classification systems.

Prison and jail systems

Definition: Government facilities that hold individuals suspected of, or convicted of, committing crimes
Criminal justice issues: Prisons; Punishment; Rehabilitation
Significance: Prison and jail systems make up the corrections arm of the criminal justice system. For many offenders, arrival in these systems signals the last step in the criminal justice process.

In American society, confinement is used for punishing individuals who have broken the law. Corporal punishment (flogging, stocks and pillory, and so on) was replaced by confinement, or incarceration, because the latter was considered to be more humane. It is not exactly known when the use of confinement for punishment began, but this method became dominant in the United States near the end of the eighteenth century. There are two types of systems that incarcerate offenders: prison and jail systems. Although there are many differences, prison and jail systems often are distinguished based on the offenders' length of sentences. Prisons, also known as correctional facilities or penitentiaries, are institutions that house offenders serving a sentence longer than one year. Jails are systems for temporary confinement and house individuals at different stages in the criminal justice process, including offenders serving sentences of less than one year.

Prison violence, overcrowding, prison health care, gang violence, prisoner rights, and prisoner suicide are some of the issues facing the management of modern prison and jail systems.

History of the Modern Prison

In ancient times, confinement was used to hold offenders until trial or until a sentence (usually some form of corporal punishment) was delivered. The beginning of the modern prison can be found in sixteenth century Britain. Although corporal punishment or banishment was the preferred method of punishment, houses of correction were built in which offenders charged with minor crimes lived and had to work under guard supervision to repay the debt. Workhouses were similar but were used to house the poor, who also had to work under guard supervision. In addition, jails were developed to detain suspects until trial.

Criminal justice reformers in Britain incited the movement toward the use of prisons for punishment as alterna-

A-Block at Alcatraz. (By Nonie, via Wikimedia Commons)

tives to the brutality of corporal punishment. These reformers argued that the punishment should be proportional to the offense, or in other words, the punishment must fit the crime. Also, the reformers protested the appalling conditions in the jails and workhouses, as well as on prison ships, where prisoners awaiting banishment to Australia were forced to live in the hulks of ships that never left the dock. The demise of the use of corporal punishment was set in motion by the reformers, and prisons were built. However, the conditions in the early prisons were still deplorable because of rampant disease, filth, and overcrowding.

Prisons did not exist in Britain's American colonies originally. Jails primarily were used to hold debtors or confine offenders until the trial or sentence of punishment. The early jails in the colonies were similar to their British counterparts as overcrowded depositories for disease. Replacing corporal punishment with confinement was an idea first postulated by William Penn, a Quaker. The founder of Pennsylvania argued that offenders should be punished by using confinement. Penn passed the Great Law of 1692, which abolished corporal punishment, except in the case of murder, and mandated the building of prisons. A visionary, Penn established prisons nearly a century earlier than Britain and the other U.S. colonies. However, the Great Law was repealed one day after his death in 1718.

After the American Revolution

Corporal punishment continued to be the primary method of punishment through the American Revolution. The Constitution and the Bill of Rights, developed as a guide for the newly independent states, included many protections for individuals suspected of crimes. The emphasis on protection from the abuses of government was influenced by the abuses the colonists had suffered under Britain's rule. The concept of the penitentiary, based on the work of William Penn, was developed and implemented by the Quakers in Pennsylvania. These penitentiaries would allow the offenders the time and solitude to repent for the crimes, to pay penance through manual labor, and to reform. The first prison under this new system was the Walnut Street Jail, opened in Philadelphia in 1790. The Walnut Street Jail served as a model for the prisons built in Pennsylvania in the 1820's.

By 1830, Western Penitentiary was opened in Pittsburgh and Eastern Penitentiary in Philadelphia. These prisons followed the philosophy of the Quakers' penitentiary and were referred to as the Pennsylvania system or the separate system. A similar system, minus the complete isolation of the inmates, was employed in the Auburn prison opened in New York in 1817. The slightly different system became known as the Auburn system, the New York system, or the congregate system. Both types of systems operated under the assumption that crime was a result of problems in the external environment.

Eventually, the Pennsylvania system was abandoned because of multiple factors, including the financial burden of operating a prison in which inmates were individually celled. The Auburn system became the model for the American penitentiary until after the Civil War. A large prison reform movement protesting the squalid prison conditions gained momentum after the war. In part because of the prison reform movement, a prison emphasizing rehabilitation was opened in Elmira, New York, during the late 1870's. The Elmira Reformatory adopted indeterminate sentencing practices whereby prison officials could determine how much of a sentence the inmate served by using reward systems for good behavior and work or educational achievements.

The Elmira model, or reformatory model, gained popularity, and by the 1920's nearly every state had adopted the system. The focus on rehabilitation continued, and new treatment programs continued to be implemented in American prisons until after World War II. By the 1950's, the number of prisoners was increasing, and the prison system experienced a wave of riots, thought to be caused by deplorable prison conditions. During the 1960's and 1970's, several landmark Supreme Court and federal court cases passed legislation that allowed certain prisoner rights and mandated improved prison conditions.

The 1970's sparked a shift in penal philosophy from an emphasis on rehabilitation to one on deterrence and incapacitation. Indeterminate sentencing was replaced with determinate sentencing systems in which the parole boards could no longer release an inmate before the sentence expired. The shift in philosophy was influenced by published research studies claiming that not one of the rehabilitation programs in place in U.S. prisons actually reduced recidivism or crime rates.

The shift from rehabilitation to deterrence and incapacitation marked the "get tough on crime" era that began during the 1970's and continued through the end of the twentieth century. The increase in availability of crack cocaine in the 1980's ensured that a continual supply of drug offenders filtered into the prison system through sentencing reforms resulting from the so-called war on drugs. These reforms included mandatory minimums for possession of certain amounts of drugs, "truth-in-sentencing" laws that forced offenders to serve the full sentence, and "three-strikes" laws that gave life sentences to inmates receiving convictions for a third felony. The impact on the prison system was profound, resulting in overcrowded conditions and millions of dollars toward new prison construction as more prisoners were incarcerated and for longer periods of time.

State Prison Systems

Currently, all fifty states operate prison systems. Operation and oversight of the state prisons falls under the state Department of Corrections. The two goals of prison systems are custody and treatment. The custody function serves to keep the inmate incarcerated so that inmates, staff, and society are safe. Vocational training, educational programs, and counseling and drug abuse programs fall under the treatment function and serve to help the inmate rehabilitate, thereby preventing future crimes. As a result of the "get tough on crime" era, custody is now the primary focus of the prison and is the prison guard's primary responsibility.

The custody function is emphasized when designing a facility. Facility designs vary across states, with factors such as financial considerations and upkeep taken into consideration during the planning. The popular prison designs of the last two hundred years offer advantages and disadvantages depending upon the style. For example, the radial-design prison, similar to the Auburn prison in New York, contains cells and areas that radiate out from a central control hub. An advantage of this type of design is that it restricts the inmates' movements, because all of the inmates must pass through the hub to travel to any other part of the facility. On the other hand, if inmates get control of the hub during a riot, then they have control of the entire facility.

In addition to prison design, the physical layout of the living units is important for administrators and staff. The linear cell design is the oldest, and many prisons still operate facilities marked by long hallways containing cells or dormitories. The cells are controlled from the end of the hallway, and officers must walk the length of the hallway to observe the insides of the cells directly. A modified version of this design was implemented in some prisons and includes clusters of individual cells that share a common living area. The more modern, "podular" design most closely resembles the modified linear design. Cells also are situated around a central living area, but the defining characteristic of the podular design is direct supervision. The prison guard works inside the pod and has direct contact with the inmates and can observe them at all times. This design has most recently been implemented in jails, known as "new generation" jails.

Inmate and Prison Classification

Upon entering prison, inmates are assessed for classification as a tool in the custody and control of inmates. The tests used for classification purposes determine the proper security level for the inmate. Classifications are made based on characteristics of inmates that may prove problematic (gang affiliation, status, race, and so on) or predictions of inmate behavior. Based on the classification, the inmate will be assigned to a maximum-, medium-, or minimum-security facility. Certain supermax prisons also exist for inmates deemed especially dangerous or at risk, but are not available in most prison systems.

The maximum-security facility, also known as the "Big House," is a colossal structure with many physical security features, including towers manned by guards, high walls, and searchlights. Facilities such as this are reserved for the inmates considered to be the most dangerous or violent in the prison system. Some programming is available to inmates in maximum-security facilities; however, the main function is custodial. One of the most famous maximum-security prisons is the San Quentin prison in California.

A medium-security facility typically houses property offenders and other inmates considered less dangerous than those housed in maximum-security facilities. In some states, the maximum- and medium-security facilities are combined. Medium-security facilities lack most of the physical security measures present in the maximum- security facilities, and guarded towers are replaced with barbed-wire fences. In some medium-security facilities, inmates reside in dormitories that are similar to military barracks.

A minimum-security facility houses property and drug offenders who are considered the least dangerous offenders and are serving the shortest sentences. Also, inmates from higher-level facilities who are close to release may serve out the end of their sentences in minimum security to ease the transition from incarceration to freedom. Minimum-security facilities rely on electronic monitoring and locked doors to prevent escape, rather than barbed-wire fences. Inmates in minimum security have access to more programs and services and are allowed greater freedom of movement.

Due to the surge in incarceration rates, some prisons and jails have undergone privatization, which involves private companies in the building or operation of prisons and jails. Arguments for and against the privatization of prisons and jails abound, and although some private prisons have been closed down, private prisons are still being used by some states to house the overflow of inmates in the state system. In addition to private prisons and jails, supermax (or maxi-max) prisons and boot camps gained popularity and continue to operate in the United States.

Federal Prison Systems

The first federal prison opened in Atlanta in 1902. Until then, federal prisoners had been housed in local jails or state prisons. The Federal Bureau of Prisons was established by President Herbert Hoover in 1930 to oversee the federal prison system. The federal prison system has seen a surge in incarceration rates since the 1970's, mainly resulting from mandatory sentencing and federal antidrug policies. The federal system operates mostly minimum-security facilities because most violent crimes fall under state jurisdiction.

Unlike state prisons, the federal system operates four different types of facilities that are related to the five security levels in the federal system: high, medium, low, minimum, and administrative. The United States penitentiaries (USP) are classified as high-security level but are comparable to maximum-security prisons in the state system. The Metropolitan Correctional/Detention Centers (MCC/MDC) are all at the administrative level. The administrative-level prisons are the jails of the federal system and house offenders at every stage in the legal process. The security level varies based one's location in the center. The federal prison camps (FPC) and satellite camps are all minimum security and house the prisoners who represent the lowest risk, including white-collar criminals or other nonviolent offenders. Finally, the federal correctional institutions (FCI), ranging from low to high security, are similar to the state correctional facilities.

Women's Prisons

Until the reformatory era of the 1870's, prisons were not segregated by gender, and abuses were common. During the late nineteenth century, three states (Indiana, New York, and Massachusetts) opened separate prison facilities for women, which were also staffed by women. By 1975, thirty-four states had opened separate facilities for women. In the states that did not have a separate facility, women and men were segregated, or the state contracted with private companies or other states to house its women inmates. In 1925, the first federal prison for women opened in Alderson, West Virginia.

The early prisons for women followed the cottage system design, which embodied the rehabilitation philosophy of the late nineteenth century. The facilities were operated by women staff, and the inmates' time of incarceration was spent learning domestic skills. When the popularity of reformatory prisons waned, a college campus design replaced the cottage system. Although these prisons offered vocational training programs, the programs were gender-specific. For example, the inmates learned job skills that would translate into secretarial positions upon release. One controversial experiment was New York's operation of a shock incarceration camp for female prisoners in the boot camp style.

Historically, women made up a small percentage of the incarcerated population. However, this number continues to rise, mainly due to the overall increase in incarceration—even for nonviolent offenders—due to the War on Drugs. Many states have only one facility for women, which houses inmates from every classification. In the modern prison, the vocational skill training often includes training considered to be traditionally male-oriented, such as firefighting. An administrative and medical issue in prisons for women is that of inmate pregnancies. Some women enter prison pregnant, and the institution must provide specialized care for these inmates. Some prisons have allowed infants to remain with the incarcerated mother for a brief period of time after the delivery.

Jail Systems

Jails are different from prisons in a number of ways. Typically, jails are operated by cities and counties, whereas prisons are run by the state Department of Corrections or the Federal Bureau of Prisons. Jails house offenders at different stages of the criminal justice system, including pretrial detention, those serving misdemeanor sentences of less than one year, felony offenders awaiting sentencing or transfer to a state or federal facility, offenders with mental illness awaiting transfer to an institution, felony offenders serving more than one year when no beds are available in the state prisons, offenders awaiting release back into the community after serving the sentence, and individuals held for other reasons such as contempt of court.

Jails also differ in design. Most jails fall into one of the following categories: traditional, second generation, or new generation. Traditional jails are similar to the linear-design prisons, with the cells situated along hallways and intermittent supervision of inmates. Second-generation jails have cells situated around a central "day room," where staff supervise inmates from a control booth. New-generation jails have a podular design and contain a separate living area, where staff supervise and interact with the inmates directly. New-generation jails have risen in popularity with a philosophy that direct supervision of the inmates allows for more control.

Tammy L. Castle

Further Reading

Allen, H. E., C. E. Simonsen, and E. J. Latessa. *Corrections in America*. 10th ed. Upper Saddle River, N.J.: Pearson/Prentice-Hall, 2004. Print.

Gido, R. L., and T. Alleman, eds. *Turnstile Justice: Issues in American Corrections*. 2d ed. Upper Saddle River, N.J.: Pearson/Prentice-Hall, 2002. Print.

Herivel, T., and P. Wright, eds. *Prison Nation: The Warehousing of America's Poor*. New York: Routledge, 2003. Print.

Johnson, Robert. *Hard Time: Understanding and Reforming the Prison*. 3d ed. Belmont, Calif.: Wadsworth, 2002. Print.

Mays, L. G., and T. L. Winfree. *Contemporary Corrections*. 2d ed. Belmont, Calif.: Wadsworth, 2002. Print.

Owen, B. *In the Mix: Struggle and Survival in a Women's Prison*. Albany: State University of New York Press, 1998. Print.

"The Prison Crisis." *American Civil Liberties Union*. ACLU, 2015. Web. 7 Dec. 2015.

Santos, M. G. *About Prison*. Belmont, Calif.: Wadsworth, 2004. Print.

Schmalleger, Frank. *Criminal Justice: A Brief Introduction*. Boston: Pearson, 2014. Print.

Scott, David Gordon. *Why Prison?* Cambridge: Cambridge UP, 2015. Print.

See also Auburn system; *Ashker v. Brown* (2016); Boot camps; Prisons, Federal Bureau of; Chain gangs; Elderly prisoners; Preventive detention; Prison escapes; Prison guards; Prison industries; Prison overcrowding; Prison violence; Supermax prisons; Walnut Street Jail; Conjugal Visitation; Pennsylvania system of corrections; Female Offenders; Medical model of offender treatment; Parole boards; Prison Rape Elimination Act (PREA) (2003); Prison inmate subculture; Prisoner rights; Privatization of Institutional and Community Corrections, including Faith-Based Prisons; Reealignment (PSR) Policy; *Roper v. Simmons* (2005); Scandinavia's prison experience; Security threat groups (STGs)/prison gangs; Technology's transformative effect; LGBTQ prisoners; History of incarceration; Prisoner Classification Systems.

Prison escapes

Definition: Unauthorized departures by lawfully incarcerated inmates from state and federal corrections facilities

Criminal justice issues: Pardons and parole; prisons

Significance: Completion of criminal sentences is an important measure of the success of the criminal justice system, so preventing prison escapes is an important goal in corrections.

Different prisons have several levels of security that vary with the size of the facilities and the types of criminals they house. The lowest level of security starts with community treatment centers, or as they are sometimes called, halfway houses. Such facilities are considered halfway between jails and prisons and full release into society. The next level up includes institutions such as prison camps, which are often located in rural areas. They typically do not have fences, and their inmates work with minimal supervision.

Escapes from halfway houses and prison camps occasionally occur; however, efficient prisoner classification systems tend to minimize such escapes by identifying the prisoners who are the greatest escape risks and sending them to facilities with higher levels of security. Prisons at the medium and maximum levels have security procedures and physical equipment designed to prevent escapes. The highest, or maximum, level of security is maintained in facilities known as supermax prisons. Designed with the goal of making escape physically impossible, these prisons house prisoners who are consider the "worst of the worst."

Prisons differ from "jails" in being designed to house criminals who are sentenced to at least a full year of incarceration. Both state and federal governments run prisons. State prisons house inmates convicted of felony violations. Federal prisons hold inmates who violate federal laws. Most federal prisoners commit felony offenses, but because the federal government does not have the equivalent of county jails, the federal prison population includes inmates convicted of misdemeanor offenses.

Security Levels and Possibilities of Escape

At the state level, departments of corrections usually determine the security levels of the institutions in which convicted prisoners serve their sentences. At the federal level, the Bureau of Prisons makes this determination. Although it is the prerogative of prison system officials to determine what types of institutions in which inmates are to serve their sentences, the recommendations of judges and prosecutors may carry some weight.

Decisions concerning the security levels of the institutions in which offenders serve their sentences take into account such factors as severity of the offenses, prior criminal histories of the offenders, and the extent and strength of the offenders' ties with their communities. The decisions are typically made while the offenders are

In 1970, radical philosopher Angela Davis made the Federal Bureau of Investigation's most-wanted list for her alleged involvement in the attempted escape of Jonathan and George Jackson, radical African American prisoners known as the "Soledad Brothers," after the name of their California prison. While the brothers were involved in a courtroom trial in Marin County, Jonathan Jackson got hold of guns and took hostages. However, in the confrontation with police that followed, both he and the judge were killed. Afterward, it was discovered that the guns he used had been purchased by Davis. Seen as Jackson's accomplice, Davis was charged with murder, kidnapping, and conspiracy, but when her case went to trial in 1972, she was acquitted of all charges. (Library of Congress)

held in classification centers. Prison officials weigh these factors with the offenders' risk of flight and the dangers they might pose to the communities if they escape back into society. The higher the levels of risk that offenders pose, the greater the levels of security that are required in the institutions in which they are to be housed.

Prisoners can and do escape from every type of prison facility. The attention that prisoner escapes attract is in proportion to the security levels of the institutions from which they flee. When a prisoner escapes from a maximum-security prison's death row, news of the escape makes national news. In December 2000, for example, seven prisoners escaped from a maximum-security Texas prison. Several of them were awaiting death sentences. Their escapes and subsequent trail of terror led law-enforcement officers from numerous state and federal agencies on a multistate chase that ended with the death of one escapee and the arrest of the others in a rural Colorado community.

Prisoners also occasionally escape while on authorized furlough releases or while they are in transit. Any furloughed prisoner who fails to return to the designated facility at the end of the furlough is considered to have escaped. Although strict security measures are usually the practice for transporting prisoners, the levels of security cannot be as strict as they are when prisoners are inside prison facilities. To escape while in transit, prisoners may use smuggled handcuff keys or makeshift weapons or have outside assistance to attack the guards escorting them.

Consequences of Escape

Recaptured escapees face felony charges for their escapes. If they are convicted, their prison sentences are extended, and they are likely to be housed in more secure facilities. Should recaptured escapees not be prosecuted for the offense of escape, they will probably lose whatever good time they have accumulated for past good behavior. The only generally accepted excuse for escape is to evade a death threat. For that defense to be successful, the escapee must not hurt anyone during or after the escape and surrender to authorities as soon as possible after escaping.

Gerald P. Fisher
Updated by Frank Salamone

Further Reading

Buck, Paul *Prison Break: True Stories of the World's Greatest Escapes* Kindle Edition John Blake Publisher, 2012

Burns, Robert E. *I Am a Fugitive from a Georgia Chain Gang.* New York: Vanguard Press, 1932. Memoir of a famous prison escapee whose story prompted calls for prison reform during the 1930's.

De Simone, Donald. *I Rob Banks, That's Where the Money Is.* New York: SPI Books, 1992. Memoir of a professional bank robber who made several successful escapes from prisons.Mullins, Richard H. Real Oklahoma Outlaws: Major Crimes, Prison Time & Jail Break - The True Story of the Justice & Davis Crime Families Paperback - Create Space Independent Publishing Platform, 2015

Simpson, Paul. *The Mammoth Book of Prison Breaks.* Running Press 2013

Elsner, Alan. *Gates of Injustice: The Crisis in America's Prisons.* Upper Saddle River, N.J.: Financial Times/Prentice-Hall, 2004. Critical analysis of the many problems faced by federal and state prisons, including the deterioration of facilities and failings in security.

Hamm, Mark S. *The Spectacular Few: Prisoner Radicalization and the Evolving Terrorist Threat.* New York: New 2013

Mullins, Richard H. *Real Oklahoma Outlaws: Major Crimes, Prison Time & Jail Breaks—The True Story of the Justice & Davis Crime Families.* Create Space Independent Publishing Platform 2015

See also Prisons, Federal Bureau of; Marshals Service, U.S.; "Not-in-my-backyard" attitudes; Prison and jail systems; Prison guards; Prison violence; Solitary confinement; Supermax prisons; Surveillance cameras.

Prison guards

Definition: Government employees responsible for custody and control of inmates
Criminal justice issues: Prisons
Significance: The role of prison guards has changed since the 1970s as a result of problems in US prisons and an increase in incarceration rates.

Prison guards, more commonly known today as correctional officers, are primarily concerned with keeping prison inmates in custody and maintaining control of the facilities. These are the two most important prison guard functions. Guards are also responsible for ensuring the safety of all staff and inmates in the prison.

Guards follow procedures in order to guarantee security in prison facilities. In addition to the standard security features such as cameras, locks, and so on, other procedures are implemented to maintain safety and control. For example, one of the primary safety concerns is the existence of contraband, which may include drugs, weapons, or other items banned within the facility. Guards attempt to control the distribution and circulation of contraband by conducting unannounced body and cell searches. However, some guards actually participate in the underground prison economy by bringing contraband into the facility and profiting by its sales.

Along with security and order maintenance functions, the role of guard involves a great degree of work in human services. Guards are responsible for tending to the daily needs of the inmates living in their cell block, which includes everything from letting the inmates out to go to work and scheduling medical appointments to helping them solve institutional problems. Sometimes prison guards are not prepared for the amount of human service work their job entails, as training can focus heavily on security measures. The illusion that guards control the prison quickly vanishes for new guards as they learn that control is primarily maintained not through force but through inmate cooperation. As there are more inmates than guards in every prison, guards may grant small privileges to inmates in exchange for good behavior.

In the past, the job of prison guard held low status and pay. Little formal education was required, and the job carried few opportunities for advancement or promotion. However, the need for a more professional guard became necessary after years of problems in the nation's prisons, the dramatic increase in incarceration rates since the 1970s, and the inability of the prison system to retain officers. The move to professionalize the prison guard incorporated more training, psychological screenings, the replacement of the title "prison guard" with that of "correctional officer," and an attempt to recruit people of color and women.

Overall, the role of prison guard can cause stress and can be very alienating. Organizational factors contribute to low job satisfaction and job stress, including a lack of supervisory support, a lack of participation in decision making, low pay, and little opportunity for advancement or promotion. Also, role conflict may contribute to stress because the officer must perform the human service functions in addition to those of custody and control. These roles often conflict, and the "people work" aspect of working with the inmates may lead to chronic stress or burnout.

Tammy L. Castle

Further Reading
Conover, Ted. *Newjack: Guarding Sing Sing*. New York: Random, 2000. Print.
Herman, Peter G., ed. *The American Prison System*. New York: Wilson, 2001. Print.
Steinberg, Eve P. *Correction Officer*. New York: Macmillan, 1997. Print.

Prison guard. (By Adam.J.W.C., via Wikimedia Commons)

See also Chain gangs; Prison and jail systems; Prison escapes; Prison overcrowding; Prison violence; Solitary confinement; Women in law enforcement and corrections; Prison inmate subculture; Privatization of institutional and community corrections, including faith-based programs; and Scandinavia's prison experience.

Prison health care

Definition: Preventive care, medical treatment, and other health services offered in correctional facilities
Criminal justice issues: Medical and health issues; Prisons and jails
Significance: Prison health care has become an increasing concern as correctional institutions across the United States have experienced significant growth in the numbers of inmates, especially those who have physical disabilities or are elderly prisoners or are chronically or terminally ill.

Prison health care presents unique challenges to the medical professionals responsible for the care and treatment of inmates. Prison health care resources are limited, and inmates are more likely than members of the general population to have serious illnesses, such as cancer, diabetes, heart disease, and HIV/AIDS. The treatments for such diseases are costly, and the financial resources of many prisons are limited. Moreover, prison health care systems are often significantly understaffed. Despite these obstacles, however, correctional facilities are constitutionally required to provide adequate medical care to their inmates. In an effort to assist the prison system with constitutional compliance, professional health care organizations have developed standards of care and ethical codes.

Legal Standards of Care

Prior to the 1960s, the judicial system practiced a judicial restraint or "hands-off" policy with regard to administration of prisons. During that period, judicial officials were reluctant to get involved in correctional issues. Many judges claimed they not only lacked the authority and expertise to intervene in correctional matters, but that court intervention might result in undermining the work of correctional administrators.

The lack of judicial intervention and court deference to prison administrators resulted in a number of abuses, especially in inmate health care. In many facilities, prisoners were routinely denied the most basic standards of medical care and treatment. However, in the landmark 1976 case of *Estelle v. Gamble*, the US Supreme Court affirmed federal jurisdiction over correctional health care systems and ruled that when constitutional rights are at risk, the courts have not the right but the duty to intervene. In addition, the Supreme Court ruled that "deliberate indifference to the serious medical needs of inmates" was a violation of the ban in the Eighth Amendment on cruel and unusual punishment. The Court reasoned that because prisoners are wholly dependent on the state for their needs, the state is obligated to provide for their serious medical needs. Therefore, correctional administrators or authorities can be held civilly liable under Section 1983 of the US Code for failing to provide adequate medical care to prisoners.

Accreditation and Professional Standards of Care

During the early 1970s, the American Medical Association (AMA) surveyed the nation's jails and found that medical services were lacking in three primary areas: adequacy, access, and availability. The AMA then developed a set of standards for the delivery of health cares services in jails and prisons and initiated a voluntary accreditation

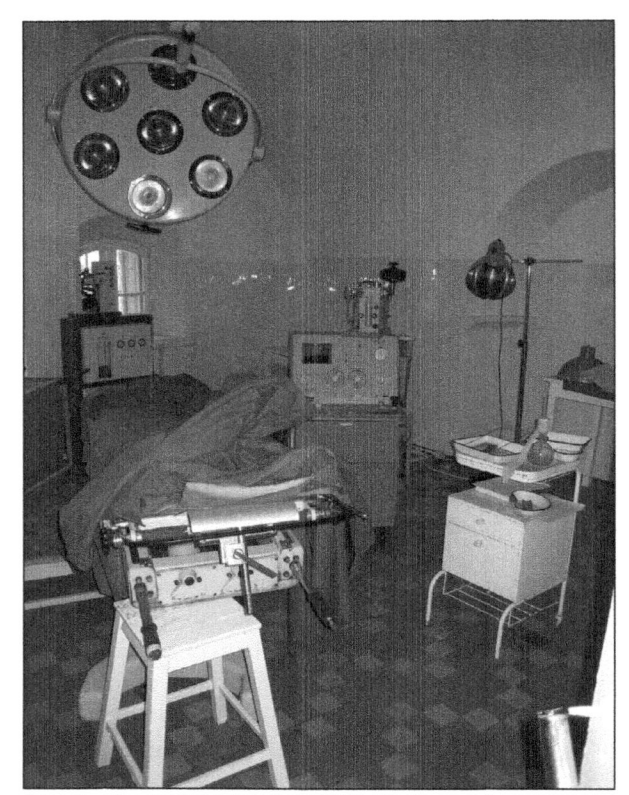

Prison hospital. (By kalev kevad, via Wikimedia Commons)

program for correctional facilities that met these standards.

Accreditation is a process in which an independent outside agency certifies that correctional institutions have met acceptable national standards for health care services. As of 2016, three national bodies offered accreditation to correctional facilities: the American Correctional Association (ACA), which accredits the entire operation of institutions, including health care services; the Joint Commission on Accreditation of Health Organizations (JCAHO), which oversees the accreditation of a variety of health care organizations, including correctional facilities; and the National Commission on Correctional Health Care (NCCHC), which sets standards of health care for jails, prisons, and juvenile facilities. Of these organizations, the NCCHC is considered the leading authority on correctional health care. NCCHC standards are wide ranging and include administrative and personnel issues, environmental and preventive health care, routine and emergency health services, and medical-legal issues.

The courts have not ruled that correctional facilities are constitutionally required to undergo accreditation. An increasing number of prisons have sought voluntary accreditation in the hope of reducing inmate litigation, but the implementation of these standards does not guarantee that result. In *Bell v. Wolfish* (1980), for example, the Supreme Court ruled that standards developed by professional associations, such as the NCCHC, are at best only advisory and do not necessarily define what is minimally required by the Constitution. Nevertheless, correctional institutions frequently set health care guidelines in accordance with NCCHC standards.

Ethical Considerations

In addition to developing standards of health care and accreditation, many professional organizations have stressed the need for prison health care providers to develop and adopt a code of professional ethics to guide the conduct of professionals and establish moral duties and obligations in relation to their clients, institutions, and society. Although a number of correctional health care organizations have adopted such codes, correctional institutions are neither constitutionally nor professionally required to do the same. However, as with accreditation, prison officials who adopt ethical standards of care and treatment of prisoners reduce the chances of inmate litigation.

Many of the ethical issues that arise for prison health care providers are similar to those encountered by health care providers practicing in the larger society. However, in contrast to the issues faced by their outside world counterparts, the ethical challenges that correctional health care providers face may be complicated by the settings in which they administer care and the clients whom they serve. For example, health care providers must disregard the criminal records of their prison patients. Providers are often aware of their patients' crimes and may have difficulty administering care because of what may be disturbing knowledge. Moreover, all patients also have a right to make autonomous decisions about their own medical care, regardless of the settings in which they receive care. Their rights includes the right to be fully informed about all medical treatments they receive and the right to refuse medical care. Finally, as in the outside world, doctor-patient confidentiality is essential, and medical staff should never discuss the medical diagnoses or treatments of prison patients with anyone other than the patients themselves.

As of 2016, debates were ongoing as to whether it was ethical for prisons to charge inmates copayments for medical services. According to a study conducted by the Brennan Center for Criminal Justice at the New York University School of Law, more than thirty states as well as the Federal Bureau of Prisons permitted this practice at state and federal prisons as of 2015. Such copayments, which can be as high as $100, are applied to both hospital visits and emergency treatment as well as routine care. Critics of this policy argue that the majority of prisoners are too poor to be able to afford such charges, deterring them from seeking medical care. Prison officials counter that these fees help prisons to raise funds to make up for the cost of having to offer medical services. In the United States in 2011, health care spending for prisons totaled $7.7 billion, according to a report by the Pew Charitable Trusts and the John D. and Catherine T. MacArthur Foundation.

Kimberly D. Dodson

Further Reading

Altice, Frederick, Peter Selwyn, and Rita Watson, eds. *Reaching In, Reaching Out: Treating HIV/AIDS in the Correctional Community.* Washington, DC: Natl. Commission on Correction Health Care, 2002. Print.

Andrews, Michelle. "Even in Prison, Health Care Often Comes with a Copay." *National Public Radio.* NPR, 30 Sept. 2015. Web. 31 May 2016.

Faiver, K. L. *Health Care Management Issues in Corrections.* Lanham: Amer. Correctional Assn., 1998. Print.

PEW Charitable Trusts, and John D. and Catherine T. MacArthur Foundation. *State Prison Health Care Spending.* Washington, DC: 2014. PDF file.

Puisis, Michael, ed. *Clinical Practice in Correctional Medicine*. St. Louis: Mosby, 1998. Print.

See also AIDS; Prisons, Federal Bureau of; Cruel and unusual punishment; Elderly prisoners; Mental illness; Preventive detention; Prison guards; Prison industries; Prison overcrowding; Prison violence; Supermax prisons; Transgender, LGBTQ prisoners.

Prison industries

Definition: Government-operated enterprises that employ and provide job training to state and federal prisoners
Criminal justice issues: Prisons; Rehabilitation
Significance: Proponents of prison industries cite reduced rates of recidivism among participants; critics, however, say the programs do not adequately compensate prisoners for their labor.

Prison industries provide work opportunities, directly or indirectly, for inmates in the prison system. Some observers view these as helpful for prisoners, while others believe that they either exploit prisoners or harm private-sector businesses.

The federal government and most states operate government-owned corporations that provide goods and services to consumers, although there are generally limitations on who can purchase those goods and services.

The government established the Federal Prison Industries (FPI) in 1934, by an act of Congress. Prisoners had previously provided goods and services through the auspices of the US Treasury Department. The new law permitted the FPI, using a trade name of Unicor, to keep surplus revenue as operating capital.

The aims of FPI are to teach employable skills to as many inmates as possible, to promote better environments at federal prisons by providing constructive opportunities for prisoners, and to produce and market high-quality goods for use by federal agencies while having minimal effects on the private sector.

The state prison industries organizations usually restrict purchases of their products to their state government or to qualified nonprofit organizations within their state. In most states, prison industries compete with private-sector business, although California requires that government organizations purchase needed materials from its Prison Industry Authority.

Prison Industries Products

Prison industries produce a wide range of products and services—not just license plates, as is popularly thought. Prison goods and services range from furniture, such as desks and other office equipment, to agricultural products to clothing. In Oregon, prisoners produce "Prison Blues" blue jeans, which have proved to be very popular. The California prison industries had sales of more than $150 million in 1998, according to a University of California at Berkeley study.

The FPI markets more than one hundred goods and services to federal agencies. Products include furniture, textiles, and electronic components. Services include data entry, engine repair, furniture refinishing, recycling, bulk mailing, and laundry services. In 2003, the FPI's revenues exceeded $700 million. In 2015, FPI reported net sales of $472 million.

Only a small percentage of prisoners are able to participate in prison industries. As of 2015, only 7 percent of eligible inmates were working in the program, according to FPI.

Studies have suggested a lower rate of recidivism among participants in these programs, compared with inmates who have not been thus employed. Proponents of prison industries argue that prison industries are not just about earning money; rather, they are a means of promoting public safety. Supporters assert that participants in prison industries are not just the prisoners deemed most likely to do well outside prison; the participants are a broad cross section of the prison population. Prisoners

James V. Bennett, leading penal reformer, served as Director of Federal Bureau of Prisons 1937-1964. (Library of Congress)

Laundry building on Alcatraz Island, San Francisco Bay. (Public domain, via Wikimedia Commons)

who participate in this programs are also said to gain skills and work experience.

Criticisms of Prison Industries

Some observers argue that the goods produced are of limited quality and thus that prison industries furnish inferior goods to government agencies. A Government Accounting Office report in 1998 described some problems with the goods produced and the inability of the FPI to meet its published deadlines. The study clearly indicated problems but stated that some improvements had already been made.

Other critics argue that prison industries interfere with the business activities of law-abiding citizens. Some in Congress have sought to require government agencies to use competitive bidding rather than purchasing from the FPI. A measure that would have enacted this change was passed by the House of Representatives in 2004, but it did not pass in the Senate.

Prisoners' net wages are typically less than $1 per hour because money is taken from their gross earnings to pay for administration of the prison industry program and for some of the expenses that the prisoners incur in confinement. Some critics of prison industries argue that this is tantamount to exploitation of prisoners. Others assert that working conditions in prisons are usually inadequate or dangerous. Still others argue that such government corporations are inefficient because of their bureaucratic structures. For example, after its creation in 1983, the California Prison Industry Authority lost money in five of its first thirteen years of operation. Despite these criticisms, it is unlikely the politicians will change the system of prison industries because they are viewed by many as cost effective and fair to prisoners.

Michael Coulter

Further Reading

Burton-Rose, Daniel, Dan Pen, and Paul Wright, eds. *The Celling of America: An Inside Look at the U.S. Prison Industry*. Monroe: Common Courage, 1998. Print.

Cardwell, Diane. "Private Businesses Fight Federal Prisons for Contracts." *New York Times*. New York Times, 14 Mar. 2012. Web. 27 May 2016.

Christie, Nils. *Crime Control as Industry: Towards Gulags, Western Style*. New York: Routledge, 2000. Print.

Goldman, George. *The Economic Impact of Production in California's Prison Industries*. Berkeley: Dept. of Agriculture and Resource Economics, U of California at Berkeley, 1998. Print.

Richmond, Kerry M. "The Impact of Federal Prison Industries Employment on the Recidivism Outcomes of Female Inmates." *JQ: Justice Quarterly* Aug. 2014: 719-45. Print.

See also Auburn system; Prisons, Federal Bureau of; Elderly prisoners; Halfway houses; Prison and jail systems; Rehabilitation; Walnut Street Jail; Work camps; Pennsylvania system of corrections.

Prison inmate subculture

Definition: A subculture consists of beliefs, customs, traditions, values, attitudes, and the way of life (lifestyles) of the people involved. This is true of prison inmates or ethnic groups.

Criminal justice issues: Criminal justice issues: Deviancy; criminology; prisons

Significance: Understanding that subcultures have similar characteristics and features is essential. People must learn a subculture's way of life and values. Prisoners must also learn the way of life and values of the penal institutions to which they are confined. Knowing the values and codes of conduct of an institution can impact inmates' survival, rehabilitation, and/or reform.

A process that is relevant for prison subcultures is prisonization. Clemmer, in his 1958 book The Prison Community, defined prisonization as "the taking on in greater or lesser degree of the folkways, mores, customs, and general culture of the penitentiary."

The process of prisonization also has been called the indigenous origins theory. Erving Goffman has termed the prison to be a total institution. Total institutions are institutions that control every aspect of the lives of their members. Total institutions have codes of behavior as well as their own language (argot). The process of prisonization enables new inmates to learn the code and argot.

Conclusion

The prison subculture is comprised of inmates. Subcultures of different prisons share basic characteristics in common. For example, the prison code tends to include the following elements: Prisoners should not trust the correction officers. They should mind their own business and not interfere with other inmates or snitch on them. Furthermore, they should not complain. They should not take advantage of other inmates and should keep their word. They also share an argot. Some examples from the argot are: fish, a new inmate; homeboy, an inmate from your home town; and a best friend is an ace dude.

Like produces like. It is not surprising that different prisons produce similar subcultures. A culture is a means for adapting to circumstances. Therefore, since inmates are adapting to similar incarceration, their subcultures strongly resemble one another. The only way to change the subculture is to change the conditions to which it is adapting. People in a deprivation situation tend to band together to ease the restrictions of deprivation. Inmates are indeed deprived —of freedom, of normal recourse for injuries and in numerous other ways. There are five deprivations of prisons: liberty; goods and services; heterosexual relationships; autonomy; and security. Thus, there are no heterosexual relationships in prison. Therefore, little, if any, stigma is attached to homosexual rape. In the outside world, rape of any kind is generally stigmatized. The importation model says that prison subcultures are formed from what inmates bring into prison from their criminal lives. It seems that a combination of these views may give a better perspective on the issue. Nothing comes from nothing. Therefore, it seems sensible to posit that people cannot but help but bring their cultures with them into prison and then adapt them to prison circumstances in the best manner possible given their situation. A large part of that situation is the deprivation of basic needs.

Frank A. Salamone

Further Reading

Alarid, L. F. "Female Inmate Subcultures." In *Correctional Contexts: Contemporary and Classical Readings*, J. W. Marquart and J. R. Sorensen, eds., 134-39. Los Angeles: Roxbury, 1997.

Bronson, Eric F. "Medium Security Prisons and Inmate Subcultures: The 'Normal Prison.'" *The Southwest Journal of Criminal Justice* 3, no. 2 (2006): 61.

Castle, T., C. Hensley, and R. Tewksbury. "Argot Roles & Prison Sexual Hierarchy." In *Prison Sex: Practice and Policy*, Edited by C. Hensley. 13-26. Boulder, Colo.: Lynne Rienner, 2002.

Clemmer, D. The Prison Community. Boston: Holt, 1958.

"Deprivation Model v. Importation Model." November 12, 2013. https://prezi.com/2oxpo58pp3vk/deprivation-model-v-importation-model/.

Goffman, E. *Asylums*. New York: Doubleday, 1961.

"Prisons: Prisoners, Inmate Subcultures and Informal Organizations." http://law.jrank.org/pages/1796/Prisons-Prisoners-Inmate-subcultures-informal-organizations.html.

"Prison Subcultures & the Deprivation Model." http://study.com/academy/lesson/prison-subcultures-the-deprivation-model.html.

Thomas, C. W. "Theoretical Perspectives on Prizonization: A Comparison of the Importation and Deprivation Models." *Journal of Criminal Law and Criminology* 68 (1977): 135-45.

Wheeler, S. "Socialization in Correctional Communities." *American Sociological Review* 26 (1961): 697-712.

See also History of incarceration; Prison/Prisoner classification systems; LGBTQ prisoners; Security Threat Groups (STGs)/Prison gangs; Prisoner rights; Prison Rape Elimination Act (PREA) (2003); Pennsylvania system of corrections; Supermax prisons; Solitary confinement; Prison violence; Prison overcrowding; Prison guards; Prison and jail systems; Elderly prisoners.

Prison overcrowding

Definition: Incarceration of more prisoners than the prisons are designed to house

Criminal justice issues: Prisons; Punishment; Sentencing

Significance: In 2000, the number of persons incarcerated in the United States was nearly six times greater than it had been in 1970. By 2012 707 out of every 100,000 people in the United States was imprisoned, by far the highest rate among the world's most populous countries. Although the numbers of both state and federal prisons also increased during this time span, the total numbers of prisoners greatly exceeded their intended maximum capacities.

From the mid-nineteenth century through around 1980, the rate of incarceration in the United States remained fairly stable. During the early 1980s, however, the rates of incarceration rose exponentially. The largest period of growth occurred between 1980 and 1995, when the rate of imprisonment grew four times larger than the rate that had been relatively stable for more than a century. Although the numbers of correctional facilities increased, the number of inmates was too great a burden for the prison system to bear. The result was many badly overcrowded prisons.

Although incarceration rates appear have leveled off since the mid-1990s, state and federal prisons still struggle to keep up with the impact of the population surge. The numbers of state and federal prisons increased by 14 percent between 1995 and 2000, expanding the total rated capacities of all prisons by 31 percent. Nevertheless, the average state prison was still operating 1 percent above its rated capacity and federal prisons were operating at a rate 34 percent over their capacities. As of 2014 almost one in two hundred people was incarcerated in the United States, a total of almost 2.3 million people.

The overcrowding problem is stronger in some states than others. According to the Bureau of Justice, by 2014 seventeen states had prison populations in excess of their prison capacities. These included Illinois (prisons operating at 151.7 percent of capacity), North Dakota (150.5 percent), California (142.7 percent), Nebraska (126.3 percent), Ohio (119.8 percent), Delaware (117.7 percent), Colorado (115.3 percent), Iowa (114 percent), and Hawaii (112.8 percent). Other states operating at or above capacity included Washington (105.7 percent), Pennsylvania (104.1 percent), Louisiana (103.7 percent), Minnesota (103.2 percent), Kansas (103.1 percent), Idaho (103 percent), Oregon (101.7 percent), Alabama (100.5 percent), and New Hampshire (100 percent).

Causes of Overcrowding

The simplest explanation for the prevalence of prison overcrowding is that there are too many inmates for the available prison beds. More substantive explanations account for what societal or criminal justice system factors led to the growth in imprisonment. From the mid-1970s through the early 1990s, the prison population expanded as courts began sentencing unprecedented numbers people convicted of less serious offenses to prison. However, the courts were merely responding to rising crime rates and public disenchantment with the criminal justice system that had begun in the 1960s and continued into the 1980s.

Rising crime rates supported the long-standing conservative argument that individualized rehabilitative treatment of offenders does not deter criminals from reoffending. As a result, a "get-tough" movement developed in which prison terms became the foremost sentencing option for the courts. Many states established mandatory sentences for repeat offenders, even for small crimes.

A second reason for the population increase followed from the first: the so-called " war on drugs," which

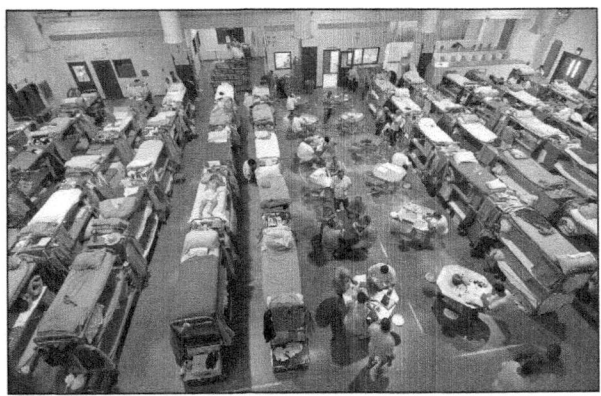

Overcrowding in California State Prison. (Public domain, via Wikimedia Commons)

prompted renewed public calls for tougher punishments. In the past, most minor drug offenders had been sentenced merely to probation and community treatment. However, from the mid-1980s through the early 1990s, increases in incarceration of drug offenders accounted for one-third of prison population growth. Although the proportion later decreased, drug offenders accounted for nearly 20 percent of the total prison population growth during the 1990s.

During the 1990s, the major cause of prison population growth shifted from the rate of admissions to longer sentences for those who were incarcerated. Lengths of sentences were increased for all major crimes, such as murder, rape, drug law violations, and burglary. These longer sentences were the result not only of the courts becoming more punitive, but also the "tough-on-crime" movement in criminal justice policy.

Criminologists have found evidence suggesting that criminal justice system factors such as structured sentencing guidelines and mandatory minimums, which force judges to impose sentences with fixed minimums for specific offenses, have contributed to prison overcrowding. In addition, many states have abolished their parole systems or limited the discretion of parole boards to decide when to release offenders. Although these systemic factors are at least indirectly the result of societal factors, they are specific policies that have contributed to increases in prison populations.

Prison Overcrowding and the Courts

Prison overcrowding has been examined in the courts as a challenge to the Eighth Amendment's cruel and unusual punishment clause, with reform advocates arguing that such conditions violate prisoner rights. The majority of the courts have held that the total conditions of an institution must be examined before the collective effects of overcrowding on inmates can be understood.

The US Supreme Court has heard several cases pertaining to prison overcrowding. In *Rhodes v. Chapman* (1981) the court allowed the housing of two inmates in cells designed for one person. In *Wilson v. Seiter* (1991) the Court found that for crowding to be considered a violation of the Eighth Amendment, plaintiffs must demonstrate deliberate indifference to basic inmate needs by prison staff that does not include the mere fact of an institution's operating above its rated capacity.

In *Farmer v. Brennan* (1994) the court defined deliberate indifference more specifically by holding that prison officials must be aware that the specific indifference may increase the risk of substantial harm to inmates. Despite making it more difficult to prove that Eighth Amendment violations result from prison overcrowding, nearly 9 percent of all state and federal prisons were under court orders to limit their populations in 2000. However, that figure was considerably less than the nearly 21 percent of prisons rated as overcrowded in 1990.

In 2011 the Supreme Court case *Brown v. Plata* marked a radical step in federal efforts to reduce prison overcrowding. The controversial ruling declared that California, long the most prominent battleground over prison issues, must allow the early release of approximately thirty-seven thousand inmates as an emergency relief measure. The close decision was made only with the swing vote of Justice Anthony Kennedy, who wrote that overcrowding indeed constituted a violation of federal rights.

Effects of Prison Overcrowding

The most significant and far-reaching effect of prison overcrowding is cost. The cost of housing a single prisoner typically ranges between twenty and eighty thousand dollars per year, but can range far higher under special circumstances. The rise in prison populations between 1982 and 1992 was reflected in a rise in annual spending in US corrections from roughly nine billion to nearly thirty-two billion dollars—the largest increase in any area of criminal justice expenditures over that time period. According to the "True Cost of Prisons" survey by the Vera Institute of Justice, in fiscal year 2010 the total cost of prisons to taxpayers in the forty states participating in the survey was $39 billion. A 2015 report by the Vera Institute found justice systems at the local level spent $22.2 billion per year on jails overall.

In addition to increasing costs, prison overcrowding affects both staff and inmates negatively. Some evidence suggests that prison overcrowding has increased staff and inmate tension and contributed to more assaults on staff and greater staff turnover. The effects on inmates are less clear. Some empirical studies have suggested prison crowding is associated with increased levels of prisoner stress, anxiety, and tension. Higher numbers of prisoners place a burden on services such as prison health care, counseling, and sanitation. Accordingly, crowded prisons have been associated with poor inmate adaptation, higher levels of prison violence such as inmate assaults, and collective actions, such as rioting. On the other hand, other studies have suggested that overcrowding has little or no negative effect on inmates, and that inmate misconduct and increases in anxiety are caused by other factors. Nonetheless, no matter which of these viewpoints is indeed the case, overcrowding, which is still prevalent in many prisons, does not have positive effects and thus must be considered a significant issue in criminal justice.

Proposed Solutions

Various methods have been proposed or tried in efforts to reduce prison overcrowding, one of the key concerns of prison reform. A 2013 report by the Urban Institute social policy research center surveyed many potential options, including some then under consideration by congress, and presented its recommended courses of action. These included reducing the number of people incarcerated for drug violations, shortening mandatory sentences for other drug offenses, allow judges more discretion in sentencing drug offenders and white-collar criminals, reducing the truth-in-sentencing requirement that inmates serve at least 85 percent of their sentence, and further reducing sentences for good behavior or enrollment in drug rehabilitation programs. Other suggested specific measures designed to reduce overcrowding include releasing elderly prisoners or certain inmates older than fifty-five years old, improving the process for transferring noncitizen inmates to their home countries, and retroactively applying the 2010 Fair Sentencing Act to reduce the sentences of those convicted for crack cocaine violations to levels comparable with powdered cocaine sentences. In 2013 the Department of Justice began its Smart on Crime program, which attemped to move away from tough-on-crime sentencing, particularly in regards to drug crimes.

More general proposed solutions include providing a variety of alternatives to prison sentences, such as community supervision, rehabilitation programs, and criminal recidivism reduction programs. Most efforts emphasize the reduced costs of such measures while arguing that they can be equally effective at keeping communities safe as high imprisonment, if not more so. More radical suggestions include decriminalization of drugs and widespread use of electronic monitoring systems to track offenders granted parole or probation, though neither has seen much support. In February 2015 the MacArthur Foundation announced its Safety and Justice Challenge, a five-year, $75 million initiative to decrease local justice systems' dependence on imprisonment.

Benjamin Steiner

Further Reading
Alarid, Leanne, and Paul Cromwell, eds. *Correctional Perspectives: Views from Academics, Practitioners, and Prisoners.* Los Angeles: Roxbury, 2002. Print.
Call, Jack. "Prison Overcrowding Cases in the Aftermath of *Wilson v. Seiter.*" *The Prison Journal* 75 (1995): 390-406. Print.
Cohen, Andrew. "The Supreme Court Declares California's Prisons Overcrowded." *Atlantic.* Atlantic Monthly Group, 23 May 2013. Web. 16 Feb. 2015.
Gaes, G. "Prison Crowding Research Reexamined." *The Prison Journal* 74 (1994): 329-363. Print.
Irwin, John, and James Austin. *It's About Time: America's Imprisonment Binge.* 3d ed. Belmont: Wadsworth, 2001. Print.
Knafo, Saki. "10 Ways to Reduce Prison Overcrowding and Save Taxpayers Millions." *Huffington Post.* TheHuffingtonPost.com, 8 Nov. 2013. Web. 16 Feb. 2015.
Stephan, James, and Jennifer Karberg. *Census of State and Federal Correctional Facilities, 2000.* Washington DC: Bureau of Justice, 2003. Print.
Tonry, Michael, ed. *The Future of Imprisonment.* New York: Oxford University Press, 2004. Print.

See also AIDS; Auburn system; Community-based corrections; Cruel and unusual punishment; Halfway houses; Mandatory sentencing; Prison and jail systems; Prison guards; Prison violence; Recidivism; Three-strikes laws; Probation, adult; Parole; Parole Officers; Prison Escapes; Prison Health Care; Prison Industries; Pennsylvania system of corrections; Auburn System; Female Offenders; Medical model of offender treatment; Parole boards; Prison Rape Elimination Act (PREA) (2003); Prison inmate subculture; Prisoner rights; Privatization of Institutional and Community Corrections, including Faith-Based Prisons; Realignment (PSR) policy; Scandinavia's prison experience; Security threat groups (STGs)/prison gangs; Technology's transformative effect; LGBTQ prisoners; History of incarceration; Prison/prisoner classification systems; Prison Guards.

Prison/prisoner classification systems

Definition: Ways to improve the prison system, especially to enhance efficiency and tackle increase in prison population and budget constraints

Criminal justice issues: Prisons; convictions; crime statistics

Significance: Various methods of prison/prisoner classification assess the risks thereby balancing security requirements with program needs, increase prison efficiency, and aid the prisoners, staff, and the public.

Need for Classification

Improving the efficiency of prisons requires tackling the rapid growth of prison population and accommodating budget constraints imposed by state legislation. An efficient classification system will also assist in minimizing prison escape, violent attacks between inmates, and institutional misconduct. Classification is also required for the safe and efficient operation of any prison facility.

Essentials for Classification of Prisons/Prisoners

The first step toward prison/prisoner classification would be to evaluate how well the existing system allocates prisoners in prison facilities. As a result of the diverse prison population, prisoners possess varied behavioral, psychological, and treatment needs. Further, various methods have to be utilized to build an efficient prison classification system.

It is advisable to follow the three basic forms of prisoner classification: the initial screening process, the initial classification form, and the reclassification form. The initial screening process is useful in identifying, especially, the emergency requirements of the prisoner when first brought into the prison. The initial classification process is used to determine the prisoner's scored custody level after being brought to the prison system. The reclassification process is a necessity to reevaluate the prisoner's requirements and conduct so as to smoothen the process of classification. All of the information gained as a result of these forms and processes need to be stored in automated data systems storage in the prison's management information system for easy access and ready monitoring.

The classification system also brings in reliability and validity. This is a result of the ability to predict the prisoner's behavior and then assigning an appropriate task, thereby enhancing validity in the accuracy of the classification system. Reliability would mean the uniformity in decision. The decisions on the housing of the prisoner, the types of services and programs to be assigned to the prisoner, and the nature of work assignment most appropriate for the prisoner, all form part of prisoner classification. Additionally, there needs to be a dedicated classification unit and staff for the prison to function efficiently. Having the desired number of dedicated, well-trained, and experienced staff ensures proper classification of prisoners in a timely manner. Sole authority of classification staff over assigning prisoners to housing units also retains prisons efficiency. Centralized control over all prison transfers is also a step forward for effective prisons, while leaving some room for staff members to recommend in emergency situations.

Most importantly, well-structured instruments, like forms, are designed and used to produce reliable assessments of the risks posed by prisoners in the objective classification systems.

The classification process does not end here as continuous monitoring and process evaluation are critical in understanding the current prison population and in enhancing the efficiency of the prison by aiding in making timely decisions.

Professionals have, over the last several decades, worked in prisons and correctional systems to improve the ability of the systems to classify offenders according to work, custody, and programming needs. The efforts have paid off as the results over the decades have shown that custody decisions are more consistent and the criteria for these decisions have been validated, reducing institutional violence and systematic prisoner program needs, among other areas where the revamping has worked. In the United States, Canada, Australia, New Zealand, and Europe, this kind of objective prison classification has worked since the 1980's.

Conclusion: Overrides and Timely and Accurate Classification

The classification of prisons/prisoners has to be executed bearing in mind that there will always be issues of overrides of around 5 to 15 percent. These will be discretionary overrides rather than the initial classification or reclassification scores. The overrides, alongwith the screening of prisoners who enter the prison systems in a timely manner, determine housing for prisoners based on threat rates, and set time frames for reclassification. These overrides go a long way in increasing the efficiency of the prison system while not compromising on security of the prisoners, staff, and the outside world.

Tania Sebastian

Further Reading

Austin, James. "Assessing the New Generation of Prison Classification Models." *Crime & Delinquency* 29 (October, 1983): 561-76.

Bench, L. Lawrence, Terry D. Allen. "Investigating the Stigma of Prison Classification: An Experimental Design." *The Prison Journal* 83 (December, 2003): 376-82.

Hardyman, Patricia L., James Austin, Jack Alexander, et. al. *Internal Prison Classification Systems: Case Studies in Their Development and Implementation.* Washington, D.C.: George Washington University, 2002. http://static.nicic.gov/Library/017381.pdf.

Hardyman, Patricia L., James Austin, and Owan C. Tulloch. *Revalidating External Prison Classification Systems: The Experience of Ten States and Model for Classification Reform.* Washington, D.C.: George Washington University, 2002.

Kupers, Terry A., Theresa Dronet, Margaret Winter, et. al. "Beyond Supermax Administrative Segregation: Mississippi's Experience: Rethinking Prison Classification and Creating Alternative Mental Health Programs." http://solitarywatch.com/wp-content/uploads/2011/08/unit-32-article-cjb2.pdf.

See also Criminal history record information; Criminal records; Elderly prisoners, prison escapes; Prison overcrowding; Prison violence; Rehabilitation; Supermax prisons; *Asker v. Brown* (2016); Prison inmate subculture; Prisoner rights; Security Threat Groups (STGs)/Prison gangs; LGBTQ prisoners; History of incarceration; Pennsylvania system of corrections; Auburn system.

Prison Rape Elimination Act (PREA) of 2003

Definition: Government mandate for correctional facilities to address prison rape

Criminal justice issues: Crime prevention; prisons; sex offenses

Significance: The passage of PREA 2003 mandates correctional facilities to address prison rape and requires the federal government to collect incidence and prevalence data on rape in adult and youth facilities.

Overview of PREA 2003

The general scope was to determine incidence and prevalence, as well as study the physical, psychological, emotional, social, medical, and even economic consequences of prison rape in the United States. Though ubiquitous throughout the correctional system, prison rape in the United States was a taboo topic and not thoroughly discussed before 2001. The general public was aware of this public health problem and even though selected scholars were investigating the issue, the government was not focused on remedying the issue.

In 2001, the Human Rights Watch (HRW) published *No Escape: Male Prisoner Rape*, which exposed several cases of sexual assault inside U.S. prisons. This paper was the main impetus behind the creation of the Prison Rape Elimination Act (PREA) in 2003. In only two months, PREA passed through the House of Representatives and the Senate, and on September 4, 2003, President George W. Bush signed it.

Multiple discussions surround the fast pace of the passage of PREA. Some scholars suggest the increase in the number of people under correctional supervision while others note the need for a humanitarian response from Congress. Other underlying factors include the increasing numbers of male-to-male cases and concerns about the short- and long-term consequences of prison rape, as well as media influence on the general public demanding the end of these cruel situations.

PREA Mandates

With the passage of PREA, a zero-tolerance policy of sexual assault was established. In general, PREA requirements are mandatory for all federal correctional institutions, and on the state and local level; facilities that do not follow the conditions can lose 5 percent of their federal funds. The PREA asked correctional facilities to make prevention of prison rape a priority. It also demanded the creation and implementation of standardized strategies to detect, prevent, reduce, and punish these cases. Other requirements of PREA include the development and maintenance of data collections to enumerate these situations, increase the accountability of staff who fail to adhere to prevention and reporting strategies, and develop a consistent definition of prison rape among all institutions.

Defining Prison Rape

With the PREA the National Prison Rape Elimination Commission (NPREC) was created, which established two main categories of prison rape: inmate-inmate and staff-inmate. For the first one, the Commission established that a sexual abuse occurs in sexual acts or penetration without the consent of the inmate, by coercion of violence, or because the inmate is unable to give consent or resist. Sexual harassment was also included. For staff-inmate rape, behaviors include sexual touching or penetration with or without the consent of the inmate, indecent exposure, and voyeurism. In summary, all sexual encounters between staff and inmates were determined to be sexual abuse because of the power component inherent in these interactions.

Government Surveys

The Bureau of Justice Statistics (BJS) is the agency responsible for collecting data on prison sexual assault across the country. Three different types of surveys gather the information. First, the Survey of Sexual Victimization (SSV) includes administrative data from all federal and state systems, institutions operated by the U.S. military, and Immigration and Customs Enforcement. It also includes juvenile facilities. The first collection of this survey was completed in 2004. Second, the National Inmate Survey (NIS) collects data reported by adult inmates in prisons and local jails. The first collection was done in 2007, and later versions include juveniles housed in adult facilities. Third, the National Survey of Youth in Custody (NSYC) gathers information about youth who report sexual abuse in juvenile institutions. The first collection of this survey was done in 2008.

Obstacles

Even though PREA establishes clear requirements on how to prevent, detect, or punish prison rape, some phenomena that promote these acts to happen cannot be stopped by the Act. Scholars have argued that correctional officers (COs) have substantial influence on sexual assault cases. Correctional officers may act as perpetrators, though they may also facilitate these situations by actively or passively creating opportunities for inmate-inmate rape through decision-making such as housing vulnerable inmates with the most violent ones, failing to provide medical and mental health assistance to victims of an assault, breaching confidentiality when a case is reported, or even refusing to provide the inmate the formal procedural requirements PREA demands.

Daniela Barberi
Eileen M. Ahlin

Further Reading

Dumond, R. W. "Confronting America's Most Ignored Crime Problem: The Prison Rape Elimination Act of 2003." *Journal of the American Academy of Psychiatry and the Law Online* 31, no. 3 (2003): 354-60.

Graham, T., and A. Hastings. "Vera and the Prison Rape Elimination Act." *Federal Sentencing Reporter* 24, no. 1 (2011): 42-43.

Henneke, E. "Prison Rape Elimination Act." *Texas Criminal Justice Coalition*, 1-6.

Jenness, V., and M. Smyth. "Passage and Implementation of the Prison Rape Elimination Act: Legal Endogeneity and the Uncertain Road from Symbolic Law to Instrumental Effects." *The Stanford Law and Policy Review* 22, no. 2 (2011): 489-527.

Schanbacher, K. "Inside Job: The Role Correctional Officers Play in the Occurrence of Sexual Assault in US Detention Centers." *DePaul Journal for Social Justice* 9 (2015): 38-66.

Smith, B. V. "The Prison Rape Elimination Act: Implementation and Unresolved Issues." *American University, Washington College of Law Research Paper*, No. 2008-49.

Struckman-Johnson, C., and D. Struckman-Johnson. "Stopping Prison Rape: The Evolution of Standards Recommended by PREA's National Prison Rape Elimination Commission." *The Prison Journal* 93, no. 3 (2013): 335-54.

Thompson, R. A., L. S. Nored, and K. C. Dial. "The Prison Rape Elimination Act (PREA): An Evaluation of Policy Compliance with Illustrative Excerpts." *Criminal Justice Policy Review* 19, no. 4 (2008): 414-37.

See also Bureau of Justice Statistics; Prison and jail systems; Prison violence; Rape and sex offenses.

Prison violence

Definition: Forms of violence and sexual assault committed on and by prison inmates
Criminal justice issues: Prisons; Sex offenses; Violent crime
Significance: Government studies have shown that assaults on staff and inmates of correctional facilities are rising across the United States, even though many assaults—especially sexual assaults—are underreported by prison officials. Trends toward making convicted offenders serve longer sentences and lose more privileges make it seem likely that prison violence will continue to increase.

Prison violence and sexual abuse may be an inevitable consequence of being locked up. Television dramas such as Home Box Office's *Oz* and popular films such as *The Shawshank Redemption* (1994) have highlighted the dangers and brutality that inmates often face from prison guards and fellow prisoners. Many people can visualize the lasting images from films in which inmates are beaten, raped, and abused for a variety of reasons. In some cases, the victims may be seen as easy targets for others; in others, violence may be a manifestation of gang activity, and some inmates resort to violence simply in order to protect themselves from others.

Many dramatic productions treat prison violence and sexual abuse as normal aspects of prison life. These productions contribute to the public expectation that violence is a natural by-product of housing criminals together under one roof. At the same time, some people charge that state and government agencies too often turn a blind eye to the abuses suffered by inmates.

Prison violence and sexual abuse are potential problems faced by all prisoners; however, many prisons are reluctant to provide adequate information about the abuse taking place within their facilities. For this reason, statistics on prison violence and abuse must be examined with caution. Statistics on violence and sexual abuse tend to underestimate incidence rates. Solid and unbiased research on prison violence is difficult to find and even more difficult to conduct because of the inherently taboo nature of the subject.

Damage leftover from a prison riot. (Public domain, via Wikimedia Commons)

Reasons for Violent Behavior

Two long-standing and competing theories have been advanced to explain prison violence. Developed during the 1950s and 1960s, the deprivation theory suggests that inmates act violently because of the "pains" they experience while incarcerated. From this perspective, prison is a harsh, degrading place that controls inmates totally. Inmates are told when to eat and when to sleep. Stripped of their identities, they become mere bodies with numbers. Under the harsher conditions imposed by many modern prisons, inmates' pains take on new forms. Many inmates spend twenty or more hours in their cells every day with few or no recreational or educational programs. Research indicates that variables such as lack of programs, higher security levels, gang activity, and prison overcrowding may all increase violent behavior.

The second major explanation for prison violence is the importation theory. It holds that inmates engage in violence because they are violent people to begin with. In fact, inmates merely carry into the prison system the same violent attitudes and behaviors they have outside prisons. This theory points to variables such as age, race, gender, and aggressive personality as causes of increased violent behavior during incarceration. Research on prison violence combines elements of both theories. It looks at how inmates with such traits as aggressive personalities react in particular prison environments.

Individual and Collective Violence

Prison violence takes several different forms. It can be individual, when it occurs between fellow inmates or between inmates and staff members. According to the Bureau of Justice Statistics, the homicide rate in state prisons rose 24 percent between 2011 and 2012, from 5 homicides per 100,000 inmates to 7 homicides per 100,000 inmates; while eighty-five state prisoners had been killed that year, almost seven hundred had been killed since 2001. Research has shown that male inmates are much more likely to be sexually and physically violent than female inmates. However, the most influential and important predictor of violent behavior is age. All research on the subject has indicated that inmates under the age of twenty-five are the most likely to behave violently. Moreover, as inmates age, they tend to commit fewer acts of violence. Other individual characteristics, such as race, education, prior criminal history, marital status, and personality, showed mixed results when predicting violent behavior.

Prior to the movement for prisoner rights of the late 1960s and 1970s, physical beatings, extended solitary confinement, strip searches, torture, and other forms of inhumane treatment by prison guards were commonplace in American prisons. Interestingly, research has indicated that staff abuse of inmates tends to occur most often in maximum-security facilities. In general, however, individual acts of staff violence against inmates were more common before the 1980s, but sporadic incidents still occur. Data on staff violence is especially difficult to find and should be looked at with an especially cautious eye.

Collective violence typically involves large groups of inmates acting out together. The most common form of collective violence is rioting. More than three hundred prison riots have occurred in US history. The most notable occurred at New York's Attica prison in 1971 and at New Mexico's state penitentiary in 1980. Both of the Attica prison riot and the New Mexico state penitentiary riot resulted in the deaths of both inmates and guards and millions of dollars in property damage. Studies of both riots emphasize issues relating to overcrowding, poor food, lack of medical facilities, guard brutality, and other forms of inhumane treatment. Most important, however, those incidents attracted public attention to the mistreatment of inmates in US prisons and helped bring about sweeping prison reforms. In 2015, a riot at a Texas prison rendered the facility uninhabitable after the inmates, who had reportedly expressed grievances regarding poor conditions and abuse for years, set the tents they were housed in on fire; all 2,800 inmates, largely convicted of immigration and nonviolent drug offenses, were moved to another facility.

Sexual Abuse

According to a survey conducted by the Bureau of Justice Statistics, 8,763 allegations of sexual victimization were reported to administrators of adult correctional facilities in 2011 alone; 10 percent of them were later confirmed to have occurred. The number of reported incidents of sexual victimization has steadily increased since 2005. Just over half of the substantiated incidents involved only inmates, while the rest included prison staff members. The rate of reported allegations had increased to 3.9 per 1,000 in 2011. For a variety of reasons, the exact numbers of inmates who suffer from this form of abuse may never be known precisely. Some inmates are reluctant to report such abuse, and some prison officials are inclined to ignore it. Moreover, many staff members may not be adequately trained to respond to incidents of sexual abuse.

Compounding the problem of quantifying sexual abuse in prisons is the fact that definitions of sexual abuse vary greatly from institution to institution. For example, some prisons classify rape, sexual harassment, and sexual abuse as the same offenses, while others classify them as separate offenses. Nevertheless, research studies do indicate which inmates are most at risk of becoming victims of sexual abuse.

The Shawshank Redemption

One of the most gripping Hollywood films about prison life is *The Shawshank Redemption*, a 1994 film adapted from a novella by Stephen King. In the film, a falsely convicted inmate (Tim Robbins), who is befriended by another inmate (Morgan Freeman), survives the brutality of prison life.

Much credible evidence has established that brutality is a fact of life in American prisons. However, *The Shawshank Redemption* does not accurately convey the presence of law within prisons. Many films have portrayed prisons as closed societies in which wardens wield absolute control. In real life, however, prison administrations are regularly the objects of litigation brought by their inmates. Litigation is also often brought against prisons by outside public-interest groups that support prisoner rights for the very reason that under the American system of criminal justice, prisoners are not thought to be outside the superintendence of law.

Timothy L. Hall

The most likely to be victimized are young first-time offenders and physically weak older inmates. Also at increased risk are inmates who fit the stereotype of educated middle-class members of outside society who lack "street smarts." At the same time, inmates with mental disabilities are also likely targets of sexual violence.

Sexual abuse among inmates has been of even greater importance over the past decades than in the past because of the threat of HIV/AIDS and other sexually transmitted diseases. According to the Centers for Disease Control and Prevention (CDC), in 2010, at least 20,093 inmates in the United States were believed to be infected with HIV/AIDS, with 91 percent being men.

To address the overlooked issue of prison violence, the US Congress passed the Prison Rape Elimination Act in 2003. This law was designed to collect more accurate and reliable data on prison violence, to protect inmates from violence, and to increase the accountability of prison staff and inmates to report these actions. A final rule in accordance with the act was released in 2012 that included a standard requiring that all allegations of sexual assault be investigated "promptly and thoroughly." As of 2016, however, debates were ongoing as to whether prison systems were actually able to live up to the standards set in the act.

Karen F. Lahm

Further Reading

Beck, Allen J., and Ramona R. Rantala. *Sexual Victimization Reported by Adult Correctional Authorities, 2009-11*. Washington, DC: US Dept. of Justice, Bureau of Justice Statistics, 2014. PDF file.

Braswell, Michael C., Reid H. Montgomery, and Lucien X. Lombardo. *Prison Violence in America*. 2nd ed. Cincinnati: Anderson, 1994. Print.

Edgar, Kimmett, Ian O'Donnell, and Carol Martin. *Prison Violence: The Dynamics of Conflict, Fear and Power*. Cullompton: Willan, 2003. Print.

"HIV Among Incarcerated Populations." *Centers for Disease Control and Prevention*. CDC, 22 July 2015. Web. 26 May 2016.

"Justice Department Releases Final Rule to Prevent, Detect and Respond to Prison Rape." *US Dept. of Justice*. US Dept. of Justice, 17 May 2012. Web. 26 May 2016.

Noonan, Margaret E. *Mortality in Local Jails and State Prisons, 2000–2012. Statistical Tables*. Washington, DC: US Dept. of Justice, Bureau of Justice Statistics, 2014. PDF file.

Ross, Jeffrey Ian, and Stephen C. Richards. *Behind Bars: Surviving Prison*. Indianapolis: Alpha, 2002. Print.

Toch, Hans. *Living in Prison*. New York: Free, 1977. Print.

Williams, Stanley "Tookie," and Barbara Cottman Becnel. *Life in Prison*. Minneapolis: Sagebrush Education Resources, 2001. Print.

See also AIDS; Cruel and unusual punishment; Elderly prisoners; Prison and jail systems; Prison escapes; Prison guards; Prison overcrowding; Solitary confinement; Supermax prisons; Prison Rape Elimination Act (PREA) (2003); Prison inmate subculture; Security threat groups (STGs)/prison gangs.

Prisoner rights

Definition: Broad term encompassing constitutional rights help by persons who have been convicted of a crime and incarcerated

Criminal justice issues: Civil rights and liberties; constitutional protections; prisons; punishment

Significance: Prisoners retain certain rights after they are incarcerated, and those rights must be preserved by correctional institutions and personnel.

Prisoners, meaning people who are incarcerated because they have been convicted of a crime, lose many of their constitutional rights at the point when they either receive court approval of their guilty pleas or are convicted through judicial proceedings in a court. However, they retain an important handful of rights related to the conditions in which they are imprisoned. The bulk of these rights arise under the Eighth Amendment protection against cruel and unusual punishment. They also retain some rights under the First Amendment, the Due Process Clause, and the Equal Protection Clause. These rights became a matter of constitutional law pursuant to the due process revolution of the 1960's and 1970's. Prisoners also may receive privileges during periods of incarceration, such as access to television, extra recreation time, or the Internet. However, most of those privileges derive from state and federal administrative laws that govern prison administration, not from any constitutional rights.

Under the Eighth Amendment, prisoners retain the right to be free from conditions and punishments that courts are inhumane. The legal standard for determining what is inhumane requires a three-pronged inquiry: (1) Does the condition that is being challenged pose a substantial risk to the inmates' health or welfare? (2) Are prison officials showing "deliberate indifference" to this known or obvious condition? and (3) Has an inmate actually been hurt by this condition or is there a high risk of future harm?

Specific definitions of proscribed prison practices evolve over time as courts review lawsuits brought by prisoners. On the whole, the United States Supreme Court has determined that it is unconstitutional to deny appropriate living conditions to inmates. Prison conditions do not have to be comfortable, but they must not pose a substantial risk of harm. Collectively, the rights retained by inmates are referred to as prisoners' "conditions of confinement." Courts regularly refine the scope of those rights through judicial opinions rendered in response to lawsuits brought to challenge conditions of confinement, including food, clothing, shelter, recreation, medical care, safety, and equal protection and due process.

Food

Food does not have to be tasty, but it must be edible and sufficiently nutritious to sustain life. For example, courts have found that food cannot be contaminated with animal feces or with mold, but cold or stale food is not unconstitutional. Short-term food deprivation is permitted under certain circumstances, and prisons in some jurisdictions are only required to serve two meals per day. Water must be potable.

Clothing

Generally, prisoners are entitled to sufficient clothing with which to cover their bodies and keep warm. They also usually are entitled to a blanket for sleeping. However, some prisons have been permitted to clothe inmates in only a paper gown with no bedsheets or blankets and no heat source.

Shelter

The conditions in which prisoners are sheltered have been the subject of extensive litigation with mixed results. Prisoners must not be chronically exposed to bugs, vermin, or other egregiously unsanitary conditions. They cannot be subjected to extreme heat or cold for prolonged periods, but broad ranges in sustained temperatures have been permitted. Claims of impermissible overcrowding in prisons led California to release many inmates to bring their prisons into compliance with a court order, but what constitutes "overcrowding" still is not clear. Short-term periods of double- or triple-capacity housing has been permitted, but sustained operations in excess of established maximums for numbers of inmates are unconstitutional. For example, prisons have been permitted to house several people temporarily in the same cell with a single toilet, and prisons may employ temporary sleeping arrangements, such as floor pads and stacked tables. There is no precise definition of the word "temporary" in these cases, and standards are defined either by administrative regulations or by the courts. Inmates can be housed in barred or walled cells, but they cannot be chained or cuffed to immobile objects, such as posts or floor grates, for extended periods of time.

Recreation

Many prisons afford inmates privileges related to exercise and recreation, but prisoners hold only a few actionable rights with respect to these activities. Most prisons provide outdoor fields or yards for sports and leisure, but the courts have found that they are not constitutionally required to do so. Prisons can suspend access to recreational opportunities in case of emergency or as short-term punishment, but inmates cannot be subjected to circumstances in which their muscles atrophy due to underuse or their health otherwise becomes impaired by lack of exercise.

Medical care

Although prisoners cannot sue for malpractice in relation to medical, dental, or mental health care they receive while incarcerated, they are entitled to a basic level of adequate care. Prisons are not required to provide the preferred type of care or the best care, but prisoners have the right to necessary care to treat all known or obvious conditions in a timely manner. The constitutional standard for medical care in prison was established in *Estelle v. Gamble*, in which the United States Supreme Court held that prisons must not be "deliberately indifferent" to a "known medical condition."

Safety

Prisoners have the right to be free from sexual and other forms of assault. Prisons have a duty to protect inmates from violence inflicted by other inmates and by prison employees.

Equal protection and due process

In addition to their Eighth Amendment rights, prisoners retain a few additional constitutional rights, including the right to be free from racial, gender, or ethnic discrimination in the manner in which prison policies are enforced. Disabled prisoners have rights of equal access to facilities. Subject to reasonable time, place, manner, and safety restrictions, prisoners retain their rights to free speech and to practice their religions pursuant to the First Amendment. They also have limited rights to be free from unreasonable deprivations of property and arbitrary disciplinary penalties.

On the whole, prisoners have the right to complain and report about any conditions of confinement. Prisoners must be advised of their right to complain and the administrative processes for pursuing those claims. Prisoners' complaints must comport with the Prison Litigation Reform Act, which means that they must exhaust all administrative remedies before they can sue in court. Prisoners are not entitled to have an attorney paid for by the government to represent them during the administrative complaint process or during subsequent litigation. However, they must be given access to necessary forms and venues for waging complaints, and they must be given access to attorneys whom they may hire or who may work pro bono for them. Prisoners must pay their own filing fees and court costs. If a court finds that a prisoner's lawsuit was frivolous or in bad faith, then the prisoner can be penalized by loss of good time credits or similar administrative penalties.

Anne S. Douds

Further Reading
Bach, G. "More on Dignity in Eighth Amendment Conditions of Confinement Claims." New England Journal on Criminal and Civil Confinement (2016): 1.
Glidden, B "Necessary Suffering: Weighing Government and Prisoner Interests in Determining What Is Cruel and Unusual." *American Criminal Law Review* 49 (2012): 1815.
Schlanger, M. "Prisoners' Rights Lawyers' Strategies for Preserving the Role of the Courts." *University of Miami Law Review* 69 (2014): 519.
Simon, J. S., and A. A. Kragen. "From Health to Humanity: Re-Reading *Estelle v. Gamble* after *Brown v. Plata*." *Federal Sentencing Reporter* 25, no. 4 (2013): _____.
Smith, C. E. "Shaping Constitutional Law: The Example of Prisoners' Rights." In *The Supreme Court and the Development of Law*, 1-13. Palgrave Macmillan US, 2016.
Tartaro, C "What Is Obvious? Federal Courts' Interpretation of the Knowledge Requirement in Post-*Farmer v. Brennan* Custodial Suicide Cases." *The Prison Journal* 95, no. 1 (2015): 23-42.

See also Prison/Prisoner classification systems; History of incarceration; Transgender, lesbian, gay and bisexual prisoners; Security Threat Groups (STGs)/Prison gangs; Scandinavia's prison experience; *Roper v/ Simmons (2005)*; Realignment (PSR) policy; Privatization of institutional and community corrections, including faith-based prisons; Prison inmate subculture; Prison Rape Elimination Act (PREA) (2003); Pennsylvania system of corrections; Parole boards; Conjugal visitation; Civil commitment; *Asker v. Brown* (2016); Work-release programs; Work camps; Supermax prisons; Solitary confinement; Punishment; Prison violence; Prison overcrowding; Prison health care; Prison and jail systems; Preventive detention; Parole; Indeterminate sentencing; Incapacitation; Elderly prisoners; Death qualification; Cruel and unusual punishment; Corporal punishment; Capital punishment; Auburn System.

Prisons, Federal Bureau of

Identification: Federal agency responsible for incarceration of prisoners convicted in federal courts
Date: Created in 1930

Significance: The creation of the Federal Bureau of Prisons to oversee the confining of criminals convicted in federal courts reflected the general expansion of federal criminal law and the growing role of federal law-enforcement agencies.

The first two federal prisons were opened in Leavenworth, Kansas, and Atlanta, Georgia, in 1905. Before that time, persons convicted of federal crimes were confined either in a facility on a military reservation or in a state or local corrections facility. Prohibition and the expansion of federal powers to combat organized crime in the 1920s and 1930s increased federal responsibilities for law enforcement and created a need for a separate federal prison system. In 1930, the Bureau of Prisons was created to administer the expanding federal corrections programs and a growing network of prison facilities. High-profile federal law-enforcement agencies, particularly the Federal Bureau of Investigation under J. Edgar Hoover's leadership, focused attention on violent crime, and new prisons were built. Alcatraz, perhaps the best known of the maximum-security facilities, was opened in 1934 and held some of the most notorious U.S. criminals until its closing in 1963.

The Bureau of Prisons, a unit of the U.S. Department of Justice, is divided into six geographical regions that have a significant amount of autonomy. The directors of the regions also serve on the executive staff of the bureau and provide national coordination of the agency's programs. The organization of the bureau includes the executive office of the director, with a general counsel and an internal affairs section. There are also divisions for administration, correctional programs (with responsibility for managing the facilities), health services, human resource management, program review, community corrections and detention, and information, policy, and public affairs. The Bureau of Prisons is also responsible for UNICOR, a public corporation and the successor to Federal Prisons Industries, founded in 1934, which provides employment and training for inmates. It produces goods and services ranging from furniture to electronics to data entry. The Bureau of Prisons also operates the National Institute of Corrections, which supports state and local corrections agencies and operates the National Academy of Corrections, an information center, and the National Jail Center. The institute has a budget separate from that of the Bureau of Prisons.

The Bureau of Prisons began to experience problems in the 1980s and 1990s because of the age of its facilities, the need for increased capacity, and the increasing costs of corrections programs. In particular, prison overcrowding, the need to accommodate a wide variety of inmate populations, and increasing costs of treating drug abuse problems and addressing health problems related to acquired immunodeficiency syndrome (AIDS) have taxed the agency. The lack of strong political constituencies in the corrections profession and the increasing unwillingness of Congress to expand funding for federal programs are making it difficult to address the growing problems, even though the need for additional resources and new programs has been noted in numerous U.S. General Accounting Office reports. The Bureau of Prisons is also facing challenges in the form of recommendations for privatization of its facilities, and it has been targeted periodically by Congress for elimination. In the mid-2010s the Bureau of Prisons was criticized in an investigative report by Seth Freed Wessler for the *Nation*, which found "at least" twenty-five questionable deaths of detainees held inside its segregated system of privatized, immigrant-only detention facilities.

William L. Waugh, Jr.

Further Reading
Alarid, Leanne, and Paul Cromwell. *Correctional Perspectives: Views from Academics, Practitioners, and Prisoners.* Los Angeles, Calif.: Roxbury, 2002.
Elsner, Alan. *Gates of Injustice: The Crisis in America's Prisons.* Upper Saddle River, N.J.: Financial Times/Prentice-Hall, 2004.
Freed Wessler, Seth. "SEPARATE, UNEQUAL, AND DEADLY. (Cover Story)." *Nation* 302.7 (2016): 12. *MasterFILE Complete.* Web. 24 May 2016.
Herman, P. G., ed. *The American Prison System.* New York: H. W. Wilson, 2001.
Johnson, R. *Hard Time: Understanding and Reforming the Prison.* 3d ed. Belmont, Calif.: Wadsworth, 2002.

See also Auburn system; Criminal justice education; Forestry camps; Model Penal Code; Parole; Prison and jail systems; Prison escapes; Prison industries; Rehabilitation; Work camps; Pennsylvania system of corrections; Privatization of institutional and community corrections, including faith-based programs; Realignment (PSR) policy; Prison Rape Elimination Act (PREA) (2003).

Privatization of institutional and community corrections, including faith-based programs

Definition: Penal institutions and community-based programs and facilities that are operated by for-profit, nongovernmental organizations with the major goal of economic gain

Criminal justice issues: Criminal justice issues: Criminology; rehabilitation; professional standards; prisons
Significance: The transfer of government programs and functions to the private sector brings about a number of concerns such as cost of incarceration, quality of services rendered, legal issues, and the role government plays in oversight.

There is a strong disagreement between those who support privatization of prisons and those who oppose it. Among the advantages that supporters list are saving the government are: time, money, and effort; creating jobs; and keeping prison population at a reasonable level. Opponents offer their own list; they note that private prisons are not as cost-efficient as their supporters claim. Moreover, they question the safety of these prisons. Finally, they note that these private prisons are for-profit organizations that need to make money. That is not always the best way to run a government organization. Moreover, it may encourage corruption and the problems that ensue from it.

It is important to know the extent of the holdings of private prisons. Currently, these for-profit companies have a total of about 16 percent of all federal inmates. Moreover, they oversee 6 percent of state prison inmates, and all prisoners in some states like Texas and Louisiana.

The first private prison in the United States was San Quentin in 1852. San Quentin is now a state-owned institution. The real expansion began in the 1980s. It peaked in the 1990's and has become contentious in the twenty-first century.

Conclusion
The dispute over private prisons is part of the dispute over the role of private industry in government services, including schools, trash pickups, and almost anything else that has routinely been done by government agencies. Those in favor of private enterprise hold that by its very nature government is inefficient and slow to change. Private enterprise, they argue, can do anything more efficiently than government. The counterargument is that private enterprise by its nature seeks to make it private. It is not concerned with the public good. It is concerned with profit. Thus, when given the choice between profit and the public welfare, it will choose profit. This argument takes place in all aspects of when the government has given in to demands to privatize essential services. Furthermore, those who oppose privatization argue that there must be oversight of the private prisons. That fact means that the government still must have a key role, one

that should routinely be found in public prisons. It costs money to provide oversight. That leads to the question of whether private enterprise will pay for that oversight or will be passed on to the taxpayer, cutting into any tax savings. Recent studies have noted major problems with private prisons and their oversight.

Frank A. Salamone

Further Reading

Beto, Dan Richard. "Contracting for Services." *Texas Probation* (July, 1987).
Borna, Shaleen. "Free Enterprise Goes to Prison." *British Journal of Criminology* 26 (1986): 321-34.
Bowditch, Christine, and Ronald S. Everett. "Private Prisons: Problems Within the Solution." *Justice Quarterly* 4 (1987): 441-53.
Bureau of Justice Assistance. *State and Local Programs: Focus on What Works*. Vol. 1. Washington, D.C.: U.S. Department of Justice, Office of Justice Programs, 1994.
Buying Influence: How Private Prison Companies Expand Their Control of America's Criminal Justice System, [PDF] In the Public Interest, October, 2016
Cikins, Warren I. "Privatization of the American Prison System: An Idea Whose Time Has Come?" *Journal of Law and Ethics and Policy* 2 (1986): 445-64.
Cody, W. J. Michael, and Andy Bennett. "The Privatization of Correctional Institutions: The Tennessee Experiment." *Vanderbilt Law Review* 40 (1987): 829-49.
Cohen, Stanley. *Visions of Social Control*. Cambridge, England: Polity. 1985.
Curran, Daniel J. "Destructuring, Privatization and the Promise of Juvenile Diversion: Compromising Community-Based Corrections." *Crime & Delinquency* 34 (1988): 363-78.
Duff, Antony, and David Garland. "Preface: E. Rotman's Beyond Punishment." In *A Reader on Punishment*, A. Duff and D. Garland, eds., 281-83. New York: Oxford University Press, 1994.
Dunham, Douglas W. "Inmates' Rights and the Privatization of Prisons." *Columbia Law Review* 86 (1986): 1475-1504.
Durham, Alexis M. "The Future of Correctional Privatization: Lessons From the Past." In *Privatizing Correctional Institutions*, G. W. Bowman, S. Hakim, and P. Seidenstat, eds., 33-49. New Brunswick, N.J.: Transaction Publishers, 1994.
Feeley, Malcolm. "The Privatization of Prisons in Historical Perspective." *Criminal Justice Research Bulletin* 6 (1991): 1-10.
Feeley, Malcolm, and Jonathan Simon. "The New Penology." *Criminology* 30 (1992): 449-74.
Field, Joseph. "Making Prisons Private: An Improper Delegation of a Government Power." *Hofstra Law Review* 15 (1987): 649-751.
Gentry, James T. "The Panopticon Revisited: The Problem of Monitoring Private Prisons." *Yale Law Journal* 96 (1986): 353-75.
Johnson, Byron R., and Paul P. Ross. "The Privatization of Correctional Management: A Review." *Journal of Criminal Justice* 18 (1990): 351-58.
McDonald, D. "Public Imprisonment by Private Means." *British Journal of Criminology* 34 (1994): 29-48
Morris, Norval, and Michael Tonry. *Between Prison and Probation*. Oxford, England: Oxford University Press, 1990.
Mullen, J. "Corrections and the Private Sector." *The Prison Journal* 65 (1985): 1-13.

Porter, Robert G. "The Privatization of Prisons in the U.S.: A Policy That Britain Should Not Emulate." *Howard Journal* 29 (1990): 65-81.
Robbins, Ira. "Privatization of Corrections: Defining the Issues." *Vanderbilt Law Review* 40 (1987): 813-28.
U.S. Department of Justice. 1974-1987. *Children in Custody*. Washington, D.C.: Government Printing Office, 1988.
U.S. Senate Committee on the Judiciary. *Ford Administration Stifles Juvenile Justice Policy*. Washington, D.C.: Government Printing Office, 1975.

See also History of incarceration; LGBTQ prisoners; Scandinavia's prison experience; Prison inmate subculture; Prison Rape Elimination Act (PREA) (2003); Pennsylvania system of corrections; Medical model of offender treatment; Solitary confinement; Rehabilitation; Prison guards; Prison violence; Prison overcrowding; Prison health care; Prison escapes; Prison and jail systems; Elderly prisons; and Auburn system.

Probation, adult

Definition: Sentencing procedure through which adults convicted of crimes are released by the court and stay out of prison, so long as they adhere to conditions set by the judges

Significance: By the end of the twentieth century, probation was the most commonly used punishment in the U.S. criminal justice system.

In 2014, approximately 3,864,100 people were on probation in the United States, compared with approximately 1,561,000 persons in state and federal correctional facilities. The number of people on probation or parole amounts to one out of every fifty-two adults; men compose 75 percent of probationers. Most people on probation have committed relatively minor crimes, such as driving with a suspended license, committing petty theft or larceny, or possessing small amounts of drugs or other controlled substances. The offenders have typically been released to the community under the supervision of a probation officer and are usually required to meet briefly with the officer once a week or perhaps only once a month for counseling.

Probationers must usually meet a series of requirements. Sometimes probationers must stay away from certain persons, such as wives or children they may have harassed or threatened, or from particular places, such as street corners at which drugs are sold. Judges may also order that probationers stay free of drugs or alcohol or that they find and hold a job. Employers generally do not need to be told that a job applicant is on probation. Breaking any of these conditions can lead to imprisonment for violating probation procedures.

According to the Vera Institute of Justice, in 2013, the average cost of probation nationwide is about $1,110 a year per offender, which compares favorably with the average $31,307 a year it costs to keep someone in prison. In many states some of the costs of probation are recovered by requiring probationers to pay part of the cost of their supervision. This cost-effectiveness is one reason that the number of persons on probation has increased dramatically in recent years.

History and Goals of Probation

Probation comes from the Latin *probatus*, which means "tested" or "proved." In the early United States, persons convicted of crimes were eligible for a suspended sentence if they promised to behave well and offered proof that they could observe the laws. The modern system began in Boston in 1841, when John Augustus, a businessman and advocate of rehabilitation, began bailing out convicted offenders, found them jobs, and gave the court monthly reports on their progress toward a better life. Augustus gained the release of more than two thousand prisoners using this method, most of whom were effectively rehabilitated. In 1878 Massachusetts became the first state to allow judges to choose probation as an alternative to a prison sentence.

By 1940 all American states allowed probation for juvenile offenders and all but six permitted adult probation. Not until the 1980s, however, did all states and the federal government provide for adult probation. The first statistics on probation were collected in 1976, when it was reported that nearly 1,000,000 adults were found to be on probation and 457,528 persons were in prison in the United States.

Probation began as an alternative to imprisonment and was justified as a method of rehabilitation that would save many people, especially nonviolent criminals, from the horrors and potential violence of prison life. Because prisons did not seem to do a very good job of reforming convicts and always seemed to be terribly overcrowded, judges would have an alternative to sending people to the penitentiary. The goal was to reduce crime by allowing offenders an opportunity to prove their goodness in society. The principal goal was rehabilitation, reforming the guilty party, rather than simply punishment, retribution, or revenge.

Central to probation is the notion that persons found to be "good risks" can be placed on probation and that they will not commit more crimes if they are given supervision and counseling. The philosophy of probation is that convicted persons can become law-abiding again. All they need is to be provided with treatment programs, employment, and other services. The focus is not on the harm done by the criminal but on the future reduction of criminal behavior, which can be achieved through proper treatment and supervision.

Violations of probation can be controlled by the ever-present threat that violators will be sent to prison if they break the rules. The idea of probation challenges the "just deserts" school of criminal justice, which proclaims that the purpose of the system is to make those convicted of crimes pay for the damage they have done by undergoing imprisonment. The goal of this method of the criminal justice system is to punish offenders, not to rehabilitate them.

Probation Decisions

The decision to place a convicted person on probation is one alternative available at a sentencing hearing. The judge is usually informed of the details of the offense in each case and makes the decision to place a person on probation after considering a variety of factors. These include the defendant's prior criminal record, social history, and family and employment record. This information is usually provided by a probation officer assigned to investigate the case. Normally, probation is given only in felony cases, not in cases involving misdemeanors.

Probation is granted by the judge in most cases if the probation officer recommends it. Two key factors are involved in this decision: the seriousness of the crime and the report on the person's prior criminal record. In most cases the seriousness of the crime is the single most important factor. Generally, persons convicted of having committed nonviolent crimes are much more likely to receive probation than those who have committed violent or drug-related criminal acts. The judge's decision is also influenced by the likelihood of rehabilitation. Persons considered "good risks" are very likely to receive probation, especially if their crimes did not involve violence.

Only a few studies have been done on the revocation of parole. Decisions to end probation and send people to prison follow no particular pattern or set of rules. There seems to be no consistent standard in revocation hearings. Judges are often inconsistent in arriving at these decisions. Generally, however, revocation depends on the nature of the probation violation. Failure to appear at meetings with parole officers is considered particularly grave. Revocation also depends on the probationer's age, prior record, and employment history. For example, the failure to find or retain a job can lead to revocation. However, any decision to revoke probation must be made by a judge, not simply by a probation officer.

Intensive Probation

One alternative to sending a violator to prison for violating probation is to order more intensive probation. This method can also be applied in cases in which a convicted person has committed a serious or violent crime. Intensive probation provides much closer supervision of offenders and is more than three times more expensive than regular probation. Offenders in intensive programs are required to contact parole officers very frequently, sometimes as often as once a day or at least once a week.

At one point, Georgia, a state with a large investment in intensive probation, required that serious nonviolent offenders have five face-to-face contacts with probation officers every week. The failure rate in this program was about 16 percent, or about one-half the failure rate for regular probationers. Prisoners on either type of probation are extremely unlikely to commit violent crimes, because most have never been convicted of violent crimes. Less than 1 percent of violent crimes in the United States are committed by probationers.

Probation Officers

The major problem with the probation system is the huge caseloads carried by most probation officers. Experts consider thirty cases per officer the best possible situation. However, the average officer in the United States has at least two hundred cases each month. Such huge caseloads prevent many officers from getting actively involved with their clients. Instead, all probationers receive the same treatment, regardless of whether they have been convicted of income tax evasion or armed robbery. Few probationers can get the individual attention they need to remain successfully employed and motivated. The problem seems not to be the idea of probation but the way the system works. There is too little money and too few probation officers to do an effective job.

Another problem since the 1980s has been the fundamental belief on the part of many criminal justice practitioners, from police officers to judges, that probation does not reduce crime. A majority of the U.S. public seems to accept this view. This has led to a major shift in how judges determine sentences. During the 1960s and 1970s, probation officers and judges believed that their mission was to reform and rehabilitate persons under their supervision and authority. Probation was supposed to help people convicted of crimes work their way back into society through employment opportunities and counseling. Probation officers saw their job as helping their clients overcome drug or alcohol dependency while meeting their family obligations.

During the 1980s, however, a much harsher form of criminal justice was instituted, with "just deserts" being the most prominent philosophy. In this view, punishment rather than rehabilitation was the goal, and parole officers responded by focusing their attention on catching probation violators and reporting them to the courts for confinement. New technologies and monitoring devices have made this practice more common. Electronic monitoring devices attached to probationers' legs or ankles enable officers to know where a subject is every minute of the day. House arrest is much more possible with such new devices, many of which have been available only since the mid-1990s. Nevertheless, probation is primarily reserved for people convicted of nonviolent crimes. The costs of normal, nonintensive probation are still about one-thirtieth the cost of imprisonment, and a majority of probationers do not commit additional crimes. Probation is a system that works well to reduce future criminal activity by providing rehabilitation for offenders. It has been shown to be the best sentencing alternative to imprisonment.

Leslie V. Tischauser

Further Reading
Abadinsky, Howard. *Probation and Parole*. 12th ed. Upper Saddle River: Prentice-Hall, 2012. Print.
Carter, Robert M., and Leslie T. Wilkins, eds. *Probation, Parole, and Community Corrections*. New York: Wiley, 1976. Print.
Bonczar, Thomas P., Danielle Kaeble, and Laura Maruschak. *Probation and Parole in the United States, 2014*. Bureau of Justice Statistics. Office of Justice Programs, 19 Nov. 2015. Web. 24 May 2016.
Henrichson, Christian, and Sarah Galgano. *A Guide to Calculating Justice-System Marginal Costs*. New York: Vera Institute of Justice, 2013. PDF file.
Hussey, Frederick A., and David E. Duffee. *Probation, Parole, and Community Field Services: Policy, Structure, and Process*. New York: Harper, 1980. Print.
Lipton, Douglas, Robert Martinson, and Judith Wilks. *The Effectiveness of Correctional Treatment: A Survey of Treatment Evaluation Studies*. New York: Praeger, 1975. Print.
Petersilia, Joan, ed. *Community Corrections: Probation, Parole, and Intermediate Sanctions*. New York: Oxford UP, 1998. Print.

See also Clemency; Community-based corrections; Drug testing; Marshals Service, U.S.; Pardons; Parole; Parole officers; Presentence investigations; Probation, juvenile; Sentencing; Suspended sentences; Technology's transformative effect.

Probation, juvenile

Definition: Sentencing procedure through which juveniles convicted of crimes are released by the court and stay out of prison, so long as they adhere to conditions set by the judges
Criminal justice issues: Convictions; Probation and pretrial release; Sentencing
Significance: As an alternative to or in addition to time spent in correctional institutions, probation is often imposed on persons who have been convicted of crimes, especially juveniles.

Probation is a general term for alternative sentencing, allowing convicted criminals to live outside prison, either in the community or in supervised residential programs. The emphasis is on rehabilitation. By the use of education, training, and counseling, it is hoped that the convict will be able to lead a useful life and not continue criminal activities. Because youthful offenders are often perceived as more likely than older ones to change their outlooks and because prison is often viewed as a "school for criminal activities," juveniles are more often sentenced to probation.

Probation has its roots in the harsh laws of the Middle Ages in Europe, where corporal or even capital punishment was imposed for crimes that would be considered minor by modern standards. Judges sometimes issued suspended sentences or imposed lesser punishments than those ordinarily called for, especially when children were involved.

The modern American system of probation began in the nineteenth century, especially in Massachusetts, where the first paid probation officer was hired in Boston in 1878. In the latter half of the twentieth century, as Americans became more interested in social problems and the welfare of underprivileged citizens, probation became increasingly widespread.

The Rationale Behind Probation

There have long been a variety of responses to antisocial activities in society. The biblical method of "an eye for an eye," combined with Christian concepts of good and evil, led to a general attitude that those who harm others must suffer pain in retribution. By the nineteenth century and the onset of the Industrial Revolution, this attitude began to change, at least in part thanks to the writings of reformers, notably Charles Dickens, whose

Brown Heatly Building in Austin—headquarters for the Texas Juvenile Probation Commission. (Public domain, via Wikimedia Commons)

novels emphasized the difficult conditions among which members of the working class were forced to live.

In the wake of the Industrial Revolution and the sudden increase of immigration to the United States by people who had few skills, little education, and little knowledge of the English language, an underclass developed, and crime became the only solution for many persons. The problem became more intense in the twentieth century, as American cities became increasingly populated by minority groups, often living in desperate conditions. Reformers became interested in improving the conditions under which such people lived rather than sending them to prison. In more recent times, there has been a great deal of concern that US prisons are overcrowded and that people convicted of relatively minor offenses should be given alternative sentences.

The result of these changes in attitude was a system of alternatives to actual jail sentences, especially for young offenders. Particularly in the latter part of the twentieth century, young criminals began to be viewed as victims of society as much as villains, and new methods were proposed.

The Mechanics and Types of Probation

In modern times the process of sentencing begins with an arraignment, at which time accused persons are brought before a judge and their alleged crimes are stated. At this stage, a probation officer may file a petition with the court if it is felt that an alternative to incarceration is advisable. The decision is based on the seriousness of the crimes, the likelihood of reform, and the environment to which the accused will be returning.

If probation is imposed, it is always conditional. Criminals are assigned probation officers, who monitor their activities. Conditions are generally imposed; persons on probation must refrain from criminal activities, attend school or training programs, and often confine themselves to a particular geographic area. Probationers are kept under regular surveillance, sometimes by electronic means. If they violate the conditions of probation, they may be resentenced to prison. After the probational period has expired, they may be released into society as free citizens.

Juvenile probation is an attempt to give youthful offenders a second chance at leading useful lives in society. There are a great many opinions as to what sort of environment is most likely to allow and encourage youth to take such a course. The first consideration is the environment in which they lived before being arrested. If they came from reasonably sound homes, they would probably be returned to the custody of their parents and be supervised by a probation officer. They would be required to attend school on a regular basis and might also be assigned to community projects. This method was common in the 1960s but was perceived as less desirable in later decades.

Intensive supervised probation, begun in the 1960s for adults and expanded to include juveniles in the 1980s, is a more structured version of community probation. Probationers are often monitored electronically and may be required to pay restitution to their victims. Intensive counseling may also be involved.

At the end of the twentieth century, residential programs for juvenile probationers became far more common. Such programs had their origins in the reform schools of the nineteenth and early twentieth centuries, but many varieties were developed. At one extreme is the boot camp system, modeled on military training methods. Probationers are given intensive physical and educational training, and their lives are very highly structured. It is hoped that such harsh discipline will be effective in teaching the youths to abide by the rules of society.

Somewhat less restrictive are group homes, in which the juveniles live together in the community, under the supervision of adults, who either live on the premises or work in shifts. The probationers may be entirely restricted to the home, may be taken on supervised outings, or may even be given limited privileges in the outside environment, depending on their behavior. The rationale behind this system is to allow offenders to gradually work their way back into the community.

Another system, which became increasingly popular in the 1980s, was to involve youths with the natural environment. This might involve something very much like a year-round summer camp, involving sports, swimming, hiking, arts and crafts, and educational programs. It may be an intensive wilderness survival program. In either case, useful work for the Forestry Service or other government agencies may be involved, including the improvement of trails and the cleanup of wilderness areas. The wilderness approach is often considered especially appropriate for juveniles from inner-city areas. It is suggested that an extreme change of environment may change youths' outlook and priorities.

If the court has determined that probationers have broken the law primarily because of an unfortunate home environment, the probationers may be placed in foster care. It is hoped that given a more supportive environment, they will change their ways. Parental visitation may or may not be granted. Along with these methods, a tactic called "shock probation" was introduced late in the twentieth century. Youths are taken to prisons, where they are shown the conditions in the hope that they will change their behavior in order to avoid going to prison themselves.

The Effectiveness of Probation

There is a great deal of controversy surrounding the effectiveness of assorted types of juvenile probation and the effectiveness of actual time in prison. Many statistical and individual studies have been conducted, but they have produced mixed results.

It is necessary to balance the welfare of juvenile offenders with the safety of the communities in which they live. At one extreme are those who believe that prisons are a bad influence in themselves. Young people who may be arrested for relatively minor offenses, such as vandalism or petty theft, will associate with hardened criminals and may learn to adopt their lifestyle. Also to be considered is that there is a great deal of violence within the prisons, including sexual abuse of young inmates, both male and female.

On the other hand, there are those who cite an apparent increase in crime among youths and stress that lawful members of the community must be protected. These people often point out that a disproportionate number of juvenile offenders come from certain regions and cities, where crime and drug use is rampant, and that if they return to these communities, they are likely to return to crime.

The use of alcohol and illegal drugs among youths confuses the situation further. The use of alcohol by someone under the legal age or the use of relatively benign drugs such as marijuana is a highly significant factor in the statistics involving youthful crime. As opinions on the law involving such offenses vary widely, the statistics are very often biased according to the viewpoints of those doing the studies.

Generally, it has been found that residential programs involving community involvement and useful training have at least some effect, although accurate figures are difficult to come by. Releasing offenders into the community is generally ineffective, especially if the community involved is an area in which both adult and juvenile crime is common.

Conclusions

The prevalence of criminal activities among young people in modern times has led to various attempts to control this problem. Beginning during the late twentieth century there was an increasing call for youths who commit serious crimes, especially violent crimes, to be tried and punished as if they were adults, even including subjecting them to capital punishment. At the same time, there were many attempts to consider alternative punishments in order to prevent young offenders from becoming lifetime criminals.

The problem is not easy to solve. On one hand, there is a natural tendency to want to treat children as gently as possible in the hope that they can overcome unfortunate environmental conditions and become useful members of society. On the other hand, the increasing presence of street gangs and juvenile delinquency causes great fear among the adult population.

Marc Goldstein

Further Reading

Bartollas, Clemens, and Stuart J. Miller. *Juvenile Justice in America*. 8th ed. Boston: Pearson, 2016. Print.

Champion, Dean John. *Probation, Parole, and Community Corrections*. 6th ed. New York: Wiley, 2007. Print.

Champion, Dean John. *Criminal Justice in the United States*. 2nd ed. Chicago: Nelson Hall, 1997. Print.

Champion, Dean John, Alida V. Merlo, and Peter J. Benekos. *The Juvenile Justice System: Delinquency, Processing, and the Law*. 7th ed. Boston: Pearson, 2012. Print.

Coffey, Alan R. *Juvenile Corrections: Treatment and Rehabilitation*. Englewood Cliffs: Prentice-Hall, 1975. Print.

Cox, Steven M., et al. *Juvenile Justice: A Guide to Theory, Policy, and Practice*. 8th ed. New York: Sage, 2013. Print.

Currie, Elliott. *Crime and Punishment in America*. New York: Metropolitan, 1998. Print.

McCord, Joan. Cathy Spatz Widom, and Nancy A. Crowell, eds. *Juvenile Crime, Juvenile Justice*. Washington, DC: National Academy, 2001. Print.

Siegal, Larry J., Frank Schmalleger, and John L. Worral. *Courts and Criminal Justice in America*. 2nd ed. Boston: Pearson, 2014. Print.

See also Juvenile courts; Juvenile delinquency; Juvenile Justice and Delinquency Prevention, Office of; Juvenile justice system; Juvenile waivers to adult courts; *Parens patriae*; Parole; Probation, adult; Sentencing; Youth authorities.

Realignment (PSR) policy

Definition: Public Safety Realignment refers to California legislation and policy designed to reduce overcrowding in state-run prisons. Assembly Bill 109, passed into law in 2011, is the centerpiece of realignment legislation. It effectively shifts, or realigns, responsibility for many low-level felons from state-level to county-level criminal justice agencies.

Criminal justice issues: Constitutional protections; political issues; prisons; punishment; rehabilitation; sentencing

Significance: Realignment has drastically altered the sentencing landscape in California, resulting in more low-level offenders serving their time in jails rather than prisons. This has led to substantial reduction in the prison population. However, questions have been raised regarding the consequences for jails as well as for crime rates, although evidence suggests that the latter is not a particular cause for concern.

California's prison population had skyrocketed since the early 1980's, increasing more than 700 percent between 1980 and 2006. Although 22 new prisons were opened during this time, this was not enough to keep up with demand. In conjunction with the growing numbers of prisoners, costs began to soar and the budget for the California Department of Corrections and Rehabilitation (CDCR) ate up an increasingly large percentage of the state's annual budget. Along with overcrowding came a series of legal challenges by state prisoners contesting that California was violating their Eighth Amendment constitutional protection from cruel and unusual punishment because the state was providing inadequate medical and mental health care due to the overcrowding.

Two legal challenges in particular received significant attention in the federal courts, *Colman v. Brown*, filed in 1990, and *Plata v. Brown*, filed in 2001. The two cases worked their way through the system, and in 2007 a three-judge district court was convened to address the overcrowding issues that the two cases raised. In 2009 that court ordered the state of California to reduce its prison population to 137.5 percent of original design capacity within two years, a reduction that would entail housing approximately 40,000 less prisoners in the system unless new prisons were built. The latter was not a viable option given the economic circumstances and time constraints. Although working on a plan to reduce overcrowding, the state appealed the ruling to the U.S. Supreme Court. In May 2011 the U.S. Supreme Court ruled in *Brown v. Plata*, upholding the District Court's order in a 5-4 decision written by Justice Anthony Kennedy.

Legislation

Given the extreme overcrowding in its state-run prison system and the connected exorbitant costs, the state of California had already created legislation to reduce its prison population ahead of the U.S. Supreme Court's ruling. In March 2011 the state legislature passed Assembly Bill 109 (AB 109), designed to lower the number of individuals sentenced to prison in part through making greater use of local jail-based sentences. Governor Edmund G. Brown Jr., who had proposed the legislation, signed AB 109 in April that year, thereby establishing the California Public Safety Realignment Act of 2011. Implementation began on October 1, 2011.

The word realignment in the legislation's title refers to the mandated shift in responsibility for many low-level felons from state to county-based criminal justice agencies. As noted above, this has a significant impact on the use of prison versus jail. Prior to October 1, 2011, convicted felons sentenced to more than a year of incarceration would be sent to a state-run CDCR prison. Following AB 109, felons convicted of most nonserious, nonviolent, nonsexual crimes worth sentences of three years or less, and without serious, violent, or sexual crimes on their record, serve that time in a county jail run by the sheriff's office, or in the community under the supervision of the county's probation department.

Additionally, the legislation makes significant changes to the penalties for parole violators facing parole revocations. Prior to AB 109, parole revocations were served in prison, a driving force behind California having the highest return-to-prison rate of all states pre-realignment. Since AB 109, parole revocations are served in a county jail for a period of no more than six months, unless the violator was originally serving a life sentence in which case they may be returned to prison.

A third important realignment involves the shift in responsibility for supervising lower-level felons post-release from prison from state-run parole to county-run probation through a system known as Post-Release Community Supervision (PRCS).

While realignment was primarily designed to reduce immediate overcrowding in prisons, further impetus came from the view that county-level supervision might lead to reduced recidivism rates among former offenders and therefore a longer-term reduction in the need for incarceration. Counties have been encouraged to use creative measures to work with offenders and one sentencing option provided for judges is a split sentence. In such cases felons serve part of their sentence in jail followed by mandatory supervision by probation officers in the community. This supervision might entail participation in rehabilitation programs.

Under realignment each county has formed a Community Corrections Partnership (CCP) consisting of the heads of local criminal justice agencies as well a representative from social services in order to oversee and orchestrate the response to AB 109. This shift to the local level means that the 58 counties in California are each adopting their own approaches to realignment resulting in greater variation in dispositions across the state than previously was the case, and varying degrees of emphasis on incarceration, rehabilitation, and reentry programming.

Along with the policy shifts, the state has directed additional funding towards the counties to support the increased responsibilities and enhanced caseloads, including provision for jail expansion. The funding is constitutionally protected, following the passage of Proposition 32 by California voters in 2012, although concern still remains as to whether each county is receiving funding commensurate with the change in workload.

Consequences

While state prisons began to see a reduction in numbers following realignment, county jails experienced increases in their population, with some seeing substantial growth in numbers. Because *Brown v. Plata* only applies to state-run prisons, concern was expressed that realignment had simply shifted the problem from the state to the county level. Many county jails faced overcrowding challenges prior to implementation of AB 109, with some subject to federal consent decrees mandating early releases of inmates when the jail population reaches a certain point. As a result, AB 109 did lead to an increase in early releases from jail in the months following implementation. This may have contributed to the erroneous but commonly held belief that AB 109 resulted in early releases from prison; it did not. Nor did AB 109 lead to the transfer of incarcerated individuals already in prison to jail. Only those sentenced for eligible felonies on October 1, 2011 or later were directed to jail instead of prison.

A separate issue for jails has been the need to manage longer-stay inmates than such facilities are generally designed to handle. Previously, jails would not expect to house inmates for more than a year, unless unsentenced defendants were involved in particularly lengthy trials. As a result, jails do not typically have substantial rehabilitative programming or recreational facilities. While these resources may be limited in prisons, customarily there are more resources in jails. This has particular significance for those individuals who receive multiple convictions for jail-eligible felonies who are ordered to serve their sentences consecutively. This can result in multiple three-year sentences adding up to very long stays in jail. Moreover, unless the inmate received a split sentence, there is no criminal justice system support or supervision following release, unlike for those released from prison. These issues, that largely surfaced after hastily passed AB 109 came into effect, have led to calls for fine-tuning the initial legislation to address these concerns.

From the outset, critics of the legislation voiced fears that public safety realignment policy would result in increased crime. However, research by the Public Policy Institute of California (PPIC) indicates that while AB 109 led to a modest increase in property offenses, most notably auto theft, this growth had begun to narrow by 2014. The PPIC has found no evidence of an increase in violent crime as a result of AB 109. In some quarters, however, concern about the impact on crime rates endures, although despite some recent upticks, California's crime rates have been in overall decline.

After the first two years of realignment, the prison population in California had decreased by approximately 25,000 people, but this was not enough to reach the required 137.5 percent of design capacity. In 2014 California voters passed Proposition 47, which downgraded certain nonviolent property and drug offenses from felonies to misdemeanors and contributed to CDCR reaching the 137.5 percent target as well as jails returning to pre-realignment numbers. In the meantime, efforts persist to find long-term solutions to prison and jail overcrowding as well as to recidivism rates that remain high. In response, increased focus is being placed on evidence-based practices including community-based treatment and rehabilitation and reentry programs in prisons and jails.

Emma Hughes

Further Reading

Brown v. Plata, 563 U.S. 493 (2011). The U.S. Supreme Court ruling in *Brown v. Plata*. https://www.supremecourt.gov/opinions/10pdf/09-1233.pdf.

Loftstrom, M., M. Bird, and B. Martin. *California's Historic Corrections Reforms*. San Francisco: Public Policy Institute of California, 2016. A thorough account of the impact of AB 109 and Proposition 47 based on current research findings.

Owen, B., and A. Mobley. "Realignment in California: Policy and Research Implications." *Western Criminology Review* 13, no. 2 (2012): 46-52. A valuable introduction to the issues raised by realignment and the research questions needing to be addressed.

Petersilia, J. "California Prison Downsizing and Its Impact on Local Criminal Justice Systems." *Harvard Law and Policy Review* 8 (2014): 801-32. An analysis of realignment's effect on county agencies including recommendations for policy alterations by one of the leading experts on California's criminal justice system.

See also Bureau of Justice Statistics; Diversion; Parole; Parole officers; Prison and jail systems; Prison overcrowding; Probation, adult; Punishment; Rehabilitation; Three-strikes laws; Medical model of offender treatment; Parole boards; Privatization of institutional and community corrections, including faith-based prisons; History of incarceration.

Recidivism

Definition: Tendency of previously convicted criminals to return to criminal behavior after release from prison, jail, or community supervision

Criminal justice issues: Crime prevention; prisons; rehabilitation

Significance: While the modern criminal justice system has been placing increased emphasis on incapacitating greater numbers of offenders and for longer periods of time, recidivist rates have also been increasing, giving rise to the perception that most offenders are being caught in an ever-revolving door from which release appears for some to be almost impossible.

During the 1998 U.S. presidential election campaign, recidivism became a national issue when Republican candidate George Bush accused his Democratic opponent, Massachusetts governor Michael Dukakis, of being "soft" on crime by calling media attention to the murderous behavior of a convict named Willie Horton whom Dukakis had released from prison. The Horton case became a national *cause célèbre* and the notion of incurably violent recidivists was imprinted in Americans' minds. That notion was reinforced by another highly publicized case in 1993, when former convict Richard Allen Davis kidnapped, sexually assaulted, and murdered a young California girl named Polly Klaas. The Polly Klaas case then gave rise to the three-strikes law movement in California. The concept of recidivism has produced a variety of definitions and special applications. However, the meaning that is most widely used defines recidivists as offenders who serve time in jails or prisons, reenter society, and then violate their parole or commit new crimes that return them to custody.

Scope of the Problem

Figures from the U.S. Bureau of Justice Statistics show that 856,900 person were on parole in the United States in 2014. In other words, just short of one million offenders had been released from prison and were residing in and roaming freely throughout the United States. Of these parolees, approximately 94 percent had originally been convicted of felonies and 31 percent had been imprisoned for drug offenses. The majority of these offenders were under the regular supervision of parole officers, but large caseloads, geographical distances, and dwindling funds have been reducing the levels and effectiveness of post-release supervision.

Research has shown that roughly 25 percent of the 404,638 parolees newly released in 2005 were successfully discharged from their parole responsibilities. A 25-percent success rate may seem alarmingly low, but may alternatively be viewed as an extraordinary success when compared to the findings of other studies of recidivism.

In 2014, the federal government released its latest comprehensive study of recidivism of prison inmates who had been released on parole in 2005. The most startling finding of that study was that within three years of their parole discharge, 67.8 percent of the former inmates had been returned to custody as the result of new crimes or parole violations.

National recidivism rates are consistent with the rate of parolee failure in California, which has the largest number of parolees in the United States. the recidivism rate is a frighteningly similar 66 percent. It would appear that California is representative of the rest of the country although the fact that the majority of its recidivists are returned for such technical violations of their parole as failing "dirty" drug tests, may indicate that particular political or social pressures are at work.

Reasons for Parole Failure

In 1974, a study on the effectiveness of correctional programs published by Robert Martinson was reduced to a public perception that "nothing works." This indictment was seized by the political proponents of the "get tough on crime" movement and used as an academically produced and research-oriented justification for dismantling and abandoning most rehabilitative efforts in corrections over the next three decades.

Since the 1970's, the United States has been fighting a continuous war on crime, drugs, and recidivism. New sentencing strategies, such as three-strikes laws, have lengthened average prison sentences. The result has been an escalating correctional population that by year-end 2014 had placed more than 1.5 million offenders in prisons and nearly another 5.5 million offenders in communities under probation or parole. Note that the rate of new incarcerations has slowed in recent years. Increased emphasis on incarcerating offenders has had both fiscal and philosophical consequences. Costs have skyrocketed as increasing numbers of offenders are incarcerated and for longer periods of time. Also, increasing numbers of prisoners are incarcerated in what are called supermax prisons, which isolate inmates as many as twenty-three hours per day. The tendency toward more severe incapacitation policies has led to reduced remedial services for inmates and further depersonalized them and alienated them from society.

Noted criminologists, such as Joan Petersilia (2003) and Jeremy Travis, have written extensively on the problems of parolees. Typical parolees are young male members of minority groups who have limited literacy and education, meager job skills, and negligible employment histories. They are often substance abusers or addicts, and many have physical, mental, and medical complications. These people tend to go through the criminal justice system without getting any help for their basic problems because of insufficient funding for treatment and rehabilitation programs and the reluctance of some prison administrators to acknowledge the need to try something new. The result is that many of these people become repeat offenders, and recidivism rates continue to climb.

Solutions

Criminologists, such as Petersilia and Travis, generally agree that the only way to combat recidivism is to return to corrections programs that provide rehabilitative services before offenders are released from incarceration. They recommend that when offenders first arrive in prison, they should be properly assessed and diagnosed—both for levels of security they require and special needs, such as professionally run literacy and education programs. Criminologists also recommend that all undereducated and illiterate inmates should be required to participate in these programs with the goal of attaining high school diplomas or the equivalent. Moreover, access to college education should not be denied to prisoners who wish to improve themselves. Similarly, substance abuse programs should be made available to all interested inmates and mandated for those identified as in need of such services. To encourage inmate participation in these programs, credits for sentence reduction could be offered.

Simultaneously, prisons must finance and support effective prerelease programs. The traditional bus ticket and two hundred dollars in "gate" money given to released prisoners is merely evidence of the system's disinterest in the offenders' successful reentry into society. Inmates should also be trained in ways that help them find housing and jobs upon their release. Indeed, job-training programs should be integral elements of the prison curriculum. Moreover, prerelease training should begin shortly after offenders are incarcerated and not be put off until shortly before they are released, as is generally done.

Upon their release, inmates should be provided with transitional housing-so-called "halfway houses"—to assist them in their transitions from total institutionalization to the free world. This is particularly important during the critical first six months after inmates are released. Halfway house programs provide structure, supervision, and services, while allowing former inmates an adjustment period before they are asked to face the demands and temptations of the free world.

While former inmates are in the community and under parole supervision, they should have immediate access to affordable and available aftercare services. Twelve-step programs are available worldwide and serve as the backbone for many substance abuse treatment programs, but other problems that involve personal, family, and social crises also require help. Providing all these services to former inmates is more cost-effective than dealing with the problems that arise when they return to criminal behavior that creates new victims and requires processing the same offenders through the criminal justice system and prisons again.

Reducing recidivism rates ultimately requires a fundamental philosophical shift in criminal justice and correctional policies. The current practice of warehousing offenders simply to incapacitate them must be modified. While it will always be necessary to protect society from truly violent and serious predators, rehabilitative services must be reinvigorated for the many nonviolent and petty criminals whose crimes are mostly related to substance abuse.

Kevin Meehan
Updated by Charles E. MacLean

Further Reading

Durose, Matthew R., Cooper, Alexia D., and Snyder, Howard N.. *Recidivism of Prisoners Released in 30 States in 2005: Patterns from 2005 to 2010.* Washington, D.C.: Bureau of Justice Statistics, 2014. Summary of the findings of the most recent federal government study of recidivism.

Kaeble, Danielle, Maruschak, Laura M., and Bonczar, Thomas P. *Probation and Parole in the United States, 2014.* Washington, D.C.: Bureau of Justice Statistics, 2015. Wide-ranging study of probation and parole populations in the United States and their characteristics.

Martinson, Robert. "What Works? Questions and Answers About Prison Reform." *Public Interest* 35 (1974): 2-35. Influential study of prisons that contributed to the belief that "nothing works."

Petersilia, Joan. *When Prisoners Come Home.* New York: Oxford University Press, 2003. Study by a noted criminologist of the wide variety of problems that former inmates face after they are released from custody.

Travis, Jeremy. "Invisible Punishment: An Instrument of Social Exclusion." In *Invisible Punishment: The Collateral Consequences of Mass Imprisonment*, edited by Marc Mauer and Meda Chesney-Lind. Washington, D.C.: New Press, 2002. Examination of the poor preparation for reentry into society provided to inmates by modern prison programs.

Travis, Jeremy, and Sarah Lawrence. *Beyond the Prison Gates: The State of Parole in America.* Washington, D.C.: Urban Institute, 2002. Important study of recidivism and parole by one of the leading criminologists in the field.

See also Boot camps; Community-based corrections; Halfway houses; Incapacitation; Mandatory sentencing; Prison overcrowding; Punishment; Rehabilitation; Sex offender registries; Supermax prisons; Three-strikes laws; Work-release programs; Medical model of offender treatment; Realignment (PSR) policy; History of incarceration.

Rehabilitation

Definition: Punishment designed to reform offenders so they can lead productive lives free from crime

Criminal justice issues: Punishment; Rehabilitation

Significance: While rehabilitation may be the most humane and progressive form of punishment, it is also the most difficult to achieve and waned in popularity in the American justice system after the 1970s.

Although rehabilitation is often considered a type of punishment for criminal offenders, its objectives are therapeutic rather than punitive. While some theories of punishment claim that criminals deserve to suffer for their crimes, the rehabilitative ideal views criminal behavior more as a disease that should be treated with scientific methods to cure offenders.

Many convicts suffer from mental and physical illnesses, drug addictions, and limited opportunities for economic success, and these problems increase their likelihood of recidivism. If the justice system simply incarcerates offenders to make them "pay their debt to society," they are likely to reenter it with all the problems that drive them to crime still in place. Moreover, they will also need to contend with the additional handicap of having a criminal record. They will also be older and still without marketable skills or education, their social relationships are likely to have deteriorated, and incarceration itself may have acclimated them to criminal culture. Thus incarcerating offenders can actually make them more likely than before to commit offenses after they are released. High rates of recidivism attest to this. A rehabilitative approach to punishment attempts to treat the underlying causes of criminals' transgressions so they can return to society to become productive citizens. Instead of exacting revenge against criminals and making their lives even worse, rehabilitation tries to help them.

Early American prisons, such as those established at Auburn and Ossining, New York, and Pittsburgh, Pennsylvania, during the 1820s, implemented rehabilitative principles. These early programs isolated convicts from one another in order to remove them from the temptations that had driven them to crime and to provide individual inmates with time to listen to their own consciences and reflect on their deeds. Those early systems, like the Auburn system, were predicated on the belief that all convicts would return to their inherently good natures when removed from the corrupting influences of society. However, those beliefs eventually gave way to more aggressive forms of treatment informed by the rise of social scientific studies into criminal behavior.

Rehabilitative Theories

Research in psychology, criminology, and sociology provided reformers with deeper understandings of deviance and sharper tools with which to treat it. Rehabilitation then became a science of reeducating criminals with the values, attitudes, and skills necessary to live lawfully. Rehabilitation has taken many forms in practice, including psychological analysis, drug and alcohol treatment, high school equivalency and other educational programs, vocational training, relationship counseling, anger-management therapy, religious study, and other services believed to meet the needs of particular offenders.

Because rehabilitation is based on the premise that every offender has different problems to overcome, programs for reform should be fashioned for individual offenders, just as doctors prescribe treatments for individual patients. Thus every sentence is individualized, and even two convicts who have committed the same crime may receive entirely different sentences. For example, an offender driven to steal because of drug addiction will require treatment different than that given to an unemployed immigrant who steals to pay for food for a family. Rehabilitative punishment is thus tailored to the offenders, rather than to the crimes.

According to rehabilitative theories, prison may not be the best venue for achieving its rehabilitative objectives because it isolates offenders from the very realities of life with which they must learn how to cope. Moreover, incarceration conditions offenders to become dependent on institutional care. Noncustodial sentences, such as parole, probation, community service, and deferred sentences serve to keep offenders functioning within their ordinary lives to some degree, while helping them learn how to manage the responsibilities they will face when their sentences expire. Such strategies are thought to be particularly important in the treatment of young offenders.

Rehabilitation seeks to reform not only individual convicts, but also the social conditions contributing to criminal culture. For example, correlations between crime, addiction, and poverty are well known. To some degree, these social ills cause crime. Treating individuals afflicted with these symptoms does not, by itself, stop the spread of the disease infecting so many others. Such problems transcend individual offenders. A complete criminal justice system, therefore, would seek to root out the structural conditions that create criminals. Under this theory, criminal behavior reflects the sickness of society, rather than simply deviant individuals.

Opposition to Rehabilitation

Rehabilitative justifications for punishment have lost popular support since the 1970s in the light of attacks coming from two fronts. While some argue that rehabilitation is fundamentally immoral, others claim it is impractical. Retributivists, who cite the ancient "eye for an eye" maxim and believe that offenders should be punished merely because they deserve to suffer as payment for their transgressions, spearhead moral critiques of rehabilitation. By providing criminals with therapy and education, retributivists argue, society fails to exact the revenge that justice demands. They further argue that this injustice is most evident in the practice of individualized sentencing, which can lead to disparate punishments for the same crimes and spare offenders from serving hard time. Such inequalities are patently unjust to retributivists.

In response to this perceived unfairness, reformers successfully lobbied for punishments to be meted out in determinate and standardized sentences corresponding to the moral desert of offenders. This movement culminated in the federal Sentencing Reform Act of 1984 and the US Sentencing Guidelines, which removed most discretion from sentencing and led to skyrocketing incarceration rates.

Retributivists also find rehabilitation morally unjustifiable because it denies the offenders' responsibility for their actions by attributing their behavior to forces beyond their control, such as their sickness or circumstances. They object to the way that rehabilitation treats offenders as if they are not ultimately accountable for the choices they made. This practice, according to retributivists, reduces offenders to the level of animals or children and leads to techniques that strip offenders of their dignity.

As Anthony Burgess explored in his 1962 novel *A Clockwork Orange*, it is unclear how far rehabilitative methods will go to reprogram individuals into obedient citizens. As it is now possible to inject drugs into sex offenders that will decrease their libido and to perform psychosurgery to reduce violent tendencies in convicts, it is now possible to create human beings who are effectively unable to choose whether to do good or evil. Because choice is so fundamental to any understanding of what it means to be fully human, such punishment is perceived as inhumane.

In *Discipline and Punish* (1979), the French philosopher Michel Foucault described the historical shift from spectacular corporal punishments, such drawing and quartering, to more subtle rehabilitative techniques as an increasingly efficient form of social control that blurs boundaries between incarceration and freedom. When punishment and education are conflated, penological methods seep into all of civilian life. Foucault claims that as a result human beings have become a "carceral" society.

Beyond these moral concerns, some doubt the practicality of rehabilitation. First, despite the boom in criminological research, little is still known about what causes crime and even less about how to reform criminal behavior. It is difficult to measure the success of rehabilitative methods, and recidivism rates have done little to change the thinking of those who doubt the effectiveness of rehabilitative techniques. Judging the progress of offenders is subject to interpretation, and offenders who are undergoing treatment have strong incentives to feign reform in order to expedite their own release. For the most serious offenders, most remain skeptical that any amount of therapy can change their ways. However, it may be that the most determinative practical concern has been economic in nature: It is expensive to administer an effective rehabilitative system, and few politicians are willing to devote funds to such a disenfranchised group as unpopular as convicted felons.

Advocates of rehabilitation respond to these criticisms by claiming that their methods have not been fairly tested because they have never been supported by adequate resources. Within the political climate of the early twenty-first century, the decline of rehabilitation provides the political right with an occasion to extend its anthem of "personal responsibility" in matters of distributive justice to justifications for punishment. Just as the poor deserve their fates and can rise from destitution by working harder, conservatives argue, criminals deserve to be held accountable for their actions. For the Left, such arguments for individual autonomy hide behind the deep social and economic injustices that segregate members of racial and economic underclasses behind prison walls.

Nick Smith

Further Reading

Allen, Francis. *The Decline of the Rehabilitative Ideal*. New Haven: Yale UP, 1981. Print.

Benko, Jessica. "The Radical Humaneness of Norway's Halden Prison." *New York Times*. New York Times, 26 Mar. 2015. Web. 31 May 2016.

Braithwaite, John. *Crime, Shame and Reintegration*. Cambridge: Cambridge UP, 1989. Print.

Foucault, Michel. *Discipline and Punish: The Birth of the Prison*. Trans. Alan Sheridan. New York: Vintage, 1979. Print.

Garland, David. *The Culture of Control*. New York: Oxford UP, 2001. Print.

Gilligan, James. "Punishment Fails. Rehabilitation Works." *New York Times*. New York Times, 19 Dec. 2012. Web. 31 May 2016.

Morris, Norval, and David Rothman. *The Oxford History of Punishment: The Practice of Punishment in Western Society*. Oxford: Oxford UP, 1997. Print.

Murphy, Jeffrie. *Punishment and Rehabilitation*. New York: Wadsworth, 1994. Print.

Rothman, David. *The Discovery of the Asylum: Social Order and Disorder in the New Republic*. Boston: Little, Brown, 1971. Print.

Woodman, Andrew. "Bringing Rehabilitation Back to Prisons." *Huffington Post*. The Huffington Post, 16 Apr. 2014. Web. 31 May 2016.

See also Auburn system; Boot camps; Community-based corrections; Deterrence; Forestry camps; Halfway houses; Incapacitation; Just deserts; Punishment; Recidivism; Restorative justice; Sentencing; Victim-offender mediation; Work camps; Work-release programs; Australia's "Reintegrative Shaming" approach; Comprehensive Addiction and Recovery Act of 2016 (CARA), Conjugal Visitation; Medical model of offender treatment; Opioid treatment breakthroughs; Pennsylvania system of corrections; Pris-

Scandinavia's prison experience

Definition: Scandinavian prisons operate under a different philosophy from American prisons. They do not face the criticism of newspapers and politicians who seek favor with the populace seeking officials to be hard on crime. Incarceration is viewed as the punishment contrast to the United States where incarceration is typically viewed for punishment.

Criminal justice issues: Criminal justice issues: Arrest and arraignment; crime prevention; criminology; prosecution

Significance: Scandinavian prisons use their correction officers as aides in rehabilitation. What comes after is, in consultation with therapists, the effort to aid in the movement back to society or reintegration of the offender back into the community.

Not all Scandinavian prisons are open prisons. However, even those that are not tend to be much less oppressive than the average American prison. In open prisons, people can leave for work or education daily, wearing a tracker, and may see their families and attend family gatherings. Moreover, there is less jailing of nonviolent and victimless crimes than in the United States. The inmates are housed in dormitory-like settings and paid for their labor (adequate enough to rent refrigerators, TVs, and purchase other niceties). They also dress in civilian clothes.

Criticisms of the System as Applicable in the United States

The question may arise that if this system seems to work so much better than that of the United States then why doesn't the United States follow the Scandinavian model. There are several reasons why this would be difficult. The first is a difference of culture. The Scandinavian countries are socialist countries that provide essential social services to their people and are egalitarian. They tax the wealthy at a high rate as a matter of course and to provide these services to all people. There is an agreement within the countries to leave criminal justice to the experts and to seek to rehabilitate prisoners. The people approve of social experiments and give experts leeway to explore them.

There is also a difference in the amount of money given to the care of prisoners and the maintenance of the system. The percentage of prisoners in Scandinavian countries is about the same as in the United States, around seven percent of the population. Moreover, the population of the Scandinavian countries is relatively homogeneous, unlike that of the United States.

In the United States, there is a range of opinion regarding crime and punishment. Politicians keep an eye on public opinion and their constituents when making policy. Newspapers find crime sells papers and crime can be reported in alarming ways to make clear policy difficult.

Conclusion

Scandinavian countries have clear objectives in their prison programs. They see the sentence as the punishment and what happens after as a means of preparing prisoners for reentry into society. The period of incarceration is used as a means for retraining and rehabilitation. The goal is to prepare the prisoner for citizenship and contributing to society. There is an awareness that brutal treatment will produce brutes and be counterproductive. There is a dependence on experts who understand the purpose of rehabilitation.

Frank A. Salamone

Further Reading

Benko, Jessica. "Radical Humanness of Norway's Halden Prison." March 26, 2015. https://www.nytimes.com/2015/03/29/magazine/the-radical-humaneness-of-norways-halden-prison.html?_r=0.

Cornwell, David J., John Blad, and Martin Wright. *Civilising Criminal Justice: An International Restorative Agenda for Penal Reform.* Hampshire, England: Waterside Press, 2013. https://play.google.com/store/books/details?id=y_99takC79YC&source=productsearch&utm_source=HA_Desktop_US&utm_medium=SEM&utm_campaign=PLA&pcampaignid=MKTAD0930BO1&gclid=CMmG8oyFytECFZF5gQodWdcOjA&gclsrc=ds-details-reviews.

Mathieson, Thomas. *Prison on Trial.* Hampshire, England: Waterside Press, 2006.

See also History of incarceration; Prison inmate subculture; Prisoner rights; Pennsylvania system of corrections; Restorative justice; Rehabilitation; Medical model of offender treatment; Prison violence; Prison overcrowding; Prison health care; Prison guards; Prison escapes; Prison and jail systems; Auburn system.

Security threat groups (STGs)/prison gangs

Definition: Formal or informal group of prison inmates, broadly known as prison gangs, who present a major threat to the safety of officials and inmates alike

Criminal justice issues: Criminal justice issues: Criminology; organized crime; prisons

Significance: Security Threat Groups, or prison gangs, control many criminal activities in prison and outside.

Law enforcement officials use the term Security Threat Group (STG) because of the desire to obscure the term "prison gang," which is more familiar to the public. No matter under what term they are known, these STGs present a major threat to the safety of officials and inmates alike. They come in many forms, but under any of them they are a threat. Some examples are the Aryan Brotherhood and the Texas Mafia. These STGs are criminal organizations and are involved in numerous criminal activities ranging from assault through murder and kidnapping and include distribution of illegal substances, extortion, and almost any other crime one can name. Although centered in prisons, they have control of criminal gangs in the general community.

Beginning in the 1950's prison gangs began to take over correctional facilities. The reason for that is that people began to be incarcerated at higher percentages and the diversity among those who were imprisoned began to grow. There began to be conflicts among members of different ethnic groups and a decrease in the maintenance of order. These factors helped lead to conditions favorable to the development of gangs, or STGs.

In many cases, these STGs provide some measure of order and the settlement of problems within prisons. Part of prison management consists of giving space to various groups and keeping their members apart. Simply put, the correctional officers often work with STGs to maintain and organize the system to keep order. Prisons have become obviously overcrowded and more difficult to control. As the "tough on crime" segment of the American population has gained the upper hand, more inmates have been crowded and overcrowded into prisons, presenting a difficulty in maintaining discipline and order. Security Threat Groups have simply stepped into the gap provided by this situation. At the same time, these STGs have gained power outside of prisons as well. The New York Daily News has cited the most powerful and dangerous gangs as being the Aryan Brotherhood, Mexican Mafia, Nazi Low Riders, Black Guerilla Family, and Nuestra Familia. These gangs have gained control of vast resources through their criminal activity and control of much criminal activity in the outside world.

Prisons have several ways to assess threats that a prisoner may present, especially if the prisoner is a member of a gang. The reason for assessing the threat level is to contain gangs and their ability to disrupt the normal and safe working of prisons. Good management has many facets but much depends on a hands-on approach by the warden who must be seen frequently and who must walk the corridors to support his or her correctional officers.

Frank A. Salamone

Further Reading

Morales, Gabriel C. *La Familia = The Family: Prison Gangs in America*. 4th ed. Independent Publishing Platform, 2015.

New York Daily News. "Aryan Brotherhood to La Eme: America's Deadliest Prison Gangs." November 20, 2015. http://www.nydailynews.com/news/crime/aryan-brotherhood-la-eme-america-toughest-prison-gangs-article-1.2441623.

Roberts, Walther. *Prison Gangs: Organized Crime Behind Bars*. Kindle Edition, 2014.

Skarbek, David. *The Social Order of the Underworld: How Prison Gangs Govern the American Penal System*. 1st ed. Oxford, England: Oxford University Press, 2014.

See also Prison and jail systems; Prison inmate subculture; Prison/prisoner classification systems; Prison violence.

Smith Act

The Law: Federal legislation, officially known as the Alien Registration Act, that required aliens to register with the U.S. government and made it a crime to advocate overthrowing the American government by force

Date: June 28, 1940

Criminal justice issues: Espionage and sedition; federal law; political issues

Significance: The Smith Act became the U.S. government's primary legal tool for attacking the American Communist Party during the early years of the Cold War.

As World War II approached, fears of foreign-inspired subversive activity grew in the United States. Concerned especially that the buildup of American defenses might be threatened by sabotage, Congress reacted by passing the Alien Registration Act, which came to be more generally known as the Smith Act for its major proponent, Congressman Howard W. Smith of Virginia.

The Smith Act had two major thrusts. The first sought greater control over aliens living in the United States. Under the act, aliens had to register with the government, be fingerprinted, carry identity cards, and report yearly. (The registration requirement was dropped in 1982.) Those involved in what were regarded as subversive activities could be deported. The other major provisions of the act were directed at disloyal activities. These made it a crime for anyone to advocate the overthrow of the federal government or other American governments by force or violence, to enter a conspiracy to advocate such a course of action, or to become a knowing member of such a group. Penalties for those convicted under the act included a ten-thousand-dollar fine, up to ten years in prison, or both.

Though a wartime measure, the Smith Act was used relatively little during World War II. As postwar tension between the United States and the Soviet Union developed into the Cold War, however, the act came to the fore as concerns about the possibility of communist subversion in the United States rose. By the late 1940's, there were increasing concerns about the activities of members of the American Communist Party and sympathetic groups, and charges of communist penetration of the government were increasingly made. The administration of President Harry S. Truman was charged with being slow to meet the communist challenge at home. Partly in response, the Truman administration used the Smith Act to attack the party's organization.

In 1948 Eugene Dennis and ten other communist leaders were arrested and charged under the act. They were convicted and sentenced to prison. They appealed, arguing that the Smith Act was an unconstitutional violation of the First Amendment's protection of free expression. Their appeal was denied by the Supreme Court in 1951.

Use of the Smith Act continued during the 1950's. Altogether, more than 140 arrests were made under the act. Later Supreme Court decisions in *Yates v. United States* (1957) and *Brandenburg v. Ohio* (1969) broadened the extent of expression protected by the First Amendment, but the Smith Act itself continued to be held as constitutional.

William C. Lowe

Further Reading
Abraham, Henry J., and Barbara A. Perry. *Freedom and the Court.* 7th ed. New York: Oxford University Press, 1998.

Ngai, Mae M. *Impossible Subjects: Illegal Aliens and the Making of Modern America.* Princeton, N.J.: Princeton University Press, 2004.

See also Clear and present danger test; Palmer raids; Seditious libel.

Solitary confinement

Definition: Confinement of prisoners in isolation from other prison and jail inmates
Criminal justice issues: Medical and health issues; prisons; punishment
Significance: A difficult challenge to prison administrators has long been how to punish inmates for offenses committed within prison walls, when extending sentences may mean nothing to prisoners already facing long sentences or possible execution. One solution has been to place prison offenders in solitary confinement. However, some critics charge that solitary confinement may merely aggravate the prisoners' problems.

Modern prisons generally have four reasons for placing inmates in solitary confinement: administrative detention, protective custody, short-term disciplinary segregation, and long-term detention in special housing units or supermax prisons. It has to be mentioned here that isolation and solitary confinement, however are not synonyms. While both are measurers imposed on a prisoner's during detention or prison sentence, solitary confinement is a disciplinary measure wherein the prisoner or detainee is completely cut off from the world. Isolation, in comparison, is a preventive measure that is used for, among other purposes, the wellbeing and health of the prisoner and other prisoners.

Inmates placed in administrative detention are put in special sections of prison segregation units when they are charged with serious rule violations, and investigations are in progress. They may also be placed in administrative detention when they voice concerns for their own personal safety because of their fears of sexual assaults by other prisoners, gang violence, or retaliation for having informed on other prisoners. When prison officers find that the prisoners' fears are well grounded, they may then place the inmates in long-term protective custody units or transfer them to other prisons.

Inmates found guilty of serious prison-rule violations, such as fighting with other inmates, assaulting staff members, or trying to escape, are placed in punitive or disci-

> **Contents of a Typical Solitary-Confinement Cell**
>
> ✓ four plain concrete walls
> ✓ one heavy metal door with a "pie flap"
> ✓ one narrow, barred window
> ✓ one stainless steel sink/toilet combination
> ✓ one bolt-down metal-frame bed or concrete sleeping slab
> ✓ one small storage container for personal items
> ✓ one bolted-down table
> ✓ one bolted-down chair
> ✓ one small bookshelf
> ✓ one reading light
>
> Inmates serving long terms in solitary confinement may also have shower stalls in their cells. Depending upon the conditions imposed on a prisoner, a cell may or may not contain a small television set, a radio, or limited amounts of reading material.

plinary segregation. Such isolation is usually limited to a maximum of sixty days at a time because of court restrictions.

The physical conditions of solitary confinement are typically spartan. Inmates are generally locked up alone for up to twenty-three hours a day in small cells.

Inmates in solitary confinement receive their food on trays passed through slots in their doors known as "pie flaps," and they eat all their meals within their cells. Inmates are permitted to exit their cells only after they have been handcuffed by extending their hands through the pie flaps in the doors. Inmates are generally allowed to exercise outside their cells for one hour per day, either alone or in small groups, in small, fenced-in units, which have been dubbed "recreation cages." Medical personnel visit periodically to attend to inmates' medical and psychological needs. The prisoners may also be allowed some educational and religious programming in their cells.

Critics of solitary confinement argue that it is unduly restrictive and punitive and creates boring claustrophobic environments that can lead to, or intensify, mental illness. Proponents of solitary confinement counter that little empirical evidence has been gathered to prove that solitary confinement causes mental disorders. They also point out that when inmates complain about solitary confinement, they typically criticize the treatment they receive at the hands of the guards, not their living conditions.

Psychologists and psychiatrists testifying in court often offer conflicting testimony on the impact of solitary confinement on mental health. Consequently, when judges examine the conditions of solitary confinement, they generally focus most of their attention on the food and physical conditions of the confinement units, not on the prisoners' psychological conditions. Contemporary challenges have emerged in the context of inmates with mental health issues and the difficulties they face in solitary confinement. In the context of mental illness, one federal judge has correctly pointed out that the solitary confinement of mental ill prisoners amounts to "..the mental equivalent of putting an asthmatic in a place with little air..." This observation arose from a constitutional challenge to segregation of inmates especially those with serious mental illness.

Most importantly, international treaty bodies and human rights experts, including the Human Rights Committee (a body of independent experts to monitor implementation of the International Covenant on Civil and Political Rights by its State parties.), the Committee against Torture (Rule 32), and the U.N. Special Rapporteur on Torture (A.63 mentions an 'Absolute ban on restraints and seclusion'),have concluded that solitary confinement of any human being may result in cruel, inhuman, or degrading treatment that is said to be in violation of the International Covenant on Civil and Political Rights, and the Convention against Torture and other Cruel, Inhuman, and Degrading Treatment or Punishment.

Robert Rogers. Updated by Tania Sebastian

Further Reading

Kupers, Terry. *Prison Madness: The Mental Health Crisis Behind Bars and What We Must Do About It.* San Francisco: Jossey-Bass Publishers, 1999.

Neal, Donice, ed. *Supermax Prisons: Beyond the Rock.* Lanham, Md.: American Correctional Association, 2003.

Toch, Hans, and Kenneth Adams. *Coping: Maladaptation in Prisons.* New Brunswick, N.J.: Transaction Books, 1989.

Metzner, Jeffrey L., and Jamie Fellner. *Solitary Confinement and Mental Illness in U.S. Prisons: A Challenge for Medical Ethics.* J Am Acad Psychiatry Law 38:104-8, 2010.

International Covenant on Civil and Political Rights. Available at: http://www.ohchr.org/Documents/ProfessionalInterest/ccpr.pdf

Convention against Torture and other Cruel, Inhuman, and Degrading Treatment or Punishment. Available at: *https://treaties.un.org/doc/Publication/UNTS/Volume%201465/volume-1465-I-24841-English.pdf*

Mendez, Juan E., Report of the Special Rapporteur on Torture and Other Cruel, Inhuman or Degrading Treatment or Punishment, UN General Assembly, 1 February 2013.

Committee against Torture: Observations of the Committee against Torture on the revision of the United Nations Standard Minimum Rules for the Treatment of Prisoners (SMR), December 2013.

Vasiliades, Elizabeth. "Solitary Confinement and International Human Rights: Why the U.S. Prison System Fails Global Standards." 21 (1) American University International Law Review, 2005, 71-99.

Shalev, Sharon, A sourcebook on solitary confinement, Mannheim Centre for Criminology London School of Economics and Political Science, 2008.

See also Auburn system; Cruel and unusual punishment; Incapacitation; Mental illness; Prison escapes; Prison violence; Supermax prisons; Walnut Street Jail; Scandinavia's prison experience; Pennsylvania system of corrections.

Supermax prisons

Definition: Control-oriented prisons designed for inmates considered so incorrigible, disruptive, escape-prone, or violent that they pose threats to the staffs and inmates of conventional maximum-security prisons

Criminal justice issues: Deviancy; Prisons; Violent Crime

Significance: Supermax prisons are a modern innovation in American corrections. By separating the most dangerous inmates from general prison populations and keeping those inmates in what amounts to long-term solitary confinement, supermax prisons appear to have reduced levels of prison violence. However, no studies have yet shown what effect the prisons are having on the inmates themselves and on crime problems generally.

Supermax prisons are based upon the concept of selective incapacitation—the notion that because most offenses are committed by a small minority of offenders, incapacitating that minority will reduce crime by an amount disproportionate to their numbers. The concept grew out of a now-classic study of juvenile offenders in Philadelphia published by Marvin E. Wolfgang, Robert M. Figlio, and Thorsten Sellin in 1972. Replications of the Philadelphia study elsewhere produced remarkably similar results. Consequently, policy analysts concluded that if this small group of chronic recidivists—both in society and in prison—could be identified and isolated, the total crime rate should drop considerably. Supermax prisons are thus designed to incapacitate these violent recidivists who do not respond well to treatment.

It has been estimated that up to 20 percent of inmates in prison are remorseless psychopaths who are not motivated to change. However, psychopaths and other dangerous repeat offenders generally "burn out," or moderate their behavior, with the passage of time. Meanwhile, less-serious offenders in traditional prisons feel safer and more secure when separated from the hard-core repeat offenders and tend to take fuller advantage of the vocational and therapeutic programs offered to rehabilitate them.

Alcatraz: The First Supermax Prison

The first supermax prison in America was Alcatraz Island. Built by the federal government on a small island in the frigid, shark-infested waters of San Francisco Bay in 1934, Alcatraz held a comparatively small number of violent and notorious criminals, including "Machine Gun" Kelly and Al Capone, in tiny cells. Alcatraz proved to be a secure facility but was expensive to operate because of its isolation. All its supplies, including fresh water, had to be shipped to it by boat, and all its waste materials had to be shipped off the island. Less than thirty years after it opened to prisoners, Alcatraz was closed down in 1963 and replaced by a federal penitentiary in Marion, Illinois.

Varner Unit Supermax, Varner, Arkansas. (By Richard apple, via Wikimedia Commons)

Marion Penitentiary soon developed problems of its own. Designed as a traditional congregate penitentiary, it was ill equipped to deal with exceptionally violent offenders placed in it. In response to the staff's ever-tightening security the prison's inmates carried out a work strike in 1980. Prison officials responded by shutting down the prison factory and terminating all education classes. After two correctional officers were killed by inmates in separate incidents in the prison's most secure housing unit in October 1983 and an inmate was found murdered in his cell four days later, federal officials from the Bureau of Prisons decided to place the penitentiary on permanent lock-down status. From that time, Marion's inmates were confined alone within their cells for more than twenty-three hours each day, and group programs were virtually eliminated.

In 1985 Marion inmates challenged their living conditions in federal court in the case of *Bruscino v. Carlson*. The judge in that case ruled that conditions in Marion met constitutional requirements. After a federal appellate court upheld that decision in 1988 and the US Supreme Court let the ruling stand in 1989 there was a rapid expansion of supermax prisons throughout the country. By the early twenty-first century, the federal government and a majority of the states were operating supermax prisons. These facilities ranged from the Bureau of Prison's Florence, Colorado, facility—which replaced the Marion Penitentiary—to California's Pelican Bay State Prison, which opened in late 1989.

Supermax Prison Design

While some supermax prisons are standalone units and others are units of larger prison complexes, virtually all supermax facilities have certain things in common as their designs seek to minimize the risk of escape and the potential for inmates to harm themselves or others. They all have tight perimeter security and severely restricted inmate movement within their walls. They all have small concrete-encased solitary cells. These cells generally measure about seven by twelve feet in area and are typically furnished with metal doors; narrow, barred windows; small steel sinks and toilets; shower stalls; small steel desks with pull-out stools; small steel bookshelves anchored to the walls; and raised concrete slabs or metal-frame beds. Radio and television receivers may or may not be allowed.

Supermax inmates typically spend twenty-three hours a day alone in their cells, eating, exercising, and taking part in whatever programming is available through video, correspondence, or written materials. Individual inmates rarely, if ever, have contacts with other inmates. Their human contacts are generally restricted to counselors, clergy members, and medical personnel who see them in their cells. When inmates leave their cells, they are handcuffed, placed in leg irons, and escorted to their destinations by at least two prison guards. When they are allowed to have visits, they are separated from their visitors by concrete, steel, and thick glass and must communicate by speakerphones or, in more extreme cases, via video screens.

Critics of the Prisons

Proponents of supermax prisons argue that they deter as well as incapacitate. Inmates housed in supermax prisons must serve a minimum of two years in solitary confinement before becoming eligible for transfer back to traditional penitentiaries.

Opponents of supermax prisons note that the facilities are more expensive to build and operate than standard maximum-security institutions. Staff-to-inmate ratios are generally higher because inmates spend so much time locked down within their cells that everything they need must be carried to them. Moreover, in contrast to most prisons, in which inmates perform many of the routine cooking, cleaning, and maintenance chores that keep the institutions running smoothly, all chores in supermax prisons must be done by staff members.

Critics also charge that the criteria for selecting inmates for supermax prisons are vaguely worded and capriciously applied. For example, some prisoners are sent to the facilities because they have become labeled as "troublemakers" for making themselves nuisances to administrators by filing frequent grievances and lawsuits. Members of gangs are sometimes sent to supermax prisons because of their gang membership, even if they have no histories of serious assault or escape.

Supermax prisons are also criticized for fostering repressive environments in which staff abuses are more likely to occur. Courts have documented abuses at Pelican Bay. Inmates who are mentally ill or prone to mental illness may deteriorate further in solitary confinement over extended periods of time. Moreover, supermax prisons typically offer inmates no work, treatment programs, or vocational training to prepare them for successful reintegration into the community.

It has also been charged that some supermax prisons have been built at the behest of politicians wanting to appear "tough on crime," even when correctional officials themselves do not think the facilities are needed. In any case, in the modern rush to build supermax prisons, little research has been conducted to prove their actual effectiveness. The Bureau of Prisons has reported that levels of violence have gone down throughout the federal prison system since supermax prisons were introduced. States such as California and Texas have also reported curbing waves of violence in their prison systems with the widespread use of solitary confinement. However, other states have not reported reductions in inmate-on-inmate assaults since the introduction of their supermax prisons. Findings on the impact of supermax prisons on inmate-on-staff assaults have also been mixed.

Robert Rogers

Further Reading
Alarid, Leanne, and Paul Cromwell. *Correctional Perspectives: Views from Academics, Practitioners, and Prisoners*. Los Angeles: Roxbury, 2002.
Briggs, Chad S., Jody L. Sundt, and Thomas C. Castellano. "The Effect of Supermaximum Security Prisons on Aggregate Levels of Institutional Violence." *Criminology* 41, no. 4 (2003): 1341-1376.
Kurki, Leena, and Norval Morris. "The Purposes, Practices, and Problems of Supermax Prisons." In *Crime and Justice: A Review of Research*, edited by Michael Tonry. Chicago: University of Chicago Press, 2001.
Neal, Donice, ed. *Supermax Prisons: Beyond the Rock*. Lanham, Md.: American Correctional Association, 2003.
Pizarro, Jesenia, and Vanja M. K. Stenius. "Supermax Prisons: Their Rise, Current Practices, and Effect on Inmates." *Prison Journal* 84, no. 2 (2004): 248-264.
Toch, Hans. "The Future of Supermax Confinement." *Prison Journal* 81, no. 3 (2001): 376-388.
Wolfgang, Marvin E., Robert M. Figlio, and Thorsten Sellin. *Delinquency in a Birth Cohort*. Chicago: University of Chicago Press, 1972.

See also Cruel and unusual punishment; Incapacitation; Mental illness; Prison and jail systems; Prison escapes; Prison violence; Recidivism; Solitary confinement; *Ashker v. Brown* (2016).

Victim and Witness Protection Act

The Law: Federal law providing guidelines for treatment of victims and witnesses in federal trials
Date: Enacted on October 12, 1982
Criminal justice issues: Crime prevention; victims; witnesses
Significance: The multiple changes enacted by the Victim and Witness Protection Act of 1982 affected the experiences of victims within the criminal justice system in a multitude of ways.

The Victim and Witness Protection Act of 1982 (VWPA) was established to address the important role crime victims and witnesses play in a federal trial and to guide criminal justice professionals in their treatment of victims and witnesses. The VWPA called for fair treatment of victims and witnesses throughout the court process and also was formulated as a model for state and local legislation.

Specifically, the VWPA called for protection of crime victims and witnesses from intimidation or retaliation by defendants, consideration of victims in regard to privacy when at trial, restitution, victim impact statements to be included in presentence reports, return of property listed as evidence, and safety when assigning bail to defendants. It also included a provision offering employer intervention services for crime victims and witnesses. To aid criminal justice professionals working with victims and witnesses, the VWPA provided for training and education for federal law-enforcement officers and government attorneys. Additionally, the VWPA prohibited federal felons from profiting from their crimes through literary or other profit-based avenues.

Subsequent amendments to the act include allowing for an oral or written statement at the hearing and assigning U.S. attorneys as federal prosecutors with the responsibility of informing victims of parole hearings.

Elizabeth Quinn DeValve

Further Reading
Karmen, Andrew. *Crime Victims: An Introduction to Victimology*. 5th ed. Belmont, Calif.: Wadsworth, 2004.
Office for Victims of Crime. *New Directions from the Field: Victims' Rights and Services for the Twenty-first Century*. Washington, D.C.: U.S. Department of Justice, 1998.

See also National Crime Victimization Survey; Organized Crime Control Act; Trials; Victimology; Victims of Crime Act.

Victim assistance programs

Definition: Advocacy and support services, often funded or administered by government, that guide victims of crime through the legal system and help them cope with emotional distress
Criminal justice issues: Domestic violence; medical and health issues; victims; women's issues
Significance: Victim assistance programs address a common criticism of the criminal justice system: that by focusing on justice for defendants and society at large, it overlooks the emotional, legal, and physical needs of crime victims.

The first victim assistance programs in the United States were created during the early 1970's. They were located in large urban areas and focused primarily on sexual assault of women. These programs offered limited support services to women for whom the criminal justice system might seem intimidating and insensitive. Since that time, victim assistance programs have expanded in number and scope. By the mid-1990's programs were in place throughout the country, addressing victims not only of sexual assault but also of child abuse, spousal battery, and other violent crimes.

Victim assistance programs typically offer services in three general areas: counseling and support, legal assistance, and public awareness and legislative reform. Counseling and support is perhaps the most common function, helping victims to cope with posttraumatic stress disorder, rape trauma syndrome, and other conditions caused by an assault. Individual and group counseling, crisis intervention, medical referrals, and relocation services are some of the resources typically available. Programs also offer legal assistance for crime victims who are testifying, seeking restraining orders, or otherwise facing the criminal justice system. Services include orientation to the justice system and courtroom assistance. Finally, victim assistance services act as advocates for crime victims generally, raising public awareness of certain crimes and how to prevent them, and advocating legislative reforms.

The federal government has promoted victim assistance programs through legislation and funding. The federal Law Enforcement Assistance Administration funded the creation of model victim assistance programs in 1974. The federal Victim and Witness Protection Act of 1982 established "fair treatment standards" for victims and witnesses of crimes. Two years later, the Victims of Crime Act (VOCA) established a fund which provides grants to states to compensate crime victims, and for state and local programs that provide direct assistance to crime victims and their families. In 1994 the Violent Crime Control and Law Enforcement Act augmented the VOCA fund and authorized funding of more than $1 billion for fighting violence against women.

National nongovernment organizations also have been established for promoting victims' rights and victim assistance. Two advocacy groups, the National Organization for Victim Assistance (NOVA) and the Victims' Assistance Legal Organization (VALOR), were created in 1975 and 1981, respectively. In 1985, the National Victim Center was established to help promote the rights and needs of crime victims by working with thousands of local criminal justice and victim service organizations around the country.

Further Reading
Karmen, Andrew. *Crime Victims: An Introduction to Victimology*. 5th ed. Belmont, Calif.: Wadsworth, 2004.
Office for Victims of Crime. *New Directions from the Field: Victims' Rights and Services for the Twenty-first Century*. Washington, D.C.: U.S. Department of Justice, 1998.

See also Criminal justice system; Domestic violence; National Organization for Victim Assistance; Rape and sex offenses; Restorative justice; Victimology; Victims of Crime Act.

Victim impact statements

Definition: Victim impact statements are written or oral statements made on behalf of the victim or by the victim at various stages of the criminal justice process (i.e., the sentencing phase, at plea-bargaining hearings, at parole hearings, and at some bail hearings), to express how the crime impacted them psychologically, physically, and financially.

Criminal justice issues: Victims; judges; juries; sentencing

Significance: Today, victims' play an important role in the criminal justice process and are afforded various opportunities to participate within the system. This has moved the system to being more victim oriented; one that acknowledges victims and attempts to reduce the impact the victimization has had on their lives. It, too, reminds judges, juries, and prosecutors that behind the "state" is a real person with an interest in how the case is resolved.

James Rowland, a probation officer in Fresno County, California, was the first person to advocate for victim impact statements (VISs). Rowland's argument for the incorporation of VISs, was to provide a balanced picture of both the offender and victim when determining the most appropriate sentence for the offender. In addition, Rowland, believed that VIS would increase compensation and restitution orders payable to victims by informing court officials of the harm they have suffered.

Currently, all fifty states provide victims the opportunity to present VISs at varying stages of the criminal justice process.

Goals

The victim's right to present a VIS has presented various moral, penological, and practical arguments for their use. Victim impact statements allow victims to describe the psychological, physical, and financial effects of the victimization beyond the visible harm they may have experienced. This opportunity is afforded to the surviving family of victims, who are able to contextualize the life of the victim to the court and the suffering experienced as a result of their loss.

In a VIS, victims generally describe the psychological and financial damages they experienced as a direct result of the victimization. Doing this is argued to aid in bringing back a sense of control to the victim's life, and allows him or her to make better sense of what happened. In the statement victims can also outline what they believe is an appropriate punishment for the crime. It is argued that by conveying his or her feelings makes the process more democratic and reflective of the community's response to crime, while recognizing the individual dignity of the victim. This is believed to increase the victim's confidence in and satisfaction with the criminal justice system.

The scale to which the criminal justice system makes use of victim impact statements today, marks a shift to want to improve the lives of those who deal with the reality of criminal victimization. However, the arguments for the use of VISs have not been accepted by all in the criminal justice system and by the public.

Shortcomings

Despite the legal advocacy victim impact statements have received, their use continues to be the subject of debate. The most noted shortcomings of VISs are their potential influence on making sentencing decisions more punitive. Over the years much research has been conducted to evaluate this argument. The growing body of literature and evidence to suggest that the inclusion of VISs at the sentencing phase does increase sentencing severity seems to outweigh the results of those that argue that the statements have little effect on sentencing outcomes.

Additionally, the content of the statements are often limited or constrained. Victim impact statements are highly regulated by the court, and designed to fit the goals of the justice system. This is done so that court officials can avoid the use of threatening language or comments made to the offender by the victim, and/or derogatory statements made about the criminal justice system. The degree to which officials limit and constrain what is included in the statement is argued to negatively affect victims' perceptions of the system, as victims are not allowed to express what they truly feel. Moreover, by only providing strong statements that depict a picture of good versus evil, VISs may serve as a strong justification for harsher punishment.

Last, whether or not VISs aid in the emotional recovery of victims is debatable. The delivery of one statement, where a person expresses his or her feelings and emotions has not provided conclusive evidence of reducing symptoms of severe emotional distress. The social sharing of emotions from a traumatic event has been argued to not have any direct effect on recovery. Additionally, the notoriously long-winded criminal justice process and the time it takes before delivering the statement may counter steps already taken to recover.

The goals of VISs are that they have a positive impact on the victim and help them to regain a sense of control over their lives. Victim impact statements also help to foster a positive perception of the criminal justice system and its willingness to take the victim seriously, balancing the rights offered to offenders with those offered to victims. Conversely, victim impact statements have shortcomings, which are that the statements are heavily regulated by court officials and may lead to more punitive sentencing decisions, and show little evidence that the statements aid in victim recovery.

Irrespective of whether or not victim impact statements meet their intended goals or are welcomed by all, their inclusion in the criminal justice system is here to stay.

Chadley James

Further Reading
Cassell, P. G. "In Defense of Victim Impact Statements." *Ohio State Journal of Criminal Law* 6 (2009): 611-48.
Englebrecht, C. M., and J. M. Chavez. "Whose Statement Is It? An Examination of Victim Impact Statements Delivered in Court." *Victims and Offenders: An International Journal of Evidence-Based Research, Policy, and Practice* 9 (2014): 386-412.
Erez, E., and P. Tontodonato. "The Effect of Victim Participation in Sentencing and Satisfaction with Justice." *Justice Quarterly* 9, no. 3 (1990): 393-415.
Johnson, I. M., and E. F. Morgan. "Victim Impact Statements: Fairness to Defendants?" In *Controversies in Victimology*, edited by L. J. Moriarty, 115-31. New Jersey: Anderson Publishing, 2008.
Lens, K. E., A. Pemberton K. Brans, J. Braeken, S. Bogaerts, and E. Lahlah. "Delivering a Victim Impact Statement: Emotionally Effective or Counter-productive?" *European Journal of Criminology* 12, no. 1 (2015): 17-34.
Paternoster, R., and J. Deise, J. "A Heavy Thumb on the Scale: The Effect of Victim Impact Evidence on Capital Decision Making." *Criminology* 49 (2011): 129-61.

See also Victim assistance programs; Victim-offender mediation; Victimology; Victims of Crime Act; Sentencing; Australia's Reintegrative Shaming Approach; Victim recovery stages; Victimization theories; Victims services.

Victim-offender mediation

Definition: Facilitated meetings between offenders and victims of their crimes with the intent to discuss the effects and triggers of the harm and to provide options of developing an agreement to repair the harm

Criminal justice issues: Justice; Probation and pretrial release

Significance: Part of the "new wave" of community justice decision-making practices known as restorative justice, victim-offender mediation emphasizes restoration and rehabilitation as opposed to traditional retributive justice system practices which highlight retribution and punishment.

Victim-offender mediation gained popularity in the United States during the 1990s, rising with the tide of the restorative justice movement, which sought alternatives to the conflict resolution practices of the (still dominant) retributive justice system. Sharing elements with other restorative practices, such as family group conferencing and circle sentencing, it appeals to community partnerships for crime control and crime prevention and represents a significant shift from the state governance of crime matters. In 2016, victim-offender mediation programs were widespread across the United States and the world. In the United States they are most often conducted by nonprofit organizations, which receive referrals from courts and probation or parole officers. Mediators are trained volunteers or paid staff members who function as facilitators so that victim and offender may exchange their experiences of the harm, and if they are agreed, help them reach a final contract, which usually involves restitution (monetary or other) and apologies for the victim, and possibly some form of assistance to the offender aimed at circumventing future offenses. This may or may not be court enforceable.

Victim-offender mediation is used in place of formal adjudication or in addition to it, or as a condition of parole or probation. It is used with lower level, moderately serious, and serious offenses, including capital murder cases. With careful preparation of both parties, mediation can register great success, as illustrated by the high rates of satisfaction reported by victims and offenders, their perceptions of fairness with both the process and the outcome, and their reports that they would choose mediation over court proceedings in the future. In addition, victims who participate in mediation are far more likely to feel that the justice system has treated them fairly and have been found to enjoy reduced fear and anxiety, while there is significant evidence that mediation is positively related to lower rates of recidivism among offenders. These results indicate that wider public policy consideration should be given to increasing the availability of victim-offender mediation services, perhaps as a basic right for all victims and offenders.

Victim-offender mediation addresses aspects of social and criminal justice that are not built into the criminal justice system: It considers public safety beyond simple imprisonment, it makes victims central to decision making, and it makes offenders accountable while simultaneously allowing them to make amends and learn about the impact of their crime, thus increasing a sense of responsibility rather than inadequacy and rejection.

Michael J. Coyle

Further Reading

Dhami, Mandeep K. "Apology in Victim-Offender Mediation." *Contemporary Justice Review* 19.1 (2016): 31-42. Print.

Miethe, Terance D., and Robert F. Meier. *Crime and Its Social Context: Toward an Integrated Theory of Offenders, Victims, and Situations*. Albany: State U of New York P, 1994. Print.

Namuo, Clynton. "Victim Offender Mediation: When Divergent Paths and Destroyed Lives Come Together for Healing." *Georgia State University Law Review* 32.2 (2016): 577-602. Print.

Ravinsky, Laura. "Reducing Recidivism of Violent Offenders through Victim-Offender Mediation: A Fresh Start." *Cardozo Journal of Conflict Resolution* 17.3 (2016): 1019-44. Print.

Umbreit, Mark S. *The Handbook of Victim Offender Mediation: An Essential Guide to Practice and Research*. San Francisco: Jossey, 2001. Print.

See also Civilian review boards; Community-based corrections; Rehabilitation; Restitution; Restorative justice; Peacemaking criminology; Australia's "Reintegrative Shaming" approach; Post-traumatic Stress Disorder; Victims services; Victim recovery stages.

Victim recovery stages

Definition: Victimization may produce a number of consequences, including emotional consequences. The emotional recovery process has been described in the victimology literature as consisting of different stages.

Criminal justice issues: Victims

Significance: It is important to acknowledge the impact of crime on victims and what support they might need to advance their recovery, both within and outside of the criminal justice system.

Consequences of victimization are manifold and diverse. Key publications on the effects of crime on individual victims, including Joanna Shapland and Matthew Hall's comprehensive article on the matter, commonly describe material, physical, and social effects as well as emotional distress as possible consequences. It is in these discourses that individual victims react very differently to victimization—their emotional reaction may, for instance, very much depend on their previous experiences, general well-being, available support, etc. Nevertheless, it is possible to distinguish some commonalities in victims' responses to victimization. For instance, from various crime victimization surveys (both on a national and international level), we know that violent crimes are more likely to have an emotional impact on victims than property crimes. However, these very same surveys also reveal that victims of burglary and victims of violent crime report similar emotional consequences: both are likely to present elevated levels of anger and fear. Furthermore, those bereaved by murder or manslaughter manifest similar emotional and psychological consequences (including depression, fear, and self-blame) as victims who directly experienced violent victimization. In short, victimization can be destabilizing—victims will feel a need to try and restore this balance.

When zooming in on emotional recovery from victimization, the victimological literature generally distinguishes between an immediate, intermediate, and final stage in the recovery process. These stages of recovery are reminiscent of Kübler-Ross' five stages of grief (denial, anger, bargaining, depression, and acceptance) and are inspired by Tyhurst's stages of recovery following natural disasters (impact, recoil, and recovery stages).

Vital publications, for instance by Ann Burgess and by Steven Berglas, describe that immediately following victimization victims might be in shock and experience disbelief at what happened, which might temporarily numb or immobilize a person. Shock and disbelief might co-occur with fear, anxiety, and depression. It has been highlighted that the reactions victims perceive in this initial phase might promote or obstruct recovery. Positive support could include informal support (from family and friends) as well as formal support (from law enforcement and professional victim support services) and may be practical or emotional in nature. Judith Herman, who is considered an authority on the emotional impact of victimization, emphasizes that ensuring the victim's safety at this stage is an essential step towards emotional recovery. She specifies that this may include particular attention to basic health needs, sleep and nourishment, living conditions, and financial security.

Next, is what is referred to as the recoil stage. The authors already mentioned previously explain that in this stage victims' emotions may fluctuate between apathy, anger, rage, and startle reactions. Victims may also be reliving the harmful incident and experience fear, anxiety, helplessness, and impaired memory and decision making. Victims may at this point experience self-blame and shame for what happened. As they are trying to adjust, victims tend to be wondering why the crime happened to them — "Why me?" — is a question many victims are plagued with, a finding that has been highlighted in Ronnie Janoff-Bulman's contributions to the field. From victim surveys, we know that victims might miss some time at work due to the physical and emotional consequences of the crime they suffered, but victims eventually resume daily activities and normal routines, which might indicate that they are coping. This might not necessarily be the case as the feelings experienced in this phase can be overpowering and affect work, school, and social life. If the crime was reported to the police, the victim might also have to deal with any formal requirements for criminal justice procedures, which in their own right can be quite overwhelming. Victims are not necessarily familiar with the criminal justice system and the formal steps, authorities and services involved; victim and witness assistance programs have been put in place to make the criminal justice process more manageable for victims. However, even if a victim did not report the crime they experienced to the police (which, as we know from crime victimization surveys, many victims do not, for a variety of reasons), they still need support, for which they again might primarily rely on relatives and friends but might also have to rely on support from health care and mental health care professionals as well as victim support services. The duration of the recoil stage seems to vary. Nonetheless, most commonly, after a short or longer time, this stage eventually results in recovery. Drawing on her extensive research on the issue, Judith Herman explains that the traumatic experience becomes a memory, not unlike other, nontraumatic events, and recalling or recounting it no longer produces the strong emotions that typify the recoil stage.

Collectively, the scholars mentioned above explain that the final stage of recovery is then marked by a sense of integration of the harmful incident and a sense of empowerment. At this stage, victims regain self-esteem and a sense of safety and manage to give the incident and the harm a place. This does not necessarily mean that things went back to the way they were before the victimization—that is simply impossible in certain cases—or that all emotional distress is resolved. What it means is that the adverse incident has been integrated and the memory of it has become bearable, Herman argues. Ronnie Janoff-Bulman, in her seminal work on meaning making following adversity, explains that the experience of adversity and trauma forces people to see the world as it really is, that is, as potentially malevolent and dangerous. She continues that coping then implies that the adverse experience and its consequences are transformed and that victims come to terms with the idea that bad things can happen. This process may produce newfound appreciation for life, self-enhancing perception of oneself as capable and strong, new wisdom, a perception of the world as not absolutely malevolent or absolutely benevolent, and even an urge to help individuals who are experiencing similar distress.

Many victimologists emphasize that most trauma survivors initially experience emotional distress (to a varying degree) but, ultimately, that most eventually demonstrate psychological adaptation as time progresses. Unfortunately, for a minority of victims the distress resulting from victimization persists. When distress does not seem to attenuate, the victim might be suffering from post-traumatic stress. According to the American Psychiatric Association, for a victim to be diagnosed with Post-Traumatic Stress Disorder (PTSD), he or she must be suffering from intrusive recollection of the harmful event (e.g., through flashbacks and nightmares), experiencing hyperarousal (e.g., hypervigilance and exaggerated startle responses) and avoiding stimuli associated with the harmful incident (e.g., avoid conversation about the trauma or avoid places). These symptoms must be occurring for at least one month and cause significant distress or impairment.

Ultimately, resilience is far from uncommon among trauma survivors, as is evidenced in a growing body of literature honing in on this phenomenon. It might require time and immediate and long-term social support seems to be important in this regard. Also respectful treatment from law enforcement, prosecutorial services, and judicial authorities has been found to advance recovery, as evidenced in Judith Herman's discourse. This finding encourages the further advancement of victim-oriented reforms in the criminal justice system.

Tinneke Van Camp

Further Reading
Berglas, S. "Why Did This Happen to Me?" *Psychology Today* (February, 1985): 44-48.
Burgess, A. W. "Rape Trauma Syndrome." *Behavioral Sciences and the Law* 1, no. 3 (1983): 97-113.Feeny, N. C, and L. A. Zoellner, eds. "Conclusion: Risk and Resilience Following Trauma Exposure." Chapter 14 in *Resilience and Recovery Following Trauma*. New York: The Guilford Press, 2013.
Herman, J. L. "Recovery from Psychological Trauma." *Psychiatry and Clinical Neurosciences* 52 (Suppl. 1998): S145-50.
Janoff-Bulman, R. *Shattered Assumptions: Towards a New Psychology of Trauma*. New York: Free Press, 1992.
Masters, R. E., L. Beth Way, P. B. GerstenfeldB. T. Muscat, M. Hooper J. P. J. Dussich, L. Pincu, and C. A. Skrapec. *CJ: Realities and Challenges* 2nd ed., Chap. 14. New York: McGraw Hill, 2013.
Shapland, J., and M. Hall. "What Do We Know about the Effects of Crime on Victims?" *International Review of Victimology* 14, no. 2 (2007): 175-217.
Tyhurst, J. S. (1957). "Psychological and Social Aspects of Civilian Disaster." *Canadian Medical Association Journal* 76, no. 5 (1957): 385-93.

See also Rehabilitation; Restorative justice; Victim-offender mediation; Victimology; Peacemaking criminology; Scandinavia's prison experience; Victims services; Victimization theories; Victim impact statements; Australia's "reintegrative shaming" approach; Crime victimization: Primary and secondary; Post-traumatic stress disorder.

Victimization theories

Definition: Theories that aim to explain who is most likely to experience (what kind of) victimization as well as theories that look at the consequences of victimization and victim needs
Criminal justice issues: Victims
Significance: In addition to looking at the causes of crime and how best to respond to crime, it is important to look at experiences and consequences of victimization.

Already in the eighteenth century scholars were studying the causes of crime. In comparison to criminology, victimology is a relatively young discipline. Early academic publications on victims of crime only emerged in the 1940's. Hans von Hentig, Benjamin Mendelsohn, Stephen Schafer, Marvin Wolfgang, and Menachem Amir are acknowledged as the pioneering victimologists in various victimology handbooks. Their work is laudable for expanding the criminological perspective from solely focusing on the offender, the causes of crime and how to deal with crime, to considering the victim of crime as well. However, these early victimologists were preoccupied with the role victims play in their own victimization, rather than with the consequences of victimization. They examined victims' actions and reactions that might have provoked, unintentionally triggered, or facilitated their own victimization.

For instance, Von Hentig, in his 1948 publication *The Criminal and His Victim*, first describes factors that he associates with the propensity for criminal behavior and then presents his analysis on what victim characteristics contribute to the genesis of crime (including age, gender, mental capacity, ethnic background, and intelligence quotient [IQ]). Mendelsohn was intrigued with the victim's behavior as a potential instigating factor to the crime and ranks victims based on the degree of their culpability, ranging from completely innocent, somewhat guilty through carelessness, equally guilty as the offender, guilty through provocation of the crime, to most guilty when victimization happened as a result of the victim committing a crime. Schafer, in his 1968 publication *The Victim and His Criminal: A Study in Functional Responsibility*, takes account of both victims' social characteristics and their behavior in the coming about of their victimization. More specifically, he distinguishes categories based on the victim's responsibility and failure to prevent victimization, including no responsibility, some degree of responsibility, shared responsibility, and total responsibility.

A more nuanced empirical approach is adopted by Wolfgang, who took a closer look at the role of the victim and offender in cases of homicide in Philadelphia between 1948 and 1952. He filtered out the cases in which the deceased was first to use a weapon or violence, which was the case in about one-quarter of all homicides in his sample. In these so-called victim-precipitated cases, often alcohol was involved and the victim had a criminal record. Wolfgang, therefore, concludes that the image of the weak and passive victim is not always correct. Wolfgang's study inspired Amir's research into incidents of rape reported to the police in Philadelphia between 1958 and 1960. Amir was interested in the extent to which victims contributed to or might have facilitated their own rape. For instance, rape incidents involving a victim who had consumed alcohol, accepted a car ride from the offender, invited the offender to their home, failed to react strongly to sexual suggestions, or had a bad reputation were categorized as potentially victim-precipitated rape incidents. While the above-mentioned early victimization theories drew criticism by focusing on the role of the victim in their own victimization and fueling victim blaming, critics argue that Amir's study seems to kick wide open the door to blaming victims (of sexual violence) for their suffering. Amir emphasizes that what matters is the offender's interpretation of the victim's actions and attitude, but this could not temper reproach to his study, especially from feminist scholars.

Subsequent victimological studies moved away from the focus on the victim's contribution to their own victimization and finally started to pay attention to who is most likely to become a victim of crime, the consequences of victimization, and victims' needs. According to victimologists, including Ezzat Fattah, the emergence of victimization surveys (including the International Crime Victims Survey and national crime victimization surveys) were key in this regard. These scientific surveys ask a sample of the general population whether they have experienced any of a number of crimes in the last six or twelve months and, if they did, whether they reported it to the police.

Findings from these surveys reveal that people are much more likely to experience minor offenses than serious offenses. Also, victimization seems to be disproportionately distributed: Young men living in urban areas are most likely to experience crime (with the exception of sexual victimization). This observation has been linked to greater propensity among these young men to engage in delinquent behavior. The work by Lauritsen and colleagues is essential in this regard: They emphasize that the greater involvement of young males in delinquent activities does not imply that they therefore deserve to be victimized, but that it is important to acknowledge that delinquent behavior poses a risk for victimization. The association between such a risky lifestyle and victimization is still explored in current theories on the causes of victimization. Such explorations include looking at factors that are mainly associated with the likelihood of committing crime to see whether they might also explain the risk of becoming a victim of crime. This includes asking questions about, for instance, the impact of witnessing domestic violence during childhood on risk of perpetrating, but also of experiencing domestic violence in adult life; witnessing such abusive relationships might negatively impact on the image these children have of what healthy relationships entail.

In addition, findings collected through the national and international victimization surveys mentioned above uncover that many crimes are not reported to the police and the reasons for such nonreporting (e.g., violent crime is less likely to be reported than property crime; a victim might think that the police will not be able to do anything about the crime and therefore not report it; previous experiences with law enforcement might have been dissatisfactory and therefore result in reluctance to reach out to the police again; or the crime might not be perceived as serious enough to be reported). This phenomenon, which in the literature is referred to as the "dark figure of crime," implies that we cannot rely on police data alone to know the prevalence of crime and victimization and who is most at risk for experiencing victimization.

Current victimological research further advances insight into the consequences of victimization. These are many-victimological literature will often refer to material, financial, and emotional consequences (such as anger, depression, self-blame, and symptoms of post-traumatic stress), as well as risk of revictimization. In the same breath, it is highlighted that some of these consequences will manifest themselves for a short time, while others might be prevalent for a long time. Meanwhile, despite a growing body of research into the impact of victimization, it is also clear that the impact of crime is highly individual, as is evidenced in Joanna Shapland and Matthew Hall's key contribution in this respect. The victimological literature emphasizes that individual reactions to adverse experiences such as victimization vary substantially and depend, for example, on the context in which a crime occurred, coping style, social support and previous adverse experiences. Also treatment by criminal justice officials matters in this regard. A growing body of research, building on procedural fairness (or procedural justice) theory, examines what victims expect from the criminal justice system and what role they wish to play in the aftermath of a crime. In these studies, it is repeatedly observed that victims want to feel involved in the formal procedures that take place in response to their victimization and to the offender.

There is also increasing research attention for resilience among victims, which is spearheaded by Patricia Frazier and Ronnie Janoff-Bulman, and potential post-traumatic growth, a term that is reportedly coined by Richard Tedeschi and Lawrence Calhoun. Several scholars highlight that a consistent observation in victimological research is that victims often prefer to describe themselves as survivors—the word "survivor" infers that one has overcome adversity and is ready to move on. Therefore, Andrew Karmen, for instance, encourages researchers to advance research into, what he dubs, "survivorology."

Tinneke Van Camp

Further Reading

Amir, M. *Patterns of Forcible Rape*. Chicago: University of Chicago Press, 1971.

Daigle, L. E. *Victimology: The Essentials*. Chap. 2. Los Angeles: Sage, 2013.

Fattah, E. A "The Evolution of a Young, Promising Discipline: Sixty Years of Victimology, a Retrospective and Prospective Look." In *International Handbook of Victimology*, S. G. Shoham, P. Knepper, and M. Kett, eds., 43-94. Boca Raton, Fla.: CRC Press, 2010.

Frazier, P., C. Greer, S. Gabrielsen, H. Tennen, C. Park, and P. Tomich "The Relation Between Trauma Exposure and Prosocial Behavior." *Psychological Trauma: Theory, Research, Practice, and Policy* 5, no. 3 (2013): 286-94.

Janoff-Bulman, R. *Shattered Assumptions: Towards a New Psychology of Trauma*. New York: Free Press, 1992.

Karmen, A. "Survivorology." In *A Companion to Crime, Harm and Victimisation*, K. Corteen, S. Morley, P. Taylor, and J. Turner, eds., 228-30. Bristol: Policy Press, 2016.

Lauritsen, J. L., R. J. Sampson, and H. Laub. "The Link between Offending and Victimization among Adolescents." *Criminology* 29, no. 2 (1991): 265-92.

Mendelsohn, B. "Une nouvelle branche de la science biopsycho-sociale: La victimologie." *Revue Internationale de Criminologie et de Police Technique* 10, no. 2 (1956): 95-109.

Mendelsohn, B. "Socio-Analytic Introduction to Research in a General Victimological and Criminological Perspective." In *The Victim in International Perspective*, edited by H. J. Schneider, 59-64. Berlin: De Gruyter, 1982.

Schafer, S. *The Victim and His Criminal: A Study in Functional Responsibility*. New York: Random House, 1968.

Shapland, J. and M. Hall. "What Do We Know about the Effects of Crime on Victims?" *International Review of Victimology* 14, no. 2 (2007): 175-217.

Tedeschi, R. G. and L. G. Calhoun. "The Posttraumatic Growth Inventory: Measuring the Positive Legacy of Trauma." *Journal of Traumatic Stress* 9, no. 3 (1996): 455-71.

Van Dijk, J. J. M., R. Manchin, R., J. N. van Kesteren, S. Nevala, and G. Hideg. *The Burden of Crime in the EU, a Comparative Analysis of the European Survey of Crime and Safety.* (2005 EU ICS). Brussels: Gallup Europe, 2005.

Von Hentig, H. *The Criminal and His Victim: Studies in the Sociobiology of Crime*. Cambridge: Yale University Press, 1948.

Wolfgang, M. E. "Victim Precipitated Criminal Homicide." *Journal of Criminal Law, Criminology, and Police Science* 48, no. 1 (1957): 1-11.

See also Restorative justice; Victimology; Peacemaking criminology; Schools of criminology; Scandinavia's prison experience; Victims services; Australia's "reintegrative shaming" approach; Criminology; National Crime Victimization Survey; Victims of Crime Act.

Victimless crimes

Definition: Legally prohibited activities or exchanges among willing parties that do not directly harm anyone except, possibly, the parties willingly involved; typical examples include gambling, prostitution, and drug use

Criminal justice issues: Criminology; Morality and public order; Victimless crime

Significance: The concept of victimless crimes—also called consensual crimes or public order offenses—is frequently applied to debates about decriminalization and the advisability of attempting to legislate morality.

Although the concept of victimless crime was suggested in the work of criminologists in the 1950s, it first found explicit statement in a 1965 study by Edwin Schur that was published under the title *Crimes without Victims*. Schur identified and discussed three types of behavior as examples of victimless crimes: abortion, drug use, and homosexuality. As he stated, "In each case the offending behavior involves a willing and private exchange of strongly demanded yet officially proscribed goods and services: this element of consent precludes the existence of a victim—in the usual sense."

Other scholars who have made use of the concept of victimless crimes include criminologist Jerome Skolnick, who applied it to offenses such as gambling, marijuana use, and prostitution, and jurist Herbert Packer, who cited fornication and narcotic use as crimes without victims. A number of other offenses, including drinking in public, vagrancy, and selling or viewing pornography, have also been called victimless crimes.

At issue is the debate over whether the law should forbid activities for which it is difficult or impossible to determine precisely who is being harmed and how. It has been argued that the law should not forbid activities if they harm no one except, perhaps, the people willingly involved in them. Some legal scholars argue that the United States has become an "overcriminalized" society. On the other hand, others point out that some supposedly "victimless" crimes indeed generate harm (for example, drug addiction leads to theft and robbery as addicts try to support their habit). There is also a widespread belief that certain activities should be prohibited because they are harmful to society at large—this is essentially a moral and philosophical position and is therefore difficult to evaluate empirically.

The concept of victimless crime has been used in efforts to reform criminal law by reducing the kinds of conduct subject to criminal penalties. Some argue that criminal offenses that lack victims in the traditional sense are good candidates for decriminalization. Decriminalization frequently entails reducing punishments from possible jail time to a fine; public drunkenness and the possession of small amounts of marijuana are offenses that have been decriminalized in some states.

Schur points out that victimless crimes often involve conduct about which there is a lack of public consensus that the conduct is seriously wrong. Moreover, the fact that many such offenses cause no measurable harm (except for possible harm to the participating individuals) gives rise to serious difficulties with enforceability. If there is no clear harm to another, there is no complainant (a crime victim who requests that an alleged criminal be prosecuted). Law-enforcement officials therefore have difficulty detecting such crimes and gathering evidence to establish the guilty parties. Thus, efforts to control more serious crimes may suffer because of the time-consuming distractions of investigating victimless crimes. Two further undesirable effects are often cited. One is that criminalizing such conduct often gives rise to illicit traffic in the goods and services legally proscribed. The conduct is not actually discouraged, and law enforcement faces the additional problem of dealing with a thriving black market. The second unwelcome consequence is that otherwise law-abiding persons are stigmatized as criminals and are thus degraded.

Examples of Victimless Crimes

No list of victimless crimes will find full acceptance by everyone. The activities listed here are merely those most commonly cited as meeting the definition of the concept.

- ✓ Alcoholism
- ✓ Breaking age-based curfews
- ✓ Bungee jumping
- ✓ Drinking in public
- ✓ Drug use
- ✓ Fornication
- ✓ Gambling
- ✓ Loitering
- ✓ Not wearing motorcycle helmets
- ✓ Not wearing seat belts
- ✓ Pandering
- ✓ Polygamy
- ✓ Prostitution
- ✓ Public nudity
- ✓ Selling or viewing pornography
- ✓ Suicide and assisted suicide
- ✓ Vagrancy

Drug addiction is a victimless crime with negative effects on society. (By Jorobeq, via Wikimedia Commons)

Despite its apparent utility, the appeal of the notion of victimless crimes has declined; by the early 1990s, criminologists were more likely to talk of consensual crimes or public-order offenses. An early manifestation of difficulty with the concept of victimless crime was that different authors provided different lists of such crimes, suggesting that the concept lacked clarity and focus. An underlying difficulty is the fact that defining "victim" or "victimization" is a complex and controversial undertaking. Being physically injured or deprived of a possession are clear-cut cases of victimization. It is also arguable, however, that damaging another person's reputation or esteem or causing mental distress or anguish through one's actions or insults should be considered as victimizing that person. Feminist critiques of pornography and prostitution, for example, condemn such practices as degrading and demeaning to the women involved. Even if meaningful consent were present, they contend, there would still be real victims of these practices.

Mario F. Morelli

Further Reading

Farley, Melissa, and Victor Malarek. "The Myth of the Victimless Crime." *New York Times*. New York Times, 12 Mar. 2008. Web. 31 May 2016.

Fernandez, Justin. *Victimless Crimes: Crime, Justice, and Punishment.* Philadelphia: Chelsea House, 2002. Print.

Hardaway, Robert M. *No Price Too High: Victimless Crimes and the Ninth Amendment.* New York: Praeger, 2003. Print.

McWilliams, Peter. *Ain't Nobody's Business If You Do: The Absurdity of Consensual Crimes in a Free Society.* Los Angeles: Prelude, 1993. Print.

Meier, Robert F., and Gilbert Geis. *Victimless Crime? Prostitution, Drugs, Homosexuality, and Abortion.* Los Angeles: Roxbury, 1997. Print.

O'Donnell, Tim. *American Holocaust: The Price of Victimless Crime Laws.* Lincoln: Writer's Showcase, 2000. Print.

Schur, Edwin M., and Hugo Adam Bedau. *Victimless Crimes: Two Sides of a Controversy.* Englewood Cliffs: Prentice-Hall, 1974. Print.

See also Breach of the peace; Commercialized vice; Drug legalization debate; Drugs and law enforcement; Mann Act; Pornography and obscenity; Prohibition; Public-order offenses; Suicide and euthanasia.

Victimology

Definition: Scientific study of victims of crime
Criminal justice issues: Criminology; Hate crime
Significance: Studying the victims of crime is an essential part of any study of criminal justice.

The discipline known as victimology emerged at a time when some of the traditional research found within the field of criminology was shifting from studies of those who commit crimes to those who are adversely affected by crimes committed against them. "Victimology" was quickly acknowledged as a branch of criminology and later became an independent discipline dedicated to studying the reasons why certain individuals and members of certain groups become victims of crime. Victimology is now a rapidly growing academic field with interests that incorporate sociology, criminology, psychology, criminal justice, legal studies, and rehabilitative sciences. Victimology differs from these other fields in developing theories about how different lifestyles can affect the chances that individuals or members of groups have of becoming victims of crime. The goal of victimology studies is to promote long-term solutions to stop victimization from occurring.

Victimologists study the effectiveness that the criminal justice system has upon the public, specifically those individuals who have had crimes committed against them. The earliest victimologists studied the effects of violent crime on victims of rape and murder. Current victimologists tend to study children, women, the elderly, immigrants, indigenous peoples, and frequently persecuted people whose sexual orientations are nonheterosexual: gay men, lesbian women, bisexuals, and those who are transgendered. Studies of hate crimes and the impact that these crimes have upon members of persecuted communities are excellent examples of research done by victimologists.

Victimologists research not only the impact of physical harm and personal loss experienced by victims, but also the handling of such victims by the criminal justice system itself. Often, the actual roles of law-enforcement officials, especially police officers, lawyers, judges, and probation officers, are studied and compared to their ideal roles. Broadly speaking, victimologists explore interactions between victims and offenders, victims and the criminal justice system, and victims and society.

Finally, victimologists study public reactions to victims of crime, as portrayed by the mass media. Victimologists research legal issues raised by the public along with new advocacy groups that emerge in response to crimes and victimization. Such advocacy groups include Mothers Against Drunk Driving (MADD), one of the largest organizations devoted to victims of crime. Other manifestations of the fruits of public campaigns undertaken by advocacy groups are laws that are named after highly publicized victims of crime. One of the best-known examples is New Jersey's Megan's Law, which requires convicted sex offenders to register with local police departments after they are released from prison.

Since the 1970s and the beginning of the victim movement, the Bureau of Justice Statistics has issued the National Crime Victimization Survey, which creates a comprehensive registry of data about the trends of the crimes being committed and the victims of those crimes. The survey is administered to roughly ninety thousand households, which translates to about 160,000 individuals. This survey is the primary source of victimology data.

Emily I. Troshynski

Further Reading

Beloof, D. *Victims in Criminal Procedure.* Raleigh, N.C.: Carolina Academic Press, 1999.

Bergen, R., ed. *Issues in Intimate Violence.* Thousand Oaks, Calif.: Sage Publications, 1998.

Johnstone, Gerry. *Restorative Justice: Ideas, Values, Debates.* Portland, Oreg.: Willan, 2002.

Karmen, Andrew. *Crime Victims: An Introduction to Victimology.* 5th ed. Belmont, Calif.: Wadsworth, 2004.

See also Battered child and battered wife syndromes; Date rape; Domestic violence; Just deserts; National Crime Victimization Survey; Rape and sex offenses; Restitution; Stalking; Victim and Witness Protection Act; Victim assistance programs; Victims of Crime Act; Victim impact statements; Victims services; Victim Recovery Stage; Victimization theories; Victims of Child Abuse Act Reauthorization (2013); Victims of Trafficking Act (2014); Jessica's Law/Jessica Lunsford Act (2005); Crime victimization: primary and secondary.

Victims of Crime Act

The Law: Federal legislation that established funding for compensating and assisting victims of crime
Date: Signed into law on October 12, 1984
Criminal justice issues: Restorative justice; victims; women's issues
Significance: The Victims of Crime Act demonstrated the federal government's commitment to assisting crime victims and encouraged the funding of victim-assistance programs throughout the United States.

Victims have existed as long as there have been crimes, and the methods and efforts of restoring the victims and their losses have been variously addressed. One of the earliest known documents that described government intervention and restoring victims was the code of the eighteenth century b.c.e. Babylonian ruler Hammurabi. In the eighteenth century, Italian criminologist Cesare Beccaria began addressing criminals' rights.

During the 1960's, various movements raised the issues of inequities in the rights of various communities in the United States. One of these communities was made up victims of crime, and the issue of their rights began gaining national attention. The developing victims' movement adopted many of the methods of the Civil Rights and women's movements and raised public awareness of victim status and treatment in the criminal justice system. As a result, some local efforts were attempted in providing assistance for crime victims, most notably in California.

During the early 1980's, President Ronald Reagan ordered the establishment of a Presidential Task Force on Victims of Crime. That initiative led to recommendations for legislative assistance and protection of crime victims and resulted in the passage of the federal Victims of Crime Act (VOCA) in 1984. The law established federal funding for the states to provide compensation and assistance to crime victims. In addition, the law established the Office for Victims of Crime (OVC) as an agency of the Department of Justice. That agency was given responsibility for administering the federal funds made possible through VOCA. In addition, the OVC was to provide advocacy and assistance for victims.

The Victims of Crime Act was a major step in changing the rights for victims of crime. By 1992, all U.S. states had established offices for victims' compensations and assistance.

Richard L. McWhorter

Further Reading
Doerner, William G. *Victimology*. Cincinnati: Anderson Publishing, 2002.
Estrich, Susan. *With Justice for Some: Victims' Rights in Criminal Trials*. Reading, Mass.: Addison-Wesley, 1995.
Karmen, Andrew. *Crime Victims: An Introduction to Victimology*. 5th ed. Belmont, Calif.: Wadsworth, 2004.

See also National Organization for Victim Assistance; Victim and Witness Protection Act; Victim assistance programs; Victimology.

Victims of Trafficking Act of 2015

Definition: Comprehensive federal legislation that expands criminal sanctions for trafficking and improves programming and funding for investigating trafficking and related crimes.

Criminal justice issues: Crime statistics; investigation; law codes; prosecution; sex offenses; victims

Significance: Creates comprehensive protections for trafficking victims and improves tools available to those who investigate and prosecute trafficking charges.

Human trafficking, sexual exploitation of children, coerced human sex trade, and "e-commerce" in trafficking are significant problems within the United States and around the world. As a comprehensive response to a growing awareness of these issues, Congress passed the Justice for Victims of Trafficking Act to establish broad protections and services for victims of sex trafficking and related crimes. The legislation endured a protracted battle in the Senate over whether funds could be used to pay for abortions for victims. The Senate was able to resolve the debate and voted 99-0 for passage of the Act. The House of Representatives previously had voted in support of the Act, and President Obama signed the law on May 27, 2015. Consistent with existing federal law, this Act recognizes pornography, child sex trafficking, adult sex trafficking, coerced prostitution, and advertising of sex with trafficked victims as violent crimes that fall within the definition of trafficking. It also amends the Victims of Child Abuse Act to include human trafficking and child pornography within the definition of child abuse. This law expands the rights of victims, improves resources for investigating and prosecuting trafficking crimes, promotes empirical data collection on trafficking and victimization, and increases penalties for persons convicted of trafficking offenses.

First, the law contains provisions related to victims. It makes it easier for trafficking victims to obtain services and treatment. It removes the requirement that trafficking victims must be certified before they can receive benefits or services from the Department of Health and Human Services (HHS). To mitigate frustrations that may arise during protracted prosecutions of abusers, the Act requires that trafficking victims must be notified of any plea bargains or deferred prosecution agreement made with defendants. It also extends the statute of limitations for civil actions against defendants to ten years from the date that victims reach the age of majority. Victims also must be told about resources available through the Victims' Rights and Restitution Act of 1990. Finally, the legislation creates the Council on Human Trafficking comprised of eight to fourteen victims of human trafficking to advise policymakers as they develop initiatives pursuant to this Act.

Next, the Act contains provisions related to prosecution and data collection. The Act creates several new programs to expand agencies' investigative and prosecutorial capacities. First, it creates a Computer Forensics Unit and a Child Exploitation Investigation Unit within Immigration and Customs Enforcement. These units enhance government's digital forensic capabilities to pursue trafficking activities on the Internet, investigate money laundering, and pursue other illicit activities that often are related to human trafficking operations.

The Act promotes inclusion of veterans in this work. Several contemporaneous Congressional initiatives incorporate veterans into criminal justice initiatives, and this Act continues that tradition by creating the Human Exploitation Rescue Operative (HERO) Child Rescue Corps. In the HERO Corps, recently returned veterans are "hired to investigate crimes of child exploitation in order to target predators and rescue children from sexual abuse and slavery." They often liaise with the investigative units described above.

The Act also establishes several critical funding streams for antitrafficking programs and services for trafficking victims. These funds are used to finance data collection efforts, investigations, and prosecutions. They also are used to provide grants for training and technical assistance for law enforcement personnel and first responders. Training topics include identification of trafficking; response to and rescue of trafficking victims; social service interventions for trafficking and victims;

eradication of child pornography; therapeutic interventions among victims of child pornography; problem-solving court programs for trafficking and related crimes; and assistance to homeless and runaway youth. All grants awarded under this Act are subject to stringent reporting requirements, including accountings and periodic, empirical program evaluations. This legislation further requires that all grant recipients take specific measures to ensure against waste, fraud, and abuse.

The Department of Justice must maintain a database for trafficking victim advocates, crisis hotline personnel, foster parents, law enforcement personnel, and crime survivors. The database contains information on counseling, housing, and legal resources. Additionally, mandatory state reports on missing children must include a recent photograph of missing children in reports when available; states must update their databases every thirty days; and states must notify the National Center for Missing and Exploited Children of all missing children reports received from foster care and childcare institutions.

Finally, the Act contains provisions related to defendants. This legislation received wide media attention because it expands the federal criminal code definition of "sex trafficking" to include solicitation of sex. This change elevates the seriousness of solicitation to make it comparable to trafficking itself, regardless of whether the defendant knew that the victim was either underage and/or coerced. It also classifies people who produce child pornography as traffickers. Relatedly, the Act increases defendants' burden of proof if they try to claim that they "reasonably believed" that a minor was over the age of eighteen. They now must provide "clear and convincing evidence" of the reasonableness of this belief.

Persons convicted of trafficking (who are not indigent) must pay a $5,000 fine, which is deposited with the Domestic Trafficking Victims' Fund. That fund provides grants to states and localities to combat trafficking and provide assistance to victims. The law imposes additional potential financial penalties on traffickers by expanding forfeiture laws to include all real or personal property that was involved in the commission of human trafficking crimes in any fashion, not just to commit the crime. Assets obtained through these forfeiture proceedings are used to satisfy victim restitution orders.

Anne S. Douds

Further Reading

Atkinson, H. G., K. J. Curnin, and N. C. Hanson. "US State Laws Addressing Human Trafficking: Education of and Mandatory Reporting by Health Care Providers and Other Professionals."*Journal of Human Trafficking* 2, no. 2 (2016): 111-38.

Congress.gov. 2015. https://www.congress.gov/bill/114th-congress/senate-bill/178/text.

Muraya, D. N., and D. Fry. "Aftercare Services for Child Victims of Sex Trafficking: A Systematic Review of Policy and Practice."*Trauma, Violence, & Abuse*. 2015. doi:1524838015584356.

Shields, R. T., and E. J. Letourneau. "Commercial Sexual Exploitation of Children and the Emergence of Safe Harbor Legislation: Implications for Policy and Practice."*Current Psychiatry Reports* 17, no. 3 (2015): 1-7.

Sneed, Tierney. "Senate Comes Together on Trafficking Bill, but Not Without One Last Fight." *US News & World Report*. April 22, 2015. http://www.usnews.com/news/articles/2015/04/22/anti-human-trafficking-bill-passes-senate-after-weeks-of-partisan-bickering.

See also Abortion; Child abduction by parents; Contributing to delinquency of minors; Criminals; Human trafficking; Kidnapping; National Organization for Victim Assistance; National Crime Victimization Survey; National Organization for Victim Assistance; Rape and sex offenses; Victim assistance programs; Victim and Witness Protection Act; Victim-offender mediation; Victimology; Victims of Crime Act; Crime victimization: Primary and secondary; Human trafficking; Post-traumatic stress disorder; Victims services; Victim recovery stages; Victimization theories; Victims of Child Abuse Act Reauthorization (2013); Victim impact statements.

Victims services

Definition: A variety of activities offered to victims in response to their victimization in relieving hardships and facilitating recovery

Criminal justice issues: Victims; professional standards; domestic violence

Significance: Services provided to crime victims from the initial crisis intervention, advocacy support throughout the criminal justice process, recovery intervention and remedies to explicitly meet the needs of victims

Victim services evolved from the victims' right movements that coincided with the women's and civil rights movement of a half century ago. California initiated the first state victim compensation program in 1965, which was soon followed by many other states. Concurrently, grassroots activism emerged from survivors of rape and domestic violence who started to create support groups and established services and shelters for those in similar situations. Numerous new programs were developed during the transition period, and considering the professionalization of the field and the need for the coordination among programs, the National Organization for

Victim Assistance (NOVA) was formed in 1975 to promote networking and to provide training opportunities for those working with victims.

Today, more than 10,000 services exist nationwide from criminal justice agencies such as the police and prosecutor's offices to other public, private, and nonprofit agencies such as hospitals, religious groups, and social services to provide assistance and support to myriad victims. The programs in the criminal justice system have the advantage of a connection to the police, the prosecutor, and the courts to provide case information, court dates, and court escort services. For victims who avoid contact with criminal justice agencies, services outside of the criminal justice system are also available.

Existing Services

Victim services include a wide array of activities such as assistance in filing compensation claims, providing criminal justice support/advocacy, crisis counseling, a 24-hour hotline, emergency financial assistance, emergency legal advocacy, information and referral, safety plan, shelter/safe house, therapy, and transportation. Some advocacy programs target special populations such as services for elder victims, children, spouse abuse victims, and human trafficking victims. Despite the size and type of the services, victim recovery is the primary objective of all victim services.

One of the greatest challenges for the service providers is to identify the necessity of victims. Victims' needs vary depending on their circumstances and socioeconomic background, but one major need that is often overlooked is information about their case—what happened to them, what is likely to happen, what their role will likely be, and information about support services such as the location and contact information of service agencies. The research shows that those who receive services are more satisfied with the criminal justice system. Furthermore, victims who are contacted immediately after a crime express greater satisfaction than those who are contacted later.

Challenges and Needs

Not all the victims access the services. In fact, according to the National Crime Victimization Survey (NCVS), less than 10 percent of victims of serious violent crime received assistance from a victim service agency from 1993 to 2009 and the percentage of victims who received assistance remained stable during that time period. Younger male victims of serious violence were less likely to receive services than older female counterparts. A lower percentage of Hispanic victims received services than other ethnic groups.

In serving victims of diverse populations, victim service providers must be mindful about active attempts to understand without negative judgments or stereotyping. Diversity extends beyond race and ethnicity and includes the impoverished; those physically, developmentally, or intellectually challenged; the lesbian, gay, bisexual, transgender, and queer (LGBTQ) population; migrants; and refugees. The elderly are an often overlooked population in advocacy and services even though the numbers of elders will increase dramatically with the coming wave of baby boomers. Nonetheless, popular culture does not acknowledge elderly sexual victims and, as a result, far fewer services are available to address their needs than those available for younger victims.

In addressing complex matters of victimization, coordinating and achieving collaborative responses among allied professionals and community leaders is crucial. Successful collaborations would not only provide cost savings by reducing the duplication of services but also benefit the service providers in increasing their own knowledge of available options and being able to respond to issues more quickly and in appropriate ways.

To enhance victim services, the areas of victim services have to expand and evolve constantly. For instance, the advancement of technology offers new tools to serve crime victims. The use of the Internet and toll-free telecommunication could help target victims in underserved or geographically isolated areas. Continuation of training and education for professionals and volunteers will help provide standard services to victims and maintain professionalism in the field. In California, to be certified as a victim advocate, employees must complete one full year of work in a comprehensive victim services program and demonstrate through education, experience, and specialized training the ability to assist victims and witnesses. In addition, the employee must complete a state-approved forty-hour training program within the first year. Finally, victim services must address such emerging crimes as white-collar fraud, hate crimes, stalking, cybercrime, human trafficking, and international terrorism and crisis response.

Yoshiko Takahashi

Further Reading

Buzawa, E., C. Buzawa, and E. Stark. *Responding to Domestic Violence: The Integration of Criminal Justice and Human Services*. 5th ed. Thousand Oaks, Calif.: Sage, 2017.

Langton, L. *Use of Victim Service Agencies by Victims of Serious Violent Crime,1993 2009.* Bureau of Justice Statistics. http://www.bjs.gov/content/pub/pdf/uvsavsvc9309.pdf.

Underwood, T. L., and C. Edmunds, eds. *Victim Assistance: Exploring Individual Practice, Organizational Policy, and Societal Responses.* New York: Springer Publishing Company Inc., 2003.

Vierthaler, K. "Best Practices for Working with Rape Crisis Centers to Address Elder Sexual Abuse."*Journal of Elder Abuse & Neglect* 20, No. 4 (2008): 306-22.

Young, M., and J. Stein.*The History of the Crime Victims' Movement in the United States.* https://www.ncjrs.gov/ovc_archives/ncvrw/2005/pg4c.html.

Walnut Street Jail

Identification: Historic U.S. penal institution
Date: Opened in 1773
Place: Philadelphia, Pennsylvania
Criminal justice issues: Prisons; rehabilitation
Significance: The Walnut Street Jail promoted the rehabilitation of criminals and was the forerunner of the modern prison system in the United States.

Designed by architect and builder Robert Smith, the Walnut Street Jail was constructed in Philadelphia in 1773. At the time, deplorable conditions existed in U.S. penal institutions. It was commonplace for men, women, and children to be incarcerated in a common locked area, where aggression and sexual exploitation frequently occurred. Encouraged by the Philadelphia Society for Alleviating the Miseries of Public Prisons, administrators of the Walnut Street Jail eventually used that jail as a model for improving the imprisonment system.

Starting during the late 1780's, instead of using the Walnut Street Jail strictly as a place for punishment of prisoners, it was redesigned to reform inmates and help prevent them from committing crimes after they were released. Men, women, and children were separated from one another in clean, solitary cells. Prisoners received basic education and religious instruction and were encouraged to treat one another humanely. Highlights of the new approach included the use of solitary confinement, special times for prisoner meditation and reflection, and training of inmates for future employment. The discipline system employed at the Walnut Street Jail became known as the Pennsylvania System.

Because of overcrowding, the Walnut Street Jail was remodeled and converted into the Walnut Street Prison in 1790, the first state prison in Pennsylvania and the birthplace of the modern U.S. prison system. Several new ideas were implemented to help rehabilitate criminals, particularly an increased focus on a variety of prison industries which included making nails, sawing rocks, weaving, and making shoes. The more hardened criminals were sentenced to hard labor during the day and at nighttime.

Alvin K. Benson

Further Reading

Blomberg, Thomas G. *American Penology: A History of Control.* New York: Aldine de Gruyter, 2000.

Peterson, Charles E. *Robert Smith: Architect, Builder, Patriot, 1722-1777.* Philadelphia: Athenaeum, 2000.

See also Criminal justice in U.S. history; Prison and jail systems; Prison health care; Prison industries; Prison overcrowding; Prison violence.

Work camps

Definition: Alternative form of incarceration that requires less security than regular prisons and offers inmates practical work experience
Criminal justice issues: Prisons; Punishment; Rehabilitation
Significance: Work camps are an alternative form of incarceration designed to meet objectives of inmates, correctional management, and society. The rehabilitative needs of inmates are served by giving them opportunities to repay their debts to society and to develop vocational and personal skills. Management needs are met as camps reduce overcrowding in secure facilities, provide placements for minimum-custody inmates, and result in costs savings associated with the use of inmate labor. Society benefits as inmates, after being punished for their crimes through involuntary work, are often returned to society with a work ethic that enhances their chances of succeeding.

The emergence of modern prison work camps can be traced to the 1970s, when prison populations began to increase dramatically. Since that time, work camps have been established throughout the United States. Typical work camps house from 40 to 250 minimum-custody inmates in barracks resembling dormitories. Most inmates in the camps have been convicted of nonviolent crimes, such as drug trafficking, white-collar crimes, and lesser property offenses. Convicted murderers are occasionally admitted to work camps, but only after they have served major portions of their sentences and have demonstrated exemplary behavior in prison. The architectural designs of most prison camps are open and are often similar to academic campuses. The camps often have perimeter fences, but their purpose is generally to provide security for the inmates themselves. When the camps are part of larger, more secure prisons, they are usually placed outside the prisons' security fences or walls. Camp living quarters are generally arranged around central buildings that contain cafeterias, recreation centers, classrooms, medical units, post offices, churches, commissaries, and administrative offices.

Specialized Camps

Some work camps are designed to serve the special needs of specific vocations, such as forestry maintenance, farming, and road maintenance. Forestry camps are usually located in national forests and state forests, where inmates assist in reforestation, fighting forest fires, clearing underbrush, and building firebreaks. Their work is usually supervised by forestry personnel, with security and discipline matters attended to by prison personnel.

Work camps in which inmates engage in farm-related tasks are usually located in rural farming communities. The specific types of farming in which they engage are usually determined by the regions and acreage available to them. For example, vegetable cultivation requires mild and wet climates, while wheat cultivation is best suited for arid climates. Pork and poultry production requires warmer climates, while beef and sheep production is best in cooler locations.

Work camps that focus on road maintenance are also suitable for rural communities, whose roads often need repair. Mild climates are best, so inmates can work outside throughout the year. When work camps are part of larger, more secure institutions, their inmates typically engage in such maintenance work as painting, carpentry, plumbing, groundskeeping, and electrical work. Camp inmates also perform service-related jobs by helping to meet the needs of higher-custody inmates, such as food preparation and service, laundry, and janitorial tasks.

Camps as Alternative Incarceration

Local, state, and federal correctional systems use work camps as an alternative form of placement for inmates. For example, the Leon County Sheriff's Department in Tallahassee, Florida, has a work camp that functions as part of the Leon County Jail. The work crews consist of inmates from the county jail who clean litter and remove undergrowth from roads. Participants in this shock-probation program are sentenced to the work camp by the court as a condition of their probation.

The Work Ethic Camp in Nebraska is an example of a state-level program. Its inmates are provided structured programming that includes work programs, vocational training, behavior management and modification, money management, substance abuse awareness, counseling, and opportunities to continue their academic educations. Inmates selected for the camp are nonviolent prison-bound offenders who are provided this plea-agreement alternative to regular incarceration to help relieve prison overcrowding and reduce recidivism. The mission of the program is the rehabilitation of program participants.

An example of a federal work camp can be found in Montgomery, Alabama. Located on a military base, inmates are required to work in the camps on the surrounding bases but have access to recreation activities on the weekends, such as crafts, fitness, and films.

Some work camps are designed for special populations, such as geriatric inmates. One such camp is Florida's River Junction Work Camp in Chattahoochee for minimum- and medium-custody inmates who are elderly. Eighty percent of camp inmates are over the age of fifty years. They work in state mental hospitals and for the city of Chattahoochee.

The success of work camps, like that of other correctional programs, is generally measured by assessing the recidivism rates of program graduates. The recidivism rates of inmates who have completed work-camp programs tend to be better than those of inmates incarcerated in traditional prison settings. In an evaluation of Florida work camps, for example, researchers found that 86 percent of 720 offenders released from work camps had not returned to state prisons, and 51 percent had not returned to the prison and jail system or any form of supervision. As is true of traditional prison inmates, recidivism rates of work-camp inmates are inversely related to the inmates' ages. As the ages of prisoners at the time of their release increase, the less likely they are to return to incarceration.

Elizabeth H. McConnell

Further Reading
Allen, Harry E., Clifford E. Simonsen, and Edward J. Latessa. *Corrections in American: An Introduction*. 10th ed. Upper Saddle River: Pearson Education, 2004. Print.
Gido, R. L., and T. Alleman. *Turnstile Justice: Issues in American Corrections*. 2nd ed. Upper Saddle River: Pearson, 2002. Print.
Haas, Kenneth C., and Geoffrey P. Alpert. *The Dilemmas of Corrections*. 4th ed. Prospect Heights: Waveland, 1999. Print.

Mays, L. G., and T. L. Winfree. *Contemporary Corrections*. 2nd ed. Belmont: Wadsworth, 2002. Print.

Murphy, Jeffrie, comp. *Punishment and Rehabilitation*. 3rd ed. Belmont: Wadsworth, 1995. Print.

Wiersma, B., and K. Siedschlaw. "Nebraska's Work Ethic Camp: The First Year." *Corrections Compendium* 28 (2004): 1-7. Print.

See also Boot camps; Prisons, Federal Bureau of; Chain gangs; Community-based corrections; Elderly prisoners; Forestry camps; Halfway houses; Prison industries; Prison overcrowding; Probation, adult; Recidivism; Rehabilitation; Work-release programs; Punishment.

Work-release programs

Definition: Alternative to traditional incarceration that places accused and convicted offenders into the community to work at jobs paying standard wages

Criminal justice issues: Probation and parole; Punishment; Rehabilitation; Sentencing

Significance: Work release is an alternative to incarceration that is expected to be used more widely in the future because of its proven benefits.

Work-release programs serve a variety of needs. They may be used as a form of pretrial release, as an option during sentencing, or as privileges awarded to incarcerated inmates with exemplary records. Accused offenders who are authorized for the programs during their pretrial release are allowed to maintain their existing jobs but must spend their nights or weekends, or both, in work-release facilities or jails. The same conditions also apply to convicted offenders who are sentenced to work release instead of prison. In addition, work release may be given as a privilege to inmates of prisons, jails, and halfway houses. In all cases, inmates in the programs are allowed to leave the facilities in which they are housed to work in the community.

Work release has been used in the United States since 1913, when Wisconsin became the first state to allow those convicted of misdemeanors to continue working at their jobs while serving short jail sentences. In 1957, North Carolina became the first state to permit those convicted of a felony to leave prison during the day to work in the community. The Federal Prisoner Rehabilitation Act, passed by the US Congress in 1965, allowed work release for prisoners of federal institutions.

Regardless of whether work release is given at the state or federal level, the working conditions of accused and convicted offenders are similar to those experienced by civilians. Job requirements are identical, and work supervision is by civilians. Moreover, like any free citizens, participants in work-release programs are usually responsible for their own transportation to and from work.

Those on work release are paid as civilians and typically receive their salaries directly from their employers. However, they usually have to turn their paychecks over to corrections officials, who extract portions of the money to reimburse the facilities for room and board. Some of the income may also be deducted to cover costs of transportation and other incidental expenses. Further deductions may also be made to pay for restitution or victim compensation. After the deductions are made, the balance of the money is deposited into the inmates' savings accounts.

Released inmates may benefit from having supervised savings accounts. Some also benefit by avoiding the risk of losing their current jobs. Those who have not worked for some time may benefit from learning new job skills and raising their self-esteem. In addition, participants in work-release programs are less adversely affected by confinement than other inmates because they can enjoy more normal societal interactions that facilitate their reintegration into the community, and their recidivism is usually reduced. Work release may also be used as an inmate-management tool. Because participation in work release is highly desired but not guaranteed, corrections administrators may use it to reward good behavior of inmates. It can also help reduce prison overcrowding.

Pauline K. Brennan

Further Reading

"Grants Totaling $30M to Help Adults in Prison Work-Release Programs Transition to the Workforce Now Available from US Labor Department." *United States Department of Labor*. Dept. of Labor, 18 Feb. 2014. Web. 24 May. 2016.

McCarthy, Belinda Rodgers, Bernard J. McCarthy, and Matthew C. Leone. *Community-Based Corrections*. 4th ed. Belmont, Calif.: Wadsworth Publishing, 2001.

"Prison Life-Work Release." *Department of Corrections Washington State*. Dept. of Corrections, 2015. Web. 24 May. 2016.

Turner, Susan, and Joan Petersilia. *Work Release: Recidivism and Corrections Cost in Washington State*. Washington, D.C.: National Institute of Justice, 1996.

Wees, Greg. "Work and Educational Release, 1996." *Corrections Compendium* (May, 1997): 8-23.

See also Arraignment; Community-based corrections; Halfway houses; Parole; Prison overcrowding; Recidivism; Rehabilitation; Sentencing; Work camps; Prison/Prisoner Classification Systems

Youth authorities

Definition: Inclusive term for the various state agencies and officials involved in juvenile justice
Criminal justice issues: Crime prevention; juvenile justice; rehabilitation
Significance: Within the criminal justice system, state youth authorities are delegated the responsibility of dealing with juvenile offenders in matters ranging from probation and parole to incarceration, education, and many other areas.

State youth authorities (SYA) are a relatively new development within the criminal justice system, as many were not created until after the 1940's. Originally, their primary responsibility was management and operation of state reformatories, as well as provision of job training and education to their juvenile charges.

After courts commit them to the care of SYAs, youths are provided services ranging from receiving educational assistance and psychological treatment for interpersonal problems to job training for specific occupations. Most youths handled by SYAs are referred by juvenile and criminal courts; however youths committed by criminal courts are transferred to the state corrections departments on their eighteenth birthday, if their sentences are not already completed.

Goals

An important difference between adult and juvenile offenders is that adults are placed in correctional facilities for the primary purpose of being punished, with rehabilitation a distant secondary goal, while the first goal for juvenile offenders is rehabilitation. The youth authorities believe that if young offenders are caught early enough, major life changes are possible for them. Hence, rehabilitation and education are primary focuses for youth authorities.

In addition to managing and administering youth correction facilities, youth authorities are also in charge of state parole and probation services for juveniles and are responsible for the care and upkeep of youth offenders remanded in their custody. Their other functions include providing improvements and any construction needed for the day-to-day running of correctional facilities.

Youth authorities are also often involved at state and local levels in efforts to prevent crime and delinquency. Youth authority officials visit schools and provide delinquency prevention advice to teachers and students, and they often address community service organizations and religious groups. In many states, youth authorities provide shelters for children aged six through seventeen, with services provided for runaways, homeless minors, and abused and neglected children. The primary goal for most of these shelters is survival—meeting the immediate needs of the children and their families for food, clothes, and safe places to sleep.

Within major urban areas such as New York City, Los Angeles, and Chicago, youth authorities work with other state agencies to combat gang violence. One strategy in this effort has been the construction of youth centers, where juveniles can receive help in job training, health, fitness, citizenship skills, pregnancy prevention, and counseling.

The philosophy behind youth centers is the belief that children need structured environments. Busy youths are expected to be less likely to experiment with drugs and alcohol, less likely to become pregnant, and less likely to get into trouble with the law. These benefits, in turn, increase youths' chances of finishing high school. Youth centers provide structured activities during nonschool hours, offering juveniles opportunities to become involved in positive activities. Other youth center services include mentoring and training in music, arts and crafts, and the culinary arts, as well as other potentially enjoyable activities.

Shortcomings

While youth authorities strive to maintain decent living conditions for the youths in their custody, problems often arise. For example, increases in the number of juvenile arrests during the early years of the twenty-first century have made overcrowding an issue. Old facilities are forced to house more youths than they are designed to accommodate. In some places, as many as three to four juveniles share rooms designed for only one person.

Another major issue has been punitive living conditions. In one center, male youths were routinely locked in bare cells for as many as eighteen hours per day. They were not allowed to keep anything of a personal nature beyond the clothes on their backs and Bibles. In addition, personal hygiene products and common items like toothpaste and soap were forbidden.

Other problems have included the use of abusive discipline without due process. Many facilities operate without offering any positive incentives for good behavior, instead relying on negative disciplinary procedures. Guards, whose own educations are often only marginally better than those of their wards, routinely administer inappropriate punishments, ranging from verbal threats to physical force. Sexual harassment and assault are also areas needing attention. Moreover, many institutions lack sufficient numbers of trained women guards for their female wards. As a result, there have been sexual assaults against girls by male staff members.

Although youth authorities assert that hiring qualified teachers for their wards is a priority, many institutions have too few educators to provide adequate schooling. This is an especially serious problem, as the wards of youth authorities have a much higher than average rate of learning disabilities.

The federal Individuals with Disabilities Education Improvement Act of 2004 provides for youths with learning disabilities in correctional facilities with special education and related services. However, providing appropriate services for these students is a challenge. Issues having an impact on the provision of appropriate special education include the transience of the student population, conflicting goals for security and rehabilitation, shortages of adequately prepared personnel, and limited interagency coordination.

Cary Stacy Smith

Further Reading

Hubner, John, and Jill Wolfson. *Ain't No Place Anybody Would Want to Be: Conditions of Confinement for Youth*. Washington, D.C.: Coalition for Juvenile Justice, 1999. Exposé of the harsh conditions provided by youth authorities to their wards by two California journalists.

Jonson-Reid, M. "Child Welfare Services and Delinquency: The Need to Know More." *Child Welfare* 83, no. 2 (2004): 157-174. Sociological study of the relationship between juvenile delinquency and the services provided by youth authorities.

Shoemaker, D. J. *Theories of Delinquency: An Examination of Explanations of Delinquent Behavior*. 4th ed. New York: Oxford University Press, 2000. Survey of theoretical approaches to explaining delinquent behavior. Clearly written evaluations of the various individualistic and sociological theories.

Siegel, L. J., Brandon C. Welsh, and Joseph J. Senna. *Juvenile Delinquency: Theory, Practice, and Law*. 8th ed. Belmont, Calif.: Wadsworth/Thomson, 2002. Comprehensive examination of juvenile justice along with policies, theories, landmark court decisions, and contemporary issues.

Tanenhaus, David S. *Juvenile Justice in the Making*. New York: Oxford University Press, 2004. Examination of three thousand juvenile case files from Chicago during the early twentieth century that are used to address fundamental questions about how juvenile offenders should be treated under the law.

Whitehead, J. T., and S. P. Lab. *Juvenile Justice: An Introduction*. 4th ed. Cincinnati: Anderson Publishing, 2003. Introductory textbook examining the history of juvenile justice in the United States, from its nineteenth century roots to the early twenty-first century.

See also Juvenile courts; Juvenile delinquency; Juvenile Justice and Delinquency Prevention, Office of; Juvenile Justice and Delinquency Prevention Act; Juvenile justice system; Probation, juvenile.

Special Issues

Adam Walsh Child Protection and Safety Act (2006)

Definition: A federal statute enacted to protect the public, especially children, from sexual exploitation and violent crime, to prevent child abuse and child pornography, to promote Internet safety and to honor the memory of Adam Walsh and other child crime victims.

Criminal justice issues: Crime prevention; deviancy; federal law; homicide; kidnapping; prosecution; punishment; sex offenses; victims; violent crime

Significance: The Walsh Act strengthened and expanded existing laws regarding sex offenders and violence against children; standardized sex offender registration nationwide and required the information be made public; created the National Child Abuse Registry; and funded a variety of grants and other initiatives to protect children from sex offenders.

On July 27, 1981, six-year-old Adam Walsh was abducted from a crowded store in Hollywood, Florida, and later found murdered. In 2008, the murderer was identified as a serial killer named Ottis Toole, who died in 1996. After Adam's death, his parents, John and Revé Walsh, became activists for missing and abused children. Their efforts helped put missing children's photographs on milk cartons, started fingerprinting programs, prompted the creation of the National Center for Missing & Exploited Children and led to the 1988 television premier of *America's Most Wanted*, which was hosted by John Walsh.

The Adam Walsh Child Protection and Safety Act (Walsh Act) was signed by President George W. Bush on July 27, 2006 (Public Law No. 109-248, 120 Stat. 587 [2006]). The Walsh Act contains a variety of provisions to protect the public, especially children, from violent sex offenders and abuse by creating national registries and increasing prison sentences.

Sex Offender Registration

The Sex Offender Registration and Notification Act (SORNA) is Title I of the Walsh Act. It revises the nationwide sex offender registration system that was put into place by the Jacob Wetterling Act (1994). The Walsh Act retains the structure of the previous system, but standardizes the reporting so it is consistent nationwide, with all states collecting the same information. Offenders are classified into three tiers, based upon the crime(s) committed. These tiers designate the reporting requirements for the offenders. Tier 3 offenders must update their location every three months for life; those in Tier 2 every six months for twenty-five years; and Tier 1 offenders annually for fifteen years. Failure to register and update is a felony. The registration information must be made publicly available online. States may choose whether or not to list Tier 1 offender information, but are required to list all Tier 2 and Tier 3 offenders.

The National Sex Offender Registry was expanded and integrates the information in state sex offender registries. This provides standardized information to law enforcement and allows them to track sex offenders even if they move from state to state. Data from this registry is available to the public online from the Dru Sjodin National Sex Offender Public Website.

Civil Commitment

The Walsh Act created a civil commitment process for federal prisoners that demonstrate they are likely to reoffend. The commitment provides for treatment options as long as the person remains a danger to others. There was a federal circuit court split on whether Congress could lawfully enact such a commitment provision. However, on May 17, 2010, the Supreme Court of the United States upheld the law in *United States v. Comstock* (130 S.Ct. 1949 [2010])). The Court held Congress did have the authority to provide for the civil commitment of sexually dangerous people whose release from federal custody is imminent.

Federal Law Amendments

The Walsh Act established new federal crimes, expanded penalties for existing crimes against children and amended federal criminal procedure to make it easier to locate, capture and incarcerate offenders. Increased penalties for existing offenses included thirty years to life, and in some cases the death penalty, for the murder of a child; a thirty-year mandatory sentence for rape of a child; and a ten-year mandatory minimum for child sex trafficking or prostitution.

Criminal procedure amendments included expanded deoxyribonucleic acid (DNA) collection for those charged or convicted of a federal crime; random searches of convicted sex offenders as a condition of parole or release; and eliminating marital privilege in abuse cases. The statute of limitations was eliminated for all federal felony offenses of sex abuse, sex trafficking, and child pornography.

Stronger record-keeping and labeling requirements were placed on pornography producers or those who produce material containing simulated sexual content.

Standardized age verification and record-keeping aimed to protect children and teenagers from being exploited. The Department of Justice may inspect any of these records on demand.

Internet Safeguards

A new mandatory minimum sentence of twenty years was created for "child exploitation enterprises," which are defined as committing at least one sex crime against children defined by the law as part of a series of three or more felony violations and more than one victim, committed with three or more other persons.

New crimes were established for Internet date rape drug trafficking and embedding words or digital images into the source code of a website with the intent of deceiving a person into viewing obscenity. The civil remedy available to children who were exploited or abused was also expanded.

Additional resources to prosecute and investigate child sex offenses were allocated, and include funding to hire at least 200 additional Assistant U.S. Attorneys, at least ten Internet Crimes Against Children Task Forces and forty-five forensic examiners to the Regional Computer Forensic Laboratories and Cyber Crimes Center.

Grants & Other Programs

The Act creates, supports, and strengthens many grant programs dedicated to child protection and safety. It includes grants to Big Brothers Big Sisters of America, the Police Athletic League and local governments for sex offender monitoring devices, treatment programs, and registration costs.

Several organizations were created, such as the Rape, Abuse & Incest National Network (RAINN), which operates a sex assault hotline and provides public education. The National Child Abuse Registry was also created and requires background checks and fingerprint criminal record checks for all prospective foster and adoptive parents. The information for the registry is collected from state databases of child abuse or neglect. The registry is intended to serve as a tool for child protective services and law enforcement, as it allows them to track the history of parents and guardians suspected of abusing children. This is intended to keep a record of any history of abuse, even if the abusive parent or guardian moves to a different jurisdiction.

Noelle Sinclair

Further Reading

Doyle, Charles. Adam Walsh Child Protection and Safety Act: A Legal Analysis. Washington, D.C.: Congressional Research Service, 2007. An analysis of the legal elements of the Adam Walsh Act.

Doyle, Charles. *United States v. Comstock*: Legislative Authority Under the Necessary and Proper Clause. Washington, D.C.: Congressional Research Service, 2012. An examination of the Adam Walsh Act's civil commitment provision as discussed in the *Comstock* case.

Ewing, Charles Patrick. Justice Perverted: Sex Offender Law, Psychology, and Public Policy. New York: Oxford University Press, 2011. The author examines the spectrum of sex offense laws and considers them based on research from the social and behavioral sciences.

Sandoval, Terrell G. *Adam Walsh Child Protection and Safety Act: Analysis and Law.* New York: Nova Science Publishers, 2013. This book contains public documents including the text of the Act, an analysis from the Congressional Research Service, and a comparison of various sex offender registration requirements.

Standiford, Les, and Joe Matthews. *Bringing Adam Home.* New York: Ecco, 2011. A former police sergeant, who worked on the Adam Walsh case for years, describes the long search for Adam's killer.

Walsh, John. *Tears of Rage-From Grieving Father to Crusader for Justice: The Untold Story of the Adam Walsh Case.* New York: Atria, 1997. Adam Walsh's father tells the story of his son's abduction and murder, as well as his own transformation from grieving parent to activist.

See also Kidnapping; Murder and homicide; Pedophilia; Rape and sex offenses; Sex offender registries; DNA yesting; Victimology; Crime victimization: Primary and secondary; Human trafficking; Mentally disordered sex offender laws; Social media; Technology's transformative effect; Civil commitment; Victims of Child Abuse Act Reauthorization (2013); Victims of Trafficking Act (2014).

Antiterrorism and Effective Death Penalty Act

The Law: Federal law expanding federal law-enforcement powers to counter terrorism and restrict appeals for those convicted of capital crimes
Date: Signed into law on April 24, 1996
Significance: The Antiterrorism and Effective Death Penalty Act granted the federal government new powers in fighting terrorism and significantly restricted post-conviction appeals brought by death-row inmates in federal court.

Following the 1993 World Trade Center bombing and the 1995 Oklahoma City bombing, the federal government was under increasing pressure to respond to terrorism taking place on American soil. At the same time, condemned inmates who filed *habeas corpus* petitions to have

Search and rescue crews work to save those trapped beneath the debris, following the Oklahoma City bombing. (Public domain, via Wikimedia Commons)

Debris from the 1993 World Trade Center bombing. (Public domain, via Wikimedia Commons)

their convictions reviewed were extending their time on death row by years, at cost to taxpayers. The Antiterrorism and Effective Death Penalty Act (AEDPA) was a response to these two situations.

The new law empowered the federal government to deny visas to people identified as belonging to terrorist groups and to deport legal resident aliens by expanding the definition of crimes that result in deportation and by eliminating judicial review of deportation orders. An important provision of the law is the authority of the federal government to designate a group as a foreign terrorist organization (FTO), allowing the group's assets to be seized and limiting their fund-raising ability in the United States. Also, the law banned the provision of support to countries that aid terrorist groups, granted Americans the ability to sue foreign countries in federal court for terrorism aimed at Americans abroad, and declared acts of participation in terrorism in the United States to be federal crimes.

The AEDPA was also designed to limit federal *habeas corpus* petitions filed by state inmates convicted of capital crimes, in an effort to prevent frivolous lawsuits. It accomplished this by requiring all inmates to exhaust their state-level appeals before filing a petition in federal court and limited the time inmates had to file a federal petition to one year after exhausting their state appeals. Also, federal petitions were effectively limited to one by requiring any successive petitions be reviewed for merit by a panel of three federal judges before being considered.

Gennifer Furst

Further Reading

Chang, Nancy. *Silencing Political Dissent.* New York: Seven Stories, 2002. Print.

Dempsey, James X., and David Cole. *Terrorism and the Constitution: Sacrificing Civil Liberties in the Name of National Security.* 3rd ed. New York: New Press, 2006. Print.

Gerken, Christina. *Model Immigrants and Undesirable Aliens: The Cost of Immigration Reform in the 1990s.* Minneapolis: U of Minnesota P, 2013. Print.

Latzer, Barry. *Death Penalty Cases.* 3rd ed. Boston: Butterworth-Heinemann, 2012. Print.

See also Attorney General, U.S.; Capital punishment; Cruel and unusual punishment; Espionage; *Habeas corpus*; International law; Terrorism.

Bloodstains

Definition: Type of biological evidence found at crime scenes that can be used to establish whether crimes have occurred, reconstruct events leading up to crimes, and solve the crimes themselves

Criminal justice issues: Evidence and forensics; investigation; violent crime

Significance: Bloodstains can be used by forensic scientists to determine if crimes have occurred in such situations as differentiating between a suicide and murder. They can also help identify perpetrators of crimes by allowing forensic scientists to reconstruct sequences of events and match DNA samples.

Before deoxyribonucleic acid (DNA) technology become widespread in law enforcement, bloodstain evidence was of only limited use to investigators, who used it mainly to match basic blood types. Blood-typing helped but generally served to narrow lists of possible suspects only slightly because of the small number of unique blood types carried by human beings. Now, with the prolific use of DNA technology, bloodstains are invaluable resources for solving crimes. By using swabs to collect small samples of blood left at crime scenes, detectives and forensic scientists can analyze their DNA and compare the results with the DNA of any suspects they take into custody.

In addition, spatter patterns of blood found at crime scenes help forensic scientists and detectives reconstruct what happens between victims and offenders. Blood drops and spatters often reveal what weapons were used, in what fashion, and in what order. For example, the amount of bleeding from puncture wounds made while victims' hearts are still beating is much greater than the bleeding that occurs when the same wounds are made after victims are already dead.

When blood traces are not apparent to the naked eye, scientists use special chemicals to test for their presence. Such chemicals can reveal the presence of blood after perpetrators try to wash away all traces with strong detergents or even bleach. One such chemical, called Luminol, emits light when it comes in contact with blood and can detect bloodstains diluted up to ten thousand times. Luminol is especially useful in forensic work because it does not interfere with DNA testing or destroy potentially valuable evidence that may be needed later. Other analyses, such as precipitin tests, can determine whether bloodstains are of human or animal origin.

Jenephyr James

Further Reading

Genge, Ngaire E. *The Forensic Casebook: The Science of Crime Scene Investigation*. New York: Ballantine, 2002.

Lee, Henry C., and Frank Tirnady. *Blood Evidence: How DNA Is Revolutionizing the Way We Solve Crimes*. Cambridge, Mass.: Perseus, 2003.

Saferstein, Richard. *Criminalistics: An Introduction to Forensic Science*. 7th ed. Upper Saddle River, N.J.: Prentice-Hall, 2001.

See also Cold cases; Crime labs; Crime scene investigation; DNA testing; Forensics; Latent evidence; Toxicology; Trace evidence.

Boston Marathon Bombing (2013)

Definition: The bombings at the Annual Boston Marathon on April 15, 2013 left three dead and more than 200 injured and wounded.

Criminal justice issues: Capital punishment; terrorism; violent crime

Significance: The Boston Marathon Bombing on April 15, 2013, by two young brothers (Tamerlan Tsarnaev and Dzhokhar Tsarnaev), using pressure cooker bombs, left many dead and injured victims. It created havoc in a long tradition of the otherwise peaceful Boston Marathon.

The Boston Marathon is an annual race that attracts runners in large numbers not just from United States, but from all over the world. In 2013, the marathon was the 117th running of the Boston Marathon. The marathon is held each year on Patriot's Day, a legal holiday in Massachusetts, commemorating the 1775 battles of Lexington and Concord that led to the American Revolutionary War.

The finish line of the Boston Marathon in 2013 was located between Exeter and Dartmouth Streets and the last leg of the marathon ran eastward along the center of Boylston Street from Hereford Street. The marathon was kept in order by the low metal barriers on both edges of the street that separated the spectators from the runners.

Two explosions occurred on the day of the Boston Marathon on April 15, 2013; the second explosion was seconds apart from the first explosion, at around 2:49 p.m. The explosions took place while the marathon was still underway on the north side of Boylston Street that was along the marathon's final stretch. The first explosion occurred in front of 671 Boylston Street and the second occurred approximately one block away in front of

755 Boylston Street. Both explosions were the result of pressure cooker bombs. The explosive devices were placed near the low metal barriers where hundreds of spectators were watching runners approach the finish line. The two explosions killed three persons and injured 270 persons, in addition to causing damage to public and private property.

As the search for the bombers began, the police availed themselves of security videotape footage. Images were released on April 18, 2016, to the public to help capture the persons involved. The two persons involved were identified as Tamerlan Tsarnaev, twenty-six years old and a lawful permanent resident of the United States, and his younger brother Dzhokhar Tsarnaev, nineteen years old. Dzhokhar Tsarnaev was a naturalized U.S. citizen. Both were seen on videotape footage carrying large knapsacks that caused the explosions.

The same night witnessed two other incidents involving the two brothers. After the Boston Marathon Bombing, at around 10:30 p.m., the Tsarnaev brothers attempted to steal the service weapon of Sean Collier, a twenty-seven-year-old police officer at the Massachusetts Institute of Technology (MIT). The officer was shot dead in his patrol car. Soon after the killings, at around midnight, a carjacking incident of a Mercedes sport-utility vehicle (SUV) at gunpoint in Cambridge, Massachusetts, was brought to the notice of the police. The man who pointed the gun at the victim had identified himself as one of the Boston Marathon bombers and would later be identified as Tamerlan Tsarnaev by the police. The carjacked victim was taken hostage and his automated teller machine (ATM) card used to withdraw money. The two brothers and the carjacked victim then drove to a gas station/convenience store in the vicinity of 816 Memorial Drive, Cambridge. When the brothers got out of the car, the victim managed to escape.

A short while later, the stolen Mercedes SUV was spotted by law enforcement officers in Watertown, Massachusetts. The brothers threw at least two small improvised explosive devices (IEDs) out of the car. Subsequently, a gunfight ensued between the brothers and law enforcement officers. Tamerlan Tsarnaev was severely injured and remained at the scene and Dzhokhar Tsarnaev managed to escape. The car was later abandoned not far away from Watertown and an intact low-grade explosive device was discovered inside it. The intact low-grade explosive device found in the abandoned car was in a plastic container and wrapped with a green-colored hobby fuse. In addition, from the scene of the shootout on Laurel Street in Watertown, the Federal Bureau of Investigation (FBI) also recovered two unexploded IEDs, as well as the remnants of numerous exploded IEDs. The explosive devices also contained metallic BBs (shot pellets) within an adhesive material as well as green-colored hobby fuses. Tamerlan Tsarnaev was taken to Beth Israel Hospital, where he was pronounced dead.

On April 19 as the search for Dzhokhar Tsarnaev continued, an individual was spotted hiding in a covered boat located at 67 Franklin Street in Watertown. After a stand-off with gunfire, the individual was wounded and removed from the boat and searched; his identity was confirmed to be that of the second marathon bomber, Dzhokhar Tsarnaev.

Dzhokhar Tsarnaev was subsequently charged in federal court for, among other charges, using and conspiring to use a weapon of mass destruction, in addition to aiding and abetting resulting in death. Dzhokhar Tsarnaev subsequently pleaded not guilty to all charges. He was found guilty on thirty charges and was found eligible for the death penalty, even though Massachusetts had ended the death penalty for state crimes. However, as Dzhokhar Tsarnaev was tried on federal charges, his case was eligible for execution. The jury recommended death by lethal injection on six of seventeen capital counts.

Tania Sebastian

Further Reading

After Action Report for the Response to the 2013 Boston Marathon Bombings, Produced by: Massachusetts Emergency Management Agency, Massachusetts Department of Public Health, City of Boston, City of Cambridge, Town of Watertown, Massachusetts Bay Transportation Authority Transit Police Department, Massachusetts National Guard, Massachusetts State Police. http://www.mass.gov/eopss/docs/mema/after-action-report-for-the-response-to-the-2013-boston-marathon-bombings.pdf.

Boston Marathon Bombing. http://www.history.com/topics/boston-marathon-bombings.

Boston Marathon website. http://www.baa.org/races/5k/event-information/course-information.aspx.

Leonard, Herman B. "Dutch," and Arnold M. Howitt. "Boston Marathon Bombing Response." *Crisis Response* 8, no. 4 ( ): 18-21.

The Road to Boston: Counterterrorism Challenge and Lessons from the Marathon Bombing, House Homeland Security Committee Report, U.S. House of Representatives, Committee on Homeland Security, Rep. Michael McCaul, Chairman, March 2014, Prepared by the Majority Staff of the Committee on Homeland Security. https://homeland.house.gov/files/documents/Boston-Bombings-Report.pdf.

Unclassified Summary of the Information Handling and Sharing Prior to the April 15, 2013 Boston Marathon Bombing, Prepared by the Inspectors General of the: Intelligence Community, Central Intelligence Agency, Department of Justice, Department of Homeland Security, April 10, 2014. https://oig.justice.gov/reports/2014/s1404.pdf.

Volpp, Leti. "The Boston Bombers." *Fordham Law Review* 82 (2014): 2209.

See also Capital punishment; Death qualification; *Gregg v. Georgia*; Crime scene investigation; Lone wolf; Surveillance cameras; Terrorism.

Bounty hunters

Definition: Bounty hunters—also known as bail-enforcement agents or bail agents—who track bail skippers, defendants who flee after bail-bond companies post their bail

Defendants; Investigation; Probation and pretrial release

Significance: In some ways, bail agents enjoy wider latitude in their enforcement powers than sworn law-enforcement officers. In addition, many bail-bond agencies have reported increasingly widespread problems with bail skippers.

To many people, the term "bounty hunter" evokes romantic visions of the Old West, with murderous men on horseback trailing escaped cattle rustlers across desolate deserts. In the modern world, however, bail-enforcement agents are professional investigators who work for private bail-bond companies that earn their incomes by charging interest on bail payments that they make for defendants who cannot afford to post bail themselves. When defendants appear for bail hearings, judges usually impose specific monetary amounts that they must post with the courts to ensure that they will return to appear in court for their trials. Defendants who fail to appear in court may forfeit the bail that they post.

Defendants who cannot post bail from their own resources engage bond companies, to whom they typically pay nonrefundable fees of about 10 or 15 percent of the total bail. For example, a defendant who must post five thousand dollars pays a bond company five hundred dollars to post the full amount. When defendants flee the jurisdiction after companies post their bail, the companies send licensed bounty hunters to track them down and deliver them to the courts, which then have the defendants incarcerated. Licensed bail-enforcement agents are legally empowered to arrest bail skippers and take them into custody.

Bounty hunters work for the bail companies and are hired to locate and apprehend those who flee the jurisdiction. Although they are legally empowered to arrest fugitives, they are not necessarily bound by the same restrictions imposed on sworn police officers. For example, they can forcibly enter fugitives' residences without search warrants and are not required to have extradition documents to take into custody defendants who flee from one state to another. Bounty hunters have this latter power because bail applicants sign extradition waivers when they apply for their bail. In some states, bail enforcers are required to register with local police before apprehending bail skippers in the local jurisdictions. Bounty hunters who fail to comply with state and local regulations can be charged with kidnapping, assault, or other offenses.

The wide powers afforded to bounty hunters are a matter of controversy in legal circles. Some jurists argue that bail enforcers are granted too much leeway to carry out their missions. Others argue that bounty hunters cannot do their jobs effectively if they are bound by the same legal restrictions as sworn law-enforcement officers.

Complaints about bounty hunters also relate to another controversial issue. Some people in the criminal justice system complain that many bail-bond agencies make poor decisions choosing to whom to grant bonds. By posting bail for untrustworthy defendants, they place greater demands on the services of bounty hunters and the courts. Moreover, these critics contend that too many defendants are skipping on their bail and are not being tracked down. Despite such criticisms, bounty hunters remain integral elements of the criminal justice system and represent examples of how private and governmental interests intersect in modern society.

David R. Champion

Further Reading
"Bounty Hunter." *The Social History of Crime and Punishment in America: An Encyclopedia*. Ed. Wilbur R. Miller. Thousand Oaks: SAGE, 2012. Digital file.
Burton, Bob. *Bail Enforcer: The Advanced Bounty Hunter*. New York: Paladin Press, 1990.
Burton, Bob. *Bounty Hunter*. New York: Paladin Press, 1984.
Devine, F. E. *Commercial Bail Bonding: A Comparison of Common Law Alternatives*. New York: Praeger, 1991.
Williams, Katie Bo. "Does the Bounty-Hunting Industry Need Reform?" *Atlantic*. Atlantic Monthly Group, July 2015. Web. 25 May 2016.

See also Bail system; Bench warrants; Criminal justice system; Manhattan Bail Project; Police corruption; Vigilantism.

Bureau of Justice Statistics

Definition: Branch of the U.S. Department of Justice that collects and disseminates statistical information about crime, criminals, victims, and the operations of the American justice system
Professional standards; Statistics
Significance: Timely and accurate information about crime is needed for decision-making at all levels of government.

The Bureau of Justice Statistics (BJS) assembles and analyzes data that were originally collected by municipal, county, state, and federal justice agencies. These data, along with information from BJS surveys, are used to prepare publications and data files on topics such as criminal victimization, law enforcement, prosecution and adjudication of crimes, jails and prisons, and capital punishment. BJS publications and data files are freely available on the World Wide Web at www.bjs.gov. The website also helps those who are unfamiliar with the justice system to find key facts in charts and tables or get answers to questions from the BJS staff.

As a member of the Interagency Council on Statistical Policy, which includes the major federal statistics agencies such as the Census Bureau, BJS establishes national standards for data collection, terminology, statistical methods, data quality, and keeping statistics independent from political influence.

National collection of statistical data about crime and justice was originally recommended by the President's Crime Commission in 1965 and was initially housed in the Census Bureau. The Census Bureau continues to administer BJS principal data collection activity, the National Crime Victimization Survey (NCVS). Crime statistics from the NCVS include some crimes not counted in the FBI's Uniform Crime Reports, which are prepared from police records. BJS also administers funds for states to improve their crime statistics keeping and criminal history records.

Jan M. Chaiken

Further Reading

"About the Bureau of Justice Statistics." *Bureau of Justice Statistics.* Office of Justice Programs, US Dept. of Justice, n.d. Web. 24 May. 2016.
Committee on National Statistics. *Principles and Practices for a Federal Statistical Agency.* Washington, D.C.: National Academy Press, 2001.
Federal Bureau of Investigation. "The Nation's Two Crime Measures." *Crime in the United States, 2002.* Washington, D.C.: U.S. Department of Justice, 2003.
Meuchel Wilson, Meagan. "Hate Crime Victimization, 2004-2012 — Statistical Tables." *Journal of Current Issues in Crime, Law & Law Enforcement* 8.1 (2015): 217-235. *Criminal Justice Abstracts with Full Text.* Web. 24 May 2016.
"U.S. Prison Population Reverses Three-Year Decline, Up Slightly in Latest Census." *Corrections Managers' Report* 21.1 (2015): 9-11. *Criminal Justice Abstracts with Full Text.* Web. 24 May 2016.

See also Attorney General, U.S.; Criminal history record information; Federal Bureau of Investigation, U.S.; National Crime Victimization Survey; President's Commission on Law Enforcement and Administration of Justice; Sex offender registries; Uniform Crime Reports; Crime victimization: primary and secondary; "Dark Figure of Crime".

Civil disobedience

Definition: A deliberate act of law breaking to protest a law or governmental policy that is regarded as immoral
Criminal justice issues: Civil rights and liberties; morality and public order
Significance: Civil disobedience is an important type of political dissent that goes beyond legal means of protest; it was widely employed by participants in the Civil Rights and anti-Vietnam War movements.

Notable discussions of the conflict between the individual and legal authority are found in Plato's *Apology* and *Crito* and Sophocles' *Antigone*. The classic discussion of civil disobedience, however, is in the essay "Civil Disobedience" by Henry David Thoreau, first presented in a public lecture at Concord, Massachusetts, in January of 1848 under the title, "On the Relation of the Individual to the State." Thoreau defended his refusal to pay the Massachusetts poll tax because of his opposition to government policies, specifically the Mexican War and governmental acceptance of slavery. He contended that the claims of individual conscience were superior to those of the state and should be followed, even if the individual must violate the law and be subject to arrest and imprisonment. Thoreau himself had been arrested for his refusal to pay taxes, and he spent one night in the Concord jail until an anonymous friend made the tax payment owed by Thoreau.

Early in the essay, Thoreau posed the question: "Must the citizen ever for a moment, or in the least degree, resign his conscience to the legislator?" His famous answer was: "I think that we should be men first, and subjects af-

Major Events in the History of Civil Disobedience

1849	Henry David Thoreau publishes "Resistance to Civil Government" (later known as "Civil Disobedience").
1906	Mohandas K. Gandhi urges Indians in South Africa to go to jail rather than accept racist policies, beginning his *satyagraha* campaign.
1919	Gandhi leads nationwide closing of businesses in India to protest discriminatory legislation.
1920-1922	Gandhi leads boycott of courts and councils in India and develops noncooperation strategies.
1928	Gandhi organizes on behalf of indigo workers in Bihar, India, and initiates fasting as a form of *satyagraha*.
1932-1933	Gandhi engages in fasts to protest untouchability.
1942	Gandhi arrested for *satyagraha* activities.
1955	Martin Luther King, Jr., leads boycott of transit company in Montgomery, Alabama.
1956-1960	King leads protest demonstrations throughout the American South.
1963	King leads March on Washington for civil rights.
1965	King leads "Freedom March" from Selma to Montgomery and organizes voter registration drive.
1968	King initiates a "Poor People's Campaign" but is assassinated before it can be carried out.

terward. It is not desirable to cultivate a respect for the law, so much as for the right. The only obligation which I have a right to assume, is to do at any time what I think right." He added the observation that "Law never made men a whit more just; and by means of their respect for it, even the well-disposed are daily made the agents of injustice." For Thoreau, the emphasis is placed on the appeal to individual conscience to justify the breaking of law.

The best-known contemporary manifesto on civil disobedience is Martin Luther King, Jr.'s "Letter from Birmingham Jail," written in April, 1963. King's letter was a response to a public appeal made by eight white Alabama clergymen who urged King and his associates not to engage in mass protests against segregation in Birmingham. Instead they recommended negotiation and dialogue. King in reply insisted that sit-ins, marches, and other forms of nonviolent direct action were a means of creating a crisis and thereby establishing "such creative tensions that a community that has constantly refused to negotiate is forced to confront the issue."

King also addressed the white ministers' criticism of King's readiness to resort to breaking the law, especially when he had urged officials in the South to obey the 1954 Supreme Court decision outlawing racial segregation in public schools. King wrote: "One may well ask, 'How can you advocate breaking some laws and obeying others?' The answer is to be found in the fact that there are two types of laws. There are *just* laws and there are *unjust* laws. I would agree with St. Augustine that 'An unjust law is no law at all.' " According to King, an unjust law is one that is out of harmony with the moral law. He thus offers what is sometimes called a "higher law" defense of civil disobedience, which differs from the appeal to individual conscience made by Thoreau.

Defining Civil Disobedience

In the writings of both Thoreau and King, one characteristic feature of civil disobedience is the deliberate violation of some established law or legal requirement. Civil disobedience is, after all, disobedience, although, as King and others have noted, the law violated may be only a putatively valid law. Especially in American legal contexts, a law may sometimes be challenged in order to test its constitutionality in court. Some have questioned whether such law-testing should be counted as civil disobedience.

Other definitional concerns have been to distinguish civil disobedience from other forms of law-breaking such as "ordinary" criminal activity and revolutionary action. One contrast is in the type of typical motivation; unlike the ordinary criminal, motivated by self-interest or malice, the civil disobedient is often moved by moral or conscientious motivation, in the sense that a moral belief prompts the illegal act. The revolutionary aims, at least ultimately, at overturning the existing political or legal order, whereas the civil disobedient seeks change within the established system. King captured these points when he affirmed that the civil disobedient must break the law "openly, lovingly..., and with a willingness to accept the penalty" and that one who does this "to arouse the conscience of his community over its injustice, is in reality expressing the very highest respect for law."

There is considerable controversy over how precisely to define civil disobedience. The philosopher John Rawls, in his book *A Theory of Justice* (1971), defined civil disobedience as a "public, nonviolent, conscientious yet political act contrary to law usually done with the aim of

Civil rights sit-in demonstration in Washington, D.C., in 1965. Throughout the Civil Rights movement, nonviolent forms of civil disobedience played a constant role. In sit-in demonstrations, protesters often went limp when they were arrested, forcing the arresting officers to carry them away. (Library of Congress)

bringing about a change in the law or policies of government." Rawls regards civil disobedience as breaking the law from motives of conscience (that is, not from self-interest) and also requires that it be nonviolent. Some critics have questioned whether nonviolence should be a defining feature of civil disobedience, suggesting instead that it is a tactical feature of civilly disobedient protest or a factor to be considered in determining whether such a protest is morally justified. Other critics have objected to requiring as part of the definition that acts of civil disobedience be public, with the likelihood of detection and arrest.

Types

Definitions such as that offered by Rawls construe civil disobedience quite narrowly. Thoreau's refusal to pay the poll tax, a pacifist's refusal to submit to military service, and a Jehovah's Witness's refusal to salute the flag are not counted as acts of civil disobedience but instead are classified as cases of "conscientious refusal." Rawls recognizes that his definition is narrower than Thoreau's but favors it because it enables him to call attention to the public and political character of those protests he chooses to label as "civil disobedience," and to relate them to political activity within a constitutional democracy.

Conscientious refusal is not primarily aimed at political change and is not made in terms of principles shared by the community. Rawls also excludes from the category of civil disobedience militant acts of resistance and disruption. An example might be animal rights activists breaking into laboratories in order to rescue the animals from experimentation. It is possible to use a more generic definition of civil disobedience, classifying under it such phenomena as conscientious refusal, militant action, and civil disobedience (in its narrow sense).

A commonly drawn distinction is between direct and indirect acts of civil disobedience. The former are acts in which the law objected to is the one violated. A clear example is the sit-ins at segregated lunch counters by civil rights protesters in the 1960's in order to protest segregation laws. They were violating the laws they were protesting. Such direct action is not always possible, since the law or policy regarded as immoral cannot be violated. Indirect acts of civil disobedience are ones in which a law violated is not the one protested. During the late 1950's, Bertrand Russell and the Committee of 100, involved in the Campaign for Nuclear Disarmament, engaged in mass demonstrations involving civil disobedience. They were arrested for violating (morally unobjectionable) trespass law during the demonstrations. In a statement on the subject, "Civil Disobedience and the Threat of Nuclear Warfare," Russell observed: "By means of civil disobedience, a certain kind of publicity becomes possible." The aim of the group was to draw attention to the dangers of nuclear weapons policy, not to protest trespass law.

Some forms of indirect civil disobedience are concerned less with publicity than with interfering with what participants in civil disobedience regard as immoral activity. This is sometimes referred to as "direct action," although that expression is used in other ways as well. Activities associated with "Operation Rescue," a campaign of abortion opponents to shut down abortion clinics in the hope of sparing the lives of the unborn who would have been aborted, constitute an example of direct action.

Justification

One of the most vexing questions is whether and when civil disobedience is morally justified. Thoreau seemed to be of the opinion that he and, presumably, others ought to do what they think is right. Many have taken a polar opposite position to the effect that, in a constitutional democracy at least, deliberately breaking the law is never justified. Others have argued that indirect civil disobedience is never justified. Former Supreme Court justice Abe Fortas, in the widely cited 1968 essay entitled "Concerning Dissent and Civil Disobedience," specifically condemned indirect civil disobedience. Fortas, writing at a time of massive protests in connection with racial discrimination, the military draft, and the Vietnam War, concluded,

> So long as our governments obey the mandate of the Constitution and issue facilities and protection for the powerful expression of individual and mass dissent, the disobedience of laws which are not themselves the target of the protest—the violation of law merely as a technique of demonstration—constitutes an act of rebellion and not merely dissent.

In the background of this issue are large questions about the nature of law, morality, and democratic government. A number of grounds have been offered for a general obligation to obey the law. In Plato's *Crito*, Socrates cites several reasons why he should not escape from jail but should instead submit to the laws of Athens. Among them are gratitude for the protection the law has afforded him as well as an implicit agreement with the state. Another common appeal has been to considerations of fairness—in a democracy, laws and policies are arrived at by procedures in which people can exert their influence.

Finally, others have cited the general value of respect for law and the threat to peaceful and orderly processes of collective decision posed by deliberate law breaking. If individuals are allowed to follow their diverse and sometimes erratic consciences, or if they are permitted to observe "higher laws," which are difficult to verify and to interpret, then the health of the democratic process is seriously jeopardized. On the other hand, many defenders of civil disobedience have held that the obligation to obey the law is not absolute, because even in constitutional democracies the political process may yield morally unacceptable outcomes. Defenders of civil disobedience cite approvingly the nineteenth and twentieth century targets of protest and civil disobedience, including slavery and fugitive slave laws, the denial of suffrage to women, laws supporting segregation and discrimination, the war in Vietnam and the military draft, and nuclear weapons policies.

Few defenders of civil disobedience see its justification as an issue that lends itself to resolution by a simple and easy formula. Complex factors relating to the type of civil disobedience, the motives and aims of the practitioners, and the circumstances in which it must be carried out must be taken into account. Among the questions that must be answered are: How gravely wrong is the law or policy being protested; what are the motives of those engaging in civil disobedience (that is, whether they are predominantly moral or are heavily mixed with less admirable motives such as fame or greed); what is the likelihood of success; what are the dangers of violence, especially injury to persons; and what is the risk of encouraging or spreading lawlessness and disrespect for law? On this latter point, the distinction between direct and indirect civil disobedience comes into play. Furthermore, significance is also given to the character of civil disobedience—that it is nonviolent, that it is done openly and with an acceptance of the penalty, and that it is done as a last resort, after available political and legal resorts have been exhausted. These are perceived as important in demonstrating that civil disobedience can be, in Rawls's words, "a form of political action within the limits of fidelity to the rule of law."

While civil disobedience may be morally justified, courts and prosecutors have seldom shown any special leniency toward those who have broken the law for reasons of conscience. As noted earlier, in the context of American law, significant constitutional issues are implicated. In particular, there is the issue of whether an apparent illegal act is really that, since the law might subsequently be declared unconstitutional by judicial review. There are also First Amendment concerns, especially the extent to which protests are protected speech. For example, the U.S. Supreme Court has held that burning a draft card is not protected speech (*United States v. O'Brien*, 1968) but that burning an American flag as a political protest is protected speech (*Texas v. Johnson*, 1989).

Mario F. Morelli

Further Reading

Bedau, Hugo. *Civil Disobedience: Theory and Practice*. New York: Pegasus, 1969. One of several excellent collections of essays that include Thoreau's famous essay.

Greenawalt, Kent. *Conflicts of Law and Morality*. New York: Oxford University Press, 1987.

Murphy, Jeffrie, ed. *Civil Disobedience and Violence*. Belmont, Calif.: Wadsworth, 1971.

Singer, Peter. *Democracy and Disobedience.* New York: Oxford University Press, 1974. Scholarly discussion of civil disobedience.

Thoreau, Henry David. *"Walden" and "Civil Disobedience": Complete Texts with Introduction, Historical Contexts, Critical Essays.* Edited by Paul Lauter. Boston: Houghton Mifflin, 2000.

Walzer, Michael. *Obligations: Essays on Disobedience, War and Citizenship.* Cambridge, Mass.: Harvard University Press, 1982. Discussion of the idea that obligation derives from consent and applies it to practical situations, including civil disobedience.

See also Marshals Service, U.S.; Nonviolent resistance; *Texas v. Johnson*; Trespass.

Clear and present danger test

Definition: The principle, articulated by Oliver Wendell Holmes, Jr., that political speech is protected unless it creates a "clear and present danger that [it] will bring about the substantive evils that Congress has a right to prevent"

Criminal justice issues: Civil rights and liberties; constitutional protections; espionage and sedition

Significance: This was the first principle used by the Supreme Court to distinguish unprotected from protected political speech; the principle is no longer used to suppress political speech but has been used to prohibit hate speech and disruptive speech.

In 1798, Congress passed the Alien and Sedition Act, which prohibited false, scandalous, and malicious publications against the United States government, the Congress, and the president. The act was particularly designed to punish newspapers which opposed President John Adams and supported Thomas Jefferson. Punishment was a fine of up to two thousand dollars and a jail sentence of up to two years. Similar prohibitions occurred in the Espionage Act of 1917, the Sedition Act of 1918, and the Smith Act of 1940, which were designed to suppress opposition to the war efforts of those times.

The first Supreme Court case to test whether a prosecution for seditious libel constituted a violation of the First Amendment occurred in 1919. Charles Schenck, the general secretary of the Philadelphia Socialist Party, published fifteen thousand leaflets protesting U.S. involvement in World War I. Schenck and several others in the party were convicted of violation of the Espionage Act; the conviction was appealed to the Supreme Court in 1919.

Justice Oliver Wendell Holmes, Jr., wrote the opinion of the Court and formulated the test which could justify suppression of speech. In ordinary times, such pamphlets might be permissible, he wrote, but the character of every act depends upon the circumstances in which it is done. "The most stringent protection of free speech would not protect a man in falsely shouting fire in a theater and causing a panic." "The question in every case," Holmes stated, "is whether the words are used in such circumstances and are of such a nature as to create a clear and present danger that they will bring about the substantive evils that Congress has a right to prevent" (*Schenck v. United States*, 1919).

The principle was used to support the conviction of more than two thousand protesters during World War I in spite of the fact that Justice Holmes dissented from these later convictions. Later, in *Whitney v. California* (1927), Justice Louis D. Brandeis formulated what was intended to be a more permissive version of the principle. Brandeis wrote that the wide difference between advocacy and incitement, between preparation and attempt, between assembling and conspiracy must be borne in mind.

This is the formulation that was adopted in *Brandenburg v. Ohio* (1969). In this case the Supreme Court overturned a conviction based on the clear and present danger test for the first time. Defendants have not been convicted of seditious libel since.

Roger D. Haney

See also Seditious libel; Smith Act.

Computer crime

Definition: Illegal intrusions into computers and the use of computers for the perpetration of other crimes

Business and financial crime; Computer crime; Fraud; Technology

Significance: Computer crimes cause immense harm and present a national problem that is difficult to control because of constantly changing technology and the inconsistent and often unenforceable national and international laws enacted to counter the crimes.

Computer crime comprises a broad range of illegal acts in which computers, other types of electronic information-processing devices, and information systems are the objects, targets, or instruments of crimes. They may also be the sites from which "attacks" are launched or the cyber environments harmed in the course of attacks on information systems.

The term "computer crime" has historically conveyed different meanings to criminal justice officials, policymakers, researchers, the media, and the general public. For example, computer crime was once regarded as any illegal act requiring knowledge of computer technology for its perpetration, investigation, or prosecution. Computers have also been conceptualized as symbols for intimidation, particularly in situations in which intended crime victims do not understand or become fearful about the functional capabilities of computers.

The absence of a widely accepted definition of computer crime has much to do with the technical and special nature of computer abuses, such as computer "hacking," the releasing into computer systems of viruses and worms, and interruptions of service. Also important are the technologically evolving nature of computers and the crimes in which they are used, the pace of computerization, and increasing adoption of computers for illicit purposes throughout the United States and other nations. As a consequence of these complexities, several different terms and labels have come into use to describe crimes in which computers—often networked and used in combination with other electronic devices—are used for criminal purposes. Terms generally considered to be synonymous with computer crime include computer-related crime, high-tech crime, information technology-related crime, information/new age crime, Internet crime, and cybercrime. In addition, computer crimes are also frequently given sensational labels in the media, such as "data rape" and "cyberstalking." These terms, too, further complicate wide acceptance of any specific term or label.

History

Computer crimes emerged in the United States with the computerizing of banking services. The first recorded instance of computer crime occurred in 1958. It involved "salami slicing," in which a bank employee in Minneapolis, Minnesota, used a computer to divert and deposit rounding errors of financial transactions into a special account. Over the years, as evolving computer technology made possible new banking services, such as personal credit cards, automatic teller machines (ATMs), and online banking, new forms of computer-enabled financial crimes arose.

Computer hacking—the unauthorized accessing of computerized information systems—also began during the late 1950s. At that time, the nation's first computer science students, at the Massachusetts Institute of Technology, were intent on discovering new uses for computers and called themselves "computer hackers."

Throughout the 1960s and 1970s the number, variety, and impact of computer abuses and crimes increased significantly. However, official estimates of such trends are not available. Nonetheless, growing concern about computer crime during the 1980s, coupled with the beginning of widespread Internet operations in 1984, resulted in several state governments and the federal government enacting special computer crime laws. In 1984, the federal government enacted the Computer Crime and Abuse Act, which made it illegal to access computer systems without prior authorization. During that same period, several new types of computer crimes arose and several famous computer crime cases occurred. For example, in 1984 Fred Cohen, a famous computer-security instructor and consultant, introduced the term "computer virus" to describe self-replicating programs capable of infecting networked computers. On November 2, 1988, Robert Morris released an infamous computer "worm"—a program that shut down significant portions of the Internet.

After 1994, the World Wide Web made online computing more accessible, versatile, and interesting to millions of computer users. The development invariably gave rise to more and increasingly imaginative forms of computer abuse. During the first decade of the twenty-first century, computer crimes included disruptions of computer services by writing and distributing malicious computer programs (viruses, worms, and trojans), and trespassing into information systems without authorization in order to explore, steal, modify, or destroy data.

Computer crimes now also include such financial crimes as embezzlement, securities fraud, unlawful use of credit card account numbers, identity theft, and fraud in online auction and retail-purchasing Web sites. Other forms of computer crime include online piracy of digitized music, film, and application files; sending of unwanted spam; online harassment and stalking; and accessing, distributing, and possessing computer media containing child pornography..

Prevalence

Computer crime now reportedly occurs throughout the United States at record rates, in more complex variations and combinations, and with increasing social and economic impacts. Computer crime also raises fears of lost, damaged, or stolen data among computer users everywhere, and is connected to rising concerns about information security throughout society, including at the highest levels of government. Nevertheless, reliable estimates of the numbers and impact of computer crimes remain largely undetermined, as few studies of the problem have been undertaken. Moreover, even when such studies are conducted, they seldom employ random sampling and other research methods capable of producing results that are scientifically valid and applicable to society as a whole. This condition is the consequence of unclear or imprecise definitions of computer crime and categorizations of offenses and offenders, the unwillingness on the part of many computer crime victims to reveal successful attacks on their information systems, the lack of criminologists specializing in computer crime issues, and a general lack of federal government funding for computer crime research.

Three basic ways of estimating the prevalence of computer crime are victimization surveys, self-report (offender) surveys, and crime reporting systems such as the Uniform Crime Report (UCR) system, which is operated by the Federal Bureau of Investigation (FBI) with voluntary participation of state and local law-enforcement agencies. None of these methods is systematically and consistently used within the United States for reporting computer crime occurrences or trends.

In 2001, the federal government began considering how best to measure the prevalence and costs of computer crime to businesses in the United States. A pilot Computer Security Survey administered in 2001 and responded to by 198 businesses revealed that 74 percent of the businesses had been victims of computer crimes, and 68 percent of the companies experiencing incidents had losses totaling $61 million. In 2002, 223 organizations surveyed reported $455,848,000 in total financial losses from thefts of proprietary information and financial fraud. The organizations surveyed also reported that their Internet connections and internal systems were the most frequent points of attack. Various high-profile attacks on major businesses throughout the 2000s and 2010s increased awareness of such crimes and led to more preventative efforts, but their frequency and cost continued to rise. According to the Ponemon Institute's 2013 Cost of Cyber Crime Study, overall costs of cybercrime had increased 78 percent from 2004 to 2013, with companies averaging annual costs to cyber crime of $11.56 million. A 2013 study by the McAfee computer security company estimated that computer crime cost $100 billion to the US economy each year, and about $300 billion worldwide. However, other studies contest these estimates both as too high and too low, reinforcing the problem of collecting accurate data, which hampers effective countermeasures.

Computer hacking. (By wardv, via Wikimedia Commons)

Internet auction fraud is a frequent form of computer crime, along with credit- and debit-card fraud, computer intrusions, unsolicited e-mail (spam), and child pornography. The Internet Crime Complaint Center (IC3) found in its 2013 annual report that out of about 290,000 total reported complaints in 2012 (causing $525 million in losses), the most common were auction fraud, scareware, and scams involving impersonation of the FBI. Auction fraud problems included nondelivery of merchandise and account payment matters.

It also appears that the levels of automation in attack tools are increasing as attack-tool developers use more advanced techniques. The number of newly discovered vulnerabilities continues to rise faster than computer security systems can be updated by systems administrators. Attack technologies are designed to bypass typical computer firewall configurations. The rise of cloud computing has also enabled easier hacking and other illegal activities, as the amount of hardware and technical knowledge required to mount a sophisticated attack has decreased. In general, greater public computer literacy and the increasing importance of the online sphere in everyday life has led to an increase in computer crime prevalence and sophistication. The security of the Internet and other systems is interdependent, as it can only be as strong as its weakest point. Attacks against critical information infrastructures are increasing concern because of the number of organizations and users on the Internet and their increasing dependency on the Internet to perform their daily functions.

Investigation

The investigation, prosecution, and punishment of computer abuse and crime began during the late 1950s as financial transactions and other types of record-keeping by banks were computerized. The first federally prosecuted case of computer crime occurred in 1966; it involved a perpetrator using a computer to manipulate computerized banking records. During the early years of computer crime, many investigators and prosecutors considered the problem to arise mainly in isolated instances in which computers were merely tools being used in innovative ways to commit already well-understood forms of white-collar and financial crimes, such as fraud and embezzlement.

The onset of computer abuse and crime also arose from establishment of the computer hacker subculture, whose participants believed in the "hacker ethic" of unconstrained discovery, exploration, and sharing of information. Although such motives may have been noble in their original intent, they underscored a considerable portion of unauthorized hacking into computer systems and remain today a justification for many acts of computer trespassing, software piracy, and illegal sharing of digitized music and film files.

Prosecution

During the 1970s and throughout the 1980s computers were increasingly used to commit other new forms of computer abuse and crime, including the creation and distribution of digitized child pornography. Fraud and exploitation of children and the elderly by means of computer bulletin boards and online information services were also commonplace during this period, as were traditional types of crimes committed with the aid of computers, such as counterfeiting, robbery, illegal gambling, kidnapping, prostitution, racketeering, drug trafficking, and homicide. Hate crimes and acts of terrorism were also facilitated by the use of computers. As a result, the US Department of Justice published the first *Computer Crime Criminal Justice Resource Manual* in 1979.

In 1987, the federal government passed the nation's first Computer Fraud and Abuse Act. The following year, Robert Morris became the first offender prosecuted under this law for releasing an Internet worm program that infected thousands of connected computers in November, 1988, and essentially shut down significant portions of the Internet throughout the eastern United States.

In 1989, the Department of Justice published a second edition of its computer crime resource book for criminal justice officials and also explained how state and local law-enforcement officials could go about creating special computer crime investigation and prosecution units. Afterward—and especially after the creation of the World

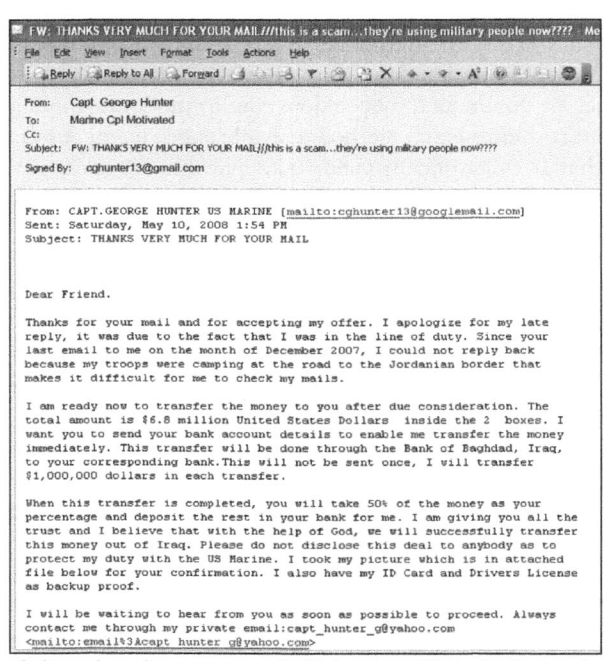

Phishing, a form of computer crime. (Public domain, via Wikimedia Commons)

Wide Web and the explosion of new forms of computer crime that ensued—numerous state and local law-enforcement agencies, as well as the federal government, established computer investigation and prosecution units. In 1994, the Computer Crime Prosecution Unit of the Department of Justice published its first set of federal guidelines for searching and seizing computers.

Several professional associations and organizations, such as the international and regional chapters of the High Technology Crime Investigation Association, the Computer Security Institute, and SANS became instrumental in developing training programs to teach and promote best practices for investigating and prosecuting computer crime, as well as enhance information-systems security. In 2000, agencies of the federal government, including the Department of Homeland Security, the National Security Agency (NSA), and the National Institute for Standards and Technology, began establishing technical standards and recommending best practices to meet the goals of improved security. These and other government agencies and private associations and organizations now routinely provide updated resource materials at no charge for law-enforcement investigators, prosecutors, and information security professionals. In 2015, following a series major data breaches against companies such as Target and Sony Pictures, the latter of which was allegedly the work of the North Korean government,

President Obama released an executive order that created the first official US program of sanctions aimed at cyberspying and cyberattacks, targeting criminals internationally as well as in the United States.

Despite such capacity-building to prevent and control computer crimes, the international and transnational aspects of investigating and prosecuting computer crimes are immensely complex and problematic for criminal justice officials. As of 2015, there was no universally accepted body of international law or treaty governing search, seizure, and the admissibility of computer evidence. There were also no universally recognized methods for effecting arrests of offenders beyond US borders or extraditing them back to the United States to stand trial for alleged crimes.

The general requirements for successful investigations and prosecutions of computer crimes do not substantially differ from those for other types of crime. However, greater understanding, curiosity, and technical knowledge about computers and other types of electronic information processing systems is required in some instances. Computer crimes range from offenses that involve little computer usage to those that involve significant usage. Evidence of computer crimes may be testimonial and either tangible or cyber, as well as circumstantial. Human factors surrounding motives, means, and opportunities to commit computer crimes, as well as the skills, knowledge, resources, and access to information systems possessed by perpetrators also matter from the standpoints of investigating and prosecuting computer crimes.

Investigations of computer crimes are subject to the same rules that govern the search, seizure, and analysis of evidence in other crimes. For example, search warrants are required to search computers for digital evidence of crimes unless exceptional circumstances exist. Ultimately, judges and juries decide on the acceptability and relative value of evidence in cases that go to trial.

Punishment

Depending on the types of computer crimes involved, suspected perpetrators may be charged with either misdemeanor or felony crimes. Adults convicted of misdemeanors are normally subject to punishment of up to one year in jail, fines of up to one thousand dollars, or both. Adults convicted of felony computer crimes may be sentenced to spend more than one year in prison, pay fines greater than one thousand dollars, or both. However, amounts of fines vary among state and federal courts. Other sanctions, such as performing community service and paying victims of crimes financial restitution may also be imposed.

Early computer criminals typically received light punishments. However as the number and seriousness of computer crimes increased, courts began imposing more severe sanctions. In an incomplete but regularly updated list of punishments imposed on convicted computer crime offenders, the Department of Justice reported that penalties ranged from five to sixty months incarceration, often combined with fines of thousands or even hundreds of thousands of dollars, depending on the circumstances of the cases.

Samuel C. McQuade III

Further Reading

"2013: The Impact of Cybercrime." *Infosec Institute*. Infosec Inst., 1 Nov. 2013. Web. 1 Apr. 2015.

Baase, Sara. *A Gift of Fire: Social, Legal, and Ethical Issues for Computing and the Internet*. 4th ed. Upper Saddle River: Prentice-Hall, 2012.

Clifford, Ralph D., ed. *Cybercrime: The Investigation, Prosecution, and Defense of a Computer-Related Crime*. 3rd ed. Durham: Carolina Academic, 2011. Print.

Grance, T., K. Kent, and B. Kim. *Computer Security Incident Handling Guide: Recommendations of the National Institute of Standards and Technology*. Washington, DC: US Dept. of Commerce, 2004. Print.

Himanen, P. *The Hacker Ethic and the Spirit of the Information Age*. New York: Random House, 2001. Print.

IC3. FBI, Natl. White Collat Crime Ctr., 2015. Web. 1 May. 2015.

Rantala, R. R. *Cybercrime Against Businesses*. Washington, DC: Bureau of Justice Statistics, 2004. Print.

Stephenson, Peter, and Keith Gilbert. *Investigating Computer-Related Crime*. 2nd. ed. Boca Raton: Taylor, 2013. Print.

Zetter, Kim. "Hacker Lexicon: What Is the Computer Fraud and Abuse Act?" *Wired*. CondÃ(c) Nast, 28 Nov. 2014. Web. 1 May. 2015.

See also Blackmail and extortion; Computer forensics; Computer information systems; Corporate scandals; Electronic surveillance; Embezzlement; Fraud; National Stolen Property Act; Privacy rights; Trespass; White-collar crime.

Computer forensics

Definition: Search of computers, networks, and communication devices for existing or deleted electronic-evidence

Criminal justice issues: Computer crime; evidence and forensics; technology

Significance: Used to detect, trace, or prove a diverse range of crimes or cause of action, including fraud, negligence, malpractice, child pornography, violent crime, money laundering, and terrorist activity.

Computer forensics is the search for electronic data or documents for use as evidence. When electronic data or documents are used as evidence, they are referred to as electronic evidence, or e-evidence. Broadly defined, e-evidence is any electronically stored information on any type of computer device that can be used as evidence in a legal action.

During computer forensics investigations, there is a search for e-evidence by analyzing electronic devices (for example, computers, personal digital assistants (PDAs), cell phones, voice mail, servers, computer discs, Zip drives, or backup tapes) and communication media (such as instant messaging or chat rooms.) Computer forensics has played a critical role in crime investigations because criminals use computers, electronic mail, and the Internet to help them plan or carry out their crimes. For example, Ramzi Yousef, the mastermind of the 1993 World Trade Center bombing, stored detailed plans to destroy U.S. airliners in encrypted files on his laptop computer. Those files were discovered and recovered using advanced computer forensics tools.

Evidence Search

Unlike physical evidence, e-evidence exists only in digital format, requiring specialized computer forensics tools and techniques for its recovery. Typically, computer forensics involves a two-stage process: the discovery, recovery, preservation, and control of electronic data or documents; and the analysis, verification, and presentation of those documents as e-evidence in court or investigations. Like all evidence collection methods, computer forensics specialists must follow legal protocols to ensure that the e-evidence is admissible. That means that the operations used to collect, analyze, control, and present e-evidence cannot modify the original item in any manner.

Any alteration to the primary source of e-evidence could contaminate it and render it inadmissible in court. Therefore, as with other types of evidence, the handling of e-evidence must follow the three "Cs" of evidence: care, control, and chain of custody. Everyone who touches the e-evidence can contaminate it, so care and control of the computer files and digital audit trails must be kept safe and secured. Chain of custody is necessary to ensure that the e-evidence presented at court is the same as that which was seized. Maintaining the chain of custody for e-evidence is more difficult than for physical evidence because it is more easily altered.

Federal Rules

In 1970, Rule 34 of the Federal Rules of Civil Procedure was amended to address changing technology and communication methods. The amended Rule 34 made electronically stored information subject to subpoena and discovery. Therefore, any communication or file storage device is subject to computer forensic searches to identify, examine, and preserve potential e-evidence—the electronic equivalent of a "smoking gun."

Clearly, this rule has far-reaching implications for electronic records and communications-gateways to evidence of a person's or organization's activities and conduct. Every computer-based activity—whether it is using the Internet for money laundering or identity theft or sending electronic mail with an incriminating or threatening message—leaves an electronic trace that computer forensics may recover. Thus, deleted or not, there is a good probability that electronic mail, Web site visits, drafts and revisions of documents, spreadsheets, or messages can be retrieved. Computer forensics is playing a growing and major role in legal cases, as new legislation is passed to combat cybercrimes, traditional crimes, and terrorism.

Types of Computer Forensics

Computer forensic investigators perform several types of e-evidence searches. There are forensics techniques based on what is searched for, such as computer disc (data) forensics, network forensics, electronic-mail forensics, Internet forensics, and portable device forensics. In data forensics, the situation under investigation is seldom live, so the data being searched for is already stored. In contrast, network forensics cases involve "live" situations, so the data capture must be done on online data feeds. Electronic mail, Internet, and portable device forensics involve the search of both live and stored data. The portable devices subject to forensics searches are flash cards, PDAs, Blackberries, electronic mail pagers, cell phones, video cameras, and instant messaging devices. Also, investigations involve forensics tools and techniques that are specific to the operating system being searched, such as Windows, Macintosh, Unix, and Linux.

Law Enforcement and Forensics Labs

The Federal Bureau of Investigation (FBI) has made computer crimes a top priority, just behind terrorism-related work, because computers are used in such a wide variety of crimes. In July, 2004, the FBI opened a new computer forensics lab in New Haven, Connecticut, for detecting computer-related crimes and training federal, state, and local police to catch Internet pedophiles, frauds, and thieves. It is the second such lab the FBI has opened in the United States, and it will serve one of fifty computer crime task forces that have been set up around the country to increase cooperation among law-enforcement agencies.

The caseload of the U.S. Department of Defense Computer Forensics Lab (DCFL) grows each year. In 2000, the DCFL investigated 148 crime and intrusion cases. In 2003, that number was 425.

Linda Volonino

Further Reading
Casey, Eoghan. *Digital Evidence and Computer Crime.* 2d ed. San Diego, Calif.: Elsevier Academic Press, 2004. Explains how computers and networks function, how they can be involved in crimes, and how they can be used as a source of evidence.
Littlejohn Shinder, Debra, and Ed Tittel. *Scene of the Cybercrime: Computer Forensics Handbook.* Rockland, Mass.: Syngress, 2002. Covers law and technology issues, including rules of evidence, control of crime scenes, and technology for fighting crime.
Prosise, Chris, Kevin Mandia, and Matt Pepe. *Incident Response and Computer Forensics.* 2d ed. New York: McGraw-Hill Osborne Media, 2003. Written by FBI insiders, this book describes the legal, procedural, and technical steps of incident response and computer forensics.
Vacca, John R. *Computer Forensics: Computer Crime Scene Investigation.* Hingham, Mass.: Charles River Media, 2002. Overview of computer forensics, including how to gather evidence, data recovery techniques, auditing methods, and terrorist cyber-attack tactics.
Volonino, Linda, and S. R. Robinson. *Principles and Practice of Information Security.* Upper Saddle River, N.J.: Prentice-Hall, 2004. Explains the legal and technical issues of computer forensics and electronic evidence.

See also Chain of custody; Cold cases; Computer crime; Computer information systems; Crime scene investigation; Criminal procedure; Cybercrime; Evidence, rules of; Search and seizure.

Computer information systems

Definition: Systems designed to bring together people, computers, and departmental rules and procedures to gather, store, retrieve, analyze, and apply information to meet organizational goals

Computer Crime; Crime Statistics; Law-enforcement organization; Technology

Significance: Modern computer technology is helping to revolutionize law-enforcement by helping police departments to deploy officers more rapidly and efficiently and enabling both departments and officers in the field to gather and assess information rapidly.

Police use of computers is a relatively recent development. The first commercially available computer was not released until 1951. Four years later, the New Orleans police adopted the first arrest and warrant computer system. The St. Louis, Missouri, police department installed the first computer-aided dispatch system in 1960. During the 1970s, law enforcement began embracing computer-based information systems even more quickly than the courts and corrections departments. However, during those early years, computer applications were generally limited to basic record keeping, crime reporting, and traffic violations.

Large police departments developed computerized data-searching capabilities during the 1980s; however, they were often disappointed that the much-anticipated benefits in productivity and efficiency were not materializing. This was due, in part, to the problem of integration: Different agencies used different types of equipment that were either incompatible with one another or could not easily be integrated into larger systems. To a lesser extent, the same problem still exists today.

By the 1990s, most police departments with one hundred or more full-time sworn officers had expanded their uses of computers to include staff allocation, dispatching, budgeting, and criminal investigations. In 1994, the U.S. Congress established the National Law Enforcement and Corrections Technology Center (NLECTC) to promote the development and production of promising technologies with law enforcement and corrections applications. In 1995, the NLECTC, in turn, created the Justice Information Network (JUSTNET) to serve as a clearinghouse for the dissemination of information about new and proven technology specifically geared for policing and corrections.

During the early stages of the information technology revolution, law-enforcement agencies relied upon computers primarily to speed up their processing of such traditional functions as crime reporting, dispatch, payroll, and traffic tickets. However, with advances in hardware and software, new ways of thinking gradually emerged. The old uses of computers were still in heavy demand. In fact, they had become indispensable. However, computers were soon expected to do more than simply gather, organize, and retrieve information. They were expected to generate new knowledge as well. Information technology is now heavily used in law enforcement in computer-aided dispatch, mobile data computing and automated field reporting, records management systems, and geographic information systems and crime mapping.

Specialized Applications

Computer-aided dispatch (CAD) is designed to handle all information relating to both mundane and emergency calls for service. Based on a "geofile," or geographic database, using map-based x and y coordinates, CAD can accurately establish the locations of callers and incidents, whether the information is provided in the form of addresses, business names, street intersections, or other fragments of information. CAD fully automates the receiving of calls and the dispatching of police vehicles. When it is used with automated vehicle location (AVL) systems that contain information on the status and location of every vehicle in a police department, CAD can help prioritize calls for service and make suggestions about which vehicles should be sent out, based upon which police officers are currently occupied and which are closest to the locations where help is needed. More advanced CAD systems can also provide officers with useful information, such as the numbers and types of prior calls made from the locations in question, whether there are any outstanding warrants on the residents who live there, and so on.

Mobile data computing allows police vehicles to become "offices" on wheels. In typical cases, officers receive dispatch information about incidents through mobile laptop computers in their squad cars. When they arrive at the scenes of incidents, they can quickly retrieve useful information electronically from remote local, state, and national databases. Officers equipped with mobile data computing can, in fact, perform a wide variety of functions using laptop and wireless hand-held units. They can, for example, access information about departmental policies and procedures, look up pertinent law in the penal code, and call up digital photographic images.

Mobile computing can significantly assist officers in on-the-spot decision making by providing them with immediate access to much-needed information. When the incidents are concluded, the officers can then prepare reports through their laptop or hand-held units. The officers then electronically submit their reports to supervisors. When the supervisors approve the reports, they can forward them electronically to their departments' records management systems. If a report requires revisions, a supervisor can send it back to the officer for corrections. Mobile data computing is enhanced by automated field reporting (AFR) software. AFR software offers time-saving features such as drop-down menus, spell-checking, error correction, pre-filled fields on the report forms, and other features.

Information Systems Technician 2nd Class Athena Stovall, assigned to Commander U.S. 3rd Fleet in San Diego, scans the network on her computer for intrusions during a cyber war training course at the Space and Naval Warfare Systems Center. (Public domain, via Wikimedia Commons)

Records management systems are designed to allow law-enforcement agencies to enter, store, manipulate, and retrieve data about virtually every aspect of police work, not merely crime reports, arrest reports, and crime analysis data. Before the 1960s, almost all law-enforcement agencies kept information of this sort in hard-copy files. Mainframe computers improved data retrieval during the 1970s but were not owned by many law-enforcement agencies themselves. Instead, police departments had to share time on the mainframes with other municipal agencies, and control of the mainframes was located outside the law-enforcement agencies. Now, advanced records management systems can be interfaced with other city, county, state, and federal law-enforcement systems, including their databases such as the National Crime Information Center (NCIC), the Interstate Identification Index (III), the Integrated Automated Fingerprinting Identification System (IAFIS), and the National Incident Based Reporting System (NIBRS). The last was the planned successor to the Federal Bureau of Investigation's Uniform Crime Reports.

State-of-the art records management systems can be integrated with other intradepartmental systems, such as computer-aided dispatch and mobile data terminals. Records management systems are not without problems, however. They are expensive to purchase and maintain and require skilled staff with extensive-and on-going-training.

Geographic information systems (GIS) are computer-based systems that store both spatial and nonspatial information in "layers" that can be called up simultaneously and depicted in the nuanced forms of maps. Replacements for the old-fashioned, color-coded pin maps traditionally used by police departments, geographic information systems can generate sophisticated maps showing, for example, relationships among illegal drug sale locations and the locations of schools, housing projects, and public telephones. GIS maps can also accurately identify "hot spots" and "hot times," enabling reallocation of police resources.

A good example of GIS usage is New York City's CompStat program. Begun in 1994, CompStat is a unit designed to analyze the statistics of daily crime reports from the city's police precincts. The data and maps generated by CompStat are used by the chief of police to evaluate the performances of precinct commanders, who, in turn, evaluate the performances of the officers on their beats.

In addition to pinpointing the locations of armed robberies over designated periods of time, a geographic information system can include information such as liquor store locations and unemployment rates in specific neighborhoods and the addresses of all probationers and parolees in the area. When combined with the satellite technology of a global positioning system, law-enforcement and correctional officials can then accurately monitor the whereabouts of known offenders in any given community.

In 2015, the RAND Corporation published its study *High-Priority Information Technology Needs for Law Enforcement*, in which it suggested several paths for improving the use of computer information services. Among its suggestions was a call for a federal coordinator for technology-related outreach, who would develop methods of maintaining and monitoring IT needs for law enforcement officials.

Robert Rogers

Further Reading

Dunworth, T. "Criminal Justice and the IT Revolution." *Federal Probation* 65.2 (2001): 52-65. Print.

Harris, K. J., and W. H. Romesburg. *Law Enforcement Tech Guide*. Washington: Dept. of Justice, Office of Community Oriented Policing Services, 2002. Print.

Hollywood, John S., et al. *High-Priority Information Technology Needs for Law Enforcement*. Washington: RAND Corporation, 2015.

Lin, C., P. J-H. Hu, and H. Chen. "Technology Implementation Management in Law Enforcement." *Social Science Computer Review* 22.1 (2004): 24-36. Print.

Reaves, B. A., and M. J. Hickman. *Law Enforcement Management and Administrative Statistics, 2000: Data for Individual State and Local Agencies with One Hundred or More Officers*. Washington: Dept. of Justice, Office of Justice Programs, 2004. Print.

Vann, Irvin B., and G. David Garson. *Crime Mapping: New Tools for Law Enforcement*. New York: P. Lang, 2003. Print.

See also Booking; Computer crime; Computer forensics; Criminal history record information; Criminal records; Fingerprint identification; Geographic information systems; Homeland Security, U.S. Department of; Interpol; Violent Criminal Apprehension Program.

Contributing to delinquency of minors

Definition: Any acts or omissions perpetrated by adults that encourage juveniles to engage in behaviors that may lead to delinquency

Crime prevention; Juvenile justice

Significance: American laws are designed to protect naive juveniles from the depredations of adults.

Contributing to the delinquency of a minor is, like the term "juvenile delinquency," relatively recent in origin. For centuries, childhood was the most precarious period in an individual's life. Scant knowledge existed concerning illnesses and bacteria, and, as a result, it was common for people to die in infancy or childhood—the central reason that married couples had big families. If children were strong enough to survive, around age seven they entered the workforce alongside their parents and older siblings, becoming "little adults."

Views regarding childhood began changing in the nineteenth century because of the paradigm shift caused by the Industrial Revolution. Instead of families working together at the farm, people began migrating into the cities. Children competed with their elders for the new jobs created by the industrial boom. Up to this point, most children could not read or write, because education was not a particularly important issue for individuals tilling the soil.

With the growth of urban populations, education became increasingly important. Most parents were happy for their children to gain educations because it meant they might not have to work twelve to fifteen hours a day in factories. In addition to providing an academic education, many reformers attempted to teach the children that certain activities or vices were unhealthy and that it would be advantageous to leave certain things alone. For example, many children enjoyed the same unhealthy habits as their parents, such as smoking, using snuff or chewing tobacco, and drinking alcohol. Once society started seeing childhood as separate from adulthood, the social and moral mores changed, and what had once been done in the open (such as smoking cigarettes) now became surreptitious. Likewise, behaviors considered normal for adults began to be seen as taboo for juveniles.

Over time, statutes and law codes were written describing the punishments, usually mild, that adults would receive if they engaged in any activities that might lead juveniles toward delinquency. Furthermore, if adults allowed juveniles to engage in behavior considered "out-of-bounds," they could face charges based on not restricting the child. For example, adults who catch children smoking cigarettes but do nothing could conceivably be brought before a judge, as tobacco use is a proscribed activity for individuals who have not reached the age of majority. Furthermore, if a parent indulges in an illegal activity, such as smoking marijuana, the state has the right to arrest the parent for setting an example that could conceivably cause the juvenile to seek out opportunities for further drug exploration.

Cary Stacy Smith

Further Reading

Champion, Dean John. *The Juvenile Justice System: Delinquency, Processing, and the Law.* 4th ed. Upper Saddle River, N.J.: Prentice-Hall, 2003.

Cox, Steven M., John J. Conrad, and Jennifer M. Allen. *Juvenile Justice: A Guide to Theory and Practice.* 5th ed. New York: McGraw Hill, 2003.

Malmgren, K. W., and S. M. Meisel. "Examining the Link Between Child Maltreatment and Delinquency for Youth with Emotional and Behavioral Disorders." *Child Welfare* 83, no. 2 (2004): 175-189.

Paternoster, R., S. Bushway, R. Brame, and R. Apel. "The Effects of Teenage Employment on Delinquency and Problem Behaviors." *Social Force* 82, no. 1 (2003): 297-336.

Shoemaker, D. J. *Theories of Delinquency: An Examination of Explanations of Delinquent Behavior.* 4th ed. New York: Oxford University Press, 2000.

Siegel, Larry J., Brandon C. Welsh, and Joseph J. Senna. *Juvenile Delinquency: Theory, Practice, and Law.* 8th ed. Belmont, Calif.: Wadsworth/Thomson Learning, 2002.

Vander Ven, Thomas. *Working Mothers and Juvenile Delinquency.* New York: LFB Scholarly, 2003.

See also Indecent exposure; Juvenile courts; Juvenile delinquency; Juvenile Justice and Delinquency Prevention, Office of; Juvenile Justice and Delinquency Prevention Act; Juvenile justice system.

Coroners

Definition: Public officials who investigate deaths when there are reasons to suspect those deaths did not occur naturally

Evidence and forensics; Investigation; Medical and health issues

Significance: A coroner is the officer responsible for finding out how a person died if that death appears to have been violent. The coroner may hold an inquest and order an autopsy to be performed if the manner of death is not obvious.

When a person dies and the manner of death is deemed either uncertain or violent, it is the coroner's job to investigate the death. A coroner is called to the scene of a crime to determine whether a death occurred by accidental, suicidal, homicidal, natural, or uncertain means. Even if law-enforcement officials feel that there already exists enough evidence to proceed with a criminal investigation, they still must wait for the coroner's decision before they act. The coroner may order an autopsy and wait until its completion before making a final decision on the manner of death.

Coroners can be elected officials who do not necessarily possess any medical or law-enforcement knowledge. Usually, though, the coroner is a mortician, doctor, or other local law-enforcement official. In big metropolitan areas such as Los Angeles, a coroner's position is a full-time job and is assisted by deputies who do the fieldwork.

Responsibilities

A coroner's responsibilities are many, including the primary one of determining whether or not enough evidence accompanies a death to justify a criminal investigation. A coroner may investigate against the will of the deceased's relatives or hospital employees; conversely, a coroner may declare the matter closed, stating there should not be an investigation at all. Coroners are also responsible for notifying the proper authorities regarding deaths and signing death certificates. A human body must be certified as legally dead before any funeral arrangements are made. If the body is eventually going to be cremated, an autopsy may be mandatory according to regional laws.

If the cause of death is not obvious at the crime scene, the coroner will usually hold an inquest and order an autopsy. For medicolegal or forensic investigations, a coroner does not have to get permission from the deceased's next of kin in order for an autopsy to be performed. The coroner will usually order a full autopsy, so as much information can be gathered as possible. The results of the autopsy will determine whether law-enforcement agencies should continue with their own investigations.

Everybody is under the jurisdiction of the coroner, from the pathologists or medical examiners who perform the autopsy to the laboratory technicians who run further tests on dissected organs (such as toxicology). The coroner can issue arrest warrants and subpoenas as needed if investigations warrant it; in some counties the coroner is legally more powerful than the sheriff. The coroner also identifies remains, testifies regarding insurance and estate claims, and warns the community about dangerous new illegal drugs as they are discovered.

History

Throughout history, there have been coroners or people like them whose job it was to say whether someone's death was intentional or not. The English were the first to establish a coroner's office: In 1194, as a way to raise ransom funds for King Richard I, knights in each county were given the task of selling the goods of hanged felons. These knights were known as "crowners," a word that eventually became "coroner" (taken from *corona*, a Latin word for "crown").

Coroner I.L. Feinberg. (Public domain, via Wikimedia Commons)

Eventually the coroner's job became that of ensuring all taxes were collected honestly by the sheriff. This meant that all deaths of a sudden or violent nature were investigated. Matters became complicated when suicide was concerned. The laws of medieval England stated that all possessions belonging to someone who committed suicide become the property of the Crown. The Church of England added that the suicide victim's soul was condemned to hell unless the victim had suffered from demoniac possession or insanity. This the coroner had to determine, and the first inquests were held.

The first written work about forensic medicine was Sung Tz'u's *Hsi Yuan Chi Lu* (washing away of unjust imputations or wrongs), written in 1247. The first university department of legal medicine opened at the University of Edinburgh, Scotland, in 1807, and in England, coroners became officials who dealt with deaths that were suspicious. The United States adopted the British coroner system but eventually began to change how it worked by using professionally trained physicians who had studied forensic pathology.

The Coroner in the United States

In the United States, a coroner was either elected or appointed to the job until 1877. In that year, a physician in Massachusetts was chosen instead to be the coroner. The job's description changed, also, so that coroners were only supposed to investigate violent deaths. In 1915, New York became the first city to give a coroner the authority to order an autopsy, and Maryland began a statewide medical examiner system in 1939.

Modern coroners are not only invaluable assets to medicolegal investigations, but they can also become celebrities in their own rights. Thomas Noguchi, Los Angeles County's chief coroner from 1967 to 1982, became

Navy Cmdr. Edward A. Reedy is one of two armed forces medical examiners outside of the United States. (Public domain, via Wikimedia Commons)

known as the "coroner to the stars" because he supervised the investigations of Hollywood celebrity deaths such as those of Natalie Wood and John Belushi. Noguchi also invented a method of trace metal identification that is now used throughout the United States.

Kelly Rothenberg

Further Reading
Blanche, Tony, and Brad Schreiber. *Death in Paradise: An Illustrated History of the Los Angeles County Department of Coroner.* New York: Four Walls Eight Windows, 2001.
Burton, Julian L., and Guy N. Rutty. *The Hospital Autopsy.* New York: Oxford University Press, 2001.
Kadish, Sanford H. *Encyclopedia of Crime and Justice.* Vol. 1. New York: Free Press, 1983.
Noguchi, Thomas T. *Coroner.* New York: Simon & Schuster, 1983.

See also Autopsies; Cold cases; Forensics; Inquests; Medical examiners; Toxicology; Trace evidence; Technology's transformative effect.

Crime labs

Definition: Facilities-mostly government-run-designed to analyze physical evidence of crimes
Evidence and forensics; Investigation; Technology
Significance: Crime labs process, analyze, and sometimes collect physical evidence from crimes and crime scenes. As the field of criminalistics has become increasingly important within the criminal justice system, crime labs have provided the expertise to use and understand scientific methods of analysis of evidence.

Most crime labs are funded and administered by governmental agencies, such as the Federal Bureau of Investigation (FBI), state departments of justice, and local law-enforcement agencies. There are also private, for-profit crime labs. The criminalists who work within crime labs typically have degrees in chemistry, biology, and other sciences, and often have masters and doctoral degrees.

Crime labs perform a wide variety of analyses. One of their most common tasks now is DNA analysis. Among other things, DNA analysis is done to identify criminal offenders and crime victims. DNA analysis can be performed on body tissues and on body fluids, such as blood, saliva, and semen. Other common crime labs tasks include fingerprint analysis; identification of trace evidence such as clothing fibers and paint particles; screening of body fluids for alcohol, drugs, and toxins; identification and matching of firearms and ammunition;

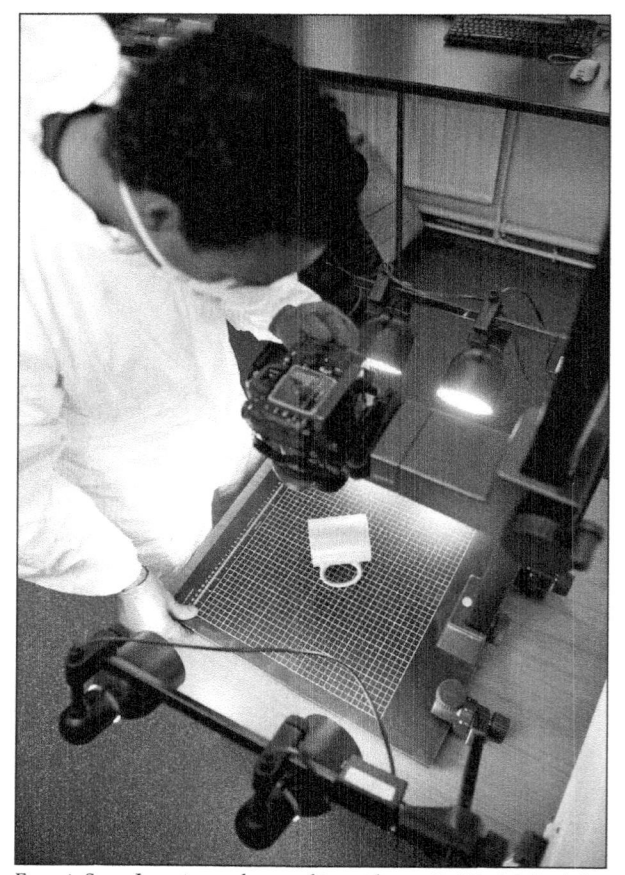

Forensic Scene Investigator photographing evidence. (By West Midlands Police (UK), via Wikimedia Commons)

identification and matching of marks made by hammers, screwdrivers, saws, and other tools; and analysis of written documents, such as matching handwriting samples to those of suspects. Depending on the types of analysis being performed, criminalists use a wide variety of scientific equipment and techniques.

Modern Challenges
As crime labs become increasingly important in the investigation of crime, they face a growing number of challenges. One of these is overwhelming caseloads and limited personnel and budgets. In 2002, for example, the fifty largest crime labs in the United States received more than 1.2 million requests for services. Although these labs had 4,300 full-time employees, they had a backlog of 270,000 requests by the end of that year. As a result of these backlogs and contrary to what is often depicted on television shows such as *CSI*, it often takes well over a month for a real-life law-enforcement agency to obtain results of scientific analysis. This contributes to slowing

down the criminal justice system's response to crimes. The delays allow some guilty people to escape justice, while innocent suspects may be detained for longer periods of time.

Another challenge that crime labs face is the quality of their work. The first years of the twenty-first century have seen a number of high-profile incidents involving crime labs and crime lab employees that have provided false and misleading results. These problems have been caused by such factors as high caseloads and inadequate personnel training and supervision. Faulty crime lab analyses are particularly troubling because they can lead to mistaken convictions of innocent people. In fact, according to the Innocence Project, defective and fraudulent science was a major contributor to the false convictions of dozens of men for crimes as serious as murder and rape. Some of these innocent men even received death sentences, and many of them spent long years in prison.

In response to the problem of bad science, there has been a recent trend toward accrediting crime labs. Under a formal accreditation process, an external agency such as the American Society of Crime Laboratory Directors audits and inspects labs. The accrediting agency checks for such things as proper employee education and training, availability of appropriate equipment and space, and correct evidence handling and analysis techniques. In addition, the U.S. Department of Justice has published several reports providing guidelines on forensic science training and techniques.

Accreditation and guidelines are likely to do little to help alleviate the backlogs in lab work. However, they should improve the accuracy and quality of the labs' work, thus leading to more accurate crime investigations.

Phyllis B. Gerstenfeld

Further Reading
Burch, Andrea M., Matthew R. Durose, and Kelly A. Walsh. "Census of Publicly Funded Forensic Crime Laboratories, 2009." *Bureau of Justice Statistics*. Office of Justice Programs, US Dept. of Justice, 2 Aug. 2012. Web. 25 May. 2016.
Bureau of Justice Statistics. *Fifty Largest Crime Labs, 2002*. Washington, D.C.: U.S. Department of Justice, 2004.
Evans, C. *The Casebook of Forensic Detection: How Science Solved One Hundred of the World's Most Baffling Crimes*. New York: John Wiley & Sons, 1998.
Genge, N. *The Forensic Casebook: The Science of Crime Scene Investigation*. Beverly Hills: Ballantine Books, 2002.
Lee, H., T. O'Neil, and C. Gill. *Cracking Cases: The Science of Solving Crimes*. 2002. Amherst: Prometheus Books, 2009.
National Institute of Justice. *Education and Training in Forensic Science: A Guide for Forensic Science Laboratories, Educational Institutions, and Students*. Washington: U.S. Department of Justice, 2004.

See also Bloodstains; Cold cases; Crime scene investigation; Criminology; DNA testing; Document analysis; Fingerprint identification; Forensics; Police detectives; Shoe prints and tire-tracks; Toxicology; Trace evidence; Technology's transformative effect.

Criminal history record information

Definition: Record, or a system of records, that includes the identification of a person and describes that person's arrests and subsequent court dispositions—also known as a rap sheet
Criminal justice issues: Arrest and arraignment; investigation; technology
Significance: Criminal history records are widely used in investigations, sentencing, licensing, background checks, and other purposes.

Typical criminal history records begin with the names, dates of birth, sex, and other identifying characteristics of persons arrested by the police, followed by listings of subsequent instances in which the persons came in contact with the criminal justice system. For example, the first event on a person's record might be an arrest on June 1, 2004, for vehicle theft, showing which law-enforcement agency arrested the suspect; the next event might be a dismissal of the charge of vehicle theft against that person on June 11, 2004, showing which court dismissed the charge.

Normally, records do not include information about arrests and dispositions that occurred when subjects were juveniles. When juvenile cases have been waived to adult court, however, the adult court disposition does appear in criminal records. Criminal history records also do not contain intelligence information on their subjects or entries about parking violations, drug abuse treatment, mental health treatment, or similar matters.

As several people may have the same name and be born on the same date (or criminal offenders may lie about their names or dates of birth), criminal history records are accompanied by a positive identification of the person, normally fingerprints. Arrests that occurred in different cities, counties, or states are linked though a computerized interstate identification index operated by the Federal Bureau of Investigation (FBI). The information from different states may be combined into a single FBI criminal history record or stored in computers in the different states, ready to be combined electronically upon request. Linking records in different states for the same person is facilitated by automated fingerprint identification systems.

A person who was never arrested does not have a criminal history record, even if the FBI or a state agency has a copy of the person's fingerprints from an employment background check or for another reason.

Originally, criminal history records were considered highly confidential, and access was restricted to employees of criminal justice agencies for specified purposes, such as trying to find perpetrators of crimes or prosecuting and sentencing offenders in accordance with law. Beginning in the 1990's, state and federal legislation has facilitated access to criminal history records (or selected portions of those records) for a variety of purposes, including background checks of applicants for purchase of a firearm, employment related to public safety, or volunteer work involving care of children or the elderly. Sex offender registries, which are completely available to the public in some states, are separate from criminal history records.

Jan M. Chaiken

Further Reading
Bureau of Justice Statistics. *Improving Criminal History Records for Background Checks*. Washington, D.C.: U.S. Department of Justice, 2003.
SEARCH, The National Consortium for Justice Information and Statistics. *Public Attitudes Toward Uses of Criminal History Information*. Washington, D.C.: Bureau of Justice Statistics, 2001.

See also Arrest; Bureau of Justice Statistics; Cold cases; Computer information systems; Criminal records; Criminals; Federal Bureau of Investigation, U.S.; Fingerprint identification; Gun laws; Juvenile justice system; Juvenile waivers to adult courts; Sex offender registries; Uniform Crime Reports.

Criminal justice education

Definition: Methods of increasing the awareness of criminal justice students with careers in their field
Criminology; Professional standards
Significance: Many undergraduate students in criminal justice are not fully aware of the wide variety of career choices available in their field. They can broaden their educations by looking beyond their regular academic course work. The broader their experiences are, the better their chances of selecting and succeeding in their criminal justice careers.

A variety of methods and techniques can be helpful in assisting undergraduate students in becoming more aware of the variety of criminal justice positions. For example, student internships are an excellent means of allowing students to find out at firsthand what various government agencies do and the services they provide. Internships usually require students to work within law-enforcement agencies, courts, corrections agencies, or forensics labs for a specific number of hours. Interns work under the supervision of staff officers and mentors in the agencies. Some internships are paid, but the main advantage offered by internships is experience. Students also usually receive college credit for their intern work.

Service learning is another means for students to gain insight, knowledge, and experience in areas that interest them. The students agree to perform certain services that agencies provide and work alongside regular staff members on projects related to the college courses in which they are registered. Such assignments may be fixed course requirements or be individual choices that the students make to complete course work. The students benefit by gaining valuable work knowledge and experience. Service-learning assignments usually entail fewer hours than internships.

Volunteering work in criminal justice agencies is another good way in which to learn more about possible careers. Voluntary work usually earns neither college credits nor payment. However, such work can be easy to get, as most criminal justice agencies rarely turn down would-be volunteers.

Many educational institutions host guest speakers from a variety of criminal justice agencies and careers to address students interested in the discipline. Such occasions can provide excellent opportunities for students to hear from practitioners in the field about the particulars of their work. They can also provide students with opportunities to make contacts for future reference.

Many educational institutions host career fairs, which as many as fifteen to thirty representatives from criminal justice agencies may attend. The agencies typically set up booths or tables to distribute information about their work. Such fairs can provide excellent opportunities for students to meet and talk directly to working criminal justice professionals. They can also make contacts for possible internships and future employment.

Campus career centers and offices are usually separate departments at most colleges. They normally maintain listings and contacts encompassing the majority of criminal justice careers available. Depending on their staffing, they can assist students with interviewing techniques,

Information Systems Technician 2nd Class Denise Darling received the certificate of recognition for completing her bachelors degree in Criminal Justice with emphasis in cyber crime. (Public domain, via Wikimedia Commons)

résumé writing, application procedures, and other job-search tasks. In addition, they can help students secure internships.

Criminal justice clubs and associations invite new members at many colleges and universities. These groups are usually operated by students majoring in criminal justice, with the help of faculty advisers from the criminal justice departments. The main goal of such groups is to disseminate information by hosting guest speakers, taking field trips, and helping organize career fairs.

Criminal justice advisory boards are another means of enhancing students' awareness of various criminal justice agencies. For example, many jurisdictions maintain youth service commissions. These bodies encompass cross sections of individual citizens—including students—who would serve as advisory groups to judiciary and juvenile justice agencies. They recommend programs and other means of dealing with juvenile offenders and juvenile delinquency. In addition, they may recommend preventive programs to agencies dealing with at-risk juveniles.

Other types of community advisory boards are youth and young-adult boards that advise criminal justice agencies. Their purpose is to communicates the ideas of young people to advise criminal justice agencies on how to deal with offenders of the same ages. A wide variety of juvenile and adult advisory groups exist that invite community participation.

John M. Paitakes

Further Reading
Bolles, Richard Nelson, and Mark Emery Bolles. *What Color Is Your Parachute? 2016: A Practical Manual for Job-Hunters and Career-Changers.* Berkeley: Ten Speed P, 2016.
Champion, Dean John. *Review of Seeking Employment in Law Enforcement, Private Security and Related Fields.* Upper Saddle River: Prentice-Hall, 1994.
Harr, Scott J., and Karen M. Hess. *Careers in Criminal Justice and Related Fields.* 6th ed. Belmont: Wadsworth, 2010.
Kanovitz, Jacqueline R. *Constitutional Law for Criminal Justice.* New York: Routledge, 2015. *eBook Collection (EBSCOhost).* Web. 25 May 2016.
Prior, Nicole M. *Graduate Study in Criminology and Criminal Justice : A Program Guide.* Hoboken: Routledge, 2015. *eBook Collection (EBSCOhost).* Web. 25 May 2016.
United States. Bureau of Labor Statistics. "Occupation Finder." *Occupational Outlook Handbook.* US Dept. of Labor, 17 Dec. 2015. Web. 25 May. 2016.

See also Prisons, Federal Bureau of; Community-based corrections; Criminal justice in U.S. history; Criminal justice system; Drug Enforcement Administration, U.S.; Judges; Neighborhood watch programs; Omnibus Crime Control and Safe Streets Act of 1968; Parole; Parole officers; Prison and jail systems; Television news.

Criminal records

Definition: Official documents that list individuals' past convictions for misdemeanors and felonies and that sometimes include arrests that do not result in convictions

Criminal justice issues: Convictions; defendants; sentencing

Significance: Criminal records allow police agencies and courts to know the histories of criminal suspects' and defendants' violations of laws and are often used as sentencing tools in evaluating convicted persons' eligibility for probation and parole.

Local, state, and federal law-enforcement agencies and courts all compile criminal records. Effective national coordination of criminal records is now a clear goal of the Federal Bureau of Investigation (FBI) and other law-enforcement agencies, but there are still holes in the system of record keeping that make it difficult to track mobile offenders, particularly low-level misdemeanants.

Data Collection

The FBI has national responsibility for the compilation of criminal records. These records are stored at the FBI's Criminal Justice Information Services (CJIS) division, which is headquartered in Clarksburg, West Virginia. The CJIS is now the world's largest fingerprint repository; it cooperates with both national and international law information agencies. From fingerprint cards to digital copies to latent fingerprints, the FBI is a repository for all. As of May, 1997, CJIS had more than 219 million fingerprint cards. Of these more than 132 million were criminal record cards and more than 187 million were civil record cards. Additionally, till 2011 the FBI has been provided with 1,50,000 latent fingerprints from the US Department of Defence.

Although submission of records to the CJIS is voluntary for state and local law-enforcement agencies, data submission increased during the late twentieth century. The CJIS also receives the fingerprints of aliens who seek permanent residence, naturalization, and asylum in the United States, as well as the fingerprints of Americans seeking to adopt children abroad. Alien residents who are convicted of felonies are automatically deported if found, and aliens with serious criminal records cannot be admitted to the United States legally.

In some states, state law requires those arrested for felonies and class A and B misdemeanors to be fingerprinted, and two sets of fingerprint records are made so that both local authorities and the state bureau of investigation can maintain appropriate records. Juveniles charged with offenses that would be felonies or class A and B misdemeanors for adults also must submit fingerprints. Minor misdemeanors slip through the cracks of states' recording systems.

Other than the use of fingerprints, today the FBI also uses latent and palm prints, facial recognition, and Combined DNA Index System to

to increase the range and quality of our biometric identification capabilities, including these three initiatives

Global Collections Program

Through the Global Collections Program, we foster national and international relationships related to biometrics in support of counterterrorism and other law enforcement efforts. Our initiatives include:

- Foreign Fingerprint Exchange
- Quick Capture Platform
- Flyaway Program

Private and Public Use of Criminal Records

In addition to law-enforcement, court, and corrections use of criminal records, private citizens increasingly seek access to criminal records. Employers must know whether they are hiring individuals with criminal histories that raise serious concern about their fitness to deal with vulnerable populations in day-care centers, schools, summer camps, and nursing homes.

If an employer fails to do a background check and hires an employee whose record would have indicated that he or she posed a potential threat, the employer can be sued for negligent hire. Judgments now average more than $1 million per case. Specialized search firms have proliferated to meet employer needs to learn of potential employees' criminal histories and other potentially damaging background information. Potential employees must often sign a consent form agreeing to a criminal record check or forfeit further consideration for employment even in low-level jobs.

Law-enforcement agencies use criminal records to track offenders over time. While juvenile records were once sealed when juvenile offenders became adults, many states now make them available to courts sentencing former juvenile felons for adult crimes.

Prosecutors and courts use criminal records in determining how serious punishment should be for particular crimes. In some states, first-time offenders may be granted a diversion that keeps them out of the criminal justice system if they accept responsibility for their offenses and honor restitution and other conditions imposed on them. The successful completion of diversion leaves persons with no formal criminal record, although prosecutors have access to records that indicate who has been granted diversions. Judges in many states use mandated sentencing guidelines that impose sentences for specific offenses based on the severity of the offense and individuals' prior criminal records. Judges must justify departures from a recommended sentencing range.

Coping with a Criminal Record

Former offenders find themselves severely handicapped by their criminal records. In addition to losing voting rights and the right to bear arms, those with felony convictions are barred from obtaining many occupational and professional licenses in most states. Sometimes criminal background checks are required for health care workers who deal directly with patients, and some states have passed laws that revoke the teaching certificates of public school teachers with felony records. It might also effect the application to immigrate to a new country, school admittance, adopting children or applying for a visa or passport. Some states have a formal process called "expungement," through which persons who can demonstrate that they have been rehabilitated can have convictions for most crimes removed from their records. Expunged records are not totally destroyed, however. In addition, expunged records can be reopened if further offenses are committed.

In 2015, the Record Expungement Designed to Enhance Employment Act, 2015 (REDEEM Act) was introduced to amend the deferral criminal code and thereby provide a process for the sealing/expungement of records that relate to nonviolent criminal or juvenile offences.

Susan A. Stussy
Updated by Tania Sebastian

Further Reading

Bureau of Justice Statistics. *Improving Criminal History Records for Background Checks.* Washington, D.C.: U.S. Department of Justice, 2004-06.

Niam, Edward, Jr. "Do You Know Who You Are Hiring?" *USA Today Magazine* 125 (July, 1997). Describes the legal problems that can confront employers who hire employees without thoroughly researching their pasts. If someone with a serious criminal record is hired and then commits a felony, the employer may be liable in tort for negligent hiring practices.

Sontag, Deborah. "U.S. Deports Felons but Can't Keep Them Out." *New York Times,* August 11, 1997. Reports on the efforts of the INS to exclude deported criminal aliens from the United States.

Vail, Kathleen. "Privacy Rights Versus Safety." *American School Board Journal* 184 (April, 1997). Reports on trends to open juvenile records of serious offenders to school superintendents and other educators.

Jacobs, James and Crepet, Tamara. "The Expanding Scope, Use and Availability of Criminal Records," *Legislation and Public Policy* (2008) 177.

Pager, Devah; Western, Bruce and Sugie, Naomi. "Sequencing Disadvantage: Barriers to Employment Facing Young Black and White Men with Criminal Records," 623(1) *Ann Am Acad Pol Soc Sci.* 195 (2009).

Kurlychek, Megan C.; Brame, Robert and Bushway, Shawn D. "Enduring Risk? Old Criminal Records and Predictions of Future Criminal Involvement," 53 *Crime & Delinquency* 64 (2007).

Jacobs, James B. "Mass Incarceration and the Proliferation of Criminal Records," 3 U. St. Thomas L.J. 387 (2006).

Mukamal, Debbie A. and Samuels, Paul N. "Statutory Limitations on Civil Rights of People with Criminal Records" 30 (5) *Fordham Urban Law Journal*, 1501 2002.

See also Booking; Computer information systems; Convictions; Criminal history record information; Criminals; Misdemeanors; Sentencing; Three-strikes laws.

Cybercrime investigation

Definition: Crimes that involve use of the Internet and computers

Business and financial crime; Computer crime; Technology; Vandalism

Significance: One of the major areas of computer crime, cybercrime is expanding rapidly, costing Americans hundreds of millions of dollars per year. Victims seldom see or know the perpetrators, and the criminal justice system is only beginning to address the problem directly.

The first useful electronic computer was built in 1946. By the mid-1960s, the term "computer crime" was in the general lexicon and in legal jargon by the 1970s. The term "cybercrime" entered general use with the development and expansion of the Internet. The two terms, cybercrime and computer crime, are often used interchangeably. This, however, is not precisely correct. A cybercrime is one that is committed using the Internet and, by definition, computers. Most observers would agree that a computer must be the tool of the attack, the object of the attack, or both. Computer crime, on the other hand, does not need the Internet to be committed.

Many crimes that have been around since before the development of computers can be committed today via computer. Computers, most of the time, add an increased shroud of anonymity to criminal acts. Crimes perpetrated over the Internet can be committed from almost any place on the planet.

Types of Cybercrime

When thinking of cybercrime, most people think of releasing so-called viruses, trojans, worms, and denial-of-service attacks. Other cybercrime includes snooping, computer hacking and cracking, spoofing, and various forms of theft and fraud. Stalking takes place on the Internet, and Internet pornography is abundant. Finally, organized crime and terrorists are using the Internet. The following discussion briefly covers prominent types of criminal activity on the Internet.

Computer viruses of many kinds have been developed, Each is able to replicate itself and to become part of another file; this is how viruses spread. Not every virus does damage, but every virus is potentially dangerous. Trojans differ from viruses in two important ways: They do not replicate themselves, and they can stand alone as files. Trojans are disguised as files that users want, such as music files, video files, games, or other software. Once inside victims' computer systems, trojans are free to release the hidden programs for which they are designed. These can be anything from harmless pranks to outright destruction of computer hard drives.

Worms spread copies or segments of themselves to other computers, usually via electronic mail. Worms differ from viruses because they do not need to attach to other files. Worms occupy increasing amounts of system resources, eventually bringing down the system. The first worm program was released in 1988. Its spread across the United States shut down a significant part of the Internet.

Computer hacking is a cybercrime. (By James Morris, via Wikimedia Commons)

A denial-of-service attack makes the computer service unavailable to authorized users. The attack hogs resources or damages resources to the extent that they cannot be used.

Web-jacking occurs when someone takes control of a site and either changes it or otherwise manipulates it. Cases have occurred in which sites have been vandalized, instructions have been altered, and other types of changes have been made.

Logic bombs are dormant until triggered by some specific logical event. This event might be a specific date and time, the removal of a person's name from the system, or some other specific event. Then the bomb delivers its payload, which can be very destructive within the computer system.

Spoofing occurs when an Internet user is redirected from a legitimate Web site to a fake site set up to look like the original. This is done to get the victim to give personal information to the "company" when transacting business.

Snooping, hacking, and cracking are all forms of unauthorized intrusion into computer systems. Snoopers are usually just curious people who enter a system to browse around. Hackers are persons with varying degrees of expertise who break into computer systems for many reasons. The challenge may merely be to see if they can do it, or it may be for more sinister reasons, such as stealing information or vandalizing the computer or Web site. Hackers also work for hire. Some consider themselves to be advanced and elegant programmers, and they consider the term "hacker" a badge of honor. These people think that hackers who ply their trade for nefarious purposes should be called "crackers," the type of hacker who should be viewed with contempt. Crackers communicate with one another online, on Web-based bulletin boards or private electronic mail lists. Sometimes crackers form groups with strange names like the Legion of Doom or the Chaos Computer Club and seek out more and more challenging exploits for their computer expertise. In 1995, the Department of Defense was subjected to more than 250,000 attacks by hackers and crackers.

Personal Crimes

A variety of thefts and fraud can take place online. The most damaging type of theft is identity theft. Hackers and crackers look for Social Security numbers and other types of personal information. Corporate and government databases are the largest sources of this kind of data. Illegal use of the victim's Social Security number, for example, can enable a criminal to borrow money, even qualify for mortgage loans, under the victim's name. Purchases of all kinds can be made, with victims unaware of it until they apply for a loan or credit card, or until they check their credit reports. It can take months, or even years, to get credit issues arising from identity theft resolved.

Fraud can take many forms, old and new. The Nigerian letter scam, formerly perpetuated by postal mail, is an example. In it, electronic mail appears in the victims' in-boxes offering to transfer large sums of money to the victims' banks if they will provide their account numbers so that the transfer can take place. Victims are offered a percentage for their cooperation. More recent examples include investment schemes and lottery or inheritance scams.

It is possible to gamble online. Players buy "chips" using a credit card, can play any game in the "house," and bet as much money as they want. Where gambling is illegal, such online gambling is illegal, too. The games may be rigged against the players. Also, some online gambling is used for money laundering.

Cyberstalking involves sending harassing or threatening electronic mail to a specific individual repeatedly and over time. It may also include visiting chat rooms frequented by victims and harassing them there. Usually, women are the victims of stalking crimes. Children may also fall victim to cyberstalkers, especially if the perpetrators are pedophiles. As many as 200,000 people stalk someone each year.

Internet pornography is another new version of an old problem. Thousands of pornographic Web sites offer pictures and videos of all kinds to anyone who can find them. All Internet sites that offer pornographic material, whether on a subscription basis or for free, are supposed to have a warning about the contents that instructs minors to exit the site. The most serious problems associated with pornography are in the area of child pornography. Child pornography can be encrypted (hidden) on computers and exchanged. In 2003, authorities in Europe and the United States uncovered an international child pornography ring leading to the arrest of hundreds of defendants.

Organized crime and terrorists also use the Internet, mainly for money laundering and transfers. The written text is encrypted to hide its meaning before it is sent over the Internet. A process called steganography hides graphic images and sends them undetected over the Internet. Gangsters operate gambling sites online as well as other illegal enterprises. Terrorists operate Web sites that incorporate elaborate symbols to deliver hidden messages. They also use the sites as recruitment tools and propaganda dissemination vehicles.

Prevalence

In 2004, a survey by the Gartner research group indicated that 1.98 million people in the United States had been victimized for $2.4 billion in checking account fraud. The same report estimates that more than fifty-seven million American Internet users received electronic mail phishing for personal information, and nearly two million people had been tricked into sending their personal data to scammers.

Criminal justice professor Marjie Britz estimated that "the vast majority of Fortune 500 companies have been electronically compromised to the tune of at least $10 billion/year." If less than 20 percent of corporate crime is reported, the number of companies and their losses could be far higher.

Internet "baby-sitter" software has been developed for use by parents to safeguard their children from deleterious Internet material and chat rooms, but it is no substitute for careful monitoring of children's online activity.

Internet crime continues to expand, and criminals find new ways to victimize people. Major companies have been founded on virus-scanning technology. Many other private companies have been formed to investigate cybercrime.

Investigation

At issue in investigating cybercrime effectively are training enough officers to conduct investigations, developing sufficient case law and knowledge among prosecutors to prosecute criminals, and establishing effective punishments to deter cybercriminals and effectively protect the private and public sectors of American society.

Since the mid-1960s, the Federal Bureau of Investigation (FBI) has effectively promoted crimefighting through the use of task forces. These have been used to fight organized crime, distribution of drugs and guns, and many other crime problems. In 1996, the FBI formed the Computer Investigations and Infrastructure Threat Assessment Center (CITAC) to coordinate computer crime initiatives. When it comes to cybercrime, the FBI continues to coordinate task forces but also offers investigative help and support, training, grants and other assistance to state and local agencies as they try to handle the growing problem.

Even though computer crime and cybercrime have been in the public consciousness since the late 1980s, the majority of police departments, and perhaps the majority of states' law-enforcement agencies, do not have well-trained, well-equipped computer crime investigation units. A few large cities, such as New York, Washington, D.C., and San Francisco, have had computer crime units since the late 1980s. These units were formed with the help of the FBI. In 2004, however, only large and well-funded departments had effective cybercrime investigative capabilities. Mid-sized and small cities had no capability for such investigations. Larger cities like the ones mentioned above and regional cooperative ventures, like the Sacramento Valley High-Tech Crimes Task Force, emerged as leaders in the field.

The Institute for Security Technology Studies at Dartmouth College convened a meeting of leading national and state agencies in 2003 to draft a coordinated research and development agenda for fighting cybercrime. Training and research were slowly being implemented to equip investigators with the necessary expertise to investigate cybercrime. The FBI and some of the larger, better-funded law-enforcement agencies offered training opportunities in the field of cybercrime. A few colleges and universities offered classes in the subject. A growing literature on cybercrime and investigations was emerging. Nevertheless, most investigation was still carried out by private sector employees of computer firms and by companies created to conduct cyber-investigations.

Most police agencies do not have the necessary resources to provide adequate training for their officers and investigators. The ability to conduct investigations of cybercrime includes not only all the training to investigate normal street crime but also a thorough knowledge of computer systems, electronic evidence collection, preservation and analysis techniques, both logical and physical analysis, and forensic analysis techniques. Most departments that do any cyber-investigation are fortunate enough to have staff members who had learned about computers before they arrived. Others have learned on the job. Organized training is still emerging and is still expensive.

Prosecution

When criminal activity on the Internet was first being recognized, it was not taken very seriously by law-enforcement agencies. Women who complained of being harassed or stalked were told to avoid particular chat rooms or to delete electronic mail messages from the harassers. Victims of fraud were told that nothing could be done to recover their money. Hackers were considered to be harmless curiosities. As the phenomenon of cybercrime gradually came to be understood, law-enforcement personnel realized the criminal justice field would be changed forever.

One of the problems with successfully prosecuting cybercrime is that of establishing jurisdiction. At issue is who should have jurisdiction when an offense occurs. Considering that the victim and the offender may be thousands of miles apart, the answer to this question has been difficult. Some have expressed the idea that cyberspace should be designated a separate and unique jurisdiction. A consensus has yet to emerge. However, the number of cases that have been tried has rapidly expanded, so the issue of jurisdiction is expected to become clearer.

Perhaps the most important computer crime statute, the Computer Fraud and Abuse Act of 1984, was the first major piece of legislation to govern cyberspace. Since its passage, a number of other laws have been enacted to address computer crime. Because there are a large number of types of such crimes, many laws are necessary. Important on the list are the Electronic Privacy Act of 1986, the Computer Abuse Amendments Act of 1994, the Electronic Espionage Act of 1996, the Electronic Theft Act of 1997, and the Digital Theft Deterrence and Copyright Damages Improvement Act of 1999.

On January 1, 2004, Congress passed a new federal antispam law in response to dramatically increasing levels of spam arriving in citizens' electronic mail in-boxes. The FBI, in cooperation with the Direct Marketing Association, launched an antispam initiative called Operation Slam-Spam. As of May, 2004, this operation had turned fifty cases over to state and federal prosecutors. In a similar case from 2003, New York State prosecutors sent Howard Carmack to prison for three-and-a-half years for sending 825 million junk electronic messages from his home. Big Internet providers have been involved in suing spammers for several years. Now federal and state agencies are also getting involved.

Along with an expanding amount of federal law to curtail cybercrime, states also have an expanding collection of statutes to deal with the issue. Among the topics covered under these laws are: computer tampering, which includes modification to programs or to the way a network or networked computer operates; computer trespassing, or unauthorized access to computer systems; disruption of computer services statutes, which seek to protect the integrity of Internet service providers; computer fraud statutes, which include all forms of fraudulent activity but specifically cover cases in which a computer is used to conduct the activity; spam-related statutes, which generally focus on using a network to falsify the header information on mass electronic mail; unlawful use of encryption statutes, which are aimed at using this technology to hide information passed between cybercriminals and increasingly among terrorists and drug traffickers.

Cyber-stalking laws make it illegal to use the Internet to harass or threaten individuals, especially for purposes of extorting money. Other broad categories of crime that have had to be covered in the cybercrime rubric include money laundering and monetary transactions, racketeering, economic espionage, theft of trade secrets, swindles, embezzlement, gambling, pornography, stalking, and terrorism.

Punishment

Early computer criminals were not punished very severely. There was little specific case law under which to punish their crimes, and most cases were novelties. When Robert Morris was convicted for releasing the first worm in 1988, the Cornell University graduate student was dismissed from school, fined $10,000 and placed on three years' probation. This was despite the fact that the worm had spread to six thousand computers and clogged both government and university systems at an estimated $100 million in damages. In 1992, Kevin Poulsen, who was wanted for other Internet crimes, rigged the phone system of a radio station in order to win a contest fraudulently. He spent five years in prison for computer and wire fraud. In 1994, Vladimir Levin was sentenced to three years in prison for stealing $10 million from Citibank.

The courts are beginning to realize that cybercrimes are at least as bad as any white-collar crimes and that they deserve to be punished accordingly. In early 2005, a federal court found nineteen-year-old Minnesota resident Jeffrey Lee Parsons guilty of "intentionally causing or attempting to cause damage to a computer." In August, 2003, Parsons had released onto the Internet a worm that affected more than seven thousand computers. Conviction for this crime can carry sentences of up to ten years in prison and $250,000 in fines, but a federal judge sentenced Parsons to the minimum term of eighteen months in prison.

According to a 2015 report by the Ponemon Institute, cybercrime costs the average American business $15 million per year, with the financial services and energy sectors being the hardest hit. Another study by Juniper Research found that the overall annual cost of cybercrime had quadrupled between 2013 and 2015 and estimated that this cost would reach $2.1 trillion by 2019. The criminal justice system is just beginning to address the issue effectively but is constantly having to catch up to the challenges posed by cybercriminals.

Donald R. Dixon

Further Reading

2015 Cost of Cyber Crime Study: Global. Traverse City: Ponemon Inst., 2015. PDF file.
Baase, Sara. *A Gift of Fire: Social, Legal, and Ethical Issues for Computers and the Internet.* 2nd ed. Upper Saddle River: Prentice-Hall, 2003. Print.
Clifford, Ralph D, ed. *Cybercrime: The Investigation, Prosecution, and Defense of a Computer-Related Crime.* Durham: Carolina Academic, 2001. Print.
Grabosky, Peter. *Cybercrime.* New York: Oxford UP, 2015. Print.
Morgan, Steve. "Cyber Crime Costs Projected To Reach $2 Trillion by 2019." *Forbes.* Forbes Media, 17 Jan. 2016. Web. 25 May 2016.
Shinder, D. L., and Ed Tittle. *Scene of the Cybercrime: Computer Forensics Handbook.* Rockland, Mass.: Syngress, 2002. Chapter 2 contains a brief history of cybercrime.
Stephenson, Peter. *Investigating Computer-Related Crime.* Boca Raton, Fla.: CRC Press, 2000. Moderately technical discussion covering types of computer crimes, their impacts, investigations, and different forensic technologies available.

See also Computer forensics; Consumer fraud; Fraud; Identity theft; Pornography and obscenity; Stalking; Telephone fraud; Terrorism; Theft; Trespass; White-collar crime.

DNA testing

Definition: Comparison of DNA samples from body tissues and fluids to identify people
DNA; Evidence and forensics
Significance: A new and highly accurate way to identify people and match evidence with victims and suspects,

DNA testing is revolutionizing investigative techniques in law enforcement and forcing major reconsiderations of the possibilities of convicting the innocent, particularly in capital cases.

DNA stands for deoxyribonucleic acid, the basic building blocks of biological genes. Because every human being has a unique pattern of genetic material, every human being has a pattern of DNA molecules that is like that of no other human being. For this reason, DNA taken from samples of human body tissues and fluids can be used to determine very accurately from what individual person those tissues and fluids come.

Criminal justice agencies have long sought better methods of linking suspects with particular crime scenes, especially when eyewitnesses to crimes are not available. Early methods of establishing such links included fingerprint analysis, blood-typing, and analyses of such trace evidence as cloth fibers and hair. Fingerprint evidence has the potential of establishing positive identifications; however, good fingerprint evidence is often difficult to obtain at crime scenes. Materials such as cloth fibers, human hairs, and blood samples can be helpful but can rarely be used to establish definitive links to any one suspect. In contrast, good DNA evidence not only is generally more readily obtainable, it is more reliable because no two human beings have exactly the same DNA patterns.

Since the mid-1980s, DNA testing has been used as a valuable tool for solving crimes. Criminalists can, for example, tell whether a single human hair or tiny blood spatter found on a victim comes from the victim or from someone else. Moreover, if the police have a suspect in the case, criminalists can determine whether the hair or blood comes from that suspect. The certainty with which tiny quantities of human tissue and fluids can be matched to criminal suspects makes it easier for prosecutors to secure convictions and lessens the chances of false convictions.

History of DNA Testing

DNA was first discovered in 1868, but it was not until 1953 that scientists discovered its physical structure. For this discovery, the American scientist James Watson and the British scientists Francis Crick and Maurice Hugh Frederick Wilkins shared a Nobel Prize in 1962.

Most DNA is identical in all humans, and much of it even matches the DNA of other animals. However, in 1983, British biochemist Alec Jeffreys discovered that certain portions of the DNA sequence vary from individual to individual. These sequences were soon dubbed

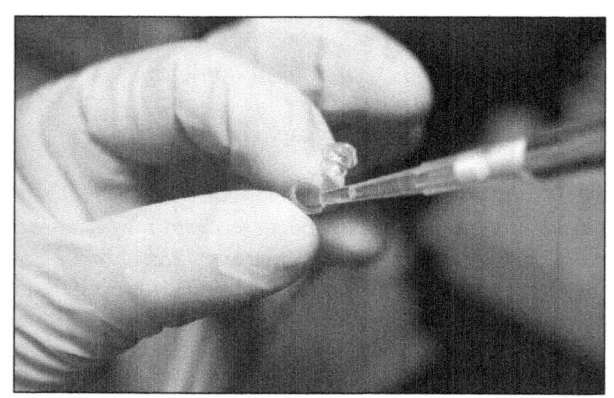

NHGRI researcher uses a pipette to remove DNA from a micro test tube. (Public domain, via Wikimedia Commons)

"DNA fingerprints," because they—like the patterns of ridges on human fingertips—were thought to be unique to individual human beings. Jeffreys and his colleagues created methods of probing DNA samples to examine the DNA fingerprints, a process that became known as DNA profiling.

Criminal justice agencies quickly realized the potential of DNA profiling as a tool for solving crimes. In 1985, Jeffreys used his techniques to help British government authorities determine whether a Ghanaian boy who wanted to come to England from West Africa to be reunited with his mother was indeed the woman's son. Jeffreys's DNA analysis proved that he was. One year later, Jeffreys helped police in Leicestershire, England, solve cases involving the rape and murder of two fifteen-year-old girls. Using traces of semen found on the victims, Jeffreys determined that both girls had been attacked by the same man. Moreover, those samples established that a suspect whom police were holding in custody could not have been the girls' assailant. After DNA samples were collected from many local men, Jeffreys was eventually able to connect a local resident to the murders.

DNA Testing Techniques

DNA is present in every part of the human body that contains nucleic cells. These include body tissues and such fluids as blood, sweat, semen, and urine. DNA cannot be collected from strands of hair that are cut, but it can be extracted from the roots and follicles of hairs that are pulled from a body or shed naturally. Material in the follicles contains DNA, as do flakes of dandruff and other minute fragments of skin that are naturally shed.

DNA typing was originally done through a process known as RFLP—which is short for "restriction fragment length polymorphisms." The process used enzymes in a fashion much like chemical scissors to cut out portions of a DNA sample. Those portions were then subjected to various electrical and chemical processes that allowed their structures to be seen. Scientists then compared the patterns observed in those portions with patterns in samples taken from materials found at crime scenes.

During criminal investigations, portions from several different sites on a DNA strand are compared. If one particular person is the source of all the samples, the patterns will match on all sites. The chance of samples from two different persons matching on all sites is minuscule.

During the mid-1990s, a new testing technique was invented: PCR, or polymerase chain reaction. Using the new PCR technique, extremely minute amounts of DNA are chemically replicated until there is a quantity large enough to analyze. Because less than one-billionth part of one gram of DNA material is sufficient for PCR analysis, it can be used to analyze DNA taken from samples as minute as the dried saliva found on cigarette butts and envelope flaps.

As of 2016, the latest form of DNA testing technology in use was called short tandem repeat (STR) analysis. Because of the types of DNA strands that STR examines, STR can be used on samples that have reached advanced states of decomposition. PCR and STR techniques are now used in combination: PCR is used to replicate DNA to enlarge the samples, which STR is then used to analyze. As few as nine human cells may be all that is needed to obtain sufficient DNA for STR analysis.

In the criminal justice system, thirteen different sites along the DNA strand are used for analysis. The chance of the DNA of any two individuals being identical in all thirteen sites is less than one in 575 trillion. Since the latter figure is roughly 40 million times greater than the number of all the human beings who have lived, it is clear that DNA testing offers an exceptionally powerful method of identifying and exonerating criminal suspects.

A final type of DNA testing that is sometimes used is mitochondrial DNA analysis, or mtDNA. Mitochondrial DNA is found outside cell nuclei, and exists in greater quantities than nuclear DNA. MtDNA testing can be done on samples in which nuclear DNA is too degraded to analyze, or on samples in which nuclear DNA is absent altogether, such as hair shafts. However, mtDNA analysis is costly and more difficult to do, and few labs are able to perform it. Moreover, all human beings have mtDNA that is identical to that of their mothers. Thus, because mtDNA patterns are not unique to each individual, mtDNA analysis is limited in its usefulness as a tool for identifying suspects.

CODIS

The Federal Bureau of Investigation (FBI) has created a computer database program called CODIS, an acronym for "Combined DNA Index System." Data from DNA evidence from unsolved crimes and from certain convicted offenders are entered into CODIS by local, state, and federal law-enforcement agencies. DNA patterns from different unsolved crimes and from known offenders can now be easily compared. In this regard, CODIS is similar to AFIS, the FBI's Automated Fingerprint Identification System. By early 2005, CODIS had produced nearly 20,000 DNA matches, or "hits," that helped solve many cold cases.

The CODIS system is not without critics. Some people have argued that mandated collection of DNA samples invades citizens' privacy. A major part of this objection is the fact that DNA, unlike fingerprints, contains information about its owners' physical, behavioral, and health characteristics. Critics are concerned about the ways such personal information might ultimately be used by the government. Some people also are concerned that in some states, such as California, DNA information is collected not only from convicted felons but also from some adults and juveniles who are simply charged with certain crimes.

The Challenges of DNA Testing

In addition to legal and ethical disputes, DNA testing also faces practical challenges. The first of these is the great care that must be used in collecting, storing, and analyzing of DNA evidence. With improper handling, DNA evidence can be contaminated easily. There are methods of detecting contamination during analysis; however, contamination makes analyses more difficult and less certain. There have also been cases in which lab employees have engaged in sloppy and improper techniques of handling and analyzing DNA that have resulted in incorrect data.

A second major challenge of DNA analysis is the time and expertise that it requires. Steadily improving technology has simplified and speeded up testing processes. Nonetheless, the demand for DNA analyses far outstrips the equipment and trained personnel of the crime labs that perform the analyses. Most crime labs have long backlogs in their work, and law-enforcement agencies may have to wait several months before they receive the results of the analyses they request. To complicate matters, the DNA evidence awaiting testing is often stored, not at crime labs, but rather at the law-enforcement agencies, which typically lack the facilities for proper storage. This fact increases the chance of evidence becoming contaminated or degraded.

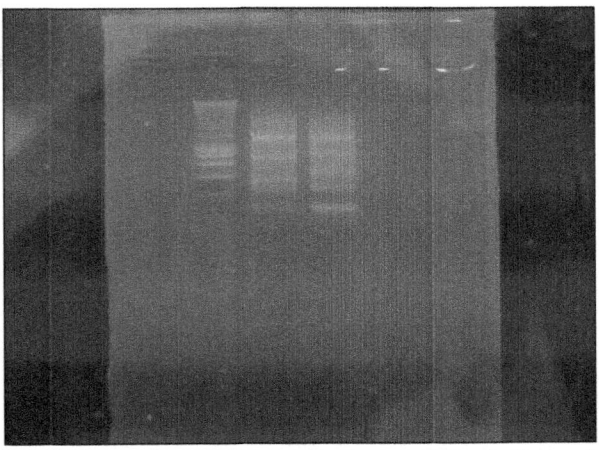

A DNA agarose gel on a UV lightbox. (By Simon, via Wikimedia Commons)

Other Uses for DNA Testing

In addition to matching suspects to crime scenes, DNA testing has found other important uses in the legal system. As often as it is used to identify offenders, it is used at least equally often to prove that suspects have not committed crimes. In 1992, the Innocence Project was created at Yeshiva University's Benjamin N. Cardozo Law School in New York City. By 2016, the Innocence Project had used DNA testing to prove the innocence of 341 people who had been convicted of serious crimes. Under new laws, states must now allow certain convicted prisoners access to DNA testing if there is any chance that it might help prove their innocence.

DNA testing is also widely used to establish paternity; that is, to determine whether two particular people are blood relatives. An instance of paternity testing that captured world headlines occurred after Asia's devastating tsunami in late 2004. In Sri Lanka, it was reported that nine different families claimed the same four-month-old infant who was found in the debris of the tsunami. DNA testing was used to identify his actual parents, with whom he was reunited. During large-scale disasters such as the Asian tsunami and the September 11, 2001, destruction of New York City's World Trade Center, DNA testing has been used to identify human remains. DNA evidence can also be used to identify human remains in missing persons cases or whenever human remains are discovered.

Phyllis B. Gerstenfeld

Further Reading

Balding, David J., and Christopher D. Steele. *Weight-of-Evidence for Forensic DNA Profiles*. 2nd ed. Hoboken: Wiley, 2015. Print.

"DNA Evidence: What Law Enforcement Officers Should Know." *National Institute of Justice Journal* 249 (2003): 10-15. Print.

Fridell, R. *DNA Fingerprinting: The Ultimate Identity*. London: Franklin Watts, 2001. Print.

Makin, David R. *DNA and Property Crime Scene Investigation: Forensic Evidence and Law Enforcement*. New York: Routledge, 2015. Print.

National Institute of Justice. *Using DNA to Solve Cold Cases*. Washington, D.C.: U.S. Department of Justice, 2002. Print.

Sallavaci, Oriola. *The Impact of Scientific Evidence on the Criminal Trial: The Case of DNA Evidence*. New York: Routledge, 2014. Print.

Scheck, B., P. Neufeld, and J. Dwyer. *Actual Innocence: Five Days to Execution, and Other Dispatches from the Wrongly Convicted*. New York: Doubleday, 2000. Print.

Shaer, Matthew. "The False Promise of DNA Testing." *Atlantic*. Atlantic Monthly Group, 17 May 2016. Web. 26 May 2016.

Wambaugh, J. *The Blooding*. New York: Bantam, 1989. Print.

See also Bloodstains; Cold cases; Crime labs; Eyewitness testimony; False convictions; Forensics; Latent evidence; Toxicology; Trace evidence; Technology's transformative effect.

Document analysis

Definition: Forensic techniques used to ascertain the authenticity of documents

Business and financial Crime; Evidence and forensics

Significance: Determining the authenticity of documents is important in the fields of both criminal law and civil law. Modern document analysis now encompasses computer documents, but even in the twenty-first century's increasingly paperless world, people and institutions continue to rely heavily on handwritten and printed documents, and the need for trained document analysts is continuing to grow.

Document analysis is a diversified area of forensics that encompasses a wide spectrum of methods of investigation. In trying to determine whether documents are legitimate, examiners employ such techniques as handwriting and signature identification; typewriter, computer, fax, and copier identification; pencil lead and ink examinations; and paper analysis. The field was pioneered by Albert S. Osborn, whose 1910 book, *Questioned Documents*, was the first major work in the field; it is still considered an important and useful work.

Handwriting and signature identification is used in the examination of such documents as letters, checks, wills, ransom notes, and suicide notes. During the Lindbergh baby kidnapping and murder trial of 1935, Osborn testified that the writing on the ransom notes was consistent with the handwriting of the defendant Bruno Hauptmann, who was convicted and later executed.

Handwriting and Signature Identification

Generally, the genuineness of any writing is established by comparing the writing on suspect documents with handwriting samples known to have been written by the purported signers of the suspect documents. Examiners prefer to have a variety of authentic writing samples to use for comparisons. Since the handwriting of individual writers tends to vary with the circumstances in which they are writing, document examiners need authentic samples that have been written under a variety of circumstances.

A skilled forger may succeed in faithfully copying a number of aspects of another person's handwriting; however, there are always noticeable differences between authentic and forged writing specimens. For example, forgeries often differ from authentic specimens in the speed with which they are written and the pressure that the forgers apply to their writing instruments. Even when there is a successful mimicry of speed and pressure, it is almost impossible for forgers to remove all traces of the peculiarities of their own writing from their forgeries.

Typed, Printed, and Copied Documents

Document examiners must sometimes question whether suspect documents originated from particular machines. Unlike human handwriting, which has numerous individual characteristics, brand-new printing devices are generally very much alike and possess only the class characteristics that make new machines of the same models produce nearly identical documents. However, after machines are used repeatedly, they begin to develop individual characteristics, the same way that shoes develop individual characteristics with increased wear. Examiners focus on these individual differences.

Manually powered typewriters were prone to having some letter keys strike their ribbons and paper with less pressure than others, and individual typists using the same machine would not all use the same force on the same keys. Photocopying machines often have imperfections in their glass plates or distribute their toner powder in ways that make them unique. All fax transmissions received by a single machine have unique identifying lines. Computer printers also develop their own individual characteristics over time.

To improve their ability to make correct identifications of typed, printed, and duplicated documents, examiners like to work with at least ten documents from each machine they examine. It is also helpful to obtain the examples as soon as possible after the suspect documents are crated, as the individual characteristics of the machines continue to change over time.

Pencil Lead, Ink, and Paper Analysis

Paper documents can be altered in many ways. They may be erased or obliterated. They may also be overwritten. Attempts may be made to completely destroy documents by burning. Document examiners are often faced the challenge of enhancing or reconstructing writing on documents. Using different light sources is often helpful in this type of work. Unless the inks used to alter documents are the same as the inks originally used on them, they will reveal different chemical and light-reflecting properties to examiners. Document reconstruction and enhancement can be done using infrared photography or digital-image processing.

Inks are especially important to identify when the ages of documents and signatures are in question. Inks are also examined when it appears that something on a document has been altered by simply writing over the document's original text. For example, forgers may simply add zeros to the dollar amounts written on checks. Ink analysis can also help determine the age of a document or the writing on it. Very old inks are easy to spot because of their chemical compositions, as the manufacture of ink products changed dramatically after 1950. Examiners must also be familiar with computer inks. The chemical compositions of inks can be revealed through the use of thin-layer chromatography.

Papers are analyzed in a variety of ways by examiners, who pay particular attention to the physical characteristics of paper. Watermarks, which are regularly used in U.S. currency, can be examined, and analyses can be conducted on the fibers, chemicals, and trace elements that make up individual papers. Examiners must also be familiar with the types of papers used by computer printers, fax machines, and copiers, as well as standard writing and typing papers.

Ayn Embar-Seddon and Allan D. Pass

Further Reading

Allen, Michael. *Foundations of Forensic Document Analysis: Theory and Practice*. Hoboken: Wiley Blackwell, 2016. Print.

Dines, Jess E. *Document Examiner Textbook*. Irvine: Pantex International, 1998. Print.

Ellen, David. *The Scientific Examination of Documents: Methods and Techniques*. 3rd ed. Boca Raton: CRC, 2006. Print.

Herbertson, Gary. *Document Examination on the Computer: A Guide for Forensic Document Examiners*. Berkeley: Wideline, 2002. Print.

Slyter, Steven A. *Forensic Signature Examination*. Springfield: C. C. Thomas, 1996. Print.

See also Circumstantial evidence; Crime labs; Criminology; Fingerprint identification; Forensics; Forgery; Latent evidence; Trace evidence; Technology's transformative effect.

Electronic surveillance

Definition: Investigative technique used to monitor telephone conversations, electronic mail, pagers, wireless phones, computers, and other electronic devices

Investigation; Privacy; Technology

Significance: Electronic surveillance significantly increases the ability of law-enforcement officers to conduct investigations of nontraditional or difficult-to-observe criminal targets.

Electronic surveillance is a tool utilized by law-enforcement agencies in the course of ongoing criminal investigations. Federal agencies have traditionally had broad legal powers to monitor telephone conversations, electronic mail, pagers, wireless phones, computers, and all other electronic devices. These powers were increased significantly after passage of the USA Patriot Act in 2001.

Popularly referred to as "tapping" in general discourse, electronic surveillance is governed by two statutes: the Federal Wiretap Act and the Foreign Intelligence Surveillance Act (FISA). The former, sometimes referred to as Title III, was initially passed in 1968 and expanded in 1986. It set procedures for court authorization of real-time surveillance in criminal investigations of all electronic communications, including voice, electronic mail, fax, and Internet.

Typically, before wiretaps can commence, court orders issued by judges must be obtained by the agencies requesting the surveillance. The government is responsible for providing the judges with affidavits detailing probable cause that crimes have been, are being, or are about to be committed. Wiretaps may be ordered for several activities, including but not limited to drug trafficking, child pornography, and terrorist activities. The Patriot Act expanded the list of criminal statutes for which wiretaps can be ordered. Wiretaps are used to prevent, as well as pun-

The U.S. Patriot Act permits all phone calls to be recorded without a warrant or notification. (By david drexler, via Wikimedia Commons)

The Patriot Act and Electronic Surveillance

A major change introduced by the Patriot Act was to allow prosecutors to use FISA for the purposes of gathering evidence in criminal investigations of national security crimes. There are also no legislative limits on electronic observation conducted overseas, as neither Title III nor FISA has any application to intelligence collection activities outside the United States.

The most common form of electronic surveillance technology used in the United States is the pen register and trap-and-trace technology. Pen registers record and decode all numbers dialed by electronic devices such as telephones, while trap-and-traces capture the originating sources of incoming calls. Together, these are commonly referred to in law-enforcement jargon as dialed number recorders, or DNR. Standards governing the use of these devices are derived from the 1986 Electronic Communications Privacy Act. The Patriot Act has also expanded permissible uses of traditional pen register and trap-and-trace devices so that they may be used to monitor not only telephonic communications, but also Internet communications.

Another form of electronic surveillance is the "roving tap." Court orders permitting roving taps do not require specific telephone lines or electronic mail accounts to be named; they allow the tapping of any phone line, cell phone, or Internet account that the targeted suspects use. Unlike the traditional trap-and-trace and pen register, which numbers thousands of uses each year, roving taps are relatively rare with only six such taps approved during all of 2003.

Although much of the Patriot Act was reauthorized when the USA Freedom Act was enacted in 2015, the Freedom Act bans the bulk collection of US phone re-

ish crimes, as the government can set up wiretaps in advance of crimes being executed. In such instances, the wiretaps are used to identify planning and conspiratorial activities related to criminal acts. Government requests for wiretaps are rarely denied.

The Foreign Intelligence Surveillance Act of 1978 allows wiretapping of aliens and citizens in the United States. Again, probable cause must be provided suggesting that the targets of surveillance are members of foreign terrorist groups or are agents of foreign powers. For American citizens and aliens who are permanent residents of the United States, there must also be probable cause to believe that the persons targeted are engaged in activities that may involve criminal violations. Suspicion of possible illegal activity is not required, however, in cases involving aliens who are not permanent residents of the United States. For such persons, membership in terrorist organizations is enough to justify surveillance, even if the activities in which they engage on behalf of their organizations are legal.

President Bush signing the Patriot Act which has expanded the permissible uses of electronic surveillance. (Public domain, via Wikimedia Commons)

cords and Internet metadata, and places limits on how much and what kind of data the government can collect.

Holly E. Ventura

Further Reading

Adams, James A., and Daniel D. Blinka. *Electronic Surveillance: Commentaries and Statutes.* Notre Dame, Ind.: National Institute for Trial Advocacy, 2003.

McGrath, J. E. *Loving Big Brother: Performance, Privacy and Surveillance Space.* New York: Routledge, 2004.

Monmonier, M. S. *Spying with Maps: Surveillance Technologies and the Future of Privacy.* Chicago: University of Chicago Press, 2002.

Stevens, Gina Marie, and Charles Doyle. *Privacy: Wiretapping and Electronic Eavesdropping.* Huntington, N.Y.: Nova Science, 2002.

"USA Freedom Act: What's In, What's Out." *Washington Post.* Washington Post, 2 June 2015. Web. 26 May. 2016.

See also Community-based corrections; Computer crime; Espionage; House arrest; *Katz v. United States*; Mafia; Organized crime; Patriot Act; Privacy rights; Search and seizure; Stakeouts; Surveillance cameras; Telephone fraud; Technology's transformative effect.

Espionage

Definition: Attempting to secure secret information from a country or a company, using illegal or covert means

Computer crime; Espionage and sedition; Technology

Significance: Protecting data about the military and technological capabilities of the United States, and discovering the intentions and capabilities of enemies, are vital to defending the national security of the country.

Espionage, counterespionage, and secret political intervention overseas are distinct operations. One actively seeks to procure secret information, the second guards against procurement of secrets by enemies, and the third, comprising clandestine operations such as assassinations and sabotage, is actually a political-military intrusion. The three are often confused with one another, a tendency encouraged by the fact that organizations such as the Central Intelligence Agency (CIA) may be concerned with all three, seeking data in foreign countries, carrying out paramilitary operations overseas, and trying to prevent attacks on the United States.

Espionage conducted by the CIA and other American government agencies against foreign powers is not a crime in the United States. Spying, sabotage, and terrorist attacks directed against the United States or its citizens are punishable crimes that the Federal Bureau of Investigation (FBI) seeks to discover and prevent as part of its national policing activity.

History of the Crime

Espionage has a lengthy genealogy. The Bible (Numbers 13) records that Moses sent agents to spy on the land of Canaan. The ancient Greeks and Romans devised ciphers to protect their communications from hostile eyes. George Washington, as commander of the American army during the Revolutionary War, employed numerous spies to keep him informed of British actions. The capture of British major John André, by alert American militiamen, with the plan of West Point in his boot and the subsequent flight of General Benedict Arnold have passed into legend, with Arnold's name becoming a synonym for traitor.

Modern American espionage and counterespionage techniques and institutions came of age during and shortly after World War II. President Franklin D. Roosevelt used a variety of secret organizations, some of which reported directly to him. William J. Donovan, a personal representative of Roosevelt, went to England in 1940 to study British antisabotage techniques and evaluate the probabilities of that country's surviving German air attacks. Donovan went on to head the Office of Strategic Services (OSS), which carried out espionage and sabotage missions inside occupied Europe and Germany. The OSS served as model when the CIA was created in 1947.

The FBI identified several German spy networks in 1941, aided by an American citizen born in Germany who had been recruited by German military intelligence against his will. The FBI arrested and convicted thirty-three operatives, effectively shutting down most German covert activity in the United States. Two separate attempts to land German saboteurs from submarines in 1942 and 1945 ended with the swift capture of ten agents, the conviction of all, and the execution of eight. The FBI was less successful in detecting atomic espionage for the Soviet Union carried out by members and sympathizers of the American Communist Party, even though the FBI was convinced the party was controlled by Moscow and had planted informants within it.

The greatest intelligence successes of the World War II were those of US cryptanalysts who deciphered Japanese diplomatic and naval codes; their example would inspire the creation of the even more technologically adept National Security Agency in 1952.

Espionage in Fiction

The spy story has become a recognized literary genre, popular with readers and attractive to Hollywood, which regularly creates films based on successful novels. The characters rarely resemble real-life spies. The protagonist of one of the earliest spy novels, John Buchan's *The Thirty-nine Steps* (1915, adapted to the screen by Alfred Hitchcock in 1935), is an amateur who stumbles upon a scheme to provoke a European war, which he successfully prevents.

Other extremely popular spy stories are often unrealistic, catering to readers' fantasies. Jack Ryan singlehandedly foils a terrorist attack on a member of the British royal family and ends up as a guest in Buckingham Palace in Tom Clancy's *Patriot Games* (1987). Interestingly, Clancy's *Debt of Honor* (1994) eerily prefigured the September 11, 2001, terrorist attacks on the World Trade Center, with its climactic description of a jumbo jet crashing into the United States Capitol. In films based on Ian Fleming's James Bond novels, the spectacular special effects became more and more fantastic as the series progressed. In contrast, novelist John le Carré effectively employed verisimilitude to express his disdain and disgust with Cold War espionage practices.

Espionage in the Twentieth Century

During World War II, Soviet spies within the United States were motivated by ideology, many being Communist Party members. Disillusionment with communism as an economic system and revelations of the excesses of Stalinism ended the ideological inspiration. Spies caught during the Cold War working for the Soviet Union were primarily motivated by cash, not idealism.

The Walker family spy ring operated for sixteen years, receiving money from the Soviet Union without showing any interest in ideology. John Walker, Jr., a US Navy officer, began selling the Soviet Union cipher keys used by the Navy in 1968, as well as descriptions of cryptographic machines, enabling the Russians to decipher American messages using their own versions of the machines. When he retired from the Navy in 1976, Walker recruited his son, his older brother, and Walker's best friend to steal data on secret American electronic systems, which they did until the spy ring's members were arrested in 1985.

From 1985 to 1994, Aldrich Ames, a senior CIA officer, received more than $4 million from the Soviets for his services. He told the Russians of every active United States espionage and counterespionage operation involving the Soviet Union; the disclosures allowed the Russians to execute at least ten spies working for the United States. He revealed the names of American intelligence officers studying the Soviet Union and described techniques used by the CIA and FBI. By telling the Russians which areas the United States particularly wanted data regarding, Ames enabled them to offer false information that the CIA welcomed and presented to the president as fact.

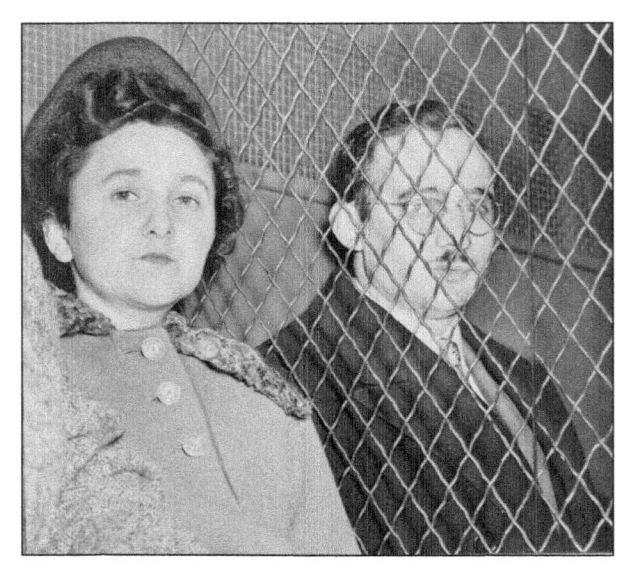

Julius and Ethel Rosenberg were found guilty of espionage. (Public domain, via Wikimedia Commons)

Robert Hanssen, an FBI agent who sold the Russians six thousand pages of secret FBI documents, claimed that he acted as a spy because of the psychological pleasure he felt in fooling his coworkers. However, he did not reject the $1.4 million dollars he was offered for his services from 1985 until he was finally apprehended in 2001.

Twenty-first Century Cases

The continued employment of Hanssen by the Russian successor organization to the Soviet spy agency testified to the reality that espionage against the American government did not cease with the demise of the Soviet Union and the end of the Cold War. Interest in acquiring military secrets and in penetrating the FBI and CIA continues. However, technological and economic espionage was of increasing importance in the last decades of the twentieth century and the beginning of the twenty-first.

Different countries used varying techniques in acquiring information. China focused on ethnic Chinese working for American companies and research institutes, appealing to pride in the resurgence of China to motivate the delivery of documents and data. Japan did not appear to have a government organization coordinating its economic espionage, but each company worked on its own to secure valuable information and patents from its competitors. France preferred using Cold War techniques, including bribery, wiretapping, thefts, and combing through trash. In May, 1991, employees of the French consul in Houston, Texas, were caught stealing garbage bags from behind the house of a technology industry executive. Russia still seemed most interested in military technology, but France, Israel, and Germany spread their efforts much wider. The International Business Machines company and Texas Instruments complained of attempts by foreign governments to steal their technology for the benefit of competitors. Corning found its fiber optics proprietary information under attack by France.

Foreign governments were not the only culprits. Domestic corporations employed espionage techniques against one another in the search for competitive advantage. A major scandal rocked the aerospace industry in July, 2003, when the U.S. Air Force discovered that Boeing Corporation had stolen thousands of documents from Lockheed Martin when the two companies competed for a rocket launch contract.

Corporate espionage cases rarely involve criminal proceedings. Many instances never become public knowledge; companies involved often prefer to suffer losses rather than admit to security failures that might adversely affect their reputations and stock prices. If diplomats are implicated, the normal procedure is simply to declare the offenders *personae non gratae* and expel them. The Boeing-Lockheed affair was unique in that two accused employees were actually indicted under the 1996 Economic Espionage Act and faced trial for theft of trade secrets. The Air Force punished Boeing by withdrawing contracts worth $1 billion and awarding them to Lockheed. However, Boeing's disgrace did not keep it from winning an even more valuable bid to build air tankers.

Counterespionage within the United States is formally part of the internal police work of the FBI, with the CIA responsible for overseas activity. Detection of espionage is difficult. Investigations can run for years without uncovering definitive answers, and success can hinge on accidental discovery of long-running penetrations of American security. Prosecution of spies sometimes becomes impossible, as the display of convincing evidence in open court conflicts with the need to avoid revealing sensitive information. Electronic counterespionage has become increasingly useful in the struggle against terrorism.

Investigation

The successful Soviet penetration of American atomic bomb research was not discovered until after the war. Information about Soviet spies came from the defection in 1945 of Igor Gouzenko, a Soviet consular official in Canada, from the testimony of Elizabeth Bentley and Whittaker Chambers in 1946 and from the partial decipherment of intercepted Soviet diplomatic messages. American code breakers had begun working on Soviet communications during World War II, but it was not until the late 1940's that they had any success. Called the Venona archive, the dispatches revealed the existence of at least two Los Alamos security breaches—one involving the Rosenberg spy ring, the other the physicist Theodore Hall. Judith Coplon, identified as a Soviet spy in the Venona transcripts, was arrested with secret documents in her possession.

The activities of the US naval officers who made up the Walker family spy ring were not discovered by counterespionage detective work but were disclosed by John Walker's estranged wife. Word of Hanssen's betrayal came from a source within the Russian intelligence community. The openly flamboyant lifestyle of Ames provided the decisive clues to his treachery; however, critics wondered why it took the CIA nine years to question how one of its employees making less than $70,000 a year got the money to charge more than $20,000 a month on his credit cards and to buy a $450,000 suburban Washington house with cash.

Prosecution and Punishment

Use of illegal wiretaps, break-ins, and mail openings by the FBI under its director J. Edgar Hoover created difficulties in securing espionage convictions. Such evidence was inadmissible in court. Of more than one hundred people named by Bentley and Chambers, only two (William Remington and Alger Hiss) were indicted and convicted—of perjury, not espionage. The Rosenbergs were prosecuted when members of their ring agreed to testify against them. Hall was never indicted because he refused to confess, and there were no witnesses to his activity; both the FBI and military intelligence objected to use of the Venona decipherment, which was not publicly disclosed until 1995. Successful prosecution of the Walkers and Hanssen involved plea bargains.

Julius and Ethel Rosenberg were convicted of espionage and executed by electrocution on June 19, 1953. David Greenglass and Harry Gold testified against the Rosenbergs; Greenglass was sentenced to fifteen years in jail, Gold to thirty. Judith Coplon escaped any jail time.

Her conviction in June, 1949, was overturned on appeal because of use of illegal wiretap evidence. The FBI opposed a retrial, which would reveal that its agents had not detected Coplon's treason, instead learning of her spying through the Venona decodes.

John Walker agreed to plead guilty in exchange for lighter punishment for his son, Michael. Michael Walker received a sentence of twenty-five years and was paroled in February 2000, after fifteen years in prison. John Walker, his brother, and Walker's friend Jerry Whitworth all received life sentences. Ames was convicted and sentenced to life in prison; his wife was jailed for five years for her share in his activity and deported in 1999. Hanssen hired a celebrity attorney who negotiated a plea bargain with the Department of Justice. In return for his wife's receiving a widow's pension of $38,000 a year, Hanssen agreed to accept a sentence of life without parole and take polygraph tests while describing all his transactions with the Soviets.

Counterespionage activity designed to combat terrorism is even more difficult than traditional spy catching. The FBI successfully pursued and convicted those responsible for the first World Trade Center attack in 1993. Detecting and preventing planned attacks is a much more challenging assignment, however, as the 9/11 *Commission Report* (2004) demonstrated. Solving that problem will be a major concern of American security and intelligence agencies in the twenty-first century.

Milton Berman

Further Reading
Fialka, John. *War by Other Means: Economic Espionage in America*. New York: W. W. Norton, 1997.
Gannon, James. *Stealing Secrets, Telling Lies: How Spies and Codebreakers Helped Shape the Twentieth Century*. Washington, D.C.: Brassey's, 2001.
Hitz, Frederick P. *The Great Game: The Myth and Reality of Espionage*. New York: Alfred A. Knopf, 2004.
Jeffreys-Jones, Rhodri. *Cloak and Dollar: A History of American Secret Intelligence*. New Haven: Yale University Press, 2002.
Owen, David. *Hidden Secrets: A Complete History of Espionage and the Technology Used to Support It*. New York: Firefly Books, 2002.
Persico, Joseph E. *Roosevelt's Secret War: FDR and World War II Espionage*. New York: Random House, 2001.
Theoharis, Athan. *Chasing Spies: How the FBI Failed in Counterintelligence but Promoted the Politics of McCarthyism in the Cold War Years*. Chicago: Ivan R. Dee, 2002.

See also Antiterrorism and Effective Death Penalty Act; Clear and present danger test; Electronic surveillance; Federal Bureau of Investigation, U.S.; Hoover, J. Edgar; National Stolen Property Act; Patriot Act; Terrorism; Treason; Fusion Centers.

Fingerprint identification

Definition: Matching of fingerprint patterns found on surfaces to those of known persons

Evidence and forensics; Investigation; Technology

Significance: Fingerprint identification is one of the longest-established and most certain methods of identifying criminal suspects and linking them to crime scenes.

Friction ridge characteristics are located on the fingers, palms, and feet of the human body. The raised ridges and furrows on tips and at the end of the first joint of the fingers have identified people for centuries. Fingerprint patterns are unique to individuals; even identical twins do not have identical fingerprints. Fingerprint patterns form in the third fetal month of human development and remain the same until death and advanced decomposition.

Ridges rise above furrows to form specific patterns that are unique to each person. Fingerprints fall into three basic patterns: arches, loops, and whorls. Subclassifications further divide the basic patterns. The pores in the skin secrete a residue that leaves traces of latent fingerprint impressions. After a person has touched a nonporous surface like glass, patent prints are visible to the eye. Plastic, or indentation, prints may be found on soft surfaces such as putty. Invisible latent prints require development with laser, powders, and chemical techniques.

Fingerprint pattern interpretation assists in the classification, searching, and suspect elimination processes. The analysis of fingerprint minutiae, such as ridge endings, dots, islands, bifurcations, and other features, allows for the specific identification of a person. Comparison of fingerprint minutiae to an individual fingerprint creates a means of personal identification.

Elimination prints help identify family members and others who have legitimate access to the crime scene. Occasionally, witnesses or police officers will touch an object at the scene of a crime. Elimination prints help isolate those of the suspect.

Developing Fingerprints

Before beginning the collection process, examiners photograph fingerprints in place, whether the prints are visible, latent, or plastic. This procedure provides a permanent record and protects the fingerprints from any damage that may ensue as a result of the collection process. When searching for latent prints at a crime scene, examiners proceed in the least intrusive manner possible.

The fingerprint identification office at a city police department. (By aeroplanepics0112, via Wikimedia Commons)

They apply nondestructive resources to the print surface, such as lasers or a long-wave ultraviolet light source. Occasionally, a simple pen light with an oblique angle may reveal patent or latent prints. Physical and chemical methods may follow, depending on the surface.

The use of dusting powders, chemicals, and lifting applications presents a health hazard to investigators. Protective safety glasses are required for viewing prints with lasers and other light sources. Examiners wear respiratory masks and rubber gloves when applying fingerprint powder and other chemicals. When possible, this work is done in a well-ventilated area with a fume hood.

Fingerprint Computer Applications

The Federal Bureau of Investigation (FBI) maintains the national fingerprint database. State and municipal law-enforcement agencies maintain independent fingerprint record systems. Automated Fingerprint Identification System (AFIS) technology has the ability to search for individual fingerprints. This electronic database links suspects with their fingerprints. The FBI's Integrated Automated Fingerprint Identification System (IAFIS) permits state and local examiners to search other state fingerprint databases. These database files contain prints of known offenders and forensic files of unsolved cases, which contain unknown fingerprints. The purpose of these forensic files is to link offenders to unsolved cases.

Formerly, searching record systems for single fingerprints could take years. The old Henry system and the former FBI extension system required all ten fingerprints for a successful search and match. As criminals rarely leave ten perfect prints at the scene of a crime, successful matches were an exceptional event in the absence of a known suspect.

Investigative Application

In one application, police were investigating serial burglary cases in a suburban community. The fingerprint expert dusted for traces of the burglar's prints. The search produced only footprints, and the same footprint patterns emerged at every case location. The preliminary and follow-up investigation centered on one known female burglar. She specialized in jewelry thefts, breaking and entering in the daytime. The offender lived less than three miles from all the crime scenes.

The fingerprint examiner obtained footprint impressions from the suspect and compared them to footprints taken from each burglary location. The expert matched twenty-four minutiae ridge characteristics from the burglar's feet to thirty other burglaries. The match involved basic minutiae ridges, such as ridge dots, endings, islands, and bifurcations. Comparisons provided a positive identification of the suspect as the one who committed the burglaries. During the subsequent interrogation process, the burglar revealed that she had worn gloves to avoid leaving fingerprint trace evidence. Furthermore, she had removed her shoes to avoid shoe impressions. Although wearing gloves did avoid a fingerprint match in the AFIS and IAFIS databases, the barefoot burglar overlooked the possibility that her foot impressions would exhibit the same points of identification as her fingers.

Thomas E. Baker

Further Reading

Becker, Ronald F. *Criminal Investigation*. Gaithersburg: Aspen, 2000. Print.

Cole, Simon A. *Suspect Identities: A History of Fingerprinting and Criminal Identification*. Cambridge: Harvard UP, 2001. Print.

Evans, Colin. *The Casebook of Forensic Detection: How Science Solved One Hundred of the World's Most Baffling Crimes*. New York: Wiley, 1998. Print.

Genge, Ngaire E. *The Forensic Casebook: The Science of Crime Scene Investigation*. New York: Ballantine, 2002. Print.

James, Stuart H., and Jon J. Nordby. *Forensic Science: An Introduction to Scientific and Investigative Techniques*. 2nd ed. Boca Raton: CRC, 2005. Print.

Saferstein, Richard. *Criminalistics: An Introduction to Forensic Science*. 8th ed. Upper Saddle River: Prentice, 2003. Print.

See also Booking; Burglary; Chain of custody; Cold cases; Computer information systems; Crime labs; Crime scene investigation; Criminal history record information; Criminal records; DNA testing; Document analysis; Evidence, rules of; Forensics; Latent evidence; Shoe prints and tire-tracks; Trace evidence; Technology's transformative effect.

Forensic accounting

Definition: Integration of accounting, auditing, and investigative skills to assist in legal investigations of possible fraud and other white-collar crimes

Criminal justice issues: Business and financial crime; evidence and forensics; fraud; white-collar crime

Significance: The specialized field of forensic accounting deals with the discovery, analysis, interpretation, summary, and presentation of financial issues or economic analysis. It involves looking beyond the numbers to detect improper, unethical, or illegal activities. Another term for forensics accounting is fraud accounting.

Forensic accounting encompasses both litigation support and investigative accounting. Litigation support is the factual presentation of economic issues related to litigation. It deals primarily with issues related to quantifying economic damages. A typical litigation support case is the calculation of economic loss resulting from a breach of contract. In these types of cases, forensic accounting professionals quantify the damages sustained by parties who are involved in legal disputes to help resolve the disputes. When unresolved disputes go to court, forensic accountants may testify as expert witnesses.

Auditing is the systematic process of objectively obtaining and evaluating evidence regarding financial matters. Investigation is the process of determining whether criminal matters, such as intellectual property theft, employee theft, identity theft, securities fraud, falsification of financial statements, or insurance fraud have occurred. As part of investigations, forensic accountants may recommend actions that can be taken to minimize risks of future losses.

Investigations may also occur in civil matters. For example, forensic accountants may search for hidden assets in divorce cases. However, investigative accounting is mostly associated with investigations of criminal matters.

When Forensic Accounting Is Needed

Forensic accountants search for evidence of criminal conduct or assist in determinations of claimed damages or rebuttals of such claims. As such, forensic accounting is required in situations needing high levels of detail or precision that are sustainable in adversarial legal proceedings. It provides an accounting analysis that is suitable to courts, thereby forming the basis for dispute resolution. Typical situations requiring forensics accounting involve white-collar crimes, insurance and securities fraud, employee theft, kickbacks, business disputes, and impaired or lost income-generating cases,

Most forensic accounting investigations involve financial theft, economic crime, bankruptcy, mergers, personal injury, and matrimonial divorce valuations. In addition, a wide range of noncriminal cases rely on forensic accounting; these include investment analyst research, litigation support, underwriting due diligence, and enterprise risk management.

Business Disputes and Fraud Investigations

The primary business disputes requiring forensic accounting investigations are professional negligence, breach of contract, warranty and products liability, patent infringements, construction claims, business valuation or dissolution, and property and income losses for insurance claim purposes, such as business interruption.

The most common investigations deal with fraud- and theft-related matters that are criminal, civil, or insurance remedies. Since the widespread corporate scandals of 2000-2004 and terrorist threats, there have been numerous investigations of financial statement manipulation, shareholder and partnership disputes, stock market fraud, supplier kickbacks, computer crime, and money laundering. Other investigations involve the search for hidden assets or unreported income for income tax, matrimonial, or related disputes.

When conducting investigations, one of the first steps that forensic accountants take is to learn as much as possible about matters such as target computers and their networks, peripheral devices, and telecommunication devices, including electronic mail, voice mail, and instant-messaging systems. Forensic accountants frequently interview information technology (IT) staff members so they can identify how and where data are stored. This part of investigations is critical to gain clear understandings of how data files, transaction data, electronic mail, and voice mail are archived. After understanding and documenting the data and telecommunication systems, forensic accountants know the dates of complete data backups. This knowledge is used to select and restore the backups most likely to contain information related to the investigation of suspected fraud.

An example of the value of forensic accounting is the case of HealthSouth Corporation, which is based in Birmingham, Alabama. Forensic accountants determined that the corporation's executives and others had committed massive accounting fraud. They discovered fraudulent entries made between 1992 and 2003 that overstated earnings by more than four billion dollars. As a result of their investigation and evidence, HealthSouth, its former investment bank, and its former audit company faced a class-action lawsuit from shareholders and bondholders. In addition, fifteen former executives pleaded guilty to taking part in the fraud scheme. HealthSouth founder Richard Scrushy faced criminal charges but was acquitted on all charges in June, 2005-possibly because the government failed to make its complex case understandable to the jury.

As a result of its effectiveness in business cases, personal injury cases are increasingly using forensic accounting to evaluate issues such as loss of earnings as well as pension or dependency claims.

Forensic accounting crosses over into criminology by the way it investigates suspicious activities. It requires special expertise, similar to the investigative skill of being able to tell when someone is being deceptive. Forensic accountants must know and be able to follow generally accepted principles, have the credentials to qualify as experts, and be competent in written and oral communications, logical reasoning, problem solving, critical thinking, and computer skills.

Linda Volonino
George F. Kermis

Further Reading

Albrecht, W. Steve, and Chad Albrecht. *Fraud Examination and Fraud Prevention.* Hoboken, N.J.: John Wiley & Sons, 2003. Discusses all phases of forensic accounting using actual examples. Explains critical accounting principles and how to implement fraud investigation processes.

Anastasi, Joe. *The New Forensics: Investigating Corporate Fraud and the Theft of Intellectual Property.* Hoboken, N.J.: John Wiley & Sons, 2003. Discusses how computers can detect fraud and other corporate criminal activities.

Crumbley, D. Larry, Lester E. Heitger, and G. Stevenson Smith. *Forensic and Investigative Accounting.* Chicago: Commerce Clearing House, 2003. Explains issues and practices associated with forensics accounting, including uncovering accounting fraud, courtroom procedures, litigation support, and cybercrime.

Friedman, Jack P., and L. Weil Roman. *Litigation Support Report Writing: Accounting, Finance, and Economic Issues.* Hoboken, N.J.: John Wiley & Sons, 2003. A collection of effective litigation reports on financial and accounting subjects. Each chapter is an actual litigation report that was submitted to court.

Silverstone, Howard, and Michael Sheetz. *Forensic Accounting and Fraud Investigation for Non-Experts.* Hoboken, N.J.: John Wiley & Sons, 2003. General guide for detecting, preventing, and prosecuting financial fraud.

See also Cold cases; Confessions; Consent searches; Conspiracy; Corporate scandals; Document analysis; Embezzlement; Forensics; Forgery.

Forensics

Definition: Applications of science to the legal arena, particularly criminal investigations
Evidence and forensics; Investigation; Technology
Significance: Forensic science and forensic medicine, as they relate to the processing of crime scene evidence, have become increasingly crucial to the resolution of cases within the criminal justice system, particularly as evolving technologies have allowed forensics to make ever greater contributions to criminal investigations.

Forensic science broadly encompasses the use of science in both criminal and civil courts. The types and variety of forensic evidence that can be presented in courtrooms are almost limitless. In criminal courts, forensic evidence is essential in drug cases. Forensic medicine is especially valuable in the handling of evidence relating to bodies in homicide and rape cases. In civil courts, forensic evidence is often presented in product-liability cases and injury cases.

Forensic Specialties

The field of forensic science includes a variety of subdisciplines. These include forensic medicine, forensic anthropology, forensic entomology, forensic odontology, forensic palynology, forensic serology, and criminalistics. Forensic medicine is further divided into the areas of forensic pathology, forensic toxicology, and forensic psychiatry.

Forensic pathology studies how and why people die and concentrates on sudden, unexpected, and violent deaths. During homicide investigations, forensic pathologists frequently perform autopsies. Forensic toxicology is concerned with chemicals-especially drugs and poisons-found in human bodies. During death investigations, forensic toxicologists may make determinations on whether victims have been killed by poisons, such as lead. Toxicology analyses can also be sued to determine whether a drug such as Rohypnol-the so-called "date-rape" drug-has been used in sexual assaults.

Forensic odontology, which is also known as forensic dentistry, deals with dental evidence. It is usually used to identify bodies or to link bite marks on victims to dental impressions of suspects. Forensic psychiatrists combine knowledge and practical experience in medicine, mental health, and the neurosciences and are called upon to testify in the courtroom regarding psychological disorders and disabilities.

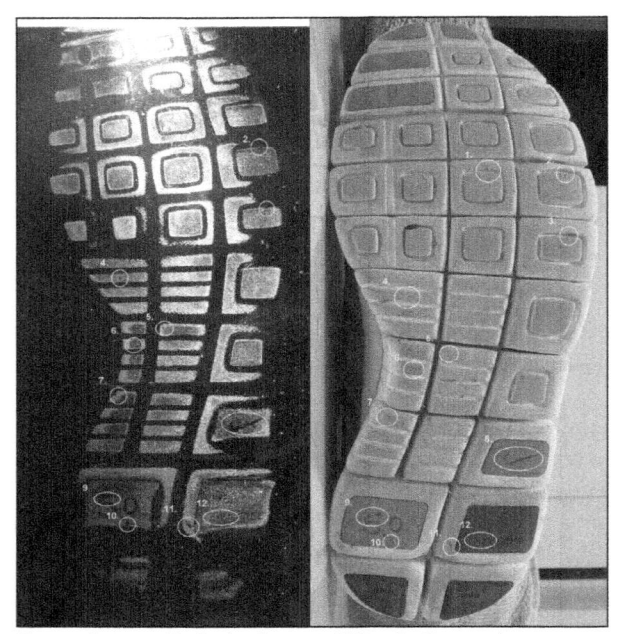

Forensic shoeprint. (By Stechondanet, via Wikimedia Commons)

Forensic anthropologists are most frequently called upon when human skeletal remains are found. Anthropologists use the remains to assist in identifying victims. They may also provide approximate dates and causes of death. Forensic entomology studies how insects colonize dead bodies. On the basis of examination of insects, estimates of times of death can be made. Forensic serologists specialize in identifying and processing blood, semen, saliva, and other bodily fluids. They may also be involved in analyses of bloodstains, blood spatters, and DNA specimens. Such evidence is often crucial in sexual assault cases and homicide investigations.

Criminalistics

Criminalistics is a broad area of forensics that is concerned with analyses of a wide variety of evidence. It encompasses questioned documents, voice examinations; ballistics and tool marks; fingerprints; tire-tracks and shoe prints; paint and glass fragments; hair, fibers, and soil; and arson and explosives. The area of questioned documents includes all types of possible forgeries of documents, papers, inks, computer copies, and handwriting analysis. Voice examination is employed to identify speakers and to ascertain whether speakers are telling the truth.

Ballistics is the study of the physics of objects in flight. In forensics, it is primarily concerned with bullets and other projectiles used as weapons. Ballistics experts can determine the angles at which projectiles strike surfaces and the damage that the projectiles cause.

Experts in firearms study all types of guns, shotguns, bullets, cartridges, and cases. Tool marks are most often found at the scenes of burglaries and other crimes at which criminals gain forcible entry into secured areas. Fingerprint experts dust for, lift, and analyze fingerprint evidence left at crime scenes. Tire-tracks and shoe prints, like fingerprints, are impressions that are often left at crime scenes and can be lifted or copied in castings made with plaster-like materials.

Many experts deal with fragment and fiber evidence and examine the microscopic differences in paints, glass, hairs, fibers, and soils. For example, through thorough examination, it may be possible to match minute samples from a crime scene with the paint or glass on a suspect's car. Paint and glass examination are frequently important in the prosecution of hit-and-run cases.

Affiliated Fields

Areas related to forensic science include forensic psychology, forensic nursing, forensic accounting, forensic engineering, and forensic computer analysis. Forensic psychology includes such activities as criminal personality profiling, child custody evaluations, and litigation consultation. Forensic nursing is an emerging specialization within nursing that concentrates on working with victims of sexual assault and domestic violence. It also contributes to evidence collection for law enforcement.

Forensic accounting utilizes accounting principles to evaluate the financial paperwork of organizations to determine if fraud is present. This specialization within accounting has become increasingly important due to highly publicized increases in financial wrongdoing among large corporations. Forensic engineering studies how structures respond to stresses. Forensic engineers explained how and why the Twin Towers of the World Trade Center collapsed during the terrorist attacks of September 11, 2001. Forensic computer analysis is the specialty within computer science that deals with analyses of computer evidence for the prosecution of individuals who steal or alter computer data.

History of Forensic Science

There are two distinct historical threads within forensic science. The first is the history of the development of law enforcement and investigation techniques. The second is the history of a variety of scientific advances that have been useful to solve cases.

The techniques used by investigators and detectives to solve cases have traditionally been called criminalistics. Has Gross, who is credited as the founder of modern criminalistics, worked as a prosecutor and judge in Austria. He was responsible for publishing the first professional paper on the application of the sciences to criminal investigation during the 1890s.

Locard's Exchange Principle, named for the French criminalist Edmond Locard, is the guiding principle behind all forensic science. It states that whenever two objects come into contact with each other, there is an exchange of materials between them. In other words, when crimes are committed and the offenders are at the crime scenes, the offenders invariably leave behind material—which may be microscopic—that can be traced back to them. Locard established an early crime laboratory in Lyons, France, in 1910.

Alphonse Bertillon developed the first system of person identification, based on body measurements, in Paris during the mid-nineteenth century. His system was soon replaced by fingerprints, which were found to be more individual than the body measurements.

The first forensic laboratory in the United States was opened by the Los Angeles Police Department during the early 1920s. During the 1930s, several state laboratories were set up throughout California. California's early start in forensics gave it an edge in the field that it retained into the twenty-first century. Meanwhile, the United States Federal Bureau of Investigation established its first forensic laboratory in 1932.

Since the field of forensics was founded, it has been advanced by numerous scientific advances. These include developments in microscopy-from Galileo's invention of the first microscope in the sixteenth century to the invention of the electron microscope during the 1930s-chemistry, biology, biochemistry, optics, microbiology, molecular biology, and DNA analysis.

In a 5-4 decision in *Melendez-Diaz v. Massachusetts*, the US Supreme Court ruled in June 2009 that defendants have the right to cross-examine forensic analysts who handle scientific evidence in criminal cases because a state forensic analyst's report used in a criminal prosecution is subject to the confrontation clause of the Sixth Amendment.

Forensic Medicine

Forensic medicine—the use of medicine to determine cause and manner of death—dates back to ancient Greece and the birth of medicine. From the inception of this discipline, medical practitioners have mastered techniques for determining the time and manner of human deaths. Forensic medical testimony is one of the oldest forms of scientific testimony and has been widely accepted in courts and legal systems across the world. With the advent of modern medicine in the sixteenth and seventeenth centuries, forensic medicine became irrevocably entrenched in the investigative process. In modern criminal justice, forensic medicine is a necessary part of any death investigation. Medical examiners oversee death investigations and may be called upon to testify in court regarding the facts surrounding deaths.

The Importance of Crime Scenes

The role of forensic science and medicine in the criminal justice system is to aid in the arrest and prosecution of criminals. When law-enforcement officers witness crimes, making arrests is easy. However, in real life, that rarely happens. Arrests that lead to successful convictions are dependent upon three things: witnesses who can testify well, crime scene evidence that can be processed and presented at court, and voluntary confessions by perpetrators. Not all three components need be present for convictions, but each component helps build the state's case against criminal defendants.

Forensic science is most concerned with the processing of crime scenes. The importance of this work cannot be overstated. Criminal investigations begin at crime scenes; if they are not handled properly, the investigations may not progress any further. All the modern scientific advances available to law enforcement cannot make up for what is lost when crime scenes are not been properly guarded and preserved for forensic analysis. Crime scenes must be kept and processed in as pristine a condition as possible.

Depending upon the size of the law-enforcement departments responding to crimes, the responsibility for collecting evidence from crime scenes may fall to the responding officers, the lead detectives, or crime scene technicians. In large jurisdictions, specialists may collect different types of evidence. For example, fingerprint specialists dust for and lift fingerprints.

Evidence from crime scenes may be examined in three different ways. Physical methods, which are often used, include measuring sizes of objects and where they are in relation to each other; physical matching and comparisons—which are common with glass fragments—and photography. Since the advent of digital photography, the first responders have been able to photograph evidence and make prints quickly and easily, thereby helping to ensure that even transitory evidence, such as wet shoe prints, can be preserved.

Chemical methods are often used—especially in the processing of drug evidence. Before convictions can be obtained in drug cases, techniques such as chromatography and spectrography are employed to determine the chemical makeups of evidence at the scenes. Chemical analyses are also performed on blood-alcohol evidence. Biological methods, including microscopy, may also be used, especially when the evidence consists of minute fibers and fragments.

Training

Training within forensic medicine and forensic science is very diverse, depending upon the particular job descriptions. Forensic medicine requires medical degrees and advanced training. Crime scene technicians generally have college degrees or certificate training. Police officers who work at crime scenes may have on-the-job-training or take specific classes. Individuals who work in crime labs generally have either master's or doctoral degrees in chemistry, biology, or other natural sciences.

Ayn Embar-Seddon and Allan D. Pass

Further Reading

Bass, William M., and Jon Jefferson. *Death's Acre: Inside the Legendary Lab—the Body Farm—Where the Dead Do Tell Tales*. New York: Putnam, 2003. Print.
Ellen, David. *The Scientific Examination of Documents: Methods and Techniques*. 3rd ed. Boca Raton: CRC, 2005. Print.
Evans, C. *The Casebook of Forensic Detection: How Science Solved One Hundred of the World's Most Baffling Crimes*. New York: Wiley, 1998. Print.
Genge, N. *The Forensic Casebook: The Science of Crime Scene Investigation*. New York: Ballantine, 2002. Print.
Lee, Henry C., Timothy M. Palmbach, and Marilyn T. Miller. *Henry Lee's Crime Scene Handbook*. New York: Academic, 2001. Print.
Lithwick, Dahlia. "Pseudoscience in the Witness Box." *Slate*. Slate Group, 22 Apr. 2015. Web. 27 May 2016.
McCrery, Nigel. *Silent Witnesses: The Often Gruesome but Always Fascinating History of Forensic Science*. Chicago: Chicago Review, 2014. Print.
Owen, David. *Hidden Evidence*. Willowdale: Firefly, 2000. Print.
Saferstein, Richard. *Forensic Science: From the Crime Scene to the Crime Lab*. 2nd ed. Boston: Pearson, 2013. Print.

See also Autopsies; Bloodstains; Circumstantial evidence; Cold cases; Coroners; Crime labs; Crime scene investigation; DNA testing; Document analysis; Fingerprint identification; Forensic accounting; Forensic psychology; Latent evidence; Medical examiners; Shoe prints and tire-tracks; Toxicology; Trace evidence; Technology's transformative effect.

Freedom of assembly and association

Definition: Right of the people to be active in self-government and to associate with those who hold similar values
Criminal justice issues: Civil rights and liberties; constitutional protections
Significance: Freedoms such as that of assembly and association are ends in themselves. Additionally, people who are not allowed a voice in their government and an opportunity for the redress of grievances will necessitate the use of force to maintain civil order.

Freedom of assembly is a right guaranteed in the First Amendment to the Constitution of the United States. The entire First Amendment could rightly be said to guarantee the freedom of association, although that right is one inherent in the right of a free people to own property, conduct business, and engage in the political process. The First Amendment says in its entirety, "Congress shall make no law respecting an establishment of religion, or prohibiting the free exercise thereof; or abridging the freedom of speech, or of the press; or the right of the people peaceably to assemble, and to petition the Government for a redress of grievances."

The denial of this freedom of petition for redress was given in the Declaration of Independence as being present in all the grievances which had been denied by the English Crown. Under U.S. law, this right is inviolable. It is only the absence of a peaceable nature, as exhibited in actual criminal behavior or in incitement to criminal behavior, that can justify dispersing an assembly.

In *United States v. Cruikshank et al.*, heard in 1875, U.S. Supreme Court chief justice Morrison R. Waite wrote:

> The right of the people peaceably to assemble for lawful purposes existed long before the adoption of the Constitution of the United States. In fact, it is, and always has been, one of the attributes of citizenship under a free government. It "derives its source," to use the language of Chief Justice John Marshall, in *Gibbons v. Ogden*, "from those laws whose authority is acknowledged by civilized men throughout the world." It is found wherever civilization exists. It was not, therefore, a right granted to the people by the Constitution. The government of the United States when established found it in existence, with the obligation on the part of the States to afford it protection.

This right is, therefore, a part of the original law of nature and of nature's god acknowledged in the Declaration of Independence and throughout the other founding documents.

Some confusion has arisen throughout American history as to the extent of freedom of assembly. One of the problems that came about was that some of the states saw this amendment as ensuring only protection from abridgement by the federal government of this right. The assertion made was that states and local governments could abridge these rights. However, the Supreme Court eventually found that the Fourteenth Amendment, ratified in 1868, settled the issue, requiring that "No State shall make or enforce any law which shall abridge the privileges or immunities of Citizenship of the United States; nor shall any state deprive any person of life, liberty, or property, without due process of law; nor deny to any person within its jurisdiction the equal protection of the laws."

Mark W. Rizzo

Further Reading
Blackstone, William. *Of the Nature of Laws in General*. Vol. 1 in *Commentaries on the Laws of England*. Chicago: University of Chicago Press, 1979.
_____. *Of Offences Against the Public Peace*. Vol. 4 in *Commentaries on the Laws of England*. Chicago: University of Chicago Press, 1979.

See also Bill of Rights, U.S.; Conspiracy; Constitution, U.S.; Due process of law; Equal protection under the law; September 11, 2001, attacks; Supreme Court, U.S.

Fusion Centers

Definition: Two or more institutions at the state or local level that pool criminal information for centralized analysis and then disseminate the end-product as criminal intelligence to an appropriate end-user
Criminal justice issues: Civil rights and liberties; crime prevention; espionage and sedition; investigation; law enforcement organization; organized crime; terrorism
Significance: At state and local levels, fusion centers are responsible for generating multisource criminal intelligence from pooled information acquired at all levels of government.

According to the US Department of Justice, a fusion center is a "collaborative effort of two or more agencies that provide resources, expertise, and information ... with the goal of maximizing their ability to detect, prevent, investigate, and respond to criminal and terrorist activity." The Office of Justice Programs adds: "A fusion center is an effective and efficient mechanism to exchange information and intelligence, maximize resources, streamline operations, and improve the ability to fight crime and terrorism by analyzing data from a variety of sources." It is helpful if the term intelligence is defined as well. The simplest (and most useful) definition is that intelligence is analyzed information, meaning that the value of intelligence is greater than the sum of its parts. In other words, analysis adds value to the intelligence product as does disseminating it to the proper enduser or client. Intelligence that is not properly disseminated and is held at the fusion center beyond its usefulness (termed a silo or bottleneck) is of no value.

Occasionally the term joint intelligence center (or JIC) is errantly equated with that of fusion center, primarily because the former is a forerunner of the latter and because their respective purposes are nearly identical. Any federal institution or agency whose purpose it is to generate intelligence from multiple informational sources is called a joint intelligence center, whether the information collected and analyzed is regarded as defense, foreign, or even criminal intelligence. However, a fusion center is differentiated from a joint intelligence center because its mission is to generate criminal intelligence (alone) at the state or local level. Otherwise, the basic tasks of fusion centers and JICs are essentially the same: to collect and analyze information, and then disseminate intelligence. To complicate matters, typically fusion centers have federal law enforcement officers on site who generate joint and fused intelligence for use across multiple levels of law enforcement. Also, certain federal agencies (non-law enforcement) routinely facilitate data access at fusion centers, notably the Defense Intelligence Agency has been working at both JIC and fusion center levels for more than a decade.

Examining the origins of fusion centers as an evolutionary product of World War II joint intelligence centers, it is important to note that early War Department (later Department of Defense) JICs weren't particularly well-received in military circles. Early failures in military intelligence were attributable to failures in joint operations among the military branches, such as the failed prisoner rescue attempts of the Son Tay Raid in Viet Nam and Operation Desert One in Iran. But by the early 1990's JICs began to assume a larger role in military intelligence, particularly during the Desert Storm era. By then the military strategy of coordinated joint operations demanded a joint and fused intelligence product. Nevertheless, after the attacks of September 11, 2001, Congress blamed failures in federal intelligence cooperation for the successes of the terrorist acts; however, the blame fell on the Federal Bureau of Investigation (FBI), the Central Intelligence Agency (CIA), and the Immigration and Naturalization Service (INS), not the military. In response to the 9-11 terrorist attacks, the Georgia Information Sharing Analysis Center (GISAC) was born, becoming the first state-operated counterterror fusion center. Initially an intelligence operation between Georgia state law enforcement and the FBI, it evolved into an all-crime intelligence center with a multitude of government participants. Since GISAC's inception in 2001, seventy state and local fusion centers have been established in the United States to process criminal intelligence.

One early issue problematic to fusion center executives was that the original purpose of the intelligence institutions was to combat terrorism. Europol, the European Union's (EU's) central criminal intelligence agency, went through a similar identity crisis years earlier, originating as a joint counterdrug intelligence operation between Germany and France, shifting its mission as an nongovernmental organization (NGO) to European counterterror intelligence, and then finally to criminal intelligence (broadly) as a function of EU governance. In the United States, fusion centers that had been established as counter-terror operations eventually evolved into all-crime intelligence centers, largely because there wasn't enough counterterror work state-by-state to keep them busy (as was exactly the case with Europol a decade before).

Opposition to Fusion Centers

Not all American institutions are supportive of government fusion centers, even in counterterror operations. The American Civil Liberties Union (ACLU), for example, argues that fusion centers have not established a place convincingly in counterterror; therefore, they are not deserving of public funds for support. Additionally, the ACLU suggests that public sector participation in information collection places corporate employees and clients at risk for theft of personal data in data mining operations (although no evidence is offered of this). They also object to the military taking part in fusion center collection citing federal prohibitions in combined operations between law enforcement and the military. Nevertheless, the ACLU observes, "not all fusion center operations raise civil liberties or privacy concerns. But some do, and the lack of a proper legal framework to regulate their activities is troublesome."

However, according to the National Criminal Intelligence Sharing Plan (NCISP), "One of the primary concerns of law enforcement agencies across the nation is the protection of the privacy, civil rights, and civil libertiesof those they serve" The NCISP is a product of the Criminal Intelligence Coordinating Council (CICC), a multijurisdictional policy coordinating body of the U.S. Attorney General's Office. The CICC, described by the Department of Justice as the cornerstone of nationwide criminal intelligence coordination, is "made up of members representing law enforcement and homeland security agencies ... to develop and share criminal intelligence for the purpose of promoting public safety and securing the nation."

As a coordinating body, the CICC collaborates with the U.S. Department of Justice, the U.S. Department of Homeland Security, the FBI, the Program Manager for the Information Sharing Environment, and the Office of the Director of National Intelligence: "The advice and recommendations of the CICC and its membership have also been sought by the Secretary of the U.S. Department of Homeland Security, members of Congress, and representatives of state government." And so, whereas, there is no federal legal framework with which to govern the operations of fusion centers, policy guidelines generated at the level of the U.S. Attorney General reach to state and local fusion centers. If a fusion center does not follow CICC policy guidelines it may lose federal cooperation in information sharing and analysis, which would be catastrophic to the fusion center process; however, the purpose of the CICC is coordination, not oversight. The government as well as state and local fusion centers appear to agree with the ACLU that privacy, civil rights, and civil liberties are issues that will follow operations in criminal intelligence into the distant future.

Kenneth Ryan

Further Reading

American Civil Liberties Union. "Executive Summary." *What's Wrong With* [sic] *Fusion Centers.* New York: ACLU, 2008. An examination of fusion centers as a new government institution that may threaten Americans.

Global Advisory Committee. *National Criminal Intelligence Sharing Plan.* Washington, D.C.: U.S. Department of Justice, 2013. Federal government plans and recommendations for coordinating fusion centers.

Lowenthal, Mark M. *Intelligence: From Secrets to Policy.* Washington, D.C.: CQ Press, 2000. A primer on the mechanics of federal intelligence.

Marchio, James D. "Support to Military Operations." *The Evolution and Relevance of Joint Intelligence Centers*. Washington, D.C.: CSI, 2008. A chronicling of the rise, fall, and rise again of JICs prominence in the military.

Office of Justice Programs. "Executive Summary." *Fusion Center Guidelines: Developing and Sharing Information and Intelligence in a New Era*. Washington, D.C.: U.S. Department of Justice, 2006. An informational brochure outlining definitions and tasks of fusion centers with guidelines and key elements.

Rosenbach, Eric, and Aki J. "Congress and the Intelligence Community." *State and Local Fusion Centers: Confrontation or Collaboration?* Cambridge, Mass.: Harvard University, 2010. A memo from the Kennedy School of Government for the U.S. Congress addressing the progress of fusion center development since 9-11.

See also Computer information systems; Crime analysis; Homeland Security, U.S. Department of; Intelligence-led policing; Lone wolf; Paris terrorist attacks (2015); Technology's transformative effect; Terrorism.

Gault, In re

The Case: U.S. Supreme Court ruling on court procedures in juvenile cases
Date: Decided on May 15, 1967
Criminal justice issues: Evidence and forensics; juvenile justice; trial procedures
Significance: This Supreme Court decision established the principle that juvenile court procedures must include the most basic procedural rights and evidentiary rules.

The *In re Gault* case arose from the 1964 arrest of Gerald Gault in Gila County, Arizona, for making a lewd telephone call to a neighbor. Gault, who was then fifteen years old, was on probation for an earlier minor offense. Although the state produced no evidence at Gault's hearing, the juvenile judge found him to be delinquent. The basis of the finding was evidently police rumors about him and statements elicited from him in the absence of his parents or his lawyer. He was committed to a state industrial school until his eighteenth birthday. Had an adult committed the same crime, the maximum penalty that could have been assessed under Arizona law would have been a fifty-dollar fine and two months' imprisonment. Gault's appeal to the Arizona Supreme Court was unsuccessful, and he brought the case to the U.S. Supreme Court.

Gault argued that the Arizona juvenile code was unconstitutional on its face because it gives the judge almost unlimited discretion to take juveniles from their parents and commit them to an institution without notice of the charges, the right to counsel, the right to confront and cross-examine witnesses, the right to a transcript of the proceedings, or the right to an appeal. Arizona argued that because the main purpose of juvenile proceedings is to protect juvenile defendants from the full rigor and consequences of the criminal law, informal procedures are required. In Arizona's view, Gault's commitment to a state institution was protective rather than punitive.

The Supreme Court decided for Gault by a vote of 8 to 1. In an opinion by Justice Abe Fortas, the Court held that the due process clause of the Fourteenth Amendment requires that juvenile defendants are at least entitled to notice of the charges, right to counsel, right to confrontation and cross-examination of witnesses, the privilege against self-incrimination, a transcript of the proceedings, and appellate review. Justice Fortas insisted that these are the minimal guarantees necessary to assure fairness. He argued that the guarantees would not unduly interfere with any of the benefits of less formal procedures for juveniles. Justice John M. Harlan wrote a separate concurrence agreeing with the result but suggesting that the crucial minimum guarantees should be limited to notice of the charges; the right to counsel, including assigned counsel for indigent families; a transcript; and the right to appeal. In dissent, Justice Potter Stewart argued that because juvenile proceedings are not adversary criminal actions, the court is unwise to fasten procedural guarantees upon them.

In re Gault forces states to provide juvenile defendants with the central procedural guarantees of the Fifth Amendment. The possibility that young defendants will be unfairly judged to have committed crimes or been delinquent was substantially reduced.

Robert Jacobs

Further Reading
Champion, Dean John. *The Juvenile Justice System: Delinquency, Processing, and the Law*. 4th ed. Upper Saddle River, N.J.: Prentice-Hall, 2003.
Cox, Steven M., John J. Conrad, and Jennifer M. Allen. *Juvenile Justice: A Guide to Theory and Practice*. 5th ed. New York: McGraw-Hill, 2003.
Feld, Bary C. *Cases and Materials on Juvenile Justice Administration*. St. Paul, Minn.: West Publishing, 2000.

See also Criminal justice system; Criminal procedure; Due process of law; Evidence, rules of; Juvenile courts; Juvenile justice system; Juvenile waivers to adult courts; *Parens patriae*; Supreme Court, U.S.; Uniform Juvenile Court Act.

Geographic information systems

Definition: Systems used to plot and analyze geographic locations of such data as crimes

Criminal justice issues: Crime statistics; investigation; technology

Significance: Improvements in the collection, mapping, and analysis of geographic data are making geographic data increasingly useful tools for crime prevention, crime investigation, and law-enforcement resource allocation.

A Geographic information system (GIS) is a set of computer-based tools that allows the user to modify, visualize, query and analyze geographic and tabular data. GIS includes the development of particular software programs to assist researchers in visualizing data, assessing human behavior over geographic space, following spatial patterns, validating theories, and examining how geography affects crime and public safety. GIS is not merely an electronic version of a push-pin map. Instead, it allows for different layers of information to be superimposed to that information about a location that can be analyzed.

Though GIS software varies in sophistication, all GIS software can run statistical programs that identify or isolate crime patterns. Many software packages include a base map that provides digital street information primarily based on US census data as well as other geographic information. Some GIS software packages merely provide data layers with street maps and a computer platform with which to manipulate and study the data.

GIS methods of plotting geographically defined locations can be used to identify various phenomena on maps of areas such as cities, counties, and states. Plotting was originally done by hand. Since the late twentieth century, plotting has been done digitally. With current technology, events such as burglaries, murders, and traffic accidents can be precisely located with geographic Global Positioning System (GPS) coordinates. Incidents plotted on digitized maps can also be displayed on computer screens or printed on paper.

GIS has existed as a field since at least 1916, when Ernest Burgess reported the results of a study of crimes reported to the Chicago police. During the 1920's, urban sociologists Clifford Shaw and Henry McKay sought to identify connections between geography and crime. They studied the distribution of incidents of adjudicated juvenile delinquents residing in Chicago and later other cities in the United States. They concluded that crime was positively correlated with economically disadvantaged areas and demonstrated a connection between delinquency rates and factors such as economic status, stability, and racial composition.

Peter and Patricia Brantingham later revolutionized GIS use for law enforcement and crime prevention. GIS computerization of GIS began around 1975. The industry was soon dominated by the ArcViewGIS and MapInfo software programs. This was also the time when the technological tools to conduct empirical studies and translate those studies to police in the field were created. They became commercially available in the late 1990s. It was only when improvements in computer software developed and technology costs decreased that law enforcement began sustained experimentation with GIS crime-mapping technology.

Crime mapping is the progressive blend of practical criminal justice issues with the research field of GIS and science. Crime mapping considers such factors as the geographical quality of crime, the residence of offenders, where are the most vulnerable communities and targets are located, and how offenders travel to crime locations.

The best known implementation of GIS technology was the CompStat system in New York City. CompStat revolutionized the policing structure of the city and created an integrated data management system for police statistics that required weekly data updates, crime-mapping, targeted police responses and an accountability mechanism that was largely data driven. Along with the adoption of Compustat were additional police practices that targeted high-crime areas with more police offers and more aggressive policing techniques.

Currently, police departments use GIS for tactical analysis, criminal investigations, statistical record keeping, strategic planning, and administrative management. The adoption of GIS were accompanied by new criminology theories.

GIS continues to be highly useful tools for law-enforcement agencies. Police departments may use GIS to plot the distribution of residential burglaries in a city, along with the characteristics of each offense, and then analyze the data to create a burglary-prevention plan. Kim Rossmo, a Vancouver, British Columbia, police officer who earned a doctorate in criminology, developed a GIS-based program to track the crimes of mobile serial offenders, particularly murderers. Rossmo's system has been used to pinpoint probable locations of serial offenders' homes to within four-square-block areas.

Lawrence M. Salinger
Updated by Christopher T. Anglim

Further Reading

Burns, R. G. (2009). Critical issues in criminal justice. Upper Saddle River, NJ: Pearson Prentice Hall.

Chainey, S., & Ratcliffe, J. (2005). GIS and crime mapping. Chichester, West Sussex, England: Wiley.

Hagan, F. E. (2003). Research methods in criminal justice and criminology. Boston, MA: Allyn and Bacon.

Hagan, F. E. (2012). Essentials of research methods in criminal justice and criminology. Boston: Prentice Hall.

Hess, K. M., Orthmann, C. M., & Cho, H. L. (2014). Police operations: Theory and practice. Clifton Park, NY: Delmar.

Johnson, E. M., & Rodriguez, M. J. (2012). Legalities of GPS and cell phone surveillance. New York: Novinka.

La Vigne, Nancy G., and Julie Wartell, eds. Crime Mapping Case Studies: Successes in the Field. Washington, D.C.: Police Executive Re- search Forum, 1998.

Leipnik, M. R., & Albert, D. P. (2003). GIS in law enforcement: Implementation issues and case studies. London: Taylor & Francis.

Paulsen, D. J., & Robinson, M. B. (2004). Spatial aspects of crime: Theory and practice. Boston, MA: Pearson A and B.

Rossmo, D. Kim. Geographic Profiling. New York: CRC Press, 2000.

Santos, R. B. (2005). Crime analysis and crime mapping. Thousand Oaks, CA: Sage Publications.

Solove, D. J., & Schwartz, P. M. (n.d.). Privacy, law enforcement and national security.

Vann, Irvin B., and G. David Garson. Crime Mapping: New Tools for Law Enforcement. New York: P. Lang, 2003.

Weisburd, David, and Tom McEwen, eds. Crime Mapping and Crime Prevention. Monsey, N.Y.: Criminal Justice Press, 1997.

Whalen, M. (2011). Technology in criminal justice: Current perspectives from Infotrac. Belmont, CA: Wadsworth/Cengage.

See also Computer information systems; Crime analysis; Criminal records; Criminal justice system; Criminology; Juvenile courts; Juvenile justice system; Juvenile waivers to adult courts; *Parens patriae*; Uniform Juvenile Court Act.

Identity theft

Definition: Crime of wrongfully obtaining and using personal data of others for one's own profit

Business and financial crime; Fraud; Robbery, theft, and burglary

Significance: Every year, millions of Americans lose access to personal accounts and lose assets when they have their identities stolen in what the federal government has called one of the nation's-fastest growing crimes.

Criminal identity theft occurs when individuals, without permission, transfer, take, or use for their own benefit the personal and financial information of others. The types of information sought by identity thieves include social security numbers, driver's license information, passport and citizenship paperwork, financial account numbers and passwords, insurance records, tax returns, and credit card numbers and account information.

Types of Identity Theft

Five main categories of identity theft have been reported in the United States since the early 1990s. These categories serve as benchmarks for the numerous subvarieties of identity theft. They fall under the broad headings of true name, or cloning, identity theft; account takeovers; criminal identity theft; Internet and telecommunications fraud; and professional identity theft.

True name, or cloning, identity theft occurs when offenders use other people's personal information to open new accounts in the victims' own names. The information sought by this type of identity thief usually focuses on social security numbers, which are used to establish lines of credit in the potential victims' names. Once thieves gain access to their victims' social security numbers, they literally begin to take over their victims' full identities.

Account takeover occurs when criminals gain access to other persons' existing accounts and use them to make fraudulent transactions. This type of identity theft is most often used to purchase merchandise, to lease cars and dwellings, and to manipulate and bleed savings accounts, retirement portfolios, and other assets.

Criminal identity theft occurs when criminals give to law-enforcement officials the identifying data of other persons in place of their own and when the impostors present counterfeit documents containing other persons' personal data. Such impostors often fraudulently obtain driver's licenses and social security cards in their victims' names and provide these false identification documents to law enforcement. When impostors lack the appropriate visual identification cards, they give law enforcement the names of friends or relatives.

Internet and telecommunications identity theft may be the fastest-growing type of identity theft in the world. Internet and telecommunications technologies allow offenders more quickly and efficiently to open new accounts, strike online merchant sites, sell and share information electronically with other criminals, and then simply disappear into the dark confines of cyberspace. Telemarketing schemes, electronic mail and regular mail offers, site cloning, using chatrooms from public lists, and various forms of fraudulent sweepstakes and prize giveaways have been some of the most common techniques used to carry out this type of identity theft. Additionally, with the rise of online banking, which can now be conducted on both personal computers and cell phones,

Dumpster diving is a technique used by criminals to commit identity theft. (Public domain, via Wikimedia Commons)

criminals have even more chances to use the Internet to find and hack into people's banking information. The prevalence of social media sites such as Facebook, which invite users to include personal information such as names, physical and e-mail addresses, and telephone numbers has also increased the ability for criminals to steal people's identities through the Internet. While most of these sites have amped up security and privacy settings over the years, many could still remain vulnerable to experienced hackers.

Professional identity theft usually consists of concerted efforts of two or more professional thieves who work together to amass as much money and merchandise as possible by stealing and using others' identities before being detected. These criminals sometimes pose as representatives of charitable organizations; volunteers in community-affiliated groups; members of social associations; and representatives of known professional organizations, such as state police or local fire department unions. In all cases, their sole purpose is to gain their potential victims' personal and financial information. In some extreme cases, these criminals create false merchant sites to elicit personal information or employ hacking and cracking methods to infiltrate directly the valid organizations they claim to represent in order to gather personal information about the organizations' donors.

Identity Theft Techniques

Several common techniques are used to conduct identity theft. Some criminals conduct what is known as "dumpster diving" expeditions, in which they literally rummage through business and residential trash cans and dumpsters to search for copies of checks, credit card and bank statements, credit card solicitations, or other records that contain personal information. After the thieves harvest such information, it becomes possible for them to assume the identities of other persons and take control of the latters' active accounts or even establish new accounts in their victims' names.

A second technique used by identity thieves has been dubbed "shoulder surfing." In this technique, offenders literally look over the shoulders of their potential victims as the latter enter personal information into telephones, computers, and automatic teller machines (ATMs). They may also wait for potential victims to leave credit card receipts on restaurant tables or in trash receptacles near automatic teller machines, banks, and residences. After the offenders get hold of codes, passwords, and account information, they begin the process of victimization.

Identity thieves who use "under the color of authority" and "skimming" fraudulently obtain credit reports by using their employers' authorized access to credit report companies without authorization and by posing as landlords, employers, and other persons who may have legitimate rights to see people's personal information. Skimming occurs when thieves steal credit and debit card account numbers when the cards are processed at restaurants, retail stores, and other business locations. Thieves employing this technique use a special data-collecting device known as a "skimmer."

Another technique used by identity theft criminals is called " phishing"—a technique used on the Internet that plays on the word "fishing." Phishing identity thieves send out large volumes of unsolicited electronic mail messages that appear to be from legitimate companies requesting personal account information. Criminals then use the data they harvest to their own advantage by robbing the unsuspecting victims' accounts. As technology has advanced, some criminals have discovered ways to send e-mails that will install a virus simply upon the opening of the message rather than just by clicking on a link or attachment. Beginning in 2012, another form of phishing became more prevalent: SMS phishing, or "smishing." In these instances, criminals send bad links and fake telephone numbers prompting victims to provide personal information through text messages on cell phones; these scams are not as easy to recognize as on a computer.

Pharming, yet another Internet technique employed by identity thieves, involves hacking into a website (such as merchant sites) and redirecting users to a different, fraudulent website. Under the impression that they are still on the correct and trusted site, victims might unknowingly submit personal and account information directly to an identity thief.

History

Identity theft is not a new crime phenomenon. Criminals have been committing similar offenses for centuries. Classic examples are petty thieves who steal wallets and purses and use the credit cards in them to go on shopping sprees. Until recent years, such crimes were categorized simply as fraud and petty theft. However, with vast advances in computing and telecommunication technologies of the late 1990s, a new wave of identity thieves emerged who were skilled at concealing both their true identities and their illicit behavior.

Fraudulent transactions on the Internet are the most common form of identity theft crimes. Before the rise of the Internet, identity theft criminals had to appear in person at banks and lending institutions to apply for accounts and faced a high risk of being caught. However, with the instant credit accounts now available on the Internet, the likelihood of identity theft criminals being caught has been significantly reduced, while the potential rewards for thievery have increased greatly.

It was not until 1998 that the federal government finally acknowledged the threat posed by identity theft and enacted legislation against it. The first federal law of its kind, the Identity Theft and Assumption Deterrence Act of 1998 served as a model for the individual states to follow in drafting their identity theft legislation.

Prevalence

The full damage done by identity theft is difficult to measure since identity theft is often the means by which criminals commit other crimes. Moreover, victims may not even know they have been victimized for more than a full year after the fact. It has been estimated that average identity theft victims do not know they have been victimized until fourteen to sixteen months after the crimes occur. Because of their consequent embarrassment or shame, they often do not file criminal complaints.

In fiscal year 2003, the federal government estimated that American financial and business institutions lost about $48 billion to identity theft, and individual citizens lost about $5 billion to the crime. The federal government has since admitted that identity theft is one of the fastest-growing categories of crime in the United States. According to the Federal Trade Commission (FTC), in 2003 an estimated ten million Americans had been victims of identity theft during the previous year; twenty-seven million had been victims during the previous five years; and close to 35 million had been victims during the previous ten years. In 2012, the Justice Department's Bureau of Justice Statistics announced that more than sixteen million people age sixteen and older had experienced at least one incident of identity theft that year. Two years later, identity theft was still landing at the top of the FTC's annual list of consumer complaints, representing 13 percent of the more than two million complaints filed. According to the FTC's report, there was an increase in complaints regarding people posing as government or Internal Revenue Service (IRS) employees in an attempt to steal identities.

Investigation

The need for stronger law enforcement against identity theft has been evident in the fact that a small amount out of hundreds of cases result in capture and successful prosecution of offenders by federal authorities. The rate is even smaller for local and state authorities. One of the most pressing issues facing law enforcement is how to investigate and successfully prosecute the often complex identity theft cases. Since the year 2000, all fifty US states have enacted identity theft laws.

Many federal, state, and local law-enforcement agencies and private institutions participate in the identity theft investigation and prosecution. These range from such federal regulatory agencies as the FTC to nonprofit organizations, such as the Identity Theft Resource Center in California, that work closely with law enforcement.

Section 5 of the federal Identity Theft Act makes the FTC a central clearinghouse for identity theft complaints. The law requires the FTC to log and acknowledge complaints, provide victims with relevant information, and refer their complaints to such entities as major national consumer reporting agencies and other state and local law-enforcement agencies.

The US Department of Justice encourages federal prosecutors to make greater use of the resources on identity theft provided by regulatory agencies and nonprofit watchdog groups. The FTC's Consumer Sentinel database, for example, is an invaluable resource for federal agents and prosecutors; it provides instant access to thousands of complaints filed about possible identity thefts. In addition, the Internet Fraud Complaint Center—a joint project of the Federal Bureau of Investigation (FBI) and the National White Collar Crime Center—provides investigators with information about Internet fraud schemes in which identity theft may figure.

The Department of Justice recognizes that all identity theft victimizations are serious offenses, even when no money is actually taken. Identity theft demands a comprehensive response that involves prosecution for identity theft and other offenses as appropriate laws prescribe. This holistic approach requires legitimate and continual cooperation among federal, state, and local law-enforcement agencies.

On the federal investigative level, violations of the Identity Theft Act are examined by such investigative agencies as the US Secret Service, the FBI, and the US Postal Inspection Service. They are then prosecuted directly by the Department of Justice.

The Department of Justice prosecutes identity theft and fraud cases under a variety of federal statutes, while also assisting various state and local district attorneys in preparing and prosecuting their cases. Federal prosecutors in various states also make use of multiagency task forces that share resources to investigate identity theft and other related white-collar crime. The Secret Service in particular recognizes the exponential growth of the electronic and computer world and developed a plan of action in late 1995 to create nontraditional task forces to assist in combating such crimes as identity theft.

In the past, traditional task forces consisted largely of law-enforcement officers and investigators to the exclusion of other parties that could make considerable contributions. This new type of nontraditional task force evolved into what the Secret Service named the Electronic Crimes Task Force. The first of its kind was established in the state of New York in 1995 and consisted of not only law-enforcement officers and analysts from various different levels, but also prosecutors, private industry professionals, and academics. By establishing new relationships with private sector organizations and numerous university scholars, the task force opened itself up to sources of information and communication lines with limitless potential. Now, task forces in every region of the United States deal with identity theft and related crimes. Although the victimization rate continues to increase, the efforts of both investigators and prosecutors continue to grow stronger and more effective, with hopes of eventually winning the war against identity thieves.

Since 1999, the US Department of Justice has chaired the Identity Theft Subcommittee of the Attorney General's Council on White-Collar Crime. The subcommittee brings together representatives from federal, state, and local law-enforcement and regulatory agencies on a monthly basis. They share data about identity theft developments and promote interagency cooperation and coordination on identity theft enforcement and prevention efforts.

In 2013, the Internal Revenue Service (IRS) expanded a pilot program designed to aid in law-enforcement efforts to track down and apprehend identity thieves in the growing area of tax fraud. The organization's Law Enforcement Assistance program grew to include all fifty states. The IRS agreed, through this program, to help law-enforcement officials get consent from taxpayers to obtain suspected fraudulent tax returns in the pursuit of an identity thief.

Prosecution and Punishment

Since Congress's enactment of the Identity Theft Act in 1998, federal prosecutors have made increasing use of the law's power and have issued sentences to convicted offenders that have ranged as high as fifteen years in prison, along with substantial fines, for offenses that net at least one thousand dollars during any twelve-month period. In July of 2004, President George W. Bush signed the Identity Theft Penalty Enhancement Act, which expanded maximum penalties for identity theft. The new legislation also defined a new offense, "aggravated identity theft," as a charge that can be added to other criminal charges in crimes that employ stolen identities, such as terrorist acts and various forms of fraud.

In addition, to ensure that persons convicted under the federal identity theft statutes receive appropriately tough sentences, the United States Sentencing Commission, with unwavering support from the Department of Justice, issued new guidelines for identity theft crimes. Even cases in which there is no monetary loss or that involve first-time offenders could result in prison sentences. The guidelines also encouraged harsher penalties for more severe offenses, such as those that seriously affect their victims' lives.

In 2008, President Bush signed the Identity Theft Enforcement and Restitution Act into law. This bill authorized victims to receive a payment equivalent to the amount of time reasonably spent resolving the complications caused by identity theft crimes, such as dealing with credit bureaus. Additionally, the law allowed federal courts to prosecute identity theft criminals if they live in the same state as their victims, made the damaging of ten or more protected computers used by or for the government or financial institutions within one year a felony, made it easier for prosecutors to bring charges against hackers and cybercriminals, and encouraged the Sentencing Commission to further review its guidelines.

According to the National Conference of State Legislatures, thirty-seven states introduced identity-theft legislation in 2013 alone. These bills, many of which were enacted, included additions to the definition of identity theft and altering the level of punishment for the crime.

Paul M. Klenowski

Further Reading

Bureau of Justice Statistics. "16.6 Million People Experienced Identity Theft in 2012." *Bureau of Justice Statistics*. Bureau of Justice Statistics, 12 Dec. 2013. Web. 22 July 2015.

Federal Trade Commission. "Identity Theft Tops FTC's Consumer Complaint Categories Again in 2014." *Federal Trade Commission*. Federal Trade Commission, 27 Feb. 2015. Web. 22 July 2015.

General Accounting Office. *Identity Theft: Prevalence and Cost Appear to Be Growing*. Washington, DC: General Printing Office, 2002. Print.

Hage, Brian S., et al. *Identity Theft in the United States*. Morgantown: Natl. White Collar Crime Center, 2001. Print.

Hammond, Robert J., Jr. *Identity Theft: How to Protect Your Most Valuable Asset*. Franklin Lakes: Career, 2003. Print.

Hayward, Claudia L., ed. *Identity Theft*. Hauppauge: Novinka, 2004. Print.

Internal Revenue Service. "IRS Expands Law Enforcement Assistance Program on Identity Theft to 50 States; Victim Assistance and Criminal Investigations Grow." *IRS*. IRS, 28 Mar. 2013. Web. 21 July 2015.

Jasper, Margaret C. *Identity Theft and How to Protect Yourself*. Dobbs Ferry: Oceana, 2002. Print.

Krebs, Brian. "New Federal Law Targets ID Theft, Cybercrime." *Washington Post*. Washington Post, 1 Oct. 2008. Web. 22 July 2015.

National Conference of State Legislatures. "Identity Theft State Legislation 2013." *National Conference of State Legislatures*. Natl. Conference of State Legislatures, 19 Feb. 2014. Web. 22 July 2015.

Sullivan, Bob. *Your Evil Twin: Behind the Identity Theft Epidemic*. New York: Wiley, 2004. Print.

Vacca, John R. *Identity Theft*. Upper Saddle River: Prentice Hall, 2003. Print.

Welsh, Amanda. *The Identity Theft Protection Guide: Safeguard Your Family, Protect Your Privacy, Recover a Stolen Identity*. New York: St. Martin's, 2004. Print.

See also Computer fraud; Criminals; Cybercrime; Forensic accounting; Forgery; Fraud; Telephone fraud; Theft; White-collar crime.

Juvenile courts

Definition: Courts specializing in cases involving juvenile offenders

Courts; Juvenile justice; Rehabilitation

Significance: Relative to adult criminal courts, juvenile courts provide a more rehabilitative and prevention-oriented approach to defendants, while observing the specific legal rights of juveniles.

In 1899, Illinois established the first juvenile court in the United States, marking a significant change in the way society dealt with youthful offenders. Prior to that time, criminal courts treated juveniles and adults similarly, and they often convicted and sentenced children as young as seven. Throughout the nineteenth century, individuals and organizations advocated for reforms in the criminal justice system. They argued that juveniles are developmentally different from adults and that the justice system should recognize this difference in its treatment and punishment of juveniles. The juvenile court was a product of these reforms.

A guiding principle of the early juvenile courts was *parens patriae*, which refers to the state acting in a parental role to care for the protection and welfare of juveniles. Under this principle, the courts treated juvenile offenders as delinquents, not criminals, and they used a variety of noncriminal sanctions in an effort to rehabilitate delinquent juveniles. Relative to criminal courts, juvenile court proceedings were less adversarial, and judges considered a larger variety of extralegal factors in making decisions. Every state had some form of juvenile court legislation by 1945, established on the premise that juveniles could be rehabilitated through appropriate treatment programs and services.

Changes in Juvenile Courts

While the early reforms fostered a more benevolent and humane system of juvenile justice, they also produced a system in which juveniles lacked many due process rights afforded to adults charged with crimes, including access to counsel. With the state acting in a parental role, these rights seemed unnecessary for juveniles. This lack of rights and protections was frequently challenged, however, and as the twentieth century progressed, juvenile courts experienced several procedural changes stemming from decisions of the US Supreme Court.

Some of the most significant changes came from the Supreme Court's 1967 decision in the case *In re Gault*, in which, among other things, the Court ruled that a juvenile has a constitutional right to a notice of charges, a right to counsel, and a protection against self-incrimination. These and other Supreme Court rulings created a juvenile court that was more formal procedurally but still focused on the unique developmental capacities and needs of juveniles.

Legislative changes also affected juvenile courts in the latter half of the twentieth century. During the 1950s and 1960s, the public became concerned with the large number of juveniles detained or imprisoned for rehabilitative treatment, especially as treatment programs generally failed to demonstrate effectiveness in reducing delinquent behavior. In 1974, Congress passed the Juvenile Justice and Delinquency Prevention Act, which required the deinstitutionalization of juvenile detention facilities. As part of this process, detention and correctional facilities began to remove status offenders and to separate juvenile and adult offenders.

During the 1980s, the public's perception that juvenile crime in the United States was rapidly increasing led to a second wave of significant legislative changes. Several states enacted punitive laws and limited the discretion and jurisdiction of the juvenile court. Some states identified certain offenses for which juveniles would be automatically transferred to adult criminal court, and other states established mandatory minimum sentences for serious offenses. In sum, these changes produced a juvenile court system that more closely resembled the adult criminal court system.

In 2004, juvenile courts varied widely from state to state. As a group, however, juvenile courts continued to reflect the public and legislative intent to get "tough on crime." During the 1990s, almost all state juvenile court systems became more punitive in their procedures regarding transfers to adult court, sentencing, and confidentiality of juvenile court records and hearings.

The Juvenile Court Process

Juvenile courts typically follow a similar pattern in processing delinquency cases. When a juvenile is accused of breaking the law, the prosecution, typically referred to as the district attorney or state attorney, must decide whether to pursue the case in court, to handle it informally, or to dismiss the case altogether. Approximately 2.1 million youths are arrested per year. Informal processing usually involves diverting the juvenile's case to community service or to some type of counseling or education program. These services and programs are often designed to prevent future delinquent behavior.

If the prosecution formally processes the case by filing a delinquency petition, the judge is then responsible for adjudicating the case. The adjudication process often requires a trial, at which the judge will determine if the juvenile is delinquent or is responsible for the offense. At the disposition stage, the judge typically has the discretion to place a delinquent juvenile on probation or in a commitment facility for a specified length of time. The juvenile court also handles cases in which delinquent juveniles violate conditions of their juvenile probation, and it determines the need to hold juveniles in secure detention during the adjudication process.

Christopher M. Hill

Further Reading

Champion, Dean John. *The Juvenile Justice System: Delinquency, Processing, and the Law*. 4th ed. Upper Saddle River: Prentice-Hall, 2003. Print.

Humes, Edward. *No Matter How Loud I Shout: A Year in the Life of Juvenile Court*. Reprint ed. New York: Touchstone, 1997. Print.

McCord, Joan, Cathy Spatz Widom, and Nancy Crowell, eds. *Juvenile Crime, Juvenile Justice*. Washington, D.C.: National Academy, 2001. Print.

Tanenhaus, David S. *Juvenile Justice in the Making*. New York: Oxford UP, 2004. Print.

Watkins, John C., Jr. *The Juvenile Justice Century: A Sociolegal Commentary on American Juvenile Courts*. Durham, N.C.: Carolina Academic, 1998. Print.

See also Blended sentences; Court types; Diversion; *Gault, In re*; Juvenile delinquency; Juvenile Justice and Delinquency Prevention Act; Juvenile justice system; Juvenile waivers to adult courts; *Parens patriae*; Probation, juvenile; Restitution; Status offenses; Uniform Juvenile Court Act; Vandalism; Youth authorities; *Roper v. Simmons (2005)*.

Juvenile delinquency

Definition: Adolescent criminal behavior
Juvenile justice; Rehabilitation; Violent crime
Significance: Juvenile delinquency is a major social concern in the United States. Every year, millions of juveniles are arrested on charges ranging from minor status offenses, such as truancy, to such serious crimes as burglary, robbery, rape, auto theft, aggravated assault, larceny, and homicide. Moreover, juvenile delinquency often carries over into adult criminal behavior.

Widely publicized school shootings during the late 1990s and first two decades of the twenty-first century have raised public concerns about rising adolescent violence and created the perception that juvenile delinquency is increasing. However, statistical studies show that juvenile crime rates are actually declining. In 2012 there were 182 violent crime arrests for every 100,000 people between the ages of ten and seventeen, a rate 38 percent below the 1980 rate and 68 percent below that of the peak year, 1994. The overall arrest rate, including nonviolent crimes, was 3,941 in 100,000, also 38 percent lower than in 1980. Nevertheless, public pressures have been mounting for wholesale reforms in the juvenile justice system, including calls for abandoning the system and treating adolescent offenders as adults. In order to understand the role of juveniles in the American criminal justice system, it is necessary to examine the root causes of juvenile delinquency.

Patterns of Delinquency

A common assumption about adolescent crime is that juveniles from lower-class families are more apt to be delinquent than those from middle- and upper-class families. However, this view has been disputed by some researchers, who claim that no connections between social class and delinquency exist, and that to infer otherwise borders on racism. Furthermore, while some scholars see connections between race and delinquency (African American juveniles were arrested at twice the rate of their white peers in 2012), other researchers disagree, stating that while black juveniles are arrested at a higher frequency, the reason is that crimes committed by African Americans are more likely to come to the attention of the police.

There are also connections between age arrests. For example, the ages of juvenile property crime offenders peak at sixteen and then decline sharply thereafter. Arrest rates for violent crimes peak at age eighteen, followed by a much slower decline. Likewise, there are also connections between gender and delinquency, with boys having higher rates of delinquency than girls. Gender differences are most evident in violent and property crimes, with boys committing most of the most serious offenses. Girls do commit similar types of crimes, but less frequently. Statistics show that boys are more likely than girls to be arrested for every category of crime except prostitution and running away.

Individual juvenile offenders tend to differ from adult offenders in the varieties of crimes that they commit. Only a small number of juvenile offenders specialize in specific crimes. A large majority of them commit a wide range of minor offenses, such as truancy, disorderly conduct, loitering, and curfew violations. However, only a small percentage commit mixtures of both minor and serious offenses.

The ages at which juveniles begin their delinquent behavior are strong indicators in predicting their future criminal behavior. The term "early onset" is applied to juveniles who begin behaving delinquently in their early childhood. Early onset delinquents usually continue their delinquent behavior into adulthood. Moreover,

Poster promoting planned housing as a method to deter juvenile delinquency. (Public domain, via Wikimedia Commons)

they commit delinquent acts at higher rates, and the crimes they commit are more often violent. The term "adolescent onset" applies to juveniles who do not begin their delinquent behavior until they reach adolescence. Adolescent onset delinquents are more common than early onset delinquents, and the crimes they commit are, on average, less serious. Adolescent onset delinquents are also more likely to stop their delinquent activities in late adolescence.

General Risk Factors

One point about juvenile delinquency that is almost undisputed is that there is a strong correlation between poverty and criminal behavior. Most scholars and juvenile justice professionals agree that adolescent violence and aggression is strongly linked to socioeconomic status, for several primary reasons. Poverty makes it difficult for parents and communities to provide the needed guidance and supervision juveniles need. Also, unemployed men in rough inner-city environments have a greater tendency than men living comfortably in middle- and upper-class communities to behave aggressively in order to assert their power and strength. Violence tends to beget violence. Juveniles growing up in dysfunctional environments in which aggressive behavior is praised are apt to engage in violence themselves.

A more controversial subject that has received major media coverage concerns biological factors: the question of how heredity, or genetics, influences antisocial behavior. Studies of genetically identical twins and biologically unrelated adopted siblings have shown that links do exist between genetics and delinquency. However, most researchers agree that criminal behavior is more likely when there are matches between juveniles' genetic predispositions toward lawbreaking and living in environments conducive to such activity.

Individual traits have also been found to correlate with delinquency, especially for high-rate and serious offenders. Studies have shown that juveniles with low verbal intelligence quotas—those who have trouble with self-expression, remembering information, and thinking abstractly—have an increased probability for delinquency. Lack of verbal skills contribute to difficulties in attaining goals in a positive manner. Juveniles suffering from attention deficit hyperactivity disorder (ADHD) are more likely to exhibit symptoms of juvenile delinquency.

A primary concern about ADHD adolescents is the hyperactivity/impulsivity continuum of the disorder. Common ADHD behaviors include being overly active for one's age, acting impulsively, focusing only on immediate events, and engaging in generally reckless behavior. ADHD also creates a greater need for stimulation that makes adolescents seek excitement, an impulse that easily bored juveniles may satisfy by turning to crime, which they may even regard as fun. Other manifestations of ADHD include reduced ability to learn from punishment, insensitivity to others, poor interpersonal problem-solving skills, and drug and alcohol use.

Family and School Factors

Family factors that play a role in breeding juvenile delinquency include having criminal parents, living in large families, growing up with little discipline, parental rejection, low socioeconomic status, and frequent changes of residence. Parents who exhibit hyper-aggressive behavior teach their children, by example, to be "strong" and "tough."

A factor that inhibits delinquent tendencies is having parents who express their love openly and take active interests in their children's daily lives. Other protective factors include attachment to parents, lack of serious family conflicts, church attendance, community support, and emphasis on academic achievement. Parental socialization is crucial, as parents teach their children not to engage in criminal behavior. When parents are indifferent to their children's development, the likelihood of delinquency increases.

School experiences correlate with juvenile delinquency as well. Low academic performance, misbehavior in and out of classrooms, weak attachments to teachers and principals, and lack of involvement in school activities are all associated with delinquency. Some schools have proven themselves successful in dealing with juvenile delinquents. Small schools with high teacher-pupil ratios and adequate supplies of needed materials, such as computers and overhead projectors, can be protective factors against adolescent criminality. Other desirable qualities in schools include clear and concise rules, absence of corporal punishment, enjoyable working conditions for both faculty and students, and, most important, teachers who care about their students.

Youth Gangs

The old adage "Birds of a feather flock together" accurately sums up the impact of youth gangs on juvenile delinquency. Gangs are perceived as distinct groups of individuals within communities. Their members see themselves as unique and different and worthy of commanding respect. A central hallmark for gang involvement, however, is myriad criminal acts leading to negative responses from both the police and community residents. Youth gangs are common throughout the United States and can be found in virtually every city, including small towns and rural communities.

Many arrests for violent acts of juvenile delinquency are gang related, and most serious juvenile violence occurs in encounters between members of rival gangs. As a means of protection, gang members frequently carry guns, which range from small handguns and shotguns to automatic assault rifles and machine guns.

Most gang members are young African Americans between the ages sixteen and twenty. Some gangs are highly organized structures, while others have little structure. Individual gang members may be classified as instigators and followers; instigators are mostly boys, and girls are mostly followers. Delinquent peers tend to reinforce each other's maladaptive behavior and allay one another's concerns about police and societal sanctions.

Reasons for joining gangs include possessing poor social skills that prohibit the delinquent from affiliating with nondelinquent adolescents, which may result from negative experiences at school. Desire for money is also a strong motivator, as most gang members come from poor families and see few alternative prospects for making money. Stressful living conditions in homes also promote gang involvement.

Illegal drugs play an important role in youth gangs, many of whose members use drugs and traffic in them. The need for money to buy drugs tends to lead gang members into other types of crime. Addicted gang members who cannot find the money to support their drug habits may even be driven to more serious crimes, including murder, to find ways to obtain their drugs. Moreover, studies have shown that many juvenile offenders are under the influence of drugs when they commit crimes. It is possible that the majority of violent crimes committed by delinquents are drug related.

Theories About Delinquency

Many theories have been advanced over the years that attempt to explain why some juveniles become delinquent while others do not. During the 1950s, Albert Bandura, a psychologist at Stanford University, formulated what he called social learning theory as a means for understanding how people learn new behaviors. In essence, his theory posits that people are more likely to repeat behaviors for which they receive positive reinforcement, while avoiding those for which they receive nothing or negative reinforcement. For a given behavior to be learned, all that is needed is the requisite level of reinforcement applied at the appropriate time. By contrast, for a behavior to be unlearned, all reinforcement should be withheld.

Bandura's theory posits that crime is a learned behavior and that what is learned can be unlearned by using sound psychological principles. According to social learning theory, the behavior of delinquent juveniles results from exposure to people with maladaptive values and attitudes toward crime. Over time, juveniles in such environments become socialized to accept antisocial behavior. Rational choice theory is another method that attempts to understand what makes juveniles delinquent. It argues that juvenile delinquency should be viewed from the perspectives of the individuals who choose to engage in criminal activity. Before initiating illegal acts, individuals weigh the chances of succeeding versus failing and being caught by authorities. After they make up their minds, they decide on courses of action, thus making logical decisions. A hallmark of antisocial behavior is lack of empathy for victims. Rational theory holds that to ameliorate juvenile delinquency, adolescents must be taught how to empathize with others. According to rational choice theory, people capable of choosing bad behaviors are equally capable of choosing legal behaviors.

Social strain theory argues that when juveniles experience mental stress or conflict, they become upset and engage in delinquent behavior because they are being inundated by negative thoughts and feelings. The theory holds that there are two major "strain" categories: failing to achieve one's goals and loss of positive stimuli or presentations of negative stimuli. The first type of strain generally centers on obtaining money, winning status and respect, and seeking personal autonomy. The second category deals with adolescents' loss of things that they value, as well as the presentation of noxious stimuli. Examples of the former might include being insulted before one's peers or becoming a victim of a crime. Examples of the latter include learning that one's parents are divorcing, having a romantic relationship end, or being arrested by police. Treatment methods involve various behavioral techniques such as self-talk, self-management, anger management, and relaxation therapy.

Punishment and Prevention

Many "get-tough" advocates feel that juvenile delinquency can be reduced if delinquents have a greater fear of being incarcerated, especially if they realize how harsh incarceration can be. However, studies of the deterrent effect of harsher punishments do not support such views. Increasing the harshness of incarceration has not been reflected in reductions of delinquent behavior, even of juveniles released from incarceration.

Among the reasons advanced for why punitive measures do not reduce delinquency is that punishments do not address the underlying causes of delinquent behavior. Moreover, while punishment might cause offenders mental and physical distress, it may also contribute to their social learning by teaching them how not to get caught. Finally, it is pointed out that the notion of deterrence is based on assumptions of rational behavior, while most juvenile delinquents, as well as their adult counterparts, do not always think rationally.

The concept of incapacitation has been promoted heavily in the media as a strategy for controlling delinquency. The principle behind incapacitation is that the best method for combating criminal behavior is to lock up the perpetrators for long periods. Delinquents who are locked up cannot cause society any further trouble. However, studies of the effectiveness of incapacitation on reducing delinquency have shown that incapacitation achieves only nominal reductions. Prevention programs attempt to prevent juveniles from becoming delinquents in the first place. Federal legislation funding juvenile justice programs has tended to favor proven prevention programs over more expensive deterrence and incapacitation programs. Well-designed programs that emphasize treating problems over punishing behavior have been found to reduce delinquency significantly. By intensively targeting the causes of delinquency, the programs often have effects that last for long periods. Their instructors rely heavily on cognitive behavioral techniques and stress changing the juveniles' ways of thinking, since a major premise in cognitive behaviorism is that one's thought processes are echoed in behavior. For example, juveniles who come into the programs thinking that the only way they can make decent livings is by engaging in criminal activity are taught how to eradicate negative cognition, replacing it with positive problem-solving skills. Research thus far indicates that the prevention programs are indeed helping juvenile delinquents.

Cary Stacy Smith

Further Reading

Agnew, Robert, and Timothy Brezina. *Juvenile Delinquency: Causes and Control*. New York: Oxford UP, 2014. Print.

Bernard, Thomas J. *The Cycle of Juvenile Justice*. New York: Oxford UP, 1992. Print.

Binder, Arnold, Gilbert Geis, and Dickson Bruce. *Juvenile Delinquency: Historical, Cultural and Legal Perspectives*. New York: Macmillan, 1988. Print.

Champion, Dean John. *The Juvenile Justice System: Delinquency, Processing, and the Law*. 4th ed. Upper Saddle River: Prentice, 2003. Print.

Cox, Steven M., John J. Conrad, and Jennifer M. Allen. *Juvenile Justice: A Guide to Theory and Practice*. 5th ed. New York: McGraw-Hill, 2003. Print.

Feld, Barry C. *Cases and Materials on Juvenile Justice Administration*. St. Paul: West, 2000. Print.

Jonson-Reid, M. "Child Welfare Services and Delinquency: The Need to Know More." *Child Welfare* 83.2 (2004): 157-74. Print.

Malmgren, K. W., and S. M. Meisel. "Examining the Link Between Child Maltreatment and Delinquency for Youth with Emotional and Behavioral Disorders." *Child Welfare* 83.2 (2004): 175-89. Print.

Paternoster, R., S. Bushway, R. Brame, and R. Apel. "The Effects of Teenage Employment on Delinquency and Problem Behaviors." *Social Force* 82.1 (2003): 297-336. Print.

Rosenheim, Margaret K., et al., eds. *A Century of Juvenile Justice*. Chicago: U of Chicago P, 2002. Print.

Shoemaker, D. J. *Theories of Delinquency: An Examination of Explanations of Delinquent Behavior*. 4th ed. New York: Oxford UP, 2000. Print.

Sickmund, Melissa, and Charles Puzzanchera, eds. *Juvenile Offenders and Victims: 2014 National Report*. Pittsburgh: Natl. Ctr. for Juvenile Justice, 2014. PDF file.

Winterdyk, John A., ed. *Juvenile Justice: International Perspectives, Models, and Trends*. Boca Raton: CRC, 2015. Print.

See also Contributing to delinquency of minors; Juvenile courts; Juvenile Justice and Delinquency Prevention, Office of; Juvenile Justice and Delinquency Prevention Act; Juvenile justice system; Juvenile waivers to adult courts; *Parens patriae*; Probation, juvenile; Status offenses; Uniform Juvenile Court Act; Vandalism; Wickersham Commission; Youth authorities; Youth gangs; Addiction; Bullying; *Roper v. Simmons* (2005).

Juvenile Justice and Delinquency Prevention Act

The Law: Federal law that was the US Congress's first major attempt to unify the treatment of juvenile offenders throughout the United States
Date: Became effective on September 7, 1974
Juvenile justice; Morality and public order
Significance: This landmark federal legislation created the Office of Juvenile Justice and Delinquency Prevention and recommended major changes to state juvenile justice systems.

The Juvenile Justice and Delinquency Prevention Act of 1974 (JJDPA) was enacted by the US Congress to provide juvenile offenders uniform treatment in every state's justice system. The act was passed with strong support from both Democrats and Republicans and a wide range of special interest groups. Because each state has independent jurisdiction over its juvenile court system, participation in the JJDPA was made optional, and the act made federal funds available to states that chose to participate. This federal funding served as strong motivation for the individual states to bring their juvenile justice systems into compliance with the new federal requirements. Under the JJDPA, states were mandated to remove status offenders from secure and correctional facilities. This movement is often referred to as the deinstitutionalization of status offenders. Another significant requirement placed on states by JJDPA was a prohibition against placing juveniles in any institutions in which they might have regular contacts with adult offenders.

Since 1974, Congress has periodically reauthorized the Juvenile Justice and Delinquency Prevention Act and appropriated funds to support the programs it created. Furthermore, Congress has responded to trends in juvenile crime in the United States by reevaluating and amending the act. For example, during the late 1980s, rising violent juvenile crime rates prompted Congress to refocus the Juvenile Justice and Delinquency Prevention

Act on serious and chronic juvenile offenders, allowing states to prosecute certain juvenile offenders as adults.

The 2004 version of the Juvenile Justice and Delinquency Prevention Act established two primary goals for the law. First, states were required to provide high-quality prevention programs that work with juveniles, their families, and communities to prevent delinquent behavior. Second, states were required to hold juveniles accountable for their actions by providing opportunities to make restitution to victims, perform community service, and develop the character qualities necessary to become productive members of their communities.

Laurie M. Kubicek

Further Reading
Champion, Dean John. *The Juvenile Justice System: Delinquency, Processing, and the Law.* 4th ed. Upper Saddle River, N.J.: Prentice-Hall, 2003.
Cox, Steven M., John J. Conrad, and Jennifer M. Allen. *Juvenile Justice: A Guide to Theory and Practice.* 5th ed. New York: McGraw-Hill, 2003.
Hess, Karen M., and Robert W. Drowns. *Juvenile Justice.* 4th ed. Belmont, Calif.: Wadsworth/Thomson Learning, 2004. Comprehensive overview of the juvenile justice system that connects theory and practice.
Olson-Raymer, Gayle. *Criminology: The Role of the Federal Government in Juvenile Delinquency Prevention-Historical and Contemporary Perspectives.* Evanston, Ill.: Northwestern School of Law Journal of Criminal Law and Criminology, 1983.

See also Contributing to delinquency of minors; Diversion; Juvenile courts; Juvenile delinquency; Juvenile Justice and Delinquency Prevention, Office of; Juvenile justice system; Juvenile waivers to adult courts; Status offenses; Uniform Juvenile Court Act; Youth authorities; *Roper v. Simmons* (2005).

Juvenile Justice and Delinquency Prevention, Office of

Identification: Branch of the US Department of Justice that provides support to states, local communities, and Native American tribal jurisdictions in an effort to treat and prevent serious juvenile delinquency, child abuse, and child neglect
Date: Established in 1974
Significance: The Office of Juvenile Justice and Delinquency Prevention, or OJJDP, was created to provide federal aid to states and local communities in a continued and comprehensive initiative to deinstitutionalize and decentralize the practices of the juvenile justice system throughout the United States.

A semiautonomous branch within the federal Department of Justice's Law Enforcement Administration Agency (LEAA), the OJJDP provides information and funding to local, state, and tribal juvenile justice agencies. Through this provision, the OJJDP aids these agencies in child service provisions, public protection, research initiatives, and specialized training for justice system officials interacting with youth.

The OJJDP was established when the US Congress passed the Juvenile Justice and Delinquency Prevention Act in 1974. Initial motivation for the creation of the office was the provision of funding to state and local jurisdictions involved in continued efforts to develop alternatives to confinement for juvenile offenders. This primary goal persisted throughout the 1980s.

During the 1990s, the OJJDP embraced a comprehensive approach to the study and treatment of juvenile delinquency, stressing prevention, assessment of risk and need, family factors, and graduated sanctions for youth. In 2002, Congress reauthorized the Juvenile Justice and Delinquency Prevention Act, which provided for continued support of the OJJDP's initial goals while increasing funding opportunities for communities and states, as well as placing a renewed focus on research, training, technical assistance, and the dissemination of information.

Courtney A. Waid

Further Reading
Champion, Dean John. *The Juvenile Justice System: Delinquency, Processing, and the Law.* 4th ed. Upper Saddle River, N.J.: Prentice Hall, 2003.
Olson-Raymer, Gayle. *Criminology: The Role of the Federal Government in Juvenile Delinquency Prevention-Historical and Contemporary Perspectives.* Evanston, Ill.: Northwestern School of Law Journal of Criminal Law and Criminology, 1983.
Tanenhaus, David S. *Juvenile Justice in the Making.* New York: Oxford University Press, 2004.

See also Contributing to delinquency of minors; DARE programs; Juvenile delinquency; Juvenile Justice and Delinquency Prevention Act; Juvenile justice system; Probation, juvenile; Restorative justice; Uniform Juvenile Court Act; Youth authorities; Peacemaking criminology; *Roper v. Simmons* (2005).

Juvenile justice system

Definition: Separate justice system developed for minors Courts; Juvenile justice; Rehabilitation
Significance: Since the turn of the twentieth century, one of the most significant developments in the American justice system has been a trend away from treating

juvenile offenders in the adult justice system by developing a largely autonomous system of justice designed for the special needs of adolescents.

The origins of America's separate juvenile justice system go back to 1899, when the state of Illinois created the first juvenile courts in Cook County, which includes Chicago. That first system had a special juvenile court and associated clinics staffed with experts in social services. Compared to traditional adult courts, that juvenile court was informal. Focusing on rehabilitating minors, it operated under the philosophy of *parens patriae*, which means the state playing the role of parent. That principle gave Illinois's court the power to intervene in the lives of any juvenile under the age of sixteen who committed delinquent or criminal acts or was thought to be in need of state help. Since then, *parens patriae* has been the cornerstone of the juvenile justice system in the United States.

The special clinics that opened in conjunction with the first juvenile court system employed experts in psychology and sociology to treat and punish juveniles. During the nineteenth century, troubled minors who were taken from their homes were generally confined in so-called houses of refuge, which attempted to reeducate youths using indeterminate sentencing, education, skills training, physical labor, religious training, parental discipline, and apprenticeships. In reality, the houses of refuge resembled harsh military training camps, in which minors were ill-treated and overworked in overcrowded conditions.

New reformatories were developed after problems with houses of refuge became apparent. Reformatory facilities were systems of cottages that resembled traditional family homes. Most of the reformatories were located in rural areas, where physical labor was emphasized. Like the houses of refuge, the reformatories tried to teach minors skills they could use to become law-abiding and contributing adults. Foster parent arrangements were also made for some juveniles, and probation became popular for juveniles during the early twentieth century.

The Philosophy of *Parens Patriae*

The principle of *parens patriae* has had a profound impact on the development of juvenile justice in the United States. Under that philosophy, minors can be confined in houses of refuge or reformatories for being incorrigible and unruly, regardless of their parents' wishes. The constitutionality of the broad government power was challenged on numerous occasions. The first challenge came as early as in 1838, when the case of *Ex Parte Crouse* reached the Supreme Court of Pennsylvania. In that case, a father challenged the constitutionality of *parens patriae* through a writ of *habeas corpus* after his daughter, Mary Ann, was sent to a house of refuge against his will. Although Mary Ann was described by her mother as wayward and disobedient, she had not actually committed a crime. Nevertheless, the courts upheld the state's decision, holding that confinement was in Mary Ann's best interests.

In 1870, an Illinois court limited *parens patriae* in *People v. Turner*. In that case, another minor was confined for a noncriminal action against the will of both of his parents. In that case, however, the court ruled that the son should be released to the care of his parents. The case was significant because it went against common practice of the day. However, it did not set a widely followed precedent and was largely ignored by other courts. *Parens patriae* was challenged again in 1905 in *Commonwealth v. Fisher*. In this case, a juvenile was sentenced to seven years confinement for a minor crime that would have received a much less severe sentence in an adult court. A court held that state intervention was necessary and in the best interests of the child. In essence, this opinion gave the courts even more discretion.

Beginning in 1966, the U.S. Supreme Court began limiting how *parens patriae* could be practiced. In *Kent v. United States* (1966) a sixteen-year-old boy was waived to an adult jurisdiction, without a hearing in juvenile court, to be tried on robbery and rape charges. As a result, the juvenile received a sentence that was harsher than he would have received if he had been tried in a juvenile jurisdiction. The case was appealed to the U.S. Supreme Court on grounds that his Sixth Amendment rights had been violated. The Court agreed, holding that the state was not acting in the boy's best interests.

In 1967, the Supreme Court handed down a landmark decision in another challenge to *parens patriae* in the case of *In re Gault*. That case originated in Arizona when fifteen-year-old Gerald Gault was taken into custody by police after allegedly making lewd phone calls and was confined in a detention facility for one week before he was granted a hearing before a juvenile court judge. Meanwhile, his parents were not even informed of the charges against him. There was no record of the hearing, and Gault's alleged victim did not make a court appearance. Nevertheless, Gault was sentenced to confinement in a reform school until he reached legal majority.

Lower courts in Arizona that heard the Gault case upheld the doctrine of *parens patriae*. On appeal, the case eventually reached the U.S. Supreme Court, whose ruling changed the way juveniles are treated in the juvenile justice system. The Court held that juveniles are entitled to due process and fair treatment and that notices of charges against them must be sent to their parents or guardians in a timely manner. The Court also held that juveniles are entitled to be represented by attorneys, and, finally, they must be interviewed in the presence of their parents or guardians. The *In re Gault* decision severely limited the power of *parens patriae* by giving juvenile offenders and their parents more rights.

The Juvenile Justice Process

The workings of the juvenile justice system differ from those of the adult justice system in processing of cases. When juveniles are detained or arrested, decisions are made whether to process their cases formally in the juvenile justice system or to divert them to less formal proceedings. Cases that are diverted may be handled by parents, school administrators, or others. Diversion is a common practice in juvenile justice and in some instances is mandatory, particularly in cases involving status offenses. Decisions to divert cases are usually made by the arresting officers, but sometimes intake officers may be consulted. Intake officers typically work on behalf of state prosecutors. Both police and intake officers have the authority to talk to juvenile offenders' family members, examine their criminal records, and talk to their teachers and others before making diversion decisions.

Juveniles who are not diverted are formally charged in petitions, the juvenile justice version of arrest warrants. In addition to specifying charges, the petitions also serve as informing documents to the juveniles' parents and guardians. Finally, the petitions specify the court jurisdictions in which the cases are to be adjudicated.

The matter of what jurisdiction in which juveniles are tried is a controversial subject in the field of juvenile justice. Juveniles may be tried in juvenile court or waived to adult jurisdictions. There are three mechanisms with which juvenile cases can be waived to adult jurisdictions. The one most commonly used is statutory exclusion. This type of waiver is used for certain serious offenses that are automatically excluded from juvenile jurisdiction. Such offenses include, most notably, murder. Most states have statutory exclusions.

The second mechanism used to waive juvenile cases to adult jurisdictions is the judicial waiver, which is simply the use of judicial discretion. Some states set lower age limits for this type of waiver. The third type of waiver is the concurrent jurisdiction, or prosecutorial, waiver. In some states, prosecutors have the authority to file cases in both juvenile and adult jurisdictions concurrently because of the nature of the offenses and ages of the offenders. However, the U.S. Supreme Court's ruling in *Breed v. Jones* (1975) ensured that juveniles cannot be tried in a juvenile court and then be waived and tried in an adult jurisdiction. This protection is the juvenile equivalent of the Fifth Amendment's double jeopardy protection.

After juveniles have been tried or adjudicated, their records are usually sealed and can be expunged when the offenders reach legal majority. The rationale behind this principle is that juveniles should be allowed to enter adulthood with clean records and not have juvenile criminal records that may impede their educational or employment opportunities. Expungement is not automatic, however, and is usually dependent upon the offenders demonstrating good behavior. Moreover, in some instances, juvenile records can be unsealed. Such a situation might arise in the case of a former juvenile offender who commits a violent crime as an adult, leading a prosecutor to suspect that his juvenile record may be relevant to his later acts.

Juvenile Dispositions

Disposition is the term given to juvenile sentencing. Dispositions for juveniles are based on the principle of least detrimental alternative, that is, what is in the best interest of the juvenile. Dispositions should also be part of an overall treatment plan for the juveniles and are based largely on predispositional reports prepared by prosecutors or intake officers. Predispositional reports contain information about such matters as the juveniles' criminal records, family backgrounds, and their academic progress. Judges consult these reports to determine what are the best sentences for the juveniles.

In addition to traditional dispositions, such as confinement and probation, a number of alternative dispositions are available for juveniles. One type that began being used widely during the mid-1980s, but that is less used now, is juvenile boot camps.

Another alternative form of disposition is wilderness programs. Like boot camps, these programs are comparatively brief in duration and are considered a form of shock incarceration. Current wilderness programs have evolved from such well-established programs as Outward Bound. Wilderness programs teach youths basic survival and dispute-resolution skills and promote self-esteem and confidence.

States that administer creative juvenile justice systems have additional alternative strategies that are implemented even before the dispositions stage. For example, during the late 1990s, Washington State began a special juvenile gun court. Although that court is technically part of the state's adult system, juveniles who are charged with certain first-time handgun-related offenses are processed through gun court and participate in the Handgun Intervention Program, which teaches them about gun safety. Numerous other states have used Washington's gun court as models for their own gun courts. Other states have drug courts for juveniles whose guidelines are similar to those of gun courts.

Washington is also known for other innovations in juvenile justice. In 1977, for example, the state passed the Juvenile Justice Reform Act, which required that all adjudicated juveniles between the ages of eight and seventeen spend at least some time in institutions. Many other states have adopted similar legislation. Experts have argued that the rationale behind such legislation was to scare juveniles straight.

Other examples of dispositions for juveniles include court-ordered school attendance, financial restitution, fines, community service, outpatient psychotherapy, drug and alcohol treatment, residential community programs, tattoo removal programs, foster home placement, sentencing circles, shaming, and restorative justice. Dispositions for juveniles may involve either indeterminate or determinate sentences. Indeterminate sentencing allows judges to order detention for indefinite periods, within certain parameters. When it is judged that the juveniles are rehabilitated, they may be released before serving the maximum periods of their indeterminate sentences.

Juvenile Appeals

Appeal is not a constitutionally guaranteed right for juveniles; however, most states provide for juvenile appeals by statute. Appeals may be made directly to appellate courts, asking them to review the facts of the cases. If successful, they result in complete retrials of the original cases. Collateral appeals use legal writs to challenge lower court decisions. Writs of *habeas corpus* are orders issued by courts to examine whether persons being held in custody are being lawfully detained. Writs of *certiorari* are orders from the U.S. Supreme Court requiring lower courts to forward the records of cases for review.

Monica L. P. Robbers

Further Reading

Benekos, Peter J., and Alida V. Merlo. *Controversies in Juvenile Justice and Delinquency*. 2nd ed. New York: Routledge, 2015. Print.

Champion, Dean John. *The Juvenile Justice System: Delinquency, Processing, and the Law*. 4th ed. Upper Saddle River: Prentice, 2003. Print.

McCarthy, F. B., W. W. Patton, and J. G. Carr. *Juvenile Law and Its Processes: Cases and Materials*. 3rd ed. Cincinnati: Anderson, 2003. Print.

Sickmund, Melissa, and Charles Puzzanchera, eds. *Juvenile Offenders and Victims: 2014 National Report*. Pittsburgh: Natl. Ctr. for Juvenile Justice, 2014. PDF file.

Tanenhaus, David S. *Juvenile Justice in the Making*. New York: Oxford UP, 2004. Print.

Watkins, John C., Jr. *The Juvenile Justice Century: A Sociolegal Commentary on American Juvenile Courts*. Durham: Carolina Academic, 1998. Print.

Whitehead, J. T., and S. P. Lab. *Juvenile Justice: An Introduction*. 4th ed. Cincinnati: Anderson, 2003. Print.

Winterdyk, John A., ed. *Juvenile Justice: International Perspectives, Models, and Trends*. Boca Raton: CRC, 2015. Print.

See also Boot camps; Criminal history record information; Criminal justice system; Diversion; *Gault, In re*; Juvenile courts; Juvenile delinquency; Juvenile Justice and Delinquency Prevention, Office of; Juvenile Justice and Delinquency Prevention Act; Juvenile waivers to adult courts; *Parens patriae*; Probation, juvenile; School violence; Status offenses; Uniform Juvenile Court Act; Youth authorities; *Roper v. Simmons* (2005); Female Offenders; Rehabilitation; Medical model of offender treatment.

Juvenile waivers to adult courts

A juvenile case can be waived through any of three major processes. The first of these is statutory waiver. For statutory exclusion, a state law specifies that for cases involving minors over a certain age who commit certain offenses, the case must be heard in adult court. In California, for example, juveniles over the age of fourteen who are accused of certain kinds of murders must be tried as adults. In 2004, about twenty-nine states had similar forms of statutory exclusion.

Definition: Formal processes of moving cases from juvenile to adult courts

Courts; Juvenile justice

Significance: Minors may be tried as adults in a number of ways, and the frequency with which this happens is on the increase.

At one time, the United States had no separate court system for juveniles, and all minors tried on criminal charges were tried as adults. However, within a few years of the establishment of the juvenile court system in 1899, virtually every US state had a separate juvenile justice system.

In contrast to the adult criminal justice systems, the systems for juveniles were meant to emphasize rehabilitation rather than punishment. Eventually, however, many people agreed that there were some cases in which it was desirable to try certain minors as adults, and so several systems evolved that allowed juvenile cases to be waived, or transferred, to adult courts. As of 2011, this means that about 250,000 juveniles countrywide are involved in the criminal court system each year.

The second type of waiver is judicial waiver. Under this system, if a person over a certain age is accused of certain offenses, a hearing (often called a "fitness hearing") is held. The judge considers several factors to determine whether the minor is amenable to treatment by the juvenile justice system. These factors might include the minor's age and intelligence, as well the degree of complexity and sophistication of the offense committed by the minor. All but four states allowed judicial waivers in 2004.

The third type, prosecutorial waiver, is also known as direct file. In states that permit this form of waiver, prosecutors may choose to file the cases of juveniles of specified ages who are accused of certain crimes in adult, rather than juvenile, courts. No hearings are required. The number of states allowing direct file is steadily increasing.

Modern Trends

In response to a publicly perceived upswing in juvenile violent crime during the early 1990s, many states began increasing the number of offenses for which juvenile cases could be waived to adult courts. They also lowered minimum ages for waivers and added additional types of waivers. As a result, increasing numbers of youths were being tried as adults. However, studies of juvenile justice have raised questions about the wisdom of this trend, as juveniles who are waived to adult courts have shown increased tendencies to become repeat offenders.

This trend also raises questions of racial justice. Cases of juveniles belonging to racial and ethnic minorities have been far more likely to be waived to adult courts than those of white juveniles—a trend that has been increasing disparities within the criminal justice system in the United States. Moreover, many critics believe that it is unethical to expose any youths to adult penalties and adult correctional facilities and to abandon rehabilitative attempts among young offenders.

Phyllis B. Gerstenfeld

Further Reading

Fagan, Jeffrey, and Frank E. Zimring, eds. *The Changing Borders of Juvenile Justice: Transfer of Adolescents to the Criminal Court.* Chicago: University of Chicago Press, 2000.

"Reducing Transfers to the Adult System." *Juvenile Law Center.* Juvenile Law Center, 10 Feb. 2015. Web. 26 May 2016.

Williams, Frank P., III, and Marilyn D. McShane, eds. *Encyclopedia of Juvenile Justice.* Thousand Oaks, Calif.: Sage, 2002.

See also Blended sentences; Criminal history record information; *Gault, In re*; Juvenile courts; Juvenile delinquency; Juvenile Justice and Delinquency Prevention Act; Juvenile justice system; Probation, juvenile; Uniform Juvenile Court Act; Violent Crime Control and Law Enforcement Act; *Roper v. Simmons* (2005).

Katz v. United States

The Case: U.S. Supreme Court ruling on electronic surveillance

Date: Decided on December 18, 1967

Criminal justice issues: Privacy; search and seizure; technology

Significance: This Supreme Court case established the principle that electronic surveillance constitutes a search subject to the Fourth Amendment's warrant and probable cause provisions.

Charles Katz was convicted of transmitting wagering information over the telephone on the basis of information he gave over a public telephone which he habitually used. The Federal Bureau of Investigation gained access to this information by attaching an external listening device to the telephone booth. The lower court concluded that since the booth had not been physically invaded, this investigative method did not constitute a "search" within the meaning of the Fourth Amendment, which requires an antecedent showing of probable cause and the issuance of a warrant. The Supreme Court, however, finding that the government had violated Katz's "legitimate expectation" of privacy, declared that the government's methods did indeed constitute a search and reversed the ruling.

Katz v. United States substituted a "reasonable expectation of privacy" test for the physical intrusion test the Court had previously used to determine if a police search and seizure was constitutional. This new test was cogently phrased in Justice John M. Harlan's concurring opinion: There "is a twofold requirement, first that a person have exhibited an actual (subjective) expectation of privacy and, second, that the expectation be one that society is prepared to recognize as 'reasonable.'" Harlan's opinion was used by lower courts to parse the meaning of *Katz*, but as he himself later recognized in *United States v. White* (1971), any evaluation of a questionable search must of necessity "transcend the search for subjective expectations." The government could, for example, defeat any expectation of privacy in telephone conversations by issuing a declaration that all such conversations are subject to third-party eavesdropping.

The reasonableness requirement may mean that an expectation of privacy in a particular realm must be shared by a majority of Americans. Yet it might also mean that although there are areas in which reasonable individuals might legitimately expect to maintain their privacy, such expectations can be superseded by more important policy considerations, such as the need for railroad engineers to give blood and urine specimens for purposes of drug testing (see *Skinner v. Railway Labor Executives Association*, 1989).

In *White*, Harlan defined searches as "those more extensive intrusions that significantly jeopardize the sense of security which is the paramount concern of Fourth Amendment liberties," but the Supreme Court has applied the *Katz* doctrine narrowly. In *United States v. Miller* (1976), for example, the Court ruled that persons do not have a reasonable expectation of privacy as to bank records of their financial transactions. In *Smith v. Maryland* (1979), the Court found that while individuals might reasonably expect the content of their telephone conversations to remain private, they cannot entertain a similar expectation as to the telephone numbers they call. In both cases, the Court based its decision on the fact that the information plaintiffs claimed to be off limits to police was already accessed by others—bank employees and telephone companies, respectively.

Lisa Paddock

Further Reading
Adams, James A., and Daniel D. Blinka. *Electronic Surveillance: Commentaries and Statutes*. Notre Dame, Ind.: National Institute for Trial Advocacy, 2003.
McGrath, J. E. *Loving Big Brother: Performance, Privacy and Surveillance Space*. New York: Routledge, 2004.
Stevens, Gina Marie, and Charles Doyle. *Privacy: Wiretapping and Electronic Eavesdropping*. Huntington, N.Y.: Nova Science, 2002.

See also Bill of Rights, U.S.; *Chimel v. California*; Electronic surveillance; Evidence, rules of; Privacy rights; Search and seizure; Stakeouts; Supreme Court, U.S.; Wiretaps.

Latent evidence

Definition: Evidence—which is typically biological material—that is left behind by fingers or other body parts that come into contact with surfaces
Evidence and forensics; Investigation; Technology
Significance: Modern techniques of recovering latent evidence offer personnel in law enforcement increased opportunities to find evidence that can be used to solve crimes.

Fingerprints, palm prints, and sole prints are examples of latent evidence composed of naturally secreted materials, such as sweat, lipids, and sebum (skin oil) that human hands and feet may deposit on surfaces with which they come into contact. Latent evidence may be deposited on both porous surfaces, such as fabrics, and nonporous surfaces, such as glass. However, evidence on porous surfaces is generally likely to last longer than that on nonporous surfaces because it may soak into the porous surfaces.

Latent prints may be distinguished from visible prints, such as bloodstains that are transferred from nonporous sources to materials such as carpeting. Latent evidence also is distinguished from what are known as plastic, or three-dimensional, prints, which are created when friction ridges come into contact with softer surfaces and

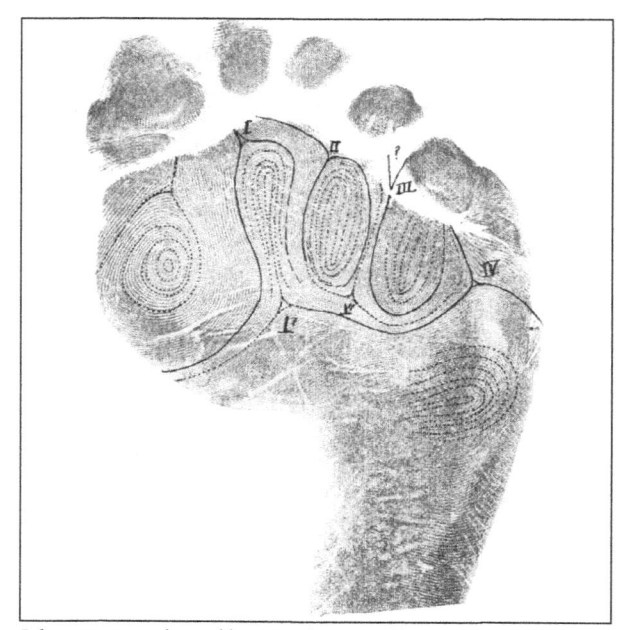

Sole prints are a form of latent evidence. (Public domain, via Wikimedia Commons)

Fingerprints are a form of latent evidence. (Public domain, via Wikimedia Commons)

make three-dimensional impressions into the softer surfaces.

Collection Techniques

Latent prints are enhanced or visualized, prior to collection, using physical, chemical, or instrumental methods. All prints are photographed prior to performing other visualization techniques. Physical methods of collection include the use of certain colored powders and brushes. Prior use of cyanoacrylate (chemical adhesives such as superglue) fuming enhances the effectiveness of physical visualization methods. Physical methods are used for dry nonporous surfaces. Once visualized, the latent prints are photographed a second time. The latent prints are then lifted, placed on backing cards and documented.

Chemical methods can be used for processing prints on both dry and wet surfaces. For dry surfaces, certain dye-staining techniques, using substances such as gentian violet, fluorescent materials, and other laser-excitable materials, are used, followed by lighting or laser excitation, followed by photography of the developed prints. On wet surfaces, small-particle reagent sprays or physical developers are used. On porous surfaces, the chemicals react with the biological evidence, not with the surfaces. Numerous techniques and substances are used, including silver nitrate and ninhydrin.

Latent prints even can be lifted from the skin of victims of a homicide. Such prints are collected using glue fuming, with or without the transfer lift technique using magnetic fingerprint powder. This technique involves directing the fumes from heated glue onto the skin.

Ronna F. Dillon

Further Reading
Baxter, Everett. *Complete Crime Scene Investigation Handbook*. Boca Raton: CRC P, 2015. *eBook Collection (EBSCOhost)*. Web. 26 May 2016.
Cole, Simon A. *Suspect Identities: A History of Fingerprinting and Criminal Identification*. Cambridge, Mass.: Harvard University Press, 2001.
Gilbert, James N. *Criminal Investigation*. New York: Prentice Hall, 2004.
James, Stuart H., and Jon J. Nordby. *Forensic Science: An Introduction to Scientific and Investigative Techniques*. Boca Raton, Fla.: CRC Press, 2003.
Kasper, Stephen P. *Latent Print Processing Guide*. London: Academic P, 2016. *eBook Collection (EBSCOhost)*. Web. 26 May 2016.
Lee, Henry C., T. Palmbach, and M. T. Miller. *Henry Lee's Crime Scene Handbook*. New York: Academic Press, 2001.

See also Bloodstains; Circumstantial evidence; Crime scene investigation; DNA testing; Document analysis; Fingerprint identification; Forensic psychology; Forensics; Shoe prints and tire-tracks; Toxicology; Trace evidence; Technology's transformative effect.

Lone wolf

Definition: An individual, acting alone, who undertakes a terrorist attack.
Criminal justice issues: Civil rights and liberties; hate crime; terrorism; violent crime
Significance: Major terrorist attacks are generally undertaken by groups with political or social agendas. Because groups are normally more visible than a single individual, law enforcement can often spot potential trouble from a group more easily than when an individual is planning an attack. Thus the successful lone wolf attacks are often a major surprise not only to law enforcement, but also to most who know the individual perpetrating the violent terrorist act.

Origins of the Term

In nature, most wolves live and hunt in packs. Their prey are used to the techniques the pack uses to hunt and responds accordingly. However, when male wolves reach maturity, they leave their pack to join or form another pack. Senior male wolves can be driven from a pack when a younger, stronger, male takes its place as the dominate one. To survive, these wolves must hunt on their own, often surprising their prey by their unorthodox style. Historically, most individuals seeking to overthrow the accepted order, whether political or social, have formed groups with similarly minded people. The potential for success seems to be better with a larger number of people involved. Throughout history there have been individuals who undertake violent acts without any warning. However, in the 1990's, two white supremacists called upon their followers to act like lone wolves in attacking the system. Since that time, this term has been adopted by the media and law enforcement to describe individuals who undertake terrorist acts without being a formal part of a group.

Previous Norm

Surveillance of individuals suspected of planning, or having undertaken, criminal conduct has always been a part of law enforcement's responsibility. Throughout most of the twentieth century, those seeking to make major political or social changes were usually affiliated with rival nations or with well-known domestic organizations. In the post-World War II era, most seeking major political or social change could depend upon the backing of the Cold War power that opposed the prevailing power within a nation. In the post-Cold War era, many groups and individuals no longer had the "automatic" support of the rival Cold War power, resulting in the need for greater self-sufficiency. While those seeking social or political change had always had some support from others who shared their ethnic, social, or religious affiliations, in this new era the incentive was to turn to these affiliations for a larger portion of the support for their cause. That being the case, law enforcement has often been able to watch emerging organizations within these groups for signs of plans for terrorist activities. Through the infiltration of these groups, or intercepting their communications, it can normally be ascertained whether these groups are planning any illegal activities.

Current Problems for Law Enforcement

However, there are times when certain individuals who have strong antigovernment or antiestablishment beliefs do not join a group of similar-minded individuals. Sometimes this is because of location and at other times, it is because of the general antisocial disposition of the individual. In places such as the United States, these individuals can be hard to track, unless they elect to use social media, or some other highly visible means, to make known their views. However, this in itself, in the United States, is not enough to make the person a criminal or terrorist. The ideals of free speech and freedom of conscience mean that law enforcement cannot interfere with all who espouse antigovernment, antisocial, or anticertain religions (and pro their own religion) points of view, although hate crime legislation has made surveillance of these views more common. Similarly, individuals have the freedom to acquire firearms. The ingredients used to make many types of explosives can also be legally purchased by individuals. All of this causes major difficulties for law enforcement in their attempt to protect the general public from terrorist attacks. Many who are planning a lone wolf terrorist attack acquire the weapons they plan to use in ways that are easily visible to law enforcement. If they do not communicate their plans to anyone else, or only make it known via unclear statements to close associates, law enforcement may not have the ability to stop the planned violence.

While the result of a lone wolf attack may not be as catastrophic as the 9/11 attacks, they do cause substantial death and destruction, as can been seen by looking at the range of terrorist actions from the Oklahoma City bombing of 1995 (two individuals involved, one planned it and forced the other to participate) to the shootings at the Orlando nightclub in 2016. Just within the United States, since the 1990's, the perpetrators of more than sixty terrorist acts have been categorized as lone wolves. While in after-the-fact statements, or messages left prior to undertaking the terrorist act, some lone wolves claim connection to various terrorist groups, or other organizations, the individuals undertook the action without any real connection to that group, or organization. The lone wolf attacker may be inspired by the rhetoric, or actions, of these groups with which they claim affiliation, but are not really members of those movements. In stopping lone wolf attacks, the fine line for law enforcement is determining when the individual has crossed the line from legal beliefs and activities to the first steps toward undertaking illegal and violent ones, since the desire is to stop the individual prior to others being harmed.

Donald A. Watt

Further Reading

Gil, Paul. *Lone-Actor Terrorists: A Behavioural Analysis (Political Violence)*. London: Routledge, 2015.

Michael, George. *Lone Wolf Terror and the Rise of Leaderless Resistance*. Nashville: Vanderbilt University Press, 2012.

National Security Critical Issue Task Force. "Report: Lone Wolf Terrorism." Security Studies Program. Washington, D.C.: Georgetown University, 2015. Simon, Jeffrey D., with Brian Michael Jenkins (foreword). *Lone Wolf Terrorism: Understanding the Growing Threat.* Amherst, N.Y.: Prometheus Books, 2013.

Worth, Katie. "Lone Wolf Attacks Are Becoming More Common—And More Deadly." *Frontline.* Boston: WGBH Foundation and the Corporation for Public Broadcasting, 2016.

See also Forensic psychology; Unabomber; Psychological profiling; Terrorism; Patriot Act; USA FREEDOM Act (2015).

Medical examiners

Definition: Officers of state and local governments who investigate and certify homicides, suicides, accidental deaths, sudden deaths, and deaths with unknown causes

Evidence and forensics; Investigation; Medical and health issues

Significance: Medical examiners are responsible for leading the investigations of all deaths that are sudden, unexpected, or violent, and they make determinations about the times, manners, and causes of the deaths.

The first government medical examiner was appointed in Boston in the late 1870s. Prior to that time, elected coroners handled death investigations. The coroner system has its roots in England, and dates back a millennium. However, because coroners were traditionally not required to have any medical training, dissatisfaction with the system arose, and medical examiner positions were created to provide an alternative. By the early twenty-first century, about one-half of the residents of the United States were living in jurisdictions with medical examiners. The jurisdictions still employing the coroner system were generally smaller and were predominantly rural areas in which sudden, unexpected, and violent deaths were uncommon. When deaths in those communities require autopsy services, medical examiners from nearby jurisdictions are often utilized.

Functions of Medical Examiners

Upon notification of a person's death, the medical examiner begins gathering facts relating to the deceased that help in making a determination as to time, manner, and cause of death. The initial call tells the medical examiner where and when the body was found and if there is any evidence of foul play. The body should not be moved until it has either been examined by a medical examiner, or a medical examiner has given permission to move the body.

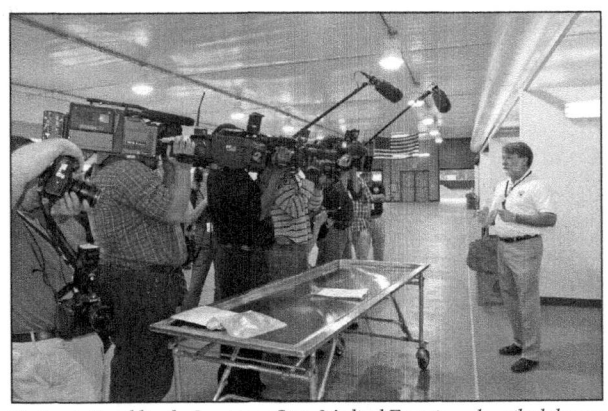

Dr. Louis Cataldie, the Louisiana State Medical Examiner, described the use of dental records in the identification of disinterred bodies during a press tour. (Public domain, via Wikimedia Commons)

Because the actual facts surrounding deaths may differ significantly from what they seem to be at first glance, medical examiners gather as much information as they can from different sources before making their determinations. The decedents' medical records are considered, and their bodies are examined externally.

Time of death is usually not in question. However, when a body is found of a person whose death has not been witnessed, determining the time of death becomes important, regardless of the cause of death. Time of death is established first by looking at the interval between the time when a person was last seen alive and the time when the person's dead body was found. The larger this interval, the more difficult it is to pinpoint the time of death.

Medical examiners take into account many factors when determining time of death, including the air temperature surrounding a dead body, where a body is found (indoors, outdoors, in water), and if a body has already stiffened in rigor mortis, or if that stage has already passed. If a body is discovered more than a day after death, decomposition may already be apparent, or insects may have begun colonizing it. By analyzing such evidence, the medical examiner can use the physical condition of the body to estimate when death has occurred.

Manner of death is the way in which a person dies: through natural causes, such as disease; through accidents; by suicide; or by homicide. Everyone dies eventually, and many people—especially older people—die of natural causes every day. However, medical examiners should not assume that merely because an individual dies while under a doctor's care or while in a hospital that the death results from natural causes. Similarly, medical examiners should not assume that merely because a death appears to be from an accident that the cause of death is accidental. Indeed, many apparent automobile accidents that involve only one vehicle are, in fact, suicides. Homicides also often appear to be accidents or suicides.

Medical examiners determine both the immediate and proximal causes of death. The immediate cause is the last event prior to a death, such as an acute myocardial infarction (heart attack), which may happen hours or days before death. The proximal cause is the first event leading up to a death, for example coronary vascular disease, which may have been evident in the decedent several years prior to death.

In homicide investigations, the victims' bodies are usually the single most important pieces of evidence that are processed. Moreover, the areas immediately surrounding the dead bodies generally contain most of the forensic evidence that is found in homicide cases.

Medical examiners also determine whether decedents have died at the scenes where they are found, or if their deaths have occurred elsewhere and their bodies have been moved. Livor mortis, the settling of blood in bodies after death and the accompanying purplish coloring (which resembles bruising), often indicates whether bodies have been moved.

Medical examiners may conduct autopsies, which include thorough interior physical examinations of the bodies and specialized laboratory tests, or forensic pathologists may do so. Medical examiners may also be called upon to testify in civil and criminal courtrooms regarding the findings from their completed investigation.

Ayn Embar-Seddon and Allan D. Pass

Further Reading

Baden, Michael M. *Unnatural Death: Confessions of a Medical Examiner.* New York: Random, 1989. Print.

Baden, Michael, M., and Marion Roach. *Dead Reckoning: The New Science of Catching Killers.* New York: Simon, 2001. Print.

Bell, Suzanne. *Encyclopedia of Forensic Science.* New York: Facts on File, 2004. Print.

Melinek, Judy, and T. J. Mitchell. *Working Stiff: Two Years, 262 Bodies, and the Making of a Medical Examiner.* New York: Scribner, 2014. Web. 25 May 2016.

Sachs, Jessica Snyder. *Corpse: Nature, Forensics, and the Struggle to Pinpoint Time of Death.* New York: Perseus, 2002. Print.

See also Autopsies; Cold cases; Coroners; Crime scene investigation; Forensics; Toxicology; Trace evidence.

National Crime Information Center

Identification: Federal agency with computerized index consisting of individuals and records
Date: Established in 1971
Criminal justice issues: Crime statistics; federal law; law-enforcement organization
Significance: The National Crime Information Center (NCIC), a powerful computer database maintained by the Federal Bureau of Investigation (FBI), provides law-enforcement agencies with access to recorded criminal justice information through its computerized records and library collection. The NCIC allows agencies to gather cross-boundary criminal justice information efficiently.

Since its creation during the early 1970's, the National Crime Information Center has amassed a substantial collection of criminal justice databases. Topics covered in the databases include missing persons, wanted persons, stolen and recovered guns, stolen securities, stolen and recovered motor vehicles, stolen license plates, and other stolen articles. NCIC users are able to access these data when they need them. Users have expressed satisfaction with NCIC and have requested enhancements over time.

To enhance the NCIC, the FBI has established NCIC-2000, which allows full on-line computer search and retrieval of crime incidents nationwide. Police officials can use it to check liens, images (such as photographs and fingerprints), license plates, and other routine items instantly. It is believed that this increased functionality helps reduce false arrests.

The FBI has merged NCIC with the National Incident-Based Reporting System (NIBRS) and Automated Fingerprint Identification System (AFIS) to create the Criminal Justice Information Services division (CJIS).

The CJIS serves as a single source for state, local, and private law-enforcement officials seeking crime analysis data, incident information, and criminal imaging data. In addition, the division provides information services for the FBI and its direct enforcement divisions. Among the stated goals of the CJIS are to develop consistent crime information collection and recording standards and to develop and implement a strategy for assisting state and other users in creating linkages to the FBI's computer systems. The CJIS also offers training and support services for federal, state, and local CJIS users.

Dale K. Nesbary

Further Reading

The National Crime Information Center and You. Washington, D.C.: U.S. Department of Justice, Federal Bureau of Investigation, 1976.

National Crime Information Center: The Investigative Tool: A Guide to the Use and Benefits of NCIC. Washington, D.C.: U.S. Department of Justice, Federal Bureau of Investigation, National Crime Information Center, 1984.

See also Booking; Computer information systems; Law enforcement; Multiple jurisdiction offenses; National Stolen Property Act; Neighborhood watch programs; Uniform Crime Reports.

National Institute of Justice

Identification: Federal research agency charged with investigating certain criminological program areas
Date: Established in 1968
Significance: Since its founding, the National Institute of Justice has been a major national and international center for criminal justice research, policy experimentation aimed at professionalizing law enforcement, and more effective ways of controlling crime.

Following recommendations from President Lyndon B. Johnson's 1967 Committee on Law Enforcement and Administration of Justice, Congress enacted the Omnibus Crime Control and Safe Streets Act of 1968. The law created, within the Department of Justice, the Law Enforcement Assistance Administration (LEAA), which in turn established the National Institute of Justice (NIJ).

The NIJ has multiple research responsibilities aimed at revising extant criminal justice policies and practices, producing new crime-control programs, encouraging the professionalization of law enforcement, sponsoring experimental training programs, and assessing law enforcement and criminal justice standards and performance. It also collects and disseminates relevant data and information. During its first decades of operations, the NIJ provided important resources for the study of violent crime in the United States, career criminals, sentencing, rehabilitation, the use of police resources, community crime prevention, and pretrial processes.

Clifton K. Yearley

Further Reading

Adams, K., et al. *Use of Force by Police: Overview of National and Local Data*. Washington, D.C.: U.S. Department of Justice, National Institute of Justice and Bureau of Justice Statistics, 1999.

Brady, T. V. *Measuring What Matters, Part One: Measures of Crime, Fear, and Disorder*. Washington, D.C.: National Institute of Justice, 1996.

National Institute of Justice. *Evaluation Plan*. Washington, D.C.: National Institute of Justice, 1991.

_____. *National Institute of Justice Journal*. Washington, D.C.: National Institute of Justice, 1992.

_____. *National Institute of Justice/NCJRS: Meeting Your Needs for Criminal Justice Information*. Washington, D.C.: National Institute of Justice, 1984.

See also Attorney General, U.S.; Justice Department, U.S.; National Commission on the Causes and Prevention of Violence; Omnibus Crime Control and Safe Streets Act of 1968; President's Commission on Law Enforcement and Administration of Justice.

Nonviolent resistance

Definition: Any deliberate refusal to comply with laws and government policies in a nonviolent manner
Civil rights and liberties; Police powers; Political issues
Significance: Nonviolent resistance has long been a central component of efforts to express political dissent and marshal the power necessary to bring about political change in the United States.

Although the term "nonviolent resistance" is a twentieth-century concept based on analysis of the strategies and conditions necessary for successful nonviolent action, its practice is deeply rooted in United States history. Religious groups from Europe such as the Amish and the Society of Friends (Quakers), who practiced a literal understanding of Jesus' teachings forbidding the use of violence, fled to North America to escape persecution.

A march is a form of nonviolent resistance. (By Jake Mohan, via Wikimedia Commons)

Boycotts are a form of nonviolent resistance. (By Calbear22, Joseph Testa, via Wikimedia Commons)

Their continued witness to principles of pacifism has influenced a tradition and philosophy of nonviolent protest. Additionally, the early colonists engaged in nonviolent resistance against British rule. In 1766, Great Britain legislated an import tax called the Stamp Act. American merchants organized a boycott of goods, causing the repeal of the act. This action marked the first organized resistance to British rule and led to the establishment of the First Continental Congress in 1774. The legal basis for nonviolent action was established in the First Amendment to the Constitution, which protects the rights of persons to "freedom of speech," peaceful assembly, and petitioning the government "for a redress of grievances." The United States has a long history of expression of such rights.

Nineteenth and Twentieth Centuries

In 1845, Henry David Thoreau was jailed for refusing to pay a poll tax in protest of the Mexican-American War. In his essay "Civil Disobedience," Thoreau proclaimed the moral necessity of resistance in the face of immoral government action. Nonviolent protest has accompanied every war in which the United States has engaged, and it was so widespread during the Vietnam War that it became a central reason for US withdrawal from Vietnam in 1974. Nonviolent protest has also been central to various movements seeking to ban and limit nuclear weapons and in wartime tax resistance movements, in which members refuse to pay taxes to support the military budget. Strategies of nonviolent resistance were also employed by the women's rights movement, which culminated in the right to vote (1920) and in greater social and economic equality for women. The labor movement has used nonviolent tactics in the form of strikes, labor slowdowns, and boycotts to force improvement of working conditions and income.

Despite strong, often violent responses by corporate owners, the Wagner Act, passed by Congress in 1935, recognized the legal right of workers to organize and use such methods. California farmworker leader César Chávez effectively used consumer boycotts in the 1970s and 1980s to win better conditions for farmworkers. Nonviolent strategies have been used by environmental groups to block construction of nuclear power plants, stop the cutting of forests, or alter policies considered to be ecologically hazardous. They have also been employed since the 1980s by antiabortion groups attempting to close abortion clinics.

The most prolonged, successful use of nonviolent resistance, however, came in the Civil Rights movement led by Martin Luther King, Jr., in the 1950s and 1960s. Drawing on the work of Mohandas K. Gandhi, the movement used marches, sit-ins, and boycotts to force an end to legal racial segregation in the South and informal (*de facto*) segregation in the North. This campaign demonstrated the ambiguity of governmental response to such tactics. Often participants were arrested and convicted under local statutes, only to have such laws ruled invalid by higher courts; this occurred during the Montgomery bus boycott. On the other hand, King and his followers were under constant surveillance by the Federal Bureau of Investigation and were considered threats to political stability by many government officials.

The debate has also focused on what constitutes "freedom of expression" and "peaceful assembly." The "plowshares eight," in 1980, protesting nuclear weapons, entered a General Electric plant in Pennsylvania and dented the nose cone of a warhead. They were sentenced to prison on grounds of trespass and destruction of private property.

Theory and Strategy

Nonviolent resistance has two distinct traditions. The religious tradition centers on the moral claim that it is always wrong to harm another and that only love of the "enemy" can transform persons and societies. Violence and hatred cannot solve social problems or end social conflict, for each act of violence generates new resentments. This spiral of violence can be ended only if some group absorbs the violence and returns only nonviolence and love. Central to this vision is a commitment to justice that requires adherents to engage injustice actively wherever they find it. The political tradition focuses on strategies for organizing political and social power to force another, usually a political authority, to change policies. As Gene Sharp, a leading analyst, notes, government requires the consent of its citizens. In nonviolent resistance, dissenters organize forms of power including economic power, labor power, and the power of public opinion in order to undermine consent and force authorities to change policies.

The use of these theories and techniques remains important in stable, democratic societies as a way of resolving conflict, generating social change, and challenging power structures, especially on behalf of the powerless, whose rights are often ignored. Without the legal sanctions that permit such protest, the only recourse becomes open societal violence and conflict, even to the point of civil war.

Charles L. Kammer

Further Reading
Ackerman, Peter, and Christopher Kruegler. *Strategic Nonviolent Conflict: The Dynamics of People Power in the Twentieth Century.* Westport: Praeger, 1994. Print.
Holmes, Robert L., ed. *Nonviolence in Theory and Practice.* Belmont: Wadsworth, 1990. Print.
King, Martin Luther, Jr. *A Testament of Hope: The Essential Writings and Speeches of Martin Luther King, Jr.* Ed. James M. Washington. San Francisco: Harper, 1991. Print.
Moses, Greg. *Revolution of Conscience: Martin Luther King, Jr., and the Philosophy of Nonviolence.* New York: Guilford, 1997. Print.
Steger, Manfred B. *Judging Nonviolence: The Dispute Between Realists and Idealists.* New York: Routledge, 2003. Print.

See also Arrest; Civil disobedience; Hit-and-run accidents; Jaywalking; Resisting arrest.

Olmstead v. United States

The Case: U.S. Supreme Court ruling on wiretaps
Date: Decided on June 4, 1928
Criminal justice issues: Privacy; search and seizure; technology
Significance: Although a majority of justices rejected the argument that government wiretaps on telephones constituted illegal searches and compelled self-incrimination, Justice Louis D. Brandeis's famous dissenting opinion laid the groundwork for the later development of a constitutional right to privacy.

During the Prohibition era, Roy Olmstead was convicted of being the general manager of a significant illegal smuggling operation that brought liquor to the United States from Canada in violation of federal law. Olmstead's illegal business had fifty employees and reportedly earned more than two million dollars each year. The evidence that produced the convictions of Olmstead and his associates was gathered through the use of wiretaps. Law-enforcement officials had attached wires to the telephone lines leading from Olmstead's residence and office. Officials had listened to and had stenographers take notes on the conversations secretly overheard through the telephone lines.

Olmstead and his codefendants challenged the use of such investigative techniques and evidence. They claimed that the wiretaps constituted an illegal search and seizure in violation of the Fourth Amendment and that the use of private conversations as evidence violated the Fifth Amendment's prohibition on compelled self-incrimination.

In an opinion by Chief Justice William Howard Taft, the Supreme Court rejected Olmstead's arguments. Taft concluded that the Fourth Amendment protected only against unreasonable searches of material things and that telephone lines running between two people's property could not be considered protected against intrusion by the government. Taft also declared that the defendants' conversations were voluntary and therefore could not be regarded as compelled self-incrimination.

In a famous dissenting opinion, Justice Louis D. Brandeis made an eloquent plea for the recognition of a constitutional right to privacy. According to Brandeis, the authors of the Constitution "sought to protect Americans in their beliefs, their thoughts, their emotions, and their sensations. They conferred, as against the government, the right to be let alone—the most comprehensive of rights and the right most valued by civilized men."

Brandeis was not the lone dissenter in the case; Justices Oliver Wendell Holmes, Jr., Pierce Butler, and Harlan F. Stone also found fault with Taft's conclusions. Brandeis, however, was the lone justice to place great emphasis on a general right of privacy. The other justices were also concerned about the definition of a search under the Fourth Amendment or the legality of police methods.

Brandeis could not manage to gain majority support for his ideas during his lifetime. Instead, his eloquent defense of a right to privacy stood for more than thirty years as the primary argument against government intrusions into citizens' private lives. Beginning in the 1960's, when the Supreme Court's composition had changed significantly, Brandeis's words were used by a generation of justices who followed his ideals and established the existence of a constitutional right to privacy in *Griswold v. Connecticut* (1965).

Christopher E. Smith

See also Electronic surveillance; Evidence, rules of; Privacy rights; Stakeouts; Supreme Court, U.S.; Wiretaps.

Parens patriae

Definition: Legal doctrine granting authority to the government to take responsibility for the welfare of those who cannot care for themselves

Juvenile justice; Legal terms and principles; Mental disorders

Significance: The principle of *parens patriae* provides the legal basis for courts to supervise and treat minors and legally incompetent adults whose families are not available or able to provide them with proper care and guidance.

The term *parens patriae* derives from the Latin for "parent of the country," and originally referred to a ruler's role as a protector and caregiver to their people before becoming part of the common law. It came to be used in English chancery courts to assist juveniles with their legal inheritances under the feudal land tenure system. It also provided legal protection for those deemed mentally incapable of caring for themselves. English common law formed the basis for the legal system of the United States, and there the concept was primarily applied to dependent, neglected, and delinquent children who were deemed in need of assistance.

During the early nineteenth century, increasing attention was given in urban areas to rapid population growth, social problems, and the placement of juvenile delinquents in the jail and prison system with adults. Concerns over these issues eventually led to the first house of refuge being opened in New York in 1825. This facility was established to house poor children and delinquents who were in need of care and guidance that was not being provided by their families. Additional houses of refuge soon opened in other major cities. In 1838 the Pennsylvania case of *Ex parte Crouse* established the doctrine of *parens patriae* as the legal basis for the government to supervise and treat children when their parents were either unable or unwilling to do so.

In Illinois, after the 1870 case of *People v. Turner* threatened the use of *parens patriae* by criminal courts, a child-saving movement in Chicago resulted in the establishment of the first juvenile court in 1899. *Parens patriae* has since been used as the legal doctrine allowing juvenile courts to adjudicate, supervise, and treat children and youth who are determined to be in need of governmental intervention.

David L. Myers

Further Reading

Champion, Dean John. *The Juvenile Justice System: Delinquency, Processing, and the Law.* 4th ed. Upper Saddle River, N.J.: Prentice-Hall, 2003.

Cox, Steven M., John J. Conrad, and Jennifer M. Allen. *Juvenile Justice: A Guide to Theory and Practice.* 5th ed. New York: McGraw-Hill, 2003.

Hess, Karen M., and Robert W. Drowns. *Juvenile Justice.* 4th ed. Belmont, Calif.: Wadsworth/Thomson Learning, 2004. Comprehensive overview of the juvenile justice system that connects theory and practice.

"Parens Patriae." *Legal Information Institute.* Cornell U Law School, 2016. Web. 26 May. 2016.

"Parens Patriae Definition." *Duhaime's Law Dictionary.* Duhaime.org, 2016. Web. 26 May. 2016.

Williams, Frank P., and Marilyn D. McShane, eds. *Encyclopedia of Juvenile Justice.* Thousand Oaks, Calif.: Sage, 2003.

See also Criminal justice system; Due process of law; *Gault, In re*; Juvenile courts; Juvenile delinquency; Juvenile justice system; Parole; Probation, juvenile; Rehabilitation; Status offenses; Uniform Juvenile Court Act.

Paris terrorist attacks (2015)

Definition: On November 13, 2015, between 9 and 10 p.m., three groups of three attackers, all wearing suicide vests, struck a total of six locations in Paris, France, causing the deaths of 130 people, plus seven of the attackers. The terrorist group, Islamic State of Iraq and the Levant (ISIL), claimed responsibility for the well-planned and coordinated attacks. Those involved were European Union (EU) citizens from France or Belgium.

Criminal justice issues: Civil rights and liberties; hate crime, terrorism, violent crime

Significance: As the deadliest terrorist attacks in Europe since 2004, the Paris attacks shook France and the world. It was the first major attempt, by ISIL, to expand the conflict from the Middle East to Europe. One goal seemed to be to cause France, and other nations, to rethink their participation in the anti-ISIL forces in the Middle East. The attacks caused great uncertainty regarding personal safety on the Continent, and in light of this, France suspended civil liberties following the declaration of a State of Emergency. However, France remained in the anti-ISIL coalition and within two days had increased the number of bombing attacks against ISIL, including some of those who participated in the Paris attacks.

France Prior to the Attack

After World War I, France was given a mandate by the League of Nations to govern what are now the countries of Lebanon and Syria, in addition to the territory it controlled in North Africa. It was the French, in consultation with the British, who decided upon the division of the territory into Lebanon (independent in 1943) and Syria (independent in 1946). Although during the Cold War, Syria often sided with the Soviet Union, the French remained more involved in that country than did other Western powers. As a result of this heritage many within those countries (obviously including ISIL) see the French as oppressors. In North Africa, although France granted independence to Tunisia and Morocco, it desired to retain Algeria, which caused a brutal war for independence, won by the Algerians. Overall, because of these historic connections, France has a sizeable Arab Muslim population, although many in that group do not feel that they have been accepted by mainstream French society. Thus, by the end of the twentieth century, there were many disaffected French citizens who responded to calls for change. In January, 2015, two French citizens, of Algerian descent, attacked the French satirical magazine Charlie Hebdo, ultimately killing twelve and wounding eleven. Prior to this attack, France basically only had to deal with lone wolf terrorists, not those equipped and supported by terrorist organizations. Thus, after this, Paris was on edge and the terror alert was raised to the highest level. Undeterred by terrorist threats, French aircraft were participating in the bombing of ISIL targets in Iraq and Syria in the days prior to the Paris attacks. However, causing concern for many was the fact that proportionately a much higher number of French citizens of Arab descent traveled to the Middle East to support Al-Qaeda or ISIL, than was the case for other Western European or North American nations.

The Attacks

The attackers choose a weekend evening, as that would be when the largest number of people would be at locations that would be easy to attack. Whether they choose November 13 because of the scheduled soccer (football) match, the anniversary of the allied (including French) occupation of Constantinople in 1981 (the last city proclaimed to be the capital of the Caliphate), or for some other reason, nine terrorists were in position to attack that evening. At least one other group had been part of the plan, but two of its members were previously arrested in Greece. The first attack was at the Stade de France, where a soccer match between France and Germany was underway. This was the least successful attack, because security guards turned away the terrorist trying to enter the stadium, wearing a suicide vest. Outside the stadium he exploded his vest, killing one other person, while the other two exploded their vests killing only themselves.

The second group attacked eating establishments, beginning about five minutes after the stadium attack. They attacked a restaurant and a bar, at one intersection, with fifteen dead and ten wounded. They then moved to another location killing five and wounding eight. Finally, they went to a third location and killed nineteen and wounded nine at another restaurant. Following this, one of the attackers killed himself, only injuring one other person. Two members of this group escaped. The most devastating attack was on a concert at the Bataclan, where the third group of three attackers killed eighty-one and wounded three hundred and twenty-two, before being killed themselves.

The Aftermath

In France, the president declared a State of Emergency and sought, and gained, legislative support to extend this for three months. However, the people of Paris, and around the world vowed to move ahead with their lives, while being vigilant. Law enforcement continued to track down any who seemed to have a connection with those who had participated in the attacks. The two attackers who escaped were killed five days later in a shoot-out with police in the Saint-Denis area of Paris. Just over two weeks after the attack, a planned multinational conference on climate change went ahead in Paris, with increased security, as a way to demonstrate that the terrorists did not affect Paris' ability to function, nor world leaders' willingness to be there. During these weeks that followed the attack, dozens of raids were conducted by law enforcement seeking those who might be sympathetic to the terrorists' cause. The French government did not lessen their support in the fight against ISIL in the Middle East.

Because the explosives came from, and some of the planners and participants lived in Belgium, raids were conducted there as well as in France. Two individuals were arrested in Belgium in March and April, 2016. For one, there was evidence linking him to the explosives used in the suicide vests. The second individual was with those involved during the time just prior to the attack, seemingly dropping off the terrorists at the Stade de France, and subsequently was involved with a terrorist attack in Brussels, in March, 2016.

While most Muslims and Arab-French citizens spoke out against the attacks, there were some silent symbolic protests and a few spoke in support of the terrorists. The attacks brought to the surface the splits within French society, and many across the society hoped that if they worked to lessen these differences, it could be a positive outcome from the tragedy. For others, these attacks only strengthened their resolve that all who live in France should live a life that reflects mainstream French culture.

Donald A. Watt

Further Reading

BBC News. "Paris Attacks: What Happened on the Night." *BBC News*. London: The British Broadcasting Corporation, 2015. Online summary of the attacks, with maps and photos of the areas where these occurred.

CNN Library. "2015 Paris Terror Attacks Fast Facts." *CNN* Atlanta: Cable News Network, 2016. This contains a summary of the events on November 13 and a chronology of relevant events over the next five months.

House of Representatives, Subcommittee on Terrorism. *The Paris Attacks: A Strategic Shift by ISIS?* Washington, D.C.: U.S. Government Publishing Office, 2015. Proceedings of the subcommittee's hearings shortly after the Paris attacks.

Iacobucci, Edward M,. and Stephen J. Toope, eds. *After the Paris Attacks: Responses in Canada, Europe, and Around the Globe*. Toronto: University of Toronto Press, 2015. Although published prior to the November attacks, this collection of papers examine many of the issues that are central to the November attacks. It was convened after the Charlie Hebdo attack.

See also Hate crime; Murders, mass and serial; Terrorism.

Patriot Act

The Law: Revision of federal laws governing warrants, electronic surveillance, access to private records, custody, and definitions of terrorism

Date: Became law on October 26, 2001

Criminal justice issues: Federal law; police powers; terrorism

Significance: A rapid response to the terrorist attacks of September 11, 2001, the Patriot Act was designed to protect the United States by making it easier to uncover and defeat foreign and domestic terrorism.

On October 26, 2001, only forty-five days after terrorists crashed skyjacked jetliners into the World Trade Center and Pentagon, President George W. Bush signed Public Law 107-56. Formally titled the Uniting and Strengthening America by Providing Appropriate Tools Required to Intercept and Obstruct Terrorism Act, the law is better known by its acronym, USA PATRIOT Act, or simply Patriot Act. The new law altered more than fifteen existing federal statutes, some in major ways, primarily to equip law-enforcement and intelligence personnel with legal tools for fighting international and domestic terrorism.

Tracking Terrorists and Their Money

The act streamlines the legal processes for obtaining authorization to perform surveillance on suspects persons and for seizing money that may be used to support terrorism. Among its measures, it requires financial institutions to report suspicious activity, identify new customers effectively, cut ties to fraudulent shell banks in foreign countries, and maintain anti-money-laundering programs. Financial institutions are encouraged to share information with law-enforcement agencies, and the federal government is empowered to confiscate the property of any person or organization that performs terrorist acts or plans to do so. The act also expanded the kinds of money-laundering and fraudulent activities—such as those involving American credit cards—that fall under the definition of supporting terrorism.

In order to catch terrorists, the act changed requirements for issuing search warrants and reduced judicial oversight. Previously, local judges—or the eleven-member Foreign Intelligence Surveillance Court in the case of suspected foreign spying—issued warrants to authorize electronic surveillance, such as wiretaps, for specific instruments or facilities. The Patriot Act permits any federal judge to issue a nationwide warrant to tap phones and electronic mail in any instruments that suspects may conceivably use. It also allows "sneak and peek" search warrants; permits delays in serving some warrants until one week after the surveillance authorized by the warrants; and requires libraries, bookstores, and Internet service providers to supply information about client use. In the case of foreign suspects, antiterrorism agents can request authorization for warrantless searches when gathering foreign intelligence is a significant reason for the searches. Before the Patriot Act was passed, foreign intelligence gathering had to be the sole reason.

Expanded Scope of Antiterrorism Efforts

The Patriot Act is designed to stop terrorists from staying in the United States. When there are reasonable grounds to believe that foreign visitors pose a threat to national security, they can be arrested and held for seven days without being charged, pending investigation or their deportation. There is no judicial review except for *habeas corpus*, and the U.S. attorney general may order aliens held indefinitely if no countries agree to accept them upon deportation.

The act makes even unknowingly associating with terrorists or terrorist organizations a deportable offense. To track and identify suspects, the act further increases rewards for information about terrorism, expands the exemptions to the Posse Comitatus Act of 1878, and permits the U.S. attorney general to collect samples of deoxyribonucleic acid (DNA) from convicted federal prisoners. It also adds a new category, domestic terrorism, applicable to any U.S. citizen who commits acts intended negatively to influence government policy or to coerce civilians by intimidation. Such acts, whether by citizens or foreigners, include attacking mass transportation, releasing biological agents, using weapons or explosives, spreading false information about terrorist attacks, or conspiring with terrorists.

The Patriot Act warns citizens not to mistreat Muslims and Arabs, and it penalizes government officials and law-enforcement agents who misuse it. The act "sunsets" many of its provisions on December 31, 2005—that is, it requires congressional reapproval by that date.

Despite its various safeguards, the act received extensive criticism from both conservative and liberal commentators. The act essentially requires citizens and legal aliens to accept reductions in civil liberties in exchange for increased security. However, critics charge that the act's infringements on civil liberties are unnecessary or excessive. Philosopher Cornel West captured the basic objection when he said that the fundamental fear is "that the present American obsession with safety may undermine freedom, that security could trump liberty, that democracy might be lost in the name of declaring war on terrorism."

Critics specifically decry the act's reduction of judicial oversight of surveillance procedures and detention of aliens, fearing that such measures give the executive branch excessive freedom and upset the balance of power in government. Although Attorney General John Ashcroft insisted in April, 2004, that neither Congress nor the courts found a single instance of abuse under the act, critics were not mollified. By then, more than two hundred local communities and four states had passed resolutions asking that the scope of the Patriot Act be narrowed. At the same time the act's supporters, including some members of Congress, argued to expand it and eliminate the sunset provision.

Roger Smith

Further Reading

Chang, Nancy. *Silencing Political Dissent*. New York: Seven Stories Press, 2002. Argues that antiterrorism policies, including the Patriot Act, threaten civil liberties and may lead to excessive executive power.

Goldberg, Daniel, Victor Goldberg, and Robert Greenwald, eds. *It's a Free Country: Personal Freedom in America After September 11*. New York: Nation Books, 2003. Forty-one articles and cartoons emphasizing civil liberties issues arising from antiterrorism efforts.

Reams, Bernard D., Jr., and Christopher T. Anglim, comps. *USA PATRIOT Act: A Legislative History of the Uniting and Strengthening of America by Providing Appropriate Tools Required to Intercept and Obstruct Terrorism Act, Public Law No. 107-56*. 5 vols. Buffalo, N.Y.: William S. Hein, 2002. Exhaustive compilation of documents and records intended as a legal resource on the Patriot Act.

Smith, Norris, and Lynn M. Messina, eds. *Homeland Security*. New York: H. W. Wilson, 2004. Twenty-eight articles reprinted from newspapers and magazines about aspects of national security, terrorism, and civil liberties.

Uniting and Strengthening America by Providing Appropriate Tools Required to Intercept and Obstruct Terrorism Act of 2001. Washington, D.C.: Government Printing Office, 2001. The complete text of the Patriot Act. The text of the law can also be found on the Government Printing Office's Web site, at purl.access .gpo.gov.

See also Attorney General, U.S.; Bill of Rights, U.S.; Drugs and law enforcement; Electronic surveillance; Espionage; Homeland Security, U.S. Department of; Illegal aliens; Money laundering; Search warrants; September 11, 2001, attacks; Skyjacking; Terrorism; Treason; Wiretaps.

Pedophilia

Definition: Adult sexual disorder that makes children sex objects

Criminal justice issues: Deviancy; juvenile justice; sex offenses

Significance: Psychiatric disorders create many difficult problems for the criminal justice system. Pedophilia is a psychiatric disorder that has entered the legal system as a major public safety issue and is being dealt with accordingly.

The term pedophilia has its roots in Greek words for child (*paido*) and love (*philos*), and the term's basic definition is childlove. The word was introduced into the English language in 1886 in a distinguished work on the psychopathology of human sexuality by psychiatrist

Richard von Krafft-Ebing. In the modern medical profession, pedophilia has long been viewed as a mental disability. Psychiatry has viewed pedophilia in a similar way—as a diagnosable disorder that should be treated medically, either through medication or psychiatric treatment, such as cognitive-behavior therapy. The American Psychiatric Association classifies pedophilia as a form of paraphilia, the general term for conditions in which one becomes sexually aroused by objects, situations, or other persons in unusual or socially unacceptable ways.

Persons diagnosed as pedophiles must be over the age of sixteen and be experiencing chronic intense sexual fantasies, urges, or behavior toward prepubescent children—those under the age of about thirteen. Moreover, the symptoms must last for at least six months and either disturb the sufferer greatly or impair the person's day-to-day functioning. Sexual attraction toward children is not related to sexual orientation and is not defined by the sex of the objects of pedophilia. Male pedophiles may be primarily attracted to prepubescent boys and at the same time be married to women and have children of their own. The prevalence rate of pedophilia is unknown, especially because many pedophiles do not seek help or acknowledge their disorder because of its taboo nature.

Pedophilic Associations

Many organizations promote the idea of sexual relations between adults and children. Such organizations are often monitored by law enforcement because of their possible links to pedophilia and sex offenses. In encouraging sexual relationships between adults and children, members of such associations advocate lowering the age of consent or legalizing all sexual acts between children and adults.

To true pedophiles, having sexual desire for children is not something to be ashamed of. They often see it as a beautiful expression of their love for a child. Pedophiles are known for surrounding themselves with children by working closely with them. Many coach sports or work as camp counselors or teachers and do not understand why society considers their sexual feelings and behaviors abnormal and wrong. Moreover, these organizations generally believe that the rights of the children themselves are being violated by not allowing them to choose to engage in sexual relationships with adults. Pedophiles who are asked about the devastating physical and emotional effects that sexual abuse has on children are apt to reply that they personally do not condone abuse and that the relationships with children they seek are purely consensual. However, the rebuttal to this assertion is that children, because of their immaturity, are incapable of consenting to such relationships. Therefore, all sexual contact between adults and children is abusive and may cause irreparable harm to children.

Pedophilia and the Criminal Justice System

Pedophilia itself is neither a crime nor a recognized legal term. The term is often applied by people in the criminal justice system to adults who commit sexual acts that involve children, but such usage may be incorrect. It is important to recognize that pedophiles are not necessarily sex offenders and that not all child sexual abusers and child molesters are pedophiles. Many pedophiles never attempt to have sexual contact with children, and not all offenders have recurrent intense feelings toward children, as diagnoses of the condition require.

Pedophiles do, however, enter the criminal justice system when they act on their sexual fantasies and urges by engaging in sexual acts with children, by intentionally exposing themselves to children for the purpose of sexual arousal, or by knowingly possessing child pornography—sexual images of children. By doing any of those things, pedophiles become sex offenders and are subject to monitoring and punishment within the criminal justice system. Although the level of monitoring varies by state, convicted sex offenders are required to register with state agencies, such as law enforcement, and may become the subjects of community notification when they are convicted.

In many states, child pornography laws are used to prosecute pedophile sex offenders. In the United States, it is illegal to produce, promote, distribute, advertise, or knowingly possess child pornography. Lawmakers and many researchers believe that handling child pornography may increase the existing propensity of pedophiles to act on their urges and fantasies. In addition, pornography is often used by pedophiles who engage in child molestation as a tool to lower the inhibitions of their young victims.

Pedophilia and the Court System

The U.S. court system has accepted psychiatric diagnoses of pedophilia as a serious mental disorder. In the case of *Kansas v. Hendricks (1997), the U.S. Supreme Court upheld Kansas's Sexually Violent Predator Act. The Kansas law permitted persons deemed to be sexually violent predators to be committed to psychiatric hospitals for control, care, and treatment until they are judged no longer to pose dangers to themselves or society.*

The Kansas case arose when the defendant, Leroy Hendricks, was due for release from prison. He had a long history of sexually molesting children, and the state judged him a sexually violent predator and civilly committed him to a state hospital. Hendricks challenged his commitment, even though at trial he had agreed not only with a state physician's diagnosis of his pedophilia but also that he continued to have sexual fantasies and urges involving children that he could not control. Finding that pedophilia qualifies as a mental disorder under the act, the Supreme Court upheld Hendricks's commitment.

In some states incarcerated offenders diagnosed as pedophiles must accept treatment as a condition of their release from prison. An example of this is California's mandatory chemical castration laws. California requires that some male sexual offenders take the drug medroxyprogesterone, which is more commonly known as Depo-Provera, to lower their testosterone levels to reduce their sexual drives. Mandatory use of this drug is being employed by other states as well.

Lisa A. Williams

Further Reading

Briere, J., and American Professional Society on the Abuse of Children. *The APSAC Handbook on Child Maltreatment.* Thousand Oaks, Calif.: Sage, 1996. Handbook of the American Professional Society on the Abuse of Children that discusses major types of child abuse, their treatment, and legal issues.

Browne, Angela, and David Finkelhor. "Impact of Child Sexual Abuse: A Review of the Research." *Psychological Bulletin* 99 (January, 1986): 66-77. Psychological study of research through the mid-1980's on sexual abuse of children.

Crosson-Tower, Cynthia. *Understanding Child Abuse and Neglect.* 5th ed. Boston: Allyn & Bacon, 2001. Textbook covering all aspects of child maltreatment, including sexual abuse, from symptoms and signs to parental motivations, and the role of the social service system.

Jenkins, Philip. *Pedophiles and Priests: Anatomy of a Contemporary Crisis.* New York: Oxford University Press, 2001. One of many studies of the widespread sexual abuse of children by priests that rocked the Roman Catholic Church during the late 1990's and early years of the twenty-first century.

McCabe, Kimberly A. *Child Abuse and the Criminal Justice System.* New York: Peter Lang, 2003. Broad study of the many forms of child abuse, including sexual abuse, and the responses of the criminal justice system to them.

Russell, Diana E. H. *Sexual Exploitation: Rape, Child Sexual Abuse, and Workplace Harassment.* Beverly Hills, Calif.: Sage, 1989. Sociological study of different forms of sex offenses, including sexual abuse of children.

See also Child abuse and molestation; Police psychologists; Pornography, child; Sex offender registries.

People v. Nidal Hasan (2013)

The Case: Military court-martial for premeditated murder of thirteen Fort Hood soldiers
Date: Decided August 23, 2013
Criminal justice issues: Military justice; terrorism
Significance: The decision of the military tribunal highlighted the need for optimizing policies for countering internal threats and enabling commanders to become attuned to behavioral indicators that signal when individuals may commit violent acts or become radicalized.

Major Nidal Hasan, the U.S. Army psychiatrist who murdered thirteen soldiers and wounded thirty-two others in November 2009, was a "ticking time-bomb." As a nation experiencing unprecedented threats of terrorism, the U.S. law enforcement and counterintelligence agencies had been warning citizens to be aware of the signals and overt behaviors that homegrown terrorists can exhibit. Unfortunately, the clear signals and overt behavior of Hasan were ignored, and, more importantly, ignored by a revered agency most likely to identify a terrorist—the U.S. Army.

Radicalization

The following is a brief review of the shooting event on November 5, 2009. Hasan, a U.S. Army psychiatrist, was assigned to the Fort Hood deployment processing center where he interviewed soldiers being deployed to Afghanistan. His job was to interview soldiers to determine their mental health fitness for deployment. By his own admission, Hasan had become radicalized by November 5, 2009. Hasan chose November 5 because it was the day the units he was to deploy with to Afghanistan were scheduled to go through the processing center, and he would have the maximum number of targets to fire at. He brought with him an FN Five-seven pistol and a Smith and Wesson .357 magnum revolver, which he used to kill thirteen soldiers and wound another thirty-two.

He was tried by court-martial during which he served as his own defense and was found guilty. At the sentencing phase of the trial, he was sentenced to death. During the trial it became clear that Hasan wanted to be found guilty and become a martyr for radical Islam. Serving as his own defense, Hasan told the jury that he was the sole shooter and that the shootings were premeditated—presumably to obviate a conviction for anything less than premeditated murder. While in military prison awaiting execution, he declared lethal injection would make him a martyr.

Hasan sent message after message of his radicalization as a Muslim jihadist well before his murderous rampage at Fort Hood. The *Washington Post* reported that as an intern at Walter Reed Army Hospital a year and a half prior to the shootings, Hasan was tasked with giving a presentation on a medical topic of his choosing as a culminating exercise of his residency program. Instead of adhering to the requirement, Hasan prepared a slide presentation, titled "The Koranic World View as it Relates to Muslims in the U.S. Military," in which he lectured on Islam, suicide bombers, and threats the military could encounter from Muslims conflicted about fighting in the Muslim countries of Iraq and Afghanistan." Ultimately, in this presentation, he advocated for the U.S. Army to offer conscientious objector status for U.S. Army Muslims who chose this option. He referred to Osama bin Laden, the Taliban, suicide bombers, and Iran. One slide read, "If Muslim groups can convince Muslims that they are fighting for God against injustices of the infidels, then Muslims can become a potent adversary, i.e., suicide bombing."

There was clear evidence that Hasan had been communicating with the Yemen-based Iman Anwar al-Awlaki, who the National Security Agency (NSA) identified as a security threat to the United States. Hasan's business cards also had the acronyms, "SoA(SWT)." U.S. intelligence agencies have identified "SoA" as "soldiers of Allah" and "SWT" as "glory to God" in Arabic. Moreover, as expressed in the special report prepared by the U.S. Senate Committee on Homeland Security and Governmental Affairs, an instructor and peer both referred to Hasan as a "ticking time-bomb." Not only was action not taken to discipline him, but also his officer evaluation reports sanitized his obsession with violent Islamist extremism into praiseworthy research on counterterrorism.

Reporting Suspicious Behavior

The question that defied logic was, "How could this officer whose evidence of radicalization was on full display to his superiors and peers slip through the Army's detection of radical Islam and murder thirteen soldiers and wound an additional thirty-two?" The answer appears to be the "fear" on the part of Hasan's Army officer superiors who believed that reporting their suspicions might result in a reprimand for religious intolerance or bias. This was revealed through interviews of Hasan's superiors. Of course, this revelation reminds that "political correctness" must be trumped when considering reporting obvious radicalization or other suspicious behavior such as rants on social media, for example.

An historical example of a citizen's suspicion paying off is the case of Bruno Hauptmann, the convicted killer of Charles Lindberg's kidnapped son. Hauptmann purchased gas with a $10 gold certificate, and the attendant thought this seemingly innocent act was strange. He wrote Hauptmann's license plate number on the back of the gold certificate, and the FBI matched the serial number on the $10 gold certificate to one of the gold certificates in the ransom. The Federal Bureau of Investigation (FBI) traced the license plate to Hauptmann's car, and he was subsequently arrested, tried, and convicted. If Hasan's superiors had reported their suspicions, it is possible that thirteen dead soldiers would be alive today, and thirty-two wounded soldiers would not be disabled.

James E. Guffey

Further Reading

Gall, J. M. *Domestic Lone Wolf Terrorists: An Examination of Patterns in Domestic Lone Wolf Targets, Weapons, and Ideologies*. 2014. ProQuest Database ID#1651237342.

Gates, R. M. *Protecting the Force: Lessons from Fort Hood. Department of the Army, Fort Hood Army Initial Review Team—Final Report*. January, 2010. http://www.defense.gov/Portal/1/Documents/pubs/DOD-ProtectingTheForce_Security_HR_13Jan10.pdf.

Kenber, B. *Nidal Hasan Sentenced to Death for Fort Hood Shooting Rampage*. August 28, 2013. http://www.washingtonpost.com/world/national-security/nidal-hasan-sentenced-to-death-for-fort-hood-shooting-rampage/2013/08/28/aad28de2-0ffa-11e3-bdf6-e4fcb77d94al_story.html?wpisrc=nl_headlines.

Platoni, K. "The Army's Fort Hood Disgrace." The Wall Street Journal. March 19, 2015. http://www.wsj.com/articles/kathy-platoni-the-armys-fort-hood-disgrace-1426806479.

Priest, D. *Fort Hood Suspect Warned of Threats Within the Ranks*. November 10, 2009. http://www.washingtonpost.com/wp-dyn/content/article/2009/11/09/AR2009110903618.html.

U.S. Government's Failure to Prevent the Fort Hood Attack. U.S. Senate Committee on Homeland Security and Governmental Affairs. http://www.hsgac.senate.gov//imo/media/doc/Fort_Hood/FortHoodReport.pdf?attempt=2.

See also Murders, mass and serial; Military justice; Terrorism.

Polygraph testing

Definition: Method of measuring physiological responses to questioning in order to detect lies

Evidence and forensics; Interrogation; Technology

Significance: Although polygraph testing has been used since the 1920s, it has failed to gain widespread acceptance as a reliable tool in criminal justice.

Also known as "lie detectors," polygraphs are instruments that record the physiological responses of persons being asked questions for the purpose of ascertaining the truthfulness of their answers. Questions are assembled in a testing format commonly called a psycho-physiological detection of deception (PDD) examination.

The word "polygraph" has Greek roots that mean "many writings." In polygraph testing, each "writing," or pen marking, on a chart paper represents a unique physiological response, such as blood pressure, upper body movement, or galvanic skin response (perspiration). Any increases in these measurements indicate that the subject of the test is being discomforted by the questions being posed. Through careful questioning, monitoring of the tests, and evaluation of the overall results, testers can generally determine the truthfulness of the subjects' responses to individual questions.

History

The Italian criminologist Cesare Lombroso is credited with developing the principles behind polygraph testing during the 1890s. A pioneer of modern scientific criminology methods, he sought to explain criminal behavior through human biology. He discovered that human blood pressure increases following deceptive responses. Later, William Marston and John Larson separately came to the conclusion that blood pressure and respiration were correlated. Larson constructed the actual recording device in 1921, but Leonarde Keeler and Walter Summers refined the direct predecessor of the modern polygraph testing device around 1924. Following their advances, investigators and employers began to use the polygraph as a matter of practice.

Legal controversies over the use of polygraph testing began around the same time. In 1923, a convicted murderer name Frye took his appeal to the US Supreme Court, arguing that he had been wrongly convicted because the trial court had refused to admit evidence in his favor that was based upon the findings of a crude precursor to the modern polygraph that involved periodic readings from a blood-pressure cuff. Because the scientific community did not accept that method, the Court found it to be unreliable and therefore ordered the evidence to be excluded in *Frye v. United States* (1923).

Although polygraph technology has advanced greatly since Frye's time, by the turn of the twenty-first century, only the state of New Mexico admitted polygraph tests into evidence at the trial level. However, in 1998, the US Supreme Court declared that individual courts have the

Grass Instruments polygraph amplifier. (By glacial23, via Wikimedia Commons)

discretion to admit such tests as evidence if they so choose.

Examination Type and Format

Polygraph examinations are most commonly used in two settings: pre-employment screening and criminal investigations. Pre-employment testing involves series of exploratory questions about job candidates' possible histories of job trouble, substance abuse, and criminal behavior. Until the practice was outlawed in 1988, private employers could require applicants to submit to polygraph examinations for purposes of job suitability and, after they were hired, could require them to take additional examinations at any time. However, passage of the federal Employee Polygraph Protection Act prohibited such testing, exempting only law-enforcement agencies, nuclear power facilities, and pharmaceutical companies.

Polygraph examinations conducted on behalf of law-enforcement agencies or defense attorneys usually focus on specific criminal issues. Depending upon the information available to them, examiners utilize one of many specific-issue question formats. One of the most commonly used is the Control Question Technique (CQT) developed by John Reid. Tests using that format begin by asking subjects "control" questions designed to elicit deceptive, or untruthful, responses from ordinarily truthful subjects. The questions that follow concern the relevant or specific issues at hand. For example, if the polygraph examination concerns the theft of money from a corporation, a control question might be, "Have you ever taken something from someone who trusted you?" The following, specific-issue question would be, "Are you the person who took the money from Company X *on the date and time in question?*"

Subjects "pass" the tests when their physiological responses to control questions are stronger than those to the specific-issue questions. Conversely, they "fail" the tests when the results are the opposite. However, contrary to the ways in which lie detectors are depicted in the popular media, there is much more to polygraph testing than simply asking questions.

The classic polygraph testing format begins with pre-test interviews that establish rapport between subjects and examiners and allows the examiners to create psychological sets—the focus of attention. Examiners formulate their questions based upon the information they gather during the interviews. After they attach the polygraph to the subjects, "stimulus tests" are conducted that require subjects to lie to certain questions. These trial tests indicate to examiners whether the subjects are testable. Next, the examiners conduct the actual examinations regarding the specific issues at hand. When the subjects are judged to have failed their tests, the examiners begin the post-interview stage and attempt to elicit admissions or confessions.

Technology, Profession, and Industry

For many years, polygraph instruments recorded responses with several ink pens moving across continuously flowing paper charts. Modern polygraph instruments are now computerized. The physiological responses of subjects received by the instruments are digitized and displayed on computer screens. Polygraph software and equipment are now commercially available to both public and private examiners.

Regulation of the polygraph industry varies throughout the United States. Some states have stringent licensing requirements regarding examiner training, test formats, and examinee fitness. Other states simply require examiner registration; many states have no licensing requirements whatsoever. In states requiring licensing, prospective polygraph examiners must attend ten-week polygraph schools, in which they receive training in psychology, physiology, interviewing and interrogation, and chart interpretation. Following their coursework, they must satisfactorily pass several examinations and, in some instances, complete academic research projects.

The American Polygraph Association (APA), the largest professional group of the trade, has attempted to standardize the industry by offering accreditation status to polygraph schools that follow standards approved in its bylaws. In addition to attending regional training sessions, APA members gather once each year to review recent research and practices.

Douglas A. Orr

Further Reading

Clifton, Charles. *Deception Detection: Winning the Polygraph Game.* New York: Paladin, 1991. Print.

Kleiner, Murray, ed. *Handbook of Polygraph Testing.* San Diego: Academic, 2001. Print.

Matte, James A. *Forensic Psychophysiology Using the Polygraph: Scientific Truth Verification, Lie Detection.* Williamsville: J. A. M., 1996. Print.

Moore, Mark H., Carol V. Petrie, and Anthony A. Braga, eds. *The Polygraph and Lie Detection.* Washington, DC: Natl. Academies, 2003. Print.

Segrave, Kerry. *Lie Detectors: A Social History.* Jefferson: McFarland, 2003. Print.

US Congress, Office of Technology Assessment. *Scientific Validity of Polygraph Testing: A Research Review and Evaluation.* Stockton: UP of the Pacific, 2004. Print.

See also Confessions; Embezzlement; Private police and guards; Suspects; Technology's transformative effect.

Pornography, child

Definition: Visual depictions of minors in sexually explicit poses

Deviancy; Juvenile justice; Sex offenses

Significance: Although adult pornography has been a tolerated, if not fully accepted, part of human culture throughout recorded history, child pornography is another matter—one that evokes nearly universal disgust across all social boundaries. However, Internet technology has added a new dimension to child pornography that presents unprecedented challenges to the efforts of the criminal justice system to combat the spread of child pornography and its associated exploitation of children.

The roots of child pornography date back to ancient Greece, and it flourished in England during the nineteenth century. However, the true birth of child pornography occurred during the mid-1960's, with an explosion in the production of sexually graphic photographs of children in Europe, Asia, Australia, and North Africa. By the late 1960's and early 1970's, child pornography was the basis of a major worldwide market. This development was partly the result of relaxation of laws against magazines containing child pornography in many countries.

The U.S. government began to take action against the widespread availability of child pornography with the Su-

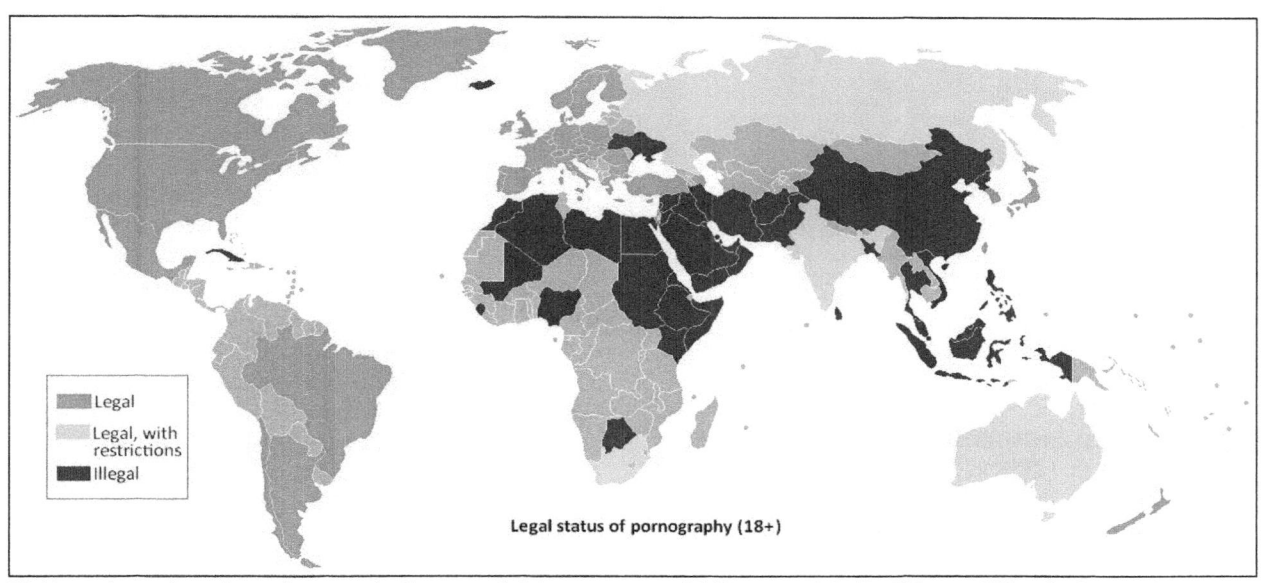

World map showing laws of general pornography (does not include laws concerning of child pornography). (By Ghibar, via Wikimedia Commons)

preme Court's 1982 ruling in *New York v. Ferber*. That case came to the Supreme Court in a challenge to a New York anti-child pornography law, which the Court upheld. The case brought child pornography to the attention of the American public. In response to a subsequent public outcry, a series of campaigns was waged against this burgeoning problem. By the mid-1980's, child pornography was virtually abolished in the United States. Its production was laborious and costly, and purchasing it was difficult and subject to severe criminal penalties.

Since then, however, technological advances, particularly in the Internet, have altered the situation by making pornographic materials convenient and inexpensive to distribute in volume. This has allowed for the almost instantaneous and anonymous dissemination of child pornography through sites on the Web, e-mail, instant messaging, bulletin boards, chat rooms, peer-to-peer file sharing networks, and social media sites. Indeed, the advent of the Internet has acted as the impetus for the resurgence of a nearly extinct subculture that has become part of a global network devoid of boundaries.

While the trafficking of child pornography literature was once limited by geography, the Internet has served as a hunting ground for sexual predators. The fact that child pornography has now found an electronic safe haven has made it one of the most controversial issues of modern law enforcement and has provoked enormous social concern.

Defining Child Pornography

Because of conflicting laws in various countries, there is considerable disagreement over definitions of child pornography. Most laws prohibit depictions of sexual activities involving children below specified ages, but the ages vary from country to country. Some countries disallow all illustrations of nude minors, some forbid written works describing sexual activities of minors, and others even prohibit simulated pornography—cartoons, paintings, drawings, and computer-generated images.

The United States Criminal Code now defines child pornography to include all photographs, films, videos, and other visual representations, regardless of how they are made, showing persons who are, or who are depicted as, being under the age of eighteen years, engaged in explicit sexual activity. The second part of the code's definition includes written materials and visual representations that promote sexual activity with persons under the age of eighteen.

The advent of sexting—the sharing of sexually explicit or suggestive, nude or seminude photographs, videos, or textual messages, primarily via text-messaging or social media—has shaken up the definition of child pornography in the United States. An increasing number of children have access to or ownership of cellphones, and studies have found that while still relatively uncommon, as many as 15 to 20 percent of adolescents and young adults have sexted at some point. Such images, when distributed beyond their intended audience (most often a romantic partner or a would-be partner), can cause shame

Warning Banner for Operation Protect Our Children. (Public domain, via Wikimedia Commons)

and ostracism; however, more importantly, the creation and sharing of that content, if it depicts the nudity or sexual activity of persons under eighteen, constitutes the creation and dissemination of child pornography while the receipt of it, whether desired or solicited or not, is considered receipt of child pornography. In many states, those caught engaging in sexting can be convicted on child pornography charges, face juvenile detention, and be required to register as a sex offender. Moreover, these situations can also quickly escalate to felonies, with images being shared across state lines.

Prevalence of Child Pornography

The incidence and prevalence rates of child pornography are difficult to ascertain given the plethora of unsubstantiated statistics and the dearth of available resources that have been allocated to measure the problem. Child pornography is an industry of high profitability that, in 2009, was estimated to generate as much as $20 billion in annual revenue globally. More than 100,000 sites offer child pornography on the Web. Moreover, it appears that more than 25 percent of youths receive sexual propositions from adults over the Internet every year.

Another Internet feature through which pornography is disseminated is the virtual chat room. The spread of Internet chat rooms created a virtually dangerous playing field for child pornography offenders and pedophiles because of the anonymity they permit. Sex offenders first encounter their child victims in chat rooms more than three-quarters of the time, according to one 2004 study. When children enter Internet chat rooms, they have an extremely high chance of coming into contact with sexual predators. Children are especially vulnerable because of their capacity for trust and may freely release sensitive personal information, such as their home addresses. Teenagers are also particularly susceptible to persuasion or coercion by their partners or online predators, who convince them to send sexual images or videos of themselves either via the Internet or their phones.

As these problems have become better known, parents have taken greater initiative in monitoring their children's online activities and educating them on safe, responsible Internet use. The Pew Research Center conducted a survey in 2015 revealing that 48 percent of parents had knowledge of their children's e-mail passwords and about one-third had access to one of their child's social media account logins. Meanwhile, fully 94 percent of parents reported discussing appropriate online behaviors, among them what should or should not be shared, acceptable content to consume, and appropriate behaviors toward others.

Prosecution and Punishment

The possible prison terms for violating federal laws against child pornography and related crimes laws are severe:

- possession of child pornography: 10-20 years
- distribution or receipt of child pornography: 5-20 years
- producing child pornography: 15-30 years

Factors such as the age of the child or children depicted, any prior sexual misconduct offenses, whether other types of violence are shown, and the number of images involved can all affect sentencing. However, the US Sentencing Commission reported in 2013 that nearly 70 percent of offenders convicted on child pornography charges receive sentences less severe than these guidelines recommend. Often, criteria such as psychological assessment of the defendant, their level of risk for contact sexual offenses, their likelihood of reoffending, the relative ages of victim and defendant, and the content itself are taken into consideration during sentencing.

Several initiatives aimed at reducing the problem were launched in 1998 in response to the public demand to end child pornography. U.S. Congress enacted the Child Online Protection Act to require online commercial pornographers to verify ages of Internet users before allowing them to view pornography. During that same year, Congress also passed the Sexual Predators Act, which required Internet service providers, such as AOL, to notify law enforcement when they discover child pornography on their Web spaces.

Cyber Tipline was also established in 1998 by the National Center for Missing and Exploited Children. This is a congressionally mandated system for reporting child sexual exploitation and is a joint venture with federal agencies, including the Federal Bureau of Investigation, U.S. Immigration and Customs, the U.S. Secret Service, the U.S. Postal Inspection Service, and state and local law-enforcement agencies.

Lisa Landis Murphy

Further Reading
Anderson, Monica. *Parents, Teens and Digital Monitoring*. N.p.: Pew Research Center, 7 Jan. 2016. PDF file.
Barnitz, L. A. *Commercial Sexual Exploitation of Children: Youth Involved in Prostitution, Pornography, and Sex Trafficking*. Washington, D.C.: Youth Advocate Program International, 1998.
Ferraro, M., and E. Casey. *Investigating Child Exploitation and Pornography: The Internet, Law and Forensic Science*. Burlington, Mass.: Academic Press, 2004.
Giacobbe, Alyssa. "Can Sexting Get You Arrested?" Teen Vogue. CondÃ(c) Nast, 22 May 2011. Web. 6 June 2016.
Jenkins, P. *Beyond Tolerance: Child Pornography Online*. New York: New York University Press, 2001.
Svedin, C. G., K. Back, and R. Barnen. *Children Who Don't Speak Out: About Children Being Abused in Child Pornography*. Sweden: Radda Barren, 1997.
Taylor, M., and E. Quayle. *Child Pornography: An Internet Crime*. New York: Brunner-Routledge, 2003.

See also Battered child and battered wife syndromes; Child abduction by parents; Child abuse and molestation; Commercialized vice; Comstock law; Pedophilia; Pornography and obscenity; Sex offender registries; Human trafficking; Victims of Child Abuse Act Reauthorization (2013); Victims of Trafficking Act (2014).

Post-traumatic stress disorder

Definition: A psychiatric condition that consists of a variety of symptoms such as flashbacks, hypervigilance, and insomnia.
Criminal justice issues: Domestic violence; mental disorders; substance abuse; victims; violent crime
Significance: Victims of crime, especially those who experience sexual violence, are often diagnosed with posttraumatic stress disorder. Police officers and other first-responders can also suffer from such symptoms. Treatments for sufferers include medications and supportive talk therapies.

Exposure to traumatic events can have life-altering consequences. Depending on the nature, severity, and frequency of the events, such incidents can lead to psychiatric symptoms that can persist for long periods. Trauma comes in many varieties and in varying doses. For example, exposure to a natural disaster can be highly traumatic, as witnessed and reported by the survivors of tornados, hurricanes, tsunamis, blizzards, and floods. Other types of trauma are human in origin, for example, wars, genocides, serious accidents, mass shootings, and criminal attacks, especially those of a violent and life-threatening character (e.g., rape, armed robbery, aggravated battery). Repeated exposures to trauma are particularly harmful to survivors. Victims of childhood sexual, physical, and emotional abuse can experience symptoms of trauma throughout adulthood. In general, events that are most likely to lead to psychological symptoms involve experiences of sexual or other types of extreme violence and other types of catastrophic events that are perceived as life threatening or lead to serious injury or disability. These adverse events also can produce the symptoms of posttraumatic stress disorder (PTSD), which has long been recognized as affecting military veterans and referred to by different terminology, such as soldier's heart and the Decosta Syndrome (Civil War), shell shock (World War I), and battle fatigue or combat stress reaction (World War II),

Definition of PTSD

Posttraumatic Stress Disorder is a mental disorder described in the psychiatric nomenclature, known as the *Diagnostic and Statistical Manual of Mental Disorders (DSM), which is published by the American Psychiatric Association and is now in its fifth edition (DSM-5). It first appeared in the third edition of the manual, and since then its definition has evolved. For example, it was initially classified as an anxiety disorder, and its diagnosis required direct exposure to a trauma-producing incident. The disorder is presently classified as a trauma- and stressor-related disorder in the DSM-5 and can be precipitated by directly experiencing a traumatic event, witnessing (direct exposure) a traumatic event, hearing about a trauma event (vicarious exposure) experienced by a loved one, such as a close family member or friend, or repeated exposure to the aftermath of traumatic events (e.g., first-responders or police officers viewing the carnage at violent crime scenes or serious accidents).*

Symptoms of PTSD

This disorder is an amalgam of symptoms that diminish people's level of functioning and cause psychological distress, which manifests itself in thoughts, feelings, and behaviors, and in social, occupational, and relational impairment. Specifically, following a traumatic event or stressor, sufferers of PTSD can experience intrusive thoughts, nightmares, and flashbacks (a dissociative reaction) in which they reexperience the event/s in vivid recollections of the sights, sounds, smells, and feelings that were present in the precipitating incident/s. They often avoid any reminders or cues related to the event/s. Such triggering stimuli (places, objects, people) can evoke anxiety and panic attacks. The trauma can elicit other symptoms of PTSD, including negative emotions, such as guilt, disgust, self-loathing and -blame, horror, and anhedonia (the inability to experience pleasure). People with PTSD can become estranged and detached from family, friends, and coworkers. They can also experience hypervigilance (i.e., continually scanning the environment for signs of danger), insomnia, diminished concentration, hyperarousal (i.e., exaggerated startle responses and irritability), and derealization (i.e., experiencing surroundings as unreal or distorted).

To be diagnosed with PTSD, an individual must have one or more symptoms of intrusive memories, including flashbacks; one or more symptoms of avoidance of reminders of the traumatic event; two or more negative emotions or cognitions, such as fear, anhedonia, self-blame, or distorted worldviews; and alterations in arousal, such as persistent jumpiness and irritability. These symptoms must persist for one month or more and can appear immediately or long after the trauma (delayed expression). Acute Stress Disorder is characterized by the same symptoms as PTSD, but these symptoms must appear within one month of trauma exposure and must persist for less than one month. This disorder occurs in approximately 8 percent of the population. More women than men are vulnerable to PTSD due to the greater likelihood of women experiencing sexual and interpersonal violence. A high percentage of people with PTSD have comorbid psychiatric disorders, such as anxiety and substance use disorders.

Treatment of PTSD

Posttraumatic Stress Disorder can be treated with a variety of interventions. For example, antidepressants and anxiolytics (antianxiety medication) are effective in alleviating anxiety and depression, particularly in controlling hypervigilance, exaggerated startle responses, and insomnia. Cognitive behavior therapy and mindfulness training can help trauma survivors process and redefine their ordeal to reframe the experience and themselves with a healthier mindset and worldview.

Developed in 1987, eye movement desensitization and reprocessing (EMDR) therapy involves patients following the lateral and vertical finger motions of the therapist while focusing on traumatic memories and visualizing painful images until they begin to weaken in their intensity and anxiety-provoking energy. Similar to other exposure-type therapies, EMDR treatments work by forcing clients to focus repeatedly on anxiety-provoking stimuli, either in their imagination (imaginal exposure) or in real life (in vivo exposure). When exposure to traumatic episodes in either type of modality is sufficiently lengthy, clients' anxiety dissipates within and across sessions, their overall symptoms diminish, and their coping ability improves. Studies have found no differences between EMDR with imaginal exposure and imaginal exposure alone in terms of reducing victims' symptoms. Service animals, especially dogs, are used to accompany people with PTSD as they venture outside their homes, which is helpful in alleviating symptoms of panic and hypervigilance.

Criminal Victimization and PTSD

Victims of crime are vulnerable to PTSD. First studied among rape victims, PTSD is especially prevalent among victims of violent attacks in which they perceived that their lives were threatened. Hence, incidents that involve a weapon-wielding perpetrator are more likely to produce the attendant symptoms of trauma. Nonetheless, victims of burglary and grand theft can also experience symptoms of PTSD. Those crime victims most vulnerable to PTSD—as with victims of all other types of trauma—had histories of mental illness or substance use disorders before the episode, previous exposures to trauma, poor coping skills, and sparse social support networks. The tendency to self-blame for the occurrence of the crime and the failure to obtain crisis intervention services can exacerbate the symptoms of PTSD.

Arthur J. Lurigio

Further Reading
American Psychiatric Association. *Diagnostic and Statistical Manual of Mental Disorders*. 5th ed. Washington, D.C.: American Psychiatric Association, 2013.
De Jong, J., T. V. M. Komproe, H. Ivan, M. von Ommeren, M. El Masri, M. Araya, N. Khaled, W. van de Put, and D. J. Somasundarem. "Lifetime Events and Posttraumatic Stress Disorder in Four Post-Conflict Settings." *Journal of the American Medical Association* 286 (2001): 555-56.
Friedman, M. J. "Finalizing PTSD in DSM 5: Getting Here from There and Where to Go Next." *Journal of Traumatic Stress* 26 (2013): 548-56.
Shiromani, P. J., T. M. Keane, and J. E. LeDoux, eds. *Post-Traumatic Stress Disorder: Basic Science and Clinical Practice*. New York: Humana Press, 2009.

Young, M. *Psychological Trauma of Crime Victimization. The Road to Victim Justice: Mapping Strategies for Service.* Arlington, Va.: National Center for Victims of Crime and National Organization of Victim Assistance, 1992.

See also Victimization theories; Victim recovery stages; Victims services; Crime victimization: Primary and secondary; Victimology; Rehabilitation; Police psychologists; Forensic psychology.

President's Commission on Law Enforcement and Administration of Justice

Identification: Federal commission established to study sequences of events in the criminal justice system
Date: Established on July 23, 1965
Criminal justice issues: Law-enforcement organization; professional standards; trial procedures
Significance: The president's commission examined the apparatus of the American system of justice from the perspective of balancing crime reduction against protection of constitutional rights.

On July 23, 1965, President Lyndon B. Johnson established the Commission on Law Enforcement and Administration of Justice through Executive Order 11236. The body was charged with examining the nature of crime and juvenile delinquency in the United States. In 1967, the commission issued its official report, *The Challenge of Crime in a Free Society*. The report detailed the commission's findings and offered a criminal justice system diagram tracing the sequence of events through the apparatus of the criminal justice system: from prosecution, and the courts, to corrections.

To understand the breadth and depth of the American system of justice, commission members worked closely with the Federal Bureau of Investigation; the Federal Bureau of Prisons; the Department of Health, Education, and Welfare; and state, local, and private entities involved in criminal justice.

While undertaking its work, the commission documented hundreds of recommendations. Among these were recommendations for organizing and expanding research of criminal justice agencies, advancing science and technology in the administration of justice, increasing the education and standards of criminal justice personnel, exploring community-based correctional alternatives for offenders, and developing a coordinated and cooperative crime prevention strategy on federal, state, and local levels. The commission's recommendations also extended to family life quality, housing and economic conditions, alcohol and narcotic addictions treatment, school system standards, and neighborhood cohesiveness and efficacy.

In its summary conclusions, the commission regarded crime as a social problem, requiring more than specialists literate in the criminal justice process for its solution. The commission suggested that the foundation for effective crime control is the "business of every American" and every American institution-religious, community, professional, business, and collegiate.

Anthony J. Luongo III

Further Reading
Federal Bureau of Investigation. *Crime in the United States (1960-2003 annual reports)*. Washington, D.C.: U.S. Department of Justice.
U.S. Department of Justice. *The Challenge of Crime in a Free Society: Looking Back Looking Forward.* Washington, D.C.: Office of Justice Programs, 1998.

See also Bureau of Justice Statistics; Criminal justice system; Federal Bureau of Investigation, U.S.; Judicial system, U.S.; Law enforcement; National Institute of Justice; Omnibus Crime Control and Safe Streets Act of 1968; Uniform Crime Reports; Wickersham Commission; Wiretaps.

Print media

Definition: Coverage of criminal justice in newspapers and news magazines
Criminal justice issue: Media
Significance: Because the print media are responsible for conveying much of the information on crime and criminal justice that the public receives, they play a significant role in helping to form public opinion on criminal justice issues. Understanding the reasons for media distortions can provide greater understanding of the relationship between media and public perception of crime.

In the twentieth century world of proliferating electronic communication, the American print media remain a booming industry. The advent of the Internet has actually increased public access to print media resources, and the print media and local and national network news sources remain important sources of information for the general public. However, the public draws on the print media's heavy coverage of crime and criminals to form its opinions, and these media often present biased views. Scholars have presented a variety of perspectives and theories concerning the processes that are at work that lead to such media distortion.

Distortions in the News

One aspect of print media coverage that has garnered attention from researchers is the issue of prevalence of crime that appears in print. To examine this issue, researchers generally use a research method known as content analysis to examine how much coverage of crime actually appears in newspapers. Studies of media content have reported that crime news represents between 4 and 28 percent of all newspaper news coverage. Some studies have placed the figure as high as 50 percent.

While it is generally well known that issues of crime and justice are popular topics in media coverage, it is not as well known how accurate this coverage is. Researchers have found that in many ways, the images of crime presented by the mass media in general, and the print media in particular, tend to distort the realities of crime, particularly in the disproportionate attention they pay to violent crime. For example, an analysis of New Orleans newspapers found that murder and robbery cases accounted for 45 percent of news items while only accounting for 12 percent of actual crimes in the region covered. Another study found that 55 percent of the stories in Canadian newspapers concerned violent offenses, whereas violent offenses represented only 6 percent of actual crimes. Another study, in 1991, found that for every two studies in the media on property crime, there were eight stories about violent crime, although property crimes outnumbered violent crimes nine to one.

Research has also suggested that changes in print media crime coverage do not necessarily reflect changes in actual local crime rates. A study made as early as 1951 found no correlations between newspaper coverage of crime and local crime rates. A study found that imbalanced crime coverage still persisted. Moreover, even as violent crime rates were declining in society, television and newspaper coverage of crime was increasing by more than 400 percent.

The Impact of Distortions on Society

There are also other, and more subtle, ways in which the print media can distort the realities of crime, such as by giving disproportionate coverage to certain types of victims, offenders, or social circumstances. For example, the print media tend to focus more attention and resources on crimes involving female victims, young victims, elderly victims, white victims, and affluent victims. At the same time, the print media emphasize cases involving offenders who are members of minority groups.

An example of skewed attention to social circumstances and contexts is the print media's emphasis on crimes involving offenses committed by strangers on local victims, while simultaneously downplaying offenses that committed by acquaintances and relatives of victims. Crimes involving multiple offenders consistently receive intensive coverage. The media also foster distorted notions about causes behind crimes by focusing on individual explanations and emphasizing crimes with unusual motives that do not match the typical patterns of the same offenses.

Media distortion of crime images potentially affects public opinion of crime and criminal justice issues. Researchers have found that people who pay the attention to entertainment and news media depictions of crime tend to hold more negative views of society. Similarly, people who consume more media news coverage are more likely to hold exaggerated views of the amount and seriousness of crime in society. They also are more likely to fear crime and support the idea of retribution. Moreover, people who consume the most media news are more likely to have negative attitudes toward African Americans and other minorities.

It is clear that news media coverage of crime can have a negative impact on social policy. This can be seen in the tendency of politicians and legislative bodies to justify "get tough" stances on criminal justice issues by citing public opinion, much of which is formed by distorted news coverage of crime.

Theories of Mass Media Behavior

Media scholar Gregg Barak has developed a theory of mass media coverage of crime that acknowledges the importance of power and interests in determining media behavior but sees power as broadly distributed. Instead of arguing for the existence of a monolithic source of power—such as the elites who own mass media outlets—as Marxist and radical media theories do, Barak sees power as more evenly dispersed among competing sources. Barak calls this "newsmaking criminology." His view holds that diverse social institutions, including the media, special interest groups, politicians, government officials, and private interests, all have power in society and all compete for the ability to shape public perception about a particular issue, such as crime. Therefore, the mass media behavior can be influenced by outside sources competing to shape public perceptions about crime. This view sees the media as conduits of information that act as middlemen to convey information to the public. Media treatment of crime is thus governed by the daily activities of the politicians, government officials, and interest groups on which the mass media subsequently report. The activities of these interest groups serve as constraints on the daily activities of journalists as they convey and report crime information to the public.

Barak's newsmaking criminology perspective also suggests that mass media reporting practices are governed by the interests of news organizations—and one overriding interest of such organizations is producing news that sells. Decisions of editors and journalists therefore reflect their interpretations of what the public wants to know about. The general assumption is that the public wants to know a great deal about crime, particularly violent crime. This view has given rise to a journalistic adage, "If it bleeds, it leads," in media coverage. The print media achieve success by selling more newspapers and magazines and increasing their advertising revenue. The broadcast media succeed by boosting their audience ratings and increasing their advertising ratings.

Another issue that news organizations consider in decisions about their news coverage is the degree to which readers can identify with stories. There is evidence suggesting that news editors and journalists make these judgments about the news items that they produce. Milwaukee journalists who were the subject of a 1997 research study confirmed this view by openly acknowledging that when they wrote stories they considered the types of people who were most likely to read them. One reporter explained, "If the reader could say 'that could have been me that was killed,' then that has more news value."

The Use of News Themes by Media

News organizations occasionally pursue interests that influence their news decisions that may have little or nothing to do with the type of information presented. These other interests typically have more to do with the gathering and synthesizing of information for presentation to the public. For example, a 1978 study found that a "crime wave" of offenses against elderly New York City residents reported in the media had nothing to do with actual increases in such crimes. The apparent "crime wave" perceived by citizens and politicians was nothing more than the continued and heavy coverage of numerous occurrences of crime that were being covered by the media as a single topic. The manner in which the media organized the news gave the public the false impression that a crime wave against the elderly was developing.

From that New York incident, a sociologist developed a theory of how media distortions can result from the ways that the media organize their news. The research coined the term "news theme" for methods of organizing and unifying massive amounts of potential news items into a single thematic framework to give them structure and reduce confusion. The practical implication of that study was that media news emphases are sometimes determined by decisions to link individual items thematically to other events occurring around the same times.

To illustrate how the generation of news themes work, the 1978 study summarized an actual package of news stories that included these segments:

- Police apprehend juveniles who mugged an elderly couple in Queens
- Police and citizens in Queens meet to discuss crimes against the elderly
- Feature segment on Senior Citizens Robbery Unit
- Police seize guns and drugs that intended for warring gangs
- Two members of a youth gang are arrested for robbery at knifepoint
- An ROTC cadet is arrested in the stabbing death of another cadet
- A city audit finds that police have been mishandling funds
- The city and the police union are working on a contract at the same time that laid-off firemen and subway cops are being rehired

This package of news items is strongly suggestive of a broader news theme of crime in general, as every item in the list covers an aspect of crime or criminal justice. However, within this broader theme, subthemes are evident as well. For example, the lists highlights crimes against the elderly, crimes committed by juveniles, and issues concerning the city police department. It seems unlikely that stories about the senior citizens robbery unit and the meeting to discuss crime against the elderly would normally be deemed newsworthy, if not for the more dramatic story about the mugging of an elderly citizen. By presenting the three stories together, the media conveyed the appearance that crime against the elderly was a serious problem that was receiving much attention by the police, even though the stories were about unrelated events.

Informational Constraints

An additional aspect of news processing that can influence print media behavior is information limitations.

News media organizations rely heavily on information that is obtained and filtered by official agencies, including the police and the courts. The amount of coverage that the media can give to stories is often limited by the amount of information they receive from those agencies. Furthermore, official agencies have different types of motives that can determine the amount of information that is released to the media. These motives can include case-management objectives, attempts to prevent organizational liability, and police attempts to legitimize their work to the public.

Mass media behavior, including the behavior of print media organizations in generating news, therefore, can be explained by considering both cultural influences and organizational influences. Cultural influences affect news organizations by providing the organization with an implicit script to follow outlining the types of news items that are considered culturally interesting, stimulating, and acceptable for news coverage. Organizational factors regarding media process in the generation of news also place considerable limitations on news organizations both in terms of how information is thematically presented, and in terms of the availability of information.

Kevin G. Buckler

Further Reading

Barak, Greg. *Media, Process, and the Social Construction of Crime: Studies in Newsmaking Criminology*. New York: Garland Publishing, 1994. Collection of eleven essays that examine various aspects of the newsmaking criminology framework. The collection includes two separate content analyses of crime appearing in newspaper coverage, as well as essays that examine the meaning and usefulness of the newsmaking criminology framework.

Chermak, Steven M. *Victims in the News: Crime and the American News Media*. Boulder, Colo.: Westview Press, 1995. Examination of the role of victims in the coverage of crime news. The central contention of the work is that victim characteristics determine how the media cover crime in the United States.

Lipschultz, Jeremy H., and Michael L. Hilt. *Crime and Local TV News: Dramatic, Breaking, and Live from the Scene*. Mahwah, N.J.: Lawrence Erlbaum Associates, 2002. Although not specifically addressing the print media, this analysis of local television news emphasizes theories of market-driven journalism and lack of interest in public affairs coverage as factors explaining media emphasis on crime.

Potter, Gary W., and Victor E. Kappeler, eds. *Constructing Crime: Perspectives on Making News and Social Problems*. Prospect Heights, Ill.: Waveland Press, 1998. Collection of fifteen essays examining media and crime. The essays examine how popular images of crime are generated, the effects of these images, and who benefits from the images that are constructed.

Prichard, D., and K. D. Hughes. "Patterns of Deviance in Crime News." *Journal of Communication* 47, no. 3 (1997): 49-67. Examination of media coverage of homicide in Milwaukee, Wisconsin, that considers four forms of deviance: statistical deviance, cultural deviance, normative deviance, and status deviance. This study provides an exceptional demonstration of how crime-related and media-related variables are measured in media research.

Surette, Ray. *Media, Crime, and Criminal Justice*. 2d ed. Pacific Grove, Calif.: Brooks/Cole Publishing, 1998. Arguably the definitive work on media and criminal justice issues, this book explores media treatments of crime and offers extensive discussions of relevant Supreme Court decisions and summaries of research on media and crime issues.

Wykes, Maggie. *News, Crime, and Culture*. Sterling, Va.: Pluto Press, 2001. Explores the links between culture, crime, and the social control of crime by emphasizing perspectives concerning how and why crime is defined. Special attention is given to how news reporting reinforces popular notions about class, race, gender, and poverty.

See also Criminals; Gag orders; Television news; Trial publicity; Social media.

Privacy rights

Definition: Constitutional protection against unlawful government intrusions on citizens' privacy

Civil rights and liberties; Constitutional protections; Police powers; Search and seizure

Significance: The increasing dependency of modern police forces and investigative agencies on electronic surveillance and search techniques presents new challenges to constitutionally protected privacy rights.

Privacy rights involve the protection of citizens against government intrusion into their personal affairs. In the criminal justice system, privacy issues arise when the police engage in surveillance of individuals and search and seizure of people and their personal effects. Nowhere in the US Constitution is privacy expressly mentioned as a protected right. However, most legal scholars conclude that the Framers of the Constitution intended citizens to have fundamental privacy rights, whose scope has been left to interpretations by the courts. This issue is an important one, as modern police often become involved in surveillance and search and seizure activities, during which they may violate the privacy of citizens. References in several amendments to the Constitution, court decisions, and legal writings have instilled the privacy concept in American law. One famous legal commentary declared that citizens have a right to be left alone by government. In its landmark decision in *Griswold v. Connecticut* in 1965, the US Supreme Court stated that citizens have a constitutional right to a certain "zone of privacy" which is free from government intrusion. In fact, during the very next year, in *Schmerber v. California*

(1966), the Court added that the "overriding function" of the Fourth Amendment is to protect personal privacy and dignity against unwarranted intrusion by the State.

In 1967, in *Katz v. United States*, the Supreme Court established the "expectation of privacy" doctrine. This principle stated that citizens are entitled to a reasonable expectation of privacy as long as they demonstrate that expectation through words or actions. In the Katz case, federal police electronically eavesdropped on Katz's public telephone booth conversation, even after he had purposefully closed the door behind him. The Court ruled that Katz's actions established a reasonable expectation of privacy, thus protecting him from government surveillance, and therefore the police in his case acted illegally.

Following the creation of the expectation of privacy rule, the courts established a "balancing of competing interests" test to weigh the needs of police to gather evidence for criminal prosecution against the right of citizens to be protected from government agents who may violate their personal privacy. Privacy protection took on a new dimension when the courts established additional exceptions to the warrant requirement of the Fourth Amendment. In 1985, the Supreme Court expanded the scope of the "special needs" exception by allowing school officials to search students and their personal effects on school premises. Any illegal contraband discovered, such as drugs or weapons, could be given to the police for possible prosecution.

Privacy in the Criminal Justice Process

Persons entering the criminal justice system forfeit some privacy protection, but courts have declared that arrested, convicted, and incarcerated persons do have a limited expectation of privacy within the system. Many courts use electronic monitoring of pretrial detainees who have been released from custody awaiting their criminal trials. These individuals consent to have electronic devices (bracelets or anklets) attached to them during their release to ensure that they comply with the court requirements restricting their movement. Also, the courts allow probation and parole officers to search, without a warrant, the homes and personal effects of individuals who are subject to community supervision. Although probationers and parolees must consent to specific conditions of their release, many requirements include drug urinalysis, warrantless searches, and electronic monitoring of their movements. Persons found through monitoring or testing to have violated their conditions of release may have their privileges revoked.

Incarcerated persons can be subject to more extensive search and confiscation of personal property in jails and prisons. One personal identification method in use within correctional institutions is obtaining and cataloging individual DNA samples from inmates. Obtaining body fluids and tissue specimens for DNA purposes is more intrusive than traditional fingerprinting because officials remove specimens directly from bodies. Correctional institutions may also monitor inmate telephone conversations and use surveillance cameras for safety purposes.

Electronic Surveillance and Privacy

Police increasingly rely on electronic technology to combat crime. As such practices become more common, they raise privacy issues. Technological applications in criminal justice cover a broad spectrum of activities. The use of surveillance cameras is increasing in an effort to identify known offenders, prevent crime, and gather information in public places. These devices have been used to monitor traffic and to cite drivers running red lights. Courts have ruled that the police can electronically monitor citizen activities in public places but cannot intrude into homes without a warrant or other legal justification.

Other devices such as pen registers, which record dialed telephone numbers, and "trap and trace" devices, which document the electronic signatures of computer transmissions, can be used by police to gather information without a warrant. However, federal law governs much of the interception of electronic telephone transmissions. These laws require the police to obtain either a warrant or consent from the one of the parties to intercept telephone wire communications. Although users of landline telephones have a lesser expectation of privacy and transmissions may be intercepted, federal laws require the police to obtain a warrant and follow guidelines in acquiring information from cellular phone service providers. the limits of these rules were tested in 2016 when, after a mass shooting in San Bernardino, California, the FBI ordered Apple to unlock the iPhone of one of the deceased gunmen. Apple refused on the grounds of protecting the privacy of all of their customers. The FBI found an alternate method of unlocking the phone, which raised many questions about privacy on private electric devices and the government's reach.

In 2001, Congress passed the Patriot Act to give law enforcement greater counterterrorism powers. The law is extensive and redefines several traditional police search procedures. It allows police to search homes and businesses without the notice typically required in conventional search warrants. It also allows the use of computer and telephone tracking devices as well as roving wiretap warrants if the investigation at hand involves counterterrorism or foreign intelligence investigations.

In 2013 the full extent of the US government's surveillance under the Patriot Act was revealed when former employee of the National Security Agency (NSA), Edward Snowden, leaked a cache of documents to journalists that revealed a number of surveillance programs that gleaned and stored information from private citizens through phone calls, e-mails, and Internet use. The NSA defended its actions, but had to do so for a congressional hearing amid public outrage at what many viewed as a violation of the privacy of the American people.

William P. Bloss

Further Reading
Del Carmen, Rolando V. *Criminal Procedure: Law and Practice*. 6th ed. Belmont, Calif.: Thomson/Wadsworth, 2004. Comprehensive and readable review of criminal procedure that includes discussions of privacy rights.
Etzioni, Amitai. *The Limits of Privacy*. New York: Basic Books, 1999. Critical consideration of the acceptable limits on constitutional protections of individual privacy rights.
Hall, John Wesley. *Search and Seizure*. 3d ed. Charlottesville, Va.: LEXIS Law Publishing, 2000. Textbook focusing on issues surrounding search and seizure, which often raises privacy rights issues.
Long, Robert. *Rights to Privacy*. New York: H. W. Wilson, 1997. Broad treatise on constitutional and legal issues relating to privacy rights.
McWhirter, Darien A. *Search, Seizure, and Privacy*. Phoenix, Ariz.: Oryx Press, 1994. Book written to make subjects such as search and seizure, the exclusionary rule, and privacy rights interesting for high school and undergraduate college students.
Monmonier, M. S. *Spying with Maps: Surveillance Technologies and the Future of Privacy*. Chicago: University of Chicago Press, 2002. Examination of the privacy rights issues arising from modern high-tech police surveillance of suspects.

See also Abortion; Bill of Rights, U.S.; Computer crime; Electronic surveillance; *Illinois v. McArthur*; *Olmstead v. United States*; Search and seizure; Surveillance cameras; Trespass; Wiretaps; Social media.

Psychological profiling

Definition: Method of identifying probable offender characteristics, including behavioral, personality, and physical attributes, based on crime scene evidence
Crime prevention; Investigation
Significance: Media portrayals have fostered a growing public fascination with the budding field of psychological profiling. Although there is debate over whether this field is more of an art than a science, it has proven particularly useful in investigations of suspects who commit serial crimes. Research confirms that at this stage in the development of psychological profiling, it should be regarded as a valuable tool for investigators, rather than a crime-solving strategy.

Variously known as criminal personality profiling, criminal profiling, crime scene analysis, and investigative analysis, psychological profiling is the technique of studying details of crimes in order to learn about the probable characteristics of the perpetrators. By examining all features of a crime, including time and location, victim characteristics, methods used, and other pertinent information, psychological profilers attempt to infer characteristics about the perpetrators. The profilers draw on their inferences to build models of possible perpetrators that include their likely psychological makeup, mental health, social adjustment, age, sex, race, height, and physical appearance. The profiles are provided to law enforcement to assist in identifying potential suspects or to aid in interrogations of already identified suspects.

History of Psychological Profiling
What may have been the first employment of psychological profiling was used in the investigation of one of the most notorious murder sprees in history—London's Whitechapel murders of the late nineteenth century whose unidentified perpetrator was dubbed Jack the Ripper. However, psychological profiling did not begin to achieve acceptance in law enforcement until after the Federal Bureau of Investigation (FBI) established its Psychological Profiling Program within is Behavioral Science Unit in 1978.

The FBI program began with the classification of information gathered through intensive interviews of thirty-six convicted sexual murderers. In 1985, psychologist David Canter of the University of Surrey in England was asked to assist in the investigation of a criminal known as the Railway Rapist. The profile that Canter produced proved useful in apprehending the rapist-murderer and helped launch Canter on a search for psychological principles that would be useful in generating other profiles. Much of his research drew on what he could learn about interactions between perpetrators and their victims. Canter later established a graduate program in "investigative psychology" at the University of Liverpool. Canter's work was followed by that of private investigator Richard N. Kocsis and his colleagues in Australia, who

Streetmap showing the locations of the first seven Whitechapel murders. Psychological profiling was first used for Jack the Ripper. (Public domain, via Wikimedia Commons)

have conducted studies on the accuracy of psychological profiling and the skills necessary to employ the method successfully.

The Process of Psychological Profiling

Although there is no single protocol, the process of developing profiles usually follows several steps. The first stage, profiling inputs, involves collecting and documenting all information that might help in solving the crimes. This information usually includes crime scene photos, police reports, results from an autopsy, and all information about victims, including age and sex.

In the second stage, known as the decision process models, collected information is organized so that preliminary analyses of the crimes are possible. In this stage, the nature of the crimes is considered, possible offender motives are inferred, and the amounts of time necessary to commit the crimes are considered.

In the third stage, crime assessment, profilers attempt to reconstruct the crimes in detail. They produce play-by-play reconstructions of the crime scene and of interactions between offenders and their victims, while considering such matters as the amount of planning needed, the extent of gratuitous aggression, types of wounds, positioning of bodies, and lengths of time for crime scene staging.

Canter's research suggests that the "criminals' shadows" should be interpreted. He uses "shadow" to mean the story, or inner narrative, of the offender that is reflected in the degree of care the offender has taken to avoid capture, the degree of expertise needed to complete the crime, personal habits, and various peculiarities of an individual crime.

In the fourth stage, the criminal profile, actual psychological profiles are completed. Complete profiles may be so detailed as to include exact age, race, sex, body type, style of clothing, occupational history, capacity for emotional intimacy, and living arrangements. Profiles might also include relationships between the offenders and their victims; the offenders' behavior before, during, and after the crimes; and their personality makeup. The final stages, investigation and apprehension, ideally consist of successful identifications, location, and arrests of suspects who match the profiles.

Psychological profiling is based on several assumptions, including the belief that criminals' crime scenes reflect their personalities. Moreover, because personality traits tend to be stable and enduring, crime scenes should reveal similar consistency. This assumption is believed to be particularly true of serial offenders, such as murderers, rapists, and arsonists, whose behaviors typically reveal continuity and consistency. For example, many serial murderers leave identifiable marks, or "signatures," at their crime scenes. Some offenders collect items or "trophies." Body positioning and crime manipulations ("staging") are usually distinctive and consistent. Another assumption of psychological profiling is that while the methods, or modus operandi (MO), of serial criminals may change somewhat over time and in different situation, other behavior patterns, such as their signatures, generally do not.

Validity of Psychological Profiling

Part of the controversy over psychological profiling stems from misunderstandings of its purpose. The FBI's own Behavioral Science Unit cautioned that although profiles occasionally lead directly to identifications of suspects, such successes are the exception rather than the rule. The chief value of psychological profiles is the direction they give to investigations to help them focus on the most likely characteristics of suspects. A study of nearly two hundred FBI profiles found that they were deemed useful in 46 percent of the cases, and in 17 percent of cases they led to actual suspects. In a majority of cases, investigators felt that the profiles provided a better focus for the process of investigating a crime.

Critics of profiling have argued that although profiles may create a wealth of information, there is currently no way of knowing what part of that information is critical. Another criticism concerns the validity of the information in the databases used to develop profiles. No central database of information on criminals exists, and the few databases that do exist draw information almost exclusively from convicted felons. Information on perpetrators who evade arrest is therefore not included. Moreover, there is also concern about the accuracy of self-reported serial offenders, the majority of whom have antisocial personalities and are proficient at lying and impression management. Finally, the requisite skills for psychological profiling are debated. Some have argued that investigative experience is essential, but recent research suggests that objectivity and logical reasoning are more important.

Richard D. McAnulty

Further Reading

Bartol, C. R. *Criminal and Behavioral Profiling*. Los Angeles: Sage, 2014. Print.
Canter, David. *Criminal Shadows: Inner Narratives of Evil*. London: AuthorLink Press, 2000. Print.
Douglas, John. *The Anatomy of Motive: The FBI's Legendary Mindhunter Explores the Key to Understanding and Catching Violent Criminals*. New York: Pocket Books, 2000. Print.
Douglas, John, and Mark Olshaker. *Mindhunter: Inside the FBI's Elite Serial Crime Unit*. New York: Scribner, 1995. Print.
Egger, Steven A. *The Need to Kill: Inside the World of the Serial Killer*. Englewood Cliffs: Prentice Hall, 2003. Print.
Holmes, Ronald M., and Stephen T. Holmes, eds. *Contemporary Perspectives on Serial Murder*. Thousand Oaks: Sage, 1998. Print.
Kocsis, Richard N., Andrew F. Hayes, and Harvey J. Irwin. "Investigative Experience and Accuracy in Psychological Profiling of a Violent Crime." *Journal of Interpersonal Violence* 17.8 (2002): 811-23. Print.
Turvey, Brent T. *Criminal Profiling: An Introduction to Behavioral Evidence Analysis*. Burlington: 2015. Print.
Ressler, Robert K., and Thomas Schachtman. *I Have Lived in the Monster: Inside the Minds of the World's Most Notorious Serial Killers*. New York: St. Martin's, 1998. Print.
Scherer, J. Amber, and John P. Jarvis. "Criminal Investigative Analysis: Practitioner Perspectives." FBI. US Dept. of Justice, 10 June 2014. Web. 20 June 2016.
White, J. H., and D. Lester, eds. "Criminal Profiling." *Encyclopedia of Crime and Punishment*. New York: Wiley, 2016. 1-5. Print.

See also Crime scene investigation; Forensic psychology; Murders, mass and serial; Police powers; Police psychologists; Racial profiling; Restorative justice; Unabomber; Technology's transformative effect.

Religious sects and cults

Definition: Religious groups that are considered nonmainstream
Criminal justice issues: Civil rights and liberties
Significance: Beliefs and lifestyle practices of groups such as the Amish, Mennonites, Jehovah's Witnesses, Seventh-Day Adventists, and others are often challenged by secular legal authorities and other critics. The U.S. Supreme Court is the final arbiter of the extent to which the practices of these religious groups are protected and to what extent.

Defining Cults and Sects

These groups are variously popularly referred to as cults, sects, New Religious Movements (NRMs), minority religions, alternative religions, spiritual or faith communities. In current usage, the terms cults and sect have negative connotations. Referring to a movement as a cult suggests that it is dangerous pseudo-religion that could be involved in financial fraud and political intrigue, to abuse women and children, and to use brainwashing methods to exploit recruits. There is a matter of particular concern when the cults are considered to be high demand, manipulative and harmful, particularly when they involve intense indoctrination into beliefs that mainstream society believe is odd or spurious.

Cults are said to be characterized by acceptance of the legitimacy claims of other groups, but a relatively negative tension with the larger society. As with sectarian collectivities, cultic groups are a form of social dissent. Their dissent, however, is likely to be less extreme because of their pluralistic position toward other groups.

How Religious Freedom is Defined in the American Context

The First Amendment of the U.S. Constitution provides that Congress may neither establish a state religion nor prohibit the free exercise of religion. These guarantees have been extended to the actions of state and local governments by the Fourteenth Amendment. The court has frequently

In *Lemon v. Kurtzman* (1970), the Supreme Court called for total neutrality of government toward religion in articulating what became known as the "Lemon test" as the standard to judge the constitutionality of government actions that may affect religious matters. Under Lemon, no law may prefer one religion over another, prefer religion to nonreligion, have a primary effect that promotes religion, or cause undue entanglement between government and religious organizations. While some religious groups applauded the Lemon test, other religious groups believed the United States is a nation founded on religion and that the wall actually favors nonreligion over religion.

In various applications of the Lemon Case, the court has ruled that Amish Mennonites are not required to obey school attendance laws, the Ten Commandments may not be posted in schools, and religious groups must be given equal access to facilities on public university campuses. In 1990, however, the Supreme Court seemed to back track from the Lemon doctrine in *Employment Division v. Smith* and ruled that government could require religious actors to obey general laws so long as the laws are not aimed specifically at religion or any particular religious institution. The case involved a Native American's right to smoke illegal hallucinogenic substances as part of religious ritual. Since the Court's ruling in Boerne v. Flores (1997), government are permitted to require religious groups and actors to obey a generally-applicable law, so long as the law is based on a compelling reason, is neutral with respect to religion, and is applied to all persons equally.

American religious freedom originated with the nation's settlement by religious dissidents in the seventeenth century, who sought freedom to worship as they pleased. Despite the ideal of religious liberty, religious intolerance was widespread throughout many of the colonies and persisted long after the Bill of Rights were adopted and affected many minority religions such as Catholics, Jews, Mormons, and Jehovah's Witnesses. Religions that have not infrequently been referred as cults or NRMs are nineteenth century sects such as the Mormons, the Plymouth Brethren, the Christadelphians, the Seventh-day Adventists, the Salvation Army, Christian Science, the Jehovah's Witnesses. Each of these sects were formed in the period from the 1820s through the 1870s.

In the late twentieth century, religious rights came under attack by non- government civilian actors in the negative reactions of established religious bodies to the New Religion movement of the 1970's and 1980's. Anti-cult groups formed and members of cults and sects, such as the Society for Krishna Consciousness (Hare Krishna) (ISKCON) and the Unification Church, were kidnapped, forced to endure deprogramming, and had their mental competency questioned in court...

It can be a matter of considerable importance whether a particular movement is considered a religion or not a religion. For example, the Science of Creative Intelligence (Transcendental Meditation) had fought (although unsuccessfully) to be recognized as a technique rather than a religion so that it could be taught in schools and prisons, which is prohibited under the contemporary interpretation of the First Amendment. The Church of Scientology, however, fought the Internal Revenue Service (IRS) successfully to be declared a religion and thus entitled to tax exempt status.

Media portrayal of these movements have tended to be negative and sensational in character, with the mass media and then the social media being the influential definers of these movements. There are also relatives and friends, encouraged by media stories and/or anti-cult groups that their (adult) children were brainwashed and that it was necessary to engage in deprogramming them (kidnapping the converts against their will until they managed to escape or convince their captors that they no longer wanted to remain in the movement. While many of these kidnappings occurred in the 1970s and 1980s, they have since become very uncommon in Western nations. Various anti-cult groups have also brought pressure on these New Religious Movements. They seek to control or bring about changes in the New Religious Movements.

Polygamous Sects

In remote communities dominated by the Fundamentalist Latter-Day Saints (FLDS) in Southern Utah/Northern Arizona such as Hildale Utah and Colorado City, Arizona, sexual and physical abuse were endemic problems. In 2016, the US Department of Justice brought federal criminal and civil rights charges against the FLDS. In March 2016, a federal jury found two FLDS run towns guilty of multiple civil rights violations. The FBI also arrested 11 sect leaders on felony welfare fraud charges. The federal jury found that these towns were still being run by Warren Jeffs, who was convicted of child molestation and bigamy charges and sentenced to life in a Texas prison. In 2008, the state of Texas took custody of 462 children who had been living on a FLDS ranch in Texas, which led to one of the largest child custody cases in US history. Jeffs reportedly has had 80 wives (some as young as 12). Jeffs continues to lead his church in a prophet role.

Violence Associated with Cults and Sects

A religious group called the Rajneeshees, who followed Bhagwan Shree Rajneesh, began a commune close to the town of Antelope, Oregon in the late 1970s. Tensions between the group and local residents seized control over the small town of Antelope, Oregon in the 1980s by mounting a relentless harassment campaign against the 43 original (and mostly elderly residents of the town to drive them out so that the Rajneesh organization could acquire their property. After years of struggle and confrontation, some of the Rajneeshees chose to begin a campaign of targeted murder attempts using poison against their opponents, including a county district attorney and a county commissioner.

The Posse Comitatus Movement began in Portland Oregon in 1969. By the late 1970s, had 78 chapters in 23 states. Its members believed that the nation's founder intended to establish a Christian Republic where the individual is sovereign and that has as its first duty to promote, safeguard, and protect the Christian faith. These groups seek to interpret God's laws with common law associations and Christian grand juries, composed of only white Christian males. Jews, racial minorities, and women may not be a part of the Posse government. The Freeman, who lived in Montana, were part of the Posse movement. Some of the Freeman were involved in an 81 day stand-off with the Federal Bureau of Investigation (FBI) from late March through mid-June 1996. After the final members of the group surrendered and left the compound, they were charged with a number of offenses including threatening public officials to financial fraud.

Several cults or sects have been involved in high-profile violent incidents. One well-publicized example was over the FBI undercover operation directed against a Christian Identity member in Deep Creek, Idaho named Randy Weaver. Weaver had been strapped for cash, so he was involved in an alteration and sale of two sawed-off shotguns in what was a government sting operation in October 1989. Weaver failed to make a court appearance in early 1991. Vicki Weaver, Randy's wife, sent a letter to the US attorney for Idaho saying that they would not obey his "evil commandments." The Weavers and their children then went to the Weaver cabin. On August 21, 1992, federal marshals killed Weaver's 14 year old son and the family dog during a failed reconnaissance mission, during which one US marshal also died. The following day, the agents killed Weaver's wife and wounded Randy Weaver and a friend who lived with them. By August 31, Harris and Weaver both surrendered which ended the confrontation. In Jun3 1993, Harris and Weaver stood trial for murder, conspiracy, aiding and abetting, and firearms violations. Weaver was convicted of failure to appear in court and violating his bail.

Another example of such violence was the FBI siege of the Branch Davidian compound near Waco Texas, which led to the deaths of 76 people, including 23 children. Agents from the Bureau of Alcohol, Tobacco and Firearms (BATF) obtained a warrant to search the Davidians' Mount Carmel community for possible firearms where leader David Koresh and his followers resided. A group of armed BATF agents raided the Mount Carmel property on February 28, 1993, only to be repelled by better-armed Davidians. This initial confrontation resulted in the deaths of four BATF agents and six Davidians as wondering twenty agents and four Davidians. The FBI quickly arrived at the site, and negotiations with the Davidians, as a 51 siege began. There was some success during the negotiations, as Koresh allowed 21 children to leave the compound. The FBI negotiators, however, began believing that Koresh was untrustworthy after he did not follow through on promises on agreements they thought he had made. One possibility is that Koresh would have never surrendered because he had sexual relations with several young girls in his group, and he knew that the government agents were aware of this.

Gordon Neal Diem
Updated by Christopher Anglim

Further Reading

Cookson, Catharine, Ed. Encyclopedia of Religious Freedom. New York: Routledge, 2003. Davis, Derek, and Barry Hankins, ed. New Religious Movements and Religious Liberty in America. Waco, Tex.: Baylor University Press, 2002.

Espejo, R. (2012). Cults. Detroit: Greenhaven Press.

Fisher, Louis. Congressional Protection of Religious Liberty. New York: Novinka Publications, 2003.

Kahaner, L. (1988). Cults that kill: Probing the underworld of occult crime. New York, NY: Warner Books.

Keiser, T. W., & Keiser, J. L. (1987). The anatomy of illusion: Religious cults and destructive persuasion. Springfield, IL, U.S.A.: Thomas.

Lucas, P. C., & Robbins, T. (2004). New religious movements in the twenty-first century: Legal, political, and social challenges in global perspective. New York: Routledge.

Miller, M. K. (2006). Religion in criminal justice. New York: LFB Scholarly Pub.

Robbins, T., Shepherd, W. C., & McBride, J. (1985). Cults, culture, and the law: Perspectives on new religious movements. Chico, CA: Scholars Press.

Rothchild, J., Boulton, M. M., & Jung, K. (2007). Doing justice to mercy: Religion, law, and criminal justice. Charlottesville: University of Virginia Press.

Snow, R. L. (2003). Deadly cults: The crimes of true believers. Westport, CT: Praeger.

Swarts, K. (2007). Are cults a serious threat? Detroit: Greenhaven Press.

Wall, E., & Pulitzer, L. (2012). Stolen innocence: My story of growing up in a polygamous sect, becoming a teenage bride, and breaking free of Warren Jeffs. New York: William Morrow.

See also Bigamy and polygamy; Bill of Rights, U.S.; Freedom of assembly and association; Hate crime.

Roper v. Simmons (2005)

Definition: Roper v. Simmons (2005) was a U.S. Supreme Court case in which the court was tasked with determining whether the execution of juveniles (i.e., individuals under the age of eighteen) was prohibited under the Constitution.

Criminal justice issues: Appeals; constitutional protections; juvenile justice

Significance: The Roper v. Simmons case overturned the court's prior decision in Stanford v. Kentucky, ruling that the execution of juveniles was forbidden under the Eighth and Fourteenth Amendment's "cruel and unusual punishment" clause.

In 1993, Christopher Simmons, a seventeen-year-old resident of the state of Missouri, concocted a plan to burglarize the home of and murder forty-six-year-old Shirley Crook. On September 9, 1993, Simmons and his teenage accomplice broke into Mrs. Crook's home, gagged her, and bound her with ropes and duct tape. The pair then drove her—in her own car—to a railroad trestle suspended over a river and threw her in. Mrs. Crook did not survive the fall. The evidence in support of Simmons' guilt was overwhelming—he had confessed to the murder, performed a videotaped reenactment at the crime scene, and evidence from his accomplice suggested that the crime had been premeditated. Simmons was tried in state court and convicted of murder. Both mitigating (i.e., factors that reduce blameworthiness) and aggravating (i.e., factors that amplify blameworthiness) factors were present in this case and considered by the jury during the sentencing phase. After weighing these factors, the jury recommended a death sentence.

Simmons appealed the court's decision to the Missouri Supreme Court following the U.S. Supreme Court ruling in *Atkins v. Virginia* (2002) in which the court overturned the death penalty for the mentally retarded. Simmons claimed that the same standards applied in the U.S. Supreme Court's ruling in Atkins, were also relevant to the consideration of the constitutionality of the provision of the death penalty for juveniles. The Missouri Supreme Court considered evidence presented showing that societal consensus had developed against the execution of juvenile offenders. This evidence was cited in the Court's decision to overturn the trial court's death sentence in Simmons' case. Simmons was instead sentenced to life imprisonment without the possibility of parole.

After an appeal by the state, the U.S. Supreme Court agreed to hear the case to determine the Constitutional permissibility of executing minors. Fifteen years earlier the Court ruled in *Thompson v. Oklahoma* that the imposition of capital punishment for those younger than sixteen was unconstitutional. However, in *Stanford v. Kentucky* and *Wilkins v. Missouri*, the Court ruled that it was constitutionally permissible to execute those older than sixteen. In Simmons the court was tasked with reviewing its previous rulings on this matter. Specifically, whether it was permissible to execute juvenile offenders who are older than fifteen but younger than eighteen at the time a capital crime was committed.

In a 5-4 decision, the Court ruled that the execution of minors violated the Eighth and Fourteenth Amendment's prohibition of "cruel and unusual punishment." This ruling overturned the Court's previous decision in

Stanford v. Kentucky, which allowed for the execution of offenders who were at least sixteen years of age at the time of the crime. In the Simmons ruling, the Court cited three lines of evidence necessitating a revised ruling from that handed down fifteen years earlier for the protection of minors against capital punishment.

First, the Court cited evolving standards of decency in the United States. Specifically, the Court discussed statistics revealing that thirty states prohibited the execution of juveniles. Furthermore, the states that did not preclude juveniles' eligibility to be sentenced to death, only infrequently applied the sentence to juveniles. Moreover, after the *Stanford* ruling, five states abandoned the use of the death penalty as punishment for juvenile offenders. Taken together, the Court determined that this provided evidence that evolving standards of decency in the United States had changed such that executing minors was no longer an accepted practice and was inconsistent with the rights afforded to citizens of the United States under the Eighth and Fourteenth Amendments.

In their ruling, the Court not only emphasized national consensus on and national standards of decency, but also considered evidence of the global acceptance (or lack thereof) of the practice of executing minors. At the time of the original ruling in the Simmons case, eight countries, including the United States, allowed the execution of minors. However, fifteen years later, the United States stood alone as the only country in the world officially permitting the death penalty for minors.

Finally, the Court cited social scientific research evidence presented to the Court in an *amicus* brief on behalf of the American Psychological Association. In the brief, research was presented highlighting deficits in cognitive control, rational thinking, consideration of future consequences, control over immediate surroundings, susceptibility to immature and irresponsible behavior, and lack of a fullydeveloped character and personal identity as compared to adults. These limitations of adolescent development were thought to reduce the culpability and blameworthiness of juvenile offenders. The Court stated that deficits inherent in youth development made the death penalty a disproportionate punishment for juveniles.

Andrea Arndorfer

Further Reading

Atkins v. Virginia, 536 U.S. 304 (2002).

Brim, M. "A Sneak Preview into How the Court Took Away a State's Right to Execute Sixteen and Seventeen Year Old Juveniles: The Threat of Execution Will No Longer Save an Innocent Victim's Life." *Denver University Law Review* 82 (2005): 739.

Furby, L., and R. Beyth-Marom. "Risk Taking in Adolescence: A Decision-Making Perspective." *Developmental Review* 12 (1992): 1-44.

Galvan, A., T. Hare, H. Voss, G. Glover, and B. J. Casey. "Risk-Taking and the Adolescent Brain: Who Is at Risk?" *Developmental Science* 10 (2006): 1-7. doi: 10.1111/j.1467-7687.2006.00579.x.

Owen-Kostlenik, J., N. D. Reppucci, and J. R. Meyer. "Testimony and Interrogation of Minors: Assumptions about Maturity and Morality." *American Psychologist* 61 (2006): 286-304. doi:10.1037/003-066X.61.4.286.

Roper v. Simmons, 543 U.S. 551 (2005).

Stanford v. Kentucky, 492 U.S. 361 (1989).

Steinberg, L. "Adolescent Development and Juvenile Justice." *Annual Review of Clinical Psychology* 5 (2009): 47-73. doi:10.1146/annurev.clinpsy.032408.153603.

Steinberg, L., E. Cauffman, J. Woolard, S. Graham, and M. Banich. "Are Adolescents Less Mature Than Adults? Minors' Access to Abortion, the Juvenile Death Penalty, and the Alleged APA 'Flip-Flop.'" American Psychologist 64 (2009): 583-94. doi: 10.1037a0014763.

Steinberg, L., and E. S. Scott. "Less Guilty by Reason of Adolescence: Developmental Immaturity, Diminished Responsibility and the Juvenile Death Penalty." *American Psychologist* 58 (2003): 1009-18. doi: 10.1037/003-066X.58.12.1009.

Thompson v. Oklahoma, 487 U.S. 815 (1988).

Wilkins v. Missouri, 492 U.S. 361 (1989).

See also Capital punishment; Death qualification; Juvenile justice system; Juvenile delinquency; Execution, forms of; Cruel and unusual punishment.

San Bernardino terrorist attack (2015)

Definition: Mass murder at Inland Regional Center, San Bernardino. Planned and executed by husband and wife duo on December 2, 2015

Criminal justice issues: Homicide; police powers; terrorism; victims; violent crime

Significance: The issue of homegrown terrorism was examined as a result of this shoot-out, with President Obama describing the shoot-out as an act of terrorism.

Syed Rizwan Farook (age twenty-eight) and his wife, Tashfeen Malik (age twenty-seven), planned and executed an attack in San Bernardino County at a Department of Public Health training event and Christmas party at a banquet hall on December 2, 2015.

For the employees of the Department of Health, it was a normal training event and Christmas party at the Inland Regional Center (IRC) in San Bernardino, California on December 2, 2015, when Farook walked in with a bag at around 8:30 a.m. Farook worked as a county environmental health specialist with the Department of Public Health. Though he looked calm, he is said to have been checking his watch now and then. He also posed for pictures at the event. Farook then left at 10:30 a.m. without his bag, which did not raise suspicion as coworkers thought he would come back later to collect it. The bag, it was later discovered, contained pipe bombs that were to be used to target emergency personnel responding to the IRC.

At 10:59 a.m. indiscriminate shooting began at the IRC. Farook had returned with his wife, both dressed in dark tactical military-style gear, and began spraying more than seventy-five rounds of .223 ammunition from assault rifles. The shooters also had two semiautomatic handguns. The shootings killed fourteen and injured another twenty-two individuals. Following the shootout, both shooters fled in a rented sport-utility vehicle (SUV).

The first officer arrived on the scene of the shooting three-and-a-half minutes after the computer-aided dispatch call went out. Subsequently, police pursued the couple and four hours later, at around 3:15 p.m., both shooters were shot dead after a fierce gun battle.

After the killings and the shoot-out, police officials investigated the small townhouse in Redlands where Farook and Malik had met after the shooting and where they lived, a few miles from San Bernardino. The house, on rent to the shooter-couple, was searched by the police using robots. Tools to make an improvised explosive device (IED), 2000 9mm handgun rounds and 2,500 .223 caliber rounds were found. The Federal Bureau of Investigation (FBI) also found nineteen types of pipes that could be converted into bombs, a correction from the earlier reported twelve pipe bombs. Searches were also made at the townhouse where Farook's father and brother lived. The couple had a six-month-old daughter who was left behind in the care of Farook's mother. Farook was an American-born U.S. citizen of Pakistani descent, and his wife was a Pakistani-born lawful permanent resident of the United States.

Farook and Malik made unsuccessful attempts to destroy their personal belongings, including mobile phones and hard drives after they met at the townhouse after the IRC shootings. One of the mobile phones found was an Apple iPhone 5C issued by San Bernardino County to its employee, Farook. Numerous attempts by the FBI to unlock the phone were made as more details of the shoot-out would emerge from the data stored in the phone, including the possibility of the involvement of a third shooter. The phone decryption for accessing the contents was halted by the advanced security features of the phone and the National Security Agency (NSA) was unable to unlock it, after which the FBI asked Apple Inc. to disable the security features. Apple Inc. declined as a result of its policy against undermining the security features of its products. Subsequently, warrants were issued against Apple, which were opposed. Other methods were also explored, including directing the owner of the phone, San Bernardino County, to reset the password using Farook's iCloud account so that the backup could be retrieved. This attempt proved unsuccessful. Subsequently, the FBI claimed to have unlocked the phone, without the assistance of Apple or the County.

During investigations conducted by the FBI, it became clear that the shooters were not part of any terrorist organization or had any past criminal behavior. They were, however, inspired by jihad (holy war) and martyrdom. In private messages between the two of them from the time of their engagement in 2013, both had spoken about jihad and martyrdom.

Further investigations revealed that they had been planning for this attack for over a year.

Earlier, in 2012, Enrique Marquez Jr., a relative by marriage and a next-door neighbor of Farook (until May 2015), on an earlier occasion did plan to carry out bombing attacks at the library or cafeteria at Riverside Community College. In 2012, when the plan was made, both Farook and Marquez were students of the college. They also planned to attack at rush hour traffic on California State Route 91 in Corona. Both plans, however, could not be executed. Marquez was subsequently, after the San Bernardino shooting, arrested and charged on three federal counts: making false statements in connection with acquisition of a firearm, conspiracy to provide material support to terrorism, and immigration fraud. Other charges were also added, including "straw-purchase" related charges. Marquez pleaded not guilty to all charges and is currently being held without bail until his next hearing scheduled in early 2017. Additionally, initial news reports and witness accounts of the involvement of a third shooter were negated by the police.

On December 3, 2015, the FBI opened an investigation and subsequently on December 6, 2015, President Barack Obama defined the shooting as an act of terrorism.

Tania Sebastian

Further Reading
Braziel, Rick, Frank Straub, George Watson, and Rod Hoops. "Bringing Calm to Chaos: A Police Foundation Review of the San Bernardino Terrorist Attacks." https://incidentreviews.org/wp-content/uploads/2016/09/ e061621766_San_Bernardino_Critical_Incident_Review_FINAL.pdf.

Baker, Peter, and Eric Schmitt. "California Attack Has U.S. Rethinking Strategy on Homegrown Terror." *The New York Times*. December 5, 2015. http://www.nytimes.com/2015/12/06/us/politics/california-attack-has-us-rethinking-strategy-on-homegrown-terror.html.

Thomas, Pierre, and Jack Date. "San Bernardino Shooters Tried to Destroy Phones, Hard Drives, Sources Say." December 3, 2015. http://abcnews.go.com/US/san-bernardino-shooters-destroy-phones-hard-drives-sources/story?id=35570286.

Horwitz, Sari. "Guns Used in San Bernardino Shooting Were Purchased Legally from Dealers." *The Washington Post*. December 3, 2015. https://www.washingtonpost.com/world/national-security/suspects-in-san-bernadino-shooting-had-a-small-arsenal/2015/12/03/9b5d7b52-99db-11e5-94f0-9eeaff906ef3_story.html.

See also Lone wolf; Murders, mass and serial; Police militarization; Terrorism; Use of force.

Schall v. Martin

The Case: U.S. Supreme Court ruling on preventive detention
Date: Decided on June 4, 1984
Criminal justice issues: Juvenile justice; probation and pretrial release; punishment
Significance: In agreeing with a New York State family court in this preventive detention case, the Supreme Court limited the application of the Fourteenth Amendment's due process clause.

Schall v. Martin was a preventive detention case involving juveniles. New York State had enacted a Family Court Act pertaining to juvenile delinquents and to juveniles arrested and remanded to the family court prior to trial. If the family court determined that pretrial release of juveniles might result in their disappearance or place them or the general public at risk, it was authorized to detain them. Detention occurred only after notice was given to parents and other authorities, a hearing was held, a statement of facts and reasons was presented, and "probable cause" that release might be harmful was established.

Juvenile detainees Gregory Martin, Luis Rosario, and Kenneth Morgan (along with thirty-three other juveniles introduced into the case) faced serious charges. Martin had been arrested in 1977, charged with first-degree robbery, second-degree assault, and criminal possession of a gun after he and two others struck another youth on the head with a loaded gun and beat him in order to steal his jacket and sneakers. He was found guilty of these crimes by a family court judge and placed on two years' probation. Martin was fourteen. Rosario, also fourteen, was charged with robbery and second-degree assault for trying to rob two men by putting a gun to their heads and beating them. He previously had been detained for knifing a student. Morgan, fourteen, had four previous arrests and had been charged with attempted robbery, assault, and grand larceny for robbing and threatening to shoot a fourteen-year-old girl and her brother.

Martin and the others brought suit claiming that their detention deprived them of a writ of *habeas corpus* and violated the due process clause of the Fourteenth Amendment. The federal district appeals court agreed that their detention "served as punishment without proof of guilt according to requisite constitutional standards." Gregory Schall, commissioner of the New York City Department of Juvenile Justice, appealed to the Supreme Court. The case reached the Supreme Court at a time when polls showed that crime was a major fear of the American public and when a relatively conservative Court was exercising judicial restraint and limiting the expansion of civil liberties.

Reading the majority 7-2 decision, Justice William Rehnquist acknowledged that the due process clause of the Fourteenth Amendment indeed applied to the pretrial detention of juveniles. He agreed with Schall, however, that when, as in these cases, there was "serious risk" involved to both the juveniles and the public by their release, the New York law was compatible with the "fundamental fairness" demanded by the due process clause.

Clifton K. Yearley

Further Reading

Champion, Dean John. *The Juvenile Justice System: Delinquency, Processing, and the Law*. 4th ed. Upper Saddle River, N.J.: Prentice-Hall, 2003.

Cox, Steven M., John J. Conrad, and Jennifer M. Allen. *Juvenile Justice: A Guide to Theory and Practice*. 5th ed. New York: McGraw Hill, 2003.

Shaughnessy, Edward J. *Bail and Preventive Detention in New York*. Washington, D.C.: University Press of America, 1982.

Singer, Richard G. *Criminal Procedure II: From Bail to Jail*. New York: Aspen, 2005.

See also Comprehensive Crime Control Act; Due process of law; Juvenile justice system; Preventive detention; Supreme Court, U.S.

School violence

Definition: Use of physical, psychological, or verbal force to threaten or harm students in the school, or prohibited juvenile social behavior that includes property damage, vandalism, excessive truancy, or prohibited gang affiliation

Criminal justice issues: Crime prevention; juvenile justice; vandalism; violent crime

Significance: The outbreak of school shootings such as those occurring in Littleton, Colorado in the 90s and Sandy Hook Elementary School in 2012 frightened students, parents, school board members, teachers, and administrators, causing them to examine what has turned out to be a growing but overlooked problem of violence in schools, ranging from bullying to school homicides.

Administrators and teachers have always faced delinquent and troubled children in the schools. The wave of school shootings at the end of the twentieth century, especially the shooting at Columbine High School in Littleton, Colorado, as well as the shooting at Sandy Hook Elementary School in Newtown, Connecticut, brought the fear of school violence onto the national agenda for education and produced an outcry for safe schools.

Police, who already were in and out of schools working off-duty security or presenting substance abuse programs, were recruited to become full-time school police; they took on the name of school resource officers (SRO). School boards enacted "zero-tolerance" weapons policies and purchased metal detectors. Campuses were closed. Dress codes, backpack and locker searches, and name badges were mandated.

Although vandalism of all kinds was an issue in schools in the 1980s and 1990s, hate related graffiti has become even more prevalent in the 2000s. In 2013, approximately 25% of students aged 12–18 reported seeing hate related graffiti at school during the school year. Hate related graffiti includes derogatory words or symbols having to do with race, ethnicity, religion, disability, gender, or sexual orientation. This hate related graffiti has been reported to be seen both inside and outside school buildings.

School violence has ranged from verbal threats that result in minor scuffles to an occasional beating leading to criminal charges of assault and battery. Knives and even guns are sometimes used. Pushed by school board policies (especially in the wake of school shootings), teachers, who had often overlooked bullying incidents in the past, began to crack down on any signs of violence—thus expanding the definition of school violence. Currently, teachers are encouraged to contact school administration regarding students who draw violent depictions of killings in any context; those who write essays or produce videos involving killing, or those who bring toy guns or anything else resembling a weapon to school. Any negative messages or threats of violence through social media are also urged to be reported to school administration, the school district and local authorities.

First National Report of Feeling Unsafe at School

In 1978, the release of the "National Safe Schools Study" to Congress included the first statistics regarding violence in American schools. The report showed that approximately 282,000 students and 5,200 teachers were physically assaulted in high schools every month. Harris and Gallup polling data during the late 1980's revealed that half of all teens believed schools were becoming more violent. By 1995, Gallup polling reported that teenagers felt safer at home and in their neighborhoods than they did at school. Nearly half of all youths in the 1993 American Teachers National Survey by Harris Polls reported they felt unsafe. A 2016 Gallup poll reports that approximately 28% of parents are concerned about school safety overall, and 13% of school students feel concern regarding their physical safety at school. These percentages have held regularly steady throughout the 2000s, except for a spike in overall school safety concerns after the 2012 mass school shooting at Newtown, Connecticut.

Rates of crimes involving physical violence rose in American middle schools, which had previously been considered immune to school violence. By 2000, twenty-two hundred representative principals of elemen-

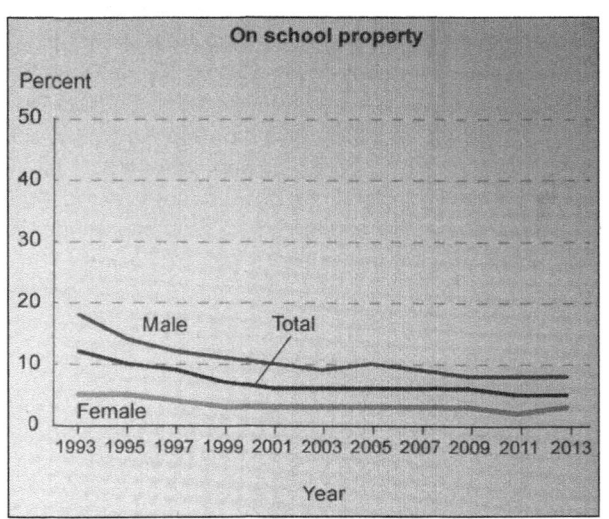

Youth Risk Behavior Surveillance System (YRBSS), 1993 through 2013. Figures reflect the percentage of students in grades 9–12 who reported carrying a weapon at least one day during the previous 30 days, by gender, between the years of 1993 and 2013. (Centers for Disease Control and Prevention, Division of Adolescent and School Health, Youth Risk Behavior Surveillance System (YRBSS))

tary, middle, and high schools were asked by the National Center for Educational Statistics of the U.S. Department of Education about the levels of violent crime, disorder, and disciplinary actions taken in their schools. The report, titled *Crime and Safety in American Public Schools*, showed the most violent school crime was experienced by 20 percent of schools, most of which were in urban areas. Such schools had experienced at least one serious incident (including rape, sexual battery other than rape, physical attacks or fights with a weapon, and threats of physical attack with a weapon and robberies).Schools experiencing serious violence were likely to have police involvement as part of their history. The majority of these schools reported at least one of these incidents to law-enforcement personnel.

Although serious violent crimes such as homicide or suicide on primary or secondary school campuses are rare, they do have lasting implications for schools and local communities.

An initial wave of school shootings in the 1990's began with a sixteen-year-old boy's attack on his schoolmates in Pearl, Mississippi, in 1997 and included a rampage by two boys at Columbine High School in Littleton, Colorado, in 1999, which left thirteen dead. In investigations, the FBI published *The School Shooter: Threat Assessment Perspective*, and the Secret Service published *Safe School Initiatives*. Both reports provide a law-enforcement behavioral profiling analysis. In December of 2012, Adam Lanza fatally shot 20 students and 6 staff members at Sandy Hook Elementary School in Newtown, Connecticut. Prior to the shooting, he killed his mother, and after the shooting, he killed himself on the grounds of the school. The incident is considered the deadliest mass shooting at a primary or secondary school in U.S. history, and prompted renewed discussion about school safety, gun laws, mandatory background checks for gun owners, and treatment for individuals who are mentally ill.

William Bourns
Updated by Gina Riley-Daly

Further Reading

Casella, Ronnie. *At Zero Tolerance: Punishment, Prevention, and School Violence*. New York: Peter Lang, 2001. Examines how the U.S. criminal justice system has responded to violence, both in communities and in schools. Based on research conducted in high schools and a prison.

Davis, Stan. *Schools Where Everyone Belongs: Practical Strategies for Reducing Bullying*. Wayne, Maine: Stop Bullying Now, 2004. A hands-on, research-based guide to intervening and preventing bullying in any school.

Devine, John. *Maximum Security: The Culture of Violence in Inner-City Schools*. Chicago: University of Chicago Press, 1997. An exposé of inner-city school violence, based on the author's experience with the School Partnership Program between New York University and New York City schools, which focused on dropout prevention strategies.

Klebold, Sue. *A Mother's Reckoning: Living in the Aftermath of Tragedy*. New York: Crown Books, 2016. This book is written by mental health and suicide prevention advocate Sue Klebold. Klebold is also the mother of Dylan Klebold, one of the two shooters at Columbine High School. It is an autobiography, but also contains significant research and writing on understanding the intersection between mental health issues and school violence.

National Center for Education Statistics. *Indicators of School Crime and Safety*. 2015. A summary of the current state of school crime and student safety in the United States. Includes statistics on violent deaths at school; student/teacher victimization; fights, weapons, and illegal substance; school fear and avoidance; and school safety and security measures.

Sexton-Radek, Kathy, ed. *Violence in Schools: Issues, Consequences, and Expressions*. New York: Praeger, 2004. Collection of essays presents a comprehensive view of the various types of school violence and preventative steps.

Wessler, Stephen. *The Respectful School: How Educators and Students Can Conquer Hate and Harassment*. Alexandria, Va.: Association for Supervision and Curriculum Development, 2003. Wessler, a former state prosecutor, describes how words can hurt as well as heal and what educators can do to create a respectful school environment that promotes positive interactions among staff members and students.

See also Campus police; Drive-by shootings; Juvenile justice system; Vandalism; Violent Crime Control and Law Enforcement Act; Youth gangs.

September 11, 2001, attacks

The Event: Terrorist hijackings of commercial jetliners that were used to kill several thousand people in attacks on New York City and Washington, D.C.

Date: September 11, 2001

Place: New York City; Washington, D.C.; rural Pennsylvania

Criminal justice issues: Homicide; international law; terrorism; violent crime

Significance: Often simply called "Nine-Eleven," the terrorist attacks on the United States of September 11, 2001, changed the attitudes of the American public and the policies of the federal government and all levels of law-enforcement regarding the threat of terrorism to American society.

In June, 2002, the Gallup Organization conducted a poll of Americans and found that terrorism, national security, and fear were the most serious problems facing the United States. The terrorist attacks of September 11,

> ### The Events of September 11, 2001
>
> At 8:45 a.m. on September, 11, 2001, an airliner flying out of Boston crashed into the north tower of New York City's World Trade Center, ripping a hole in several upper floors and starting a fire so intense that people on higher floors could not evacuate the building. At first, the crash was believed to be an accident. However, when a second airliner struck the Trade Center's south tower eighteen minutes later, it was clear that neither crash had been accidental. Fearing that a large-scale terrorist attack was underway, government agencies shut down local airports, bridges, and tunnels. Less than one hour after the first crash, the Federal Aviation Administration ordered—for the first time in history—a stop to all flight operations throughout the United States. Only moments later, a third airliner crashed into the Pentagon Building outside Washington, D.C.
>
> Meanwhile, the intense fires in the Trade Center towers—fed by the airliners' jet fuel—so weakened the buildings that they could no longer support their upper floors. At 10:05 a.m., the entire south tower collapsed; twenty-three minutes later, the north tower collapsed. Between those events, a fourth airliner crashed in a field outside Pittsburgh, Pennsylvania.
>
> As was later determined, all four airliners had been hijacked by operatives of a shadowy Middle Eastern organization known as al-Qaeda that was determined to kill as many Americans and do as much damage to the United States as possible. By any measure, the scheme was a great success. The cost of the physical damage of the attacks could be measured in billions of dollars. Although the extent of human fatalities was not as great as was initially feared, about three thousand people lost their lives—a number greater than all the American fatalities during the Japanese attack on Pearl Harbor on December 7, 1941. In addition, the sense of security from outside threats that Americans had long enjoyed was shattered. The impact of the terrorist attacks on American criminal justice would be profound.

2001, had changed the attitudes of many Americans, making them more fearful and concerned about the world than ever before.

Americans began demanding more from law enforcement, whose agencies are expected to protect and defend Americans against any future terrorist attacks. Crimes involving political and religious motives and international organizations became the most important policy issue for many Americans. Because terrorism is a form of crime, it draws the attention and resources of the entire criminal justice system. In the twenty-first century, criminal activity in the form of international terrorism dominates other policy issues, such as drugs, the economy, and education. Because of Nine-Eleven, terrorism and national security are thus the most fundamental issues facing Americans.

Homeland Security and the Patriot Act

In response to Nine-Eleven attacks. the U.S. Congress created the Department of Homeland Security to consolidate the administration and coordination of law-enforcement agencies. The National Strategy for Homeland Security and the Homeland Security Act of 2002 served to activate and organize the United States to stop terrorist attacks. The main purpose for the establishment of the Department of Homeland Security was to unite the large number of law-enforcement organizations and institutions involved in efforts to provide safety for citizens. Federal agencies, including the Federal Bureau of Investigation (FBI), were brought together under the unified control of the Homeland Security Department and were required to divert their resources and efforts toward investigating and preventing terrorist attacks. Federal agencies immediately began tightening security at airports and national borders.

In 2001, Congress also passed the USA Patriot Act (an acronym for "Uniting and Strengthening America by Providing Appropriate Tools Required to Intercept and Obstruct Terrorism") to provide more power and discretion for federal law-enforcement agencies to investigate, especially through the use of electronic surveillance against suspected terrorists. Under that law, law-enforcement officers can use roving wiretaps against terrorist suspects who attempt to evade law enforcement by changing locations and communication devices. They can also employ "delayed notification search warrants" to prevent suspected terrorists from being tipped off about investigations. They can also access business records and monitor computer activity on Internet servers more easily. Finally, the Patriot also made punishments more severe for terrorists or those who aid them and their activities.

One of the most important consequences of the government response to Nine-Eleven was the large-scale diversion of federal law-enforcement resources to investigating possible terrorist activities. In fact, as early as October, 2001, so many FBI agents were focusing their attention upon preventing new terrorist attacks, that some observers feared that the bureau's traditional investigative responsibilities were being dangerously neglected.

Indeed, it is possible that a long-term consequence of the Nine-Eleven attacks may be a significant reduction in the federal role in traditional law-enforcement activities. If so, criminal investigations traditionally handled by federal agencies may be transferred to state and local agencies.

Preventing Future Attacks

The attacks on the World Trade Center and the Pentagon demonstrated that major cities within the United States were not safe, and law-enforcement officials have realized the need for increased awareness of the activities of such international criminal organizations. Since September 11, 2001, the entire American criminal justice system and U.S. intelligence agencies have increased their efforts to gather information that may help avert future attacks. Many international terrorist organizations use criminal activities such as credit card fraud and drug trafficking to secure resources for their operations. For example, one year after the September 11 attacks, the federal government uncovered an illegal cigarette smuggling operation based in North Carolina that was suspected of raising funds for a terrorist organization.

Because organizations that employ terrorist tactics for political purposes are closely connected to international crime networks, the United States has devoted additional personnel and resources in efforts to cut off their supplies of money and weapons. Most important, law-enforcement agencies work to prevent the acquisition of nuclear materials and weapons by al-Qaeda and other terrorist groups. The law-enforcement agencies of many other countries have increased their levels of communication and cooperation with the United States in this work.

Balancing National Security and Freedoms

In the aftermath of Nine-Eleven, the U.S. criminal justice system entered a new phase in which suspects have been detained and prosecuted based upon evidence of their connections to organizations responsible for terrorism. For example, the federal government created a list of both citizens and noncitizens deemed "enemy combatants" and confined many of them to military facilities with no concrete plans for their formal prosecution. Many people, including legal scholars, charged that this practice is a denial of the basic constitutional rights that are accorded to suspects in civilian criminal courts. Many people also charged that Muslims have been discriminated against because of their religious and political beliefs and associations.

Since Nine-Eleven, the U.S. Supreme Court has ruled that American citizens can challenge the government's actions in federal court, but that right has not been granted to noncitizens. It is therefore clear that the Nine-Eleven attacks have significantly altered constitutional protections, government power, and attitudes toward political crimes in the criminal justice system.

Scott P. Johnson

Further Reading

Chang, Nancy, and Howard Zinn. *Silencing Political Dissent: How Post-September 11 Anti-Terrorism Measures Threaten Our Civil Liberties.* New York: Seven Stories Press, 2002. Critical examination of the effect on civil liberties of post-Nine-Eleven antiterrorism legislation, such as the Patriot Act.

Cronin, Audrey, and James M. Ludes. *Attacking Terrorism: Elements of a Grand Strategy.* Washington, D.C.: Georgetown University Press, 2004. Outline of a strategy for fighting future terrorism with a warning that the battle will be a long and arduous process.

Leone, Richard C., Greg Anriq, Jr., and Greg Anriq. *The War on Our Freedoms: Civil Liberties in an Age of Terrorism.* New York: BBS Public Affairs, 2003. Three experts on civil liberties warn of the consequences of the war on terrorism to American freedoms, while documenting how each generation of Americans has witnessed struggles between order and liberty.

Lyon, David. *Surveillance After September 11.* Cambridge, England: Polity Press, 2003. Lyon examines the changes in the security atmosphere such as the integration of databases containing personal information, biometric identifiers, such as iris scans, and how consumer data is being merged with data obtained for policing and intelligence, both nationally and internationally.

Schulhofer, Stephen J. *The Enemy Within: Intelligence Gathering, Law Enforcement, and Civil Liberties in the Wake of September 11.* New York: Century Foundation Books, 2002. Examination of the wide-ranging new surveillance and law-enforcement powers acquired by the federal government that have eroded civil liberties.

See also Border patrols; Electronic surveillance; Freedom of assembly and association; Hate crime; Homeland Security, U.S. Department of; Patriot Act; Skyjacking; Terrorism.

Sex discrimination

Definition: Unequal treatment of similarly situated individuals based on their sex

Business and financial crime; Civil rights and liberties; Women's issues

Significance: Strong federal legislation has made it illegal for employers and institutions to treat men and women differently in such matters as employment and access to educational opportunities.

Discrimination is the treatment of individuals with similar abilities and potential in a different manner because of some distinguishing characteristic. Sex discrimination is the use of gender as the basis for such unequal treatment. Federal and state anti-discrimination laws, most of which were enacted during the 1960s and 1970s, prohibit sex discrimination, as do federal and state constitutions. Sex discrimination laws cover a wide array of issues, including employment rights and education opportunities.

Civil Rights Act of 1964

Title VII of the federal Civil Rights Act of 1964 is titled "Equal Employment Opportunity" and expressly prohibits employment discrimination based on several criteria, including sex. The act applies to certain private employers, employment agencies, and labor organizations. Title VII also prohibits discriminatory and unlawful employment practices, including the use of gender as the basis for hiring and firing decisions. Thus, when equally qualified male and female candidates apply for the same job, gender may not be the determining factor of which of them is hired.

Likewise, Title VII forbids sex discrimination in compensation, working conditions, employment terms, and privileges afforded employees. Moreover, test scores used for selection or referral of persons for jobs may not be adjusted or altered based on sex. People with the same qualifications must therefore receive equal pay, equal opportunities for obtaining jobs and promotions, and equal benefits. However, even more than five decades after the passage of the Civil Rights Act of 1964, women are estimated to receive about 20 to 25 percent less compensation than equally qualified men holding the same kinds of jobs. Sex discrimination still exists in the twenty-first century.

Title VII also prohibits the unlawful employment practice of classifying, limiting, or segregating employees based on gender in a manner that might deprive employees of various employment opportunities, such as advancement and training opportunities. job. In addition, employment agents and labor unions may not make gender-based decisions to refer clients and members for employment, and it is unlawful for labor organizations to make membership decisions on the basis of gender.

Title VII does, however, permit good-faith employment qualification and ability test exceptions that may result in discrimination based on sex. Under these exceptions, employers may impose specific job qualifications that can be shown to be necessary for job performance. For example, an employer might set as a job qualification the ability to lift a minimum weight that would disqualify most women from the job. If, however, a woman applicant were able to lift the required weight, then gender could not be used to disqualify her. Courts have also held that arbitrary weight and height requirements for employment are illegal.

Women want equal pay for equal work. (Public domain, via Wikimedia Commons)

The Civil Rights Act of 1991 added a disparate impact category to unlawful employment practices. Under this provision, if a complaining party were to show that an employment practice would have a disparate gender impact, then the employer would have to show that the practice is job related and required by business necessity. Such a defense is not, however, available in intentional sex discrimination cases. Complaining parties may also demonstrate that alternative employment practices are available to employers that do not result in disparate impacts based on sex.

Title VII of the Civil Rights Act of 1964 does not require preferential treatment of members of any gender group in order to correct imbalances that may exist, but this fact does not prevent voluntary attempts to correct the imbalance. Reverse discrimination claims have met with some success in the courts when men have claimed to be victims of general discrimination in hiring, firing, and promotion practices designed to increase the numbers of women workers. Employers may also provide different levels of compensation, terms, conditions, and privileges of employment at different locations as long as they are not based on sex discrimination. For example, the cost of living may be higher in one area of the country than in another, and the same employer could provide disparate pay for the same job in the two separate locations.

The Equal Employment Opportunity Commission (EEOC) is the federal law enforcement agency responsible for upholding anti-discrimination legislation. In 2011 it expanded Title VII's protections against employment discrimination to make stereotyping of lesbian, gay, and bisexual people illegal, and in 2012 it further prohibited discrimination of transgender individuals or due to gender identity. In September 2014 the first federal lawsuits regarding transgender discrimination were filed against two private companies.

Penalties for Violating the Civil Rights Act

Intentional violations of Title VII may subject violators to a variety of punishments and sanctions, such as having to pay compensatory and punitive damages, based on the size of the employer; injunctions to terminate unlawful employment practices; orders that may require reinstatement or hiring of employees; awards of back pay; and payment of attorney and expert witness fees.

Because intentional violations may subject violators to monetary damages, jury trials are also available. When employers prove they have not intentionally discriminated, then sanctions may be limited to equitable relief to stop their discrimination and the payment of attorney fees alone.

Officers and employees of the EEOC are also subject to penalties under Title VII for failing to maintain the confidence of parties who file discrimination claims. Moreover, any employee who makes such information public may be charged with a misdemeanor and made to pay a fine or be subject to imprisonment.

The fact that a person may be subject to penalties under the federal Civil Rights Act does not relieve such a person from compliance with anti-discrimination laws adopted by states and their political subdivisions. Furthermore, it is unlawful for employers to retaliate against employees who oppose employment practices that constitute sex discrimination or who file claims, provide testimony, or otherwise participate in investigations of sex discrimination cases under Title VII.

The Education Amendments of 1972

Title IX of the Education Amendments of 1972 prohibits gender discrimination with respect to education programs and related activities that receive federal financial assistance in the form of grants, loans, or contracts. However, several types of educational institutions are exempt from Title IX, such as single-gender schools and military training facilities. Title IX requires that both sexes have equal opportunities to seek education programs, and anything that might discriminate based on gender and interfere with this opportunity would be in violation of Title IX. Educational institutions may, however, require separate living facilities for each gender, and they are not required to provide benefits related to abortions.

The rights under Title IX also include equal access to sports opportunities. Educational institutions do have some flexibility in complying with the law, however, and are not required to offer exactly the same sports or even equal numbers of sports for both genders. However, educational institutions are required by the Title IX regulations to accommodate the athletic interests and abilities of each gender when selecting sports to support. Similar to Title VII, Title IX does not require preferential treatment of a person or group of persons on the basis of gender in order to correct any imbalance that may exist. Failure to comply with this act could result in termination of federal financial assistance.

Constitutional Protections and the ERA

The Fifth and Fourteenth amendments to the US Constitution and comparable provisions under state constitutions require governments to provide equal protection for all their citizens. In interpreting the Constitution in gender-based discrimination cases, the US Supreme Court has imposed a heightened standard of review, sometimes referred to as a middle-tier scrutiny, in which governmental entities imposing gender-based classification must demonstrate an "exceedingly persuasive justification" by proving that the classification meets two requirements: an important governmental purpose for the classification, and a substantial relationship between the purpose and the means used to achieve it. The Supreme Court has held that this heightened scrutiny does not apply in gender-based discrimination claims under the Civil Rights Act, as private entities are not subject to constitutional requirements.

In 1972, Congress approved the Equal Rights Amendment (ERA) to the US Constitution and submitted it to the states for ratification. That amendment would have

> ### Seeking Equal Pay for Equal Work
>
> American women have struggled for equal pay for many years, and thousands of women have joined together to file class-action sex-discrimination suits against large corporations. The first major victory came in 1973 in a suit against American Telephone and Telegraph (AT&T); the giant communications company paid out $38 million to more than 13,000 women. In a classaction suit filed against Wal-Mart during the first years of the twenty-first century, hourly and salaried female employees of the world's largest retailer sought lost wages and punitive damages. Both sex discrimination cases were based on claims of unequal pay when compared with men in similar positions and failure of the companies to promote women to management positions.

expressly prohibited government from denying or abridging equal rights based on sex, but it eventually failed because of lack of timely ratification by at least thirty-eight states. However, advocates continued to promote the idea, and the issue was maintained in congress as supporters pushed to remove the ratification deadline. The ERA was frequently reintroduced, including to the 113th Congress in 2013, and remained a topic of debate.

Other Sex Discrimination Issues

Prior to passage of the Civil Rights Act of 1964, Congress enacted the Equal Pay Act of 1963. That law prohibits gender-based discrimination with respect to compensation in situations in which men and women perform substantially similar work under the same working conditions in the same locations. Since the early 1990s, the Department of Labor has found violations of anti-discrimination laws, such as the Equal Pay Act, among approximately one-half of all companies whose federal contracts have been audited. These audits have resulted in multimillion-dollar settlements because of gender-based pay disparities and lack of management opportunities for women. A proposed extension of the Equal Pay Act, known as the Paycheck Fairness Act, was introduced in an attempt to further reduce the male-female wage gap. It was originally passed by the House of Representatives in 2009, but strong opposition from the Republican Party led to the bill's failure to pass through the Senate on repeated attempts in 2010, 2012, and 2014, despite the support of President Barack Obama's administration.

In 1978, Congress passed the Pregnancy Discrimination Act as an amendment to Title VII of the Civil Rights Act. Under this act, it is illegal for employers to deny the use of sick leave to employees because of pregnancy or childbirth or to exclude such conditions from health benefit plans. Likewise, the 1991 Civil Rights Act defined the terms "discrimination on the basis of sex" and provided that this means any discrimination based on "pregnancy, childbirth, or related medical conditions." One gender-based exception under the Civil Rights Act, however, is that employers are not required to pay for health benefits for abortions, unless a pregnant woman's life is endangered or medical complications arise after an abortion. In the 1991 act, Congress also appointed a Glass Ceiling Commission to study artificial barriers to advancement in the workplace for women and minorities (known as the glass ceiling).

In 2015 the Department of Labor released a proposal for updates to regulations regarding sex discrimination by federal contractors dating back to 1970. The changes would bring policy and legal precedent up to date with Title VII.

Parties continue to raise gender discrimination issues in many venues in order to change laws to meet the needs of modern society. Arguments have concerned matters such as abortion and reproductive rights; access to Medicaid; same-sex marriage, adoption, and inheritance rights; domestic abuse and the battered woman's syndrome defense; pregnancy, health care, and family care; and marriage, divorce, alimony, and child custody. If the past is any example, future changes in the law to correct discrimination are likely to remain controversial and move forward at a slow pace.

Carol A. Rolf

Further Reading

Ficks, Barbara J. *American Bar Association Guide to Workplace Law: Everything You Need to Know About Your Rights as an Employee or Employer.* New York: Random House, 1997. Print.

Gavora, Jessica. *Tilting the Playing Field: Schools, Sports, Sex, and Title IX.* San Francisco: Encounter, 2003. Print.

Lindgren, J. Ralph, Nadine Taub, Beth Anne Wolfson, and Carla M. Palumbo. *Law of Sex Discrimination.* 3d ed. Belmont: Wadsworth, 2004. Print.

Macklem, Timothy, and Gerald Postema, eds. *Beyond Comparison: Sex and Discrimination.* Cambridge: Cambridge U P, 2003. Print.

Rowland, Debran. *The Boundaries of Her Body: A History of Women's Rights in America.* Naperville: Sphinx, 2004. Print.

"Sex/Gender Discrimination." *Workplace Fairness.* Workplace Fairness, 19 Dec. 2008. Web. 16 Feb. 2015.

"Sex-Based Discrimination." *US Equal Employment Opportunity Commission.* EEOC, n.d. Web. 16 Feb. 2015.

Simon, Rita J. *Sporting Equality: Title IX Thirty Years Later.* Emeryville: Transaction, 2004. Print.

Stockford, Marjorie A. *Bellwomen: The Story of the Landmark AT&T Sex Discrimination Case.* Piscataway: Rutgers U P, 2004. Print.

See also Abortion; Constitution, U.S.; Equal protection under the law; Privacy rights; Sexual harassment; Victimology; Female offenders; Feminist criminology; LGBTQ prisoners; Prison Rape Elimination Act (PREA) (2003); Victims services; Victimization theories; Black Lives Matter Movement/Blue Lives Matter Movement.

Shoe prints and tire-tracks

Definition: Prints and impressions left by shoes and vehicle tires at crime scenes
Criminal justice issues: Evidence and forensics; investigation; technology
Significance: Evidence left by shoe prints and vehicle tires is commonly found at crime scenes and frequently contributes to solving investigations by helping to identify the suspects and vehicles involved in the crimes.

Shoes and tires are surprisingly complex and have many identifiable characteristics. Shoes are made up of many parts, but investigators are generally concerned only with the shoes' outsoles, which are commonly known simply as soles. Many types of modern shoes—especially those manufactured for sports—have identifying logos or motifs on their soles. They may also have distinct grooves and divisions designed for specialized uses.

Vehicle tires are also complex and are commonly identified by their unique ridges and grooves. Because tire manufacturers patent the treads on their products, each unique tread pattern can appear on one manufacturer's tires.

A key concern of the first investigators to reach crime scenes is preservation of possibly transient evidence. Shoe-print evidence can be especially sensitive to disintegration or contamination. Moreover, shoe prints are easily susceptible to destruction because they are often found outside primary crime scenes. To preserve such evidence, it is important to strictly control access to crime scenes and to establish entry and exit paths from the scenes that do not interfere with print evidence.

Shoe-print and tire-track evidence should be photographed as soon as possible. Shoe prints found in dust can be lifted with a technique known as electrostatic lifting. Both shoe prints and tire-tracks made in soft surfaces, such as mud, can be cast in a variety of materials. Prints and tracks made in snow can be preserved with colored aerosols and photographed, or they can be cast with special materials.

Items of evidence found at crime scenes possess either class or individual characteristics. Evidence with individual characteristics—such as human fingerprints—can be matched to its source with a high degree of certainty. Evidence with class characteristics can be matched only to groups and not to particular sources. Both shoe-print and tire-track evidence possess class characteristics. However, as shoes and tires are used over time, they take on individual characteristics, such as nicks and scrape marks. Eventually, tires and shoes may develop distinctive wear patterns and leave impressions that indicate to investigators exactly which particular shoes or tires of the same types have made the impressions.

Ayn Embar-Seddon
Allan D. Pass

Further Reading
Adams, T., A. Caddell, and J. Krutsinger. *Crime Scene Investigation.* 2d ed. Upper Saddle River, N.J.: Prentice-Hall, 2004.
Genge, Ngaire E. *The Forensic Casebook: The Science of Crime Scene Investigation.* New York: Ballantine, 2002.
Houck, Max M., ed. *Mute Witnesses: Trace Evidence Analysis.* San Diego, Calif.: Academic Press, 2001.
_____. *Trace Evidence Analysis: More Clues in Forensic Microscopy and Mute Witnesses.* San Diego, Calif.: Academic Press, 2003.

See also Crime labs; Crime scene investigation; Fingerprint identification; Forensic psychology; Forensics; Latent evidence; Trace evidence.

Social media

Definition: Internet communications technology that allows users to connect via the Internet to engage in sharing content online. Some examples include platforms such as Facebook, Twitter, Instagram, LinkedIn, Snapchat, Reddit, and Pinterest.
Criminal justice issues: Crime prevention; media; technology
Significance: Social media has opened new avenues for criminal activity via the Internet.

Cybercrime is a twenty-first century phenomenon causing concern with what tools are used to perform online crime and where cybercriminals exist. Law enforcement agencies use social media to fight traditional and online crime. However, there is no overarching federal legislation to address the use of social media or the increasing problem of cybercrime.

The advent of social media can be found in the 1990's. Early social media consisted of online community boards that allowed anyone with Internet access to create a user profile to meet and make friends though social media websites. Technology's evolution and proliferation into all personal and economic aspects of society took traditional crime online. Traditional crimes that are committed in a physical location can take place via social media. Cybercrimes are any online activity with malicious intent. Examples include bullying, organized groups of hackers taking down government infrastructures, bank thefts, and identity theft.

The United States Department of Justice and state and local law enforcement agencies have added social media to their arsenal of tools to fight online and traditional crime. In the twenty-first century, the number of users on social media has reached more than 200 million. Law enforcement has been forced to adapt to the cyber-environment to investigate different crimes.

Goals

Preventing, investigating, solving, and mitigating crimes are incorporated goals in law enforcement's mission of public safety. Law enforcement's use of social media has become an integral part of mitigating and fighting crime. Social media gives law enforcement the power to interact in real-time to locate or anticipate crime. For example, in an age of mass shootings, law enforcement can use social media databases to identify crime suspects with the use of photos posted on social media websites. Saving lives by following tips disseminated through social media sites can assist in halting crimes in progress. Law enforcement's ability to alert the public is enhanced by using social media to provide alerts and advisories instantaneously.

Social media has already been used in court cases to identify suspects and to verify behavior. In the case of *Bradley v. Texas* (2012), Michael Bradley was identified as a suspect in a robbery and convicted. The victim of the robbery identified Bradley from Facebook photos. Bradley attempted to appeal his conviction based on the Facebook photos not being him. The court denied his appeal, ruling that Facebook provided more than enough sufficient photos of Bradley. Online photo databases will continue to play an important role in prosecuting criminals. In the case of *Hoffman v. State of Delaware* (2012), Nicole Hoffman was convicted of vehicular manslaughter based on photos from her Myspace page glamorizing alcohol abuse.

Shortcomings

The federal government, in addition to state and local governments, have different policies on how to handle social media and the use of data collection. Illegal use of social media in the United States may breach individual rights protected under the Fourth Amendment. Keeping pace with existing social media sites and increasing new sites pose huge challenges for law enforcement agencies. Comprehensive information on cybercrimes is not yet available due to technology's rapid evolution. There are currently no overarching federal, international, state or local legal provisions, policies, or standards in place to articulate the use of social media by law enforcement. Preserving and collecting evidence in social media is critical to use in prosecuting cases. Training staff to decrease barriers such as infringement on the civil liberties or civil rights of groups and individuals becomes problematic if specific policies and procedures are not outlined. Social media crime can occur from any platform with the ability to connect to the Internet. For law enforcement, sharing of personal identifiable information can compromise a victim's personal financial future if not handled properly. In using social media to combat crime, one must adhere to the same confidentiality, integrity, and availability policies found in cybersecurity policies.

Kimberly A. Harper

Further Reading

Anderson, P. *WEB 2.0 and Beyond: Principals and Technologies*. Boca Raton, Fla.: Taylor & Francis Group, 2012. *Discussed framework of WEB 2.0 technology and how business, law, media studies, and other multidisciplinary perspectives regard the implications of computers and science.*

Fischer, Eric A. *Cybersecurity Issues and Challenges: In Brief*. Washington, D.C.: Congressional Research Service Report to Congress, 2016. R43831. *Discusses information and communication technologies' growth and the risk associated with cybersecurity. Lists more than fifty statutes that address cybersecurity and the federal role involved in securing systems.*

The United States Federal Bureau of Investigation (FBI). *Cyber Crime. What We Investigate.* https://www.fbi.gov/investigate/cyber. *Gives a good overview of cybercrime and how the FBI engages in investigations in the United States and globally.*

See also Community-oriented policing; Cybercrime; Evidence, rules of; Privacy rights.

Status offenses

Definition: Offenses such as truancy, incorrigibility, or running away from home that are considered crimes when they are committed by juveniles but are not considered crimes when committed by adults

Juvenile justice; Victimless crime

Significance: Although status offenses generally pose no immediate threats to public safety, they may create cases difficult to resolve, require significant expenditures of court and community resources, and result in the removal of children from their homes.

Juvenile courts have jurisdiction over a broad range of behaviors including some behaviors that are illegal for minors but not illegal for adults. Indeed, part of the reason that the juvenile justice system was originally established arose from the fact that adult courts lacked authority to deal with youths who ran away from home, refused to obey their parents, or failed to attend school. Most modern juvenile courts continue to handle status offense cases.

DC Police Truancy and Curfew enforcement vehicle. (Public domain, via Wikimedia Commons)

There are a number of reasons for enforcing status offenses. Some people believe that juvenile court involvement is needed because status offenders place themselves at risk or because status offense behaviors will lead to more serious types of juvenile delinquency and criminal activity. Also, because juvenile courts are often sensitive to community demands for assistance, they are frequently willing to support parental or school authorities in their efforts to deal with problem behaviors exhibited by children.

Although there are compelling arguments for court involvement in status offense cases, not all courts have the resources or expertise necessary to deal effectively with such cases. Status offense cases can be complex and may be the products of years of family dysfunction, child abuse and neglect, or ineffective parenting. Because of these complications, some courts limit their involvement in status offense cases or avoid them even when legal intervention is possible. Effective community resources for handling these cases do not always exist.

Preston Elrod

Further Reading

Elrod, Preston, and R. Scott Ryder. *Juvenile Justice: A Social Historical and Legal Perspective.* Gaithersburg, Md.: Aspen, 1999.

Lemmon, John H. "Invisible Youth: Maltreated Children and Status Offenders in the Juvenile Justice System-Politics, Science, and Children's Issues." In *Controversies in Juvenile Justice and Delinquency*, edited by Peter J. Benekos and Alida V. Merlo. Cincinnati: Anderson Publishing, 2004.

See also Alcohol use and abuse; Juvenile courts; Juvenile delinquency; Juvenile Justice and Delinquency Prevention Act; Juvenile justice system; *Parens patriae*.

Surveillance cameras

Definition: Video cameras mounted on elevated locations in public areas such as highways, parking lots, and spaces within or between buildings

Civil rights and liberties; Crime prevention

Significance: Widely practiced throughout the United States, the electronic monitoring of people in public areas represents an important application of technology in the face of increasing concern about crime in such areas. Moreover, surveillance cameras can deter crime while reducing demands on personnel time. At the same time, criminal courts have found that evidence from surveillance cameras increases guilty pleas.

The commission of crimes in public spaces has long been a focus of concern, especially to law-enforcement authorities. Much of the impetus for the development and implementation of closed-circuit television surveillance (CCTV) has come from Great Britain, which has the most extensive CCTV monitoring in the world—including tens of thousands of surveillance cameras in London alone. The data firm IHS estimates that as of 2014, there were more than 245 million surveillance cameras installed globally.

CCTV monitoring is usually operated remotely from central stations that are typically police headquarters. The actual monitoring of the cameras themselves is done by police or civilian personnel, who make surveillance recordings that are kept on file for various periods. The amounts of personnel time that different agencies allot to monitoring cameras and recordings vary greatly.

The impact of CCTV monitoring the commission of crimes is difficult to measure, as reported results vary greatly: Changes in crime rates range from reductions as high as 90 percent to increases of up to under 20 percent. Interpreting figures for crime increases is complicated. If one by-product of surveillance cameras is better detection of crime, then increases may actually be signs of success.

The problem of interpreting these figures reflects a duality in the basic goal of CCTV: deterring crime, while facilitating the detection and prosecution of crime. There is some evidence that surveillance cameras are more effective in deterring property crimes than violent crimes, as the latter are more likely to be impulsive and to be committed under the influence of alcohol and drugs. Under those conditions, offenders are less aware of the presence of surveillance cameras.

Another question about the impact of surveillance cameras is whether they actually help with crime prevention or merely displace it to other locations that lack surveillance. There is some evidence that this may be the case.

First image of two showing a speed camera catching a speeding violation in Mt. Rainier, Maryland. (Public domain, via Wikimedia Commons)

Three camera surveillance unit. (By Thomas R Machnitzki, via Wikimedia Commons)

Public Concerns

A 2013 *New York Times-CBS News* public opinion poll about surveillance cameras found approval among 78 percent of respondents. Moreover, surveillance cameras can enhance communications among police agencies and area businesses, while helping to revive businesses located in "trouble" areas. The police can also demonstrate their acquisition of the most up-to-date technology.

Despite the apparent effectiveness of surveillance cameras in combating crime, the use of cameras has raised several concerns about violations of citizens' civil rights and civil liberties. For example, the unfettered discretion of CCTV operators has led some analysts to speculate that minority group members may be disproportionately represented among those being monitored. There are also concerns that the monitoring itself may be used for controversial purposes beyond the scope for which it is initially approved. The right of people to know when they are being monitored has also been emphasized.

There is also a potential for abuses arising from inaccurate or misinterpreted video-recorded information. Sound tracks are often not part of the tapes, pictures may be out of focus, and people in the videos may be difficult to identify definitively. Nevertheless, the use of CCTV is steadily rising.

Law enforcement officials have used surveillance camera footage to identify the suspects in the 2005 London subway bombings and the 2013 Boston Marathon bombing. The latter investigation served as a renewed reminder of both the limitations of the technology and its advances. A tremendous amount of collected evidentiary data must be analyzed, deterrence of crime remains difficult to prove, and the monitoring system is costly to run. Meanwhile, the speed with which analysis of video footage can be performed has greatly increased, and ever-improving facial and object recognition software can provide much more specific results. Debate as to the proper use of the technology continues, however.

Eric W. Metchik

Further Reading
Gill, Martin, ed. *CCTV.* Leicester, England: Perpetuity Press, 2003.
Goold, B. J. *CCTV and Policing: Public Area Surveillance and Police Practices in Britain.* New York: Oxford University Press, 2004.
Kelly, Heather. "After Boston: The Pros and Cons of Surveillance Cameras." CNN. *Cable News Network,* 26 Apr. 2013. Web. 3 June 2016.
McGrath, J. E. *Loving Big Brother: Performance, Privacy and Surveillance Space.* New York: Routledge, 2004.
Newburn, Tim, and Stephanie Hayman. *Policing, Surveillance and Social Control: CCTV and Police Monitoring of Suspects.* Portland, Oreg.: Willan Publishing, 2002.
Vlahos, James. "Surveillance Society: New High-Tech Cameras Are Watching You." *Popular Mechanics.* Hearst Digital Media, 30 Sept. 2009. Web. 3 June 2016.

See also Electronic surveillance; Prison escapes; Privacy rights; Robbery; Shoplifting; Stakeouts; Wiretaps; Body-worn cameras; Technology's transformative effect.

Technology's transformative effect

Definition: Evolution of Web technology platforms and the adoption of digital and Web technologies to generate, process, share, and transact information in criminal justice
Criminal justice issues: Courts; law enforcement organization; probation and pretrial release; technology
Significance: Within the criminal justice system, digital technologies have transformed policing, courts, and corrections practices. In a broader sense technology is assisting to enforce the law, mitigate crime, solve crimes, and provide public safety.

Technology's transformative effects have led to new tools that assist criminal justice agencies in their efforts to battle crime. As society becomes more technology savvy, technological efforts to fight crime have increased. Historically, law enforcement agencies have relied on technological advances to assist in their effectiveness. Radios, telephones, and crime labs are examples of early technological tools used in law enforcement.

Goals

Critical to the role of criminal justice is the use of technologies to mitigate, solve, and prevent crime. For example, within policing, CompStat (pioneered by the New York Police Department [NYPD]) is a predictive policing system that uses mathematical, predictive, and analytical tools toward the goals of reducing crime and managing police operations. CompStat's tools for predicting crime include: (1) timely and accurate information or intelligence; (2) rapid deployment of resources; (3) effective tactics; and (4) relentless follow-up. Police departments in the United States, Canada, and other countries have adopted CompStat and other predictive policing systems after the NYPD drastically reduced serious crime within a five-year period by more than 50 percent. The predictive policing strategy is driven by the time of crimes' occurrence, locations of crimes, and nature of crimes. Data gathered instructs law enforcement on how to best use resources to detect, mitigate, and solve crimes. The science behind predictive policing is a mathematical model type of software that evaluates crime data to predict where crimes may occur, which enables deployment of preventive resources accordingly.

Body-worn video devices, also referred to as body cameras, are worn by law enforcement to gather information on a variety of police interactions. For example, traffic stops, crime scenes, and parking enforcement are some areas in which law enforcement uses video to gather evidence. Video of police and citizen encounters can be used as firsthand evidence. Officers who abuse powers can be quickly identified in cases of questionable police behavior.

Technology has improved courtroom operations. Video displays monitor courtroom activity, are used for lawyers to present cases and serve as displays for each juror. Some courtroom judges allow broadcasting of trials, as well as video to present evidence and record proceedings. Also, technology has aided in monitoring prisoners, probationers, and parolees. Electronic ankle monitors assist courts and probation officers with the supervision of convicted individuals. Monitors keep track of offenders on house arrest and can detect drug and alcohol consumption.

Shortcomings

Ethics, civil liberties, and lack of resources create concerns for predictive policing. Ethical issues regarding CompStat and other predictive policing tools can produce biased data resulting from unethically constructed software. For example, innocent victims can be targeted by police through unwarranted tracking. Surveillance of images on software containing face recognition can also produce privacy issues when identifying suspects. Minorities are at risk of racial profiling from data collected in high-crime areas. Predictive policing can be flawed with problems of not responding to data quickly. Lack of resources can lead to an inability to stop crimes occurring and those on the rise. Safely transmitting secure and accurate data is a huge concern in an age of cybersecurity threats.

Privacy and First Amendment protections are of concern with body cameras. For example, freedom of information laws govern use of camera footage. State laws can limit what police departments can release, and in court cases footage is not used unless requested. Other concerns have come into question in events where cameras have been found turned off.

Electronic monitors are questionable under privacy laws. Some global positioning system (GPS) monitors are designed to allow the probation officer to communicate with an offender. Issues arise when communications allow for invasion of a probationer's or parolee's privacy without knowledge. Financial cost and maintenance of electronic monitors is the responsibility of the offender, which can create a hardship for families with little economic resources.

Kimberly A. Harper

Further Reading
Bach, Lance. "How to Take Advantage of Courtroom Technology." *Litigation News*. American Bar Association. https://apps.americanbar.org/litigation/litigationnews/trial_skills/022814-tips-courtroom-technology.html. Discusses federal courtrooms' integration of video, computers, digital technology, and other presentation devices.

Eterno, John A., and Eli B. Silverman. "The NYPD's Compstat: Compare Statistics or Compose Statistics?" *International Journal of Police Science and Management* 12, no. 3 (2010): 1-24. Study and results on NYPD pressures managers face regarding using unethical crime reporting.

Friend, Zach. "Predictive Policing: Using Technology to Reduce Crime." *Law Enforcement Bulletin*. https://leb.fbi.gov/2013/april/predictive-policing-using-technology-to-reduce-crime. Overview of technology efforts to reduce crime using predictive policing methods.

Haberman, Corey P., and Jerry H. Ratcliffe. "The Predictive Policing Challenges of Near Repeat Armed Street Robberies." *Policing: Journal of Policy and Practice* 6, no. 2 (____): 151-66. Article reviews methodologies of the near repeat phenomenon used in predictive policing. Philadelphia is used to identify and quantify multiple events near repeat chains.

National Institute of Justice. Office of Justice Programs. *Predictive Policing*. 2016. https://www.nij.gov/topics/law-enforcement/strategies/predictive-policing/Pages/welcome.aspx. Overview of NIJ programs using predictive policing in law enforcement.

National Institute of Justice. "Research on Body-Worn Cameras in Law Enforcement." 2013, 2014. https://www.nij.gov/topics/law-enforcement/technology/pages/body-worn-cameras.aspx. Overview of body-worn camera use by law enforcement.

U.S. Department of Justice. "Electronic Monitoring Reduces Recidivism." Office of Programs. National Institute of Justice. 2016. https://www.ncjrs.gov/pdffiles1/nij/234460.pdf. Study funded by the National Institute of Justices looks at Florida offenders placed on electronic monitoring and found reduction in risk of failure compared to those not under electronic monitoring.

Walter, Perry L., Brian McInnis, Carter C. Price, and S. Smith. *Predictive Policing: The Role of Crime Forecasting in Law Enforcement Operations*. Arlington, Va.: Rand Corporation, 2013. http://www.rand.org/content/dam/rand/pubs/research_reports/RR200/RR233/RAND_RR233.pdf. Research and report conducted by RAND Safety and Justice Program that addresses all aspects of public safety and the criminal justice system.

See also Body-worn cameras; Computer information systems; Crime analysis; Electronic surveillance; Predictive policing; Surveillance cameras.

Terrorism

Definition: Coercive use, or threat, of violence to terrorize a community or society to achieve political, economic, or social goals

Criminal justice issues: International law; political issues; terrorism; violent crime

Significance: Long a significant factor in other parts of the world, large-scale terrorism suddenly became a primary law-enforcement issue in the United States after the surprise terrorist attacks of September 11, 2001. Since that time, threats of terrorism have reshaped US criminal justice and continue to do so.

Defining terrorism is difficult for several reasons. The first reason is the problem of perspective: One person's terrorist may be another person's freedom fighter. For example, many people in the Middle East regard the al-Qaeda operatives who carried out the September 11, 2001, attacks on the United States as heroes. By contrast, the British regarded the "Sons of Liberty" (an American

Patriot group) as terrorists during the American Revolution.

A second problem is the type of analytical confusion that can lead to circular thinking. For example, if an organization or group is labeled as "terrorist," then its actions are automatically viewed as "terroristic," even though it was labeled terrorist because of its earlier terroristic actions and statements. A third problem is that "terrorism" can be meaninglessly overinclusive. Some commentators have argued that the definition of terrorism used in the USA Patriot Act of 2001 is overly broad, and poses a danger to individual rights. Thus, developing an authoritative definition of the term "terrorism" has been one of the most difficult issues in conceptualizing terrorism as a crime. Because of difficulties including the inherent biases, clarity of purpose, and disagreements about which phenomena to include, no one definition can be completely relied upon.

Federal and state legislation do not explicitly state "terrorism" as such. Instead, the various criminal provisions outlaw a large number of specified crimes that are commonly though t of as terrorism-related offenses. Terrorism-related crimes can fall into categories such as: 1) legislation that focus on the technical means used to conduct the attack, i.e., bombs, or, 2) legislation establishing several different crimes that would be considered terrorism only if there is evidence that they were carried out with the intent to intimidate or coerce a civilian population. Most of the statutory amendments following the 9-11 attacks made almost no changes to substantive federal law (which would define particular crimes), and focused instead on the areas of procedure, investigations, authorization, and punishment enhancement.

Thus, the definition of terrorism is controversial and contentious. There exists no consensus on how terrorism should be defined. The term is also used in different ways in different contexts.

For our purposes terrorism almost always involves some form of coercion, through either actual or threatened violence. Not all violence need be against human targets. For example, the Weather Underground, a radical leftist organization of the late 1960's and 1970's, attacked mainly structures and attempted to limit harm to human life. Similarly, the Narodnaya Volya (People's Will) of nineteenth century Russia was adamant about the protection of the innocent and targeted only the czar and his support system.

At its core, terrorism is a technique of communication. Acts of terror are designed to communicate messages to audiences larger than those targeted by the acts themselves. When the Provisional Wing of the Irish Republican Army blew up police stations in Belfast, it did so not to deliver a message to the police officers who are attacked, but to send a message to the wider audiences of the British and Ulster Protestant authorities.

Because terrorist target selection is often symbolic, terror is sometimes called "propaganda of the deed." Allied with this point, the message communicated is often a sociopolitical one; some form of change is desired. For example, the Zapatista rebels of Mexico desire agrarian reform and attracted the attention of the national government by taking hostages and capturing key government facilities.

Finally, terrorism can be practiced by either insurgents or governments. Insurgent organizations often try to place their issues before wider, perhaps national, audiences to bring about changes in how things are done. In contrast, governmental terror usually strives to quiet dissent or to oppress some within governmental control. In addition to these general types of terror, there are also variations on these themes, including transnational terror, cyberterrorism, ethnonational terror, and narcoterrorism.

Historical Antecedents

Violent oppression and opposition may be endemic to the leadership of humans by other humans, but some of the earliest accounts of activities that would now be recognized as terrorism come from the ancient Holy Land of the Middle East. During the Roman occupation of what was then called Judea, in what is now Israel, Jewish Zealots known as Sicarii killed Jewish moderates, burned financial records, and staged other assaults on Roman/Jewish order. Their goal was to provoke Roman authorities to commit counter- atrocities that would turn all Judeans against Roman rule. The name of the Sicarii comes from their choice of weapon: a dagger or short sword called the sica that they used to dispatch enemies in crowded public places in broad daylight. Attackers would strike their victims, then feign horror at what they were seeing and thereby escape detection. The Sicarii campaign of terror made all Judeans feel unsafe and helped to incite Jews to open rebellion against the Romans.

Another early Middle Eastern terrorist movement was that of the Hashishim, or Assassins, who operated from the eleventh through the thirteenth centuries. Their name literally means "hashish eaters," so called because they were known to ingest hashish before making their attacks. The Assassins desired to invoke the coming of the Messiah, as well as to protect their religious autonomy from Seljuk oppression, by killing government officials. Again, daggers were the weapon of choice, largely for religious reasons.

The Thuggee, or Thugs, of India were professional assassins in a cult that operated for several centuries, until British rule was firmly implanted in India. The Thugs killed mostly randomly, paying homage to their god Kali. In contrast to other organizations of terror, the Thugs used silk ties to strangle their victims, an artistic flourish rarely employed before or since.

The first use of the term "terrorism" in the modern sense of the word comes from the time of the French Revolution. The Jacobins were the first to use the term and used it with affection, but the positive connotations they invested in the term did not last very long. However, the rapid evaporation of positive connotations of "terrorism" should not be read to indicate that since the French Revolution all terrorists have been regarded as monsters.

One of the most significant and fascinating terrorist organizations of the nineteenth century was Russia's Narodnaya Volya, whose "Narodniki" members were anticzarist socialists. Possessing an egalitarian organization and a well- read membership, the Narodniki aimed at achieving a "blow at the center." Even more interesting than their organization is their commitment—uncommon in the modern world—to protecting the innocent. The Narodniki targeted specific individuals and would, at their own peril, protect nontargets from the violence they sought to visit upon the czarist regime. They wrestled philosophically with their right to resort to violence for the furtherance of their political aims and concluded that they could secure this right only by forfeiting their own lives.

Modern Trends

The twentieth century witnessed many important changes in the application and perception of terrorism. For example, the struggle against European imperialism in the developing world saw the creation of several terrorist organizations, including the Jewish Irgun, which fought against the British administration of Palestine, and the Irish Republican Army, which sought to end British of Ireland.

Since the mid-twentieth century, religiously inspired terrorism has proliferated greatly, especially in the Middle East. Religious purposes, however, blended with more secular ambitions. Organizations such as Hezbollah, Hamas, Palestinian Islamic Jihad, al-Gama'a al Islamiyya, al-Asqa Martyrs' Brigade have commingled religious and political agendas, sometimes cooperating, sometimes clashing. Many newer groups have formed from divisions from older groups. These divisions often occur over religo-political disagreements,

The impact of Middle Eastern terrorism on American criminal justice takes several forms. First, the United States has been involved in the region for many years—most prominently in its support of the Jewish state of Israel, which has been almost constantly in conflict with its predominantly Muslim neighbors since its creation in 1948. One result of American involvement in the Middle East has been to make the United States itself a target of some of the region's jihadist organizations. Al-Qaeda, the organization behind the September 11, 2001, attacks, is but one notable example.

A second point is that in the pursuit to understand criminal behavior, Middle Eastern terrorism presents an opportunity to study morally justified violence achieve a just and lasting peace worldwide. Finally, it is in the best interests of all the world's peoples to end terrorism's violence, regardless of whether Americans are targets.

Leftist Terror

Many organizations on the left side of the political spectrum have sought to launch workers' revolutions with terrorist violence. Notable examples have included Russia's Red Army Faction, Italy's Red Brigades, Mexico's Zapatistas, Peru's Tupac Amaru and Sendero Luminoso, and America's own Weather Underground. Such groups attempt to raise the consciousness of the proletariat in order to bring about revolutions against the upper classes and replace existing regimes with Marxist or socialist governments.

After the end of the Cold War and the dissolution of the Soviet Union during the early 1990's, a major funding and ideology source for Marxism- motivated terror groups dried up, and leftist organizations were weakened. The Weather Underground collapsed due to a perceived failure to bring about the desired changes in consciousness in the American underclass.

Single-Issue and Domestic Terrorism

Some organizations form around single socio- political issues and employ terror to further their cause. For example, radical opponents of abortion bomb abortion clinics, hoping to end abortions through violence because they believe they are protecting unborn people by doing so. Groups such as Earth First! use coercive means to, in their view, protect the environment.

Far from being less significant due to their narrower platforms, single-issue terror organizations may be more problematic for law enforcement than ideologically broader groups precisely because they are more focused. Although target selection by such groups may be more predictable, the members' fervent beliefs and commitments to their causes may make them even more vicious and tenacious than other types of terrorism.

Terrorism has been a part of American history from the inception of the nation. The Sons of Liberty and the Minutemen of the American Revolution were prototerrorists and insurgents, respectively. On the political Left are groups such as the Weather Underground and the Symbionese Liberation Army, and on the political Right are groups such as the Order; the Covenant, Sword, and the Arm of the Lord; and other organizations of the Christian Identity movement. Also on the Right are groups such as the Ku Klux Klan, Posse Comitatus, Aryan Nation, and others with neo-Nazi and hate-based ideologies

Prevalence of Terrorism

It may not be an exaggeration to say that there is no place on Earth in which human beings live in any numbers that is not, or has not been, affected by terrorism. Terror has been the resort of groups as diverse as Earth First! the Jewish Defense League, Hamas, and the Liberation Tigers of Tamil Eelam of Sri Lanka.

With a few notable exceptions, before 2001, Americans observed terrorism only from afar, on television and through other media. The events of September 11 gave Americans a jarring wakeup call regarding the threat of terrorism. While the United States has become increasingly more secure from terrorist attacks since 9-11, it is impossible to guarantee complete safety from any and all terrorist attacks. The 9-11 and subsequent terrorist attacks effectively ended the illusion of many Americans that they were somehow immune from terrorist attacks.

Investigation

Inadequate and ineffective government responses to nonstate terrorism may be the most important factor in the success and continuation of terrorism. If national governments respond either repressively or with too little force they may encourage terrorists and worsen their own situations. However, finding a proper balance between strong armed response and diplomacy is inherently difficult and made even more so by the fact that every case may require a unique and unprecedented solution.

Two major issues confront the investigation of terrorism in the United States. First, intelligence gathering and analysis is crucial to prevent terrorism. Second, resources including additional officers and equipment are needed to extend the blanket of coverage and enhance response capabilities of local law enforcement.

The best way to meet terrorist threats is to be forewarned and prepared. Having and understanding information regarding preparations, funding sources, travel, and connections help facilitate the interdiction of terrorism possible. Local law enforcement has a major role in this undertaking by being a major source of valuable information that, when combined with other intelligence, enables agencies responsible for intelligence analyses to determine threat levels.

Logically, then, to prevent terrorism, all that would be required would be total scrutiny of all activities and sufficient personnel to analyze intelligence as it is received. In an authoritarian state, this solution may be possible, provided there are sufficient resources. However, aside from the inherent logistic difficulties, another major problem exists in this model. In a democracy, the wholesale invasion of privacy entailed to total surveillance would not be tolerated. In the United States, the Fourth Amendment to the Constitution of the United States guarantees that Americans are protected search and seizure of their homes and persons except in cases in which warrants have been issued upon probable cause that a crime had been committed. The goal and challenge for law enforcement in this regard is to provide the maximum amount of protection to citizens that is compatible with constitutionally guaranteed civil liberties.

Despite constitutional limitations on the intelligence gathering ability of law enforcement and by policies, laws, and regulations issued under the constitution's authority, law enforcement has a great deal of leeway to investigate potential terrorists. For example, records that can be obtained without warrants—but through subpoenas—includes bank records, flight itineraries, telephone records, and credit card transactions. In addition, recording of conversations with third parties, vehicle tracking, and observing buildings from the air are all permissible investigative activities that do not require demonstration of probable cause.

Resources

As the first line of defense and as an important source of intelligence, local law-enforcement agencies must have sufficient resources and training to provide the high-quality service Americans need from them. Long after the 9-11 attacks, needed resources were slow in getting to local law enforcement. Local police were required to carry additional duties without additional personnel. These increased demands have meant that already thinly stretched police force was further strained, which detrimentally affected the service they sought to perform.

Only since September 11, 2001, has there been a concerted effort to bridge communication barriers among U.S. law-enforcement agencies, to provide the necessary resources, and to enhance cooperation among different agencies. One key problem is that the American criminal justice system is a patchwork of different agencies. Organizations at the same jurisdictional levels have traditionally not had to cooperate, so coordination across jurisdictional levels likely will be that much more of a challenge.

Prosecution and Punishment

Those individuals suspected of terrorism are prosecuted by federal agencies, rather than state agencies, because terrorism is a federal crime. Punishments for terrorists, in the United States and abroad, have varied from nothing or home detention to summary execution. Leading figures of the Weather Underground were released from custody because of the illegal means used by the FBI to gather intelligence against them. In Italy, the "pentiti" (repentant) law allowed many Red Brigades members to escape significant punishment in exchange for information that was used against other members of the organization. In the United States, Timothy McVeigh was executed for his role in the terrorist bombing of the federal office building in Oklahoma City, Oklahoma, in 1995.

These wide variations in punishments are due in part to at least three factors. First, the threats offered by different terrorist organizations are not all of the same level; some are more dangerous than others. Second, when terrorist organizations enjoy some measure of popular support within their own countries, their governments may wish to avoid appearing repressive by "over punishing" them. Finally, in cases in which security forces overstep their authority by conducting illegal searches or seizures, the evidence they collect may be deemed inadmissible—as in the case of the Weather Underground in the United States.

Responses to Terrorism by Democracies

Because of their need to preserve civil liberties, democracies face the greatest challenges in dealing with terrorism. As has been discussed, how a government responds to terror may be one of the most significant determinants of whether terrorism continues. Weak responses may encourage terrorists to continue their campaigns, while overly violent responses by a government may polarize citizens and strengthen the position of terrorists.

The "hardline" approach to fighting terrorism advocated by Paul Wilkinson in Terrorism Versus Democracy (2001) makes several important points. First, security forces in democratic states must act within the scope of their own authority and abide by relevant laws and democratic principles. Second, intelligence is central to success. Third, despite the importance of intelligence, security forces must be fully accountable to democratic institutions of government. Fourth, terrorist propaganda efforts must be countered as fully as possible. Finally, under the most circumstances, governments should avoid inasmuch as possible, from conceding to terrorist demands.

Although Wilkinson's model has considerable merit, it also has weaknesses, as it tends to paint with a broad brush. For example, acting aggressively to counter propaganda may make a government appear as if it wishes to conceal something. Additionally, cases have arisen in which making concessions to terrorists has led to cessations of hostilities.

The use of military forces in the pursuit of terrorists can be problematic. In a domestic context, a full military response to a terrorist threat would involve martial law, which often requires government action such as the suspension of civil liberties, establishment of curfews, censorship, and summary punishments. Using the military to aid civil power can be effective, provided the troops have proper training. The military, however, is not a proper tool for peacekeeping and is not appropriate to resolve domestic crises. Thus, using an army for domestic terror response should be undertaken with care and circumspection, and only under the most compelling of circumstances.

Anti-Terrorism legislation takes several forms. It may be preventive by attempting to address the underlying issues that have given rise to terrorists' grievances. It may be aimed at deterrence by making punishments so harsh as to discourage would-be terrorists from risking capture. Finally, it may be enforcement-based, aiming to equip law enforcement with sufficient powers to detect, prevent, arrest, and successfully prosecute terrorists. Laws themselves do not guarantee victory; many terrorists fight against the governments that draft and implement the laws. Also, humans interpret and enforce law, and so the law is only as effective a tool as its users make it.

Terrorism: War or Crime?

Since the 9/11 attacks, terrorism has generally been treated as a form of "war" rather than a "crime". Both the criminal justice and military models have their strengths. Many of those who frequently argue that terrorism should be treated as "war" because terrorism is a threat to the entire nation, rather than individual persons. The US government also operated under the assumption that hostilities against it would continue and that these hostilities require self-defense.

Those who argue that terrorism should be treated as a crime argue that by using the criminal justice system to hear terrorism cases, the United States would be able to increase the strength of the rule of law, incorporate international humanitarian law into US courts, and deny the terrorists at least one opportunity to legitimize their objectives. The use of the criminal justice system may also increase the legitimacy of government, provide greater transparency, provide more consistent and equitable legal provisions, and decrease the number of motivated offenders.

During the so-called "War on Terror" which followed the 9-11 attacks, some of the leading issues regarding terrorism suspects included the indefinite detention of so-called "enemy combatants at Guantanamo Bay, the use of controversial interrogation methods at Abu Ghraib and elsewhere, and the 'extraordinary rendition'" of alleged terrorists.

One of the most controversial aspects of the war on terror was the Patriot Act, which was intended to hasten the search and seizure, and if warranted execution of enemy belligerents that carried out the attacks. The Patriot Act has been criticized particularly for its authorization to indefinitely detain suspected and certified alien terrorists, particularly on issues such as how long an individual can be incarcerated and whether this provision violates the convict's due process rights. The United States government also has refused to describe the individuals captured during hostilities as "prisoners of war", but instead describes them as "unlawful enemy combatants," a phrase that is not clearly defined in international humanitarian law.

There is also ample precedence for processing terrorism suspects through the criminal justice system including the prosecuting of the Oklahoma City bombers, Timothy McVeigh and Terry Nichols, the Unabomber Ted Kaczynski, Ramzi Yousef, the 1993 World Trade Center bomber, and Zachariah Moussaoui, who was one of the 9-11 conspirators. One drawback, however, in the use of criminal justice process, is that is very time-consuming and expensive.

The Politicization of Terrorism

The Bush administration claimed that the US government was incarcerating known terrorists and dangerous enemy combatants, claiming authority to do so under the Authorization for Use of Military Force (2001). The majority of the inmates at Guantanamo, however, were not captured by US military forces, but were turned over by bounty hunters and then transferred to that base.

Criticisms of Using the Criminal Justice System to Try Terrorism Cases

The underlying premise of US antiterrorism law is that terrorism presents a significant threat to the national security of the United States. Those who criticize using the criminal justice to handle terrorism cases argue first that politically motivated crimes that inflict (or intended to inflict) a great deal of harm on a large number of people, and are intended to coerce governments to change their actions or policies, should severely prosecuted and punished under specialized terrorism offenses. They specifically criticize the criminal justice system for 1) failing to make the accused's political motivation in carrying out the crime an element of the terrorism crime, and 2) placing the authority to make this classification solely at the discretion of prosecutors, who may misuse the existing terrorism statutes in cases related to terrorism.

Michael J. DeValve
Updated by Christopher Anglim

Further Reading

Hoffman, B. Inside Terrorism. London: Victor Gollancz, 1998. Broad conceptual review of issues relating to world terrorism.

Kushner, H., ed. Essential Readings on Political Terrorism: Analyses of Problems and Perspec

tives for the Twenty-first Century. New York: Gordian knot Books, 2002. Collection of articles written by leading scholars on terrorism. Laqueur, Walter. No End to War: Terrorism in the Twenty-first Century. New York: Continuum International Publishing, 2003. Up-to- date survey of world terrorism that attempts to project future trends.

Mack, R. L. Equal Justice: America's Legal Response to the Emerging Terrorist Threat. Ann Arbor: University of Michigan Press, 2004. Study of post-September 11 legislative and judicial responses to terrorism, with a discussion of the challenge of balancing of civil liber ties protections and national security needs.

Rapoport, David C., and Yonah Alexander, Eds. The Morality of Terrorism: Religious and Secular Justifications. 2d ed. New York: Columbia University Press, 1989. Collection of essays that includes several classic readings on justifications of terrorism and historical perspectives that are invaluable for understanding current terrorism issues.

Smith, B. Terrorism in America: Pipe Bombs and Pipe Dreams. Albany: State University of New York Press, 1994. Detailed review of domestic terrorism through the early 1990's that is perhaps the finest source on that subject.
Wilkinson, Paul. Terrorism versus Democracy: The Liberal State Response. Portland, Ore.: Frank Cass, 2001. Presents an enlightened review of issues facing democracies in responding to terrorism.
Lichtblau, E. (2008). Bush's law: The remaking of American justice. New York: Pantheon Books.
Roth, M. P. (2011). Crime and punishment: A history of the criminal justice system. Australia: Wadsworth/Cengage Learning.
Siegel, L. J. (2011). Essentials of criminal justice. Belmont, CA: Wadsworth Cengage Learning.
Smith, C. E., McCall, M. M., & McCluskey, C. P. (2005). Law & criminal justice: Emerging issues in the twenty-first century. New York: Peter Lang.
Sulmasy, G. M. (2009). The National Security court system: A natural evolution of justice in an age of terror. Oxford: Oxford University Press.

See also Antiterrorism and Effective Death Penalty Act; Cybercrime; Espionage; International law; Patriot Act; September 11, 2001, attacks; Skyjacking; Treason; Unabomber.

Toxicology

Definition: Science concerned with the effects of harmful and toxic substances on living organisms
Criminal justice issues: Evidence and forensics; investigation; technology
Significance: Toxicology plays a prominent role in many investigations of homicides, accidental deaths, and suicides.

In its most elementary form, toxicology is the study of poisons. However, scientific advances and research have complicated definitions of toxicology. Some scientists regard toxicology as the study of chemistry and chemical composition, while others regard it as the study of biological poisoning. Here, toxicology is defined as the study of the chemical composition, symptoms, identification, and treatment of foreign substances (to include poison, alcohol, industrial chemicals, poisonous gas, and illegal drugs) on living organisms.

The study of toxicology encompasses many scientific disciplines, including chemistry, biochemistry, epidemiology, pathology, physiology, and pharmacology—all of which are concerned with substances that can be ingested or inhaled or that can make direct contact with skin and eyes. The adverse effects of these toxins—which are commonly known as poisons—may include illness, injury, and death, depending on the types and amounts of the toxins that enter the body.

History of Toxicology

The scientific field of toxicology is comparatively modern, but study and use of toxic substances has a long and well-documented history in human societies. In fact, knowledge of dangerous toxins can be traced back to prehistoric humans, who used their senses of touch and taste to recognize poisonous plants and animals. Early humans extracted the poisons they found for use in medicinal healing and the manufacture of poison-tipped weapons for hunting and warfare.

Scientific toxicology began to take shape during the Renaissance. During the early sixteenth century, the Swiss scientist Paracelsus, who is regarded as the founder of biochemistry, instituted what is now called the dose-response relationship, a significant tenet in toxicology. He posited that everything had the potential to imitate a poison and it was the dosage that dictated the body's response. Small doses yielded harmless effects, while larger doses resulted in higher degrees of toxicity.

The first important work on toxicology was published in 1813 by the Spanish physician and chemist Mathieu Orifila, who is now regarded as the founder of the field of toxicology. He was the first person to established connections between the chemical and biological properties of poisons.

Forensic Toxicology

Forensic toxicology was developed to solve the "invisible" crime of poisoning. Poisoning has been a popular method of committing murder for millennia. In the ancient world, the many illustrious figures who were victims of poisoning included the Greek philosopher Socrates, Egypt's Queen Cleopatra, and several Roman emperors. Not only were carefully selected and administered poisons impossible to identify, but the very fact that they had been administered might also go undetected.

The first murder trial to showcase toxicological testimony occurred in England in 1751, when the medical testimony of four doctors resulted in a woman being found guilty of murdering her father with arsenic. The verdict in that case was later criticized because the doctors had used sensory data rather than scientific measures to identify the presence of arsenic in the murdered man's food. The first scientific use of toxicology in the courtroom occurred in 1840, when traces of arsenic were found in the body of a man, whose wife was subsequently found guilty of poisoning him.

Throughout history, detection of poisoning crimes and identification of the poisons used have posed difficult challenges to investigators. The effects of most poisonous substances can be misdiagnosed as symptoms of common medical diseases, thereby rendering the toxins virtually untraceable. In modern crime investigation, toxicological sections have become commonplace parts of crime labs. Their task is to identify foreign substances in bodies and communicate their findings to law-enforcement investigators.

Toxicological Analyses

A standard toxicological procedure includes preliminary examinations of blood and urine samples and sometimes strands of hair. In some cases, full autopsies are needed so that tissue samples can be removed from various organs. Tests of the samples can detect the presence of chemicals and other foreign substances that have been ingested into the body.

In early times, the poison of choice for murder was arsenic, as it was readily available as a rat poison. Its effects on humans vary with the amounts ingested. Large doses are fast-acting and cause damage to the brain, liver, and spinal cord. Conversely, small doses ingested over extended periods of time show subtle effects such as nerve damage, headaches, nausea, numbness, and muscle weakness. Both methods of ingestion ultimately kill, but smaller doses are less detectable.

Lisa Landis Murphy

Further Reading
Klassen, C. D., and J. B. Watkins. *Casarett and Doull's Essentials of Toxicology.* New York: McGraw—Hill, 2003. Detailed explanations of the basic concepts and principles associated with toxicology.
Levine, B. *Principles of Forensic Toxicology.* Washington, D.C.: AACC Press, 2003. Book designed for use in one—semester undergraduate courses that explores the principles and theories associated with forensic toxicology.
Olson, K. R. *Poisoning and Drug Overdose.* New York: McGraw—Hill, 2003. Accessible reference guide to aid clinicians in the diagnosis and treatment of toxic poisoning and drug overdose.
Rudin, N., and K. Inman. *An Introduction to Forensic DNA Analysis.* 2d ed. New York: CRC Press, 2001. Comprehensive reference guide to DNA for lay readers.
Timbrell, J. A. *Introduction to Toxicology.* New York: CRC Press, 2001. User—friendly introductory text for students that serves as an outline to the basic tenets and origins of toxicology.
Trestrail, J. H. *Criminal Poisoning: An Investigational Guide for Law Enforcement, Toxicologists, Forensic Scientists, and Attorneys.* Totowa, N.J.: Humana Press, 2000. Comprehensive guide to the identification of toxic poisons used in homicides.
Williams, P., R. James, and S. Roberts, eds. *The Principles of Toxicology: Environmental and Industrial Applications.* New York: John Wiley & Sons, 2002. Guide for health professionals in the fundamentals of toxicology in both occupational and environmental settings.

See also Autopsies; Bloodstains; Coroners; Crime labs; DNA testing; Drug testing; Forensics; Latent evidence; Medical examiners; Sobriety testing; Trace evidence.

Trace evidence

Definition: Forms of physical evidence at crime scenes that are usually not visible to the naked eye
Criminology; Evidence and forensics; Investigation; Technology
Significance: Trace evidence is an integral part of many police investigations because it employs scientific methods to establish direct links between suspects and crime scenes. Trace evidence can provide powerful clues for reconstructing crimes for which little other evidence exits.

During the early part of the twentieth century, Edmond Locard, a French scientist who directed the world's first crime laboratory, articulated a principle of criminology that became known as Locard's exchange principle. It holds that when two physical objects come into contact with each other, each leaves particles on the other. Locard observed that no crime scene can ever be completely free of evidence; although no evidence may be seen by the naked eye, some evidence is always left behind. Locard's principle has served as the foundation for the forensic study of trace evidence.

Trace evidence alone may be inadequate to build cases against criminal suspects, but it can establish links between suspects and crime scenes or victims of crimes. The types of trace evidence analyzed most often at crime scenes are hair and fibers. Large amounts of hair found at a crime scene often indicate a struggle; they are commonly found on floors near weapons or points of contact between victims and their assailants. Rooted hair may provideDNA evidence. Carpet and clothing fibers are also commonly found in places where assailants and their victims come into contact with one another.

Other important types of trace evidence include paint residue, dust and dirt, and firearm residues. Chips of paint from vehicles, doors, and furniture are often found on weapons and clothes. Paint chips from vehicles can often be used to identify the vehicles' production years and makes and models. Dust and dirt residue can be used to determine places where people have been, where they reside, and what kinds of animals they have come into contact with. Other, similar organic materials that form trace evidence might include pollen, wood, or fungal spores.

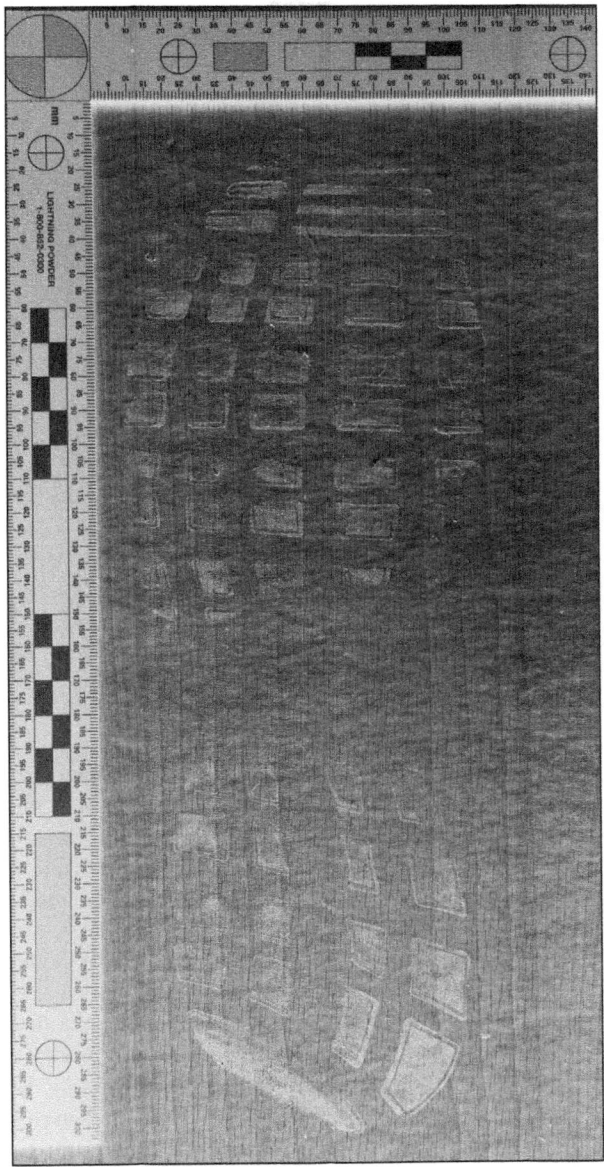

Photo of dust residue impression left on the floor of a crime scene. (By Zalman992, via Wikimedia Commons)

Residues left by ammunition can indicate whether suspects have fired firearms, but tests for such residues must be conducted within six hours of the time that weapons are fired. Explosive materials and propellants can likewise leave behind identifiable residues.

Another broad category of trace evidence is used to identify the characteristics of persons involved in crime scenes. This type of evidence includes bodily fluids, bite marks and other wounds, shoe prints, and tool marks. Bodily fluids, which can provide useful evidence whether they are fresh, coagulated, or dry, include blood, semen, saliva, and sweat. The dryness of blood specimens can be used to estimate how much time has passed since crimes have been committed. Bite marks—which might be found on either victims or suspects—can be particularly useful in identifying suspects, as every person's teeth leave unique impressions. Likewise, every person has a walk that leaves shoe prints that are unique because of both the way in which people walk and the distinctive wear on their shoes. Wounds made by weapons can often be used to determine the size, shape, and length of the weapons. Even tools leave identifying marks that can be used to link suspects with crime scenes.

Research also suggests that the microbiome—an individual's unique makeup of bacteria, both internal and external—may also one day serve as a reliable, cost-effective means of identifying suspected criminals. Each person leaves some of their bacteria behind wherever they go, and these microbes remain viable for up to seventy-two hours afterward. Furthermore, bacteria samples are comparatively easier to analyze than inorganic residues such as fibers or paint.

Lisa Landis Murphy

Further Reading
Houck, M. *Mute Witnesses: Trace Evidence Analysis.* San Diego, Calif.: Academic Press, 2001.
Houck, M. *Trace Evidence Analysis: More Clues in Forensic Microscopy and Mute Witnesses.* San Diego, Calif.: Academic Press, 2003.
Lee, H., H. C. Lee, and T. Timedy. *Blood Evidence: How DNA Is Revolutionizing the Way We Solve Crimes.* Cambridge, Mass.: Perseus Publishing, 2004.
Oaklander, Mandy. "A Strange New Way to Solve Crimes." *Time* 31 Aug. 2015: 44-47. Academic Search Complete. Web. 31 May 2016.
Stoney, David A., and Paul L. Stoney. "Critical Review of Forensic Trace Evidence Analysis and the Need for a New Approach." *Forensic Science International* 251 (2015): 159-70. Web. 31 May 2016.

See also Autopsies; Bloodstains; Crime labs; DNA testing; Fingerprint identification; Forensic psychology; Forensics; Latent evidence; Medical examiners; Shoe prints and tire-tracks; Toxicology; Trace evidence; Technology's transformative effect.

Uniform Juvenile Court Act

The Law: Federal model law outlining significant changes recommended for state juvenile courts
Date: Enacted in 1968
Criminal justice issues: Constitutional protections; courts; juvenile justice

Significance: The Uniform Juvenile Court Act served as a model that the individual states could follow to make their own juvenile justice systems more uniform in their purposes, scopes, and procedures.

After years of criticism regarding the lack of procedural safeguards afforded juveniles in state courts, the Uniform Juvenile Court Act was drafted by the National Conference of Commissioners on Uniform State Laws. With the express goal of developing a model juvenile justice system that could be used as a blueprint for state juvenile courts, the law addressed the issues of decreasing the stigmatization of delinquent youth and helping to maintain family units. The act also addressed the need to preserve recently recognized constitutional rights of youth. These rights included the right to legal counsel, articulated in the U.S. Supreme Court's *In re Gault* ruling in 1967, and the right to due process, articulated in *Kent v. United States* in 1966.

Additionally, the model law outlined how state courts might accomplish these goals. Philosophically, the model system aimed to blend the original juvenile courts' goal of treating children as capable of reform and rehabilitation while still holding them accountable for their misdeeds. In short, it outlined the need for judicial intervention when necessary for the care of dependent children and for the treatment and rehabilitation of juvenile delinquents, while ensuring fair and constitutional procedures.

Rachel Bandy

Further Reading
Champion, Dean John. *The Juvenile Justice System: Delinquency, Processing, and the Law.* 4th ed. Upper Saddle River, N.J.: Prentice-Hall, 2003.
Cox, Steven M., John J. Conrad, and Jennifer M. Allen. *Juvenile Justice.* 5th ed. New York: McGraw-Hill, 2002.
Hess, Karen M., and Robert W. Drowns. *Juvenile Justice.* 4th ed. Belmont, Calif.: Wadsworth/Thomson Learning, 2004.

See also Counsel, right to; *Gault, In re*; Juvenile courts; Juvenile delinquency; Juvenile Justice and Delinquency Prevention Act; Juvenile Justice and Delinquency Prevention, Office of; Juvenile justice system; Juvenile waivers to adult courts; *Parens patriae*.

USA FREEDOM Act (2015)

Definition: Popular name for United States Public Law No. 114-23, extending USA PATRIOT Act provisions into 2019 while also limiting the government's ability to collect telecommunications data and other business records in bulk

Criminal justice issues: Privacy; search and seizure; terrorism; federal law; investigation

Significance: Prior to the USA FREEDOM ACT, American intelligence agencies had been utilizing Section 215 of the USA PATRIOT Act to collect all phone data from telephone service providers. The USA FREEDOM Act prohibited the government from conducting such mass data surveillance on citizens at large, and also provided for additional transparency and oversight for the Foreign Intelligence Surveillance Court (FISC), which approves search orders under Section 215.

The Uniting and Strengthening America by Fulfilling Rights and Ensuring Effective Discipline Over Monitoring (USA FREEDOM) Act of 2015 was signed into law by President Barack Obama on June 2, 2015. This Act modified previous procedures for obtaining business records originally put in place by the Foreign Intelligence Surveillance Act of 1978 and modified by the USA PATRIOT Act of 2001, which had both been codified at 50 U.S. Code, Sections 1801-1885(c).

Legal History

In 1978, Congress passed the Foreign Intelligence Surveillance Act (FISA) of 1978, which outlined specific procedures for authorizing electronic surveillance to obtain foreign intelligence information. In an attempt to expand judicial and congressional oversight of foreign intelligence operations, FISA allowed for the chief justice of the Supreme Court to designate seven district court judges to hear applications and grant electronic surveillance orders, with three additional judges from the district courts or courts of appeal appointed as an appellate body, with the Supreme Court as the highest level of appeal. Each year, the attorney general would prepare an annual report for Congress and the Administrative Office of the United States Courts.

Most importantly, under FISA a judge was only to grant an order allowing electronic surveillance of American citizens or legal residents if the court found probable cause that the surveillance target was a foreign power or agent of a foreign power. When FISA was amended by the Intelligence Authorization Act for Fiscal Year 1999 (Public Law No. 105-272), the legislature added language allowing upper-level Federal Bureau of Investigation (FBI) directors or agents to apply to FISC judges for orders authorizing four specific types of businesses to release their business records to the FBI. These types of businesses were common carriers (e.g., railroads or airlines), physical storage facilities, public accommodation facilities (e.g., hotels or motels), and vehicle rental facilities. These businesses were not permitted to disclose that they had produced the records to the FBI. However, following roughly the same standard set by the original FISA, a proper application had to include specific and articulable facts giving reason to believe that the person to whom the records pertained was a foreign power or an agent of a foreign power.

After the terrorist attacks of September 11, 2001, many lawmakers called for new legislation that would facilitate law enforcement and the intelligence community as they investigated the attacks. Among many other changes, FISA was amended again by Section 215 of the USA PATRIOT Act, now allowing the same upper-level FBI agents to apply to the FISC judges for "the production of any tangible things (including books, records, papers, documents, and other items)," expanding far beyond the business records of the four specific business categories. Also, instead of the previous probable cause requirement, the FBI now simply had to specify that the records concerned were "for an authorized investigation [...] to obtain foreign intelligence information not concerning a United States person or to protect against international terrorism or clandestine intelligence activities."

Development

In June, 2013, former defense contractor and Central Intelligence Agency (CIA) employee Edward Snowden leaked a document showing that a FISC judge had approved an order requiring Verizon to provide the National Security Agency (NSA) with electronic copies of all call detail records for phone calls where at least one participant was within the United States. Verizon was ordered to produce this information "on an ongoing daily basis" while the order was in effect. Later it was revealed that other large telecommunications providers including AT&T and Sprint had also provided the NSA with bulk call data.

On March 27, 2014, President Barack Obama announced that his administration had been working with Congress, the private sector, and privacy and civil liberties groups to discuss alternatives to the NSA's bulk metadata program that would appropriately protect the privacy of the American public while also providing intelligence and law enforcement agencies with the tools they needed. President Obama also stated that he thought the best approach was for the government to no longer collect metadata in bulk, with the data remaining at the phone companies for a standard amount of time and the FISC approving specific requests. President Obama urged Congress to pass appropriate legislation to achieve those aims, which resulted in the USA FREEDOM Act of 2015.

At the same time, Section 215 and two other surveillance laws stemming from the PATRIOT Act were set to expire or "sunset" on June 1, 2015 unless reauthorized by Congress. The other two sections concerned roving wiretaps—or wiretap orders that focus on an individual rather than a particular phone number—and the "lone wolf" provision of Section 6001 of the Intelligence Reform and Terrorism Prevention Act of 2004. According to a May 19, 2015 memorandum prepared by the Congressional Research Service for the House Judiciary Committee, if Section 215 was not reauthorized by 12:00 a.m. on the morning of June 1, 2015, then Sections 501 and 502 of FISA would read as they read on October 25, 2001 before the implementation of the PATRIOT Act. The Legislature was unable to pass a version of the USA FREEDOM Act in the 113th Congress, but the potential sunsetting of the three surveillance provisions motivated Congress to pass a reintroduced version. The House of Representatives passed the Act on May 13, 2015, and the Senate officially passed the Act on June 2, 2015, which caused the three provisions to temporarily sunset.

Effect

The USA FREEDOM Act prohibits the government from collecting business records or other tangible things in bulk. The USA FREEDOM Act added language requiring FISA applications to include "specific selection terms." Section 107 of the Act describes these specific selection terms as "a term that specifically identifies a person, account, address, or personal device, or any other specific identifier." Specific selection terms also have to limit the scope of the search as much as possible. For example, a county, state, or zip code without an additional term is not sufficient. An application must now include a statement of facts showing that there are "reasonable grounds" to believe the specific selection term is relevant to the investigation and associated with a foreign power engaged in international terrorism. This is slightly more limiting than the previous standard, but not as limiting as the original probable cause requirement.

Additionally, under Section 402 of the USA FREEDOM Act, the director of National Intelligence and the attorney general will conduct a declassification review for each order of FISC opinion that "includes a significant construction or interpretation of any provision of the law," including the interpretation of "specific selection term." This will serve as a check on the FISC, and will theoretically prevent the law from broadening past what the Legislature intended.

After reauthorization from the USA FREEDOM Act, the three PATRIOT Act surveillance provisions are set to sunset again on December 15, 2019.

Savanna L. Nolan

Further Reading

Berman, Emily. "The Two Faces of the Foreign Intelligence Surveillance Court." Indiana Law Journal 91 (2016): 1191. Discusses the dual "gatekeeper" and "rule maker" functions of the FISC and how the USA FREEDOM Act falls short because its reforms fail to fully take the rule-making function into account.

Forsyth,. "Banning Bulk: Passage of the USA FREEDOM Act and Ending Bulk Collection." Washington & Lee University Law Review 72 (Summer, 2015): 1307. Discusses the political development of the USA FREEDOM Act and argues against the idea that Congress tacitly agreed to the Obama Administration's interpretation of the statute because Congress reauthorized the statute after the bulk metadata program was approved by the FISC.

McGowan, Casey J.. "The Relevance of Relevance: Section 215 of the USA PATRIOT Act and the NSA Metadata Collection Program." Fordham Law Review 82 (April, 2014): 2399. Provides legal background on the NSA's surveillance programs under Section 215, including prior Fourth and First Amendments' case law concerning the search and seizure of technological information.

Peterson, Kristina, and Damian Paletta. "Congress Reins In Spying Powers." *The Wall Street Journal*, June 3, 2015, A1. Reports on the final passage of the Act.

See also Federal Bureau of Investigation, U.S.; Fusion centers; Homeland Security, U.S. Department of; Lone wolf; Probable cause; Search warrants; September 11, 2001, attacks; Terrorism; Wiretaps.

Victims of Child Abuse Act Reauthorization Act (2013)

Definition: Federal legislation to restore funding for state and local programs for child abuse investigations, prosecutions, and treatment

Criminal justice issues: Courts, investigation; law codes; sex offenses; victims

Significance: Several empirically grounded programs, including children's advocacy centers and court-appointed special advocate programs, rely upon federal funding to investigate and provide child abuse treatment services at the state and local level.

The Victims of Child Abuse Act Reauthorization Act of 2013 (VOCAA), which became law on August 8, 2014, reauthorizes various funding conduits for programs that serve child victims of abuse. This legislation primarily concerns funding for children's advocacy centers (CACs); court-appointed special advocate (CASA) programs; and state and federal programs that provide technical and training assistance to state and federal court professionals.

The original VOCAA passed Congress as part of the 1990 Crime Control Act. The legislation was introduced in response to the story of eight-year-old Leilani who fearfully disclosed to her teacher that she was being sexually abused. Leilani begged the teacher not to allow her uncle to pick her up after school, explaining that he "bothers her" and requires her to keep quiet about the abusive behavior. Eventually, Leilani and her family received therapy, and the uncle was convicted and sent to prison. Leilani's story encapsulates the scourge of child abuse that plagues society. According to the National Child Abuse (NCA) and Neglect Training and Publications Project in 2014, 679,000 children were victims of abuse and neglect.

The Victims of Child Abuse Act Reauthorization Act received bipartisan support as part of a national initiative to address the pernicious problems of child abuse and neglect and ease some pressure on the court systems that prosecuted those cases. Congress acknowledged that juvenile and family courts were overwhelmed with abuse and neglect litigation, and they recognized that federal funding for CAC, CASA, and other state and local initiatives could ameliorate some of the burdens arising from the heavy caseloads.

All states host at least one CAC, which are child-centric, facility-based programs that provide a one-stop process for child abuse investigation. A multidisciplinary team, including a forensic interviewer, conducts joint interviews and reaches a consensus on how best to develop evidence and manage the prosecution of child abuse cases. The CAC model evolved from a program that began in Alabama in 1985. Court advocacy centers first received federal funding in 1990 as part of VOCAA. Funding for CACs lapsed in 2005. The 2013 reauthorization of VOCAA restored those funds, expanded some resources, and imposed increased accountability and reporting requirements upon CACs. It also increased resources available to CACs' partner organizations, such as the umbrella National Network of Children's Advocacy Centers, which develops standards and guides empirical program evaluations. At the local level, the Act provides funding for CAC to training their personnel and development practice protocols.

In 2013, CACs served 295,000 children, the majority of whom were seen in relation to charges of sexual abuse. Court advocacy centers provide prompt, comprehensive support to child victims. Team members work together and respond to the impacts of the abuse, manage child victims' interactions with criminal justice professionals, and mitigate potential secondary victimization that may arise during the investigatory process. They also provide support for child victims' nonoffending family members.

According to federal guidance, all CACs must have child-appropriate facilities; multidisciplinary teams; a designated legal entity (such as a nonprofit organization) for program and fiscal operations; culturally competent policies and practices; appropriate forensic-interviewing capabilities; medical evaluation and treatment capabilities; resources for therapeutic interventions; resources for victim support; resources for victim advocacy; and a formalized case review and tracking system. The 2013 reauthorization of VOCAA requires CACs that receive federal funds to undergo periodic audits; establish procedures to prevent waste, fraud, or abuse; prescribe reasonable compensation structures for officers and employees; and seek approval from the deputy attorney general before expending funds for conferences.

Court-appointed special advocates are specially trained volunteers who are appointed by courts to investigate child abuse allegations. Originally intended to serve as fact finders for overburdened social workers and court personnel, CASAs now provide a multitude of services for the children they serve. The first CASA programs began in the 1970's in Seattle, Washington in response to demands of the burgeoning foster care system. These programs, and their close cousins known as guardian ad litem (GAL) programs, link children with emergency and social services, investigate allegations of abuse, conduct home studies for short- and long-term placement, and advocate for abused children throughout the criminal justice process. Court-appointed special advocates often work within CAC multidisciplinary teams, but they also may work independent of CACS, or they may provide services in jurisdictions that do not have CACs. Today, there are approximately 76,000 CASAs nationwide who serve over 250,000 children. It is not known how many more volunteer advocates serve abused and neglected children through GAL and other advocacy programs that do not use the formal CASA designation.

The Victims of Child Abuse Act Reauthorization Act provides resources to CASA programs through direct and indirect funding streams. The National CASA Association receives the bulk of the federal funds allocated to CASA programs and awards subgrants to state and local programs. VOCAA allocates funding for training and technical assistance programs that enhance CAC, CASA, and other organizations concerned about child abuse and neglect.

The VOCAA funding also distributes monies to state and federal courts to refine and expand their processing of abuse and neglect cases. For example, the original VOCAA provides funds to a permanency planning program sponsored by the National Council of Juvenile and Family Court Judges (NCCJC). The 2013 reauthorization increases funding to judicially sponsored programs that support integration of CASAs into court proceedings; conducts seminars for lawyers and judges; and provides training materials to advocates and criminal justice personnel who interact with abused and neglected children.

Anne S. Douds

Further Reading
Faller, K. C., and V. J. Palusci. "Children's Advocacy Centers: Do They Lead to Positive Case Outcomes?" *Child Abuse & Neglect* 31, no. 10 (2007); 1021-29.
Jones, L. M., T. P. Cross, W. A. Walsh, and M. Simone. "Do Children's Advocacy Centers Improve Families' Experiences of Child Sexual abuse Investigations?" *Child Abuse & Neglect* 31, no. 10 (2007): 1069-85.
National Child Abuse and Neglect Training and Publications Project. *The Child Abuse Prevention and Treatment Act: 40 Years of Safeguarding America's Children.* Washington, D.C.: U.S. Department of Health and Human Services, Children's Bureau, 2014.
Petersen, A. C., J. Joseph, and M. Feit, eds. *New Directions in Child Abuse and Neglect Research.* Washington, D.C.: National Academies Press, 2014.
Piraino, M. S. "Lay Representation of Abused and Neglected Children: Variations on Court Appointed Special Advocate Programs and Their Relationship to Quality Advocacy." *Journal of the Center for Children and the Courts* 1 (1999): 63-71.
Weisz, V., and N. Thai. "The Court-Appointed Special Advocate (CASA) Program: Bringing Information to Child Abuse & Neglect Cases."*Child Maltreatment* 8, no. 3 (2003): 204-10.

See also Adam Walsh Child Protection Act; Battered child and battered wife syndromes; Child abduction by parents; Criminals; *Jaycee Lee Dugard case (2009); Jessica's Law/Jessica Lunsford Act (2005);* National Organization for Victim Assistance; National Crime Victimization Survey; Pedophilia; Rape and sex offenses; Victim assistance programs; Victim-offender mediation; Victimology; Victims of Crime Act; Crime victimization: Primary and secondary; Human trafficking; Post-traumatic stress disorder; Victims services; Victim recovery stages; Victimization theories; *Victims of Trafficking Act (2014);* Victim impact statements.

Wiretaps and criminal justice

Definition: Electronic surveillance method of eavesdropping by a third party to monitor or record communications of individuals or groups under investigation
Investigation; Privacy; Technology

Significance: Wiretaps can be effective law-enforcement tools for gathering information that helps identify criminal activity and often lead to successful prosecutions; however, they are controversial because they have often been used illegally and pose the threat of increasing government intrusions on privacy.

As of 2014, federal law-enforcement agencies, such as the Federal Bureau of Investigation and the Drug Enforcement Administration, and forty-four states allowed electronic interception of conversations. Intercepted conversations may include oral, wired, or cellular transmissions. During the early 2010s, the number of court-ordered interceptions ranged from 2,732 to 3,576 per year. All such intercepted conversations are legally required to be reported to the administrative office of the U.S. Courts, which makes an annual report to the Congress. A device called a pen register, which records the telephone numbers called and requires judicial approval, is often used to provide probable cause for the wiretap.

By the 1960's, technology had been developed that was being used frequently by both law-enforcement officers and private detectives to monitor telephone conversations of individuals who had a reasonable expectation of privacy. In response to complaints about such activity, Congress passed Title III of the Omnibus Crime Control and Safe Streets Act of 1968. That law established guidelines and standards for both federal and state law enforcement and still governs actions of court-ordered wiretaps.

In 2001, Congress passed the Patriot Act, which expanded powers granted to law-enforcement agencies by the Foreign Intelligence Surveillance Act of 1978 to gather foreign intelligence information. Title III of the new law allowed wiretaps to be used to investigate possible terrorism within the United States. These powers included roving wiretaps, which allow electronic surveillance to continue even after suspects change their telephones, venues, or Internet accounts. Title III also prohibits all private wiretaps.

Enforcement

The President's Commission on Law Enforcement and Administration of Justice, the President's Commission on Organized Crime in 1983, the Pennsylvania Crime Commission, and the McClellan Committee of the late 1950's all concluded that traditional law-enforcement methods were not effective against complex criminal organizations such as the Mafia, South American drug cartels, triads, outlaw motorcycle gangs, and—in the twenty-first century—terrorists. Wiretaps have been successful, when combined with traditional law-enforcement methods, against such crime bosses as John Gotti (the head of the Mafia's Gambino family) and Pablo Escobar (the head of Colombia's Medellin drug cartel).

Leaders of criminal organizations have traditionally been skilled at insulating themselves against arrest and prosecution, typically by having others in their organizations carry out their criminal acts. The leaders usually engage in conversations with their subordinates only when giving them orders or discussing criminal activities. Telephones are frequently used as communication devices and thus are excellent sources of evidence that can be intercepted by wiretaps.

Wiretaps can be very expensive, owing to the legal requirements requiring the presence of two monitors, in addition to the officers who actually conduct the surveillance of the suspects. The monitors are necessary for the corroboration and identification of callers. Electronic monitoring also often entails overtime wages, expensive equipment and training, and the costs of transcribing recordings. Monitors also take notes that are part of the record and are used to verify what is said on the communi-

Mark Klein is a former AT&T technician who blew the whistle on the telecom giant for their cooperation with the Bush Administration's illegal warrantless wiretapping program. (By EFF, via Wikimedia Commons)

cation devices. Monitors must be alert to noticing when conversations are not criminal so that they can stop recordings when conversations have no evidentiary value.

Wiretapping is a complex operation requiring analytical, legal, and technological expertise. Moreover, because many conversations are conducted in codes, analysts experienced in decoding may be required. Intelligence analysts synthesize information to develop probable cause to obtain judicial approval of a wiretap order/warrant. Targets of wiretaps must be notified that their conversations have been intercepted within ninety days after termination of the judicial orders. Most orders permit wiretaps for thirty days and require judicial reviews for extensions.

Wiretaps often collect valuable evidence that is used against major violators, but they sometimes produce little or no useful evidence. They can be potent tools in the arsenal of criminal investigation, but tools that require considerable thought and planning before they are implemented.

Stephen L. Mallory

Further Reading
Adams, James A., and Daniel D. Blinka. *Electronic Surveillance: Commentaries and Statutes.* Notre Dame, Ind.: National Institute for Trial Advocacy, 2003.
Brzezinski, Matthew. *Fortress America: On the Frontline of Homeland Security-An Inside Look at the Coming Surveillance State.* New York: Bantam Books, 2004.
Diffie, Whitfield, and Susan Landau. *Privacy on the Line: The Politics of Wiretapping and Encryption.* Cambridge, Mass.: MIT Press, 1999.
Keefe, Patrick Radden. *Chatter: Dispatches from the Secret World of Global Eavesdropping.* New York: Random House, 2005.
Schulhofer, Stephen J. *The Enemy Within: Intelligence Gathering, Law Enforcement, and Civil Liberties in the Wake of September 11.* New York: Century Foundation Books, 2002.

See also Comprehensive Crime Control Act; Electronic surveillance; Espionage; Omnibus Crime Control and Safe Streets Act of 1968; Organized crime; Organized Crime Control Act; Patriot Act; Privacy rights; Surveillance cameras; Body-worn cameras; Technology's transformative effect.

Youth gangs

Definition: Self-defined group of adolescents whose value systems and activities encourage deviant behavior
Juvenile justice; Vandalism; Violent crime

Significance: Although juvenile crime has tended to decline since the mid-1990s, crimes associated with youth gangs have continued to increase as gangs have proliferated across the United States and as gang members have engaged in more serious forms of crime.

Youth gangs have received considerable attention in criminal justice since the beginning of the twentieth century, but no universally accepted definition of what constitutes a gang has yet emerged. The consensus among scholars and people in criminal justice is that a gang is a group with at least three members who engage in delinquent behavior. Gangs are more than merely groups of delinquent peers; they are unique in that the values of their members support the deviant behavior of both the individual members and the gang as a whole. Many researchers also agree that an important element of youth gangs is their adoption of distinctive identifying names. Moreover, gang members also tend to identify themselves by wearing distinctive clothing and tattoos and by marking neighborhoods with distinctive graffiti-all of which reinforces group cohesiveness.

History and Theory

The first documented youth gangs emerged in the Five Points District of New York City at the beginning of the twentieth century. Members of these early gangs were predominantly white and included many newly arrived immigrants from Europe. These early gangs were forerunners to organized crime groups—a fact that makes them different from their modern gang counterparts. Early attempts to explain the criminal behavior of youth gangs focused on social disorganization. However, during the 1920s, researchers took on the challenge of specifically explaining the gang phenomena.

It was not until the mid-twentieth century that Los Angeles and Chicago saw the emergence of what would become modern youth gangs. These later gangs were similar to the earlier gangs in that their membership was made up of mostly new immigrants. These new gangs also included groups whose members were moving throughout the United States. Most of their members were African Americans and Hispanics. The modern gangs developed in response to conditions of poverty, discrimination, and other social problems in developing urban areas in big cities. Research on gangs during the mid-twentieth century leaned toward "strain theory"—an emerging explanation of general criminal behavior that focused on lack of legitimate opportunities in society and the resulting need for value adaptation.

A major difference between these modern gangs and earlier gangs is that instead of dissolving or seeing their members move into organized crime, the modern gangs have tended to become more deeply entrenched in street crime. Part of the reason for this development researchers have found has been the inability of gang members to gain access to legitimate employment opportunities.

The continuity of gangs has been reinforced by the continued involvement of members into their adulthood, and twenty-first century gangs have their roots in the mid-twentieth century gang movement. The perpetuation of gangs has encouraged a resurgence of scholarly interest in gang theory. A notable development in theory has been the application of general criminological theory to explain why individuals join gangs. Money, gang members in the family, friendship, respect, protection, and self-esteem are among the reasons that have been noted for joining gangs.

The late twentieth century saw increased levels of gang violence and a proliferation of gangs across the United States. Cities that had never had youth gangs before the 1980s suddenly had to deal with gangs. Much of this change has been attributed to deindustrialization and a consequent need to rely more on criminal activities, especially drug sales. Large gangs expanded across the United States, and entirely new gangs emerged in many cities.

One of the most visible changes in modern gangs has been their trend toward multiracial membership. Also, many gangs are taking in female members. The age structures of gangs are also changing. Gangs are taking in more younger members than ever before, and increasing numbers of members are remaining active in their gangs into their young adulthood. There also seem to be growing connections between street gangs and prison gangs that were not evident in earlier years.

Structure and Behaviors

The evolution of gangs over time has brought with it variety in the structure of the groups and the criminal behaviors of its members. The structures of gangs appear to be related to the gangs' behaviors. For example, gangs lacking cohesion are generally less organized than others are and are more likely to engage in random deviant behavior. More cohesive groups have tighter structures and engage in more organized criminal activities. The longer gangs are in existence, the more cohesive they become. Gangs whose members stay in longer are also more likely to develop greater cohesion and stronger organization. However, most gangs are not formally organized, and most members are transitional and do not stay in gangs for life.

Emergent gangs with low levels of cohesion tend to have weak leadership. Their members tend to engage in random and diverse deviant behaviors that are individually based and do not benefit the gangs as a whole. Many members of such gangs engage only in minor forms of juvenile delinquency. Members of gangs of this type are the most likely to quit before they reach adulthood, and the gangs themselves are prone to disband. Many gangs in the United States can be classified as emergent.

When emergent gangs continue to evolve, they become more cohesive. They often have initiation rituals that test members' loyalty and strength. Eventually, formal rules develop, and members who violate the rules may face consequences. Meanwhile, more leadership structures develop, and the deviant behaviors of individual members may monetarily benefit a gang as a whole.

Most gangs never become solidified and tightly organized, but a few "supergangs," such as the Latin Kings, have reached advanced levels of organization. Gangs of this nature have intricate leadership structures with multiple tiers and elaborate rules for members to follow. Highly organized groups often have branches dispersed throughout the United States, and their criminal activities are well structured. Such gangs tend to operate as organizations and often benefit from the criminal activities of their individual members. Their members generally avoid outward displays of their gang affiliation to avoid attracting the attention of police.

Criminal Activities

Criminal activity of gangs range from minor delinquent behaviors, such as shoplifting and drinking, to such serious crimes as robbery and homicide. Most gang members engage in deviant behavior before joining their gangs, but their deviant behaviors increase after they join. Reasons for this tend to revolve around the common value systems and group mentalities of the gangs.

Among the most common criminal activities of gangs are graffiti marking, drug trafficking, and seemingly random violence, such as homicides and drive-by shootings. A traditional gang behavior, graffiti marking serves multiple purposes, including creating artistic displays (tagging), marking territory, honoring fallen members, and communicating with rival gangs. However, increasing violence in gang-ridden urban areas has overshadowed this relatively minor deviant behavior. Gang violence takes the form of intergang wars and drive-by shootings. The result has been staggering death rates among young urban male members of minority groups.

Much of modern youth gang violence is due partly to increased availability of guns and personal transportation, which has expanded rivalry areas. It has also been suggested that this violence is a function of increased drug sales, which rely heavily on tough enforcement of street-level rules.

Prevention and Intervention

As law enforcement and scholars have tackled problems of youth gangs and street crime, strategies for preventing gang violence have proliferated. Some of these strategies are implemented at the individual level to keep youths from joining gangs and to encourage those already in gangs to renounce their gang lifestyles. Prevention and intervention are important because of both the short and long-term consequences of gang membership.

The effect of gang membership stays with many members long after they leave their gangs. Gang-prevention programs strive to raise awareness of the effects of gangs and give youths the skills necessary to resist membership. Those at higher risk for gang membership may require more intensive efforts, including family counseling and mentoring programs. For youths who are already gang involved, outreach and street-worker programs provide job skills training and guidance to help with the transition to legitimate adulthood activities.

Gang membership affects not only individual members but also entire communities, which suffer from gang activities. Several prevention and intervention efforts aim to strengthen communities and reduce criminal behavior in high-crime areas. Community organization efforts encourage community efforts to combat the effects of social disorganization. Working together ultimately strengthens communities and helps to protect them against escalating crime. An example of this type of approach is neighborhood watch programs. Other avenues for organization utilize key community stakeholders, such as religious leaders and business owners.

The criminal justice system also plays a role in the reduction of gangs and gang activity. While community-oriented policing is an important endeavor in community relations, law enforcement also plays a role in suppressing the criminal gang activities. The toughest police approaches to gangs may include zero-tolerance enforcement and specialized gang units.

In some instances, tough police policies have backfired and strengthened gangs. The U.S. Supreme Court seems to recognize the potentially negative effects of hard-core gang enforcement in its 1999 ruling in *Chicago v. Morales*, which limited police discretion in handling suspected gang members. At the same time, programs such as Boston's Ceasefire Program, which combines suppression with other intervention efforts, have shown favorable results.

Efforts to control youth gang activity have also been strengthened as a result of administrative and legislative changes that include civil injunctions, enhanced sentencing, and gang-specific prosecutions. However, enhanced sentencing and more efficient detection and criminal prosecution of gang activity have also led to problems within correctional institutions. Increases in gang activity on the streets have been accompanied by the increased presence of gangs in correctional facilities, which have been accompanied by growing connections between street and prison gangs.

Kimberly Tobin

Further Reading
Brotherton, David. *Youth Street Gangs: A Critical Appraisal*. New York: Routledge, 2015. Print.
Esbensen, Finn-Aage, Larry K. Gaines, and Stephen G. Tibbetts. *American Youth Gangs at the Millennium*. Long Grove: Waveland, 2004. Print.
Franzese, Robert J., et al. *Youth Gangs*. 4th ed. Springfield: Charles C. Thomas, 2016. Print.
Miller, Jody, Cheryl Maxson, and Malcolm Klein, eds. *The Modern Gang Reader*. 2nd ed. Los Angeles: Roxbury, 2000. Print.
"National Youth Gang Survey Analysis." *National Gang Center*. Dept. of Justice, n.d. Web. 21 June 2016.
Pedersen, Traci. "Study Finds 1 Million Juvenile Gang Members in US." *Psych Central*. Psych Central, 6 Oct. 2015. Web. 21 June 2016.
Rodriguez, Luis J., et al. *East Side Stories: Gang Life in East LA*. New York: Powerhouse, 2000. Print.
Shakur, Sanyika. *Monster: The Autobiography of an L.A. Gang Member*. New York: Grove, 2004. Print.
Sheldon, Randall G., Sharon K. Tracy, and William B. Brown. *Youth Gangs in American Society*. Belmont: Wadsworth, 2003. Print.
Valdez, Al. *Gangs: A Guide to Understanding Street Gangs*. 3rd ed. San Clemente: Law Tech, 2000. Print.

See also Drive-by shootings; Graffiti; Juvenile delinquency; Juvenile justice system; Neighborhood watch programs; Organized crime; School violence; Vandalism; Violent Crime Control and Law Enforcement Act.

Appendices

Bibliography of Basic Works on Criminal Justice

General

Albanese, Jay S. *Professional Ethics in Criminal Justice: Being Ethical When No One Is Looking.* 4th ed. Boston: Pearson, 2016. Print.

Barkan, Steven. *Criminology: A Social Understanding.* 3d ed. Upper Saddle River, N.J.: Prentice Hall, 2005. This edition provides readers with a sociological perspective on crime. The central theme of this book focuses on social inequality as a correlate of crime, and interactive scenarios at the close of each chapter will actively engage readers on integral issues concerning society's treatment of criminals. Topics unique to this edition include the following: death penalty, terrorism, stalking, identity theft, computer crime, and white collar crime.

Brown, Brittni. "Is the Media Altering Our Perceptions of Crime?" *International Policy Digest.* International Policy Digest, 11 Mar. 2015. Web. 26 May 2016.

Brown, Stephen E., Finn-Aage Esbensen, and Gilbert Geis. *Criminology: Explaining Crime and Its Context.* 9th ed. New York: Routledge, 2015. Print.

CADCA. "Comprehensive Addiction and Recovery Act (CARA)." *CADCA: Building Drug-Free Communities.* Alexandria Va.: Community Anti-Drug Coalitions of America, 2016. Lembke, Anna. *Drug Dealer, MD.* Baltimore: Johns Hopkins University Press, 2016.

Farley, Melissa, and Victor Malarek. "The Myth of the Victimless Crime." *New York Times.* New York Times, 12 Mar. 2008. Web. 31 May 2016.

Freiburger, Tina L., and Catherine D. Marcum. *Women in the Criminal Justice System: Tracking the Journey of Females and Crime.* Boca Raton: CRC, 2016. Print.

Jacoby, Joseph, ed. *Classics of Criminology.* 3d ed. Long Grove, Ill.: Waveland Press, 2004. Collection of sixty-five of the most influential writings from the past 240 years that attempt to explain crime. Presented chronologically in three sections: classic descriptions of crime, theories of causation of crime, and social responses to crime.

Office of the Surgeon General. *Facing Addiction in America: The Surgeon General's Report on Alcohol, Drugs, and Health.* Washington, DC: U.S. Department of Health and Human Services, 2016. The first comprehensive, historic, and up-to-date government report that acknowledges addiction as a major public health challenge in the country. The report also includes state-of-the art treatments, preventive measures, and research for this chronic disease.

Pollock, Joycelyn M. *Ethical Dilemmas and Decisions in Criminal Justice.* 8th ed. Belmont: Wadsworth, 2014. Print.

Corrections

Abadinsky, Howard. *Probation and Parole.* 12th ed. Boston: Pearson, 2015. Print.

Allen, Harry E., Edward J. Latessa, and Bruce S. Ponder. *Corrections in America: An Introduction.* 14th ed. Upper Saddle River: Pearson Education, 2015. Print.

Fenton, Jenifer. "Is the Report: Jail Suicide Leading Cause of Death of US Inmates." *Al Jazeera.* Al Jazeera America, 5 Aug. 2015. Web. 31 May 2016.

Irwin, John. *The Warehouse Prison: Disposal of the New Dangerous Class.* Los Angeles, Calif.: Roxbury, 2005. Thorough examination of the implementation of new technology and prison regimes from 1980 to 2000.

Johnson, Ida. "Women Parolees' Perceptions of Parole Experiences and Parole Officers." *American Journal of Criminal Justice* Dec. 2015: 785-810. Print.

Kaeble, Danielle, Maruschak, Laura M., and Bonczar, Thomas P. *Probation and Parole in the United States, 2014.* Washington, D.C.: Bureau of Justice Statistics, 2015. Wide-ranging study of probation and parole populations in the United States and their characteristics.

Lens, K. E., A. Pemberton K. Brans, J. Braeken, S. Bogaerts, and E. Lahlah. "Delivering a Victim Impact Statement: Emotionally Effective or Counter-productive?" *European Journal of Criminology-* 12, no. 1 (2015): 17-34.

Masters, R. E., L. Beth Way, P. B. GerstenfeldB. T. Muscat, M. Hooper J. P. J. Dussich, and C. A. Skrapec. *CJ: Realities and Challenges* 3nd ed., Chap. 14. New York: McGraw Hill, 2017.

Morales, Gabriel C. *La Familia = The Family: Prison Gangs in America.* 4th ed. Independent Publishing Platform, 2015.

Namuo, Clynton. "Victim Offender Mediation: When Divergent Paths and Destroyed Lives Come Together for Healing." *Georgia State University Law Review* 32.2 (2016): 577-602. Print.

Paluch, James A., Jr., T. J. Bernard, and R. Johnson. *A Life for a Life: Life Imprisonment (America's Other Death Penalty).* Los Angeles, Calif.: Roxbury, 2003. Firsthand account of the realities and culture of prison life by a convict serving a life sentence.

Petersilia, J. "California Prison Downsizing and Its Impact on Local Criminal Justice Systems." *Harvard Law and Policy Review* 8 (2014): 801-32. An analysis of realignment's effect on county agencies including recommendations for policy alterations by one of the leading experts on California's criminal justice system.

Phelps, M. S. "Rehabilitation in the Punitive Era: The Gap between Rhetoric and Reality in U.S. Prison Programs." *Law Soc Rev 45*, no. 1 (March, 2011): 33-68.

Pollock, Joycelyn M. *Prisons and Prison Life: Costs and Consequences*. New York: Oxford UP, 2013. Print.

Reamer, Frederic G. *On the Parole Board: Reflections on Crime, Punishment, Redemption, and Justice*. New York: Columbia University Press, 2016. Reflections of an individual, a professor of social work, who served on the Rhode Island parole board for twenty-four years.

Reiter, Keramet. *23/7: Pelican Bay Prison and the Rise of Long-Term Solitary Confinement*. New Haven, Conn.: Yale University Press, 2016. This book describes how Pelican Bay was created, how easily prisoners can be sentenced to solitary, and the psychological and social costs of years in isolation.

Roberts, Walther. *Prison Gangs: Organized Crime Behind Bars*. Kindle Edition, 2014.

Russ, J. I., and S. C. Richards. *Convict Criminology*. Belmont, Calif.: Thomson/Wadsworth, 2003. Mixture of autobiographical accounts with research that presents convict perspectives on prison life and the problem of re-entrance into the community.

Schanbacher, K. "Inside Job: The Role Correctional Officers Play in the Occurrence of Sexual Assault in US Detention Centers." *DePaul Journal for Social Justice* 9 (2015): 38-66.

Schenwar, Maya. "The Quiet Horrors of House Arrest, Electronic Monitoring, and Other Alternative Forms of Incarceration." *Mother Jones*. Mother Jones and the Foundation for Natl. Progress, 22 Jan. 2015. Web. 26 May 2016.

Skarbek, David. *The Social Order of the Underworld: How Prison Gangs Govern the American Penal System*. New York: Oxford University Press, 2014. The author uses economics to explore how gangs form alternative governance institutions to facilitate illegal activity, and why they have influence outside prison walls.

Criminal Law

Caldwell, H. M. "Everybody Talks about Prosecutorial Conduct but Nobody Does Anything About It: A 25-Year Survey of Prosecutorial Misconduct and a Viable Solution." *University of Illinois Review* (forthcoming 2016).

Corley, Pamela C., Artemus Ward, and Wendy L. Martinek. *American Judicial Process: Myth and Reality in Law and Courts*. New York: Routledge, 2016. Print.

Del Carmen, Rolando V. *Criminal Procedure: Law and Practice*. 10th ed. Boston: Cengage, 2017.

Gifis, Steven H. *Dictionary of Legal Terms: A Simplified Guide to the Language of Law*. Hauppauge: Barron's, 2015. Print.

Lippke, Richard. "The Prosecutor and the Presumption of Innocence." *Criminal Law & Philosophy* 8.2 (2014): 337-352. Legal Source. Web. 27 May 2016.

Merlone, A. P., and A. Karnes. *The American Legal System: Foundations, Processes, and Norms*. Los Angeles, Calif.: Roxbury, 2003. Thorough introduction to the relationship between private and public law that aids in understanding the legal system.

Nemeth, C. P. *Law and Evidence: A Primer for Criminal Justice, Criminology, Law, and Legal Studies*. Upper Saddle River, N.J.: Prentice Hall, 2001. Review of the various forms of evidence, with advice on how best to utilize it.

Robinson, Paul H., and Markus D. Dubber. "The American Model Penal Code: A Brief Overview." *New Criminal Law Review* 10.3 (2007): 319-41. Web. 27 May 2016.

Domestic Violence

Buzawa, E., C. Buzawa, and E. Stark. *Responding to Domestic Violence: The Integration of Criminal Justice and Human Services*. 5th ed. Thousand Oaks, Calif.: Sage, 2017.

Conte, Jon R. *Child Abuse and Neglect Worldwide*. 3 vols. Santa Barbara: Praeger, 2014. Print.

Crosson-Tower, Cynthia. *Understanding Child Abuse and Neglect*. 9th ed. Boston: Allyn, 2014. Print.

Giardino, Angelo P., and Eileen Giardino. *Recognition of Child Abuse for the Mandated Reporter*. 4th ed. St. Louis: STM Learning, 2015. Print.

Mills, Linda G. *Insult to Injury: Rethinking Our Responses to Intimate Abuse*. Princeton, N.J.: Princeton University Press, 2003. Critique of the failure to consider racial, ethnic, and religious issues in domestic violence theories.

Roberts, Albert, ed. *Handbook of Domestic Violence Intervention Strategies: Policies, Programs, and Legal Remedies*. New York: Oxford University Press, 2002. Book designed to provide professionals with the tools necessary to address the specific needs of women and children falling victim to domestic violence.

Homicide and Capital Punishment

Baker, David V. *Women and Capital Punishment in the United States: An Analytical History.* Jefferson: McFarland, 2016. Print.

Del Carmen, Rolando V., et al. *The Death Penalty: Constitutional Issues, Commentaries, and Case Briefs.* Cincinnati, Ohio: Anderson, 2005. Survey of the history and foundation of the death penalty followed by the constitutional issues associated with its successful implementation.

Hatch, Virginia Leigh, and Anthony Walsh. *Capital Punishment: Theory and Practice of the Ultimate Penalty.* Oxford: Oxford UP, 2015. Print.

Hood, Roger, and Carolyn Hoyle. *The Death Penalty: A Worldwide Perspective.* 5th ed. New York: Oxford UP, 2015. Print.

Hickey, Eric. *Serial Murderers and Their Victims.* 4th ed. Belmont, Calif.: Thomson/Wadsworth, 2005. Detailed examination of the biological, cultural, historical, psychological, and religious factors influencing more than four hundred serial murderers throughout the world. The book features updated statistical information and profiles of some of the most famous serial killers.

Shipley, S. L., and B. A. Arrigo. *The Female Homicide Offender: Serial Murder and the Case of Aileen Wuornos.* Upper Saddle River, N.J.: Prentice Hall, 2005. Thorough examination of female criminality with special attention to the case of Aileen Wuornos.

Vollum, Scott, et al. *The Death Penalty: Constitutional Issues, Commentaries, and Case Briefs.* 3rd ed. Boston: Anderson, 2015. Print.

Juvenile Justice

Agnew, Robert, and Timothy Brezina. *Juvenile Delinquency: Causes and Control.* New York: Oxford UP, 2014. Print.

Barrington, Richard. *Juvenile Court System.* [N.p.]: Rosen Publishing Group, 2015. eBook Collection (EBSCOhost). Web. 24 May 2016.

Bartollas, Clemens, and Stuart J. Miller. *Juvenile Justice in America.* 8th ed. Boston: Pearson, 2016. Print.

Benekos, Peter J., and Alida V. Merlo. *Controversies in Juvenile Justice and Delinquency.* 2nd ed. New York: Routledge, 2015. Print.

Franzese, Robert J., et al. *Youth Gangs.* 4th ed. Springfield: Charles C. Thomas, 2016. Print.

Howell, James C. *The History of Street Gangs in the United States: Their Origins and Transformations.* Lanham: Lexington, 2015. Print.

National Center for Juvenile Justice. *Juvenile Offenders and Victims: 2014 National Report.* Pittsburgh: Natl. Center for Juvenile Justice, 2014. Print.

Nellis, Ashley. *A Return to Justice: Rethinking Our Approach to Juveniles in the System.* Lanham: Rowman, 2016. Print.

Sanborn, J. B., and A. Salerno. *The Juvenile Justice System: Law and Process.* Los Angeles, Calif.: Roxbury, 2005. Comprehensive overview of the history of juvenile justice in the United States, jurisdiction of the courts, prevalence and incidence of delinquent behavior, trial and sentencing phases, community and institutional corrections, and recommendations for the future.

Siegel, L. J., B. C. Walsh, and J. J. Senna. *Juvenile Delinquency: Theory, Practice and Law.* 9th ed. Belmont, Calif.: Thomson Learning, 2005. Overview of all facets of the juvenile justice system, including theories; social, community, and environmental influences; and the organization of the system itself.

Law Enforcement

Ariel, Barak, Farrar, William, and Sutherland, Alex. "The Effect of Police Body-Worn Cameras on Use of Force and Citizens' Complaints against the Police: A Randomized Controlled Trial." *Journal of Quantitative Criminology*, 31, no. 3 (2015): 509-35. Examination of the impacts of body-worn cameras on use of force and citizen complaints.

Brantingham, Jeffrey. *Research Brief: Predictive Policing, Forecasting Crime for Law Enforcement.* Santa Monica, Calif.: RAND Corporation, 2013.

Caldero, M. A., and J. P. Crank. *Police Ethics: The Corruption of Noble Cause.* 3rd ed., revised. London: Routledge-Taylor & Francis Group, 2015.

Goldstein, Joseph. "Judge Rejects New York's Stop-and-Frisk Policy." *New York Times.* New York Times, 12 Aug. 2013. Web. 30 May 2016.

Jones, Phill. "August Vollmer: Police Reformer." *History Magazine* 12.5 (2011): 12-13. Print.

Kiker III, C.R. (2015). From Mayberry to Ferguson: The militarization of American policing equipment, culture, and mission. Washington & Lee Law Review, 71(4/5), 282-298.

Lersch, Kim Michelle. *Policing and Misconduct.* Upper Saddle River, N.J.: Prentice Hall, 2002. Examination of the various aspects of the historical development of appropriate police conduct and ethical behavior.

Li, Victor. "50-year Story of the Miranda Warning Has the Twists of a Cop Show." *ABA Journal* (August, 2016). Discussion of Miranda warnings popularized in television and movies and its impact on actual practice.

Lum, C., C. S. Koper, and C. W. Telep. "The Evidence-Based Policing Matrix."*Journal of Experimental Criminology* 7, no. 1 (2011): 3-26.

Martinelli, Ron. *The Truth Behind the Black Lives Matter Movement and the War on Police*. Temecula, Calif.: Martinelli & Associates, 2016.

Mazerolle, L., E. Sargeant, A. Cherney, S. Bennett, K. Murphy, E. Antrobus, and P. Martin. *Procedural Justice and Legitimacy in Policing*. Switzerland: Spring International Publishing, 2014.

Panditharatne, Mekela. "When Is the Use of Force by Police Reasonable?" *Atlantic*. Atlantic Monthly Group, 17 July 2015. Web. 31 May 2016.

Rahr, S., and S. K. Rice. *From Warriors to Guardians: Recommitting American Police Culture to Democratic Ideals*. Harvard Kennedy School, New Perspectives in Policing. April, 2015. https://www.ncjrs.gov/pdffiles1/nij/248654.pdf.

Ratcliffe, J. H*Intelligence-Led Policing*. 2nd ed. London: Routledge: Taylor & Francis, 2016.

Schultz, Paul D. "The Future Is Here: Technology in Police Departments." *Police Chief*. International Association of Chiefs of Police, June 2016. Web. 20 June 2016.

Miscellaneous

2013: The Impact of Cybercrime. *Infosec Institute*. Infosec Inst., 1 Nov. 2013. Web. 1 Apr. 2015.

DNA Exonerations in the United States. *Innocence Project*. Innocence Project, 2016. Web. 27 May 2016.

Drug Courts. *National Institute of Justice*. Dept. of Justice, 13 May 2016. Web. 31 May 2016."

Federal Trade Commission. "Identity Theft Tops FTC's Consumer Complaint Categories Again in 2014." *Federal Trade Commission*. Federal Trade Commission, 27 Feb. 2015. Web. 22 July 2015.

Fischer, Eric A. *Cybersecurity Issues and Challenges: In Brief*. Washington, D.C.: Congressional Research Service Report to Congress, 2016. R43831. Discusses information and communication technologies' growth and the risk associated with cybersecurity. Lists more than fifty statutes that address cybersecurity and the federal role involved in securing systems.

Haj, Tabatha Abu El-. "Defining Peaceably: Policing the Line between Constitutionally Protected Protest and Unlawful Assembly." *Missouri Law Review* 4 (2015): 961.

Lithwick, Dahlia. "Pseudoscience in the Witness Box." *Slate*. Slate Group, 22 Apr. 2015. Web. 27 May 2016.

Marion, Nancy E., and Joshua B. Hill. *Legalizing Marijuana: A Shift in Policies across America*. Durham: Carolina Academic, 2016. Print.

Mattick, Richard P., et al. "Buprenorphine Maintenance versus Placebo or Methadone Maintenance for Opioid Dependence." *Cochrane Library*. New York: Wiley Online Library, 2014. A summary of various studies regarding the treatment of opioid addiction.

Morgan, Steve. "Cyber Crime Costs Projected To Reach $2 Trillion by 2019." *Forbes*. Forbes Media, 17 Jan. 2016. Web. 25 May 2016.

Saferstein, Richard. *Criminalistics: An Introduction to Forensic Science*. 8th ed. Upper Saddle River, N.J.: Prentice Hall, 2004. Examines the latest technological advances employed in the use of trace evidence to link offenders to crime scenes that in turn lead to eventual apprehension and prosecution.

Salter, Ann. *Predators: Pedophiles, Rapists, and Other Sex Offenders-Who They Are, How They Operate, and How We Can Protect Ourselves and Our Children*. New York: Basic Books, 2003. The authors use case histories to investigate varying types of predators and offer strategies to be employed in minimizing risks of victimization.

Terry, Karen J. *Sexual Offenses and Offenders: Theory, Practice, and Policy*. Belmont, Calif.: Thomson Learning/Wadsworth, 2005. Discussion of the history of sexual offenses, definitions, incidence, and prevalence, with information on offender typologies. The book examines such issues as Megan's law and legislation designed to combat sexual offenses.

The Prison Crisis. *American Civil Liberties Union*. ACLU, 2015. Web. 7 Dec. 2015.

UNODC. "Human Trafficking." *United Nations Office on Drugs and Crime*, 2016.

U.S. Department of Justice. *Electronic Monitoring Reduces Recidivism*. Office of Programs. National Institute of Justice. 2016. https://www.ncjrs.gov/pdffiles1/nij/234460.pdf. Study funded by the National Institute of Justices looks at Florida offenders placed on electronic monitoring and found reduction in risk of failure compared to those not under electronic monitoring.

Vera Institute of Justice. *The Potential of Community Corrections: To Improve Communities PDF and Reduce Incarceration.* New York: Vera Inst. of Justice, 2013. file.

Weston, Paul B., and Charles A. Lushbaugh. *Criminal Investigation: Basic Perspectives.* 10th ed. Upper Saddle River, N.J.: Prentice Hall, 2006. With a combined fifty years of law-enforcement experience, the authors present a comprehensive review of the basic concepts concerning all aspects of criminal investigation.

Theories

Agnew, Robert. *Why Do Criminals Offend? A General Theory of Crime and Delinquency.* Los Angeles, Calif.: Roxbury, 2004. The author integrates past and current research to develop a general theory of crime that incorporates theories of social learning, social control, self-control, strain, labeling, and social support.

Akers, R. L., and C. S. Sellers. *Criminological Theories: Introduction, Evaluation and Application.* 4th ed. Los Angeles, Calif.: Roxbury, 2004. Exhaustive review of the leading theories influencing the field of criminology, with empirical evaluations of each theory.

Bernard, T. J., J. B. Snipes, and A. L. Gerould *Vold's Theoretical Criminology.* Oxford and New York: Oxford University Press, 2016.

DeKeseredy, W. S., D. Ellis, and S. Alvi. *Deviance and Crime: Theory, Research, and Policy.* 3d ed. Cincinnati, Ohio: Anderson, 2005. Comprehensive examination of the discordance among the academic community, policymakers, and the population at large concerning the construction of social policies aimed at preventing social deviance.

Gottfredson, Michael R., and T. Hirschi. *A General Theory of Crime.* Palo Alto, Calif.: Stanford University Press, 1990. Controversial book that dismisses classical sociological theories and focuses on control theory and successful socialization as being predictors of subsequent criminality.

Thornberry, Terence P. *Developmental Theories of Crime and Delinquency.* Somerset, N.J.: Transaction, 2004. The author describes the evolution of criminal behavior that typically begins in adolescence and carries forward throughout the life course.

Vold, G. B., T. J. Bernard, and J. B. Snipes. *Theoretical Criminology.* 5th ed. New York: Oxford University Press, 2002. Overview of a wide range of theories addressing crime, including classical theory, positivism, biological and psychological theories, mainstream sociological theory, and theoretical integration.

Terrorism

Benjamin, Daniel, and Steven Simon. *The Age of Sacred Terror: Radical Islam's War Against America.* New York: Random House, 2003. Nearly a year before the September 11, 2001, attacks on the United States, the director and senior director of the National Security Council began writing this book in an attempt to warn the public about a newly emerging breed of terrorists determined to kill large numbers of Americans.

Gall, J. M. *Domestic Lone Wolf Terrorists: An Examination of Patterns in Domestic Lone Wolf Targets, Weapons, and Ideologies.* 2014. ProQuest Database ID#1651237342.

Gil, Paul. *Lone-Actor Terrorists: A Behavioural Analysis (Political Violence).* London: Routledge, 2015.

Posner, Gerald. *Why America Slept: The Failure to Prevent 9/11.* New York: Random House, 2003. Attempt to uncover the truth behind the failed U.S. intelligence investigations during the time leading up to the September 11, 2001, attacks.

Unclassified Summary of the Information Handling and Sharing Prior to the April 15, 2013 Boston Marathon Bombing, Prepared by the Inspectors General of the: Intelligence Community, Central Intelligence Agency, Department of Justice, Department of Homeland Security, April 10, 2014. https://oig.justice.gov/reports/2014/s1404.pdf.

USA Freedom Act: What's In, What's Out. *Washington Post.* Washington Post, 2 June 2015. Web. 26 May. 2016.

Criminal Behavior and Typologies

Andrews, Donald A., and James Bonta. *The Psychology of Criminal Conduct.* 5th ed. 2010. New York: Routledge, 2015. Print.

Bartol, C. R., and A. M. Bartol. *Criminal Behavior: A Psychological Approach.* 7th ed. New York: Prentice Hall, 2005. Examination of behavioral, emotional, and cognitive aspects of criminals in an effort to uncover the causes, classification, and intervention of criminals and crime.

Cassel, E., and D. A. Bernstein. *Criminal Behavior.* New York: Allyn & Bacon, 2000. Detailed exploration of the origins of criminal behavior and its development over the life courses of offenders; also includes a typology of all violent and property crimes from the perspectives of both offenders and victims.

Dabney, Dean A., ed. *Crime Types: A Text/Reader.* Belmont, Calif.: Thomson/Wadsworth, 2004. Compilation of original essays exploring typologies of homicide and assault, violent sex crimes, robbery, burglary, common property crimes, public order crimes, and organizational crime.

Glenn, Andrea L., and Adrian Raine. *Psychopathy: An Introduction to Biological Findings and Their Implications.* New York: New York UP, 2014. Print.

Violence

Barnett, O., C. L. Miller-Perrin, and R. Perrin. *Family Violence Across the Lifespan: An Introduction.* 2d ed. Thousand Oaks, Calif.: Sage Publications, 2005. Provides readers with a better understanding of the methodology, etiology, prevalence, treatment, and prevention of family violence. The chapters chronologically address the following areas as they relate to violence over the life course: child physical, sexual, and emotional abuse; courtship violence; date rape; spousal abuse; battered women; batterers; and elder abuse.

Gilbert, P. R., and K. K. Eby. *Violence and Gender: An Interdisciplinary Reader.* Upper Saddle River, N.J.: Prentice Hall, 2004. Multidisciplinary approach to understanding violent behavior in order to develop strategies for its reduction.

Gosselin, Denise Kindschi. *Heavy Hands: An Introduction to the Crimes of Intimate and Family Violence.* Boston: Pearson, 2014. Print.

Lopata, H. Z., and J. A. Levy. *Social Problems Across the Life Course.* Lanham, Md.: Rowman and Littlefield, 2003. Study of how society develops social problems through personal hardships confronted by individuals at varying stages in life.

Meadows, Robert J. *Understanding Violence and Victimization.* 3d ed. New York: Prentice Hall, 2003. Provides a multitude of varying perspectives on causes surrounding victimization, the dynamics of victim-offender relationships, and legal and behavior responses to victims.

Toch, Hans. *Violent Men: An Inquiry into the Psychology of Violence.* Washington, D.C.: American Psychological Association, 1992. Portrayal of the motivational factors, attitudes, assumptions, and perceptions among chronic violent offenders and others with established propensities toward violence.

Careers in Criminal Justice

Most of these books are similar in approach, offering descriptions of criminal justice jobs, the qualifications necessary to obtain them, and practical advice on applying for the jobs. Persons considering careers in criminal justice would do well to make sure they get hold of the latest editions of any of these books they wish to consult.

Peat, Barbara. *From College to Career: A Guide for Criminal Justice Majors.* Boston: Allyn & Bacon, 2004.

Prior, Nicole M. *Graduate Study in Criminology and Criminal Justice : A Program Guide.* Hoboken: Routledge, 2015. eBook Collection (EBSCOhost). Web. 25 May 2016.

Stephens, W. Richard. *Careers in Criminal Justice.* 2d ed. Boston: Allyn & Bacon, 2003.

Stinchcomb, James. *Opportunities in Law Enforcement and Criminal Justice Careers.* 2d ed. New York: McGraw-Hill, 2002.

Lisa Landis Murphy
Updated by the Editors

Glossary

abuse of discretion. Standard that an appellate court uses to reverse actions or decisions of a lower court that are clearly wrong.

accessory. Person who secondarily assists in the commission of a crime.

Adam Walsh Child Protection and Safety Act (2006). A law containing a variety of provisions to protect the public, especially children, from violent sex offenders and abuse by creating national registries and increasing prison sentences.

accomplice liability. Liability for assisting someone else commit a crime.

accused/accused person. Person formally charged with having committed a crime; a defendant.

acquittal. Judgment of a criminal court-based on the verdict of a jury or, in cases without a jury, on the court's decision, that a criminal defendant is not guilty of the crimes charged against that defendant.

actus reus. Act that violates the law; a guilty act.

adjudication. Arrival by a court at a decision.

adversary system. System-such as prevails in the United States-in which the opposing parties in a case rather than the judge have the primary responsibility for presenting evidence necessary to decide the case.

advocate-witness rule. Rule of legal ethics that generally prohibits an attorney from acting both as an advocate and a witness in the same case.

affidavit. Written statement made under oath.

aggravation/aggravating circumstances. Circumstances relating to the commission of a crime that cause it to be treated more seriously than average instances of the same crime.

alcohol. A volatile flammable liquid that is the intoxicating constituent of wine, beer, spirits, and other drinks.

alias. Alternative name under which a person is known.

American Bar Association. Most prominent national association of lawyers in the United States.

ACLU. American Civil Liberties Union, an organization devoted to protecting individual rights.

Alexander Maconochie. A British administrator who is credited with one of the first attempts to introduce the ideas of rehabilitation and treatment of prisoners as people with personal dignity into the penal system.

amicus curiae **brief.** Brief filed with a court by persons or organizations who are interested in the issues raised by a case even though they are not official parties to the case.

amnesty. Pardon granted to a person guilty of having committed a political crimes.

annotated codes. Statutes organized by topic and accompanied by brief descriptions of cases referring to the statutes.

antitrust law. Legislation that provides for civil and criminal penalties against businesses that act or conspire unreasonably to limit competition in the marketplace.

appeal. Request to a higher court to review the decision of a lower court.

appearance. Act of coming into a court and submitting to that court's authority.

appellant. Person who is appealing the decision of a lower court to a higher court.

appellate jurisdiction. Authority of a higher court to hear a case appealed from a lower court.

appellee. Person who receives a favorable decision in a lower court that is being appealed by another person, an appellant, to a higher court.

arraignment. Point in criminal proceeding when the accused of a crime is brought before a court to be informed of the charges against the person and to enter a plea as to those charges.

arrest. Act of taking a person into custody for the purpose of charging that person with having committed a crime.

arrest warrant. Document issued by a judicial officer directing a law-enforcement officer to arrest a person accused of committing a crime.

arson. Unlawful destruction of property by fire or explosion.

assault. Attempt to inflict bodily harm on another, even if such harm is not inflicted. When combined with actual physical harm, it becomes assault and battery.

Assembly Bill 109. California legislation and policy to reduce overcrowding in state-run prisons that is the centerpiece of realignment legislation. The law was designed to lower the number of individuals sentenced to prison in part through making greater use of local jail-based sentences.

asset forfeiture. Government seizure of personal property derived from, or connected to, criminal activity.

assignment of error. Points made by party appealing a case that specify the mistakes allegedly made by a lower court.

attempt. Effort to commit a crime that may be punished even if crime is not carried out.

attorney. Person who, with appropriate education and training, is admitted to practice law in a particular jurisdiction and thus authorized to advise and represent other persons in legal proceedings.

Auburn Prison. A prison system of corrections that began in Auburn, New York in 1817 and developed a silent system of confinement that allowed prisoners to assemble with each other.

authenticate. To demonstrate that an item is genuine.

Autopsy. Medical examination of a dead body undertaken to determine the cause and other circumstances of a death.

aver. To allege or assert.

background check. Search undertaken to verify the identity of, and information about, an individual.

bail bond. Agreement made by one party to procure the release of a criminal defendant that specifies that the party will pay a specified amount if the defendant thereafter fails to appear in court.

bail. Money or other property given to obtain the release from custody of a criminal defendant and to guarantee that the defendant will thereafter appear in court.

bail-enforcement agent/bail agent. *See* **Bounty hunter**

bailiff. Person assigned to keep order in a courtroom and superintend arrangements for the jury.

ballistics. Analysis of firearms, ammunition, and explosive devices.

bar exams. Comprehensive tests of legal knowledge given to persons desiring to become lawyers as a condition to earning the right to practice law.

battered child and battered wife syndromes. Reactions to violence perpetrated by parents, guardians, or spouses that lead victims to adopt coping mechanisms that may lock them into cycles of violence.

battery. Harmful touching of another.

bench warrant. Order issued by a court directing that a law-enforcement officer bring the person named in the warrant before the court, usually because that person has failed to obey a previous order of the court to appear.

beyond a reasonable doubt. Degree of proof required to convict a person accused of having committed a crime.

bifurcated trial. Legal proceeding in which two or more separate hearings, or trials, are held on different issues of the same case.

bigamy. Crime of marrying a person while a previous marriage to another person is still in effect; usually characterized by deceit.

Bill Cosby. An entertainer who came to the forefront of national attention as his prosecution for scores of alleged assaults facilitated by drugs began.

bill of attainder. Unconstitutional action by a legislature that singles out particular persons for punishment without a trial.

bill of attainder. Legislative act that assigns a penalty to a person or group of people.

bill of particulars. Detailed document itemizing charges against a defendant.

Bill of Rights, U.S. First ten amendments to the United States Constitution, which safeguard various individual liberties, including rights for persons suspected, or accused, of having committed crimes.

billable hours. Hours spent working on a client's matter, for which a lawyer bills an agreed upon hourly rate.

Black Lives Matter Movement. A movement that focusses attention on the perceived mistreatment of African Americans by law enforcement.

Black Nationalist Movement. A movement that came to the forefront in the 1960s whose proponents advocated racial pride, separatism, and economic self-sufficiency for African Americans.

Black's Law Dictionary. Foremost American dictionary of legal terms.

blackmail. Attempt to extort money by the threat of inflicting violence upon or exposing some wrongdoing of another; closely related to extortion.

blended sentences. Types of sentences in which judges simultaneously impose both juvenile and adult sanctions on juvenile offenders.

blue laws. State and local regulations banning certain activities, particularly on Sundays.

Blue Lives Matter Movement. A movement in the United States that was founded by law enforcement officers and others who honor the actions of police and work against slander, illegitimate complaints, frivolous legal suits, and physical attacks against them.

body-worn cameras. Video-recording cameras that are mounted somewhere on a police officer's body, used for recording what happens during police-citizen encounters.

booking. Official entry of a record of detention after the arrest of a person identifying the person arrested.

boot camps. Alternative form of incarceration using rigid discipline modeled on military training camps.

boot camps. Alternative form of incarceration using rigid discipline modeled on military training camps.

border patrols. Units of a federal agency that oversees the coastal and land boundaries of the United States.

bounty hunter/bail-enforcement agent/bail agent. Person who tracks bail skippers, defendants who flee after bail-bond companies post their bail.

breach of the peace. Disturbance of public order.

bribery. Attempt to influence some public person in the discharge of a public duty by offering something of value to the person.

brief. Concise statement of the facts and arguments in a case, or a written document presenting an argument to a court about some matter.

broken windows. Theory that posits a relationship between neighborhood disorder and serious crime.

Brown v. Plata **(2011).** A US Supreme Court decision that held a court-mandated population limit was needed to remedy a violation of prisoners' Eighth Amendment Rights.

bullying. A type of physical, verbal, and/or psychological aggression that generally occurs within or outside of school.

buprenorphine. An opioid derivative drug used in the treatment of opioid addiction.

Burden of proof. Duty of prosecution to prove a particular issue in a case; in criminal cases, for example, the duty of the prosecutor to prove beyond a reasonable doubt that an individual has committed a crime.

burglary. Entrance into a building for the purpose of committing a felony such as theft.

campus police. Law-enforcement departments based on college and university campuses.

capital crime. Crime punishable by death.

capital punishment. Punishment by death.

carjacking. Theft of a vehicle that is committed while the vehicle owner is inside or near the vehicle.

case law. Law derived from the decisions of courts.

cease-and-desist order. Order from court or agency prohibiting certain persons or entities from continuing certain conduct.

certiorari, **writ of.** Application to the United States Supreme Court, or a state appellate court, seeking review of a lower court decision.

Cesare Beccaria. An Age of Enlightenment Italian thinker and founder of the classical school of criminology who proposed that prison sentences would be a more appropriate response to crime and would have the benefit of deterring further offending and encouraging offenders to reform.

chain gang. Group of prisoners who are chained together while performing manual labor outside a prison or work camp.

chain of custody. Account of the possession of the evidence from its discovery and initial possession until it is offered as evidence in court.

change of venue. Relocation of a trial from one jurisdiction to another.

chambers. Private office of a judge.

charge. Claim that an individual has committed a specific criminal offense.

check kiting. Unlawful use of two or more checking accounts to write worthless checks.

child abduction. The kidnapping of a child.

child abuse. An act or failure to act on that results in a child's serious physical or emotional harm, sexual abuse, exploitation or death.

child pornography. Depiction of erotic behavior focusing on children that is intended to arouse sexual excitement.

children's advocacy centers. Child-friendly, safe and neutral locations in which law enforcement and Child Protective Services investigators may conduct and observe forensic interviews with children who are alleged victims of crimes, and where the child and non-offending family members receive support, crisis intervention services etc.

Christopher Simmons. A juvenile offender who was convicted of murder and sentenced to death but it was overturn and he instead was sentenced to life imprisonment without the possibility of parole.

circumstantial evidence. Evidence from which a primary issue may be inferred.

citation. Order issued by a court or law-enforcement officer requiring a person to appear in court.

cite. To order someone to appear in court; to refer to legal authority in support of one's argument.

citizen's arrest. Taking of a person into physical custody by a witness to a crime other than a law-enforcement officer, for the purpose of delivering the person into the physical custody of law-enforcement officials.

civil commitment. The legal process allowing the involuntary hospitalization and treatment of a person with mental illness who is dangers to self or others.

civil disobedience. Deliberate act of law breaking undertaken to dramatize or protest a law or governmental policy that the offender regards as immoral.

civilian review board. Official group of citizens who examine the merits of complaints against members of the local police department.

clear and present danger test. Principle holding that political speech is protected unless it creates a "clear and present danger" to the nation.

clearance rate. Ratio of crimes reported as to the number of crimes solved.

clemency. Act of an executive official reducing a criminal sentence as a matter of leniency.

clerk of the court. Court official who maintains the court's official records and files.

closing argument. Summary of the arguments in a case made by the prosecution and the defense at the conclusion of a trial.

code of silence. Police officers covering for each other's unethical conduct by not informing on each other.

club drugs. Designer drugs (also called synthetic drugs) manufactured for recreational use.

COINTELPRO. Secret federal government counterintelligence programs designed to neutralize radical political organizations in the United States during the late 1950's and 1960's.

cold case. Unsolved criminal case, usually involving a homicide, on which active police work has ceased.

collaborative responses. Joint reactions among allied professionals and community leaders to provide victims services.

Colman v. Brown **(1995).** A federal court in Sacramento, CA held that California Department of Corrections and Rehabilitation violated the cruel and unusual punishment clause of the Constitution because they did not supply adequate mental health care.

color of law. Action that has the appearance of authority and legality but is actually unauthorized and illegal.

commercialized vice. Business enterprises catering to various human desires that lead to statutory crimes; examples include prostitution, gambling, and pornography.

common law. Body of law, going back into early English history, that arises from judicial decisions, rather than from written statutes, that reflect customs, tradition and precedent.

community-based corrections. Use of sentencing options that permit a convicted offender to remain in a community under conditional supervision rather than serve a sentence in prison.

community-oriented policing. Philosophy of law enforcement that encompasses aspects of social service as police officers work with members of the communities.

community service. Sentencing arrangement that requires criminal offenders to spend time performing public service supervised by a community agency.

competency, legal. Capacity to understand and to act rationally.

Comprehensive Drug Abuse Prevention and Control Act (1970). The act created a five-level classification tier that placed marijuana in the most severe Schedule 1 drug category.

CompStat. Use of computerized data to identify crime hot spots and facilitate resource deployment and accountability for crime control.

compulsory process. Right of a person charged with a crime to summon witnesses to court on his behalf.

computer crime. Illegal intrusions into computers and the use of computers for the perpetration of other crimes.

computer forensics. Search of computers, networks, and communication devices for existing or deleted electronic-evidence.

computer information system. System designed to bring together people, computers, and departmental rules and procedures to gather, store, retrieve, analyze, and apply information to meet an organizations' goals.

concurrent jurisdiction. Authority of two or more courts to hear the same case.

concurrent sentence. Sentence imposed after conviction of a crime that is to be served at the same time as a sentence for another crime.

concurring opinion. Judicial opinion that agrees with the result in the case reached by other judges but states different reasons for this result.

conditions of confinement. The scope of those rights through judicial opinions rendered in response to lawsuits brought to challenge conditions of living while incarcerated, including food and clothing.

confession. Admission of guilt.

conjugal rights. Rights of married couples including companionship and sex.

conjugal visit. A visit for a prisoner who is permitted to spend time in private in which sex is permitted.

consecutive sentence. Sentence served in sequence after a sentence for another crime, thus increasing the maximum to an offender is incarcerated.

consequences of victimization. The diverse material, physical, social, and emotional effects of crime upon individual victims.

consent decree. Court decree based upon the agreement of the parties to a case.

consent search. Search by law enforcement that is based on permission, usually given by the party who is the object of the search.

conspiracy. Agreement among two or more parties to commit a criminal act.

Constitution, U.S.. Law: Foundation document representing the supreme law of the United States of America, as applied to the body of law dealing with offenses against the state, which may be penalized by fine or imprisonment.

Constitutional issues. Important questions about the meaning of the Constitution that stimulates disagreement.

consumer fraud. Intentional deception of consumers with untruthful or misleading information about goods, services, and other aspects of business.

contempt of court. Conduct that disobeys a court order, disrupts court proceedings, or undermines the dignity of a court.

contingency fees. Fee (not generally permitted in criminal cases) payable to a lawyer only if the lawyer achieves some successful result.

continuance. Delay of court proceedings until some future date.

contributing to delinquency of minors. Acts or omissions perpetrated by adults that encourage juveniles to engage in behaviors that may lead to delinquency.

controlled substance. Drug proscribed by law, such as marijuana, cocaine, and heroin.

conviction. Final determination that a criminal defendant is guilty made as a result of a trial or a plea bargain.

coroner. Public official who investigates the circumstances of violent or suspicious deaths; may or may not also be a medical examiner.

corporal punishment. Physical punishment.

corpus delicti. Meaning literally, "the body of crime," and referring to facts that demonstrate a crime has occurred.

corrections. A term frequently referring to prison and jail confinement, and community-based programs for offenders.

corroborate. To support or confirm.

categorical imperative. The viewpoint of the criminal justice system that nonviolence and social justice are the foundations of the system

Council on Human Trafficking. A group of eight to 14 victims of human trafficking to advise policymakers as they develop initiatives pursuant to the Victims' Rights and Restitution Act of 1990.

counsel, right to. Entitlement provided for criminal defendants by the U.S. Constitution to receive representation by an attorney during a criminal proceeding.

counterfeiting. Copying something and illegally passing the copy off as an original.

Court Appointed Special Advocates (CASA). A national association in the United States that supports and promotes court-appointed advocates for abused or neglected children in order to provide children with a safe and healthy environment in permanent homes.

court reporter. Person who creates a verbatim record of proceedings in court.

court-martial. Military tribunal convened to try members of the armed forces accused of violating the Uniform Code of Military Justice.

crime. Any violation of a criminal law that bans or commands acts whose commission or omission are subject to penalties.

crime analysis. Use of methodological strategies for analyzing crime data and other data to facilitate deployment of resources.

Crime Index. Part of the Federal Bureau of Investigation's annual Uniform Crime Reports that is the most complete compilation of national reported crime statistics for the eight most serious types of crime, as determined by the FBI.

Crime Control Act (1990). This was a large law enacted by Congress during the George H.W. Bush administration that had considerable impact on the juvenile crime control policies of the 1990s.

crime lab. Facility-mostly government-run-designed to analyze physical evidence of crimes.

crime of passion. Crime committed under the influence of strong emotion.

crime scene investigation. Meticulous preservation of physical evidence at specific locations by use of photographs, sketches, and collection and preservation.

criminal. Perpetrator of criminal offenses.

criminal history record information. Record, or a system of records, that includes the identification of a person and describes that person's arrests and subsequent .

criminal intent. Wrongful or guilty purpose.

criminal justice system. Interrelationships among all law-enforcement bodies, the courts, corrections, and juvenile justice through the United States.

criminal law. Body of law that defines criminal offenses and sets out appropriate punishments for convicted offenders.

criminal liability. Accountability under criminal law.

criminal negligence. Act that fails to exercise the appropriate care needed to avoid foreseeable harmful consequences.

Glossary

criminal procedure. Stages and points at which particular decisions are made in the criminal justice process that are mandated by statutes and constitutional judicial decisions.

criminal record. Official documents that list an individual person's past convictions for misdemeanors and felonies and that sometimes include arrests that do not result in convictions.

criminal victimization. Those who are made into victims as a result of someone who commits a crime.

criminology. Interdisciplinary field that relies heavily on scientific methods to study crime phenomena, including patterns and rates of crime and victimization, etiology of crime, social responses to crime, and crime control.

cross-examination. Questioning of a witness called by an opponent in a court proceeding.

cruel and unusual punishment. Punishment that is disproportionately severe in relation to a crime or otherwise excessive.

cryptology. Science of enciphering and deciphering codes, ciphers and cryptograms.

culpable. Worthy of criminal sanction.

cultural defense. Legal defense designed to diminish or eliminate criminal responsibility by establishing that the cultural traditions of the defendants have led them reasonably to believe in the propriety of their otherwise criminal acts.

cyber bullying. Bullying that occurs online.

cybercrime. Crimes that involve use of the Internet and computers.

dark figure of crime. Crimes unknown to the police, usually because they were not reported by the victim or a witness.

date rape. Rape committed by a person with whom the victim is voluntarily engaging in a social outing.

de minimus. Legal matter that is considered trivial or unimportant.

deadly force. Killing of people by police officers through the use of choke holds, firearms, or other methods of physical control.

death certificate. Official document recording the fact of an individual's death.

death qualification. Procedure used in selecting jury members to try death-penalty cases.

death-row attorney. Lawyer who specializes in representing criminal defendants sentenced to death in appeals of their convictions.

declaratory judgment. Court order declaring the rights or obligations of parties without awarding monetary relief or specifically ordering any party to act or not act in particular ways.

decriminalization. Process of lessening or removing penalties for violations of specified laws.

default. Failure to perform some legal duty.

defendant. Person accused of having committed a crime in a criminal case.

defendant self-representation. Situations in which criminal defendants reject professional legal counsel and represent themselves.

defense attorneys. Attorneys who are engaged to represent criminal defendants and are usually paid by the clients.

defenses to crime. Justifications and excuses offered by criminal defenses in attempts to win cases or have charges dropped or reduced.

deportation. Removal of a person from a country.

deposition. Questioning of a witness under oath outside of court that is transcribed by a court reporter or otherwise recorded.

desistance from crime. The cessation of crime commission.

determinate sentence. A prison or jail sentence that has a defined length and cannot be changed by a parole board or other agency.

deterrence. Effect of discouraging individuals from future involvement in criminal conduct that is produced-or believed to be produced-by harsh punishments of convicted offenders.

dictum. Language in a court opinion that is not necessary to the decision.

dilatory tactics. Attempts to delay the progress of a legal proceeding.

diminished capacity. Defense tactic used to reduce the culpability of a criminal defendant.

diplomatic immunity. Legal immunity that exempts foreign diplomats and their families from the laws of the host countries in which they work.

direct examination. Questioning of a witness by the party who called the witness.

diplomatic immunity. Freedom of diplomatic personnel from prosecution for crimes in the country in which they are posted.

discovery, pretrial. Procedures for allowing parties to a court case to exchange and discover relevant information prior to the trial.

discretion. Flexibility allowed to the police and the courts to make decisions such as whether to arrest and prosecute individuals and the s.

discrimination. Treating persons or matters differently when no reasonable grounds exists for doing so.

dismiss, motion to. Motion made by defense in a criminal case arguing that grounds exist to discontinue charges against a defendant without a trial, or-in some cases after a trial has begun-without submitting case to a jury for a verdict.

dismissal. Formal termination of a legal proceeding.

disorderly conduct. Illegal conduct that disturbs the public peace.

dissenting opinion. In cases, such as appeal cases, decided by more than one judge, an opinion written by one or more judges who believe a case should have been decided with a different result than that adopted by a majority of the court.

district attorney. Prosecuting attorney who represents the government within a particular judicial district.

diversion. Decision that may be made at several stages of the juvenile justice process to avoid formal court processing.

DNA testing. Comparison of DNA (deoxyribonucleic acid) samples from body tissues and fluids to identify people.

docket. Brief record of the proceedings in a case.

document analysis. Forensic techniques used to ascertain the authenticity of documents.

domestic violence. Emotional, sexual, or other physical abuse committed by a spouse, intimate partner, or other relatives living in the same household.

double jeopardy. To expose a criminal defendant a second time to prosecution for an offense for which the defendant has already been acquitted or that has already been finally dismissed.

Dr. Benjamin Rush. A signer of the Declaration of Independence who also established the Philadelphia Society for Alleviating the Miseries of Public Prisons.

drive-by shooting. Use of firearms to shoot at people from a moving vehicle passing through a neighborhood; typically associated with gang violence.

drug court. Less formal alternative to regular criminal courts in which drug-related offenses are adjudicated.

"drug czar". Nickname for the federal government official in charge of the Office of National Drug Control Policy.

Drug Enforcement Agency. A federal drug law enforcement organization.

drunk driving/DUI. Operating or controlling a motor vehicle while under the influence of intoxicants; also known as "driving under the influence" (DUI).

due process of law. Constitutional requirement that individuals be accorded legal procedures consistent with the orderly operation of law and with fundamental rights.

DUI. *See* **drunk driving/DUI**

due process of law. Fundamental principle of fairness in all legal matters, both civil and criminal, especially in the courts. All legal procedures set by statute and court practice, including notice of rights, must be followed for each individual so that no prejudicial or unequal treatment will result.

due process revolution. A movement of the 1960s and 1970s that allowed prisoners to receive privileges during incarceration, such as access to television, extra recreation time etc.

duress. Condition under which a person is forced to act against his or her will.

Eastern State Penitentiary. A Pennsylvania prison opened in 1829 (also known as Cherry Hill State Prison) designed by John Haviland in the panoptican prison style.

e-commerce. A transaction of buying or selling online.

effective counsel. Legal representation of clients by fully qualified attorneys who are committed to providing their clients with the best possible.

electronic surveillance. Investigative techniques used to monitor telephone conversations, electronic mail, pagers, wireless phones, computers, and other electronic devices.

Eighth Amendment. A part of the Bill of Rights that offers protection against cruel and unusual punishment.

embezzlement. Unlawful appropriation of money or property held in trust by one person for another.

emotional recovery from victimization. Victimization recovery is a process that generally progresses from an immediate, to an intermediate, and then to a final stage.

en banc. Decision of a case by all of the judges who serve on court.

enjoin. To command that something be done or not done.

entrapment. Unlawful or improper inducement of one to commit a crime.

Glossary

environmental crimes. Violations of environmental laws, such as the dumping and discharging of pollutants into the atmosphere and water and the illegal production, handling, use, and disposal of toxic substances and hazardous wastes.

equal protection of the law. Constitutional requirement that persons similarly situated be accorded the same treatment under law.

espionage. Attempting to secure secret information from a country or a company, using illegal or covert means.

ethics. Sets of moral principles and values that differentiate between good and bad behavior.

euthanasia. Intentional taking of the life of another or allowing, through intentional neglect, another life to end.

evidence-based policing. Empirically based approach to crafting policing strategies.

evidence, rules of. Rules governing the admissibility of all forms of evidence at trial.

ex parte. Communication, typically with a judge, by only one side of a case without the other side's knowledge or participation.

ex post facto laws. Laws enacted "after the fact" of actions or occurrences that retrospectively alter the legal consequences of those original actions or occurrences.

exclusionary rule. Rule of constitutional criminal procedure that prevents the use of evidence in a criminal trial that was obtained illegally.

Execution. Carrying out of death penalty.

execution of judgment. Process of carrying into effect the orders, judgments, or decrees of courts.

expert witness. Person who offers testimony in a legal proceeding based on a specialized knowledge of a subject.

extended family visit. This phrase is the current term for conjugal visits to preserve family life for prisoners.

extortion. Use of illegal threats by one party to obtain money or property from another; closely related to blackmail.

extradition. Surrender by one country to another of a person accused or convicted of a crime in the other country.

Eye Movement Desensitization and Reprocessing (EMDR). A therapeutic modality frequently used with those suffering from post-traumatic stress disorder.

eyewitness testimony. Account given by a person who have directly observed a crimes or an action related to a crime.

frankpledge. Ancient system of policing in which communities policed themselves under the auspices of an often absentee noble.

false conviction. Occasion in which an innocent person os convicted of a crimes that the person did not commit.

felony. Serious crime, as distinguished from a misdemeanor, normally punishable by death or a prison sentence rather than a jail sentence.

female offenders. Women and girls who commit crime.

feminist criminology. A discipline that examines women's position in relation to authority structures, both public and private, as a way both to explain lower rates of crime by women as well as to explain the crimes that women do commit.

feminism. A gender based distinction begun only by late 20th century.

fiduciary. Person with special obligation to act on another's behalf.

fine. Monetary payment required of a defendant that provides compensation to either the government or the victim of the defendant's crime.

firearm. Small weapon that uses gunpowder to fire lethal projectiles.

First Amendment. A part of the Bill of Rights prohibiting making law against free exercise of religion, speech, freedom of the press, right to peaceably assemble, or prohibit the petitioning for governmental redress of grievances.

first-degree murder. Willful, premeditated murder.

forensic accounting. Integration of accounting, auditing, and investigative skills to assist in legal investigations of possible fraud and other whit.

forensic anthropology. Analysis and identification of human skeletal remains that sometimes uses archaeological methods to recover buried remains.

forensic entomology. Use of insects and their by-products as evidence in legal investigation, prosecution, and defense.

forensic odontology. Examination of teeth to identify human remains, or to match bite marks to the teeth of an individual.

forensic palynology. Use of pollen and spore data to help solve crimes.

forensic psychology. Application of psychology to legal issues.

forensics. Application of science to the legal arena, particularly criminal investigations.

forestry camp. Minimum-security facility in which low-risk adult and juvenile offenders work with local, state, and federal forestry departments to maintain public forests.

forgery. Illegal creation of a document or alternation of an existing document to accomplish a fraudulent purpose.

Foucha v. Louisiana **(1992).** A Supreme Court case where the court ruled that dangerousness alone, without the presence of a serious and severe mental illness was not enough to support civil commitment.

Fourteenth Amendment. A Constitutional amendment that addresses citizenship rights and equal protection of the laws.

fraud. Intentional misrepresentation or distortion of facts.

fugitive. Person who flees from justice to avoid being tried or serving a sentence.

fusion centers. Two or more institutions at the state or local level that pool criminal information for centralized analysis and then disseminate the end-product as criminal intelligence to an appropriate end-user.

gag order. Court order that prevents parties, attorneys, or others from discussing matters pertaining to a case.

gambling. Playing of games and placing of bets to win money or other prizes; may be legal or illegal, depending on the jurisdiction and the form that the gambling takes.

gang validation. A process whereby prisoners could be assigned to solitary confinement simply for being associated with a gang by means of reliance on confidential informants, tattoos, certain types of literature and/or passing acquaintances.

gangster. Member of a professional crime organization; the term is most closely associated with criminals during the Prohibition era of the 1920's and early 1930's, when organized crime profited from the sale of illegally alcohol.

George Zimmerman. A neighborhood watch leader who shot and killed Trayvon Martin.

guardian ad litem. A person or program appointed by the court to link children with emergency and social services, investigate allegations of abuse, conduct home studies for short and long term placement, and advocate for abused children throughout the criminal justice process.

geographic information system. System that is used to plot and analyze geographic locations of such data as crimes.

gendered structures. Understanding gender as a part of our social structure.

good time. Reduction of prison sentences based on good behavior or participation in some kind of program by inmates.

graffiti. Unauthorized drawing, writing, or painting on a surface in a public space.

grand jury. Citizens appointed to here evidence relating to crimes and to determine whether criminal indictments should be brought against particular individuals.

habeas corpus, **writ of.** Application to a court to consider whether a person held in custody is being held lawfully.

halfway house. Supervised-living facility, usually in an urban area, that provide an alternative to incarceration that midway between incarceration and release.

harmless error. Legal mistake made during the course of a defendants' progress through the justice system that is not considered to be damaging.

hate crime. Crime perpetrated against a person because of the person's race, ethnicity, religion, sexual orientation, or other group characteristic.

hate crime statutes. Laws that impose penalties or increase penalties for crimes motivated by racial prejudice or other specified forms of hatred.

hearing. Legal proceeding other than a trial in which evidence is taken or legal arguments presented.

hearsay. Out-of-court statement offered to prove the truth of some matter at issue in a legal proceeding.

heroin. A highly addictive opiate drug typically used recreationally for its euphoric effects.

high-speed chase. Vehicular pursuit by law-enforcement officers of a suspected or known criminal or traffic law violator.

highway patrol. State government law-enforcement agency whose primary responsibilities are traffic management and traffic law enforcement.

hit-and-run accident. Vehicular accident in which the responsible driver leaves the scene prior to the arrival of police.

homicide. Killing of another person.

house arrest. Intermediate form of sanction that allows offenders to remain in their homes under specific restrictions.

human sex trade. A type of slavery that involves the transport or trade of people for the purpose of work in the commercial sex industry.

human trafficking. The recruitment, transport, transfer, harboring, or receipt of a person by such means as threat or use of force or other forms of coercion, of abduction, of fraud or deception for the purpose of exploitation.

hung jury. Jury that cannot agree to the extent specified by law-whether unanimously or otherwise-on a verdict.

identity theft. Crime of wrongfully obtaining and personal data of others for one's own profit.

ignorance of the law. Criminal defense based on defendants' claims to have been ignorant of the laws they have broken.

illegal alien. Colloquial term for a foreign-born person who enters the United States without legal authorization or one who enters legally but violates the terms of admission or fails to acquire permanent residence status.

immunity from prosecution. Legally binding promise not to prosecute a potential defendant, typically offered in exchange for testimony.

impanel. To select and install the members of a jury.

impeach. To discredit the testimony of a witness, or, of judges or other public officials, to accuse of wrongdoing.

importation model. A paradigm indicating that prison subcultures are formed from what inmates bring into the prison from their criminal lives.

in forma pauperis. Latin phrase, meaning "as a poor pauper," that is applied to legal matters involving poor persons.

inalienable. Incapable of being transferred or surrendered, such as inalienable rights.

incapacitation. Aim or rationale of punishment that seeks to control crime by rendering a criminal unable, or less able, to commit crimes, such as incarceration of the offender.

inchoate crime. Crime that is intended to lead to another crime, such as the crime of solicitation to commit murder.

incompetent to stand trial. Condition, often the result of a mental illness, under which a criminal defendant is unable to understand the charges and proceedings against him or to assist in the preparation of his own defense.

incorporation doctrine. Process through which the U.S. Supreme Court has extended U.S. Bill of Rights protections to the states.

incorrigible. Not capable of being reformed.

indecent exposure. Unlawful and intentional exposure in public places of one's normally covered body parts.

incriminate. To provide evidence that would implicate someone, including one's self, in having committed a crime.

indeterminate sentencing. System of awarding prison sentences whose terms are defined by minimum and maximum lengths.

indictment. Formal accusation made by a grand jury that a particular individual has committed a crime.

indigent. Poor.

information. Formal accusation by a public official such as a judge that an individual has committed a crime, used in many states as an alternative to a grand jury indictment.

injunction. Order by a court for someone to do or not do something.

illicit drugs. Include a broad category of substances such as marijuana, heroin, crack/cocaine, methamphetamines, hallucinogens, and others.

inquest. Official investigation of whether a crime has occurred, especially in connection with a death.

insanity. In criminal law, the state of being either temporarily or permanently unaware of one's actions, or unable to determine whether one's actions are right or wrong.

insanity defense. Defense tactic used to reduce the culpability of a criminal defendant.

insider trading. Purchase or sale of securities by persons who have access to information that is not available to those with whom they deal or traders generally.

insurance fraud. Willful misrepresentations or fabrications by claimants or providers of facts concerning accidents, injuries, or thefts for the purpose of monetary gain.

intelligence-led policing. Law enforcement strategy in which data are used to help target crime fighting resources to the areas of greatest need.

internal affairs. Units within police departments that investigate charges of police misconduct.

international law. Body of international norms and practices established by national governments to deter and to punish criminal acts of international consequence.

international tribunal. Court established by countries at the regional or global level to try war criminals.

interpol. International Criminal Police Organization, the largest international police organization in the world.

involuntary manslaughter. Unintentional killing that is not murder but for which criminal liability is imposed.

interlocutory. Temporary or provisional action, such as a court order pending a final determination of some matter or an appeal pending the conclusion of a trial.

J.D. Doctor of jurisprudence; a post graduate degree normally necessary to practice law in the United States.

jails. Facilities normally under the jurisdiction of a local government that lawfully confines people who are convicted of minor crimes or who are confined while awaiting trial.

James Rowland. The first person to advocate for victim impact statements to provide a balanced picture of both the offender and victim when determining appropriate sentences for offenders.

Jaycee Lee Dugard. Was freed and released to her family after 18 years in captivity.

jaywalking. Crossing of public streets at illegal locations.

Jeremy Bentham. An Age of Enlightenment English thinker and founder of the classical school of criminology who proposed that prison sentences would be a more appropriate response to crime and would have the benefit of deterring further offending and encouraging offenders to reform.

Jim Crow laws. Discriminatory laws of the past that were designed to disfranchise and segregate African Americans in the South.

John Howard. An English prison reformer who campaigned for improved conditions in prisons and jails.

judge. Appointed or elected public official who is charged with authoritatively and impartially resolving disputes presented in a court of law.

judicial review. Power of courts to review the constitutionality of actions taken by other branches of government.

jurisdiction. Authority of a court to hear and decide a particular case.

jurisprudence. Philosophy of law.

jury duty. Obligation of citizens to respond to summonses to serve the legal system by hearing evidence and rendering decisions in trials.

jury nullification. For a jury to render a verdict inconsistent with law.

jury sequestration. Confinement of a jury during a trial or jury deliberations to prevent jury members from being improperly influenced by contact with others.

just deserts. Concept that punishments for crimes should match the severity of the crimes themselves.

justice. Administration of rewards and punishments according to rules and principles that society considers fair and equitable.

justifiable homicide. Killing of another person, as in self-defense, that is permitted by law.

juvenile court. Court specializing in cases involving juvenile offenders.

juvenile death penalty. The Roper v. Simmons (2005) case held that the execution of juveniles was forbidden under the Eighth and Fourteenth Amendment's cruel and unusual punishment.

juvenile delinquent/juvenile offender. Minor who has committed a crime.

juvenile waiver to adult courts. Formal process of moving a case from a juvenile court to an adult court.

Kansas v. Hendricks **(1997).** A United States Supreme Court case ruling that the Sexually Violent Predator Act permitting the indefinite, involuntary civil commitment of offenders convicted of sex offenses the state regards as dangerous due to a mental defect was constitutional.

kidnaping. Unlawful detention of a person by force against the person's will.

larceny. Illegal taking of another's personal property with the intent to steal it.

latent evidence. Evidence that is left behind by fingers or other body parts that come into contact with; such evidence is typically biological material.

law enforcement. Component of the criminal justice system that is responsible for such functions as crime prevention and fighting, order maintenance, conflict management, and other services.

LGBTQ. An acronym referring to lesbian, gay bisexual, transgender, and questioning individuals who do not identify as heterosexual.

Lifetime electronic monitoring (LEM). The Jessica Lunsford Act of 2005 mandates a minimum sentence of 25 years in prison and lifetime electronic monitoring for adults who have been convicted for certain sex crimes against children less than 12 years old.

LSAT. Law School Admission Test; a standardized test used to measure the qualifications of potential law students.

leading question. Question asked during the examination of a witness that suggests the answer desired; generally permitted during cross examination of a witness but not the direct examination of a witness.

Lindbergh law. Congressional legislation making kidnapping for ransom and carrying victims across state lines a federal crime.

lesser-included offense. Crime necessarily proven by proof that a more serious crime has been committed.

loitering. Standing idle or wandering about aimlessly without a lawful purpose.

lone wolf. An individual, acting alone, who undertakes a terrorist attack.

lynching. Extralegal means of social control in which individuals-typically members of mobs-take the law into their own hands to inflict physical punishment or even death upon persons seen as violating local customs and mores.

magistrate. Judicial official with authority to decide preliminary matters or minor cases.

mail fraud. Use of government postal services to conduct fraudulent schemes.

mala in se. Action that is considered wrong in itself.

mala prohibita. Action, such as driving on the wrong side of the road, that is considered wrong only because the law defines it as such.

malfeasance. Wrongful or illegal conduct.

malice. Intent to commit a wrongful act.

malice aforethought. Predetermined intent to commit a wrongful act.

malicious mischief. Spiteful destruction of personal property.

mandamus, **writ of.** Court order requiring a lower court or government agency to carry out its lawfully mandated duties.

mandatory sentencing. Laws requiring judges to impose predetermined penalties for certain specified crimes or third felony convictions.

manslaughter. Negligent or otherwise unlawful killing of a person without malice aforethought.

Marihuana Tax Act. A 1937 law that banned all forms of marijuana by imposing an exorbitant tax.

martial law. Use of armed forces or National Guard units to help maintain public order during emergencies.

McNaughton **rule.** Legal test for insanity in criminal cases, that asks whether a defendant knew the nature of his actions and whether those actions were right or wrong.

medical examiner. Official responsible for investigating the circumstances of suspicious or violent deaths.

Medication-assisted treatments (MAT). Drugs used in combination with advanced counseling techniques that help in the initial treatment and recovery maintenance of drug addiction.

mens rea. Criminal intent.

mental disorders. Conditions that are classified and detailed in the Diagnostic and Statistical Manual of Mental Disorders (DSM-5) published by the American Psychiatric Association.

mental illness. Illness, disease, or condition that substantially impairs sufferers' thought processes, perceptions of reality, and sense of judgment, while grossly impairing their behavior and emotional well-being.

methadone. A relatively inexpensive heroin replacement drug used to treat addiction.

Michael Jackson. A popular celebrity who died from an overdose of chemically altered fentanyl.

military justice. System of justice designed to maintain order and discipline within the armed forces.

minor. Person who has not reached age of adulthood defined by law.

Miranda rights. Requirement that individuals be advised of certain constitutional protections at the time of their arrest.

miscarriage of justice. Legal act, verdict, or punishment that is clearly unfair or unjust.

misdemeanor. Minor crime punishable by a fine or imprisonment for a relatively brief period, generally less than one year in most jurisdictions, and generally in a local jail as opposed to a prison.

misprison of felony. Concealment of or failure to report a felony under circumstances where the law requires one to report the felony.

missing persons. Persons who is abducted or who inexplicably leaves home or remains away from home for an extended period.

mistrial. Premature termination of a trial because of some misconduct or other unusual occurrence.

mitigating circumstances. Circumstances relating to violations of law that may cause decreases in the sentences.

Model Penal Code. Code of criminal provisions developed by the American Law Institute and intended to standardize criminal law among the various states.

money laundering. Methods of concealing the source of illegally obtained money.

modus operandi. Method by which a crime is carried out.

moral turpitude. Act characterized by dishonesty or depravity.

motion. Request for a court to take some action.

motive. Reason a person commits a crime.

multidisciplinary teams. A group of health care workers who are members of different disciplines, each providing specific services to individuals.

multiple jurisdiction offense. Criminal offense that is subject to prosecution in more than one jurisdiction.

murder. Unlawful killing of another person with malice aforethought.

murder, mass. Killing of multiple victims in a short period of time.

murder, serial. Killing of multiple victims over a period of time, often using the same methods.

naloxone. A drug that blocks or reverses the effects of opioids.

naltrexone. A non-opioid drug that blocks the effects of opioids.

Nancy Garrido. One of the persons who abducted Jaycee Lee Dugard.

National Child Abuse Registry. The Adam Walsh Child Protection and Safety Act created the registry and funded a variety of grants and other initiatives that protect children from sex offenders.

National Crime Victimization Survey (NCVS). A statistical sampling of households and individuals who have been personally victimized by specific crimes.

National Sex Offender Registry. Integrates the information in state sex offender registries and provides standardized information to law enforcement and allows them to track sex offenders even if they move from state to state.

National Institute on Drug Abuse. A U.S. federal government research institute whose mission is to lead the country in bringing the power of science to affect drug abuse and addiction.

National Organization for Victim Assistance (NOVA). An organization formed in 1975 to promote networking and to provide training opportunities for those working with victims.

natural law. Legal principles derived from general moral intuitions.

naturalization. Process by which a person not born a citizen is granted citizenship in a country.

negligence. Failure to act with due care.

night court. Court holding its sessions during evening hours.

noble cause. A form of abuse of authority where unethical means are used to achieve just ends.

no-knock warrant. Written order allowing police to enter a structure without first announcing their presence.

nolle prosequi. Announcement made into a court record that a plaintiff or prosecutor will not proceed forward with a lawsuit or indictment.

***nolo contendere* plea.** Plea according to which a criminal defendant neither denies nor admits guilt.

nonlethal weapon. Weapon designed to control living persons and animals when used properly, without killing or causing serious bodily injury.

nonviolent resistance. Active use of nonviolent strategies to resist laws and policies regarded as unjust and to promote social and political chang.

O'Connor v. Donaldson. A U.S. Supreme Court ruling that a state connot confine a non-dangerous mentally ill person against his/her will who is capable of surviving safely in the community.

objection. Challenge to testimony or other evidence offered in court, or to other action taken in court.

obscenity. Patently offensive sexual material lacking serious literary, artistic, political, or scientific value.

obstruction of justice. Crime of interfering with the administration of justice such as by improperly influencing a witness or destroying evidence.

offender. Perpetrator of a crime.

offer of proof. Means of preserving a record of evidence not admitted in a trial, so that an appellate can determine whether the evidence was improperly excluded from the trial record.

Olweus Bullying Prevention Program. The oldest and most used program to address bullying in the United States. It is geared to students ages 5 - 15.

opinion. Written statement of a judge or court summarizing facts of a case, the issues raised in the case, and the reasons for the court's decision.

opioids. Substances that act on opioid receptors to produce morphine-like effects.

ordinance. Law adopted by a local political body such as a city council.

organized crime. Syndicated enterprises characterized by pyramidal structures, specialization of functions, and unity of command that engage in ongoing criminal activities.

original jurisdiction. Authority of a court-such as a trial court-to make the initial determination of a particular issue, in contrast with appellate jurisdiction.

overrule. For a court to deny an objection in a case or to overturn the legal authority of a prior case.

oyez. Meaning literally "Hear Ye," a phrase used to call a judicial proceeding to order.

pandering. Encouraging another person to engage in prostitution.

paradigms. Frameworks containing the basic assumptions that underlie theories.

paralegal. Nonlawyer with legal skills who works under the supervision of an attorney.

pardon. Exempting, by the U.S. president of the governor of a state, of one accused of a crime from punishment.

Glossary

parens patriae. Legal doctrine granting authority to the government to take responsibility for the welfare of children.

parole. Release of a prisoner, generally subject to conditions, prior to the time a sentence has been completed.

parole officer. Government employee charged with supervising parolees, convicted criminals who have been released, or exempted, from incarceration.

parole violation. Violation of one or more of the conditions of parole, for which parole may be revoked an a person who has been released on parole returned to incarceration.

pathways perspective. A viewpoint arguing that marginality and victimization are major risk factors correlating with criminal behavior.

pedophilia. Adult sexual disorder that makes children sex objects.

Peacemaking criminology. An approach that promotes mediation, conflict resolution, reconciliation and community which is not based on retribution and punishment.

penal code. Collection of laws defining criminal conduct.

penal reform. Effort to improve conditions inside prisons, launch a more successful penal system, or apply alternatives to incarceration.

penitentiaries. Penal institutions that incarcerated offenders because of the belief that prisoners might be encouraged through religious means to repent and express penitence, or remorse, for their crimes.

peremptory challenge. Objection to the seating of a particular person on a jury that need not be supported by specific reasons.

Performance enhancing drugs (PEDs). Substances taken by athletes and others seeking to improve their physical capabilities.

perjury. Deliberate false statement made under oath.

personal recognizance. Pretrial release of criminal defendant without bail, on the basis of defendant's reasonably relied upon promise to appear for trial.

Phillip Garrido. One of the persons who abducted Jaycee Lee Dugard.

pickpocketing. Form of larceny that involves the sudden or stealthy stealing of property directly from persons, usually in public places.

plain error rule. Rule allowing an appellate court to reverse a trial court decision on some issue even if the person appealing did not complain about the issue at trial, as is normally required.

plain view doctrine. Rule allowing law-enforcement personnel to seize items in plain view even if they do not have a proper search warrant.

plea bargain. Agreement between a prosecutor and a criminal defendant disposing of a criminal matter.

plea. Response of a criminal defendant to the charge or charges contained in an indictment.

police. Officers of municipal law-enforcement agencies whose primary mission is to protect their communities from crime and other threats.

police academy. Training school for new police recruits.

police brutality. Abuses of authority that amount to serious and divisive human rights violations involving the excessive use of force that may occur in the apprehension or retention of civilians.

police chief. Top officer in an urban police department.

police civil liability. Police officers' obligations to refrain from acts within the course of duty that may cause undue harm to another.

police corruption. Unethical, dishonest, and other criminal conduct or deviant behaviors by police officers that involve abuses of their authority.

police detective. Police officer who specializes in criminal investigations.

police dog. Dog used by law-enforcement professionals to help find missing persons and criminal suspects and to sniff out controlled substances.

police lineup. Investigative tool used by police to identify possible suspects of a crime by lining them up, side by side, as victims and eyewitnesses attempt to pick out perpetrators.

police militarization. Deployment of military-style equipment by police to employ in meeting their local law enforcement duties.

police powers. Authority conferred on law-enforcement officers to enforce the law.

Police subculture. Shared attitudes, values, and norms within certain police officers, which can contribute to degrading organizational integrity.

political corruption. Misuse of public office for personal gain.

polling a jury. Asking each member of a jury whether he or she agrees with the verdict that the jury has announced.

polygamy. Condition of having more than one spouse at the same time; differs from bigamy in not being undertaken deceitfully.

polygraph. Device used to conduct to test whether a person is telling the truth.

pornography. Depiction of erotic behavior that is intended to arouse sexual excitement.

positive law. Law created or enacted by an appropriate law making authority, such as a legislature or a court, in contrast with natural law.

posse comitatus. Group of people pressed into service to help civilian officials enforce the law.

post mortem. Official examination of a body after death has occurred.

precedent. Decision of a court that is used to resolve a subsequent legal case.

predictive policing. Analysis of data from a variety of sources and using the results to anticipate and deploy resources to locations where crime is expected to occur.

preemption. Doctrine of constitutional law, based on the Supremacy Clause, that stipulates that federal laws on a subject (including the U.S. Constitution) are superior to and override inconsistent state and local laws.

preliminary hearing. In criminal proceedings that do not involve a grand jury indictment, a court hearing to determine whether there is probable cause to believe that an accused person has committed a crime.

presentence investigation. Report drafted by a probation officer or court officials that details significant information that may be used in sentencing a defendant.

preponderance of the evidence. Standard for deciding whether a person who brings a civil lawsuit will prevail, which requires evidence sufficient to suggest that it is more likely than not that an asserted claim is true. Contrasted with the more demanding standard used for deciding whether a government has proved that an individual has committed a crime, which requires proof beyond a reasonable doubt.

presumption of innocence. Requirement that government affirmatively prove that an individual has committed a crime.

preventive detention. Confinement of a criminal defendant before final conviction and sentencing.

preventive patrol. A policing strategy dependent on officers' visible presence in communities to serve as a deterrent to street-level crimes.

price fixing. Agreement between competitors establishing prices, generally prohibited by state or federal antitrust laws.

Prince. A popular celebrity who died from an overdose of chemically altered fentanyl.

prima facie case. Presentation of evidence sufficient to prevail in a case absent some response from an opponent.

primary victimization. Occurs when someone suffers as a direct result of the commission of a crime.

prison code. A system of words, phrases, and norms prisoners use that enables them to communicate with others in the prison environment.

Prison/Prisoner Classification Systems. A management tool that evaluates an inmates custody and program needs while balancing security requirements.

Prisonization. When inmates internalize the folkways, mores, customs, and culture of a penal institution.

Prison Rape Elimination Act (2003). Federal legislation which led to the 2012 publication of National Standards to Prevent, detect, and Respond to Prison Rape.

prisoner. A person legally held in prison for crimes committed or while awaiting trial.

prisons and jails. Government facilities that hold individuals suspected of, or convicted of, committing crimes.

private detectives. Nongovernment investigators who hire out to attorneys, companies, and private citizens.

private police and guards. Nongovernment security personnel who provide protective services that supplement law-enforcement protection.

Privatization. The transfer of government programs and functions to the private sector.

privileged communication. Communication between two individuals, such as an attorney and a client or a physician and a patient, whose confidentiality the law protect, made in circumstances in which the individuals intend for the communication to remain secret. This communication cannot be admitted into evidence in a judicial proceeding without the permission of the parties to the communication.

pro bono legal work. Legal services provided by an attorney without charge.

pro se **representation.** Representation of one's self in a legal proceeding, in contrast with being represented by an attorney.

probable cause. In criminal proceedings that do not involve a grand jury indictment, information sufficient for a judge to conclude that it is likely enough that an accused person has committed crime to justify proceeding with a trial; in the case of search warrants, information sufficient for a judge to conclude that evidence relating to a crime may be found at a particular location.

procedural fairness. Also called procedural justice examines what victims expect from the criminal justice system and what role they wish to play in the aftermath of a crime.

probation. Sentencing procedure through which offenders convicted of crimes are released by courts and remain out of prison, so long as they adhere to conditions set by the judges.

problem-oriented policing. A policing strategy that focuses on the underlying dynamics of crime problems.

procedural justice. Degree of due process guaranteed to every criminal suspect under the U.S. Constitution, the practice of which enhances perception of the criminal justice system as fair and legitimate.

Progressive Era. A period of social and political reform and activism.

Prohibition. Historical period during which a federal constitutional amendment banned the production, sale, and distribution of alcoholic beverages throughout the United States, thereby enabling organized crime to make large profits through the sale of contraband alcohol.

proof, burden of. *See* **Burden of proof**

prosecutor. Lawyer, such as a district attorney or a United States attorney, who represents the government in cases against persons accused of having committed crimes.

prosecutorial abuse. Misuse or abuse of authority by officials charged with prosecuting crime.

prostitution. Criminal act of engaging in the sale of sexual services.

proximate cause. Action that results in an event, particularly an injury or damage even, due to negligence or intentionally wrongful behavior.

psychiatric diagnosis. The act by a psychiatrist of identifying a disease from its signs and symptoms as detailed in the Diagnostic and Statistical Manual of Mental Disorders published by the American Psychiatric Association.

psychological disorders. The act by a mental health professional of identifying a disease from its signs and symptoms as detailed in the Diagnostic and Statistical Manual of Mental Disorders published by the American Psychiatric Association.

psychological profiling. Method of identifying probable offender characteristics, including behavioral, personality, and physical attributes, based on crime scene evidence.

psychopathy/sociopathy. Psychological disorder marked by a constellation of personality traits, including dishonesty, guiltlessness, and callousness.

PTSD. Post-Traumatic Stress Disorder.

public defender. Attorney appointed by government to defend a person accused of crime when that person cannot afford to hire a lawyer.

public nuisance. Unlawful interference with a community's use of public property.

public defender. Attorney appointed by government to defend a person accused of crime when that person cannot afford to hire a lawyer.

public-order offense. Act that interferes with the operations of society and its ability to maintain order.

public prosecutor. Attorney serving as the public official responsible for overseeing the prosecution of criminal cases by setting charges, conducting plea negotiations, and presenting evidence in court on behalf of the government.

Public Safety Realignment Act of 2011. Law that shifts or realigns responsibility for many low-level felons from state-level to county level criminal justice agencies.

punishment. Intentional infliction of harm by government on individuals for offenses against law.

punitive damages. Money awarded in civil tort actions to punish intentional wrongdoers and to deter them and others from engaging in similar such behavior in the future.

race riot. Short-lived but violent conflict-usually in an urban area-that pits members of different racial groups against each other.

racial profiling. Police practice of using race or ethnicity as a primary reason for stopping, questioning, searching, or arresting potential suspects.

rape. Criminal act of engaging in sexual intercourse with an individual against his or her will.

reasonable doubt. Absence of moral certainty of a defendant's guilt.

reasonable doubt, proof beyond a. Standard of proof required in criminal cases according to which the government must offer proof such as to preclude the reasonable possibility of innocence.

reasonable force. Amount of physical force that police officers may use while making arrests.

reasonable suspicion. Amount of certainty that illegal actions are taking place that law-enforcement officers must have to stop suspects in public-the standard amounts to something greater than mere hunches but less than probable cause.

The Criminal Justice System — Glossary

receiving stolen property. Crime of accepting possession of property when it is known to be stolen.

recess. Temporary adjournment of legal proceedings in a case.

recidivism. Possessing the characteristic of having repeatedly engaged in criminal conduct.

reckless endangerment. Willful engaging in conduct that shows a conscious disregard for safety and welfare of others.

recovery. The processes of change whereby people improve their health, live self-directed lives, and attempt to reach their full potential.

recuse. For a judge to withdraw from consideration of a matter because of some prejudice or conflict of interest.

Reefer Madness. A film depicting marijuana as leading to sexual orgies, murder, suicide, and psychological devastation.

Rehabilitative Penology. An alternative term for the medical model of offender treatment.

Registered sex offenders. Males or females who has been convicted of a crime involving a sexual act where federal, state, or local laws require that they be placed on the sexual offender registry after they served their sentences or when released on parole.

regulatory crime. Business practices that banned under regulatory law instead of criminal or civil law.

rehabilitation. Punishment designed to reform offenders so they can lead productive lives free from crime.

reintegration. Transition from criminal functioning to well-adjusted and lawful functioning in the community.

reintegrative shaming. An approach to working with offenders that entails expressions of support and tightening of bonds with supporters that make offenders want to avoid disappointing supporters and as such refrain from offending behavior in the future.

Reintegrative Shaming Experiments Study (RISE). A famous study conducted in Canberra, Australia between 1995 and 2000 that compared offender experiences with police-run restorative conferencing and traditional court hearings.

relativity of crime. What is defined as criminal behavior varies widely across time and space.

release. Liberation from incarceration.

remand. Order by a higher court returning a proceeding to a lower court for further action consistent with the higher court's decision in the case.

reprieve. Postponement of the execution of a criminal sentence.restorative conferencing. The victim and offender of a particular crime, who are accompanied by their respective supporters and often a police or community representative, are brought together by a trained facilitator to talk about the crime and its consequences.

restorative justice. Justice that is characterized by (face-to-face), written or mediated) communication between the victim and offender of a particular crime, who voluntarily agree to participate in an intervention, in search of conciliation and perhaps reparation.

residency restrictions. Controls that prevent sex offenders from living in certain locations such as close to schools or parks.

resisting arrest. Crime arising out of the preventing of law-enforcement officers from detaining or arresting suspects.

restitution. Legal remedy requiring someone to restore property or money to the person from whom it was originally taken or obtained.

restorative justice. Philosophy of justice that focuses on repairing harm caused by offenses.

restraining order. Court order in the form of an injunction, usually temporary, that forbids a specified party or parties from doing specified acts.

retainer. Fee for legal services paid in advance.

reversible error. Significant error committed by a trial court sufficient to justify an appellate court to overrule the result obtained at trial.

right to bear arms. Right of citizens to own and carry guns.

Risk assessment. The accurate prediction of future dangerousness by relying on empirically validated factors to estimate the likelihood of offender recidivism

robbery. Taking on one's property within one's presence by force or the threat of force.

SARA model. Scanning, Analysis, Response, and Assessment (SARA) problem-solving methodology used in conjunction with the problem-oriented policing strategy.

Scandinavian prisons. A prison system that operates under a different philosophy from American prisons where incarceration is viewed as punishment and not for punishment and where the primary purposes of prisons are to prepare offenders for rehabilitation and reentry back into society.

Schools of criminology. Collective viewpoints of thought which provide structure for theoretical development in criminology. Typically criminological schools are referred to as classical and positivist.

schools of thought. A framework containing the basic assumptions that underlie theories in criminology.

scienter. Knowledge.

search and seizure. Law-enforcement practice of searching people and places in order to seize evidence or suspects.

search warrant. Judicial order allowing law-enforcement personnel to enter and search a particular location.

secondary victimization. Arises as an adverse consequence of crime victims' negative interactions with people and institutions in the aftermath of crime.

security threat groups. Gangs within prisons.

seditious libel. Criminal act of undermining government by publishing criticism of it or of public officials.

self incrimination. Testimony by an individual that tends to suggest that the individual has committed a crime.

self-defense. Protection of one's person or property from attack by another.

self-incrimination, privilege against. Privilege found in the Fifth Amendment to the U.S. Constitution that protects persons from being compelled to be witnesses again.

sentencing. Pronouncing of punishment on a person convicted of having committed a crime.

sex offenders. Persons who commit crimes involving a sexual act.

sexual battery. Act of having sexual intercourse with one who is unable to consent to the intercourse because, for example, he or she is intoxicated or unconscious.

sex discrimination. Unequal treatment of similarly situated individuals based on their sex.

Sex Offender Registration and Notification Act (SORNA). Revised the nationwide sex offender registration system that was put into place by the Jacob Wetterling Act (1994) and standardized reporting so it is consistent nationwide.

sex offender registries. Law-enforcement databases that contain the names, crimes, and current addresses of convicted sex offenders released from custody.

sex trafficking. When a commercial sex act is induced by force, fraud, or coercion or when the person induced to perform the act is under 18 years of age.

sexual harassment. Unwelcome gender-based treatment of individuals in workplaces and other arenas.

sheriff. Chief law-enforcement administrator of a county; usually an elected official.

shoplifting. Stealing goods from a retail establishment.

side bar. Discussions between a judge and attorneys in a case that cannot be heard by the jury or spectators.

skyjacking. Hijacking of aircraft in flight by armed persons or groups, usually for the purpose of perpetrating other crimes.

slave patrol. Summoned body of citizens charged with enforcing laws restricting the activities and movement of slaves in the antebellum South.

sobriety testing. Methods of determining whether drivers are operating vehicles while under the influence of alcohol or drugs.

Social media. Internet communications technology that allows users to connect via the Internet to engage in sharing content online.

solicitation to commit a crime. Enticing or inducing someone to commit a crime.

solicitation. The act of offering, or attempting to purchase goods or services.

solicitor general of the United States. Lawyer appointed by the U.S. president to represent the United States in cases argued before the Supreme Court.

solitary confinement. Confinement of prisoners in isolation from other prison and jail inmates.

sovereign immunity. Doctrine that prevents suits against the government for damages unless the government has previously authorized such suits.

spam. Unsolicited and usually unwanted electronic mail.

special weapons and tactics teams (SWAT). Specialized police units designed to resolve dangerous crises.

speedy trial requirement. Right provided to criminal defendants by the Constitution's Sixth Amendment to be tried without excessive delay.

stare decisis. Principle that courts should generally follow the decisions of previous cases in the interest of consistency of legal stability.

stakeout. Tactical deployment of law-enforcement officers to a specific location for the purpose of surreptitiously observing criminal suspects.

stalking. Willful, malicious, or repeated following of another person.

standards of proof. Rules determining how much and what sort of evidence is enough to win cases in courts of law.

Stand Your Ground. A doctrine that allows people who believe they or someone else is in danger of being seriously harmed to use deadly force against the perpetrator.

stare decisis. Deciding of cases on the basis of judicial precedent in similar cases.

state police. Law-enforcement organizations that operate directly under the authority of state governments, rather than under municipalities.

status offense. Offense such as truancy, incorrigibility, or running away from home that is considered a crime when is it committed by a juvenile.

statute. Law enacted by the legislative branch of government, whether at the federal or state level.

statutes of limitations. Laws that disallow prosecution of crimes after specified periods of time elapse.

statutory rape. Crime of having sexual intercourse with an underage female.

sting operation. Undercover police operation in which police officers pose as criminals in order to trap law violators.

stop and frisk. Power of police to stop and search suspects or their property when there is reason to believe that the suspects have committed crimes or may be carrying concealed weapons.

strict liability offenses. Offenses for which people are responsible, whether they mean them to occur or not.

subornation of perjury. Crime of inducing another to commit perjury.

subpoena. Order for a witness to appear in court to testify.

substance abuse. Behavior when individuals use substances that can harm themselves and others.

Substance disorders. Prolonged, repeated, and uncontrolled substance misuse that is medically based.

suicide. Voluntary taking of one's own life.

summons. Judicial instrument used to initiate a legal proceeding or to command the appearance of persons before courts or other bodies.

supermax prison. Modern innovation in American corrections that separate the most dangerous inmates from general prison populations and keep them what amounts to long-term solitary confinement.

surveillance cameras. Video cameras mounted on elevated locations in public areas such as highways, parking lots, and spaces within or between buildings for the purpose of spotting and recording criminals in action and collecting video evidence for possible prosecution.

suspect. Person under investigation for possible criminal activity who has not yet been charged.

suspended sentence. Postponement of the execution of a sentence handed down by a court.

sustain. For a court to agree with an objection made by a lawyer or for a higher court to uphold the ruling of a lower court.

SWAT team. *See* **special weapons and tactics teams**

synthetic drugs. Designer drugs (also called club drugs) manufactured for recreational use.

Synthetic Drug Abuse Prevention Act of 2012. Law that changed the details of how designer drugs are managed legally.

tax evasion. Deliberate failure to pay legally due income taxes or to submit required returns and other documents.

telephone fraud. All uses of telephones to defraud or cheat victims.

ten-most-wanted lists. Federal Bureau of Investigation program that publicizes the names and images of the most dangerous and sought-after criminal fugitives.

terrorism. Coercive use, or threat, of violence to terrorize a community or society to achieve political, economic, or social goals.

testimony. Statement made in a legal proceeding by a witness under oath.

theft. Taking of a person's property without that person's consent.

three-strikes law. Statute that requires repeat criminal offenders to be punished with long prison terms, regardless of the severity of any of the three offenses.

Total institution. An organization that controls every aspect of the lives of its members.

toxicology. Science concerned with the effects of harmful and toxic substances on living organisms.

trace evidence. Forms of physical evidence at crime scenes that are usually not visible to the naked eye.

traffic court. Special court that deals only with infractions of traffic laws that are considered less serious than misdemeanors and felonies.

traffic fine. Monetary penalty imposed for a traffic violation.

traffic law. Branch of law comprising rules for the orderly and safe flow of pedestrian and vehicular traffic.

transcript. Official record of a legal proceeding.

trauma. Events that have life-altering consequences.

treason. Crime consisting of rebellious action toward one's government.

trespass. Crime of interfering with the property rights of another.

trial. Formal process of adjudication, from arraignment through verdicts.

trial transcript. Official record of a trial proceeding.

Trayvon Martin. A young man who was shot and killed by George Zimmerman, a neighborhood watch leader.

Uniform Crime Reports. National crime statistics compiled from government law-enforcement records.

use of force continuum. Learning aid for training police in use of force policy.

United States v. Comstock. Held Congress had the authority to provided for the civil commitment of sexually dangerous people whose release from federal prison is imminent.

United States Supreme Court. The highest federal court in the United States that has final appellate jurisdiction over all courts in the nation.

vacate. In criminal justice proceedings, to set aside or rescind a court order or decision.

vandalism. Crime of willfully destroying property.

vehicle checkpoint. Stoppages of motorists by police for such purposes as apprehending criminals, preventing criminal behavior, and obtaining information.

venire. List of those who have been summoned for jury duty.

verdict. Formal decision, or finding, made by a jury or a judge upon matters of fact submitted to them for deliberation and determination.

venue. Jurisdiction in which a legal action, such as a trial, arises.

verdict. Decision of a jury in a trial.

vicarious liability. Legal concept that someone in a supervisory role, such as an employer or parent, may be held liable for harm done by their subordinates.

victim assistance program. Advocacy and support services, often funded or administered by government, that guide victims of crime through the legal system.

victim-offender mediation. Facilitated meetings between offenders and victims of their crimes with the intent to discuss the effects and triggers of the harm.

victimless crime. Legally prohibited activities or exchanges among willing parties that do not harm anyone except, possibly, the parties willingly.

victimization. Causing someone to be treated unfairly or made to feel as if one is in a bad position.

victimology. Study of the relationships among victims, offenders, the criminal justice system, and society.

Victims of Child Abuse Act (2013). A bill that reauthorized funding the Victims of Child Abuse Act of 1990 through 2018 to help child abuse victims.

Victims' right movements. Organizational efforts to support victims that coincided with the women's and civil rights movements.

vigilantism. Illegal assumption of law-enforcement responsibilities by organized groups of private citizens.

voir dire. Examination of potential jurors to determine whether they should be seated on a jury or the preliminary examination of a witness to determine whether the witness is competent to testify.

voting fraud. Use of illegal tactics and practices to influence political elections.

war crimes. Crimes against humanity that go beyond the acts normally considered permissible in international armed conflicts.

warrant. Order permitting an official to take some action, such as an order permitting law-enforcement personnel to arrest someone or to search certain property.

warrior versus guardian mentality. Police officers with a warrior mentality view themselves as warriors, poised to fight to combat crime; police officers with a guardian mentality view themselves as protectors of the public, due process, and procedural fairness.

watch system. In antiquity, patrol of communities by watchmen-citizens who issued a "hue and cry" to summon aid in the event of a crime or security concern.

white-collar crime. Nonviolent crimes committed by professional workers.

wiretap. Surreptitious monitoring of telephone conversations by law-enforcement officials.

witness. Person who offers testimony in a legal proceeding.

witness protection program. Government program designed to ensure the safety of key witnesses during and after court proceedings.

work camp. Alternative form of incarceration that requires less security than regular prisons and offers inmates practical work experience.

work-release program. Alternative to traditional incarceration that places accused and convicted offenders into the community to work at jobs paying standard wages.

Xanax. A prescription drug that has been used as a date rape drug.

youth authorities. Inclusive term for the various state agencies and officials involved in juvenile justice.

Zebulon Brockaway. Introduced a system for imprisoned offenders at Elmira Penitentiary which would allow them to eventually gain release from prison

Timothy L. Hall
Updated by the Editors

Crime Rates and Definitions

Accurate measurement of crime is of vital importance for public and private agencies in determining priorities and policies regarding crime and for the evaluation of existing programs. The two main sources of crime data in the United States are the Uniform Crime Reports (UCR) of the Federal Bureau of Investigation (FBI) and the National Crime Victimization Surveys (NCVS) of the U.S. Census Bureau.

The FBI's Uniform Crime Reporting (UCR) program, which began in 1929, collects, publishes, and archives crime data provided by law-enforcement agencies across the United States. The data collected represent well over 90 percent of the U.S. population. The UCR program classifies offenses into two groups. Part I crime counts are based on crimes reported to the police, and Part II crime counts are based on arrests made. In counting crimes, the FBI uses a hierarchical rule: In multiple-offense situations—those in which several offenses are committed at the same time and place—only the highest-ranking offense is scored, after classifying all Part I offenses. All other crimes are ignored, regardless of the numbers of offenders and victims.

Each year since 1973, the U.S. Census Bureau (under the U.S. Department of Commerce) on behalf of the Bureau of Justice Statistics (under the U.S. Department of Justice) has collected data on the frequency, characteristics, and consequences of crime victimizations. These data are collected from a nationally representative sample of roughly 49,000 households in the United States that contain more than 100,000 persons twelve years of age and older. The survey collects information not only on crimes and their circumstances but also on such characteristics of victims as age, sex, race, ethnicity, income, and marital status. Victims are also asked whether they have reported the crime incidents to police and, in cases of personal violent crimes, they are asked about their relationships to the offenders and characteristics of the offenders.

The UCR calculates crime rates by dividing the numbers of crimes by the population of an area—for example, city, region, and country—and then multiplying by 100,000, yielding rates per 100,000 persons. The NCVS reports two types of rates: crimes against persons and crimes against households. Person crime rates are equal to the numbers of person crimes divided by the numbers of people and then multiplied by 1,000; the resulting figures are rates per 1,000 people. Household crime rates are calculated by dividing the numbers of household crimes by the numbers of households and multiplying those results by 1,000 to determine the rates per 1,000 households.

Uniform Crime Reports: Crime Definitions and Rates per 100,000 Population in 2015

Part I Offenses

2015	Offense	Definition
4.9	Criminal homicide	Murder and non-negligent manslaughter: the willful (non-negligent) killing of one human being by another.
38.6	Rape	Penetration, no matter how slight, of the vagina or anus with any body part or object, or oral penetration by a sex organ of another person, without the consent of the victim.
101.9	Robbery	Taking or attempting to take anything of value from the care, custody, or control of persons by force or threat of force or violence and/or by putting the victims in fear.
237.8	Aggravated assault	Unlawful attack by one person upon another for the purpose of inflicting severe or aggravated bodily injury. This type of assault usually is accompanied by the use of a weapon or by means likely to produce death or great bodily harm. Simple assaults are excluded.
491.4	Burglary (breaking or entering)	Unlawful entry of a structure to commit a felony or a theft. Attempted forcible entry is included.

Crime Rates and Definitions

2015	Offense	Definition
1,775.4	Larceny/theft	Unlawful taking, carrying, leading, or riding away of property from the possession or constructive possession of another. Examples are thefts of bicycles or automobile accessories, shoplifting, pocket-picking, or the stealing of any property or article which is not taken by force and violence or by fraud. Attempted larcenies are included. Motor vehicle theft, embezzlement, confidence games, forgery, worthless checks, and similar offenses, are excluded.
220.2	Motor vehicle theft	Theft or attempted theft of a motor vehicle—any self-propelled vehicle that runs on solid surfaces and not on rails. Motorboats, construction equipment, airplanes, and farming equipment are specifically excluded from this category.
13.6	Arson	Willful or malicious burning or attempt to burn—with or without intent to defraud—a dwelling house, public building, motor vehicle or aircraft, personal property of another, and so forth. Although arson is included in Part I offenses, insufficient data are available to calculate rates.

Part II Offenses

2015	Offense	Definition
336.8	Other assaults (simple)	Assaults and attempted assaults in which no weapons are used and which do not result in serious or aggravated injury to the victim.
17.3	Forgery and counterfeiting	Making, altering, uttering, or possessing—with intent to defraud—anything false in the semblance of that which is true. Attempts are included.
41.4	Fraud	Fraudulent conversion and obtaining money or property by false pretenses. Confidence games and bad checks, except forgeries and counterfeiting, are included.
5.0	Embezzlement	Misappropriation or misapplication of money or property entrusted to one's care, custody, or control.
27.7	Stolen property offenses	Buying, receiving, and possessing stolen property, including attempts.
59.6	Vandalism	Willful or malicious destruction, injury, disfigurement, or defacement of any public or private property, real or personal, without consent of the owner or persons having custody or control. Attempts are included.
45.1	Weapons offenses	All violations of regulations or statutes controlling the carrying, using, possessing, furnishing, and manufacturing of deadly weapons or silencers. Attempts are included.
12.8	Prostitution and commercialized vice	Sex offenses of a commercialized nature, such as prostitution, keeping a bawdy house, procuring or transporting women for immoral purposes. Attempts are included.
16.0	Other sex offenses	Statutory rape and offenses against chastity, common decency, morals, and the like. Attempts are included. Forcible rape, prostitution, and commercialized vice are excluded.
463.3	Drug abuse violations	State and/or local offenses relating to the unlawful possession, sale, use, growing, and manufacturing of narcotic drugs. Specified drug categories: opium or cocaine and their derivatives (morphine, heroin, codeine); marijuana; synthetic narcotics—manufactured narcotics that can cause true addiction (Demerol, methadone); and dangerous non-narcotic drugs (barbiturates, Benzedrine).
1.5	Gambling	Promoting, permitting, or engaging in illegal gambling.
29.3	Offenses against the family and children	Nonsupport, neglect, desertion, or abuse of family and children. Attempts are included.
337.7	Driving under the influence	Driving or operating any vehicle or common carrier while drunk or under the influence of liquor or narcotics.
82.9	Liquor laws	State and/or local liquor law violations, except drunkenness and driving under the influence. Federal violations are excluded.

2015	Offense	Definition
127.5	Drunkenness	Offenses relating to drunkenness or intoxication. Driving under the influence is excluded.
120.8	Disorderly conduct	Breach of the peace.
7.9	Vagrancy	Begging, loitering, and so forth. Includes prosecutions under the charge of suspicious person.
1,000.9	Other offenses	All violations of state and local laws not listed above and traffic offenses.
0.4	Suspicion	No specific offense; suspect released without formal charges being placed.
13.7	Curfew and loitering laws	Offenses relating to violations by persons under the age of eighteen of local curfew or loitering ordinances where such laws exist.
n/a	Runaways	Limited to juveniles (under the age of eighteen) taken into protective custody under provisions of local statutes.

National Crime Victimization Survey: Crime Rates per 1,000 Population for Violent Crime and Property Crime in 2015

As much as their different collection methods permit, both the UCR and NCVS measure the same subset of serious crimes, defined alike.

Type of Crime	Rate per 1,000 Persons Age 12 or Older
Violent crime	
Rape/Sexual Assault	1.6
Robbery	2.1
Aggravated Assault	3.0
Simple Assault	11.8
Intimate Partner Violence	3.0
Stranger Violence	6.8
Violent Crime Involving Injury	4.8
Serious Violent Crime	
Serious Intimate Partner Violence	1.2
Serious Stranger Violence	2.6
Serious Violent Crime Involving Weapons	3.6
Serious Violent Crime Involving Injury	2.4
Type of Crime	Rate per 1,000 Households
Property Crime	
Burglary	22.0
Motor Vehicle Theft	4.3
Theft	84.4

Composite Rates

Both the UCR and the NCVS construct composite rates that are used to track changes and trends in amounts of crime more often than are individual rates. The UCR constructs a violent crime rate, which incorporates murder, forcible rape, robbery, and aggravated assault, and a property crime rate that incorporates burglary, larceny-theft, and motor vehicle theft. Similarly, the NCVS constructs a violent crime rate that incorporates rape, robbery, aggravated assault, and simple assault and a property crime rate that incorporates burglary, theft, and motor vehicle theft.

The UCR also creates the Crime Index, which is the sum of selected offenses used to indicate changes in the overall rate of crime reported to law enforcement. Offenses included in the Crime Index total include the violent crimes of murder and non-negligent manslaughter, forcible rape, robbery, and aggravated assault, and the property crimes of burglary, larceny-theft, and motor vehicle theft.

Comparing UCR and NCVS Rates

The NCVS was created to complement the UCR. Each has its advantages, and each has its flaws. The UCR measures only crimes reported to law-enforcement agencies, and research indicates that fewer than 40 percent of crimes are reported in a given year. By interviewing victims, the NCVS measures both reported and unreported crimes. However, the NCVS excludes homicide, arson, commercial crimes, and crimes against children under the age of twelve, all of which are included in UCR rates. Furthermore, being based on a sample of American households, the NCVS is subject to sampling error, meaning a different sample might yield different results.

The UCR data are, in most cases, based on actual counts of offenses reported by law-enforcement jurisdictions. However, officers in law-enforcement agencies responsible for compiling data for the UCR can and do make errors. Similarly, another source of error in the NCVS is that victims may not accurately recall how many times they were crime victims in the six-month reference period, either forgetting some victimizations or including some that occurred prior to the reference periods.

The basic counting units of the NCVS are individual victimizations. Victimizations are reported by victims, and thus each person victimized is counted as a victimization. The basic counting unit for the UCR is the offense. An offense can have one or more victims. If two people are robbed in a single incident, the UCR would count this as one offense, while the NCVS would count it as two victimizations.

Neither crime measure is necessarily better than the other. Together they give a better idea as to crime volume and trends than either alone could. The UCR is likely to be a better measure for more serious offenses, since these are more likely to be reported to the police. This is especially the case for murder as it cannot be included in the NCVS, and virtually all murders come to the attention of the police. The NCVS is likely to be the better measure for less serious offenses, which often go unreported.

Jerome L. Neapolitan
Updated by Frank Salamone and the Editors

Crime Trends

Policy makers such as legislators, mayors, and police chiefs need up-to-date, accurate information to make their decisions. In recognition of that need, the Federal Bureau of Investigation (FBI) created the Uniform Crime Reports (UCR) to collect information from the states about the numbers of crimes reported to the police. The basic crime categories tracked most regularly since the late twentieth century are known as Part I, or Index offenses. They include murder and non-negligent manslaughter, forcible rape, robbery, aggravated assault, burglary, larceny theft, motor vehicle theft, and arson. Because of special rules surrounding the reporting of arson, arson rates are generally not reported along with other Part I crimes. To control for variations over time in the numbers of crimes due to changes in the population, this information is often reported in the form of rates: numbers of offenses per 1,000 or 100,000 population.

Recognizing that not all crimes are reported to the police, the U.S. Department of Justice began the National Crime Victimization Survey (NCVS) in 1973. This survey, conducted annually through telephone calls to a random sample of 90,000 households, asks all persons of the age of twelve and older in each household about their victimization experiences. Generally, the NCVS expresses victimization rates as numbers of victimizations per 1,000 population—also of persons aged twelve and older.

In the 2014 Criminal Victimization report, figure 1 compares the rate of both property victimization and violent victimization between 1993 and 2014. Both rates have dropped dramatically since the early 1990s, with temporary spikes in 2006 and 2012. As UCR data in has shown, crime rates in the United States rose steadily throughout the 1960s and 1970s and peaked in 1980, when 5,950 offenses per 100,000 population were reported. The victimization data show a slightly earlier peak, with 602 victimizations reported per 1,000 population aged twelve and older.

After a brief decline through the early 1980s, the crime rate again approached its 1980 peak in 1991. Between then and 2003, the overall crime rate dropped by slightly more than 30 percent, approaching lows not seen since the early 1970s. In 2014, the rates per 1,000 people 12 or older hovered around 25. The trends in victimizations reported in the survey data largely match those recorded in the official report data.

The Composition of the Crime Rates

In the NCVS data, violent crimes include forcible rape, robbery, assault, and domestic violence. The violent crime rate for 2014 was 20.1 per 1,000 people. Property crimes include burglary, theft, and motor vehicle theft. The vast majority of offenses reported to police since 1960 have been property crimes; the rate in 2014 was 118.1 per 1,000 households, down from 159.5 in 2005.

Reported incidents of violent crime in the United States steadily rose to a 596.6 incidents per 100,000 population in 1980. Then, after a brief decline, they again rose to reach a high of 758.1 in 1991. The national victimization survey data closely track the official report trend, though they did not reflect as steep a post-1980 increase.

Further examining the violent crime composition reveals that not all violent crimes equally contribute to the rate. In 2014, the bulk of violent crimes reported to police were assaults (8.9 per 1,000); rape and sexual assault accounted for less than 1 per 1,000 of the violent crime rate.

Similar patterns can be observed in the property crime data. Reported incidents of property crime in the United States followed the same trend seen in the violent crime rates, steadily rising to a peak rate of 5,353.3 incidents per 100,000 population in 1980. After a brief decline, they rose to a new high of 5,139.7 in 1991. As with violent crime, the national victimization survey data closely tracks the official report trend. Again, the victimization data show a peak victimization rate of 553.6 per 1,000 population (age twelve and older) in 1975, five years before the UCR peak in 1980. According to the NCVS, the overall property crime rate in 2014 was 72.8 per 1,000.

Further examining property crime composition reveals that, while not all property crimes contribute equally to the rate, the distribution is not nearly as uneven as that seen in violent crime. The major contributor to the nation's property crime rate is theft, accounting for 85 percent of total property crimes. The rate of motor vehicle theft makes the smallest contribution (0.7 per 1,000, a significant decline since 2005, when the rate was 7.2 per 1,000).

Timothy M. Bray

Further Reading

Blumstein, Alfred, and Joel Wallman. *The Crime Drop in America*. Rev. ed. New York: Cambridge UP, 2006. Print.

Shahidullah, Shahid M. *Crime Policy in America: Laws, Institutions and Programs.* 2nd ed. Lanham: UP of America, 2016. Print.

Truman, Jennifer L., and Lynn Langton. "Criminal Victimization, 2014." *Bureau of Justice Statistics.* US Dept. of Justice, 29 Sept. 2015. PDF file.

Supreme Court Rulings on Criminal Justice

Cases marked with asterisks (*) are subjects of essays within the main text.

Year	Case	Relevance to criminal justice
1884	Hurtado v. California*	Held that due process under the Fourteenth Amendment does not require indictments by grand juries in state murder prosecutions.
1900	Maxwell v. Dow	Held that trial by jury in state courts is not a necessary requisite of due process of law.
1908	Twining v. New Jersey	Held that protection against self-incrimination is not required in state trials under the Fourteenth Amendment due process clause.
1914	Weeks v. United States*	Established the exclusionary rule whereby illegally obtained evidence may not be used in federal prosecutions.
1927	Tumey v. Ohio	Ruled that due process is denied when suspects are tried before judges who have direct, personal, substantial, and pecuniary interests in deciding against them.
1928	Olmstead v. United States*	Held that the Fourth Amendment does not preclude use of wiretapping by federal agents.
1932	Powell v. Alabama*	In this first Scottsboro case, ruled that the due process clause of the Fourteenth Amendment requires that defendants in state capital cases are entitled to counsel.
1935	Norris v. Alabama	In this second Scottsboro case, held that systematic exclusion of African Americans from service on grand and trial juries denies black defendants equal protection guaranteed by the Fourteenth Amendment.
1936	Brown v. Mississippi*	Held that due process under the Fourteenth Amendment prohibits the use of confessions coerced by physical torture.
1937	Palko v. Connecticut*	Held that due process under the Fourteenth Amendment may incorporate Bill of Rights protections that are "the very essence of a scheme of ordered liberty"; double jeopardy is not one of those provisions.
1938	Johnson v. Zerbst	Ruled that the Sixth Amendment requires appointment of counsel for all felony defendants in federal courts.
1940	Chambers v. Florida	Held that the Fourteenth Amendment's due process clause prohibits admissibility of confessions coerced by psychological or nonphysical means.
1942	Betts v. Brady	Held that the appointment of counsel for indigents in state felony cases depends upon the special circumstances of the cases.
1942	Skinner v. Oklahoma ex rel. Williamson	Held that equal protection is violated by state laws requiring sterilization of habitual criminals.
1943	McNabb v. United States	Voided a conviction, not on grounds of unconstitutional self-incrimination, but because prisoners had not been taken before the nearest judicial officer without unnecessary delay for hearing, commitment, or release on bail, as required by statute.
1947	Adamson v. California	Self-incrimination clause of the Fifth Amendment does not apply to the states; dissent in this case articulated total incorporation doctrine.
1947	Louisiana ex rel. Francis v. Resweber	Held that the Eighth Amendment ban against cruel and unusual punishment does apply to states; however, defendant in this case had to face the electric chair a second time, even though it malfunctioned during the first attempt to execute him.
1948	In re Oliver	Incorporated the Sixth Amendment right to a public trial to apply to the states.
1948	Cole v. Arkansas	Incorporated the Sixth Amendment notice clause to apply to the states.

Supreme Court Rulings on Criminal Justice

Year	Case	Relevance to criminal justice
1949	Wolf v. Colorado	Incorporated the Fourth Amendment search and seizure protections to apply to the states but did not incorporate exclusionary rule.
1957	Mallory v. United States	Broadened the 1943 McNabb rule to invalidate even a voluntary confession made before arraignment.
1961	Mapp v. Ohio*	Applied the exclusionary rule to the states.
1962	Robinson v. California*	Incorporated Eighth Amendment protections against cruel and unusual punishment to apply to the states while finding that narcotics addiction is not in itself a crime.
1963	Gideon v. Wainwright*	Required counsel for indigent defendants in all state felony cases.
1964	Escobedo v. Illinois*	For first time, recognized suspects' right to counsel during police interrogations in states.
1964	Malloy v. Hogan	Incorporated Fifth Amendment protection against self-incrimination to apply to the states.
1964	Massiah v. United States*	Held that incriminating statements elicited by federal agents during the absence of the defendant's attorney deprived the defendant of his right to counsel under the Sixth Amendment; the statements collected could not be used as evidence in trial.
1965	Pointer v. Texas	Incorporated the confrontation clause of the Sixth Amendment to apply to the states.
1966	Parker v. Gladden	Incorporated Sixth Amendment right to an impartial jury to apply to the states.
1966	Miranda v. Arizona*	Announced Miranda rule requiring specific procedures for police to follow during interrogations and declared that any statements elicited in violation of these procedures would be inadmissible.
1967	In re Gault*	Held that minors are entitled to certain procedural rights including adequate notice, right to counsel, privilege against self-incrimination, and the rights of confrontation and sworn testimony.
1967	Katz v. United States*	Held that because the Fourth Amendment protects people, not places, electronic surveillance is an unreasonable intrusion into privacy.
1967	Klopfer v. North Carolina	Incorporated Sixth Amendment right to a speedy trial to apply to the states.
1967	United States v. Wade	Allowed accused suspects to be compelled to participate in police lineups and to utter the words attributed to offenders in crimes.
1967	Washington v. Texas	Incorporated Sixth Amendment compulsory process clause to apply to the states.
1968	Chimel v. California*	Held that arresting suspects does not empower police officers to conduct widespread searches of the arrestees' homes without search warrants.
1968	Duncan v. Louisiana	Incorporated Sixth Amendment jury trial protections to apply to the states.
1968	Harris v. United States*	Established plain view exception to search warrant requirements.
1968	Witherspoon v. Illinois*	Held that excluding jurors opposed to capital punishment results in an unrepresentative jury on the issue of guilt or substantially increases the risk of conviction.
1969	Benton v. Maryland	Incorporated Fifth Amendment protection against double jeopardy to apply to the states.
1970	Brady v. United States*	Approved most forms of plea bargaining, in which defendants agree to plead guilty in return for reduced charges or sentences.
1970	Illinois v. Allen	Allowed disruptive defendants to be removed from courtrooms without violating their constitutional right to be present and to confront witnesses against them.

Supreme Court Rulings on Criminal Justice

Year	Case	Relevance to criminal justice
1970	Williams v. Florida	Held that the right of trial by jury does not require state to provide defendants with twelve-person juries in noncapital cases.
1971	Bivens v. Six Unknown Named Agents*	Held that plaintiffs can—under certain conditions—seek damages when federal officials violate their Fourth Amendment protection against unreasonable searches.
1971	Santobello v. New York*	Held that when defendants rely on prosecutors' plea bargain promises, due process requires that the promises be kept or that the defendants be given some form of relief, such as withdrawal of their guilty pleas.
1971	Schilb v. Kuebel	Incorporated Eighth Amendment protection against excessive bail to apply to the states.
1972	Apodaca v. Oregon	States may allow nonunanimous jury verdicts in noncapital cases.
1972	Argersinger v. Hamlin*	Requires counsel for indigent defendants in all state misdemeanor cases in which imprisonment in jail is the penalty for conviction.
1972	Barker v. Wingo*	Developed a "balancing test" in applying Sixth Amendment speedy trial protections, thus requiring such cases to be approached on an ad hoc basis.
1972	Furman v. Georgia*	Invalidated the death penalty as then administered as a violation of the cruel and unusual punishment clause of the Eighth Amendment applied to the states by the Fourteenth Amendment.
1973	Roe v. Wade	Decriminalized abortions under certain conditions.
1975	Faretta v. California*	Held that defendants have a constitutional right to proceed *pro se*, that is, to represent themselves in criminal trials.
1976	Gregg v. Georgia*	Reversed the 1972 *Furman* decision, finding that the death penalty is a constitutionally permissible punishment for carefully defined categories of murder; required carefully controlled discretion of sentencing authority, with bifurcated trial procedures.
1977	Coker v. Georgia*	Held that death sentences for the crime of rape are grossly disproportionate and excessive punishment and are therefore forbidden by the Eighth Amendment as cruel and unusual punishment.
1978	Ballew v. Georgia	Held that juries for state criminal trials must have at least six members.
1979	Burch v. Louisiana	Held that when juries have only six members in state criminal trials for nonpetty offenses, nonunanimous verdicts violate the Sixth and Fourteenth Amendments.
1980	Rummel v. Estelle*	Ruled that Texas's mandatory life sentence for a three-time recidivist felon did not constitute cruel and unusual punishment under the Eighth and Fourteenth Amendments.
1983	Illinois v. Gates*	Adopted the "totality of the circumstances" approach for determining whether an informant's tip establishes probable cause for issuance of a warrant.
1983	Solem v. Helm*	Held that the Eighth Amendment's cruel and unusual punishments clause prohibits sentences that are disproportionate to the crimes and that a state's sentence of life imprisonment without the possibility of parole for recidivist criminals violates that clause.
1984	United States v. Leon*	Created the good faith exception to the exclusionary rule, holding that evidence gained by officers acting in good faith is admissible even when their search warrants prove to be invalid.
1984	Massachusetts v. Sheppard*	Held that police officers are not required to disbelieve judges who advise them that the warrants they possess authorize them to conduct the searches they request.

Supreme Court Rulings on Criminal Justice

Year	Case	Relevance to criminal justice
1984	*Nix v. Williams*	Held that evidence obtained in violation of the *Miranda* decision need not be suppressed if the same evidence would have been inevitably discovered by lawful means.
1984	*Schall v. Martin**	Upheld a state preventive detention statute authorizing pretrial detention of juveniles as a legitimate protection of society from the hazards of pretrial crime.
1985	*New Jersey v. T.L.O.**	Permits school officials to search students who are under their authority without warrants.
1985	*Tennessee v. Garner**	Held that a state law authorizing police officers to use deadly force against apparently unarmed and nondangerous fleeing suspects violates Fourth Amendment protections; such force may not be used unless necessary to prevent the escape and officers have probable cause to believe that suspects pose a significant threat of death or serious physical injury to them or others.
1986	*Batson v. Kentucky**	Held that states excluding persons from jury service on account of race are in violation of the equal protection clause of the Fourteenth Amendment.
1986	*Bowers v. Hardwick**	Upheld Georgia's antisodomy law, finding no fundamental right for homosexual offenders.
1986	*Ford v. Wainwright**	Held that the Eighth Amendment prohibits state from inflicting the death penalty upon prisoners who are mentally ill.
1986	*Terry v. Ohio**	Authorized the "stop and frisk" exception to warrant requirements.
1987	*Illinois v. Krull**	Held that the Fourth Amendment exclusionary rule does not apply to evidence obtained by a police officer who acted in objectively reasonable reliance upon a state statute authorizing a warrantless administrative search of an automobile wrecking yard that was subsequently found to violate the Fourth Amendment.
1987	*McCleskey v. Kemp**	Rejected claims based on statistical studies that Georgia's capital punishment process discriminated on the basis of the race of the murder victim, in violation of the Eighth and Fourteenth amendments.
1987	*United States v. Salerno*	Upheld the Bail Reform Act of 1984, which authorized judges to deny bail to defendants to ensure the safety of other persons and the community.
1987	*Tison v. Arizona**	Created a flexible Eighth Amendment standard for applying the death penalty to felony-murder accomplices who demonstrate reckless disregard for human life even though they do not directly participate in killing victims.
1987	*Turner v. Safley*	Announced a four-pronged test to determine whether prison regulations impinging on inmates' constitutional rights are reasonable, concluding that regulations are valid if they are reasonably related to legitimate penological interests.
1988	*Coy v. Iowa*	Struck down a state law permitting children who claim they are victims of sexual abuse to testify in court from behind screens.
1989	*Graham v. Connor**	Established the "objective reasonableness" standard for use of force by police. Each application of force should be based upon a standard of objective reasonableness under the totality of circumstances. Three determinants are (1) severity of the crime at issue, (2) whether a suspect poses an immediate threat to the safety of officers or others, and (3) whether a suspect is actively resisting arrest or attempting to evade arrest by flight.
1989	*Stanford v. Kentucky**	Sustained the constitutionality of imposing the death penalty on individuals for crimes committed at the age of sixteen or seventeen.
1989	*Texas v. Johnson**	Struck down a state flag-desecration law because it is not viewpoint-neutral.

Supreme Court Rulings on Criminal Justice

Year	Case	Relevance to criminal justice
1990	Maryland v. Buie*	Held that the Fourth Amendment permits properly limited protective sweeps in conjunction with in-home arrests when the searching officers possess reasonable beliefs, based on specific and articulable facts, that the areas to be swept harbor persons posing dangers to those on the arrest scenes.
1990	Maryland v. Craig*	Held that the Sixth Amendment's confrontation clause does not guarantee criminal defendants an absolute right to face-to-face meeting with the witnesses against them at trial.
1990	Minnick v. Mississippi*	Held that when suspects request counsel, their interrogation must cease, and officials may not reinitiate interrogations without counsel present—whether or not the accused consult with their attorneys; the requirement that counsel be "made available" to the accused refers not to the opportunity to consult with attorneys outside the interrogation room, but to the right to have the attorney present during custodial interrogation.
1991	Arizona v. Fulminante*	Held that tainted testimony erroneously admitted as evidence at trial need not overturn convictions if sufficient independent evidence supporting guilty verdicts also is introduced.
1991	Harmelin v. Michigan*	Held that the Eighth Amendment does not prohibit imposing mandatory life sentences without possibility of parole for possessing more than 650 grains of cocaine.
1991	Payne v. Tennessee*	Upheld use of victim impact evidence and emotional impact of crimes on victims' families by juries in capital sentencing procedures.
1992	United States v. Alvarez-Machain*	Held that the forcible abduction of a defendant in Mexico did not prohibit his trial in a U.S. court for violations of U.S. criminal laws; defendant may not be prosecuted in violation of the terms of an extradition treaty; however, when a treaty has not been invoked, a court may properly exercise jurisdiction even though the defendant's presence is procured by means of a forcible abduction.
1992	Jacobson v. United States	Employed federal approach to entrapment defense requiring proof that accused was disposed to commit a criminal act prior to first being approached by government agents.
1992	R.A.V. v. City of St. Paul*	On the basis of the First Amendment, invalidated a municipal ordinance outlawing fighting words (hate speech) because it involved viewpoint-based distinctions among different topics.
1993	Wisconsin v. Mitchell*	Upheld a state-enhanced penalty for aggravated battery hate crimes that are unprotected by the First Amendment.
1995	United States v. Lopez*	Held that the Gun-Free School Zones Act of 1990 exceeded Congress's commerce clause authority because possessing guns in local schools is not an economic activity that might have a substantial effect on interstate commerce; characterized the law as a criminal statute that has nothing to do with "commerce" or any sort of economic enterprise.
1995	Wilson v. Arkansas*	Held that the common-law knock-and-announce principle forms a part of the Fourth Amendment reasonableness inquiry when police enter a suspect's residence.
1996	Whren v. United States*	Found that the temporary detention of motorists upon probable cause to believe that they have violated the traffic laws does not violate the Fourth Amendment's prohibition against unreasonable seizures, even if reasonable officers would not stop the motorists absent some additional law-enforcement objective.
1997	Hudson v. United States	Held that the double jeopardy clause permits government to fine persons for fraud and other regulatory law violations and later use the criminal process to prosecute the same persons for the same offenses.

Supreme Court Rulings on Criminal Justice

Year	Case	Relevance to criminal justice
1998	United States v. Balsys	Held that resident aliens may not invoke the self-incrimination clause to withhold information from the U.S. government out of fear that disclosure might lead to prosecution by a foreign nation.
1998	California v. Greenwood*	Held that the Fourth Amendment does not prohibit warrantless search and seizure of garbage left in plastic bags for collection on street curbs.
1998	Knowles v. Iowa*	Held that a police officer's search of an automobile with neither the driver's consent nor probable cause, after the driver was issued a citation for speeding, violates the Fourth Amendment.
2000	Dickerson v. United States	Ruled that the Miranda case is so embedded in routine police practice that the warnings have become part of American national culture.
2000	Illinois v. Wardlow*	Held that police officers stopping suspects and conducting protective pat-down searches for weapons on public streets in areas known for heavy narcotics trafficking do not violate the Fourth Amendment.
2001	Atwater v. City of Lago Vista*	Held that the Fourth Amendment does not forbid warrantless arrests for minor criminal offenses, such as misdemeanor seatbelt violations punishable only by fines.
2001	Illinois v. McArthur*	Ruled it permissible under the Fourth Amendment for police officers who have probable cause to believe that suspects have hidden marijuana in their homes to prevent the suspects from reentering their homes for up to two hours while they obtain search warrants.
2001	Kyllo v. United States*	Held that using thermal imaging devices, which are not in general public use, to explore details of private homes that would be unknowable without physical intrusion constitutes a Fourth Amendment "search" and is presumptively unreasonable without a warrant.
2002	Atkins v. Virginia	Held that executing murderers with mental disabilities violates the Eighth Amendment.
2002	United States v. Drayton	Ruled that during random searches for drugs or weapons on buses, police are not required to inform passengers that they may refuse to be searched.
2002	Ring v. Arizona	Held that the Eighth Amendment requires that only juries—not judges—can award the death penalty.
2003	Ewing v. California	Held that the Eighth Amendment does not prohibit sentencing repeat felons to prison terms of twenty-five years under a "three-strikes" law, as the sentence of the appellant in the case was not grossly disproportionate.
2003	Lawrence v. Texas	Struck down state antisodomy law as violation of liberty guarantees of due process.
2003	Virginia v. Black*	Upheld a state law prohibiting cross burning when it is undertaken with the intent to intimidate.
2004	Blakely v. Washington	Held that the Sixth Amendment's guarantee of trial by jury prevents judges from making factual findings that increase defendants' sentences beyond the usual ranges for the crimes under state sentencing guidelines; juries must find such facts beyond a reasonable doubt.
2004	Crawford v. Washington	Reaffirmed that the Sixth Amendment's guarantee that defendants have the right to face their accusers has few exceptions and that prosecutors cannot introduce statements from absent witnesses (for example, on tape), unless defendants have opportunities to cross-examine such witnesses at earlier hearings or in previous trials.
2004	Hamdi v. Rumsfeld	Held that U.S. citizens captured on foreign battlefields in the war on terrorism have a due process right to a "meaningful opportunity" to contest the factual basis for their detention.

Supreme Court Rulings on Criminal Justice

Year	Case	Relevance to criminal justice
2004	Hiibel v. Sixth Judicial District Court of Nevada	Held that police are entitled to obtain the names of persons they suspect are involved in crimes, even in the absence of the probable cause normally necessary to make arrests.
2004	Missouri v. Seibert	Ruled that police cannot withhold Miranda warnings during initial phases of questioning in order to induce inadmissible confessions that the suspects might be persuaded to repeat after receiving their Miranda warnings; in such cases, the second confessions are not admissible either.
2005	Roper v. Simmons*	Ruled that it is unconstitutional to impose capital punishment for crimes committed while under the age of 18.
2005	Gonzales v. Raich	Ruled that under the Commerce Clause of the Constitution, Congress may criminalize production and use of homegrown cannabis even if states approve its use for medicinal purposes.
2006	Gonzales v. Oregon	Held that the federal Controlled Substances Act did not prevent physicians from being able to prescribe the drugs needed to perform assisted suicides under state law.
2006	Georgia v. Randolph	Held that police cannot conduct a warrantless search in a home where one occupant consents and the other objects.
2006	Hamdan v. Rumsfeld	Held that the military commissions set up by the Bush administration to try detainees at Guantanamo Bay are illegal because they lack the protections required by the Geneva Conventions and the Uniform Code of Military Justice.
2006	Lopez v. Gonzales	An aggravated felony includes only conduct punishable as a felony under the federal Controlled Substances Act, regardless of whether state law classifies such conduct as a felony or a misdemeanor.
2007	Gonzales v. Carhart	Upheld the Partial-Birth Abortion Ban Act of 2003.
2007	Panetti v. Quarterman	Held that criminal defendants sentenced to death may not be executed if they do not understand the reason for their imminent execution, and that once the state has set an execution date death row inmates may litigate their competency to be executed in habeas corpus proceedings.
2008	Boumediene v. Bush	Held that foreign terrorism suspects held at Guantanamo Bay have the constitutional right to challenge their detention in United States courts.
2008	Baze v. Rees	Held that the three-drug cocktail used for performing executions by lethal injection in all of the states using lethal injection at the time is constitutional under the Eighth Amendment.
2008	Kennedy v. Louisiana	Ruled the death penalty is unconstitutional in all cases that do not involve murder or crimes against the state, such as treason.
2008	District of Columbia v. Heller	Held that the Second Amendment applies to federal enclaves in protecting an individual's right to possess a firearm unconnected with service in a militia and to use it for traditionally lawful purposes such as self-defense within the home.
2008	United States v. Williams	Ruled that a federal statute prohibiting the "pandering" of child pornography (offering or requesting to transfer, sell, deliver, or trade the items) does not violate the First Amendment to the United States Constitution, even if a person charged under the code does not in fact possess child pornography with which to trade.

Supreme Court Rulings on Criminal Justice

Year	Case	Relevance to criminal justice
2008	*Kennedy v. Louisiana*	Held that the Eighth Amendment's Cruel and Unusual Punishments Clause does not permit a state to punish the crime of rape of a child with the death penalty; more broadly, the power of the state to impose the death penalty against an individual for committing a crime that did not result in the death of the victim is now limited to crimes against the state (e.g., espionage, treason).
2009	*Montejo v. Louisiana*	Overruled its prior decision in *Michigan v. Jackson* (1986) that held that a defendant may waive his or her right to counsel during a police interrogation even if the interrogation begins after the defendant's assertion of his or her right to counsel at an arraignment or similar proceeding.
2009	*Herring v. United States*	Held that the good-faith exception to the exclusionary rule applies when a police officer makes an arrest based on an outstanding warrant in another jurisdiction, but the information regarding that warrant is later found to be incorrect because of a negligent error by that agency.
2009	*United States v. Hayes*	Interpreted Section 921(a)(33)(A) of the federal Gun Control Act of 1968, as amended in 1996, holding that a domestic relationship is not necessarily a defining element of the offense to support a conviction for possession of a firearm by a person previously convicted of a misdemeanor crime of domestic violence.
2010	*Graham v. Florida*	Held that a sentence of life imprisonment without the possibility of parole may not be imposed on juvenile non-homicide offenders.
2010	*McDonald v. Chicago*	Ruled that the individual right to keep and bear arms for self-defense is fully applicable to the states through the Due Process Clause of the Fourteenth Amendment.
2010	*Abbott v. United States*	Addressed the mandatory sentencing increase under federal law for the possession or use of a deadly weapon in drug trafficking and violent crimes. The Court ruled a minimum five-year prison sentence is to be imposed in addition to any other mandatory sentence given for another crime, including the underlying drug-related or violent offense. The only exception to the five-year addition applies only when another provision required a longer mandatory term for conduct.
2010	*Padilla v. Kentucky*	Held that criminal defense attorneys are required to inform non-citizen clients about the deportation risks of a guilty plea or conviction.
2011	*Brown v. Plata*	Ruled that a court-mandated population limit was necessary to remedy a violation of prisoners' Eighth Amendment constitutional rights. The Court orders California to reduce its prison population to 137.5% of design capacity within two years.
2011	*J.D.B. v. North Carolina*	Held that age is relevant when determining police custody for Miranda purposes.
2012	*Miller v. Alabama*	Ruled that a sentence of life imprisonment without the possibility of parole may not be a mandatory sentence for juvenile offenders.
2012	*Arizona v. United States*	Arizona law enforcement may inquire about a resident's legal status during lawful encounters, but the state may not implement its own immigration laws.
2012	*United States v. Jones*	Held that attaching a GPS device to a vehicle and then using the device to monitor the vehicle's movements constitutes a search under the Fourth Amendment.
2013	*Salinas v. Texas*	Ruled that the Fifth Amendment's protection against self-incrimination does not protect an individual's refusal to answer questions asked by law enforcement before he or she has been arrested or given the Miranda warning. A witness cannot invoke the privilege by simply standing mute; he or she must expressly invoke it.

Year	Case	Relevance to criminal justice
2014	*Riley v. California*	Ruled that the police need warrants to search the cell phones of arrestees.
2014	*Hall v. Florida*	Rejected Florida's IQ cutoff as too rigid to decide which mentally disabled people must be spared the death penalty.
2015	*Obergefell v. Hodges*	Guaranteed the fundamental right to marry to same-sex couples.
2015	*Holt v. Hobbs*	Found that Arkansas corrections officials had violated the religious liberty rights of Muslim inmates by forbidding them to grow beards over security concerns.
2016	*Betterman v. Montana*	Found that the Sixth Amendment does not guarantee a right to a speedy sentencing after conviction. The Sixth Amendment's "speedy trial clause" only applies to the trial portion of criminal proceedings.
2016	*Foster v. Chatman*	Evidence was sufficient to establish that there was purposeful discrimination in that prosecutors discriminated against Timothy Foster when they removed all black potential jurors from his jury pool, violating the Equal Protection Clause of the 14th Amendment. The 1986 Batson v. Kentucky precedent was upheld.

Theodore M. Vestal
Updated by the Editors

Famous American Trials

Date	Trial	Charge or Issue	Result or Significance
1634	Roger Williams	Religious dissent	Williams was found guilty of blasphemy and exiled from Massachusetts Bay Colony; he subsequently founded Rhode Island.
1636	Anne Marbury Hutchinson	Religious dissent	Hutchinson was convicted of sedition and contempt and exiled; she founded Portsmith, Rhode Island.
1690	Rebecca Nurse and others	Witchcraft	During the Salem witchcraft trials, Rebecca Nurse and five others (all old men and women) were convicted of witchcraft and hanged.
1735	John Peter Zenger	Seditious libel	Zenger published a newspaper opposed to the New York colonial government. He was arrested and imprisoned. Defended by Alexander Hamilton, Zenger proved that his statements were true and was acquitted. His trial set the pattern for freedom of the press in America.
1770	William McCauley and others	Manslaughter	McCauley and six other British soldiers were tried for killing five men in a riot on Boston Commons in March, 1770 (the "Boston massacre"). Future president John Adams defended them. Four were acquitted and two were convicted. The latter were branded and released.
1804	Samuel Chase	Impeachment	Associate Justice Chase was impeached by Jeffersonian Democrats for his opposition during sedition trials, but the Senate refused to convict him.
1807	Aaron Burr	Treason	Burr planned to create a personal empire in the Mississippi Valley. President Thomas Jefferson charged him with treason. The judge, Chief Justice John Marshall, narrowly defined the charge, and Burr was quickly acquitted. Popular sentiment was so much against Burr, however, that he was forced into European exile for a number of years.
1859	John Brown	Treason and murder	Brown's trial on charges stemming from his abolitionist raid on the federal arsenal at Harpers Ferry lasted four days. Supporters' plans to free him failed. The jury convicted him in forty-five minutes, and he was hanged two months later.
1862	Rda-in-yan-ka, Big Eagle, and others	Murder	After a Sioux uprising in 1862 in Minnesota in which more than four hundred white settlers were killed, a mass trial was held. Three hundred and six Indians were sentenced to death and eighteen to prison. President Abraham Lincoln commuted all but thirty-nine of the death sentences. Rda-in-yan-ka was hanged and Big Eagle was imprisoned.
1865	Mary Surratt	Conspiracy to murder and treason	Linked to the assassination of President Abraham Lincoln because the conspirators stayed at her boardinghouse, Surratt was found guilty and hanged although there was no direct evidence against her.
1866	Samuel A. Mudd	Conspiracy to murder	A physician, Mudd treated John Wilkes Booth after he killed Lincoln. Although he claimed he did not know of the assassination, he was sentenced to life imprisonment.
1868	Andrew Johnson	Impeachment for high crimes and misdemeanors	A southern pro-Union Democrat, Johnson became president after Lincoln's assassination. The Republican Congress passed a law limiting his ability to control his cabinet. When he refused to abide, an impeachment trial in the Senate began. Johnson was acquitted when seven Republicans refused to join the others in a guilty verdict: The charge failed by one vote to reach the required two-thirds majority.

Famous American Trials

Date	Trial	Charge or Issue	Result or Significance
1873	Susan B. Anthony	Illegal voting	After voting in Rochester, New York, in a federal election, Anthony was arrested for illegal voting because she was a woman. When she was later tried, the judge would not let her testify and instructed the jury to find her guilty. She was convicted and fined one hundred dollars and court costs, but she refused to pay. She petitioned Congress to remit her unjust fine, but Congress ignored her petition.
1875	John Doyle Lee	Murder	A Mormon and Indian agent, Lee was involved in a dispute with a band of California-bound settlers. He encouraged a group of Paiute Indians to kill them and participated in the massacre at Mountain Meadows, Utah. After two trials he was executed.
1881	Charles J. Guiteau	Murder	The assassin of President James Garfield, Guiteau was convicted and executed.
1886	August Spies and others	Accessory to murder	Spies and seven others were tried for abetting the murder of policemen killed by a bomb during a labor demonstration in Chicago (the Haymarket Riot). Although their connection to the crime could not be proved, they were charged because they were labor leaders and outspoken anarchists. They were convicted—seven sentenced to hang and one, Oscar Neebe, to life imprisonment. One committed suicide. Two death sentences were commuted. Four of the men were hanged, including Spies. The remaining three were pardoned by Illinois governor John Peter Altgel in 1893.
1893	Lizzie Borden	Murder	When Borden was thirty-two years old, her father and stepmother were brutally killed by blows from an axe in their Massachusetts home in 1892. The circumstantial evidence against Borden was strong, but she was acquitted of murder in a jury trial. Nevertheless, her name was ever afterward associated with her parents' murder.
1901	Leon Czolgosz	Murder	Czolgosz was the anarchist assassin of President William McKinley. He was rapidly tried and convicted in Buffalo, New York, where the assassination took place. He was executed by electrocution.
1906	William Dudley ("Big Bill") Haywood	Murder	Haywood was accused with others of murdering Frank Steunenberg, the governor of Idaho. They were defended by Clarence Darrow and acquitted.
1907	Harry Thaw	Murder	A wealthy socialite married to the dancer Evelyn Nesbit, Thaw shot and killed Nesbit's lover, prominent architect Stanford White. He was acquitted on grounds of insanity.
1911	J. J. and J. B. McNamara	Murder	The McNamara brothers bombed the *Los Angeles Times* building during a labor dispute, killing twenty-one persons. Their attorney, Clarence Darrow, pleaded guilty to save their lives. They were sentenced to long prison terms.
1914	Joe Hill (Joe Emmanuel Hagglund)	Murder	A Swedish-born labor organizer and composer, Hill was falsely charged with murder. He was convicted on doubtful evidence and executed despite widespread appeals for reconsideration, including one from President Woodrow Wilson.
1917	Margaret Sanger	Creating a public nuisance	A nurse and advocate of artificial birth control, then illegal in most states, Sanger was arrested and convicted of creating a public nuisance. She was sentenced to thirty days in jail.
1917	Emma Goldman	Hindering conscription	An anarchist and pacifist, Goldman opposed American entry into World War I. She was tried for impeding conscription, denaturalized, and returned to her native Russia in 1919.

The Criminal Justice System — Famous American Trials

Date	Trial	Charge or Issue	Result or Significance
1918	Eugene V. Debs	Sedition	A labor leader and pioneer American socialist, Debs was tried and convicted of violating the Espionage Act. Sentenced to ten years, he was pardoned by President Warren G. Harding in 1921.
1921–1922	Roscoe "Fatty" Arbuckle	Manslaughter	A comedic film star, Arbuckle was arrested after the death of a young actress at a Hollywood party. After three trials he was acquitted, but his film career was ruined because of the scandal.
1924	Nicola Sacco and Bartolomeo Vanzetti	Murder and robbery	Sacco and Vanzetti were Italian-born anarchists who were tried and convicted of armed robbery and murder in 1924. Although the evidence against them was flimsy and some evidence pointed toward other possible culprits, the authorities refused appeals and new trials. Sacco and Vanzetti were convicted largely because of their anarchist political beliefs. The case provoked worldwide condemnation and mass demonstrations. Sacco and Vanzetti were executed in 1927. Fifty years later, Massachusetts governor Michael Dukakis issued a proclamation formally exonerating them of any guilt or stigma.
1924	Nathan Leopold and Richard Loeb	Murder	This celebrated case involved the brutal homosexual rape and murder of young Bobby Franks by two wealthy young men, Leopold and Loeb. Clarence Darrow successfully argued against the murderers' execution in a bench trial, and they were given life imprisonment. Loeb was killed in prison in 1936; Leopold was paroled in 1968 and died three years later.
1925	John T. Scopes	Teaching evolution	In what was dubbed the "monkey trial," Scopes, a high school teacher, deliberately broke Tennessee's law against teaching Darwinian evolution. The trial gained national publicity because it pitted William Jennings Bryan as prosecutor against Clarence Darrow for the defense. Scopes was convicted and given a nominal fine. The U.S. Supreme Court overturned Scopes's conviction, but the statute remained.
1926	Albert Fall	Accepting bribes	The secretary of the interior under President Warren G. Harding, Fall was at the center of the Teapot Dome scandal, giving out generous leases on public land. He was convicted and served one year in prison.
1927	Harry Daugherty	Conspiracy to defraud the government	President Harding's attorney general, Daugherty was also involved in the Teapot Dome scandal. His two trials ended in hung juries.
1931	Haywood Patterson and others	Rape	Patterson and eight other African Americans were falsely charged with rape in Scottsboro, Alabama. All-white juries quickly convicted them in three trials, and all nine were sentenced to execution. The "Scottsboro" case drew national attention and involved complex political and racial issues. The U.S. Supreme Court overturned the convictions because the defendants were denied due process and the right to counsel.
1931	Al Capone	Income tax evasion	A notorious gangster involved in the illegal manufacture and sale of alcohol and other rackets, Capone had long evaded arrest. Federal authorities finally charged him with violating the tax laws. He was convicted and sentenced to eleven years in prison and fined $80,000.
1936	Bruno Hauptmann	Kidnapping and murder	Hauptmann was charged in the sensational Lindbergh kidnapping case. He was accused of kidnapping and murdering the son of famous aviator Charles Lindbergh. Although the evidence was circumstantial, he was convicted and executed. The media reporting of the event was extremely controversial.
1941	Louis (Lepke) Buchalter	Murder	The leader of Murder Incorporated, Buchalter's organized crime assassination ring in 1930's New York, was convicted in one of a series of trials against racketeers that brought District Attorney Thomas E. Dewey to prominence. Buchalter was executed.

Famous American Trials

Date	Trial	Charge or Issue	Result or Significance
1948	Caryl Chessman	Kidnapping	Chessman forced his victim from one car to another and raped her. In a trial in which he defended himself, he was convicted on the technical charge of kidnapping, rather than rape, and was sentenced to death. His execution was postponed for twelve years, during which time he wrote a number of successful books. The controversial nature of the charge, the length of the delay, and his personal publicity made his case a *cause célèbre*.
1949	Julius and Ethel Rosenberg	Espionage	The Rosenbergs were convicted of passing atomic secrets to the Soviet Union in a controversial trial. Despite many appeals for their sentences to be commuted to life imprisonment, they were executed.
1950	Alger Hiss	Perjury	Hiss was tried and convicted in a second trial after a first one ended in a hung jury. He was charged with lying about his communist connections. The trials were public sensations, contributing to the hysteria of the McCarthy period.
1951	Elizabeth Gurley Flynn	Smith Act (membership in the Communist Party)	A prominent radical labor leader and Communist Party member, Flynn was convicted under the Smith Act of 1940.
1954	Sam Sheppard	Murder	Sheppard was convicted of murdering his wife and sentenced to life imprisonment. The U.S. Supreme Court in 1965 overturned the conviction because the publicity associated with the case had denied him a fair trial.
1964	Jack Ruby	Murder	The killer of President John F. Kennedy's alleged assassin, Lee Harvey Oswald, Ruby was defended by attorney Melvin Belli. He was convicted and sentenced to death, but the conviction was reversed in 1966 on appeal, and he died while awaiting a new trial.
1967	Jimmy Hoffa	Jury tampering and mishandling union funds	The leader of the mob-ridden Teamsters Union, Hoffa was an object of the U.S. Department of Justice's war on union corruption. He was convicted in 1967 after several trials and then pardoned in 1971.
1968	James Earl Ray	Murder	Ray was convicted of murdering civil rights leader Martin Luther King, Jr., and sentenced to life imprisonment.
1969	Angela Davis	Accessory to murder	Charged because her guns were used in a prison escape attempt, Davis was acquitted in a case that brought international publicity. Her membership in the Communist Party was thought to be part of the reason behind the charge.
1969-1970	Rennie Davis and others	Conspiracy and intent to incite riot	The "Chicago eight" (later seven), were arrested for disrupting the 1968 Democratic convention. Conspiracy charges were dismissed, but five were convicted of intent to incite riot; they were sentenced to five years and fined. Prominent attorney William Kunstler defended them. The convictions were reversed in 1972.
1971	Charles Manson and others	Murder	The leader of a counterculture commune known as the "Manson family," Charles Manson was charged with the murder of actor Sharon Tate and more than six others. Although the murders were carried out by his followers, and he was not present at any of them, he was seen as primarily responsible. Manson was sentenced to death, but later the sentence was commuted when California overturned its death penalty. The trial attracted international attention.
1971	William J. Calley	Murder	A U.S. Army lieutenant, Calley commanded a platoon that massacred women and children in the South Vietnamese village of My Lai during the war. The publicity about the event forced a court-martial of Calley. He was convicted and sentenced to twenty years, but he served little time before being pardoned.

Date	Trial	Charge or Issue	Result or Significance
1971	Daniel Ellsberg	Theft, espionage, and conspiracy	Ellsberg leaked the Pentagon Papers, secret documents that contained information on U.S. violations of international law in the Vietnam War. He was indicted, but the charges were dismissed because of improper government actions in preparing their case.
1973	Spiro Agnew	Accepting bribes	Charged with accepting bribes and other wrongdoing while he had held public offices—including the governorship—in Maryland, Vice President Agnew pleaded no contest and was sentenced to three years' probation and a $10,000 fine. He resigned as vice president.
1973	John Dean	Perjury	A key figure in the Watergate scandal, Dean pleaded guilty of perjury in the cover-up and was sentenced to prison.
1974	G. Gordon Liddy	Burglary, conspiracy, and wiretapping	One of the principal "plumbers" in the Watergate affair, Liddy was convicted of burglarizing and bugging the Democratic headquarters and was sentenced to seven to twenty years.
1974-1975	John Mitchell, H. R. Haldeman, John Ehrlichman, and others	Conspiracy	Seven high-ranking members of the Nixon administration, White House staff, and Republican National Committee were indicted for illegal conspiracy relating to the 1972 election. Five, including Mitchell, Haldeman, and Ehrlichman, were convicted and given sentences ranging from two and one-half to eight years.
1974	E. Howard Hunt and others	Burglary, conspiracy, and wiretapping	Along with G. Gordon Liddy, Hunt directed the Watergate burglary. He and his four codefendants actually carried out the burglary. Hunt pleaded guilty and was sentenced to thirty months to eight years.
1975	Patricia Hearst	Armed robbery	Kidnapped by the radical terrorist Symbionese Liberation Army, Hearst, the daughter of a newspaper magnate, joined the group and participated in its bank robberies. Her criminal career, capture, and trial were a media sensation. She claimed to have been "brainwashed" but was convicted and sentenced to seven years, commuted by President Jimmy Carter after two and one-half years.
1976	Gary Gilmore	Murder	Gilmore was convicted of two murders and sentenced to death. His case became controversial when he requested (and received) execution rather than following up the appeals process, and his 1977 execution was the first in the United States since the U.S. Supreme Court had ordered executions halted in 1972.
1982	Claus von Bulow	Attempted murder	A financial consultant married to a New England socialite, von Bulow was convicted of trying to kill her by administering an insulin overdose. He was sentenced to thirty years. The conviction was overturned in 1985 when von Bulow was represented by attorney Alan Dershowitz.
1984	Raymond James Donovan	Falsifying documents, business records	President Ronald Reagan's secretary of labor, Donovan was hounded through his tenure of office by charges of corruption linked to organized crime. He was indicted, tried, and acquitted.
1984, 1986	John DeLorean	Drug trafficking, racketeering, and fraud	In two trials, automobile entrepreneur DeLorean was acquitted on all counts.
1986	Jim Bakker	Conspiracy and fraud	A television evangelist, Bakker lost his ministry because of a sex scandal and then was convicted of diverting donations from his ministry to his personal use and other frauds. He was sentenced to forty-five years in prison. His conviction was upheld in appeal, but his sentence was reduced to eighteen years and he was released even sooner.

Famous American Trials

Date	Trial	Charge or Issue	Result or Significance
1989	Oliver North	Conspiracy to defraud and obstruction of Congress	A staff member on the National Security Council, North was a key figure in the Iran-Contra scandal (the Reagan administration's illegal trading of arms for hostages). He was convicted of covering up the affair and sentenced to a three-year suspended sentence, probation, a fine, and community service.
1990	John Poindexter	Conspiracy, perjury, and obstruction of Congress	As secretary of the Navy, Poindexter lied during the congressional investigation of the Iran-Contra scandal. He was convicted on all counts and sentenced to six months. The conviction was reversed on appeal.
1990	Marion Barry	Drug possession	The mayor of Washington, D.C., Barry was convicted of cocaine possession and sentenced to six months. After serving his term he was again elected mayor.
1992	Jeffrey Dahmer	Murder	A serial killer, Dahmer enticed his victims to his apartment, murdered them, and saved parts of their bodies. He also engaged in cannibalism. The gory nature of his crimes made his trial a sensation. He was ruled sane, convicted of murder, and sentenced to sixteen life terms. He was killed in prison in 1994.
1992	Mike Tyson	Rape	The heavyweight boxing champion was accused and convicted of raping a participant in a beauty contest in which he was a judge.
1992	William Kennedy Smith	Rape	A member of the prominent Kennedy family, Smith was accused of rape by a woman he invited to the family's compound in Florida. He was acquitted after a televised trial.
1992, 1993	Stacey Koon, Laurence Powell, and others	Police misconduct, violation of civil rights	Four Los Angeles police officers were charged with using excessive force in arresting African American motorist Rodney King for a traffic violation. The beating of King was videotaped by a witness. The police officers were acquitted by a suburban jury, causing five days of rioting in Los Angeles. In a second trial in federal court, Koon and Powell were convicted of civil rights violations and sentenced to two-and-a-half years.
1993	Lorena Bobbitt	Malicious wounding	Bobbitt cut off her husband's penis in retaliation for spousal abuse. (Doctors were able to restore the organ surgically.) She was acquitted and became a feminist icon for standing up to male abuse.
1993-1994, 1995-1996	Erik and Lyle Menendez	Murder	In a much-publicized case, the Menendez brothers, who were accused of murdering their wealthy parents, pleaded innocent on the basis that they had been abused as children. Their first trial was declared a mistrial. In their second trial, they were both convicted of first-degree murder and sentenced to life in prison without the possibility of parole.
1994	Byron de la Beckwith	Murder	Beckwith assassinated prominent civil rights activist Medgar Evers in 1963. Although he was known to have committed the crime, racial prejudice in Mississippi—where the murder occurred—resulted in two hung juries. A new trial took place in 1994. He was convicted and sentenced to life imprisonment.
1995	Susan Smith	Murder	After murdering her two young sons, Smith claimed that they were kidnapped. She was convicted and sentenced to life imprisonment.
1995	O. J. Simpson	Murder	In a sensational, nationally televised trial lasting almost a year, celebrity and former football star Simpson was charged with murdering his former wife and her friend. A jury took less than a day to acquit him in a decision that had racial overtones and divided the nation.

Date	Trial	Charge or Issue	Result or Significance
1996	Timothy McVeigh	Bombing	Two days after the bomb blast that killed 168 people in a federal office building in Oklahoma City, Oklahoma, McVeigh and his friend Terry Nichols were arrested. A federal grand jury later indicted them for first-degree murder, conspiracy to use a weapon of mass destruction, and destruction by explosives. McVeigh was later tried by himself, found guilty on all counts, and executed.
1999	Jack Kevorkian	Murder	A medical doctor and outspoken practitioner of assisted suicide, Kevorkian repeatedly challenged state laws by assisting with more than one hundred suicides until he was convicted of second-degree murder in Michigan and sentenced to ten to twenty-five years in prison.
1999	Bill Clinton	Impeachment	In late 1998, the House Judiciary Committee approved four articles of impeachment against President Clinton: perjury before a grand jury, obstruction of justice, perjury in a civil deposition, and abuse of power. After the full House approved two of the articles, the impeachment trial opened in the Senate in January. The trial ended with the Senate voting 45 to 55 for conviction on the perjury count and 50 to 50 on the obstruction of justice count. As conviction requires a two-thirds vote, the president was acquitted.
2002	Andrea Yates	Murder	Suffering from severe mental disorders, Yates drowned all five of her young children in a bathtub. A Texas jury rejected her insanity defense and convicted her of murder but sentenced her to life in prison. In 2005, her conviction was overturned because of faulty expert testimony in her trial, but she remained in prison under psychiatric care.
2002	Winona Ryder	Shoplifting	The shoplifting charges against Ryder were comparatively minor, but her fame as an actor attracted great public interest in her case, particularly because of the apparent senselessness of the crime of shoplifting by a wealthy person. Convicted on two counts of felony theft, she was sentenced to paying restitution and community service, but her felony convictions were later reduced to misdemeanor convictions.
2004	Martha Stewart	Conspiracy, making false statements, obstruction of justice, and securities fraud	Stewart was investigated for insider trading but was tried for only a variety of technical offenses. Because of her fame as a television and publishing personality, her trial was closely watched by the media. In early 2004, she and her stockbroker were convicted on all charges, and she was sentenced to five months in a federal prison.
2004	Scott Peterson	Murder	Four months after Peterson's pregnant wife, Laci, disappeared, Peterson was charged with both her murder and the murder of her unborn child. Peterson's subsequent trial attracted wide interest because of public curiosity about how such an attractive and apparently loving couple's marriage could end in murder and because of legal questions about whether the killing of a fetus could constitute murder.
2004-2005	Jayson Williams	Manslaughter	A wealthy former basketball star, Williams shot to death his chauffeur in what was apparently a drunken accident in 2002. The charge against Williams was manslaughter, but the issue was whether the homicide was aggravated manslaughter or merely negligent manslaughter. In Williams's first trial, a jury acquitted him of aggravated manslaughter, but afterward, a judge ordered that he be retried for reckless manslaughter.
2005	Robert Blake	Murder	Blake was tried for murdering his wife and for attempting to solicit murder. The circumstantial evidence against him was strong, but the prosecution failed to prove its case beyond a reasonable doubt, and he was acquitted by a jury.

Famous American Trials

Date	Trial	Charge or Issue	Result or Significance
2005	Michael Jackson	Child molestation	A decade after a scandal in which the famous pop singer was alleged to have paid millions of dollars to silence a child who had charged him with sexual molestation, Jackson was brought to trial in another molestation case that turned into a true media circus. After a trial that heard the testimony of more than 130 witnesses over the course of fourteen weeks, a jury deliberated for seven days and then ruled Jackson not guilty on all counts.
2006	Andrea Yates	Capital murder	Andrea Yates drowned her five children, one by one, in a bathtub at their Clear Lake, Texas home. Yates who had a history of mental illness (postpartum depression and psychosis) thought the only way of prohibiting her children from eternal damnation was to kill them. She plead not guilty by reason of insanity. In her first trial she was found not guilty by reason of insanity in 2002 and was sentenced to life in prison and then in a second trial in 2006 was ordered to a mental hospital.
2006	Sadam Hussein	Crimes Against Humanity	On November 5, 2006 the Iraq Special Tribunal sentenced the President of Iraq, Saddam Hussein, to death by hanging for the killing of 148 Shiites from Dujail, Iraq, a small town in the Saladin Province, in retaliation for a 1982 assassination attempt on his life. Hussein was executed on December 30, 2006 within 30 days of the sentence. According to Human Rights Watch, Hussein's death resulted in a "flawed trial and marks a significant step away from the rule of law in Iraq."
2007	Brian Gall	Federal Sentencing Guidelines	Brian Gall, while a student at the University of Iowa, was a member of an ongoing enterprise distributing the drug "ecstasy." He withdrew from the conspiracy after seven months. He thereafter used no drugs and worked steadily, eventually becoming a master carpenter. He subsequently became the focus of a criminal investigation regarding his past drug sales, and ultimately pleaded guilty. A presentence report recommended a sentence of 30 to 37 months in prison. However, the District Court judge sentenced Gall to 36 months probation, finding that imprisonment was unnecessary due to his voluntary withdrawal and post-offense conduct and no longer being a danger to society. The Eighth Circuit reversed on the ground that a sentence outside the Federal Sentencing Guidelines range must be supported by extraordinary circumstances, which were not present in the Gall matter. The Supreme Court then held that the sentence imposed by the District Court was reasonable based upon the totality of circumstances and that the Eighth Circuit's decision could not stand. A federal appeals court may not presume a sentence falling outside the range recommended by the Federal Sentencing Guidelines is unreasonable.
2008	Patrick O'Neal Kennedy	Limitation on Capital Punishment	In 2003 a Louisiana court found Patrick Kennedy guilty of raping his eight-year-old stepdaughter, which under Louisiana law was punishable by the death penalty. The prosecutor sought, and the court imposed, the death penalty. The defendant appealed to the Louisiana Supreme Court, affirming the imposition of the death penalty when the victim was a child. In a subsequent landmark decision, the U.S. Supreme held that the Eighth Amendment's Cruel and Unusual Punishments Clause did not permit imposition of the death penalty for commission of a crime that did not result in the death of the victim or a crime against the state, such as treason or espionage.

Date	Trial	Charge or Issue	Result or Significance
2008	Sean Bell	First- and Second-degree Manslaughter, First- and Second-degree Assault, and Second-degree Reckless Endangerment	In 2006 in Queens, New York three males were shot a total of 50 times by New York Police Department plainclothes and undercover officers who were present because the club owners were being investigated by undercover police for claims of fostering prostitution. The incident took place at a strip club where Bell was hosting a bachelor party the morning before he was to be married. Sean Bell was killed and two of his friends, Trent Benefield and Joseph Guzman, were severely wounded. Public outcry harshly condemned the police for force thought by many as excessive and three of five detectives involved in the shooting went to trial and were found not guilty.
2009	Ali Saleh Kahlah al-Marri	Indefinite Detention Absent Charges	Ali Saleh Kahlah al-Marri, a citizen of Qatar but a legal resident of the United States, was arrested, classified as an enemy combatant, and transferred to military custody where he was detained for 6 years in solitary confinement at the Naval Consolidate Brig at Charleston, South Carolina. Ultimately, he was entitled to contest his detention in federal court where it was ruled that he needed to be charged and tried, or released. He pleaded guilty to one count in a plea bargain after his case was transferred in 2009 to the federal court system. He is the only non-citizen known to have been held as an enemy combatant within the continental United States since the September 11 attacks.
2010	Van Chester Thompkins	Miranda Rights	Van Chester Thompkins was a suspect in a fatal shooting on January 10, 2000. Thompkins remained silent after being advised of his Miranda Rights, not expressing that he wanted to rely on his right to remain silent, nor that he did not want to talk to the police nor speak with an attorney. Officers then interrogated him and for a three-hour period he remained almost completely silent, uttering a few comments that did not have a bearing on the case. The officers then changed their approach to a spiritual one and through this approach elicited incriminating responses. Thompkins made a motion to suppress his statements, claiming he had not waived his rights. The U.S. Supreme Court opined that a suspect's silence did not invoke his right to remain silent; the invocation of that right must be unambiguous, and silence is not enough to invoke it.
2010	Lindsey Lohan	Violation of Probation	Actress Lindsey Lohan was sentenced to 90 days in jail for missing alcohol counseling sessions and was ordered to spend 90 days in a drug and alcohol rehabilitation program after her incarceration. This case illustrates that the court system normally strives to deal with celebrities and non-celebrities equitably.
2010	Oscar Grant III	Murder	On New Year's Day 2009 Bay Area Rapid Transit (BART) police officer Johannes Mehserle responded to reports of a fight on a BART train returning from San Francisco to Oakland, California. Oscar Grant was detained on a train platform lying face down and handcuffed when he was shot in the back and eventually died. The incident was caught on digital video and cell phone cameras. Public outrage, protests, and riots followed and the incident was condemned by some as a summary execution. Grant's shooter, Mehserle, was found guilty of involuntary manslaughter and was sentenced to two years incarceration minus credit for time served.
2011	Tom Delay Trial	Money Laundering and Conspiracy Charges Related to Illegal Campaign Finance Activities	In January 2011 Delay was sentenced to three years in prison on the charge of conspiring to launder corporate money into political donations and received ten years probation for money laundering. In 2013 Delay's convictions were overturned on the basis of not having sufficient evidence to sustain his convictions.

Famous American Trials   The Criminal Justice System

Date	Trial	Charge or Issue	Result or Significance
2011	Rod Blagojevich	Corruption	Rod Blagojevich, a politician and former Governor of Illinois, was found guilty of approximately 17 charges some of which included wire fraud, attempted extortion, conspiracy to solicit bribes, and conspiracy to commit mail fraud. The case involved the request of personal benefit in exchange for an appointment to the United States Senate as a replacement for Barack Obama after his resignation when he was elected President of the United States. Blagojevich was sentenced to 14 years incarceration.
2011	Casey Anthony	Capital Murder	Casey Anthony was found not guilty of first-degree murder and the other most serious charges against her in the 2008 death of her 2-year-old daughter, Caylee Marie Anthony. However, the jury convicted her on four misdemeanor counts of providing false information to law enforcement officers. She was sentenced to four years in jail for lying to law enforcement but she received credit for the time she served. Two of the convictions for providing false information to police were thrown out by an appeals court in 2013.
2011	Conrad Murry	Involuntary Manslaughter	Conrad Murry, a cardiologist, was the personal physician of Michael Jackson, pop singer, before his death from a massive overdose of the general anesthetic propofol. Dr. Murry was convicted, and then sentenced to four years in jail of which he served two.
2011	Zacarias Moussaoui	Terrorism	A federal grand jury indicted Zacarias Moussaoui in December 2001for conspiracy related to the "9/11" attacks. Minnesota FBI agents had arrested Moussaoui on immigration charges, alerted by a flight instructor of his unusual involvement in flight training. Moussaoui admitted his involvement with al-Qaeda but claimed he was not involved with the "9/11" attacks. He also said he was aware of the "9/11" attacks but did nothing to stop them; he added that he was preparing for another attack. He subsequently pleaded guilty to all terrorism-related charges. He was sentenced to life without parole in May 2006.
2011	Joanna Yeates	Murder	The English Yeates' trial involved a 25 year old female victim who was a landscape architect from Bristol, England. She was declared missing in December 17, 2010 and her body was found fully clothed in the snow on December 25, 2010. It was eventually determined she was strangled to death by a Dutch engineer named Vincent Tabak. In October 2011, Tabak was sentenced to jail for life, with a minimum term of 20 years. The Yeates murder inquiry was codenamed Operation Braid and one of the largest police investigations in the Bristol area, resulting in extensive international news coverage.
2012	Antoine Jones	Search and Seizure	Antoine Jones was suspected of drug trafficking. Police received a warrant to attach a GPS tracking device to his vehicle. A warrant was issued, authorizing installation of the device in the District of Columbia and within 10 days. In reality, the GPS was installed on the 11th day while the vehicle was parked in a public lot in Maryland. Jones was subsequently arrested and charged with distribution of cocaine. Recognizing the attachment of the GPS constituted a search and thus required a valid warrant, i.e., one which was compliant in terms of both time and geography, the search was deemed invalid by the federal trial court and the U.S. Court of Appeals for the District of Columbia.

The Criminal Justice System

Famous American Trials

Date	Trial	Charge or Issue	Result or Significance
2012	Anders Behring Breivik	Mass Murder and Terrorism	In 2011 Breivik, a Norwegian citizen, killed eight people by detonating a van bomb in Oslo, then shot dead 69 participants of a Workers' Youth League (AUF) summer camp on the island of Utøya. In 2012 in Oslo, Breivik was found sane and guilty of murdering 77 people. He was sentenced to 21 years in prison in preventive detention requiring a minimum of 10 years incarceration and the possibility of one or more extensions for as long as he was deemed a danger to society. Breivik received the maximum penalty in Norway.
2013	Ethan Couch (Affluenza Defense)	Intoxication Manslaughter	Ethan Couch, a 19-year-old male from Texas, killed four passengers and seriously injured two others who were driving with him while he was under the influence of alcohol. A Texas judge sentenced Couch to ten years of probation and then ordered him to a long-term in-patient facility for therapy. Couch's attorneys successfully argued that the teen was the product of affluenza (the unhealthy and unwelcome psychological and social influences of an affluent life) and he needed rehabilitation instead of incarceration. Eventually Couch violated his probation, fled to Mexico with his mother, and eventually in 2016 was sentenced to two years in jail. The affluenza defense and probation sentence set off a media firestorm, strong negative reactions from the public, and a national conversation about sentencing equity.
2014	David Leon Riley	Search and Seizure	David Leon Riley was accused of firing at a rival gang member's car in August 2009. Riley was subsequently pulled over for driving with expired license tags. In an inventory search of his car, police found weapons, for which he was arrested. Riley's cell phone was taken from him and the contents accessed without a warrant to determine whether he might be gang-affiliated. This led to information that tied him to the shooting. He was convicted and sentenced to 15 years to life in prison. Riley moved to suppress the evidence acquired through his cell phone. The ultimate finding of the U.S. Supreme Court was that evidence admitted at trial from Riley's cell phone was discovered through a search that violated his Fourth Amendment right.
2015	Jodi Arias	First-Degree Murder	In 2008 Jodi Arias killed her ex-boyfriend, Travis Alexander, by inflicting multiple stab wounds and a gunshot to the head. She claimed her actions were a result of self-defense. In 2015 she was sentenced to life in prison. The Arias trial received widespread media attention.
2015	Amanda Knox	Murder	The Amanda Knox trial was an Italian case that came to be known worldwide as the 'Trial of the Century." In 2007 Amanda Knox, an American student, and her Italian boyfriend, Raffaele Sollecito, were arrested for the killing Amanda's housemate, Meredith Kercher, a 21-year-old British student studying in Perugia, Italy. Knox was then placed in solitary confinement for the murder, primarily because of illegal interrogation and junk profiling behavior. In 2015 Italy's highest court finally ruled that she and her boyfriend were innocent of murder charges and ended the case. Knox was then able to return to the United States.
2015	Odin Lloyd	First-degree Murder	Odin Lloyd, a semi-pro linebacker for the Boston Bandits, was fatally shot. Aaron Hernandez, tight end for the New England Patriots, Carlos Ortiz, and Ernest Wallace were convicted in Lloyd's death. Aaron Hernandez was found guilty of first-degree murder, and Ortiz and Wallace were found guilty of accessories after the fact. Hernandez was sentenced to life imprisonment without the possibility of parole and both Ortiz and Wallace were sentenced to 4.5 to 7 years in prison. This case was high profile and made international headlines.

Date	Trial	Charge or Issue	Result or Significance
2016	Brock Allen Turner (Stanford Rape Case)	Rape/Felony Sexual Assault/Attempted Rape	Turner was a student athlete at Stanford University when he sexually penetrated an intoxicated and unconscious 22-year-old woman with his fingers. Specifically, he was found guilty of assault with intent to rape an intoxicated woman, sexually penetrating an intoxicated person with a foreign object, and sexually penetrating an unconscious person with a foreign object. In 2016 he was sentenced to six months in jail followed by three years of formal probation. Turner was released after three months jail time and is permanently registered as a sex offender. He was also required to participate in a sex offender rehabilitation program.
2016	Oscar Pistorius	Murder	Oscar Pistorius, a leading South African Summer Olympic athlete with prosthetic legs, shot and killed his girlfriend, model Reeva Steenkamp, claiming he mistook her for an intruder. In 2016 Pistorius was sentenced to six years in prison. This trial was broadcast live via television and came to international attention.

Frederick B. Chary
Updated by the Editors

Time Line

Year	Event
1692	Salem witchcraft trials result in the execution of twenty people in Massachusetts.
1773	Walnut Street Jail opens in Philadelphia.
1776	Continental Congress approves the Declaration of Independence, which formally begins the American Revolution.
1783	Treaty of Paris formally ends the American Revolution.
1787	U.S. Constitution is framed in Philadelphia in 1787 and becomes effective in 1789.
1789	The first U.S. Congress passes the First Judiciary Act to provide for an attorney general, the Supreme Court, and the establishment of the U.S. Marshals; Federal Crimes Act, the first law to define federal crimes.
1790	U.S. Supreme Court holds its first session.
1791	Ratification of the Bill of Rights adds major new rights protections to the U.S. Constitution.
1792	Congress passes the Uniform Militia Law, which authorizes creation of the National Guard.
1803	U.S. Supreme Court's *Marbury v. Madison* decision establishes the Court's power of judicial review over congressional legislation.
1804	Associate Justice Samuel Chase is impeached but is acquitted by the Senate.
1807	Former vice president Aaron Burr is tried and acquitted for treason on charges of attempting to lead a secessionist movement.
1820's	New York State opens Auburn and Sing Sing prisons.
1824	Society for the Reformation of Juvenile Delinquents is founded.
1830	First U.S. race riots occur against abolitionists and African Americans.
1831	Downtown Bank of New York City is the first in the United States to be robbed.
1843	M'Naghten rule establishes the use of the insanity defense in a criminal court.
1845	Macon B. Allen is the first African American lawyer admitted to the bar, in Worcester, Massachusetts.
1845	Federal government begins publishing the United States Statutes at Large.
1851	First of several San Francisco vigilante groups forms to combat lawlessness brought on by the California gold rush.
1859	John Brown is convicted of treason after leading an abolitionist raid on the federal arsenal at Harpers Ferry, Virginia; he is hanged in December.
1861-1865	Civil War; President Abraham Lincoln declares martial law and suspends the writ of *habeas corpus* in Washington, D.C., and Confederate territories occupied by Union troops during the war.
1862	Internal Revenue Service is established.
1865	Mary Surratt is the first woman to be executed in the United States after being convicted of participating in the conspiracy to assassinate President Abraham Lincoln.
1865	U.S. Secret Service is established to combat counterfeiting of currency.
1866	Ku Klux Klan is organized.
1868	Andrew Johnson is the first president to be impeached by the House of Representatives but is acquitted by the Senate.
1868	Ratification of the Fourteenth Amendment establishes, among other things, the principle of equality before the law, strengthens constitutional protections of due process, and creates a basis for incorporating the protections of the Bill of Rights to the states.

Time Line   The Criminal Justice System

Year	Event
1870	Ratification of the Fifteenth Amendment guarantees voting rights to African American men, prompting southern states to manipulate their voting laws to exclude black voters.
1870	Organizations founded: U.S. Justice Department; American Correctional Association; National Prison Association.
1873	Congress passes the Comstock law, which amends postal regulations prohibiting the use of the mails to send sexually suggestive material, including birth-control information.
1878	American Bar Association is established.
1879	President Rutherford B. Hayes signs a bill allowing female attorneys to argue cases before the Supreme Court.
1881	Charles J. Guiteau shoots President James Garfield, who dies two and one-half months later; Guiteau is convicted of murder and hanged the following year.
1883	Congress passes the Pendleton Civil Service Reform Act, which requires positions within the federal government to be awarded on the basis of merit rather than political affiliation. States and cities subsequently adopted the civil service system for selection and promotion of police officers and other members of the criminal justice system work force.
1884	In *Hurtado v. California*, the Supreme Court finds, for the first time, that the due process clause of the Fourteenth Amendment might apply some provisions of the Bill of Rights to the states.
1889	New York law legalizes the use of the electric chair for execution; William Kemmler becomes the first person to be executed by electric chair, despite a legal appeal to have electrocution ruled cruel and unusual punishment.
1890	Congress passes the Sherman Antitrust Act to prohibit restraints on trade.
1891	Federal Immigration and Naturalization Service is established.
1893	Lizzie Borden is tried for the axe-murder of her father and stepmother and is acquitted.
1893	International Association of Chiefs of Police is established.
1894	Yale University hires two New Haven, Connecticut, police officers, who become the forerunners of the first campus police in the United States.
1896	In *Plessy v. Ferguson*, the Supreme Court upholds a Louisiana segregation law and articulates the principle of "equal but separate," which governs legal tests of segregation over the next six decades
1896	The first documented American serial killer, "Dr. H. H. Holmes," is hanged.
1899	Illinois establishes the first juvenile court in the United States.
1901	Anarchist Leon Czolgosz assassinates President William McKinley; after a rapid trial, is executed by electrocution.
1907	National Council on Crime and Delinquency is established.
1907	New York City's police are the first in the United States to use police dogs.
1908	The forerunner of the Federal Bureau of Investigation, the Bureau of Investigation is established under the U.S. Department of Justice.
1909	Congress passes the Opium Exclusion Act, which bans the importation of opium and opium compounds, except those used expressly for medicinal purposes
1910	Congress passes the Mann Act to prohibit the interstate transportation of women for immoral purposes.
1912	National Automobile Theft Bureau is founded.
1914	Congress passes the Clayton Antitrust Act, which strengthens the Sherman Antitrust Act by regulating practices such as price discrimination, and the Harrison Narcotic Drug Act, the first federal antidrug act.
1914	In *Weeks v. United States*, the Supreme Court establishes the exclusionary rule to prohibit the use of illegally obtained evidence in federal criminal trials.
1914	Federal Trade Commission (FTC) is established to protect consumers.

The Criminal Justice System — Time Line

Year	Event
1915	The forerunner of the federal Drug Enforcement Administration is established as a branch of the Bureau of Internal Revenue.
1915	Police Activities League program begins in New York City.
1917	Congress passes the Espionage Act, which imposes twenty-year prison terms for offenders; anarchist Emma Goldman is convicted under the Espionage Act and is later deported to Russia.
1917	Major race riot erupts in East St. Louis, Illinois.
1918	Congress passes the Sedition Act, which outlaws spoken and printed attacks on the U.S. government, constitution, and flag.
1918	Socialist labor leader Eugene V. Debs is convicted of violating the Espionage Act and is sentenced to prison; President Warren G. Harding pardons him two years later.
1919	Most of Boston's police go on strike for ten days, and a crime wave sweeps the city.
1919	Race riots erupt in twenty cities, including Charleston, South Carolina; Washington, D.C.; Knoxville, Tennessee; and Chicago.
1919	Ratification of the Eighteenth Amendment to the Constitution and passage of the Volstead Act outlaw the manufacture, sale, and transportation of intoxicating liquors, beginning in January, 1920.
1919	The forerunner of the modern Bureau of Alcohol, Tobacco, Firearms and Explosives, the federal Alcohol Prohibition Unit, is established.
1920's	Scandal unfolds as high-ranking officials in President Warren G. Harding's administration are found to have profited from the illegal awarding of oil leases to federal lands at Teapot Dome, Wyoming and Elk Hills, California.
1920	Nineteenth Amendment to the Constitution gives women the right to vote in federal elections.
1920	In the so-called Palmer raids, federal law-enforcement agents sweep through dozens of American cities to arrest alien residents suspected of being radicals.
1920	League of Nations establishes the International Court of Justice, later known as the World Court.
1920	American Civil Liberties Union is established to protect constitutional rights.
1921-1922	Film star Roscoe "Fatty" Arbuckle is acquitted on manslaughter charges in the death of a young woman at a Hollywood party.
1923	Interpol, the International Criminal Police Organization, is created.
1924	U.S. Border patrol is established.
1924	Italian-born anarchists Nicola Sacco and Bartolomeo Vanzetti are convicted of armed robbery and murder in Massachusetts; despite worldwide protests, they are executed in 1927.
1924	Nathan Leopold and Richard Loeb are convicted of the rape and murder of young Bobby Franks in Chicago and are sentenced to life imprisonment.
1925	In *Carroll v. United States*, the Supreme Court finds that search warrants are not necessary when police officers have probable cause to search vehicles for contraband or evidence of crimes.
1925	Tennessee schoolteacher John T. Scopes is convicted of violating a state law against teaching evolution in what becomes known as the "Scopes monkey trial"; live radio broadcasts from the trial inaugurate radio coverage of crime.
1926	Federal government compiles the first United States Code.
1928	In *Olmstead v. United States*, the Supreme Court finds that wiretaps placed outside suspects' homes do not violate Fourth Amendment rights to privacy because the interiors of the homes are not trespassed upon.
1929	Gangsters under Al Capone's command gun down seven men from a rival Chicago gang in the St. Valentine's Day massacre.
1929	International Association of Chiefs of Police begins issuing the Uniform Crime Reports.

Time Line — The Criminal Justice System

Year	Event
1929	National Commission for Law Observance and Enforcement is established.
1929	President Herbert Hoover appoints the Wickersham Commission to review law enforcement throughout the United States; the commission issues its final report in 1931.
1930	U.S. Department of Justice creates the United States Board of Parole (later renamed the United States Parole Commission).
1930	Federal Bureau of Prisons is established.
1931	Gangster leader Al Capone is convicted of federal income tax evasion and is sent to prison.
1931-1937	Nine young African American men falsely accused of rape in Scottsboro, Alabama, are convicted by all-white juries and subjected to years of incarceration.
1931	International Association of Auto Theft Investigators is founded.
1932	In *Powell v. Alabama*, the Supreme Court rules that the concept of due process requires states to provide effective counsel in capital cases when indigent defendants are unable to represent themselves.
1932	Federal Bureau of Investigation's Scientific Crime Detection laboratory opens in Washington, D.C.
1932	In response to the kidnapping and murder of aviator Charles Lindbergh's infant son, Congress passes the Lindbergh law, making kidnapping a federal offense when kidnappers cross state boundaries; Congress also passes the Fugitive Felon Act, designed to prevent interstate travel to avoid prosecution.
1933	Ratification of the Twenty-first Amendment to the Constitution repeals Prohibition.
1933	Federal Securities and Exchange Commission is established.
1934	Alcatraz receives its first federal prisoners, who are regarded as America's "most dangerous."
1934	Congress passes the Anti-racketeering Act, making it unlawful to engage in acts interfering with interstate commerce; the National Stolen Property Act, which prohibits trafficking of stolen property; and the National Firearms Act, which imposes a tax on the transfer of machine guns, short barreled rifles, and shotguns.
1935	Bureau of Investigation is renamed the Federal Bureau of Investigation (FBI).
1936	In *Brown v. Mississippi*, the Supreme Court finds that coerced confessions violate the due process clause of the Fourteenth Amendment.
1936	Bruno Hauptmann is convicted of kidnapping the Lindbergh baby and is executed.
1937	In *Palko v. Connecticut*, the Supreme Court establishes an influential test for determining which fundamental rights contained within the Bill of Rights are incorporated into the Fourteenth Amendment's due process clause.
1937	Congress passes the Marijuana Tax Act, which levies fines on possession of untaxed marijuana.
1937	National Council of Juvenile and Family Court Judges is founded.
1938	Congress passes the National Firearms Act to regulate interstate commerce in firearms.
1939	Congress passes the Hatch Act to combat political corruption among government employees.
1940	Congress passes the Alien Registration Act—also known as the Smith Act—making it illegal to advocate overthrowing the government, and the Selective Service Act, which allows African Americans to serve in the military.
1941	After the surprise Japanese attack on Pearl Harbor, the governor of Hawaii declares martial law, with President Franklin D. Roosevelt's endorsement.
1945	Federal Rules of Criminal Procedure establish all rules governing criminal proceedings.
1945-1946	Associate Justice Robert H. Jackson serves as chief U.S. prosecutor in the Nuremberg War Trials after World War II.
1946	Association of Trial Lawyers of America is established.
1946	World Court holds its first session at The Hague, the Netherlands.

The Criminal Justice System — Time Line

Year	Event
1947	Congress passes the Hobbs Act to enhance federal antiracketeering legislation and the National Security Act, which establishes the Central Intelligence Agency.
1949	International Association of Arson Investigators is founded.
1950	FBI publishes its first ten-most-wanted list.
1950	One of the most sensational robberies in U.S. history takes nearly three million dollars in cash and securities from Boston's Brinks Bank.
1950	Alger Hiss is convicted of perjury for lying to Congress about his communist connections.
1950	National District Attorneys Association is established.
1952	Institute for Judicial Administration is founded.
1953	Julius and Ethel Rosenberg, who have been convicted of espionage, become the first Americans executed for that crime during peacetime.
1954	Congress passes the Espionage and Sabotage Act to make engaging in these acts during times of peace a capital offense; the Communist Control Act, which outlaws the Communist Party in the United States; and the Immunity Act, which requires witnesses to appear in national security cases.
1954	U.S. Court of Appeals decision establishes the Durham rule, which provides an insanity test to prove an accused person has a mental disorder at the time of committing a crime.
1954	Ohio physician Sam Sheppard is convicted of murdering his wife and sentenced to life imprisonment—a decision that the U.S. Supreme Court overturns in 1965.
1956-1971	Federal government's secret counterintelligence programs (COINTELPRO) are conducted to neutralize radical political organizations in the United States.
1957	Organized Crime and Racketeering Section (OCR) is created.
1958	Congress passes the Federal Aviation Act, which makes it a crime to board or attempt to board aircraft with concealed weapons.
1958	International Association of Campus Law Enforcement Administrators is founded.
1959	First Peace Officers Standards and Training (POST) programs begin.
1960	Convicted rapist Caryl Chessman is executed in California after spending twelve years on death row and becoming a national symbol in the fight against capital punishment through his writings.
1960	International Narcotic Enforcement Officers Association is founded.
1961	President John F. Kennedy appoints Thurgood Marshal a judge in the U.S. Circuit Court of Appeals.
1961	In *Mapp v. Ohio*, the Supreme Court rules that illegally obtained evidence must be excluded from criminal trials in state courts, a rule that previously had been applied to federal trials in 1914.
1961	Manhattan Bail Project is undertaken to identify what kinds of defendants are the best risks for pretrial release.
1961	Center for the Study of Crime, Delinquency, and Corrections is founded.
1962	In *Robinson v. California*, the Supreme Court finds that narcotics addiction by itself is not a crime and incorporates the Eighth Amendment's protection against cruel and unusual punishment to the states.
1962	American Law Institute publishes the Model Penal Code.
1963	Civil rights leader Medgar Evers is assassinated in Mississippi; Byron de la Beckwith is tried for Evers's murder in 1964 but is released after two hung juries; in 1994 Beckwith is tried again and convicted.
1963	President John F. Kennedy is assassinated in Dallas, Texas; Lee Harvey Oswald is arrested for the crime but is himself assassinated by Jack Ruby before he can be tried. President Lyndon B. Johnson appoints the Warren Commission to investigate the assassination.
1963	Federal prison on Alcatraz Island closes after sending all its inmates to other federal facilities.

Time Line   The Criminal Justice System

Year	Event
1963	In *Gideon v. Wainwright*, the Supreme Court finds that all indigent offenders are entitled to have court appointed counsel represent them in felony cases.
1963	Organizations founded: Academy of Criminal Justice Sciences; Center for Criminology Library; International Association for Police Professors.
1964	Rioting erupts in New York City's Harlem district.
1964	In *Escobedo v. Illinois*, the Supreme Court finds that law-enforcement questioning has shifted from investigatory to accusatory; the suspect has a right to counsel and can refrain from speaking until counsel is present.
1964	In *Massiah v. United States*, the Supreme Court finds that a taped conversation between an indicted suspect and his friend constituted an interrogation and violation of rights because the friend was acting on the instructions of government, and the suspect was without counsel during the interrogation.
1964	Organizations founded: International Brotherhood of Police Officers; International Halfway House Association.
1965	Six-day riot ravages Los Angeles's Watts district.
1965	Malcolm X is assassinated.
1965	President Lyndon B. Johnson establishes the President's Commission on Law Enforcement and Administration of Justice to study sequences of events in the criminal justice system.
1965	Organizations founded: Institute for Law and Criminal Procedure; Office of Law Enforcement Assistance.
1966	In *Miranda v. Arizona*, the Supreme Court makes a landmark ruling by requiring police officers to inform suspects of their right not to incriminate themselves, thereby limiting police interrogations and inaugurating a revolutionary change in arrest procedures.
1966	Organizations founded: Americans for Effective Law Enforcement; American Federation of Police; Vera Institute of Justice; National Polygraph Association; Black Panther Party.
1967	Teamsters Union president Jimmy Hoffa is convicted on federal corruption charges; he is pardoned in 1971.
1967	New rioting erupts in Newark, New Jersey; Tampa, Florida; Cincinnati, Ohio; Atlanta, Georgia; and Detroit, Michigan.
1967	In *In re Gault*, the Supreme Court establishes the right of juvenile defendants to counsel, the right of cross-examination of witnesses, sufficient notice of charges when punishments are involved, and protection against self-incrimination.
1967	In *Katz v. United States*, the Supreme Court establishes the principle that electronic surveillance constitutes a search subject to the Fourth Amendment's warrant and probable cause provisions.
1967	Congress passes the Freedom of Information Act, which allows private citizens to obtain confidential government files.
1967	Organizations founded: Center for Administration of Criminal Justice; National Crime Information Center; Federal Judicial Center.
1968	Civil rights leader Martin Luther King, Jr., is assassinated in Memphis, Tennessee; James Earl Ray is convicted of his murder and is sentenced to life in prison.
1968	In *Bruton v. United States*, the Supreme Court finds that defendants have the right to cross-examine their accusers, even if they are accomplices.
1968	In *Chimel v. California*, the Supreme Court rules that in searches incidental to arrests, arrest warrants entitle police only to search the persons and areas within their immediate vicinity, unless proper search warrants are issued.
1968	In *Harris v. United States*, the Supreme Court finds that anything in plain view in an automobile is subject to seizure and admissible in a court of law.
1968	In *Witherspoon v. Illinois*, the Supreme Court finds that prospective jurors cannot be excluded as part of the *voir dire* process for voicing objections to the death penalty as long as they can make fair and impartial decisions.

The Criminal Justice System — Time Line

Year	Event
1968	Congress passes the Uniform Juvenile Court Act, a precursor to the Juvenile Justice and Delinquency Prevention Act of 1974, and the Omnibus Crime Control and Safe Streets Act, which is designed to reform the criminal justice system.
1968	President Lyndon B. Johnson appoints the National Commission on the Causes and Prevention of Violence to investigate the causes, consequences, and prevention of violence in American society.
1968	Organizations founded: Law Enforcement Assistance Administration; National Juvenile Detention Association; National Institute of Justice; Afro-American Police League.
1969	Weather Underground Organization, an American militant radical left-wing organization, emerges from a faction of Students for a Democratic Society with the goal of creating a revolutionary party for the takeover of the U.S. government.
1969	Center for Criminal Justice is established at Harvard University.
1969-1970	"Chicago Seven" are tried for conspiracy, inciting to riot, and other offenses relating to protest demonstrations at the 1968 Democratic Party National Convention.
1970	Congress passes the Comprehensive Drug Abuse Prevention and Control Act, which creates a single system of control for both narcotic and psychotropic drugs for the first time; the Organized Crime Control Act, which establishes the Witness Protection Plan; and the Racketeer Influenced and Corrupt Organizations Act, which authorizes asset forfeiture in the war on organized crime.
1970	New York City creates the Knapp Commission, which issues its report in 1972.
1970	In *Brady v. United States*, the Supreme Court acknowledges the validity of plea bargaining by asserting that it offers a "mutuality of advantage" for both defendant and the state.
1970	Organizations founded: Environmental Protection Agency; Insurance Crime Prevention Institute.
1971	Forty-two inmates and guards die in the Attica prison riot in New York State.
1971	Charles Manson and his followers are convicted of the murder of actor Sharon Tate and others; Manson is sentenced to death, but his sentence is later commuted when California overturns its death penalty.
1971	U.S. Army lieutenant William J. Calley is convicted in a court-martial for his role in commanding an Army platoon that massacred women and children in the Vietnamese village of My Lai in 1968; Calley's life sentence is reduced to twenty years, but he ultimately serves only three and one-half years.
1971	In *Bivens v. Unknown Named Agents of Federal Bureau of Narcotics*, the Supreme Court finds that in certain federal actions, plaintiffs have the right to claim civil damages when federal officials violate the Fourth Amendment protection against unreasonable search and seizure.
1971	In *Santobello v. New York*, the Supreme Court confirms the binding nature of plea-bargaining agreements made by prosecutors and defendants in criminal proceedings.
1971	Organizations founded: National Crime Information Center (branch of the Federal Bureau of Investigation); National Computerized Criminal History System; Institute for Court Management; National Center for State Courts; National Disabled Law Officers Association.
1972	In *Furman v. Georgia*, the Supreme Court finds that administration of the death penalty constitutes a form of cruel and unusual punishment because of its random and unpredictable application.
1972	In *Argersinger v. Hamlin*, the Supreme Court finds that indigent defendants have a right to counsel if they are charged with offenses punishable by incarceration.
1972	In *Barker v. Wingo*, the Supreme Court finds that defendants must request speedy trials to ensure compliance with the speedy trial provision of the Sixth Amendment.
1972	Division of Alcohol, Tobacco, and Firearms separates from the Internal Revenue Service and is renamed the Bureau of Alcohol, Tobacco, and Firearms.
1972	Organizations founded: Citizens United for Rehabilitation of Errants; National Association of Blacks in Criminal Justice.

Time Line   The Criminal Justice System

Year	Event
1972-1974	A break-in at the Democratic national headquarters in Washington, D.C.'s Watergate Hotel by Republican Party operatives and the subsequent cover-up by the Nixon administration leads to the criminal prosecution of top administration officials and the resignation of President Richard M. Nixon.
1973	Vice President Spiro Agnew pleads no contest to charges of corruption while he was an elected official in Maryland; he is sentenced to three years' probation, a fine, and restitution, and he resigns the vice presidency.
1973	In *Roe v. Wade*, the Supreme Court decriminalizes abortion by ruling that a woman's right to abortion falls within the right of privacy implied by the Fourteenth Amendment.
1973	Organizations founded: Drug Enforcement Administration; Institute for Law and Social Research; International Association of Bomb-Technicians and Investigators; National Crime Survey (later becomes known as the National Crime Victimization Survey); Academy for Professional Law Enforcement.
1974	Newspaper heiress Patricia Hearst is kidnapped by the Symbionese Liberation Army, which later involves her in its robberies; Hearst is eventually caught and convicted of bank robbery.
1974	Congress passes the Juvenile Justice and Delinquency Prevention Act, which creates the Office of Juvenile Justice and Delinquency Prevention and promotes the development of community treatment programs for youthful offenders; Congress also passes the Speedy Trial Act (amended in 1979 and 1984) to ensure that defendants are brought to trial within seventy days of the time that formal charges are brought against them.
1974	Organizations founded: National Clearinghouse on Child Abuse and Neglect Information; Commission on Accreditation for Corrections; Criminal Justice Statistics Association; National Military Intelligence Association; Office of Juvenile Justice and Delinquency Prevention (OJJDP).
1975	Teamsters Union president Jimmy Hoffa disappears near Detroit, Michigan; his disappearance remains unexplained thirty years later.
1975	In *Faretta v. California*, the Supreme Court finds that defendants have a right to self-representation in criminal proceedings.
1975	Organizations founded: National Association of Legal Assistants; Task Force on Juvenile Justice and Delinquency Prevention; National Organization for Victim Assistance (NOVA).
1976	In *Gregg v. Georgia*, the Supreme Court rules that the death penalty itself is not a cruel and unusual punishment, but that procedural safeguards are required to prevent its use in an arbitrary and unpredictable manner.
1976	Organizations founded: American Law Enforcement Officers Association; Integrated Criminal Apprehension Program; National Center for the Prevention and Control of Rape.
1976	Crime Stoppers is founded to gain community involvement by offering monetary rewards for information leading to the capture and conviction of criminals.
1976	United States Board of Parole is renamed the United States Parole Commission.
1977	Convicted murderer Gary Gilmore is the first person executed in the United States since the Supreme Court's 1972 ban on capital punishment.
1977	Congress passes the Foreign Corrupt Practices Act, which establishes antibribery provisions from foreign entities, and the Juvenile Justice Reform Act, which imposes mandatory sentencing on juveniles based on age, previous criminal activity, and the nature of their crimes.
1977	In *Coker v. Georgia*, the Supreme Court rules that the death penalty is an inappropriate punishment in rape cases when the victims' lives are not taken.
1978	Ted Kaczynski—who publicly calls himself the "Unabomber"—begins his terrorist bombing campaign.
1978	Serial killer David Berkowitz, better known as "Son of Sam," is sentenced to twenty-five years to life for each of the six murders he has committed.
1978	Organizations founded: International Union of Police Administration; National Coalition of Jail Reform; National Forensic Center.
1979	Organizations founded: Commission on Accreditation for Law Enforcement Agencies (CALEA); Office of Justice Assistance, Research, and Statistics.

The Criminal Justice System — Time Line

Year	Event
1980	Seventeen people are killed during three days of racially charged rioting in Miami, Florida, after the criminal justice system fails to convict police officers for the death of a black businessman.
1980	Inmates in the New Mexico state penitentiary seize control of the prison for thirty-six hours, killing thirty-three inmates and taking twelve guards hostage before surrendering to authorities.
1980	In *Rummel v. Estelle*, the Supreme Court rules that application of Texas's mandatory life-imprisonment statute on a habitual small-time offender does not constitute cruel and unusual punishment.
1980	National Crime Prevention Council creates McGruff the Crime Dog.
1980	Organizations founded: Aid to Incarcerated Mothers; Mothers Against Drunk Driving.
1981	President Ronald Reagan is wounded in a failed assassination attempt by John Hinkley, Jr.
1981	Sandra Day O'Connor becomes the first woman justice on the U.S. Supreme Court.
1981	Organizations founded: International Association of Law Enforcement Intelligence Analysts; National Center for Community Anti-Crime.
1982	Congress passes the Victim and Witness Protection Act, which protects victims and witnesses in criminal proceedings.
1982	Law Enforcement Assistance Administration is abolished.
1983	In *Illinois v. Gates*, the Supreme Court finds that when the totality of circumstances suggests that a crime has been committed and suspects are identified, police are not in violation of the Fourth Amendment by obtaining search warrants.
1983	In *Solem v. Helm*, the Supreme Court finds that the Eighth Amendment's prohibition on cruel and unusual punishments limits states' power to impose life sentences for multiple convictions on nonviolent felony charges.
1983	First DARE program is founded to help deter schoolchildren from taking up drug use.
1983	Criminal Justice National Council on Crime and Delinquency is founded.
1984	Congress passes the Comprehensive Crime Control Act, revising bail and forfeiture procedures; the National Narcotics Act, which establishes a government board to coordinate law-enforcement efforts in the federal war on drugs; the Victims of Crime Act, which improves services to crime victims; the Sentencing Reform Act, which creates the United States Sentencing Commission; the Bail Reform Act, which establishes procedures for the release or detention of suspects under arrest; the Trademark Counterfeiting Act to combat trafficking in counterfeit goods; the Insanity Defense Reform Act, which shifts the burden of proof for insanity pleas from the prosecution to the defense; and the Missing Child Act, which establishes a hotline for information reporting and coordination of public and private programs in the location of missing children.
1984	In *United States v. Leon*, the Supreme Court establishes a good faith exception to the exclusionary rule, ruling that evidence may be admissible in court if officers act in good faith, believing the search warrants they use are valid.
1984	In *Massachusetts v. Sheppard*, the Supreme Court finds that police officers acted in good faith by executing a revised and re-written search warrant because the judge advised that the warrant was valid.
1984	In *Schall v. Martin*, the Supreme Court finds that detention of a juvenile based on false information given by him to law enforcement does not violate due process.
1984	Organizations founded: National Bureau of Document Examiners; Office of Justice Programs (OJP); Community Patrol Officer Program.
1985	The city of Philadelphia's attempt to evict illegal squatters belonging to an organization called MOVE culminates in a bombing that kills eleven people and destroys sixty-one homes.
1985	In *New Jersey v. T.L.O.*, the Supreme Court finds that school officials only need reasonable suspicion to search students and their possessions on school property.
1985	In *Tennessee v. Garner*, the Supreme Court nullifies the fleeing felon rule for using deadly force, finding that deadly force may only be applied to fleeing suspects if they pose threats to the lives of law-enforcement officers or others.

Time Line   The Criminal Justice System

Year	Event
1985	The Violent Criminal Apprehension Program (ViCap) is launched on the Internet.
1986	In *Terry v. Ohio*, the Supreme Court establishes acceptable "pat and frisk" procedures for police searches of suspects.
1986	In *Ford v. Wainwright*, the Supreme Court holds that the criminally insane cannot be executed and that Florida's procedures for determining competence are inadequate.
1986	In *Bowers v. Hardwick*, the Supreme Court upholds a Georgia sodomy law criminalizing homosexual relations—a decision that the Court will overturn in *Lawrence v. Texas* in 2003.
1986	In *Batson v. Kentucky*, the Supreme Court rules that peremptory challenges used to exclude prospective jurors must not be racially discriminatory.
1986	Organizations founded: International Law Enforcement Instructors Agency; American Crime Prevention Institute.
1987	In *McCleskey v. Kemp*, the Supreme Court finds that Georgia's death penalty is not arbitrary, capricious, or discriminatory.
1987	In *Tison v. Arizona*, the Supreme Court finds that accomplices who do not actually murder others but assist in murders can receive the death penalty.
1987	In *Illinois v. Krull*, the Supreme Court establishes the "good-faith exception," which allows evidence gathered from warrantless searches to be admitted at trial when investigators act in good faith.
1987	U.S. Sentencing Guidelines are created to guide discretionary power of judges.
1987	International Association for Asian Crime Investigators is founded.
1988	In *California v. Greenwood*, the Supreme Court determines that warrantless searches of garbage are permissible because the right to privacy is relinquished when things are placed in public areas.
1989	Serial killer Ted Bundy is executed.
1989	In *Stanford v. Kentucky*, the Supreme Court finds that the Eighth Amendment's prohibition against cruel and unusual punishment does not forbid executions of offenders who are juveniles at the time they commit their capital crimes.
1989	In *Texas v. Johnson*, the Supreme Court upholds symbolic forms of expression, including flag burning in political demonstrations.
1990	Washington, D.C., mayor Marion Barry is convicted of cocaine possession and sentenced to six months in prison; after his release, he is reelected mayor.
1990	In *Maryland v. Buie*, the Supreme Court rules that contraband goods or evidence of crimes seen in plain view during an arrest is a reasonable seizure under the Fourth Amendment.
1990	In *Minnick v. Mississippi*, the Supreme Court rules that a reinitiated interrogation of a murder suspect who was advised of his Miranda rights and received counsel still violated the suspect's Fifth Amendment rights because it was conducted without counsel being present.
1990	In *Maryland v. Craig*, the Supreme Court finds that the Sixth Amendment right to cross-examine accusers is not violated when children testify via closed circuit television.
1991	Los Angeles police officers stop motorist Rodney King and savagely beat him. The incident is recorded on videotape, prompting criticisms of the police department that lead to the establishment of the Christopher Commission to investigate and report on the police misconduct.
1991	In *Arizona v. Fulminante*, the Supreme Court rules that coerced confessions wrongly admitted as evidence cannot be subjected to "harmless error" analysis and may not be grounds for automatic invalidation of criminal convictions.
1991	In *Payne v. Tennessee*, the Supreme Court finds that victim impact statements are not in violation of an offender's Eighth Amendment rights at sentencing hearings.
1991	In *Harmelin v. Michigan*, the Supreme Court upholds a Michigan drug possession law carrying a mandatory term of life imprisonment, rejecting the plaintiff's argument that the sentence is "cruel and unusual punishment," in violation of the Eighth Amendment.

The Criminal Justice System — Time Line

Year	Event
1992	Serial killer Jeffrey Dahmer is sentenced to life in prison in Milwaukee, Wisconsin.
1992	Federal agents raid the communal home of Randy Weaver—who is wanted for illegal gun sales—at Ruby Ridge, Idaho; in the ensuing shootout, Weaver's wife and son are killed.
1992	Rioting erupts in Los Angeles after the four police officers responsible for beating Rodney King are acquitted in a criminal trial.
1992	California executes Robert Alton Harris for a 1978 double murder, marking the first time in twenty-five years the state has put a man to death.
1992	Kathleen Hawk Sawyer becomes the first woman director of the federal Bureau of Prisons.
1992	In *United States v. Alvarez-Machain*, the Supreme Court finds that the abduction of criminal offenders from other countries is legal for the purpose of returning them to the United States for trial.
1992	In *R.A.V. v. City of St. Paul*, the Supreme Court holds that a local ordinance criminalizing cross-burning for the purpose of racial harassment is unconstitutional, even though such acts motivated by hate are reprehensible.
1992	National Insurance Crime Bureau is founded.
1992	Operation El Dorado is formed by U.S. Customs and the Department of Treasury as one of the nation's most successful money-laundering task forces.
1993	Terrorist bombing damages one of the World Trade Center towers in New York City, killing six people and injuring more than one thousand.
1993	Agents of the federal law-enforcement agencies, National Guard troops, and local law-enforcement officers destroy the compound of the Branch Davidian cult outside Waco, Texas, raising questions about the use of excessive force.
1993	Congress passes the Brady Handgun Violence Prevention Act, which imposes five-day mandatory waiting periods for handgun purchasers.
1993	In *Wisconsin v. Mitchell*, the Supreme Court upholds the constitutionality of state laws increasing punishments of offenders who target their victims on the basis of race.
1993-1996	Brothers Erik and Lyle Menendez are tried for the murder of their parents; their first trial ends in a mistrial; they are convicted in their second trial.
1994	The U.S. prison population reaches more than one million inmates for the first time in history.
1994	Congress passes the Violent Crime Control and Law Enforcement Act to provide funding for law enforcement and crime prevention initiatives, such as the establishment of a three-strikes provision for violent offenders.
1994	New Jersey passes Megan's Law, which requires convicted sex offenders to register with local law-enforcement agencies so that they may inform the public.
1994	Office of Community Oriented Policing is founded.
1995	Terrorist bomb blast destroys the Murrah Federal Building in Oklahoma City, Oklahoma, killing 168 people; Timothy McVeigh is quickly arrested and is later convicted and executed.
1995	Former football star O. J. Simpson is acquitted of the murder of his former wife and another man in Los Angeles; Simpson later loses a wrongful death suit brought against him in civil court by the murder victims' families.
1995	In *Wilson v. Arkansas*, the Supreme Court holds that police officers, when conducting searches, are normally expected to knock and announce their presence before entering private homes, except in special circumstances.
1995	In *United States v. Lopez*, the Supreme Court finds that possession of a firearm in a school zone does not violate the interstate commerce clause since it is not considered an economic activity.
1996	Congress passes the Anti-Terrorism and Effective Death Penalty Act, which imposes limits on *habeas corpus* claims filed by inmates on death row and reduces lengths of appeals in capital cases.
1996	In *Whren v. United States*, the Supreme Court upholds the authority of police officers to stop automobiles whenever there is probable cause of minor traffic violations, even if circumstances suggest that the officers are motivated by considerations of race or physical appearance of the motorists.

Time Line — The Criminal Justice System

Year	Event
1998	Ramzi Ahmed Yousef is sentenced to life imprisonment for his role in the 1993 World Trade Center bombing.
1998	International tribunal makes the Rwandan Jean-Paul Akayesu the first person in world history to be convicted of genocide.
1998	In *Knowles v. Iowa*, the Supreme Court limits the authority of police to search cars while conducting routine traffic stops.
1999	President Bill Clinton is acquitted by the Senate after the House of Representatives impeaches him on charges of perjury and obstruction of justice.
1999	Two teenage boys enter Littleton, Colorado's Columbine High School with an assortment of firearms and homemade bombs and kill thirteen people, including themselves.
1999	Physician Jack Kevorkian is convicted of second-degree murder in Michigan and is sentenced to ten to twenty-five years in prison after assisting more than one hundred people to commit suicide.
1999	Organizations founded: Academy of Experimental Criminology; National Center for Analysis of Violent Crime (under FBI).
2000	In *Illinois v. Wardlow*, the Supreme Court expands the powers of police to stop and frisk suspects by holding that taking flight in high-crime areas gives police enough evidence to undertake such actions.
2001	On September 11, Middle Eastern terrorists hijack four U.S. airliners; they fly two of the planes into New York City's World Trade Center towers, which later collapse; one plane is flown into Washington, D.C.'s Pentagon Building; and the fourth plane crashes into a western Pennsylvania field—apparently because of an effort by passengers to retake the plane.
2001	In response to the hijackings, the United Nations adopts a resolution to establish measures to combat terrorism, and the U.S. Congress passes the Patriot Act to increase the authority of federal officials to track and intercept communications relating to international and domestic terrorists.
2001	In *Atwater v. City of Lago Vista* the Supreme Court rules that warrantless arrests for misdemeanor traffic violations do not violate the Fourth Amendment right to be free from unreasonable search and seizure.
2001	In *Illinois v. McArthur*, the Supreme Court permits police officers with probable cause to believe that criminal evidence is located within private homes to use reasonable means to prevent destruction of that evidence while they await search warrants.
2001	In *Kyllo v. United States*, the Supreme Court rules that government use of technology not commonly employed by the public to sense images, sounds, or smells coming from homes is a form of search and thus requires a warrant.
2002	Congress passes the Homeland Security Act, which calls for the reorganization of government law-enforcement and investigative agencies under the new U.S. Department of Homeland Security, which is established in 2003.
2003	In *Virginia v. Black*, the Supreme Court finds that a ban on burning of a cross violates the First Amendment right to freedom of expression, except when such acts are undertaken for the purpose of intimidation.
2003	In *Lawrence v. Texas*, the Supreme Court overturns its 1986 *Bowers v. Hardwick* ruling on homosexuality.
2004	Media mogul Martha Stewart is convicted on federal charges of perjury, conspiracy, obstruction of justice, and securities fraud stemming from an investigation of possible insider trading; she is sentenced to five months in a federal prison.
2004	Congress passes the Justice for All Act to enhance protections of victim rights in federal crimes, increase resources to combat crimes with DNA technology, and reduce the risk of conviction and execution of innocent persons.
2005	Pop singer Michael Jackson is tried and acquitted on child molestation charges in Southern California.
2006	Enron Corporation scandal results in the largest bankruptcy reorganization in American history and the de facto dissolution of Arthur Andersen audit and accountancy partnership.

The Criminal Justice System   Time Line

Year	Event
2006	In *Gonzales v. Oregon* the Controlled Substances Act does not prevent physicians from being able to prescribe the drugs needed to perform assisted suicides under state law.
2006	In *Georgia v. Randolph* police cannot conduct a warrantless search in a home where one occupant consents and the other objects.
2006	In *Hamdan v. Rumsfeld* the military commissions set up by the Bush administration to try detainees at Guantanamo Bay are illegal because they lack the protections that are required by the Geneva Conventions and the Uniform Code of Military Justice.
2006	In *Lopez v. Gonzales* an aggravated felony includes only conduct punishable as a felony under the federal Controlled Substances Act, regardless of whether state law classifies such conduct as a felony or a misdemeanor.
2007	Virginia Tech University English major Seung-Hui Cho goes on a murderous rampage within campus buildings, killing 32 people before committing suicide. Cho had previously been removed from a creative writing class due to the graphic, violent nature of his essays.
2007	The United Nations adopts General Assembly Resolution 62/149, which calls for a worldwide moratorium on the use of the death penalty. The United States voted against the resolution.
2007	In *Gonzales v. Carhart*, a United States Supreme Court case, upheld the Partial-Birth Abortion Ban Act of 2003.
2007	In *Panetti v. Quarterman* criminal defendants sentenced to death may not be executed if they do not understand the reason for their imminent execution, and that once the state has set an execution date death-row inmates may litigate their competency to be executed in habeas corpus proceedings.
2008	In *Boumediene v. Bush*, the Supreme Court holds that foreign terrorism suspects held at Guantanamo Bay have the constitutional right to challenge their detention in United States courts.
2008	In *Al-Marri v. Wright*, the Fourth Circuit Court of Appeals decides that A-Marri, a legal resident arrested in the United States, was entitled to contest his detention in federal court and rules he needed to be charged, tried, and released.
2008	In *Baze v. Rees* the three-drug cocktail used for performing executions by lethal injection in all of the states using lethal injection at the time is constitutional under the Eighth Amendment.
2008	In *Kennedy v. Louisiana*, the death penalty is unconstitutional in all cases that do not involve murder or crimes against the state such as treason.
2008	In *District of Columbia v. Heller* the Second Amendment protects an individual right to possess a firearm unconnected with service in a militia and to use it for traditionally lawful purposes such as self-defense within the home.
2008	In *United States v. Williams* a federal statute prohibiting the "pandering" of child pornography (offering or requesting to transfer, sell, deliver, or trade the items) does not violate the First Amendment to the United States Constitution, even if a person charged under the code does not in fact possess child pornography with which to trade.
2008	*Kennedy v. Louisiana* holds that the Eighth Amendment's Cruel and Unusual Punishments Clause does not permit a state to punish the crime of rape of a child with the death penalty; more broadly, the power of the state to impose the death penalty against an individual for committing a crime that did not result in the death of the victim is now limited to crimes against the state (e.g., espionage, treason).
2009	Phillip Garrido, a parolee, and his wife Nancy are arrested for the kidnapping, false imprisonment, and rape of Jaycee Dugard who was kept captive in Antioch, California for almost 18 years.
2009	Bernard Madoff pleads guilty to 11 federal felonies and admits turning his wealth management business into a Ponzi scheme.
2009	In *Montejo v. Louisiana* a defendant may waive his or her right to counsel during a police interrogation even if the interrogation begins after the defendant's assertion of his or her right to counsel at an arraignment or similar proceeding.

Time Line   The Criminal Justice System

Year	Event
2009	*Herring v. United States* held that the good-faith exception to the exclusionary rule applies when a police officer makes an arrest based on an outstanding warrant in another jurisdiction, but the information regarding that warrant is later found to be incorrect because of a negligent error by that agency.
2009	*United States v. Hayes* interprets Section 921(a)(33)(A) of the federal Gun Control Act of 1968, as amended in 1996 holding that a domestic relationship is not necessarily a defining element of the offense to support a conviction for possession of a firearm by a person previously convicted of a misdemeanor crime of domestic violence.
2010	The Cruise Vessel Security and Safety Act is enacted and establishes requirements to ensure the security and safety of passengers and crew on cruise vessels.
2010	The website WikiLeaks makes international headlines after releasing a video showing a U.S. helicopter gunship in Iraq allegedly firing indiscriminately, killing a dozen people, including two Reuters newspersons. It later publishes almost 400,000 classified military documents on the Iraq War.
2010	In *Graham v. Florida* a sentence of life imprisonment without the possibility of parole may not be imposed on juvenile non-homicide offenders.
2010	In *McDonald v. Chicago* the individual right to keep and bear arms for self-defense is fully applicable to the states through the Due Process Clause of the Fourteenth Amendment.
2010	*Abbott v. United States* addresses the mandatory sentencing increase under federal law for the possession or use of a deadly weapon in drug trafficking and violent crimes. A minimum five-year prison sentence is imposed in addition to any other mandatory sentence given for another crime, including the underlying drug-related or violent offense. The only exception to the five-year addition applies only when another provision required a longer mandatory term for conduct.
2010	In *Padilla v. Kentucky* criminal defense attorneys are required to inform non-citizen clients about the deportation risks of a guilty plea or conviction.
2011	The "Occupy Wall Street" movement begins in New York City's Zuccotti Park, with thousands massing and protesting corporate bailouts and economic inequality.
2011	*Brown v. Plata* holds that a court-mandated population limit was necessary to remedy a violation of prisoners' Eighth Amendment constitutional rights. The Court orders California to reduce its prison population to 137.5% of design capacity within two years.
2011	In *J.D.B. v. North Carolina* the Supreme Court of the United States holds that age is relevant when determining police custody for Miranda purposes.
2012	The Sandy Hook Elementary School shooting occurs in Newtown, Connecticut. Adam Lanza fatally shoots 20 children aged between six and seven years old and six adult staff members. This becomes the deadliest mass school shooting in U.S. history.
2012	Approximately 30 minutes into the screening of "The Dark Knight Arises, James Earl Holmes enters Theater 9 at Century 16 in Aurora, Colorado, and sprays the audience with deadly gunfire from his arsenal of weapons. Holmes later expresses to a court-appointed psychiatrist that his "self-worth would increase by one 'value unit' for each person he killed."
2012	In *Miller v. Alabama* a sentence of life imprisonment without the possibility of parole may not be a mandatory sentence for juvenile offenders.
2012	In *Arizona v. United States* Arizona law enforcement may inquire about a resident's legal status during lawful encounters, but the state may not implement its own immigration laws.
2012	In *United States v. Jones* attaching a GPS device to a vehicle and then using the device to monitor the vehicle's movements constitutes a search under the Fourth Amendment.
2013	The U.S. Department of Justice unseals two counts of violating the Espionage Act of 1917 and theft of government property against Edward Snowden for copying and leaking classified information from the National Security Agency.

Year	Event
2013	Explosive devices are detonated at the Boston Marathon, instantaneously transforming one of the nation's most cherished events into a scene of gruesome carnage.
2013	George Zimmerman is rendered a not guilty verdict on all counts in the shooting of Trayvon Martin, an African-American, whom Zimmerman confronted and shot dead while Martin was committing no crimes.
2013	In *Floyd v. City of New York*, a federal court finds the New York City Police Department's stop-and-frisk practices to be unconstitutional, in violation of the Fourth Amendment right to be free from unreasonable searches and seizures and also in violation of the Equal Protection Clause of the Fourteenth Amendment.
2013	In *United States v. Windsor* the federal government must provide benefits to legally married same-sex couples.
2013	In *Shelby County v. Holder* states and localities do not need federal approval to change voting laws.
2013	In *Salinas v. Texas* the Fifth Amendment's protection against self-incrimination does not protect an individual's refusal to answer questions asked by law enforcement before he or she has been arrested or given the Miranda warning. A witness cannot invoke the privilege by simply standing mute; he or she must expressly invoke it.
2013	In *Evans v. Michigan* if a person accused of a crime receives a directed acquittal, the Double Jeopardy Clause bars a second trial of that person for the same crime, even if the person was acquitted in error.
2013	*Chaidez v. United States* holds that the ruling in *Padilla v. Commonwealth of Kentucky* that criminal defense attorneys are required to inform non-citizen clients about deportation risks of a guilty plea or conviction cannot be applied retroactively.
2013	*Millbrook v. United States* holds that the Federal Tort Claims Act waives the sovereign immunity of the United States for certain intentional torts committed by law enforcement officers.
2014	African American robbery suspect Michael Brown is shot to death in Ferguson, Missouri by white police officer Darren Wilson. The shooting of Michael Brown, despite the eventual exoneration of the involved officer, exposed a broader breakdown in civic trust.
2014	The "Black Lives Matter" movement becomes nationally recognized through its street demonstrations following the officer-involved deaths of African Americans Michael Brown, in Missouri, and Eric Garner, in New York.
2014	The "Blue Lives Matter" movement launches in the wake of the ambush slayings of NYPD officers Rafael Ramos and Wenjian Liu.
2014	On April 13, 2014, three people are killed by a gunman, 73-year old Frazier Glenn Miller, Jr., at the Jewish Community Center and Village Shalom Retirement Center in Overland Park, Kansas. In November 2015 Miller, a Neo-Nazi, was convicted of murder and other crimes, and sentenced to death.
2014	The Clemency Project came into being to help reduce the problem of mass incarceration within federal prisons and to restore equity in sentencing. To be eligible for clemency project consideration federal prisoners would have to receive a markedly lower sentence if convicted of the same crime(s) today. Other requirements are prisoners must be low-level, non-violent offenders without ties to large-scale criminal organizations, gangs or cartels; have served at least 10 years of their sentence; have demonstrated good behavior while incarcerated; and have had no record of violence before or during their current term of imprisonment. If prisoners meet the criteria they are assigned lawyers to help fill out and submit the clemency petition for commutation. To date President Barak Obama released 1715 prisoners, more than any other president in U.S. history.
2015	The Charleston Church Shooting or Massacre takes place at the Emanuel African Methodist Episcopal Church in Charleston, South Carolina during a prayer service killing nine people. The shooter, Dylann Roof, confesses and indicates his motive of hoping to ignite a race war.
2015	President Barack Obama's 11-member task force on 21st century policing releases its *Final Report of the President's Task Force on 21st Century Policing*, creating a road map for the future of policing and providing direction on how to build trust with the public.
2015	President Barack Obama begins to grant clemency to thousands of federal prisoners serving sentences for non-violent crimes.

Time Line   The Criminal Justice System

Year	Event
2015	In *Obergefell v. Hodges* the fundamental right to marry is guaranteed to same-sex couples.
2015	Amanda Knox is acquitted of the murder of Meredith Kercher, a British student, in Italy's Supreme Court of Cassation after finding the case was without foundation.
2016	Major riots break out in the City of Baltimore following the funeral of African American Freddie Gray, who succumbed to a fatal spinal injury incurred in the course of being taken into police custody for alleged possession of an illegal knife.
2016	A series of coordinated terrorist attacks strike Paris and a northern suburb, resulting in 130 deaths. The Islamic State of Iraq and the Levant (ISIL) claims responsibility, saying the attacks were retaliation for French airstrikes on ISIL targets in Syria and Iraq.
2016	Two assailants armed with AR-15 weapons invade and fire on a meeting of San Bernardino County employees, killing 14 before fleeing. Subsequent investigation of the assailants, a husband and wife, reveals the couple were homegrown violent extremists inspired by foreign terrorist groups.
2016	Pulse, a gay nightclub in Orlando, Florida is attacked by 29-year old Omar Mateen, a security guard, killing 49 people and wounding 53 others who are mostly Latino. The massacre becomes the deadliest mass shooting by a single shooter and the deadliest incident of violence against LGBTQ people in the United States.
2016	A minivan packed with explosives blows up and kills 143 people in central Baghdad. The attack is the third mass slaughter during Ramadan in three countries in less than a week. Two days earlier, two police officers and 20 hostages were killed by gunmen in a restaurant in Dhaka, Bangladesh. In Turkey, a suicide attack on Istanbul, Turkey's main airport left more than 40 people dead. The Islamic State of Iraq and the Levant claimed responsibility for the Baghdad and Dhaka attacks.
2016	A truck intentionally drives into a crowd celebrating Bastille Day in Nice, France, killing 84 people. The Islamic State of Iraq and the Levant claims responsibility, but there is no evidence the extremist group directed it.
2016	Eight police officers are murdered in two separate ambushes occurring in Dallas and Baton Rouge. Coincidentally, both shooters are military veterans, and the shootings occurred in the wake of unrest in both cities.
2016	The federal Justice Department decides to stop using private corporations to manage the federal prison population.
2016	Missouri legislation prohibits shackling of pregnant inmates and juveniles.
2016	Notorious drug lord and prison escape artist Joaquin Guzman (also known as El Chapo) is captured for the third time after escaping incarceration and is awaiting extradition to the United States for trial on charges of murder, money laundering, drug trafficking, racketeering, and organized crime.

Lisa Landis Murphy
Updated by the Editors

Topics by Subject Category

Appeals 1048
Arrest and Arraignment. 1048
Attorneys 1048
Business and Financial Crime. 1048
Capital Punishment 1048
Civil Rights and Liberties. 1049
Computer Crime. 1049
Confessions. 1049
Constitutional Protections 1049
Convictions. 1050
Courts 1050
Crime Prevention 1050
Crime Statistics. 1051
Criminology 1051
Defendants 1051
Deviancy. 1052
Domestic Violence 1052
Espionage and Sedition 1052
Evidence and Forensics 1052
Federal Law. 1052
Fraud. 1053
Government Misconduct. 1053
Hate Crime. 1053
Homicide 1053
Immunity 1054
International Law. 1054
Interrogation. 1054
Investigation. 1054
Judges 1054
Juries 1055
Jurisdictions 1055
Juvenile Justice 1055
Kidnapping 1055
Law Codes. 1055
Law-Enforcement Organization. 1056
Legal Terms and Principles, 374. 1056

Media 1057
Medical and Health Issues 1057
Mental Disorders 1057
Military Justice 1057
Morality and Public Order 1057
Organized Crime. 1057
Pardons and Parole 1058
Police Powers. 1058
Political Issues. 1058
Prisons. 1058
Privacy 1059
Probation and Pretrial Release. 1059
Professional Standards 1059
Prosecution. 1059
Punishment. 1059
Rehabilitation. 1060
Restorative Justice 1060
Robbery, Theft, and Burglary 1060
Search and Seizure 1060
Sentencing 1061
Sex Offenses 1061
Substance Abuse. 1061
Technology 1061
Terrorism. 1062
Testimony 1062
Traffic Law 1062
Trial Procedures 1062
Vandalism 1063
Verdicts. 1063
Victimless Crime. 1063
Victims 1063
Violent Crime 1064
White-Collar Crime 1064
Witnesses 1064
Women's Issues 1064

Topics by Subject Category **The Criminal Justice System**

APPEALS
Stare decisis, 709
Appellate process, 554-555
Certiorari, 579
Clemency, 584
Court types, 593-594
Double jeopardy, 320
False convictions, 629-630
Habeas corpus, 639-640
Harmless error, 642
Judicial review, 652
Opinions, 672
Reversible error, 695
Scottsboro cases, 699
Supreme Court, U.S., 711-713
Supreme Court, U.S., and criminal rights, 711-713
Trial transcripts, 720

ARREST and ARRAIGNMENT
Arraignment, 557
Arrest, 278-281
Arrest warrants, 282
Bail system, 564-566
Booking, 424
Chimel v. California, 294
Citations, 581
Citizen's arrests, 296
Criminal history record information, 867
Criminal procedure, 310-313
Escobedo v. Illinois, 327
Habeas corpus, 639-640
Illinois v. Wardlow, 345
Information (written accusation), 347
King beating case, 472-473
Manhattan Bail Project, 361
Minnick v. Mississippi, 668
Miranda rights, 369-371
Miranda v. Arizona, 372
Pleas, 677
Preliminary hearings, 680
Probable cause, 383-384
Reasonable force, 526
Resisting arrest, 527
Search warrants, 393-394
Sobriety testing, 219-220
Suspects, 229
Tennessee v. Garner, 538

ATTORNEYS
Brady v. United States, 572

Attorney ethics, 557-558
Counsel, right to, 591
Cross-examination, 598
Defendant self-representation, 604
Defense attorneys, 607
Discovery, 612
District attorneys, 614
Effective counsel, 619-621
Faretta v. California, 631
Gideon v. Wainwright, 635
Massiah v. United States, 666
Objections, 671
Privileged communications, 382
Public defenders, 683-685
Public prosecutors, 686-687

BUSINESS and FINANCIAL CRIME
Antitrust law, 273-276
Blackmail and extortion, 21-23
Bribery, 25-26
Computer crime, 855
Conspiracy, 44
Consumer fraud, 49-50
Corporate scandals, 51-54
Counterfeiting, 55-58
Cybercrime, 871-874
Document analysis, 878
Environmental crimes, 103
Forensic accounting, 886
Forgery, 109
Fraud, 110
Identity theft, 895-898
Insider trading, 128
Insurance fraud, 129-130
Internal Revenue Service, U.S., 465
Money laundering, 154
Organized crime, 170
Regulatory crime, 201
Secret Service, U.S., 527-528
Sex discrimination, 948-951
Sherman Antitrust Act, 213
Shoplifting, 214-216
Sports and crime, 221-224
Tax evasion, 230-232
Telephone fraud, 233
Treasury Department, U.S., 241
White-collar crime, 261

CAPITAL PUNISHMENT
Antiterrorism and Effective Death Penalty Act, 846-

847
Capital punishment, 573-577
Coker v. Georgia, 585
Death qualification, 603-605
Execution, forms of, 622-623
Ford v. Wainwright, 633
Furman v. Georgia, 634
Gregg v. Georgia, 638
McCleskey v. Kemp, 667
Murder and homicide, 160-165
Powell v. Alabama, 678
Punishment, 688-691
Stanford v. Kentucky, 708
Tison v. Arizona, 717
Witherspoon v. Illinois, 727

CIVIL RIGHTS and LIBERTIES
Batson v. Kentucky, 569
Bill of Rights, U.S., 287
Civil disobedience, 851
Clear and present danger test, 855
Cultural defense, 314
Equal protection under the law, 326
Freedom of assembly and association, 890
Furman v. Georgia, 634
Hate crime, 117-119
Illegal aliens, 124-125
Jim Crow laws, 354-356
Ku Klux Klan, 139
Lynching, 141
Magna Carta, 359
McCleskey v. Kemp, 667
Nonviolent resistance, 915-916
Police ethics, 507-508
Privacy rights, 934-935
Racial profiling and criminal justice, 523-525
Right to bear arms, 202-203
Scottsboro cases, 699
Sex discrimination, 948-951
Sexual harassment and criminal justice, 211-212
Slave patrols, 530
Supreme Court, U.S., 711-713
Supreme Court, U.S., and criminal rights, 711-713
Surveillance cameras, 954-955
Virginia v. Black, 257
Women in law enforcement and corrections, 546-549

COMPUTER CRIME
Computer crime, 855
Computer forensics, 859

Computer information systems, 861-862
Cybercrime, 871-874
Espionage, 881-883
Fraud, 110
Internal Revenue Service, U.S., 465

CONFESSIONS
Arizona v. Fulminante, 277
Arrest, 278-281
Brown v. Mississippi, 291
Confessions, 301-302
Corporal punishment, 589
Escobedo v. Illinois, 327
Massiah v. United States, 666
Minnick v. Mississippi, 668
Miranda rights, 369-371
Miranda v. Arizona, 372
Police ethics, 507-508
Self-incrimination, privilege against, 701-702

CONSTITUTIONAL PROTECTIONS
Barker v. Wingo, 568
Bill of Rights, U.S., 287
Bivens v. Six Unknown Named Agents, 290
Breach of the peace, 24
Brown v. Mississippi, 291
Certiorari, 579
Clear and present danger test, 855
Color of law, 297-298
Constitution, U.S., 46-48
Counsel, right to, 591
Defendants, 606
Double jeopardy, 320
Due process of law, 321-323
Effective counsel, 619-621
Equal protection under the law, 326
Escobedo v. Illinois, 327
Ex post facto laws, 328
Faretta v. California, 631
Freedom of assembly and association, 890
Furman v. Georgia, 634
Gregg v. Georgia, 638
Gun laws, 336-339
Hate crime, 117-119
Hurtado v. California, 341
Incorporation doctrine, 346
Jim Crow laws, 354-356
Judicial review, 652
Justice, 134-135
Magna Carta, 359

Mapp v. Ohio, 362
Maryland v. Craig, 364
Miranda v. Arizona, 372
No-knock warrants, 378
Palko v. Connecticut, 672
Pornography and obscenity, 181-184
Privacy rights, 934-935
R.A.V. v. City of St. Paul, 190
Reasonable doubt, 387
Right to bear arms, 202-203
Search and seizure, 391-392
Solem v. Helm, 706
Speedy trial right, 707
Supreme Court, U.S., 711-713
Supreme Court, U.S., and criminal rights, 711-713
Texas v. Johnson, 237
Uniform Juvenile Court Act, 251
United States v. Lopez, 409
Wilson v. Arkansas, 415
Wisconsin v. Mitchell, 266

CONVICTIONS
Acquittal, 553
Amnesty, 553
Arizona v. Fulminante, 277
Blended sentences, 571
Convictions, 588
Criminal records, 869
Cruel and unusual punishment, 599-602
Death qualification, 603-605
Execution of judgment, 624
False convictions, 629-630
Felon disfranchisement, 334
Harmless error, 642
Misdemeanors, 372-373
Mitigating circumstances, 374
Parole, 773-776
Plea bargaining, 676
Probation, adult, 806-808
Probation, juvenile, 809-810
Restitution, 692
Reversible error, 695
Sentencing, 703-704
Suspended sentences, 714

COURTS
Appellate process, 554-555
Bailiffs, 567
Case law, 578
Cease-and-desist orders, 579

Certiorari, 579
Clerks of the court, 584
Contempt of court, 587
Court reporters, 592
Court types, 593-594
Criminal justice in U.S. history, 65-69
Criminal justice system, 70-74
Criminal prosecution, 595-597
Depositions, 610
Discretion, 443
Drug courts, 617-618
Drug testing, 95-96
Execution of judgment, 624
Incorporation doctrine, 346
Judicial review, 652
Judicial system, U.S., 652-654
Jurisdiction of courts, 655-656
Jury system, 659-662
Juvenile courts, 899
Juvenile justice system, 905-907
Juvenile waivers to adult courts, 908
Mandamus, 664
Military justice, 367
Night courts, 670
Objections, 671
Obstruction of justice, 671
Precedent, 679
Subpoena power, 710
Summonses, 711
Supreme Court, U.S., 711-713
Supreme Court, U.S., and criminal rights, 711-713
Traffic courts, 718
Uniform Juvenile Court Act, 251

CRIME PREVENTION
Attempt to commit a crime, 18
Community-oriented policing, 434-435
Contributing to delinquency of minors, 863
DARE programs, 440
Deterrence, 611
Drug courts, 617-618
Drug legalization, 92-94
Incapacitation, 764
Inchoate crimes, 126
Just deserts, 663
Juvenile delinquency, 900-903
Juvenile justice system, 905-907
Motor vehicle theft, 156-159
Neighborhood watch programs, 484
Omnibus Crime Control and Safe Streets Act of 1968,

168
Private police and guards, 519-520
Psychological profiling, 936-937
Psychopathy, 187-188
Punitive damages, 386
Recidivism, 813-814
Reckless endangerment, 199
Restorative justice, 693
Restraining orders, 695
School violence, 944-945
Sex offender registries, 396-397
Shoplifting, 214-216
Stakeouts, 533
Surveillance cameras, 954-955
Vehicle checkpoints, 542
Victim and Witness Protection Act, 824
Victimology, 833
Violent Crime Control and Law Enforcement Act, 412
Violent Criminal Apprehension Program, 256
Witness protection programs, 728
Youth authorities, 841

CRIME STATISTICS

Geographic information systems, 894
Bureau of Justice Statistics, 851
Computer information systems, 861-862
Crime index, 64
National Crime Information Center, 914
National Crime Victimization Survey, 767
National Institute of Justice, 915
Uniform Crime Reports, 249-250
Violent Criminal Apprehension Program, 256

CRIMINOLOGY

Crime, 59-63
Criminal justice education, 868-870
Criminology, 78
Forensic psychology, 107
Trace evidence, 964
Uniform Crime Reports, 249-250
Victimless crimes, 832
Victimology, 833

DEFENDANTS

Brady v. United States, 572
Appellate process, 554-555
Argersinger v. Hamlin, 556
Arrest, 278-281
Bail system, 564-566
Bill of particulars, 571

Bounty hunters, 850
Brown v. Mississippi, 291
Competency to stand trial, 585-586
Convictions, 588
Counsel, right to, 591
Crimes of passion, 64
Criminal intent, 304
Criminal liability, 309
Criminal records, 869
Criminals, 75-77
Cultural defense, 314
Defendant self-representation, 604
Defendants, 606
Defense attorneys, 607
Defenses to crime, 315-318
Diminished capacity, 319
Duress, 324
Entrapment, 325
Excuses and justifications, 331
False convictions, 629-630
Faretta v. California, 631
Ford v. Wainwright, 633
Gideon v. Wainwright, 635
Ignorance of the law, 342
Immunity from prosecution, 644
In forma pauperis, 645
Insanity defense, 347-349
Massiah v. United States, 666
Mens rea, 366
Minnick v. Mississippi, 668
Mitigating circumstances, 374
Motives, 375
Nolo contendere, 670
Palko v. Connecticut, 672
Plea bargaining, 676
Pleas, 677
Powell v. Alabama, 678
Presumption of innocence, 380
Preventive detention, 381
Principals (criminal), 185
Public defenders, 683-685
Reasonable doubt, 387
Santobello v. New York, 698
Self-defense, 395
Self-incrimination, privilege against, 701-702
Strict liability offenses, 403
Suspects, 229
Trials, 721-724

DEVIANCY
Animal abuse, 9-11
Commercialized vice, 38-40
Criminals, 75-77
Indecent exposure, 127
Mass and serial murders, 145-149
Murders, mass and serial, 145-149
Pedophilia, 921
Pornography, child, 926-928
Psychopathy, 187-188
Sex offender registries, 396-397
Stalking, 225
Supermax prisons, 822-823
Vagrancy laws, 410

DOMESTIC VIOLENCE
Alcohol use and abuse, 6-8
Animal abuse, 9-11
Assault and battery, 15-17
Battered child and battered wife syndromes, 744-745
Child abduction by parents, 32
Child abuse and molestation, 33-37
Cultural defense, 314
Date rape, 83
Domestic violence, 86-90
Kidnapping, 136
Rape and sex offenses, 193-198
Restraining orders, 695
Stalking, 225
Victim assistance programs, 824

ESPIONAGE and SEDITION
Clear and present danger test, 855
Deportation, 608
Diplomatic immunity, 319
Espionage, 881-883
Palmer raids, 773
Seditious libel, 210
Smith Act, 819
Treason, 241

EVIDENCE and FORENSICS
Autopsies, 19
Bloodstains, 848
Chain of custody, 580
Circumstantial evidence, 295
Computer forensics, 859
Coroners, 864-865
Crime labs, 866
Crime scene investigation, 438
DNA testing, 875-877
Document analysis, 878
Evidence, rules of, 388-390
Exclusionary rule, 329
Eyewitness testimony, 626-628
Fingerprint identification, 884-885
Forensic accounting, 886
Forensic psychology, 107
Forensics, 887-889
Gault, In re, 893
Hearsay, 340
Latent evidence, 910
Mapp v. Ohio, 362
Medical examiners, 913
Payne v. Tennessee, 378
Police detectives, 504-505
Police lineups, 509
Polygraph testing, 924-925
Rules of evidence, 388-390
Shoe prints and tire-tracks, 952
Standards of proof, 707
Testimony, 715
Toxicology, 963
Trace evidence, 964
Weeks v. United States, 413
Witnesses, 730

FEDERAL LAW
Alcohol, Tobacco, Firearms and Explosives, U.S. Bureau of, 419-420
Anti-Racketeering Act of 1934, 12
Antiterrorism and Effective Death Penalty Act, 846-847
Asset forfeiture, 283-284
Attorney General, U.S., 559-560
Bill of Rights, U.S., 287
Comprehensive Crime Control Act, 300
Comprehensive Drug Abuse Prevention and Control Act, 42
Comstock law, 43
Counterfeiting, 55-58
Drug Enforcement Administration, U.S., 444
Drugs and law enforcement, 445-447
Environmental crimes, 103
Federal Bureau of Investigation, U.S., 450-453
Federal Crimes Act, 334
Hobbs Act, 121
Homeland Security, U.S. Department of, 459-461
Hoover, J. Edgar, 121
Illegal aliens, 124-125

Internal Revenue Service, U.S., 465
Judicial system, U.S., 652-654
Justice Department, U.S., 467-471
Kidnapping, 136
Law Enforcement Assistance Administration, 479
Lindbergh law, 358
Mandamus, 664
Mann Act, 143
Marshals Service, U.S., 480
National Crime Information Center, 914
National Guard, 482-483
National Institute of Justice, 915
National Narcotics Act, 167
National Stolen Property Act, 168
Omnibus Crime Control and Safe Streets Act of 1968, 168
Opium Exclusion Act, 169
Organized Crime Control Act, 173
Parole Commission, U.S., 779
Patriot Act, 920
Prisons, Federal Bureau of, 804
Racketeering Influenced and Corrupt Organizations Act, 191
Secret Service, U.S., 527-528
Sherman Antitrust Act, 213
Smith Act, 819
Treasury Department, U.S., 241
United States Code, 407
United States Sentencing Commission, 725
United States Statutes at Large, 407
United States v. Lopez, 409
Violent Crime Control and Law Enforcement Act, 412

FRAUD
Arson, 12-14
Computer crime, 855
Conspiracy, 44
Consumer fraud, 49-50
Corporate scandals, 51-54
Counterfeiting, 55-58
Document analysis, 878
Forensic accounting, 886
Forgery, 109
Fraud, 110
Identity theft, 895-898
Insider trading, 128
Insurance fraud, 129-130
Internal Revenue Service, U.S., 465
National Stolen Property Act, 168
Organized crime, 170

Political corruption, 177-180
Racketeering Influenced and Corrupt Organizations Act, 191
Rummel v. Estelle, 697
Tax evasion, 230-232
Telephone fraud, 233
Theft, 238
Treasury Department, U.S., 241
Voting fraud, 258

GOVERNMENT MISCONDUCT
Bribery, 25-26
Civilian review boards, 431
Color of law, 297-298
Cruel and unusual punishment, 599-602
Deadly force, 441-442
Exclusionary rule, 329
Hoover, J. Edgar, 121
Impeachment of judges, 645
Internal affairs, 463-464
Jim Crow laws, 354-356
King beating case, 472-473
Knapp Commission, 474
MOVE bombing, 481
Miscarriage of justice, 669
Palmer raids, 773
Pardons, 673-674
Police brutality, 493-497
Police civil liability, 498-499
Police corruption, 500-503
Political corruption, 177-180
Proximate cause, 385
Racial profiling and criminal justice, 523-525
Sting operations, 536
Voting fraud, 258
White-collar crime, 261
Wickersham Commission, 545

HATE CRIME
Ku Klux Klan, 139
Lynching, 141
R.A.V. v. City of St. Paul, 190
Victimology, 833
Virginia v. Black, 257
Wisconsin v. Mitchell, 266

HOMICIDE
AIDS, 740
Abortion, 3-4
Cold cases, 432-433

Topics by Subject Category — The Criminal Justice System

Crimes of passion, 64
Deadly force, 441-442
Drive-by shootings, 91
Inquests, 648
Manslaughter, 144
Mass and serial murders, 145-149
Murder and homicide, 160-165
Murders, mass and serial, 145-149
Self-defense, 395
September 11, 2001, attacks, 946

IMMUNITY
Amnesty, 553
Diplomatic immunity, 319
Immunity from prosecution, 644
Police civil liability, 498-499
Self-incrimination, privilege against, 701-702

INTERNATIONAL LAW
Border patrols, 425-426
Deportation, 608
Diplomatic immunity, 319
Extradition, 331-333
Illegal aliens, 124-125
International law, 350-353
Interpol, 466
September 11, 2001, attacks, 946
Skyjacking, 217
United States v. Alvarez-Machain, 408
War crimes, 259-260
World Court, 733

INTERROGATION
Arrest, 278-281
Confessions, 301-302
Corporal punishment, 589
Cross-examination, 598
Escobedo v. Illinois, 327
Forensic psychology, 107
Massiah v. United States, 666
Minnick v. Mississippi, 668
Miranda rights, 369-371
Miranda v. Arizona, 372
Police ethics, 507-508
Police psychologists, 514
Polygraph testing, 924-925
Self-incrimination, privilege against, 701-702

INVESTIGATION
Geographic information systems, 894
Autopsies, 19
Bloodstains, 848
Bounty hunters, 850
Chain of custody, 580
Circumstantial evidence, 295
Cold cases, 432-433
Coroners, 864-865
Crime labs, 866
Crime scene investigation, 438
Criminal history record information, 867
DNA testing, 875-877
Document analysis, 878
Electronic surveillance, 879-880
Federal Bureau of Investigation, U.S., 450-453
Fingerprint identification, 884-885
Forensic psychology, 107
Forensics, 887-889
Grand juries, 636-637
Hearings, 642
Inquests, 648
Latent evidence, 910
Medical examiners, 913
Missing persons, 152-153
Police detectives, 504-505
Police dogs, 506
Police lineups, 509
Presentence investigations, 681
Psychological profiling, 936-937
Reasonable suspicion, 387
Secret Service, U.S., 527-528
Shoe prints and tire-tracks, 952
Stakeouts, 533
Stop and frisk, 401-402
Suspects, 229
Toxicology, 963
Trace evidence, 964
Vehicle checkpoints, 542
Violent Criminal Apprehension Program, 256
Wiretaps and criminal justice, 970

JUDGES
Arrest warrants, 282
Bench warrants, 570
Case law, 578
Cease-and-desist orders, 579
Concurrent sentences, 587
Execution of judgment, 624
Gag orders, 635
Impeachment of judges, 645
Judges, 650-651

Mandatory sentencing, 664-665
Opinions, 672
Precedent, 679
Subpoena power, 710
Three-strikes laws, 716
United States Sentencing Commission, 725

JURIES
Voir dire, 727
Batson v. Kentucky, 569
Change of venue, 581
Death qualification, 603-605
Hung juries, 643
Jury nullification, 657
Jury sequestration, 658
Jury system, 659-662
Powell v. Alabama, 678
Scottsboro cases, 699
Witherspoon v. Illinois, 727

JURISDICTIONS
Change of venue, 581
Court types, 593-594
Extradition, 331-333
Habeas corpus, 639-640
Judges, 650-651
Jurisdiction of courts, 655-656
Lindbergh law, 358
Martial law, 363
Multiple jurisdiction offenses, 376
Night courts, 670
Sheriffs, 529

JUVENILE JUSTICE
Blended sentences, 571
Boot camps, 746-747
Contributing to delinquency of minors, 863
Criminal justice system, 70-74
DARE programs, 440
Diversion, 616
Drive-by shootings, 91
Gault, In re, 893
Graffiti, 116
Juvenile Justice and Delinquency Prevention Act, 904
Juvenile Justice and Delinquency Prevention, Office of, 905
Juvenile courts, 899
Juvenile delinquency, 900-903
Juvenile justice system, 905-907
Juvenile waivers to adult courts, 908

Kidnapping, 136
New Jersey v. T.L.O., 377
Parens patriae, 918
Pedophilia, 921
Pornography, child, 926-928
Schall v. Martin, 944
School violence, 944-945
Shoplifting, 214-216
Stanford v. Kentucky, 708
Status offenses, 954
Uniform Juvenile Court Act, 251
Vandalism, 252-253
Youth authorities, 841
Youth gangs, 971-973

KIDNAPPING
Child abduction by parents, 32
Kidnapping, 136
Lindbergh law, 358
Lynching, 141
Missing persons, 152-153
United States v. Alvarez-Machain, 408

LAW CODES
Stare decisis, 709
Accomplices and accessories, 271
Annotated codes, 273
Common law, 299
Comprehensive Crime Control Act, 300
Criminal law, 305-308
Decriminalization, 314
Ex post facto laws, 328
Federal Crimes Act, 334
Felonies, 335
Gun laws, 336-339
International law, 350-353
Judicial system, U.S., 652-654
Loitering, 140
Mala in se and *mala prohibita*, 359-360
Misdemeanors, 372-373
Moral turpitude, 375
Precedent, 679
Statutes, 400
Statutes of limitations, 401
Strict liability offenses, 403
Traffic law, 404
United States Code, 407
United States Statutes at Large, 407
Vicarious liability, 411

Topics by Subject Category — The Criminal Justice System

LAW-ENFORCEMENT ORGANIZATION

Alcohol, Tobacco, Firearms and Explosives, U.S. Bureau of, 419-420
Attorney General, U.S., 559-560
Attorneys general, state, 561
Border patrols, 425-426
Boston police strike, 427
Campus police, 429-430
Community-oriented policing, 434-435
Computer information systems, 861-862
Criminal justice in U.S. history, 65-69
Criminal justice system, 70-74
Criminal law, 305-308
Drug Enforcement Administration, U.S., 444
Drugs and law enforcement, 445-447
Federal Bureau of Investigation, U.S., 450-453
Highway patrols, 459
Homeland Security, U.S. Department of, 459-461
Hoover, J. Edgar, 121
Interpol, 466
Justice Department, U.S., 467-471
Juvenile Justice and Delinquency Prevention, Office of, 905
Law Enforcement Assistance Administration, 479
Law enforcement, 475-478
Marshals Service, U.S., 480
Multiple jurisdiction offenses, 376
National Crime Information Center, 914
National Guard, 482-483
Omnibus Crime Control and Safe Streets Act of 1968, 168
Police, 488-490
Police academies, 491-492
Police chiefs, 498
Police psychologists, 514
Posse comitatus, 516
President's Commission on Law Enforcement and Administration of Justice, 931
Private police and guards, 519-520
Sheriffs, 529
Slave patrols, 530
State police, 534-535
Strategic policing, 537
Uniform Crime Reports, 249-250
Wickersham Commission, 545

LEGAL TERMS and PRINCIPLES, 374

Stare decisis, 709
Voir dire, 727
Accomplices and accessories, 271
Amicus curiae briefs, 272
Annotated codes, 273
Arraignment, 557
Attempt to commit a crime, 18
Bifurcated trials, 570
Burden of proof, 292
Certiorari, 579
Chain of custody, 580
Color of law, 297-298
Common law, 299
Concurrent sentences, 587
Conspiracy, 44
Crime, 59-63
Crime index, 64
Criminals, 75-77
Criminology, 78
Depositions, 610
Deterrence, 611
Diminished capacity, 319
Discovery, 612
Discretion, 443
Dismissals, 613
Diversion, 616
Double jeopardy, 320
Due process of law, 321-323
Duress, 324
Ex post facto laws, 328
Exclusionary rule, 329
Felonies, 335
Gag orders, 635
Good time, 757
Habeas corpus, 639-640
Harmless error, 642
Hearsay, 340
In forma pauperis, 645
Incapacitation, 764
Inchoate crimes, 126
Information (written accusation), 347
Jury nullification, 657
Just deserts, 663
Justice, 134-135
Lesser-included offenses, 358
Mala in se and *mala prohibita*, 359-360
Malice, 361
Mandamus, 664
Mens rea, 366
Mitigating circumstances, 374
Multiple jurisdiction offenses, 376
Nolle prosequi, 670
Nolo contendere, 670

Parens patriae, 918
Principals (criminal), 381
Probable cause, 383-384
Proximate cause, 385
Reasonable doubt, 387
Reasonable force, 526
Vicarious liability, 411

MEDIA
Change of venue, 581
Gag orders, 635
Jury sequestration, 658
Murders, mass and serial, 160-165
Print media, 931-933
Seditious libel, 210
Sports and crime, 221-224
Television news, 235-236
Trial publicity, 246

MEDICAL and HEALTH ISSUES
AIDS, 740
Abortion, 3-4
Alcohol use and abuse, 6-8
Animal abuse, 9-11
Autopsies, 19
Battered child and battered wife syndromes, 744-745
Child abuse and molestation, 33-37
Comprehensive Drug Abuse Prevention and Control Act, 42
Coroners, 864-865
Corporal punishment, 589
Cruel and unusual punishment, 599-602
Defenses to crime, 315-318
Domestic violence, 86-90
Drug Enforcement Administration, U.S., 444
Drug courts, 617-618
Elderly prisoners, 755
Execution, forms of, 622-623
Inquests, 648
Insanity defense, 347-349
Insurance fraud, 129-130
Medical examiners, 913
Mental illness, 150-151
National Organization for Victim Assistance, 768
"Not-in-my-backyard" attitudes, 769
Police psychologists, 514
Prison health care, 790-791
Solitary confinement, 820-821
Suicide and euthanasia, 226-228
Victim assistance programs, 824

MENTAL DISORDERS
Competency to stand trial, 585-586
Diminished capacity, 319
Ford v. Wainwright, 633
Mental illness, 150-151
Parens patriae, 918
Psychopathy, 187-188

MILITARY JUSTICE
Court types, 593-594
Martial law, 363
Military justice, 367
National Guard, 482-483
War crimes, 259-260

MORALITY and PUBLIC ORDER
"Not-in-my-backyard" attitudes, 769
AIDS, 740
Adultery, 5
Breach of the peace, 24
Bribery, 25-26
Civil disobedience, 851
Commercialized vice, 38-40
Comstock law, 43
Disorderly conduct, 85
Drug legalization, 92-94
Gambling, 113-115
Indecent exposure, 127
Juvenile Justice and Delinquency Prevention Act, 904
Law Enforcement Assistance Administration, 479
Martial law, 363
Moral turpitude, 375
Pornography and obscenity, 181-184
Posse comitatus, 516
Prohibition, 186
Public-order offenses, 189
Reckless endangerment, 199
Special weapons and tactics teams (SWAT), 531-532
Vandalism, 252-253
Victimless crimes, 832
Vigilantism, 254-255

ORGANIZED CRIME
Anti-Racketeering Act of 1934, 12
Gambling, 113-115
Mafia, 143
Money laundering, 154
Organized Crime Control Act, 173
Organized crime, 170
Prohibition, 186

Racketeering Influenced and Corrupt Organizations Act, 191

PARDONS and PAROLE
Amnesty, 553
Clemency, 584
Pardons, 673-674
Parole, 773-776
Parole Commission, U.S., 779
Parole officers, 780
Prison escapes, 787-788
Suspended sentences, 714

POLICE POWERS
Atwater v. City of Lago Vista, 285
Automobile searches, 285-286
Boston police strike, 427
Campus police, 429-430
Chimel v. California, 294
Civilian review boards, 431
Color of law, 297-298
Deadly force, 441-442
Discretion, 443
Entrapment, 325
Harris v. United States, 340
High-speed chases, 457-458
Illinois v. Wardlow, 345
Internal affairs, 463-464
King beating case, 472-473
Knapp Commission, 474
Knowles v. Iowa, 357
Law enforcement, 475-478
Loitering, 140
MOVE bombing, 481
Maryland v. Buie, 363
Massachusetts v. Sheppard, 365
Nonviolent resistance, 915-916
Patriot Act, 920
Peace Officer Standards and Training, 487
Plain view doctrine, 379
Police, 488-490
Police brutality, 493-497
Police chiefs, 498
Police civil liability, 498-499
Police corruption, 500-503
Police detectives, 504-505
Police dogs, 506
Police powers, 511-513
Posse comitatus, 516
Privacy rights, 934-935

Probable cause, 383-384
Racial profiling and criminal justice, 523-525
Reasonable force, 526
Reasonable suspicion, 387
Search warrants, 393-394
Sobriety testing, 219-220
Special weapons and tactics teams (SWAT), 531-532
State police, 534-535
Sting operations, 536
Stop and frisk, 401-402
Strategic policing, 537
Tennessee v. Garner, 538
Whren v. United States, 414

POLITICAL ISSUES
Antitrust law, 273-276
Attorney General, U.S., 559-560
Felon disfranchisement, 334
Jim Crow laws, 354-356
Magna Carta, 359
Mala in se and *mala prohibita*, 359-360
National Commission on the Causes and Prevention of Violence, 166
Nonviolent resistance, 915-916
Palmer raids, 773
Pardons, 673-674
Political corruption, 177-180
Public prosecutors, 686-687
Seditious libel, 210
Smith Act, 819
United States v. Lopez, 409
Voting fraud, 258

PRISONS
Auburn system, 743
Boot camps, 746-747
Elderly prisoners, 755
Forestry camps, 756
Good time, 757
Mandatory sentencing, 664-665
Prison and jail systems, 783-786
Prison escapes, 787-788
Prison guards, 789
Prison health care, 790-791
Prison industries, 792
Prison overcrowding, 794-796
Prison violence, 800-801
Prisons, Federal Bureau of, 804
Recidivism, 813-814
Solitary confinement, 820-821

Supermax prisons, 822-823
Walnut Street Jail, 838
Work camps, 838-839

PRIVACY
Abortion, 3-4
DNA testing, 875-877
Electronic surveillance, 879-880
Katz v. United States, 909
Mapp v. Ohio, 362
New Jersey v. T.L.O., 377
Olmstead v. United States, 917
Search and seizure, 391-392
Surveillance cameras, 954-955
Trespass, 244, 539-540
Weeks v. United States, 413
Wilson v. Arkansas, 415
Wiretaps and criminal justice, 970

PROBATION and PRETRIAL RELEASE
Arrest warrants, 282
Bail system, 564-566
Barker v. Wingo, 568
Bench warrants, 570
Booking, 424
Bounty hunters, 850
Community-based corrections, 749
Criminal procedure, 310-313
Drug testing, 95-96
Halfway houses, 758
House arrest, 763
Manhattan Bail Project, 361
Parole officers, 780
Presentence investigations, 681
Presumption of innocence, 380
Preventive detention, 381
Probation, adult, 806-808
Probation, juvenile, 809-810
Schall v. Martin, 944
Sentencing, 703-704
Speedy trial right, 707
Victim-offender mediation, 827
Work-release programs, 840

PROFESSIONAL STANDARDS
Attorney ethics, 557-558
Bureau of Justice Statistics, 851
Civilian review boards, 431
Criminal justice education, 868-870
Due process of law, 321-323

Effective counsel, 619-621
Internal affairs, 463-464
Judges, 650-651
National Institute of Justice, 915
Peace Officer Standards and Training, 487
Police academies, 491-492
Police brutality, 493-497
Police chiefs, 498
Police corruption, 500-503
Police ethics, 507-508
Police powers, 511-513
President's Commission on Law Enforcement and Administration of Justice, 931
Privileged communications, 382
Public defenders, 683-685
Public prosecutors, 686-687
Standards of proof, 707
Strategic policing, 537
Wickersham Commission, 545
Women in law enforcement and corrections, 546-549

PROSECUTION
Attorneys general, state, 561
Bill of particulars, 571
Burden of proof, 292
Convictions, 588
Criminal intent, 304
Criminal law, 305-308
Criminal liability, 309
Criminal prosecution, 595-597
Discovery, 612
Dismissals, 613
District attorneys, 614
Double jeopardy, 320
Grand juries, 636-637
Harmless error, 642
Indictment, 647
Information (written accusation), 347
Mens rea, 366
Nolle prosequi, 670
Public prosecutors, 686-687
Statutes of limitations, 401

PUNISHMENT
Aggravating circumstances, 271
Boot camps, 746-747
Breach of the peace, 24
Capital punishment, 573-577
Community service, 750
Community-based corrections, 749

1059

Concurrent sentences, 587
Contempt of court, 587
Corporal punishment, 589
Criminal justice in U.S. history, 65-69
Criminal justice system, 70-74
Criminal law, 305-308
Cruel and unusual punishment, 599-602
Deterrence, 611
Execution, forms of, 622-623
Felon disfranchisement, 334
Fines, 632
Forestry camps, 756
Gregg v. Georgia, 638
Halfway houses, 758
Harmelin v. Michigan, 641
House arrest, 763
Incapacitation, 764
Indeterminate sentencing, 646
Just deserts, 663
Mandatory sentencing, 664-665
Misdemeanors, 372-373
Parole, 773-776
Parole Commission, U.S., 779
Parole officers, 780
Prison and jail systems, 783-786
Prison overcrowding, 794-796
Prisons, Federal Bureau of, 804
Punishment, 688-691
Punitive damages, 386
Rehabilitation, 815-817
Restitution, 692
Robinson v. California, 696
Rummel v. Estelle, 697
Schall v. Martin, 944
Sentencing, 703-704
Sentencing guidelines, U.S., 705
Solem v. Helm, 706
Solitary confinement, 820-821
Three-strikes laws, 716
Traffic fines, 719
Vigilantism, 254-255
Work camps, 838-839
Work-release programs, 840

REHABILITATION
Auburn system, 743
Community-based corrections, 749
Elderly prisoners, 755
Forestry camps, 756
Good time, 757

Halfway houses, 758
Juvenile courts, 899
Juvenile delinquency, 900-903
Juvenile justice system, 905-907
Parole, 773-776
Prison and jail systems, 783-786
Prison industries, 792
Recidivism, 813-814
Rehabilitation, 815-817
Walnut Street Jail, 838
Work camps, 838-839
Work-release programs, 840
Youth authorities, 841

RESTORATIVE JUSTICE
Clemency, 584
Community service, 750
Fines, 632
Restorative justice, 693
Victim-offender mediation, 827
Victims of Crime Act, 834

ROBBERY, THEFT, and BURGLARY
Burglary, 29-30
Carjacking, 31
Crime, 59-63
Hobbs Act, 121
Identity theft, 895-898
Mafia, 143
Motor vehicle theft, 156-159
National Stolen Property Act, 168
Pickpocketing, 177
Robbery, 204-207
Shoplifting, 214-216
Theft, 238

SEARCH and SEIZURE
Asset forfeiture, 283-284
Atwater v. City of Lago Vista, 285
Automobile searches, 285-286
Bivens v. Six Unknown Named Agents, 290
California v. Greenwood, 293
Chimel v. California, 294
Consent searches, 303
Harris v. United States, 340
Illinois v. Gates, 343
Illinois v. Krull, 343
Illinois v. McArthur, 344
Illinois v. Wardlow, 345
Katz v. United States, 909

Knowles v. Iowa, 357
Kyllo v. United States, 475
Maryland v. Buie, 363
Massachusetts v. Sheppard, 365
New Jersey v. T.L.O., 377
No-knock warrants, 378
Olmstead v. United States, 917
Plain view doctrine, 379
Privacy rights, 934-935
Racial profiling and criminal justice, 523-525
Reasonable suspicion, 387
Search and seizure, 391-392
Search warrants, 393-394
Stop and frisk, 401-402
Terry v. Ohio, 404
United States v. Leon, 409
Vehicle checkpoints, 542
Weeks v. United States, 413
Whren v. United States, 414
Wilson v. Arkansas, 415

SENTENCING

Aggravating circumstances, 271
Blended sentences, 571
Concurrent sentences, 587
Criminal records, 869
Execution of judgment, 624
Fines, 632
House arrest, 763
Indeterminate sentencing, 646
Just deserts, 663
Mandatory sentencing, 664-665
Mitigating circumstances, 374
Presentence investigations, 681
Preventive detention, 381
Prison overcrowding, 794-796
Probation, adult, 806-808
Probation, juvenile, 809-810
Punishment, 688-691
Restitution, 692
Rummel v. Estelle, 697
Sentencing, 703-704
Sentencing guidelines, U.S., 705
Suspended sentences, 714
Three-strikes laws, 716
Tison v. Arizona, 717
United States Sentencing Commission, 725
Work-release programs, 840

SEX OFFENSES

AIDS, 740
Adultery, 5
Bigamy and polygamy, 20
Child abuse and molestation, 33-37
Coker v. Georgia, 585
Date rape, 83
Domestic violence, 86-90
Indecent exposure, 127
Mann Act, 143
Pandering, 174
Pedophilia, 921
Pornography and obscenity, 181-184
Pornography, child, 926-928
Prison violence, 800-801
Rape and sex offenses, 193-198
Sex offender registries, 396-397
Sexual harassment and criminal justice, 211-212

SUBSTANCE ABUSE

Alcohol use and abuse, 6-8
Alcohol, Tobacco, Firearms and Explosives, U.S. Bureau of, 419-420
Asset forfeiture, 283-284
Comprehensive Drug Abuse Prevention and Control Act, 42
DARE programs, 440
Decriminalization, 314
Drug Enforcement Administration, U.S., 444
Drug courts, 617-618
Drug legalization, 92-94
Drug testing, 95-96
Drugs and law enforcement, 445-447
Drunk driving, 97-99
Harmelin v. Michigan, 641
Hit-and-run accidents, 120
Kyllo v. United States, 475
Mothers Against Drunk Driving, 155
National Narcotics Act, 167
Opium Exclusion Act, 169
Prohibition, 186
Public-order offenses, 189
Robinson v. California, 696
Sobriety testing, 219-220
United States v. Leon, 409

TECHNOLOGY

Arson, 12-14
Autopsies, 19
Cold cases, 432-433

Computer crime, 855
Computer forensics, 859
Computer information systems, 861-862
Counterfeiting, 55-58
Crime labs, 866
Crime scene investigation, 438
Criminal history record information, 867
Cybercrime, 871-874
DNA testing, 875-877
Drug testing, 95-96
Electronic surveillance, 879-880
Environmental crimes, 103
Espionage, 881-883
Execution, forms of, 622-623
Expert witnesses, 625
Fingerprint identification, 884-885
Forensics, 887-889
Geographic information systems, 894
Katz v. United States, 909
Latent evidence, 910
Motor vehicle theft, 156-159
Olmstead v. United States, 917
Polygraph testing, 924-925
Shoe prints and tire-tracks, 952
Stakeouts, 533
Telephone fraud, 233
Toxicology, 963
Trace evidence, 964
Wiretaps and criminal justice, 970

TERRORISM
Antiterrorism and Effective Death Penalty Act, 846-847
Blackmail and extortion, 21-23
Border patrols, 425-426
Deportation, 608
Extradition, 331-333
Homeland Security, U.S. Department of, 459-461
Illegal aliens, 124-125
International law, 350-353
Interpol, 466
Ku Klux Klan, 139
Money laundering, 154
Patriot Act, 920
September 11, 2001, attacks, 946
Skyjacking, 217

TESTIMONY
Evidence, rules of, 388-390
Hurtado v. California, 341

Rules of evidence, 388-390

TRAFFIC LAW
Citations, 581
Drunk driving, 97-99
High-speed chases, 457-458
Highway patrols, 459
Hit-and-run accidents, 120
Jaywalking, 133
Mothers Against Drunk Driving, 155
Proximate cause, 385
Reckless endangerment, 199
Sobriety testing, 219-220
State police, 534-535
Traffic courts, 718
Traffic fines, 719
Traffic law, 404
Vehicle checkpoints, 542

TRIAL PROCEDURES
Acquittal, 553
Amicus curiae briefs, 272
Argersinger v. Hamlin, 556
Arizona v. Fulminante, 277
Arraignment, 557
Bailiffs, 567
Barker v. Wingo, 568
Bench warrants, 570
Bifurcated trials, 570
Bill of particulars, 571
Burden of proof, 292
Case law, 578
Change of venue, 581
Competency to stand trial, 585-586
Contempt of court, 587
Criminal justice in U.S. history, 65-69
Criminal procedure, 310-313
Criminal prosecution, 595-597
Cross-examination, 598
Defendant self-representation, 604
Defendants, 606
Defense attorneys, 607
Defenses to crime, 315-318
Diminished capacity, 319
Discovery, 612
Dismissals, 613
Equal protection under the law, 326
Evidence, rules of, 388-390
Excuses and justifications, 331
Expert witnesses, 625

Gag orders, 635
Gault, In re, 893
Grand juries, 636-637
Hearings, 642
Hung juries, 643
Hurtado v. California, 341
Ignorance of the law, 342
Immunity from prosecution, 644
Indictment, 647
Indictment, 647
Insanity defense, 347-349
Jury nullification, 657
Jury sequestration, 658
Jury system, 659-662
Lesser-included offenses, 358
Lesser-included offenses, 358
Manhattan Bail Project, 361
Miscarriage of justice, 669
Nolle prosequi, 670
Nolo contendere, 670
Nolo contendere, 670
Objections, 671
Obstruction of justice, 671
Opinions, 672
Perjury, 176
Plea bargaining, 676
Plea bargaining, 676
Pleas, 677
Preliminary hearings, 680
President's Commission on Law Enforcement and Administration of Justice, 931
Presumption of innocence, 380
Reversible error, 695
Rules of evidence, 388-390
Santobello v. New York, 698
Speedy trial right, 707
Standards of proof, 707
Stare decisis, 709
Subpoena power, 710
Summonses, 711
Testimony, 715
Trial publicity, 720
Verdicts, 726
Voir dire, 727
Witness protection programs, 728
Witnesses, 730

VANDALISM
Animal abuse, 9-11
Arson, 12-14
Burglary, 29-30
Cybercrime, 871-874
Graffiti, 116
School violence, 944-945
Trespass, 246
Vandalism, 252-253
Youth gangs, 971-973

VERDICTS
Acquittal, 553
Convictions, 588
Dismissals, 613
False convictions, 629-630
Hung juries, 643
Judges, 650-651
Jury nullification, 657
Jury sequestration, 658
Jury system, 659-662
Miscarriage of justice, 669
Pleas, 677
Reasonable doubt, 387
Reversible error, 695
Verdicts, 726

VICTIMLESS CRIME
Bigamy and polygamy, 20
Commercialized vice, 38-40
Disorderly conduct, 85
Gambling, 113-115
Moral turpitude, 375
Public-order offenses, 189
Sports and crime, 221-224
Status offenses, 954
Vagrancy laws, 410
Victimless crimes, 832

VICTIMS
Missing persons, 152-153
National Crime Victimization Survey, 767
National Organization for Victim Assistance, 768
Payne v. Tennessee, 378
Punitive damages, 386
Restorative justice, 693
Restraining orders, 695
Stalking, 225
Victim and Witness Protection Act, 824
Victim assistance programs, 824
Victimology, 833
Victims of Crime Act, 834
War crimes, 259-260

VIOLENT CRIME

Aggravating circumstances, 271
Alcohol use and abuse, 6-8
Assault and battery, 15-17
Battered child and battered wife syndromes, 744-745
Bloodstains, 848
Carjacking, 31
Drive-by shootings, 91
Felonies, 335
Juvenile delinquency, 900-903
Mafia, 143
Malice, 361
Murder and homicide, 160-165
National Commission on the Causes and Prevention of Violence, 166
Prison violence, 800-801
Right to bear arms, 202-203
Robbery, 204-207
School violence, 944-945
Self-defense, 395
September 11, 2001, attacks, 946
Special weapons and tactics teams (SWAT), 531-532
Sports and crime, 221-224
Supermax prisons, 822-823
Violent Crime Control and Law Enforcement Act, 412
Youth gangs, 971-973

WHITE-COLLAR CRIME

Antitrust law, 273-276
Blackmail and extortion, 21-23
Conspiracy, 44
Consumer fraud, 49-50
Corporate scandals, 51-54
Fines, 632
Forensic accounting, 886
Fraud, 110
Insider trading, 128
Insurance fraud, 129-130
Regulatory crime, 201
Tax evasion, 230-232
Telephone fraud, 233
White-collar crime, 261

WITNESSES

Circumstantial evidence, 295
Cross-examination, 598
Depositions, 610
Evidence, rules of, 388-390
Expert witnesses, 625
Eyewitness testimony, 626-628
Hearsay, 340
Maryland v. Craig, 364
Perjury, 176
Police lineups, 509
Rules of evidence, 388-390
Subpoena power, 710
Testimony, 715
Victim and Witness Protection Act, 824
Witness protection programs, 728
Witnesses, 730

WOMEN'S ISSUES

Abortion, 3-4
Adultery, 5
Battered child and battered wife syndromes, 744-745
Child abuse and molestation, 33-37
Comstock law, 43
Crimes of passion, 64
Date rape, 83
Domestic violence, 86-90
Mann Act, 143
Mothers Against Drunk Driving, 155
Pandering, 174
Pornography and obscenity, 181-184
Rape and sex offenses, 193-198
Sex discrimination, 948-951
Sexual harassment and criminal justice, 211-212
Victim assistance programs, 824
Victims of Crime Act, 834
Women in law enforcement and corrections, 546-549

Index to Court Cases

A
Adams v. Texas, 603
Adamson v. California, 697
Aguilar v. Texas, 296, 343
Alberts v. California, 181
United States v. Alvarez-Machain, 408
Apodaca v. Oregon, 313, 644
Argersinger v. Hamlin, 556-557, 592
Arizona v. Fulminante, 277-278
Atkins v. Virginia, 319, 575, 602
Atwater v. City of Lago Vista, 285

B
Barker v. Wingo, 568-569, 707
Barnes v. Glen Theatre, 183
Barron v. Baltimore, 47, 323
   and incorporation doctrine, 346
Batson v. Kentucky, 569-570, 682
Bell v. Wolfish, 791
Bethel School District No. 403 v. Fraser, 184
Betts v. Brady, 636
Bivens v. Six Unknown Named Agents, 290-291, 392
Blanton v. North Las Vegas, 312
Booth v. Maryland, 378
Bowers v. Hardwick, 39
Boyd v. United States, 413
Bradley v. Texas, 953
Brady v. Maryland, 682
Brady v. United States, 572-573, 698
Brandenburg v. Ohio, 820, 855
Breed v. Jones, 907
Brewer v. Williams, 667
Brinegar v. United States, 384
Brown v. Board of Education, 356, 710
   and forensic psychologists, 108
Brown v. Mississippi, 291-292, 701
   and incorporation doctrine, 347
Brown v. Plata, 766, 812
Brown v. Texas, 346, 543
Bruscino v. Carlson, 823
Burch v. Louisiana, 313
Burlington Industries v. Ellerth, 411

C
Calder v. Bull, 328
California v. Acevedo, 394
California v. Greenwood, 293-294
Carroll v. United States, 285, 357, 384
Carter v. Carter Coal Company, 410
Chaplinsky v. New Hampshire, 181
Chapman v. California, 278
Chicago v. Morales, 973
Chimel v. California, 294-295
City of Renton v. Playtime Theaters, 183
Cohen v. California, 39, 184
Coker v. Georgia, 585, 602
Colman v. Brown, 811
Commonwealth v. Fisher, 906
Connick v. Thompson, 682
County of Riverside v. McLaughlin, 312
Cramer v. United States, 243
Cruikshank v. United States, 337, 890
Cumming v. County Board of Education, 355

D
Denver Area Educational Consortium v. Federal Communications Commission, 184
Dickerson v. United States, 302
Douglas v. California, 313, 592
Drope v. Missouri, 586
Duke lacrosse case, 682
Duncan v. Kahanamoku, 363
Dusky v. United States, 586

E
Edwards v. Arizona, 668
Edwards v. South Carolina, 25
Elkins v. United States, 382, 414
Employment Division v. Smith, 939
Enmund v. Florida, 602, 718
Ernst and Ernst v. Hochfelder, 52
Erznoznik v. Jacksonville, 183
Escobedo v. Illinois, 327-328, 667
Escott v. BarChris Construction Corporation, 52
Estelle v. Gamble, 790, 803
Estelle v. McGuire, 745
Ewing v. California, 717
Ex Parte Crouse, 906, 918

F
Faragher v. City of Boca Raton, 411
Faretta v. California, 604, 631-632
Farmer v. Brennan, 796

Federal Communications Commission v. Pacifica Foundation, 184
Florida v, Royer, 512
Florida v. Bostick, 303
Florida v. Royer, 346
Floyd v. City of New York, 402
Fong Yue Ting v. United States, 608
Ford v. Wainwright, 602, 633-634
Foucha v. Louisiana, 583
Frye v. United States, 925
Furman v. Georgia, 575, 601, 634-635, 638

G
Garcia v. San Antonio Metropolitan Transit Authority, 410
Garland, Ex parte, 674
Garrity v. New Jersey, 464
Gault, In re, 893, 906, 966
Gebhart v. United Railways Company., 382
Geders v. United States, 621
Gibbons v. Ogden, 890
Gideon v. Wainwright, 336, 592, 604, 635-636, 646, 683, 712
  and public defenders, 683
Gitlow v. State of New York
  and incorporation doctrine, 346
Glossip v. Gross, 47
Godinez v. Moran, 605
Graham v. Connor, 507
Graham v. Connor (1989), 455
Gregg v. Georgia, 575, 601-602, 634, 638-639, 714
Griswold v. Connecticut, 3, 934
Guinn v. United States, 356

H
Hall v. de Cuir, 355
Harmelin v. Michigan, 641-642, 697
Harper v. Virginia, 356
Harris v. United States, 294, 340
Haupt v. United States, 243
Helvering v. Hallock, 709
Henry v. United States, 667
Herrera v. Collins, 602
Herring v. New York, 620
Hiibel v. Sixth Judicial District Court of Nevada, 229
Hoffman v. State of Delaware, 953
Hurtado v. California, 323, 341-342, 637, 647

I
Illinois v. Gates, 343
Illinois v. Krull, 343-344

Illinois v. Lidster, 543
Illinois v. McArthur, 344-345
Illinois v. Rodriguez, 392
Illinois v. Wardlow, 345
Indiana v. Edwards, 605
Indianapolis v. Edmond, 543
Ingraham v. Wright, 590

J
Jackson v. Bishop, 590
Jackson v. Indiana, 586
Jacobellis v. Ohio, 39, 181
Jacobson v. United States, 325
Jaycee Lee Dugard case (2009), 131
Johnson v. Zerbst, 592

K
Kansas v. Hendricks, 398, 922
Kastigar v. United States, 637, 644
Katz v. United States, 294, 909-910, 935
Kawakita v. United States, 243
Kent v. United States, 906, 966
Kentucky v. Dennison, 332
Ker v. California, 340
Kirby v. Illinois, 509
Klopfer v. North Carolina, 707
Knowles v. Iowa, 357
Kyles v. Whitley, 682
Kyllo v. United States, 475

L
Lafler v. Cooper, 622
Lochner v. New York, 652
Lockyer v. Andrade, 717
Loewe v. Lawlor, 680
Louisville, New Orleans and Texas Railroad v. Mississippi, 355

M
Mabry v. Johnson, 698
McCleskey v. Kemp, 667-668
Mack v. United States, 337
Malloy v. Hogan, 701
Mapp v. Ohio, 295, 328-329, 362, 392, 394, 409, 414, 696, 713
Marbury v. Madison, 652, 712
Maryland v. Buie, 363-364
Maryland v. Craig, 364-365
Massachusetts v. Sheppard, 330, 362, 365-366
Massiah v. United States, 277, 303, 666-667

McDonald v. City of Chicago, 204
McKaskle v. Wiggins, 604
McMann v. Richardson, 620
Meritor Savings Bank v. Vinson, 211
Michigan v. Long, 364
Miller v. California, 39, 182
Miller v. Texas, 337
Miller v. United States, 337
Minnesota v. Dickerson, 393
Minnick v. Mississippi, 668-669
Miranda v. Arizona, 277, 279, 302, 370, 372, 667, 712
Monroe v. Pape, 298
Morissette v. United States, 304
Moyer v. Peabody, 363
Murphy v. Ford, 674

N
National Organization for Women v. Scheidler, 192
Neil v. Biggers, 230, 509
New Jersey v. T.L.O., 377
New York Times Company v. Sullivan, 211
New York v. Ferber, 182
New York v. Quarles, 371
New York vs. Ferber, 927
Nix v. Williams, 330
Norris v. Alabama, 700
Northern Securities v. United States, 214

O
O'Connor v. Donaldson, 582
Olmstead v. United States, 917-918
Osborne v. Ohio, 182

P
Palko v. Connecticut, 48, 323, 672-673, 696
Papachristou v. City of Jacksonville, 411
Paris Adult Theatre v. Slaton, 182
Payne v. Tennessee, 378-379, 753
Payton v. New York, 283
Pennsylvania State Police vs. Suders, 212
Penry v. Lynaugh, 575
People v. Carpenter, 319
People v. Court, 331
People v. George Zimmerman (2013), 675
People v. Nidal Hasan (2013), 923
People v. Terry, 18
People v. Turner, 906, 918
Plessy v. Ferguson, 355, 710
Powell v. Alabama, 592, 635, 678-679, 699
  and incorporation doctrine, 347

Powell v. Texas, 696
Printz v. United States, 337
Prison Rape Elimination Act (PREA) of 2003, 798
Puerto Rico v. Branstad, 332

R
R.A.V. v. City of St. Paul, 118, 190-191, 257
Redrup v. New York, 182
Reed v. Reed, 547
Regan v. Time Inc., 56
Reno v. American Civil Liberties Union, 184
Rhodes v. Chapman, 796
Riley v. California, 47
Robinson v. California, 696-697
Rochin v. California, 327
Roe v. Wade, 652
Roper v. Simmons (2005), 941
Ross v. United States, 384
Roth v. United States, 39, 181-182
Rummel v. Estelle, 697-698, 706

S
Sable Communications v. Federal Communications
  Commission, 184
Santobello v. New York, 698
Schall v. Martin, 944
Schenck v. United States, 855
Schmerber v. California, 934
Segura & Colon v. United States, 330
Sherman v. United States, 325
Sibron v. New York, 404
Silveira v. Lockyer, 204
Slaughterhouse cases, 346
Smith v. Allwright, 356
Smith v. Maryland, 910
Solem v. Helm, 697, 706-707
South Dakota v. Opperman, 286
Spano v. New York, 667
Spinelli v. United States, 343
Stack v. Boyle, 565
Stanford v. Kentucky, 576, 602, 708-709
Stanley v. Georgia, 182
Sterling v. Constantin, 363
Strickland v. Washington, 621
Swain v. Alabama, 569

T
Tennessee v. Garner, 442, 495, 507, 538-539
Tennessee v. Garner, 542
Tennessee v. Garner, 471 U.S. 1 (1985), 456

Index to Court Cases

Terry v. Ohio, 229, 364, 402, 404, 513
Texas v. Johnson, 237-238
Thompson v. Oklahoma, 576
Tison v. Arizona, 602, 717-718
Trop v. Dulles, 575, 600-601, 634, 713

U

United States v. Addyston Pipe and Steel Company, 213
United States v. Aluminum Company of America, 214
United States v. Comstock, 845
United States v. Doremus, 40
United States v. E. C. Knight Company, 213
United States v. Emerson, 203
United States v. Jackson, 572
United States v. Leon, 330, 344, 392, 409
United States v. Lopez, 409-410, 468
United States v. Miller, 204, 910
United States v. Peoni, 271
United States v. Price, 298
United States v. Rabinowitz, 294
United States v. Reidel, 182
United States v. Salerno, 566
United States v. White, 910

V

Verdugo-Urquidez v. United States, 337

Victor v. Nebraska, 387
Virginia v. Black, 118, 257-258

W

Wainright v. Witt, 603
Webb v. United States, 40
Weeks v. United States, 292, 295, 329, 362, 391, 394, 413-414
Weems v. United States, 575
Weems, United States v., 600
Welsh v. Wisconsin, 345
Whitney v. California, 855
Whren v. United States, 414-415
Wilkerson v. Utah, 575, 600
Williams v. United States, 637
Wilson v. Arkansas, 415
Wilson v. Seiter, 796
Winship, In re, 708
Wisconsin v. Mitchell, 191, 266-267
Witherspoon v. Illinois, 603, 727-728
Wolf v. Colorado, 327, 329, 362, 392, 414
Woodson v. North Carolina, 601

Y

Yates v. United States, 820
Young v. American Mini Theaters, 183

Index to Laws and Acts

A
Adam Walsh Act, 397
Adam Walsh Child Protection and Safety Act (2006), 845
Alien Registration Act of 1940, 819
Alien and Sedition Acts of 1798, 210, 608
Anti-Car Theft Act of 1992, 158, 160
Anti-Drug Abuse Act of 1988, 283, 665
Anti-Racketeering Act of 1934, 121
Anti-Racketeering Act of 1946, 121
Antiterrorism and Effective Death Penalty Act of 1996, 846-847
Aviation and Transportation Security Act of 2001, 218

B
Bail Reform Act of 1966, 361-362, 565
Bail Reform Act of 1984, 565
Bank Secrecy Act of 1970, 465
Beer and Wine Revenue Act of 1933, 187
Bill of Rights, 46
    enumerated rights, 46
    incorporation doctrine, 47-48, 311, 323, 341, 647, 673, 696
Bill of Rights, U.S.
    and incorporation doctrine, 346-347
Bipartisan Campaign Reform Act of 2002, 179
Boggs Act of 1952, 665
Boggs Act of 1956, 444
Brady Handgun Violence Prevention Act, 203
Brady Handgun Violence Prevention Act of 1993, 337

C
Celler-Kefauver Anti-merger Act of 1950, 214
Child Online Protection Act of 1998, 928
Civil Asset Forfeiture Reform Act of 2000, 284
Civil Rights Act of 1875, 355
Civil Rights Act of 1964, 356, 546, 948-951
    and sexual harassment, 211
Civil Rights Act of 1991, 212, 949, 951
Clayton Antitrust Act, 274
Clean Air Act of 1970, 103
Clean Water Act of 1977, 103
Communications Decency Act of 1996, 184
Communist Control Act of 1954, 451
Comprehensive Addiction and Recovery Act of 2016 (CARA), 41
Comprehensive Crime Control Act and the Sentencing Reform Act of 1984, 665
Comprehensive Crime Control Act of 1984, 300-301, 481, 729
Comprehensive Drug Abuse Prevention and Control Act of 1970, 42-43, 201, 444, 445, 665
Comprehensive Environmental Response, Compensation, and Liability Act of 1980, 104
Computer Abuse Amendments Act of 1994, 874
Computer Crime and Abuse Act of 1984, 856
Computer Fraud and Abuse Act of 1984, 874
Computer Fraud and Abuse Act of 1987, 858
Comstock law, 43-44
Constitution U.S.
    and incorporation doctrine, 346-347
Constitution, U.S., 46-48
    commerce clause, 410
    and federal crimes, 334
    and jury system, 659
Controlled Substances Act of 1970, 444-445
Counterfeiting
    and Federal Crimes Act of 1790, 334

D
Digital Theft Deterrence and Copyright Damages Improvement Act of 1999, 874
Dyer (Motor Vehicles Theft) Act, 450
Dyer Act of 1919, 156

E
Economic Espionage Act of 1996, 883
Education Amendments of 1972, 950
Eighteenth Amendment, 178, 186-187, 290, 419
Eighth Amendment
    and three-strikes laws, 717
    cruel and unusual punishment clause, 599-603, 641-642, 696-697, 706-709
    excessive bail clause, 47, 311, 381, 564
    and prison health care, 790
    and prison overcrowding, 795
Electronic Communications Privacy Act of 1986, 880
Electronic Espionage Act of 1996, 874
Electronic Privacy Act of 1986, 874
Electronic Theft Act of 1997, 874
Employee Polygraph Protection Act, 102
Employee Polygraph Protection Act of 1988, 925
End Racial Profiling Act of 2001, 524

Index to Laws and Acts

End Racial Profiling Act of 2004, 525
Equal Opportunity Employment Act of 1972, 546-547
Equal Pay Act of 1963, 951
Espionage Act of 1917, 210, 243, 450, 452, 855
Expanded War Crimes Act of 1997, 261
Explosives Control Act of 1970, 419
Extradition Act of 1793, 332
Extradition clause of the U.S. Constitution, 332

F
Federal Computer Fraud and Abuse Act of 1986, 376
Federal Crimes Act of 1790, 334
Federal Insanity Defense Reform Act of 1984, 349
Federal Kidnapping Act, 572
Federal Prisoner Rehabilitation Act of 1965, 749, 840
Federal Wiretap Act of 1968, 879
Fifth Amendment, 289
    and *Miranda v. Arizona*, 372
    and defendant rights, 606
    and double jeopardy, 320-321
    due process clause, 321-324, 381, 599
    and grand juries, 47, 310, 341, 636
    and incorporation doctrine, 347
    and military law, 367
    and right to trial by jury, 659
    and self-incrimination, 301, 303, 369-371, 572, 644, 667, 701-702, 731, 917
Firearms Owners' Protection Act of 1986, 420
First Amendment
    and civil disobedience, 854
    and clear and present danger, 855
    and free press, 210, 237-238, 267
    and free speech, 499, 679, 820
    and freedom of assembly, 140, 890, 916
    and hate crime, 118, 190-191
    and hate speech, 257
    and incorporation doctrine, 346
    and pornography, 39
First Judiciary Act of 1789, 480
Foreign Corrupt Practices Act of 1977, 53
Foreign Intelligence Surveillance Act of 1978, 879-880, 966, 970
Fourteenth Amendment, 47-48, 323, 355
    due process clause, 277, 291-292, 311, 323, 341-342, 672 - 673, 696, 707, 891, 944
    equal protection clause, 569
    and incorporation doctrine, 346-347
    and right to trial by jury, 659
Fourth Amendment, 288
    and *Whren v. United States*, 414-415
    and knock-and-announce principle, 415
    and privacy rights, 934-936
    and probable cause, 383, 909-910
    and search and seizure, 543
    search and seizure clause, 46, 290-291, 293-295, 310, 322, 327, 340, 344-345, 357, 364-366, 377-378, 391-393, 401-402, 404, 413-414, 442
    and search warrants, 393-395
Freedom of Information Act of 1967, 122
Fugitive Slave Act of 1793, 480

G
Geneva Convention of 1949, 368
Geneva Convention on the High Seas of 1958, 218
Geneva Conventions, 259-261
Great Law of 1692, 759
Gun Control Act of 1968, 203, 338, 419-420

H
Hague Convention of 1899, 260
Harrison Narcotic Drug Act of 1914, 40, 169, 444-446
Health Insurance Portability and Accountability Act of 1996, 112
Hobbs Act of 1946, 12, 121
Homeland Security Act of 2002, 460, 947
    and Treasury Department, U.S., 244, 539
    and illegal aliens, 125

I
Identity Theft Penalty Enhancement Act of 2004, 898
Identity Theft and Assumption Deterrence Act of 1998, 112, 897-898
Immigration Act of 1918, 450
Immigration Reform and Control Act of 1986, 125
Immigration and Nationality Act of 1952, 609
Individuals with Disabilities Education Improvement Act of 2004, 842
Insecticide, Fungicide, and Rodenticide Act of 1948, 103
Insider Trading Act of 1984, 128
Intelligence Authorization Act for Fiscal Year 1999, 966
Internal Revenue Code, 230
Internal Revenue Service Restructuring and Reform Act of 1998, 465

J
Jessica's Law/Jessica Lunsford Act (2005), 648
Judges' Bill, 712
Judiciary Act of 1789, 559, 664

Judiciary Act of 1925, 712
Juvenile Justice and Delinquency Prevention Act of 1974, 900, 904-905
    and forestry camps, 757

L

Lindbergh law, 358
Lindbergh law of 1934, 137
Lyncher Act, 397
Lyncher Act of 1996, 397

M

Magna Carta, 321, 359
Mann (White Slave Traffic) Act of 1910, 38, 143-144, 450, 452
Marihuana Tax Act, 201
Marijuana Tax Act of 1937, 444
McCarran (Internal Security) Act of 1950, 451
Megan's Law, 397, 834
Metropolitan Police Act, 66
Michael Morton Act in 2013, 682
Military Justice Act of 1968, 367
Military Justice Act of 1983, 367
Missing Children's Act of 1982, 137
Money Laundering Act, 465
Motor Vehicle Theft Law Enforcement Act of 1984, 158

N

Narcotics Drugs Import and Export Act of 1922, 444
National Child Search Assistance Act of 1990, 138, 153
National Firearms Act of 1934, 337, 419
National Minimum Drinking Age Act of 1984, 155
National Motor Vehicle Theft Act of 1919, 168
National Narcotics Act of 1984, 167-168
National Narcotics Leadership Act, 167
National Stolen Property Act of 1934, 168
1990 Crime Control Act, 968
Nineteenth Amendment, 178

O

Omnibus Crime Control Act of 1984, 445
Omnibus Crime Control Act of 1988, 665
Omnibus Crime Control and Safe Streets Act of 1968, 73, 168 - 169, 289, 451, 476, 479
    and National Institute of Justice, 915
    and wiretaps, 970
Opium Exclusion Act, 169-170
Organized Crime Control Act of 1970, 173, 191

P

Parole Commission and Reorganization Act of 1976, 779
Partial-Birth Abortion Act of 2003, 4
Patriot Act of 2001, 243, 508, 920-921, 947, 962
    and electronic surveillance, 879-880, 970
    and illegal aliens, 125
    and money laundering, 155
    and privacy rights, 935
    and skyjacking, 218
Porter Act of 1930, 445
Posse Comitatus Act of 1878, 483, 921
Pregnancy Discrimination Act of 1978, 951
Prison Rape Elimination Act of 2003, 765, 802
Protect Act of 2003, 397, 725
Pure Food and Drug Act of 1906, 40

R

Racketeer Influenced and Corrupt Organizations Act of 1970, 12, 143, 173, 191-193, 446, 451, 480
    and Justice Department, U.S., 469
    and corporate fraud, 53
    and extortion, 24
    and motor vehicle theft, 158
Resource Conservation and Recovery Act of 1976, 103

Robinson-Patman Act of 1936, 274

S

Safe Drinking Water Act of 1974, 103
Sarbanes-Oxley Act of 2002, 54, 266
Second Amendment, 203
    and gun laws, 336-339
Section 215 of the USA PATRIOT Act, 967
Securities Act of 1933, 111
Securities Exchange Act of 1934, 128
Securities and Exchange Act of 1933, 52
Securities and Exchange Act of 1934, 52, 239
Sedition Act of 1918, 450, 773
Selective Service Act of 1917, 450
Sentencing Reform Act of 1984, 69, 725, 779, 817
Seventeenth Amendment, 178
Seventh Amendment, 347
Sex Offender Registration and Notification Act (SORNA), 397
Sexual Predators Act of 1998, 928
Sherman Antitrust Act of 1890, 213-214, 273-277
Sixteenth Amendment, 230
Sixth Amendment, 47, 289, 310, 322, 364-365, 659, 710, 720

Index to Laws and Acts

and *Miranda v. Arizona*, 372
and arraignment, 557
and cross-examination, 598
and defendant rights, 606
and incorporation doctrine, 347
and right to counsel, 303, 327, 370, 556, 635-636, 678, 683, 702, 704
right to counsel clause, 591
and self-representation, 631-632
and speedy trial right, 721
Smith Act of 1940, 211, 243, 452, 819-820
Stamp Act of 1766 (Great Britain), 916
Stanford, Leland, Sr., 256
Superfund, 104
Synthetic Drug Abuse Prevention Act of 2012, 85

T
Telephone Consumer Protection Act of 1991, 234
The Adam Walsh Child Protection and Safety Act (Walsh Act), 845
The Sex Offender Registration and Notification Act (SORNA), 845
Toxic Substances Control Act of 1976, 103
Twenty-first Amendment, 187

U
USA PATRIOT Act, 966
Unborn Victims of Violence Act of 2004, 4
Uniform Controlled Dangerous Substances Act of 1974, 40
Uniform Criminal Extradition Act, 332
Uniform Militia Law of 1792, 482-483
United States Code, 334, 407
and skyjacking, 218
United States Code Annotated, 407

V
Victim and Witness Protection Act of 1982, 824-825
Victims of Child Abuse Act, 835
Victims of Child Abuse Act Reauthorization Act (2013), 968
Victims of Crime Act of 1984, 825, 834-835
Violent Crime Control and Law Enforcement Act of 1990, 445
Violent Crime Control and Law Enforcement Act of 1994, 338, 412-413, 445, 491
Volstead Act, 187
Volstead Act of 1919, 40, 186, 450
Voting Rights Act of 1965, 356, 661

W
Wagner Act of 1935, 916
War Crimes Act of 1996, 261
Wetterling Act of 1994, 397

Indexes

Personages Index

A

Abel, Rudolf I., 452
Adler, Mortimer, 60
Africa, John (Vincent Leaphart), 481
Agnew, Spiro, 179
Alvarez-Machain, Humberto, 408
Ames, Aldrich H., 453
Andersen, Arthur, 54
Araujo, Gwen, 119
Aristotle, 202
Arnold, Benedict, 881
Arrigo, Bruce, 63
Ashcroft, John, 453
    and Patriot Act, 921
Ashurst, Hy, 12
Augustus, John, 807

B

Bandura, Albert, 903
Barker, Willie, 568
Barkley, Charles, 222
Barrow, Clyde, 452
Batson, James Kirkland, 569
Becarria, Cesare, 689, 781, 834
Becker, Howard, 62
Jeremy Bentham, 781
Bentham, Jeremy, 629, 689, 764
Bertillon, Alphonse, 889
Bertuzzi, Todd, 224
Bianchi, Kenneth, 146
Billington, John, 161
Binet, Alfred, 108
Black, Hugo L., 636
    on due process, 696
    on incorporation doctrine, 48, 323
Blackmun, Harry, 344
    on cruel and unusual punishment, 709
    on free expression, 191, 237
Blackstone, William, 109, 299, 328
Blakey, G. Robert, 191
Boesky, Ivan, 128, 263
Bonaparte, Charles J., 450
Borchard, Edwin, 629-630
Borden, Lizzie, 161
Boucha, Henry, 223
Bradley, Tom, 473
Brady, Robert M., 572
Branch, Elmer, 634
Brandeis, Louis D., 855, 917
Brennan, William J., 181-182
    on Fourth Amendment, 291
    on capital punishment, 601, 634, 639
    on cruel and unusual punishment, 575
    on exclusionary rule, 409
    on free expression, 237
Brockaway, Zebulon, 777
Brooks, Pierce, 256
Brown, Michael, 494, 510, 542
Brown, John, 242
Bryant, Kobe, 199, 222
Buchalter, Louis "Lepke", 452
Bundy, Ted, 146
Burger, Warren, 713
Burger, Warren E., 182
    appointment of, 295
    on exclusionary rule, 392
    on plea bargaining, 698
Burgess, Anthony, 691, 817
Burr, Aaron, 242
Bush, George, 813
    and Intro-Contra scandal, 674
    and Supreme Court, U.S., 713
Bush, George W., 898
    and Homeland Security, U.S. Department of, 460
    and Mexico, 125
    and Patriot Act, 920
    on racial profiling, 524
Butler, Pierce, 917
Byrd, James, 119
Byrnes, Thomas, 505

C

Calder, Ronald, 332
Callahan, Harry, 47
Canter, David, 936
Capone, Al, 452, 465, 822
    bootlegging of, 186
Capriati, Jennifer, 215
Cardozo, Benjamin, 673
Carlin, George, 184
Castile, Philando, 542
Castro, Fidel, 217, 219
Chambers, Whittaker, 883
Chambliss, William, 79
Chaney, James E., 453
Chaplin, Charles, 375
Chavis, Benjamin, 769
Christopher, Warren, 473
Chávez, César, 916
Claiborne, Harry, 645
Clark, Tom, 362
    on police interrogation, 372
Clarke, Edward Y., 452
Cleckley, Hervey, 188
Clinard, Marshall, 263-264
Clinton, Bill
    and Violent Crime Control and Law Enforcement Act, 412
Cohen, Fred, 856
Cohen, Stanley, 62
Colescott, James A., 140
Collier, James, 187
Comstock, Anthony, 43-44
Conyers, John, 525
Coolidge, Calvin, 427
    and Prohibition, 186
Cooper, D. B., 217
Copeland, Royal, 12
Coplon, Judith, 452, 883
Cornwell, Patricia, 470
Coster, Donald, 53
Crane, Stephen, 144
Cressey, Donald, 101
Crick, Francis, 875
Crofton, Walter, 775
Cunanan, Andrew, 149

D

Dahrendorf, William, 79
Darrow, Clarence., 161
Dasch, George John, 452
Daschle, Tom, 224
Davis, Jefferson, 243
Davis, Richard Allen, 813
De Angelis, Anthony, 53
Dennis, Eugene, 820
Dershowitz, Alan M., 176
Dickens, Charles, 505, 809
Dillinger, John, 452
Dingell, John, 54
Dirty Harry, 47
Dorr, Thomas, 242
Douglas, William O.
    attempted impeachment of, 645
    on Fourth Amendment, 404
    on incorporation doctrine, 48, 323
Dracula, Vlad III, 146
Dreiser, Theodore, 144
Dugard, Jaycee Lee, 132
Dukakis, Michael, 813
Duke, David, 140
Duquesne, Fritz, 452
Durk, David, 474
Durkheim, Ã‰mile, 60

E

Edmunds, George F., 213
Eisenhower, Dwight D., 484

1075

Personages Index

Eisenhower, Milton S., 167
Elliott, William, 475
Escobar, Pablo, 970
Estes, Billie Sol, 53
Ethelred I, 662
Evans, Hiram Wesley, 140
Evers, Medgar, 453

F

Faubus, Orville, 484
Fay, Michael, 590
Feingold, Russ, 525
Ferguson, Colin, 605
Ferracuti, Franco, 79
Fielding, Henry, 66
Figlio, Robert M., 822
Fleming, Ian, 882
Floyd, Charles "Pretty Boy", 452
Forbes, David, 223
Ford, Alvin Bernard, 633
Ford, Gerald R., 554
    and Douglas, William O., 645
    amnesty of war resisters 1974, 554
Forrest, Nathan Bedford, 139
Fortas, Abe, 636, 893
    on political dissent, 854
Fox, Vicente, 125
Franklin, Benjamin, 57
Freud, Sigmund, 108, 194
Fugate, Caril Ann, 149
Fulminante, Oreste C., 277
Furman, William, 634

G

Gacy, John Wayne, 146
Gandhi, Mohandas K., 76, 691, 916
Garfield, James A., 528
Garner, Eric, 542
Garrido, Phillip, 132
Garvey, Marcus, 450
Gates, Daryl, 472, 531
Gault, Gerald, 893, 906
Gideon, Clarence, 646
Goldman, Emma, 452
Goldstein, Herman, 521
Goldstein, Herman, 435
Goode, Wilson, 482
Goodman, Andrew, 453
Gotti, John, 452, 970
Gouzenko, Igor, 883
Gratian of Bologna, 202
Graves, Bibb, 700
Gray, Freddie, 542
Greenwood, Billy, 293
Gregg, Troy, 638
Groome, John C., 534
Gross, Has, 889

H

Hagan, John, 63
Hagerman, Amber, 138
Haldeman, H. R., 494
Hale, Matthew, 193
Hall, Jerome, 59
Hall, Theodore, 883
Hamilton, Alexander, 245, 539
Hammurabi, 16, 239, 834
Hand, Learned, 271
Hanssen, Robert, 882-883
Harding, Warren G.
    and Prohibition, 186
    and scandals, 121
Hare, Robert, 188
Harlan, John M. (I), 341
Harlan, John M. (II), 184, 294, 893, 909-910
Harlan, John Marshall (II), 39
    on police interrogation, 372
Harmelin, Ronald Allen, 641
Harris, James H., 340
Harris, Thomas, 470
Hasan, Nidal, 923
Hastings, Alcee, 645
Hauptmann, Bruno, 136, 162, 359, 452
    and handwriting analysis, 878
Haywood, William D. "Big Bill", 452
Hearst, Patricia, 453
Hebdo, Charlie, 919
Helm, Jerry, 706
Henry II, 239
Henry VIII, 113
Henry, Stuart, 63
Hinckley, John, 349
Hinckley, John, Jr., 301, 307
Hirsch, Andrew von, 664
Hiss, Alger, 452
Hoar, George F., 213
Hobbs, Carl, 121
Hoffa, Jimmy, 179
Hoffman, Abbie, 215
Holliday, George, 472
Holmes, H. H., 146
Holmes, Oliver Wendell, Jr., 855, 917
Hoover, Herbert, 487, 545, 786
    and Prohibition, 186-187
Hoover, J. Edgar, 76, 121-122
    and Federal Bureau of Investigation, 804
    and Federal Bureau of Investigation, U.S., 450-453
    eccentric behavior, 453
    and wiretaps, 883
Horton, Willie, 813
Howard, John, 781
Huberty, James, 146
Hughes, Charles Evans, 292

Hurtado, Joseph, 341
Hussein, Saddam, 352

J

Jack the Ripper, 146, 936
Jackson, Michael, 85
Jackson, Lucious, 634
Jackson, Robert H., 243
Jefferson, Thomas
    and Sedition Act, 210
Jeffreys, Alec, 875
John Paul II, Pope, 3
John, King, 359
Johnson, Andrew
    amnesty of Confederate officers, 554
Johnson, Gregory Lee, 237
Johnson, Jack, 452
Johnson, Lyndon B.
    and Estes, Billie Sol, 53
    and National Commission on the Causes and Prevention of Violence, 166-167
    and President's Commission on Law Enforcement and Administration of Justice, 931
    and voting fraud, 259

K

Kaczynski, Theodore J., 146, 249-250, 453, 605
Kane, General Kathleen, 682
Kanka, Megan, 397
Kant, Immanuel, 664, 691
Karpis, Alvin, 452
Katz and Kahn, 486
Keenan, Joseph B., 12
Kelly, George "Machine Gun", 452, 822
Kempe, Henry C., 745
Kemper, Edmund, 146
Kennedy, Anthony, 668
    on cruel and unusual punishment, 642
    on free expression, 237
Kennedy, Edward, 300
Kennedy, John F.
    and voting fraud, 259
Kennedy, Joseph, 259
Kennedy, Robert F., 480
    and Hoover, J. Edgar, 122
    assassination of, 167
Rodney King, 494
King Charles II, 203
King James II, 203
King, Martin Luther, Jr., 76, 916
    and Federal Bureau of Investigation, U.S., 453
    and Hoover, J. Edgar, 122

"Letter from a Birmingham Jail", 852
assassination of, 166, 484
King, Rodney, 472-474
Klockars, Carl, 486
Knapp, Whittman, 474
Kocsis, Richard N., 936
Korbut, Olga, 215
Krafft-Ebing, Richard von, 922
Kreuger, Ivar, 52
Kyllo, Danny, 475

L
Landru, Henri., 146
Lanier, Mark, 63
Le Carré, John, 882
Leaphart, Vincent, 481
Lennon, John, 375
Leon, Alberto, 409
Lidster, Robert, 543
Lightner, Candace, 98, 155
Lightner, Cari, 98
Lincoln, Abraham
    and Internal Revenue Service, U.S., 465
    assassination of, 161, 528
    and martial law, 363
Lindbergh, Charles, 162, 358, 452
Lindbergh, Charles A., 136
Lindsay, John, 474
Liuzzo, Viola, 453
Locard, Edmond, 889, 964
Locke, John, 395
Lombroso, Cesare, 77, 925
Lopez, Alfonso, Jr., 409-410
Lynch, Edward, 255

M
Maconochie, Alexander, 775, 777
Madison, James, 134
Mafia
    and Kennedy, Robert F., 122
Mann, James Robert, 144
Manning, Silas, 568
Manson, Charles, 146, 148
Mapp, Dollree, 362
Marshall, John, 242, 652, 890
Marshall, Thurgood
    on capital punishment, 379, 601, 634, 639
    on cruel and unusual punishment, 575, 709
    on exclusionary rule, 409
    on free expression, 237
    on juries, 569
Martin, Trayvon, 675
Martinson, Robert, 68, 814

McCarthy, Joseph R.
    and Hoover, J. Edgar, 122
McCleskey, Warren, 667
McConnell, William John, 256
McFadden, Martin, 404
McKinley, William, 528
McNaghten, Daniel, 319
McSorley, Marty, 224
Meese, Edwin, 167
Metadata, 967
Michael, Jerome, 60
Michalowski, Raymond, 63
Mickelson, Phil, 129
Milken, Michael, 128, 263
Milovanovic, Dragan, 63
Minnick, Robert S., 668
Miranda, Ernesto, 372
Mitchell, Todd, 267
Mondale, Walter, 675
Montgomery, Olen, 699
Morris, Robert, 856, 858, 874
Mottl, Ronald, 224
Munsterberg, Hugo, 108, 627
Murphy, Frank
    on incorporation doctrine, 48, 323
Musica, Philip, 53

N
Ng, Charles, 147
Nixon, Richard M.
    and African Americans, 494
    Ford's pardon of, 554
    and Supreme Court, 295, 392
    and Supreme Court, U.S., 713
    and Watergate scandal, 638, 674
    pardon of, 674
Nixon, Walter, 645
Norris, Clarence, 699, 701

O
O'Connor, Sandra Day
    on cruel and unusual punishment, 642, 708
    on free expression, 237
    on police powers, 285
    on witnesses, 365
Olmstead, Roy, 917
Orifila, Mathieu, 963
Osborn, Albert S., 878
Owens, Marie, 546

P
Packer, Herbert, 832
Palko, Frank, 672-673
Palmer, A. Mitchell, 773
Paracelsus, 963
Parker, Bonnie, 452

Parsons, Jeffrey Lee, 875
Partridge, G. E., 188
Patterson, Haywood, 699, 701
Payne, Pervis Tyrone, 379
Peacock, Kenneth, 65
Peel, Robert, 66, 319, 487, 491
Peltier, Leonard, 453
Pelton, Ronald, 453
Penn, William, 784
Pennypacker, Samuel W., 534
Petersilia, Joan, 814
Peterson, Luci, 4
Peterson, Scott, 635
Pinkerton, Allan J., 505, 519
Pius IX, Pope, 3
Plato, 854
Poindexter, Joseph, 363
Pol Pot, 352
Ponzi, Charles, 50
Pound, Roscoe, 79
Powell, Lewis F., Jr., 568
    on capital punishment, 585, 668
    on cruel and unusual punishment, 697
Powell, Ozie, 678, 699, 701
Prince, 85

Q
Quinney, Richard, 62, 263-264

R
Raj Rajaratnam, 129
Rawls, John, 852
Reagan, Ronald
    and Iran-contra scandal, 674
    and National Narcotics Act, 167-168
    assassination attempt on, 301, 307, 349
    and crime victims, 834
    drug policy, 665
Reagan, Ronald W.
    and Supreme Court, U.S., 713
Rehnquist, William H., 183, 346, 713
    on capital punishment, 634
    on confessions, 277
    on due process, 944
    on extradition, 408
    on free expression, 237, 267, 697
    on police powers, 410
    on police searches, 357
    on sentencing rules, 725
Reid, Jerame, 542
Remington, William, 452
Rice, Tamir, 542
Roberson, Willie, 699
Rockefeller, John D., 213

Personages Index

Rokitansky, Karl, 20
Roosevelt, Franklin D.
    and Prohibition, 187
    and crime bills, 12
    and espionage, 881
    and martial law, 363
    and social justice, 136
Roosevelt, Theodore, 223
Rosenberg, Ethel, 122, 452, 883
Rosenberg, Julius, 122, 452, 883
Rowland, James, 825
Rummel, William, 697
Rumrich, Guenther Gustav, 452
Rush, Dr. Benjamin, 781
Russell, Bertrand, 853
Rutledge, Wiley B.
    on incorporation doctrine, 48, 323
Ryan, George, 576
Ryder, Winona, 215

S
Salekin, Randall, 188
Sambor, Gregore, 482
Sanders, Wilbur Fiske, 256
Santobello, Rudolph, 698
Scalia, Antonin, 365
    on free expression, 237
    on search and seizure, 414
    on warrantless searches, 475
Schenck, Charles, 855
Schur, Edwin, 832
Schweindinger, Herman, 62
Schweindinger, Julia, 62
Schwerner, Michael, 453
Scott, Walter, 542
Scrushy, Richard, 887
Seles, Monica, 221
Sellin, Thorsten, 60, 79, 822
Serpico, Frank, 474
Shepard, Matthew, 119
Sheppard, Osborne, 365
Sheppard, Samuel, 162
Lawrence Sherman, 449
Simmons, Christopher, 941
Simpson, O. J., 222, 293
    and double jeopardy, 320
    and miscarriage of justice, 669
Skolnick, Jerome, 832
Smith, Al
    and Ku Klux Klan, 140
    and Prohibition, 187
Smith, Benjamin Nathan, 149
Smith, Robert, 838
Edward Snowden, 967
Socrates, 854, 963
Souter, David
    on cruel and unusual punishment, 642

Speck, Richard, 146, 148
Stanford, Kevin Nigel, 576, 708-709
Starkweather, Charles, 149
Steffens, Lincoln, 144, 178
Stephenson, David C., 140
Sterling, Alton, 542
Stevens, John Paul, 184, 408
    on cruel and unusual punishment, 709
    on free expression, 191
Stewart, Martha, 129, 263
Stewart, Potter, 181, 362, 639, 728, 893
    on capital punishment, 575
    on police interrogation, 372
Stone, Harlan F., 917
Sullivan, Dennis, 63
Sutherland, Edwin, 60, 63, 262
Sutherland, George, 678
Sutton, Willie the "Eel", 452

T
Taft, William Howard, 917
Tappan, Paul, 60, 262
Thomas, Clarence
    on Fourth Amendment, 415
Thoreau, Henry David, 851, 916
Thurmond, Strom, 300
Tifft, Larry, 63
Till, Emmett, 142
Toguri, Iva ("Tokyo Rose"), 243
"Tokyo Rose" (Iva Toguri), 243
Topinard, Paul, 79
Travis, Jeremy, 814
Truman, Harry S.
    and civil rights, 142
    and communism, 820
Tweed, "Boss" William Macy, 178
Tyson, Mike, 222

U
Unabomber (Theodore J. Kaczynski), 146, 249-250, 605
    and Federal Bureau of Investigation, U.S., 453
Unruh, Howard, 146
Urschel, Charles F., 452

V
Valachi, Joseph P., 452
August Vollmer, 449
Vollmer, August, 498

W
Waite, Morrison R., 890
Waksal, Samuel, 129
Walker, John, Jr., 882-884
Walker, Lenore, 745

Wallace, George, 701
Walsh, Adam, 137
William T. Walters, 129
Warren, Earl, 712
    and *Miranda v. Arizona*, 372
    and Nixon, Richard M., 295
    criticisms of, 696
    on incorporation doctrine, 48, 323, 697
    on police searches, 404
    on speedy trials, 707
Washington, George, 242, 480, 881
    and Whiskey Rebellion, 554
    and attorney generals, 559
Watson, James, 875
Weaver, Randy, 420, 453
Webster, John, 161
Weems, Charlie, 699-700
Weinberger, Casper, 674
Wells, Alice Stebbins, 546
West, Cornel, 921
White, Byron R., 183
    on capital punishment, 575, 585
    on confessions, 277
    on deadly force, 538
    on exclusionary rule, 409
    on free expression, 191, 237
    on police interrogation, 372
    on police searches, 365
Whitman, Charles, 146, 531
Wickersham, George, 187, 545
Wigmore, John Henry, 382, 598
Wilkins, Maurice Hugh Frederick, 875
Willey, David M., 129
William the Conqueror, 662
Williams, Eugene, 699
Williams, G. Mennen, 701
Williams, Wayne, 146
Wilson, O. W., 507
Wilson, Sharlene, 415
Wilson, William, 773
Wolfgang, Marvin, 79
Wolfgang, Marvin E., 822
Wright, Andrew, 699-700
Wright, Leroy, 699
Wundt, Wilhelm, 108
Wuornos, Aileen, 146

Y
Yates, Andrea, 148
Yousef, Ramzi, 860

Z
Zenger, John Peter, 210
Zimmerman, George, 675

Subject Index

A

AIDS (acquired immunodeficiency syndrome), 740-741
    and prisons, 756, 790, 802, 805
Abortion, 3-5
    and Comstock law, 44
    Roe v. Wade, 652
    and civil disobedience, 853, 916
    protests, 247
    and victimless crimes, 832
Abortions
    and labor law, 951
Abscam scandal, 181, 263, 537
Abuse of authority, 500
Abuse of power, 431
Academic field, 833
Accessories, 271, 306
    and conspiracy, 44-46
    vs. principals, 185-186
Accomplices, 271
    and capital punishment, 717-718
    and capital punishment, 602
    and immunity, 644
    vs. principals, 185-186
Account takeover, 895
Accountability, 495
Accreditation, 791
Acquittal, 553
Acquittals, 669
Acts or omissions, 309
Actus reus, 60, 198, 304-305, 316, 366, 403
Addiction, 737, 816
Administrative discretion, 443
Administrative regulation, 59
Adult probation, 808
Adultery, 5-6
    in Colonial America, 66
Adversary system, 652-654, 721
    and plea bargaining, 616
    and discovery, 612-613
    and drug courts, 618
    and expert testimony, 625
    and forensic accounting, 886
    and judges, 650
    and juvenile justice, 893
    and prosecutors, 688
    and public defenders, 685
Advertising, 233
    and kleptomania, 215
    and child pornography, 922
    deceptive, 49, 263
    and federal law, 245, 539
Advocacy groups, 834

Aerial pursuit, 458
Affidavits, 282, 393
African Americans, 525
    and Jim Crow laws, 354-356
    Scottsboro cases, 699-701
    and capital punishment, 577
    and equal protection under the law, 326
    and hate crime, 118
    and homicide, 162
    and juries, 569
    and lynching, 141-142, 161
    and police brutality, 493-497
    and print media, 932
    and punishment, 690
    and racial profiling, 414-415, 523-525
    and rape, 196
    and slave patrols, 530-531
    and suicide, 227
Aggravated assault, 75
Aggravating circumstances, 271-272, 374
    and bias, 118
Aggressive personality, 800
Agreement, 677
Aguilar-Spinelli test, 343
Alabama
    Powell v. Alabama, 678-679
    political corruption, 180
Alaska
    political corruption, 180
    prosecutors, 686
    sex offender registry, 397
    state police, 535
Alcatraz Island, 804, 822
Alcohol, 737
    and Alcohol, Tobacco, Firearms and Explosives, U.S. Bureau of, 419-421
    and Prohibition, 186-187
    and homicide, 163
    and police academies, 492
    and rape, 198
    and sobriety testing, 219-220
Alcohol Administration Act of 1935, 419
Alcohol Prohibition Unit, 419
Alcohol abuse, 6-8, 40
    and suicide, 227
Alcohol and Tobacco Tax and Trade Bureau, 244, 539
Alcohol use and abuse, 6
Alcohol use disorder (AUD), 8

Alcohol, Tobacco, Firearms and Explosives, U.S. Bureau of, 419-421
    and Branch Davidians, 420
    and Treasury Department, U.S., 244, 539
Alcohol, Tobacco, Firearms and Explosives, U.S. Bureau of (ATF), 471
Alcoholics Anonymous, 618
Alcoholism
    and child abuse, 34
    and psychopathy, 188
Algorithms, 517
Alibis
    and dismissals, 614
Aliens
    criminal records of, 870
Alliance Against Fraud in Telemarketing, 234
Allied Crude Vegetable Oil Refining Corporation, 53
Alternative dispute resolution, 108
Alternative sentencing, 809
Aluminum Company of America, 214
American Correctional Association, 791
American Federation of Labor, 427
American Law Institute, 304
American Medical Association, 790
American Polygraph Association, 926
American Society for the Prevention of Cruelty to Animals, 9
American Telephone and Telegraph, 214
Amicus curiae briefs, 272-273
Amnesty, 553-554
    and pardons, 554
Amnesty International, 261
Analysis, 960
Anger-management therapy, 816
Animal abuse, 9, 11, 40, 314
Animal and Plant Health Inspection Service, 460
Annotated codes, 273
Anti-Defamation League, 120
Anti-Drug Abuse Act of 1988, 283
Anti-Racketeering Act of 1934, 12
Anti-money-laundering laws, 155
Anti-Racketeering Act of 1934, 12
Anti-Saloon League, 144
Anti-horse thief movement, 255
Antisocial personality disorder, 188
Antistalking laws, 225
Antiterrorism and Effective Death

1079

Subject Index

Penalty Act, 846-847
Antitrust law, 273-277
    and Justice Department, U.S., 470
    Sherman Antitrust Act, 213-214
    and attorneys general, 561
    cases filed, 265
Appeals, 941
    and *habeas corpus*, 640
Appellate courts, 71, 555, 594, 653
Appellate process, 313, 554-556, 653, 724
    and evidence, 653
    and testimony, 653
    and clemency, 584
    federal courts, 655
    and harmless error, 642
    and jurisdiction, 656
    and juvenile justice, 908
    and military justice, 368-369
    and military law, 367
    and reversible error, 695-696
Arabs
    and Patriot Act, 921
Arizona
    Gault, In re, 893
    Miranda v. Arizona, 372
    Tison v. Arizona, 717-718
    boot camps, 747
    border patrols, 426
    and illegal aliens, 125
Arkansas
    Wilson v. Arkansas, 415
Armed, 488
Armed conflicts, 259
Arms dealing, 466
Arraignment, 380, 557, 643
    and clemency, 584
Arraignments, 312
Arrest, 278-282, 443, 488
    booking, 424-425
    and probable cause, 383-385
    resisting, 527
    and sobriety testing, 219-220
    and suspects, 229-230
Arrest and arraignment, 421, 818
Arrest data, 754
Arrest warrants, 282-283
    and juvenile justice, 907
Arrests
    and shoplifting, 216
Arson, 12-14, 60, 64, 192, 308, 336
    and animal abuse, 10
    and psychological profiling, 938
Article I, section 9, 46
Article II, section 2, 46
Article III of the U.S. Constitution, 659
Articles of Confederation, 407, 411
Articles of War, 367

Aryan Brotherhood, 819
Ashker v. Brown (2015), 741
Asian Americans
    and Ku Klux Klan, 140
Asporation, 177
Assassinations, 166
Assault, 308
    and HIV, 741
    and sports, 224
Assault and battery, 15-18
Assault weapons, 337-338, 412
Assembly Bill 109, 811
Asset forfeiture, 283-284
Assistance of counsel, 47
Athlete Crimes, 222
Attempt to commit a crime, 18-19, 126-127, 306
Attendant circumstances, 271, 374
Attention deficit hyperactivity disorder, 902
Attitudes, 548
Attorney General's Council on White-Collar Crime, 898
Attorney general, 469
Attorney general, U.S., 559-560
    and Organized Crime Control Act, 173
    and Patriot Act, 921
    and deportation, 609
    establishment of, 467
Attorney generals, state, 535, 562, 596, 686
Attorney-client privilege, 382
Attorneys
    and depositions, 610-611
    ethics of, 557-559
    and false convictions, 631
    and juries, 661
    and plea bargaining, 676-677
    and privileged communications, 382-383
Attorneys general, state, 561
    and antitrust law, 275
    and telephone fraud, 234
    and white-collar crime, 264
Attorneys, U.S., 468-469, 686
    and treason, 243
Auburn Prison, 782
Auburn system, 690, 743-744, 760, 784-785, 816
Australia's "Reintegrative Shaming" approach, 562
Automated Fingerprint Identification System, 877, 885, 914
Automated field reporting (AFR), 862
Automatic teller machines, 856, 896
Automobile exception, 285
Automobile searches, 285-287, 542-

544
Automobiles
    and carjacking, 31, 157
Autopsies, 19-20, 165, 914
    and coroners, 19, 864-865
    and inquests, 648

B

Background checks
    and suspects, 229
Bad checks, 239
Bail bondsman, 566
Bail skippers, 850
Bail system, 564-567
    Manhattan Bail Project, 361-362
    and bounty hunters, 850
    and parole, 777
    and preventive detention, 381-382
Bailiff, 480
Bailiffs, 567-568
    and juries, 659
"Bait and switch", 50, 233
Baldus study, 667
Ballistics, 888
Banishment, 759
Bank robberies
    and federal law, 468
Bank robbery, 205-206
    and motor vehicle theft, 157
Bankruptcy courts, 595, 655
Banks
    Federal Reserve Bank, 56
Barricaded suspects, 531
Bataclan, 510, 919
Battered child syndrome, 744-746
Battered wife syndrome, 744-746
Battered women, 657
Battery, 308
Bench trials, 312-313, 620, 653
Bench warrants, 282, 570
Berkeley, 498
Beyond a reasonable doubt, 305, 387
Bias, 492
Bible
    and theft, 239
Bicycles
    and drunk driving, 97
Bid-rigging, 274
Bifurcated trials, 570-571
    and capital punishment, 575
Bigamy, 20-21
Bigamy and polygamy, 20
Bilateral treaties, 333
Bill of Rights, 46, 522
    and Supreme Court, U.S., 712
Bill of Rights, English, 203, 564
Bill of Rights, U.S., 287-290
    criminal justice provisions, 310-311,

322, 701
Bill of particulars, 571
Bills of attainder, 46
Biological theory of criminality, 209
Biometric identification, 433
Bipartisan bill, 412
Birth control, 43-44
Birth of a Nation, The (film), 139
"black codes", 354
Black Guerilla Family, 819
Black Lives Matter movement, 421, 442
Black Nationalist movement, 421
Black Panthers, 531
   and Hoover, J. Edgar, 122
Blackmail, 21-24
   and rape, 193
Blackmail and extortion, 21
Bleak House (Dickens), 505
Blended sentences, 571-572
Block meetings, 485
Bloodstains, 17, 848
Blue code of silence, 523
Blue-collar crimes, 263
Blue wall of silence, 497
Body cameras, 494, 957
Body-worn cameras, 422
Boeing Corporation, 883
Bombings
   and MOVE, 481-482
Bombs, 249
Bombs and explosives, 419-421
   and Unabomber, 249-250
   and terrorists, 353
Booking, 279, 424-425
Boot camps, 703, 746-747, 786, 907
   and forestry camps, 757
   military discipline, 746, 810
Border Safety Initiative, 426
Border and Transportation directorate, 460
Border patrols, 425-426
   and Homeland Security, U.S. Department of, 460
   and and illegal aliens, 125
Bosnia, 352
Boston
   police, 66
   youth gangs, 973
Boston Marathon Bombing (2013), 848
Boston police strike, 427, 483
Bounty hunters, 296, 500, 566, 850
Brady Bill, 413
Brainwashing., 318
Branch Davidians, 420
Breach of contract
   and punitive damages, 386
Breach of peace, 527

and citizen's arrests, 296
and guns, 339
and loitering, 140
Breach of the peace, 24-25, 85-86
Breath tests, 220
Breath-analyzer equipment, 219
Brennan, William J.
   on cruel and unusual punishment, 709
Bribery, 25-27, 263-264, 500-501
   and extortion, 22
   and federal law, 334
   and police, 68, 474
Broadcast technology, 720
Broken windows theory, 427
Bulgaria
   counterfeiting in, 57
Bullying, 27
Buprenorphine, 772
Burden of persuasion, 292
Burden of production, 292
Burden of proof, 292-293, 380, 588, 716, 723
   and child abuse, 37
   and due process, 322
   and insanity defense, 347-349
   and presumption of innocence, 380-381
   and self-defense, 395
   and traffic law, 405
Bureau of Justice Statistics, 851
   and criminology, 80
   and recidivism, 814
   and sexual victimization, 193
Bureau of Justice Statistics (BJS), 799
Burglary, 29-30, 239
   and trespassing, 358
   and common law, 308
   and motor vehicles, 240
   neighborhood watch programs, 484
Business and financial crime, 100-102

C
COINTELPRO, 122
COMPuter STATistics (COMPSTAT), 462
California
   Chimel v. California, 294-295
   DNA collecting, 877
   Faretta v. California, 631-632
   Highway Patrol, 535-536
   Hurtado v. California, 341-342
   Indian casinos, 115
   King beating case, 472-474
   Klaas murder, 813
   National Guard, 484
   Operation Pipeline, 524
   Peterson murder trial, 635

Robinson v. California, 696-697
boot camps, 747
border patrols, 425
castration laws, 923
drunk driving standards, 97
forensic laboratories, 889
gambling in, 114
hate crime, 118
illegal aliens, 125
juvenile justice, 908
mandatory sentencing, 665
police, 487
police chiefs, 498
police ethics, 507
political corruption, 180
prisons, 74, 823-824
private detectives, 505
racial profiling, 524
recidivism in, 814
sex offender registry, 396
three-strikes laws, 716-717, 813
victims' rights, 834
vigilantism in, 255-256
California Public Safety Realignment Act of 2011, 812
Cambodia, 493-497
Campaign for Nuclear Disarmament, 853
Campus police, 429-431
Canada
   Gouzenko case, 883
   Law Commission of, 61
   Royal Canadian Mounted Police, 254
   and U.S. Prohibition, 917
   borders, 425
   newspapers, 932
   restorative justice programs, 694
Capital punishment, 573-578, 848-849
   and *Coker v. Georgia*, 585
   and sex offenses, 585
   Supreme Court on, 667-668
   and Supreme Court, U.S., 713-714
   and accomplices, 717-718
   application of, 634-635
   and bifurcated trials, 570
   and civil rights, 667-668
   and clemency, 584
   cruel and unusual punishment clause, 634-635, 638-639
   and death qualification, 603-605
   electrocution, 600, 623
   and extradition, 334
   and false convictions, 630
   firing squads, 600, 623
   forms of execution, 574, 622-624
   gas chambers, 623
   hanging, 600, 623

Subject Index

and hate crime, 118
history of, 68
and juries, 727-728
and juveniles, 576, 708-709
lethal injection, 574, 600, 624
and mental disorders, 633-634
and military justice, 367
and psychopathy, 189
and theft, 239
Car stops, 380
Carjacking, 31, 157
Case law, 578-579
Cash bond, 566
"Castle doctrine", 396
Castration, 690
Cease-and-desist orders, 579
Cell block, 789
Censorship
  and Comstock law, 43-44
  gag orders, 635
Census Bureau, U.S.
  crime statistics, 767, 851
Certified, 507
Certiorari, 556, 579-580, 712
Chain of custody, 580, 860
  and rape, 197
  and sobriety testing, 220
Challenge of Crime in a Free Society, The (1967), 168, 931
Change of venue, 581, 721
  and King beating case, 473
Character evidence, 389-390
Charges, 347, 686
Check kiting, 239
Checks and balances
  and Supreme Court, U.S., 712
  and pardon power, 673-674
Chest-mounted, 423
Chicago
  gangsters, 143
  juvenile courts, 34
  juvenile justice, 74
  police, 345, 505, 546
  police department, 457
  riots, 167
  voter fraud in, 259
  youth authorities, 841
  youth gangs, 971
Child Abduction, 133
Child Abuse Prevention and Treatment Act of 1974, 34, 36
Child-Savers movement, 34
Child abduction, 32, 136-139, 153
Child abduction by parents, 32
Child abuse, 33-38, 835
  pedophilia, 921-923
  and runaways, 154
  and statutes of limitations, 401

Child abuse and molestation, 33
Child custody, 729
  and adultery, 6
  and child abduction, 32, 137
  and courts, 594
  and restraining orders, 695
Child endangerment, 33
Child molestation, 33-38
  and rules of evidence, 389
  and sex-offender registries, 397
Child neglect, 33
  prevalence, 34
Children's advocacy centers (CACs), 968
Chile
  counterfeiting in, 57
China
  counterfeiting in, 58
  espionage of, 882
  gambling in, 113
Chiseling, 50, 501
Choke holds, 441
  and deaths, 442
Christopher Commission, 473, 494
Chromatography, 95, 879, 890
"Chop shops", 157-158
Church of Jesus Christ of Latter-day Saints, 21
Circumstantial evidence, 295-296, 389
Citations, 581
Citizen behavior, 423
Citizen involvement, 484
"Citizen soldier", 483
Citizenship and Immigration Services, 460
Citizen's arrests, 296-297
Civil Asset Forfeiture Reform Act, 284
Civil Courts, 594
"Civil Disobedience" (Thoreau), 851, 916
Civil Rights Division, 471
Civil Rights movement, 916
  and Ku Klux Klan, 140
  and National Guard, 484
Civil War
  and Internal Revenue Service, U.S., 465
  and counterfeiting, 56, 527
  martial law during, 363
  slave patrols during, 531
  treason cases during, 242
Civil commitment, 399, 582
Civil disobedience, 851-855
Civil law
  and liability, 309
  statutes of limitations, 401
  summons, 711
Civil liability, 526

Civil liberties, 508, 961
  and Constitution, U.S., 46-48
  and Magna Carta, 359
  and Patriot Act, 921
  and asset forfeiture, 284
  double jeopardy, 320-321
  exclusionary rule, 329-331
  and grand juries, 638
Civil litigation, 497
Civil procedure, 135
Civil rights, 464
  and Federal Bureau of Investigation, 470
  and Jim Crow laws, 354-356
  and Justice Department, U.S., 470
  and "color of law", 297-298
  and equal protection under the law, 326-327
  and indeterminate sentencing, 646
  and police brutality, 493-497
Civil rights and liberties, 117, 398-399, 427-428, 439, 455-456, 544, 748, 752-753, 765, 802-803, 891-892, 918-919
Civil rights cases, 298
Civil rights legislation, 326
Civil rights violations, 472
Civilian confidence, 511, 523, 545
Civilian oversight, 431
Civilian review boards, 431-432, 495, 502-503
  and police brutality, 496
Civilly liable, 790
Clear and present danger test, 855
Clear signals, 923
Clemency, 584
Cleric-penitent privilege, 383
Clerks of the court, 584-585, 593
Clockwork Orange, A (Burgess), 691, 817
Closed-circuit television surveillance (CCTV, 954
Cloud computing, 857
Club drugs, 84
Coast Guard, U.S.
  and Homeland Security, U.S. Department of, 461
  and drug trafficking, 446
Cocaine, 68, 92, 171, 425, 444-446, 502-503, 665, 784
  detection of, 95
  and mandatory sentencing, 665
  and punishments, 62
Coercive force, 488
Cold Case Squad, 432
Cold War era, 912
Cold cases, 432-433
  and DNA testing, 877

Collaborative responses, 837
College campuses
　stalking on, 226
Colombia
　counterfeiting in, 57-58
　drug cartels, 57, 170, 172, 970
Color of law, 297-298, 499
　and extortion, 23
　and vigilantism, 517
Color of the law
　and police brutality, 495
Colorado, 534
　Columbine High School killings, 146, 944-946
　boot camps, 747
Columbine High School killings, 146, 944-946
Comity, 639
Commercial bribery, 26
Commercialized vice, 38-41
　and gambling, 113-115
Commission for Accreditation of Law Enforcement Agencies, 481
Commission for the Accreditation of Law-enforcement agencies, 478
Committee of 100, 853
Common law, 299-300, 708
　and Second Amendment, 336
　and accessories, 271, 306
　and bail, 381
　and bribery, 25-26
　and burglary, 308
　and case law, 578-579
　and citizen's arrests, 296
　and competency, 586
　courts of, 593
　and criminal intent, 304
　and criminal liability, 307
　and criminal principals, 185
　and effective counsel, 556
　and homicide, 161
　and ignorance of the law, 342
　and indecent exposure, 128
　and indictments, 647
　and kidnapping, 139
　and malice, 361
　and police powers, 538
　and precedent, 680
　and rape, 193-194
　and reversible error, 696
　and robbery, 204
　search and seizure clause, 391
　and seditious libel, 210
　and self-defense, 395
　stare decisis, 709-710
　vs. statutory law, 400
　and theft, 238
　and treason, 241, 243

and vagrancy, 410-411
and witnesses, 730
Communication devices, 970
Communication skills, 548
Communism
　and Federal Bureau of Investigation, U.S., 452
　and Hoover, J. Edgar, 122
　and Smith Act, 819-820
Communist Party
　and Scottsboro cases, 699
Community Oriented Policing Services, 431
Community-based corrections, 74, 749-750
Community-oriented policing, 434-436, 476, 478
　and civilian review boards, 503
　and youth gangs, 973
Community policing, 428, 455, 490
Community policing, 462
Community safety, 716
Community service, 750-751
　and forestry camps, 756-757
　and rehabilitation, 816
　and restitution, 693
　and vandalism, 253
Community-oriented policing
　and illegal aliens, 125
Community-policing, 545
Commutation of sentences
　and clemency, 584
CompStat, 894, 956
Compensatory damages, 386
Competency hearing, 586
Competency to be executed, 634
Competency to stand trial, 585-586
Competent, 620
Competition, 274
Complaint procedures, 464
Complicity, 306
Composite drawing, 250
Comprehensive Crime Control Act of 1984
　and bail, 565
Comprehensive Drug Abuse Prevention and Control Act of 1970, 42
Computer
　viruses, 247, 856
Computer crime, 855-859, 871-875
　and extortion, 23
　and forensic accounting, 886
Computer crimes, 376
Computer forensics, 859-861
Computer information systems, 861-863
Computer models, 517

Computer-aided dispatch, 862
Computer-enabled financial crimes, 856
Computers
　and cryptology, 860, 873
　and polygraph testing, 926
　viruses, 856, 871
Comstock law, 43
"Concerning Dissent and Civil Disobedience" (Fortas), 854
Concurrent jurisdiction, 656
Concurrent sentences, 587-588
Conditions of confinement, 803
Confessions, 289, 301-303, 370
　Supreme Court on, 291-292, 327-328
　coerced, 277-278, 291-292
　and corporal punishment, 589
　and police ethics, 508
Conflict of interest, 620
Congress
　and political corruption, 181
Congress, U.S.
　and Justice Department, U.S., 467-469
　and attorney generals, 559
　environmental legislation, 103
　and interstate commerce, 409-410
　and military law, 367
　and police corruption, 503
　and political corruption, 178
　and wiretaps, 970
Conjugal visitation in prison, 751
Connecticut
　Palko v. Connecticut, 672-673
　Yale university police, 430
　and contraceptives, 3
　state police., 535
Consensual crimes, 76, 832-833
Consensual encounter, 303
Consent, 317
Consent searches, 303-304
Consequences of victimization, 828
Consequences of victimization., 831
Conspiracy, 18, 44-46, 185, 306
　and Watergate scandal, 638
　and antitrust law, 213-214, 274-275
　and drug laws, 665
　and inchoate crimes, 126
　and organized crime, 192
　and terrorism, 45, 921
Constables, 455
Constitution, 321
Constitution, U.S., 46
　Bill of Rights, 287-290
　and Supreme Court, U.S., 711-714
　and capital punishment, 634
　on extradition, 332

Subject Index   The Criminal Justice System

extradition clause, 332
and income tax, 230
and military law, 367
and pardon power, 673-675
and police powers, 511
and privacy rights, 934
and treason, 241
Constitutional issues, 766
Constitutional law, 679
Constitutional protections, 398-399, 455-456, 541, 582-583, 741-742, 765, 802-803, 811-812, 941
Constitutional rights, 525
Consumer fraud, 49-51, 192, 596-597
   cost of, 264
Contempt of court, 587-588
Continental Congress, 367, 916
Contraband, 789
Contracts
   and duress, 324
Contributing to delinquency of minors, 863-864
Control Question Technique (CQT), 925
Controlled Substances Act, 43
Controlled substances, 445
   and Drug Enforcement Administration, U.S., 444-445
   and jurisdictions, 376
   and police dogs, 506-507
Convictions, 588-590, 686, 797
   appeal of, 313
   and concurrent sentences, 587-588
   and criminal records, 869, 871
   and effective counsel, 622
   and miscarriage of justice, 669
   and plea bargaining, 596
   and reversible error, 695-696
   and standards of proof, 707-708
   wrongful, 628-631
Coroners, 165, 505, 864-866
   and autopsies, 19
   and inquests, 648
   juries, 142, 660
   and medical examiners, 865, 913
Corporal punishment, 589, 591, 689, 703, 759, 783-784
   in schools, 590
Corporal punishments, 589
Corporate Lenience Policy, 277
Corporate crime, 263
Corporate scandals, 51-55
Correctional facilities, 790
Correctional officers, 789
Corrections, 781
   and criminology, 81
Corrections, community-based, 749-750

Corruption, 431
Cosby, Bill, 85
cottage system, 760
Council on Human Trafficking, 835
Counsel, right to, 327-328, 556-557, 591-592, 636, 666-669
   Gideon v. Wainwright, 635-636
   and defendant self-representation, 604, 606
   and military justice, 369
Counter-Intelligence Program, 122
Counterfeiting, 55-58, 244, 539
   and Interpol, 466
   and Marshals Service, U.S., 480
   and National Stolen Property Act, 168
   and Secret Service, 55-58, 527-529
   and identity theft, 233, 895
County jails, 529
Court of Federal Claims, 655
Court of International Trade, 655
Court reporters, 592-593, 710
   and grand juries, 715
   and hearings, 643
Court-appointed special advocate (CASA), 968
Court-martials
   and military justice, 367-369
Courts, 582-583, 593, 652-655, 675, 956, 968-969
   appellate courts, 594
   appellate process, 554-556
   bankruptcy courts, 595, 655
   and case law, 578-579
   and criminology, 81
   drug courts, 617-619
   execution of judgment, 624-625
   hearings, 642-643
   and judicial review, 652, 711-714
   jurisdictions, 655-657
   and jury system, 659-663
   juvenile, 899-900
   juvenile courts, 594
   and juveniles, 908-909
   mediation courts, 594
   night courts, 594, 670
   persuasive authority, 578
   police courts, 594
   probate courts, 594
   state, 653
   subpoena power, 710-711
   traffic, 718-719
   types, 593-595, 655-657
Courts of appeal, 593
Courts of general jurisdiction, 336
Courts of limited jurisdiction, 593
Courts of specialized jurisdiction, 593
Crashes, 457

Credentials, 626
Credibility, 599
Credit cards, 240
Crime, 59-63, 106, 403
Crime analysis, 436
Crime analysts, 754
Crime control, 513
Crime data, 437
Crime incidence rates, 768
Crime index, 64
Crime labs, 165, 432, 477, 506, 866-867, 889
   DNA testing, 875-877
   and crime scene investigation, 438
   and state police, 459, 536
   and toxicology, 964
Crime mapping, 437, 462, 490, 861, 894
Crime prevention, 174-175, 421, 427-428, 436-437, 462, 484, 517-518, 521, 737-739, 766, 770-772, 777-778, 798-799, 818, 845, 891-892, 952-953
   and community-oriented policing, 434-436
   and attempt to commit a crime, 18-19
   and drug courts, 617-619
   and juvenile delinquency, 903
   and police powers, 72
Crime scene investigation
   and forensics, 889
Crime scene investigation (CSI), 438-439
Crime statistics, 436-437, 517, 754, 797, 835, 894
   Uniform Crime Reports, 251
   and Wickersham Commission, 546
   and abortion, 3
   and animal abuse, 10
   and criminology, 79
   and homicide, 162
   reliability of, 80
Crime Victim Bill of Rights, 753
Crime victim compensation, 768
Crime victimization surveys, 828
Crime victimization: primary and secondary, 752
Crimes Without Victims (Schur), 832
Crimes against humanity, 351
Crimes against property, 308
Crimes of passion, 64-65
   manslaughter, 144
Crimes reported to the police, 754
Criminal Courts, 594
Criminal Investigation, 504
Criminal Investigation division, 465
Criminal Justice Information Services,

1084

869-870
Criminal activity, 393
Criminal complaint, 680
Criminal courts of general jurisdiction, 593
Criminal history record information, 867-868
Criminal intent, 304, 315-318, 375, 403
    and Model Penal Code, 304
    and motives, 375-376
    and traffic violations, 718
Criminal investigation, 534
    and psychologists, 514
Criminal justice
    history of, 65-70
Criminal justice education, 169, 868-870
Criminal justice issues: Domestic violence, 761-762
Criminal justice system, 70-75, 870
    and criminology, 81
Criminal law, 59, 305-309, 374
Criminal laws, 656
Criminal liability, 231, 309
    and due process, 324
    and excuses, 331
Criminal personality profile, 250
Criminal personality profiling, 936
Criminal procedure, 310-313
Criminal procedure laws, 656
Criminal prosecution, 321, 496, 595-598
Criminal psychology
    vs. forensic psychology, 107
Criminal records, 869, 871
Criminal sanction, 608
Criminal statistics
    National Crime Victimization Survey, 767-768
Criminal trials, 627
Criminalistics, 866-867, 888-889
Criminals, 75-78
    and deterrence, 690
    and psychological profiling, 936-938
Criminology, 76, 78-83, 104-106, 174-175, 200, 208-209, 421, 793, 805, 818-819
    and burglary, 30
    and graffiti, 116
    study of, 498
    and trace evidence, 964-965
    and victimless crime, 832
Critical race theory, 209
Critical theory, 208
Cronyism, 177
Cross burning, 118, 191, 257-258
Cross-examination, 722

Cross-examination, 598-599
Cruel and unusual punishment, 47, 290, 599-603, 696-698, 741, 748, 941
    and capital punishment, 638-639
    and mental disorders, 575, 602
    Supreme Court on, 706-707
    and capital punishment, 575, 634-635
    and diminished capacity, 319, 634
    and execution, 574
    and execution of juvenile offenders, 576, 708-709
    and prison health care, 790
    and prison overcrowding, 795
    and schools, 590
Cryptology
    and computers, 860, 873
    in World War II, 881
Cultural defense, 314
Culture, 492
Curfews
    and halfway houses, 758
    and house arrest, 763
Customs Service, U.S., 481, 505, 524
    and Treasury Department, U.S., 244, 539
    and motor vehicle theft, 160
Customs and Border Protection, 425-426
Cyber Tipline, 929
Cyberbullying, 27
Cybercrime, 855-859, 871-875
    and Federal Bureau of Investigation, 470
    and Federal Bureau of Investigation, U.S., 451
    and Secret Service, 528
    and computer forensics, 859-861
    and extortion, 22
Cybercrime investigation, 871
Cyberspying, 859
Cyberstalking, 226

D

DARE programs, 440-441
DNA
    and Patriot Act, 921
    and adultery, 6
    and bloodstains, 848
    and cold cases, 433
    and hair, 964
    and sex offenders, 397
DNA testing, 875-877
    and crime labs, 866
    and false convictions, 629-631
    and homicide, 164
    and juries, 663

    and prisoners, 935
    and rape, 197
DSM-5, 8
Dachau War Crimes, 261
Dallas and Baton Rouge police officer attacks (2016), 439
"Dark figure of crime", 34, 437, 754, 831
Dark figure of pursuits, 458
Databases
    sex offender registries, 396-398
Date rape, 83-84, 193, 196, 198
    and drugs, 887
De facto arrests, 371
De facto police, 531
Deadly force
    and self-defense, 307
Deadly force, police use of, 441-442, 478, 495-496, 538-539
Death
    causes of, 914
    and coroners, 864-866
    manner of, 864-865, 913
    and medical examiners, 913-914
Death investigations, 913
Death qualification, 603-605
Deception, 508
Declaration of Independence, 135-136, 659
    and petition of redress, 890
Decriminalization, 314-315
    and drugs, 40
    and gambling, 115
    and victimless crime, 40, 832
Defendant self-representation, 604, 606
Defendants, 606-607, 675
    and appellate process, 554-556
    and bill of particulars, 571
    and effective counsel, 619-622
    and right to counsel, 591-592
    rights of, 73
    and summonses, 711
Defense Department, U.S.
    Computer Forensics Lab, 861
Defense attorney, 677
Defense attorneys, 312-313, 558, 607-609
    and prosecutors, 612-613
    and district attorneys, 615
    ethics of, 558
    and grand juries, 637
    origins of, 66-67
    and polygraph testing, 925
    and prosecutors, 686-688
    and trials, 721-724
    and *voir dire*, 727
Defenses, 315-318

diminished capacity, 318-319
duress, 317, 324-325
entrapment, 318, 325
insanity, 318, 347-349
self-defense, 395-396
Defenses to crime, 299, 307, 331
Deferred sentences, 816
Delaware
    prosecutors, 686
Deliberate indifference, 790
Democracy
    and capital punishment, 573-577, 601
    and civil disobedience, 853-854
    and judicial review, 652
    and pardons, 673, 675
    and police powers, 488, 495, 500-503, 525
    and political corruption, 177-180
    and protest, 917
    and public-order offenses, 190
    and sedition, 210
    and trial publicity, 720
    and voting fraud, 258-259
    and war on terrorism, 921
Denial-of-service, 871
Deportation, 608-609
    and Antiterrorism and Effective Death Penalty Act, 847
    Palmer raids, 773
    and Patriot Act, 921
    and border control, 413
    and diplomatic immunity, 320
Depositions, 610-611
    cross-examination, 598
Depression era
    Federal Bureau of Investigation, 122
    and Prohibition, 187
    forestry camps, 757
    prisoner parole, 775
    vagrancy laws, 411
Deprivation theory, 800
Deprogramming, 939
Desegregation, 710
    and Marshals Service, U.S., 480
Designer and date rape drugs, 84
Desistance from crime, 562
Destruction of evidence, 378
Detectives, 504-506, 848
    and arson, 14
    and cold cases, 432-433
    and forensics, 887-890
    and homicide, 163
Detention, 820
Determinate sentences, 703, 778
Deterrence, 362, 611, 748, 764
    and attempt to commit a crime, 18-19

and capital punishment, 576
and contempt of court, 587
and fines, 632
and punishment, 689, 691-692, 703
and punitive damages, 386-387
and reckless endangerment, 200
and restorative justice, 694
and strict liability offenses, 403
and supermax prisons, 823
and surveillance cameras, 954-955
and traffic fines, 719
Deterrence, 428
Detroit Pistons, 221
Deviancy, 200, 208-209, 793, 845
Diagnosis, 929
Diagnostic and Statistical Manual of Mental Disorders, 188
Digital technologies, 956
Diminished capacity, 307, 318-319
    and bifurcated trials, 570
    and false convictions, 631
Diplomatic immunity, 319-320
Direct examinations, 598
Directed verdict, 292
Dirty Harry, 47
Disasters, 648
    and Homeland Security, U.S. Department of, 460
    victim assistance, 768
Discovery, 612-613
    and bill of particulars, 571
    and depositions, 610
Discretion, 443-444, 495, 513, 558, 657
    and indeterminate sentencing, 646-647
    and suspended sentences, 714-715
Discretionary powers, 686
Discrimination, 354
Disfranchisement of felons, 334-335
Dismissals, 613-614
Disorder, 428
Disorderly conduct, 24-25, 85-86, 373
    and alcohol, 7
    and vagrancy, 411
    and loitering, 140
Dispositions
    and child abuse, 36
    and juvenile justice, 907
    nolle prosequi, 670
District attorney
    and juvenile justice, 900
District attorneys, 596, 614-616, 686
    and inquests, 648
District of Columbia
    adultery laws, 5
    bail, 565
    courts, 655

parole in, 779
preventive detention, 565
prisoner rights, 335
victim assistance in, 768
Diversion, 253, 598, 616, 870, 907
    and community-based corrections, 74
Divorce
    and adultery, 6
    and bigamy, 21
    and child abduction, 32
    and courts, 594
    and privileged communications, 383
Document analysis, 866, 878-879, 888
Domestic Preparedness, Office of, 460
Domestic violence, 86-90, 744-746, 752-753, 761, 836-837, 929-930
    and alcohol abuse, 8
    and animal abuse, 10
    and assault, 17
    and homicide, 163
    and restraining orders, 695
    and stalking, 226
Double jeopardy, 47, 289, 320-321, 672
    and acquittal, 553
    and dismissals, 614
    and juvenile justice, 907
Double-blind police lineups, 509
Draft evaders
    and forestry camps, 757
Drive-by shootings, 91-92, 972
Drone aircraft, 426
"Drug czar", 167
Drug Enforcement Administration, 408, 445-446, 471
    and wiretaps, 970
Drug Enforcement Administration, U.S., 444-445
Drug Enforcement Agency (DEA), 84
Drug abuse, 440
Drug and alcohol treatment, 816
Drug courts, 617-619, 908
Drug laws
    and Alcohol, Tobacco, Firearms and Explosives, U.S. Bureau of, 420
    and Drug Enforcement Administration, 471
    and mandatory sentences, 664-666
Drug testing, 95-97, 219-220, 910
    and drug courts, 618-619
    and parole, 777
    and recidivism, 814
Drug traffic
    in Canada, 573
    Opium Exclusion Act, 169-170
    and drive-by shootings, 91
    interdiction, 447
    and juvenile delinquency, 903

and law enforcement, 445-448
and sting operations, 536-537
and "war on drugs", 93
and youth gangs, 972
Drug trafficking, 466
and organized crime, 171
Drug use
and DARE programs, 440-441
and HIV, 741
decriminalization of, 40, 314-315
and juvenile delinquency, 903
and law enforcement, 445-448
legalization, 92-94
and mandatory sentences, 641-642
and property crimes, 76
and punishment, 62
and shoplifting, 215
and sobriety testing, 219-220
Drugs, 507
Drunk driving, 7, 97-100, 405-406
and hearings, 643
and sobriety testing, 219-220
and traffic fines, 719
Drunkenness, 85
and hit-and-run accidents, 120
and sports, 221
Due Process Clause, 802
Due Process Clauses, 682
Due process, 68, 321-325, 486, 557
and bifurcated trials, 570
and deportation, 608
and dismissals, 614
and drug testing, 96
and exclusionary rule, 329
and *habeas corpus*, 640
and hearings, 643
and indeterminate sentencing, 646
and juvenile courts, 75
and juvenile justice, 907
and juvenile offenders, 893
and perjury, 176
and police powers, 512
and preventive detention, 944
Due process clause, 370
Due process of law, 278
Due process of the law, 47
Due process revolution, 802
Dueling, 66, 310
Duress, 307, 317, 324-325, 331
and Model Penal Code, 331
Durham rule, 307, 348

E
Early warning systems, 497
Easement, 249
Education
and campus police, 429-431
and forensic psychology, 108

and juvenile delinquency, 902
and police, 489
and sex discrimination, 950
Educational programs, 816
Effective counsel, 619-622
and self-representation, 631-632
Eighth Amendment, 523, 741, 802
Eighth and Fourteenth Amendment, 941
Elderly prisoners, 755-756
Elected, 529
Electrocution, 600, 623
Electronic Crimes Task Force, 898
Electronic interception, 970
Electronic mail
and computer forensics, 860
and Patriot Act, 920
and cybercrime, 871-874
and electronic surveillance, 879-880
Electronic monitoring, 970
Electronic signatures, 935
Electronic surveillance, 879-880, 909-910, 917-918
and Patriot Act, 920
cameras, 954-955
and organized crime, 172
and privacy rights, 935
and stakeouts, 533
wiretaps, 970-971
Elmira model, 760
Elmira prison model, 784
Elmira system, 775
Embezzlement, 308
and theft, 238
Emergency Preparedness and Response directorate, 460
Emotional recovery from victimization, 828
Empaneling jurors, 727
Employment
and crime, 434
and sex discrimination, 948-951
Employment-sanctioned, 411
England
posse comitatus, 65, 516
Scotland Yard, 505
capital punishment, 66
history of, 65
homicide laws, 161
police, 66, 505
right to bear arms, 203
sheriffs, 529
Enhanced Border Security and Visa Entry Reform Act of 2002, 125
Enron Corporation, 54, 262, 264
Entitlement, 223
Entrapment, 307, 318, 325
and Alcohol, Tobacco, Firearms and

Explosives, U.S. Bureau of, 420
and "reverse sting" operations, 448
and sting operations, 536-537
Environmental Protection Agency, 103-104, 201
Environmental crimes, 103-104, 171, 247, 263, 265
and Federal Bureau of Investigation, 103
and Federal Bureau of Investigation, U.S., 452
and Justice Department, U.S., 470
Environmental racism, 770
Equal Employment Opportunity Commission, 201, 212, 950
Equal Protection Clause, 802
Equal Rights Amendment, 950
Equal protection clause, 48
Equal protection under the law, 326-327
Equality under the law, 326
Equity Funding Corporation of America, 53
Equity courts, 593, 708
Escape, 378
Espionage, 881-884
and death penalty, 573
Espionage and sedition, 891-892
Established law, 679
Ethics, 536-537
attorneys, 557-559, 619-622
and criminology, 82
police, 507-509
and prison health care, 791
and punishment, 692
Euthanasia, 228
Evidence, 295-296, 347, 394, 613, 722
and appellate process, 653
and burden of proof, 292
and child abuse, 37, 745
and discovery, 612-613
and dismissals, 614
exclusionary rule, 329-331
"good-faith" exception, 343-344
hearsay, 340-341, 390
planting of, 631
rules of, 340, 388-390, 730, 732
shoe prints, 952
and testimony, 715-716
tire-tracks, 888, 952
victim-impact, 378-379, 731
Evidence suppression, 681
Evidence, rules of, 340, 365-366, 413-414
and juveniles, 893
Evidence-based policing, 448
Evidentiary hearing, 680
Ex post facto laws, 328-329

1087

Subject Index

and Lindbergh kidnapping, 359
Excessive bail, 290, 564
Excessive force, 455, 473, 499, 526-527
Exclusionary rule, 295, 328-331, 345-346, 391-392, 413-414
   and Supreme Court, U.S., 713
   "good faith" exception, 343-344, 409
   and search warrants, 394
Exclusionary rule., 318
Exclusive dealing contract, 274
Excuse defense, 314
Excuses and justifications, 331
Execution drug, 47
Execution of judgment, 624-625
Execution, forms of, 622
Executions
   by firing squad, 600
   forms of, 574, 622-624
   history of, 67
   and incapacitation, 764
   public, 589
   violence of, 600
Executive branches, 71
Executive orders, 367, 931
Exigencies, 378
Expectation of privacy rule, 935
Expert witnesses, 625-626
   and battered woman syndrome, 746
   and cross-examination, 599
   and false convictions, 631
   forensic accountants, 886
   and rules of evidence, 389
Explosives, 507
Expungement, 870
Expungement of records, 670, 907
Extended family visits, 752
Extortion, 21-24
   and Hobbs Act, 121
   and police brutality, 501
   and robbery, 205
Extradition, 331-334
   and *habeas corpus*, 333
   and Justice Department, U.S., 468
   and Marshals Service, U.S., 470, 481
   and Mexico, 408
   and bounty hunters, 850
   and capital punishment, 334
Extremist groups, 119
Exxon Valdez, 263
"Eye for an eye, an", 691, 809, 816
Eyewitness testimony, 296, 509, 626-628
   and false convictions, 631

F

Facebook, 952
Fair hearing, 321
Fair trial procedures, 46
Fair trials, 48
False arrest, 499
False arrests
   and National Crime Information Center, 914
False convictions, 576, 629-631
False imprisonment, 136-139, 308, 502
False pretenses, 110, 238
Families
   battered child and battered wife syndromes, 744-746
   and child abuse, 36-37
   and child-protective agencies, 36
Fatality Analysis Reporting Systems, 458
Federal Bureau of Investigation, 68, 470, 936, 938
   and Abscam, 181
   Automated Fingerprint Identification System, 877, 885, 914
   Combined DNA Index System, 877
   Crime index, 64
   Criminal Justice Information Services, 869-870
   and Hoover, J. Edgar, 121-122
   and identity theft, 897-898
   and King, Martin Luther, Jr., 916
   and Lindbergh kidnapping, 359
   and Marshals, U.S., 480
   National Computer Crime Squad, 376
   National Crime Information Center, 424, 535, 914-915
   Organized Crime Drug Enforcement Task Force, 446
   and President's Commission on Law Enforcement and Administration of Justice, 931
   and Prohibition, 187
   and terrorism, 470
   Uniform Crime Reports, 251, 768
   and child pornography, 929
   and color of law violations, 298
   and computer forensics, 860
   and espionage, 881
   forensic laboratories, 889
   and fraud, 112
   investigators, 505
   and kidnapping, 137
   and motor vehicle theft, 158, 160
   and narcotics, 446
   national sex offender registry, 397
   and organized crime, 446
   and police brutality, 496
   and rape, 196
   renaming of, 121
   and serial killers, 146
   and skyjacking, 217-218
   and sting operations, 536
   and treason, 243
   and white-collar crime, 264
   and wiretaps, 883, 970
   and women, 547
Federal Bureau of Investigation, U.S., 450-453
   National Crime Information Center, 451
   and narcotics, 451-452
Federal Bureau of Investigations informants, 277
Federal Bureau of Narcotics, 291
Federal Bureau of Prisons, 805
Federal Communications Commission, 184, 201, 595
   and telephone fraud, 234
Federal Emergency Management Agency, 460
Federal Law Enforcement Training Center, 244, 460, 539
Federal Prison Industries, 792
Federal Protective Service, 460
Federal Rules of Criminal Procedure, 557
Federal Rules of Evidence, 388-390, 730, 732
Federal Support for Local Law Enforcement Equipment Acquisition, 532
Federal Trade Commission, 49, 275
   and identity theft, 897
   Telemarketing Sales Rule, 234
   and fraud, 111
   and identity theft, 239
   and regulatory crime, 201
   and telephone fraud, 234
Federal bribery, 181
Federal courts, 593
Federal criminal code, 300
Federal facilities, 528
Federal firearms licenses, 337
Federal law, 84, 765, 845, 966-967
Federal prosecutors, 596
Federalism, 593
Federalist Papers, 134
Federalists, 210
Felon disfranchisement, 334-335
Felonies, 306, 335-336, 373
   and Clean Air Act, 103
   and antitrust law, 275
   arraignment, 312
   blackmail, 22, 24
   bribery, 26
   and citizen's arrests, 296-297
   computer crimes, 859
   defendants, 312, 556, 592

drunk driving, 100
extortion, 22, 24
kidnapping, 139
and mandatory sentencing, 664-666
and military court-martials, 369
robbery, 204-207
and telephone fraud, 234
theft, 238
and trespass, 248
Felony, 60, 680
Felony-murder rule, 200, 717
Female offenders, 104
Feminine fragility, 492
Feminism, 106
Feminist criminology, 105-106
Ferguson, 525
Ferguson, Missouri, 494, 542
Ferguson, Missouri, 510
Fifth Amendment, 321, 370, 522, 701
Films
   Goodfellas, 173, 730
   Mississippi Burning, 266
   Serpico, 474
   Shawshank Redemption, The, 800
Financial Crimes Enforcement
   Network, 244-245, 539-540
Financial crimes, 25, 465, 528
   and Secret Service, 527-529
Fines, 632-633
   and regulatory crime, 202
Fingerprint, 869
Fingerprints, 875, 884-885, 888, 910
   and National Crime Information
     Center, 914
   and kidnapping, 138
Firearms, 888
   and crime labs, 866
   and homicide, 162, 165
   and right to bear arms, 202-204
   and robbery, 206
   and suicide, 227
Firing squads, 600, 623
First Amendment, 802
   and cross burning, 257-258
   and hate crime, 119
   and pornography, 181-185
First-offender programs, 253
First-time offenders, 715
Flag burning, 237-238
Fleeing felons, 442
Florida
   boot camps, 747
   capital punishment, 633
   courts, 556
   drug laws, 597
   gun laws, 337
   house arrest in, 750
   investigatory agency, 535

segregation, 356
vagrancy laws, 411
work camps, 839
Foils, 509
Follow-up, investigations, 506
Ford, Gerald R.
   pardon of Nixon, 674
Foreign Corrupt Practices Act, 55
Foreign terrorist organization (FTO), 847
Forensic accounting, 886-888
Forensic analysis, 433
Forensic anthropology, 164, 888
Forensic engineering, 888
Forensic entomology, 888
Forensic medicine, 889
Forensic nursing, 888
Forensic odontology, 161, 887
Forensic pathology, 165, 887
Forensic psychiatry, 887
Forensic psychology, 107-109, 888
Forensic serology, 888
Forensic toxicology, 887
Forensics, 887-890
   and arson, 14
   bloodstains, 848
   computer, 859-861
   document analysis, 878-879
   trace evidence, 964-965
Forestry camps, 756-757, 839
Forfeiture Endangers American Rights, 284
Forfeiture hearings, 284
Forgery, 109, 239, 336
   and Secret Service, 528
   and document analysis, 878-879, 888
   and white-collar crime, 265
Foster care, 37
   and child abuse
   and probationers, 810
Fourteenth Amendment, 298, 311, 322, 326, 355, 387, 473, 741
   and Supreme Court, U.S., 712
   equal protection clause, 326-327
Fourteenth Amendments, 402
Fourth Amendment, 282, 377-379, 384, 391, 394, 401, 455, 458, 473, 522
   and arrest warrants, 282-283
   and police powers, 513
42 U.S. Code, Section 1983, 456
France
   espionage of, 883
Frankpledge and watch system, 454
Fraud, 100-102, 110-113
   and bigamy, 20-21
   and computer crime, 856

corporate, 62
corporate scandals, 51-55
counterfeiting, 55-58
and forensic accounting, 886-887
identity theft, 895-898
Fraud Triangle, 101
Free speech
   and counterfeiting, 56
Freedom of assembly and association, 890-891
   and loitering laws, 140
   and nonviolent resistance, 916
   and police, 499
Freedom of conscience, 912
"Friend of the court" briefs, 272-273
Frisk, 402
Frontier, American, 396, 517, 529
Fugitives, 481
   and Marshals, U.S., 470
   and bounty hunters, 850
Fundamental fairness, 323
Fusion Centers, 511, 891
Fusion center, 891

G

Gag orders, 635, 721
   and contempt of court, 587
Gambling, 40, 113-115, 189-190, 376, 873
   on Internet, 872
   and organized crime, 12, 114, 122, 143, 173, 192
   and victimless crime, 832
   and vigilantism, 255
Gang validation, 742
Gangs
   drive-by shootings, 91-92
   youth, 162, 902, 971-973
Gangsters
   and drive-by shootings, 91
Garrity warning, 464
Gas chambers, 623
Gatekeepers, 488
Gender, 105
Genetics
   DNA testing, 875-877
   and criminal behavior, 150, 902
Geneva Conventions, 260
Genocide, 351-352
Geographic information systems, 490, 861-862
Georgia
   Coker v. Georgia, 585
   Furman v. Georgia, 634-635
   Gregg v. Georgia, 638-639
   boot camps, 747
   capital punishment, 68
Germany

Subject Index

espionage of, 883
Get-tough-on-crime, 716
Global Positioning System (GPS, 894
Global positioning system (GPS), 957
Go ahead, make my day!, 47
Good time, 757-758, 775
  and indeterminate sentencing, 646
  and prison escapees, 788
Gossiping, 665
Government misconduct, 485-486, 514-515, 541, 681-682
Government responses, 960
Governors
  and extradition, 332-333
  pardon power, 554, 674
Graffiti, 116-117, 252-253
  and youth gangs, 971-972
Grand juries, 636-638, 660
  and Fifth Amendment, 289
  and Organized Crime Control Act, 173
  and attorneys, U.S., 469
  and incorporation doctrine, 347
  and indictments, 310-312, 341-342, 596, 647-648
  and military justice, 369
  and organized crime, 172
  origins of, 66
  and political corruption, 180
  and public prosecutors, 687
  secrecy of, 380, 715
  testimony before, 715
Grand jury, 596
Grandfather clauses, 356
Grass-eaters, 474
Gross Commission, 503
Gross criminal negligence, 309
Group homes, 810
Guardian ad litem (GAL), 969
Gun-Free School Zones Act, 410
Gun laws, 336-339
  and Alcohol, Tobacco, Firearms and Explosives, U.S. Bureau of, 419-421
  and drive-by shootings, 92
  and mental disorders, 338
  and right to bear arms, 202-204
Guns
  and assault, 15
  and youth gangs, 902

H

HIV (human immunodeficiency virus), 740-741
Habeas corpus, 313, 622, 639-640
  and Constitution, U.S., 46
  Lincoln's suspension of, 363
  and Magna Carta, 359

and Patriot Act
and extradition, 333
and martial law, 363
Habeas corpus
  and Antiterrorism and Effective Death Penalty Act, 640
  and juvenile justice, 908
Hacking, computer, 247, 856, 858, 871-872, 874, 896
Halfway houses, 749, 758-759, 815
  and NIMBY attitudes, 769
  and parole, 776
  security of, 787
Hallucinogens, 445
Hands-off policy, 790
Handwriting analysis, 866, 878, 888
Hanging, 600, 623
  and lynching, 141
Hard-core repeat offenders, 822
"Hardline" approach, 961
Harmful behaviors, 59
Harmless error, 642
  and reversible error, 696
Harmless errors, 277-278
Hate crime, 60, 117-120, 266-267, 675, 918-919
  and religion, 948
  and Secret Service, 528
  and cross burning, 257-258
  and First Amendment, 190-191
  lynching, 141-142
  and police brutality, 493
  and terrorism, 119
  and victimology, 833
Hatred, 118
Hawaii
  and gambling, 113-115
  political corruption, 180
Head-mounted, 423
Headline cases, 720
Health and Human Services Administration for Children and Families, U.S. Department of, 34, 36
Health care
  in prisons, 790-791
HealthSouth, 55
HealthSouth Corporation, 886
Hearings, 642-643
  and grand juries, 660
Hearings, preliminary, 680
Hearsay evidence, 340-341, 390, 730
Heroin, 42, 95-96, 169, 171, 315, 444-446, 665
  and organized crime, 40
  criminalization of, 444
  detection of, 95
High-speed chases, 386, 457-458, 478
  and motor vehicle theft, 157

Highway patrols, 459, 534-536
Himmelsbach, Ralph, 218
Hired guns, 625
Hiring, 514
Hispanics, 525
History of incarceration, 759
Hit-and-run accidents, 120-121, 406
  and forensic evidence, 888
Holliday's tape, 472
Holocaust, 351
Homeland Security, U.S. Department of, 459-462
  and Interpol, 466
  and Nine-Eleven attacks, 947
  Transportation Security Administration, 218
  and Treasury Department, U.S., 244, 539
  and border patrols, 425-426
  and computer crime, 858
  and law enforcement, 73
Homeland defense, 483
Homeland security, 463
Homeless women and victimization, 761
Homicide, 160-166, 307, 675, 845, 942-943
  and HIV, 740
  and abortion, 3-5
  and euthanasia, 228
  and federal law, 334
  and hate crime, 118
  investigations, 914
  and kidnapping, 139
  manslaughter, 144-145
  and self-defense, 395-396
  and television news, 236
Homosexuality
  and hate crime, 118, 833
  and sexual harassment, 212
  and victimless crime, 832
Hoovervilles, 411
Horizontal gaze nystagmus (HGN) test, 220
Hostage
  and terrorism, 353
Hostages
  and SWAT teams, 531
Hostile workplaces, 548
Hot pursuit
  and indictments, 647
House arrest, 750, 763
  and probation, 808
Houses of correction, 759
Hue-and-cry system, 66
Human Rights Watch, 261, 493-497
Human exploitation, 122
Human rights, 261

Human sex trade, 835
Human trafficking, 466
Hung juries, 568, 643-644, 661, 724
Hunting, 202-203, 338, 963
Husbands and Wives, 383
Hypnosis, 108, 305

I
ISIL, 918
Identifiable residues, 965
Identification, 628
Identity fraud
 and theft, 239
Identity theft, 76, 111-112, 239-240, 528, 872, 895-898
 and Secret Service, 528
 and computer crime, 856
 and telephone fraud, 233
Ignoramus, 637
Ignorance of the law, 342
Illegal Source Financial Crimes Program, 232
Illegal aliens, 124-126
Illicit drugs, 737
Illinois
 Escobedo v. Illinois, 327-328
 Witherspoon v. Illinois, 727-728
 capital punishment, 576
 juvenile justice, 71, 74, 899, 906, 918
 political corruption, 180
 prisons, 823
 rape laws, 195
 sports violence in, 222
 vigilantism in, 255
Immigration, 608
 and Homeland Security, U.S. Department of, 460
 and Ku Klux Klan, 140
 and border patrols, 425-426
 and child labor, 34
 and "color of law", 298
 and cultural norms, 61
 and culture defense, 314
 and deportation, 608-609
 and gun laws, 337
 and illegal aliens, 124-126
 and political corruption, 178
Immigration and Customs Enforcement, Bureau of, 69, 447
Immigration and Naturalization Service, 124-126, 425
Immoral acts, 360
Immunity, 681-682
 and witnesses, 469
Immunity from prosecution, 644
 and organized crime, 172
Impartiality, 651

Impeachment
 and pardons, 674
Impeachment of judges, 645
Importation model, 794
Importation theory, 800
In forma pauperis, 372, 645-646
In loco parentis, 377, 430
In re Winship, 387
Incapacitation, 690, 764-765
 and executions, 764
 and three-strikes laws, 716-717
 and juvenile delinquency, 903
 selective, 822
Incarceration, 774
 and community service, 750-751
Incarceration rates, 689
Inchoate Crimes, 306
Inchoate crimes, 18-19, 126-127, 306
 and conspiracy, 44-46, 126
Incivilities, 428
Incommensurability, 691
Incompetence, 620
Incorporation doctrine, 346-347, 712
Indecent exposure, 127-128
Indefinite commitment, 586
Indeterminate sentencing, 646-647, 664-665, 703, 749, 906
 and Elmira system, 775, 784
 and juvenile justice, 908
Indian casinos, 40, 115
Indiana
 Ku Klux Klan in, 140
 prisons, 786
Indictment, 69, 636
Indictments, 647-648
 and dismissals, 613
 and due process, 341-342
 and grand juries, 596
Indigent defendants, 556-557, 645-646, 678-679
 and bail, 567
 and public defenders, 683
 and vagrancy laws, 410-411
Individual liberties, 508
Industrial Workers of the World, 452
Ineffective assistance of counsel, 620
Infanticide, 34
Informal prosecutorial disclosure, 613
Informal social control, 484
Informant, 296
Informants, 384
 and organized crime, 143, 172
 and sting operations, 447-448
Information (written accusation), 347
Information Analysis and Infrastructure Protection directorate, 461
Informational probable cause, 384

Infractions, 373
Inherently dangerous, 403
Initial appearance, 69, 425
Injunctions
 and restraining orders, 695
Inmate pregnancies, 761
Inmates, 820
Innocence
 and acquittal, 553
Innocence Project, 867, 877
Inquests, 648
 and coroners' juries, 660
Insanity, 375
Insanity defense, 301, 318, 347-349
 and burden of proof, 293
 and bifurcated trials, 570
 and criminal liability, 307
 and defendant self-representation, 605
 and diminished capacity, 319
 history of, 319
 and mass murder, 148
Insider trading, 111, 128-129, 143, 263
Inspector General, Office of, 246, 540
Inspector General, Office of the, 244, 539
Instagram, 952
Insurance fraud, 129-131, 264
 and arson, 12-14
 and motor vehicle theft, 160
Integrated Automated Fingerprinting Identification System, 862
Integration stage, 155
Intelligence, 891
Intelligence gathering, 960
Intelligence-led policing, 462
Intention, 309
Intentional torts, 499
Intermediate sanctions, 549
Internal Revenue Service, U.S., 230, 244-245, 465, 539, 595
 Web site, 154
 and tax evasion, 230-232
Internal affairs, 463-464
 and police brutality, 495, 497
 and police corruption, 503
International Association of Chiefs of Police, 251, 478, 487, 491, 498
 and ethics, 507
International Court of Justice, 260
International Criminal Court, 260, 352-354, 734
International Red Cross, 261
International courts, 260
International humanitarian laws, 259
International law, 122-123, 350-354, 957-962
 and Federal Bureau of Investigation,

1091

Subject Index

U.S., 451
and Interpol, 466-467
and Justice Department, U.S., 471
and terrorism, 353, 466-467
World Court, 733-734
diplomatic immunity, 319-320
and extradition, 331-334, 408
and military justice, 368
and war crimes, 259-261, 350
International notices, 466
International tribunals, 261
Internet, 856, 871, 927
and identity theft, 895, 897
and organized crime, 871
auction fraud, 857
and child pornography, 926-929
cybercrime, 871-875
and gambling, 115
and hate groups, 119
phishing, 896
and print media, 931
sex offender registries, 397
Internet Crime Complaint Center (IC3), 857
Internet Fraud Complaint Center, 112
Internet communications technology, 952
Internet fraud, 111-112
Interpol, 444, 466-467, 481
and Justice Department, U.S., 470-471
and homicide rates, 162
Interrogation, 371
and Miranda rights, 369-371
Interrogations
and police ethics, 508
Interstate Identification Index, 862
Interstate commerce
and Hobbs Act, 121
and National Stolen Property Act, 168
and Racketeer Influenced and Corrupt Organizations Act, 173
Intervening situational factors, 386
Investigation, 278, 521, 835, 891-892, 894, 966-969
Investigations
and bounty hunters, 850
cold cases, 432-433
and legislative bodies, 643
mass murders, 148
and serial killings, 147-148
Investigative stops, 371
Iowa
Knowles v. Iowa, 357
political corruption, 180
state police, 534
Iran-Contra scandal, 674

Iraq, 352
Irresistible impulse, 348
Israel
espionage of, 883

J
Jackson, Andrew, 255
Jail matrons, 548
Jails, 786, 811
Japan
in World War II, 452
espionage of, 882
Japanese American internment
and martial law, 363
Jaywalking, 133-134
Jews
and Ku Klux Klan, 139-140
gangs, 143
and hate crime, 118
and Holocaust, 351
Jim Crow laws, 354-356
Jjoint intelligence center (or JIC), 891
Joint Commission on Accreditation of Health Organizations, 791
Joyriding, 156
Judges, 650-651, 825-826
and adversary system, 650
and appellate courts, 555
and case law, 578-579
and contempt of court, 587-588
and convictions, 589
and defendant self-representation, 604
and district attorneys, 615
and drug courts, 618
and evidence, 723
execution of judgment, 624-625
federal, 654
gag orders, 635
impeachment of, 645
and jury nullification, 657-658
and mandatory sentencing, 664-666
and objections, 671
opinions, 672
state courts, 653
and trials, 721-724
Judicial activists, 709
Judicial balance, 651
Judicial discretion, 271, 443
Judicial review, 652
and Supreme Court, U.S., 711-714
and *certiorari*, 579-580
Judicial system, U.S., 652-655
Judiciary Acts of 1789, 564
Juries, 825-826
and bifurcated trials, 570
and capital punishment, 727-728
and change of venue, 581

and conspiracy, 45
and convictions, 589
and death qualification, 603-605
and evidence, 388-390
and gag orders, 635
hung, 643-644
and judges, 657-658
and peremptory challenges, 569-570, 727
selection, 722
and trials, 722-724
Jurisdiction, 593, 653
Jurisdiction of courts, 653-657
Supreme Court, U.S., 712
World Court, 733
and common law, 732
and judges, 651
juvenile courts, 900, 904, 907, 954
and military justice, 367-368
multiple jurisdiction offenses, 376
night courts, 670
and precedent, 680
and public defenders, 684
and sentencing guidelines, 705
Juror incompetence, 626
Jury behavior, 657
Jury deliberations, 644
Jury duty and summonses, 711
Jury nullification, 643, 657-658
Jury sequestration, 568, 658-659, 663, 723, 731
and trial publicity, 721
Jury system, 312-313, 659-663
voir dire, 727
Jury tampering, 681
Jury trial, 310
Just deserts, 576, 663-664, 807
and probation, 808
and retribution, 691
Just war, 360
Justice, 134-136
Justice Assistance, Bureau of, 169
Justice Department, U.S., 467-471
and antitrust law, 273-277
and attorney general, 559-560
Bureau of Narcotics and Dangerous Drugs, 446
and computer crime, 858
corporate lenience policy, 277
creation of, 560
and crime labs, 867
Criminal Division, 469
and hate crime, 118
Homeland Security, U.S. Department of, 125
and identity theft, 897
independent counsel, 469
Juvenile Justice and Delinquency

Prevention, Office of, 905
National Institute of Justice, 915
and Omnibus Crime Control and Safe Streets Act, 168
and police brutality, 496
Prisons, Federal Bureau of, 74
Public Integrity Section, 179
and restorative justice, 693
and treason, 243
and Treasury Department, U.S., 246, 541
Victims of Crime Act, 834
Justice Information Network (JUSTNET), 861
Justice of the peace, 594
Justice Statistics, Bureau of
National Crime Victimization Survey, 767-768
Justice of the peace, 455
Justices of the peace, 529, 581, 653
Juvenile Death Penalty, 942
Juvenile Justice and Delinquency Prevention, Office of, 904-905
Juvenile courts, 594, 899-900
Uniform Juvenile Court Act, 965-966
blended sentences, 571-572
and criminal liability, 307
history, 34, 67
and *parens patriae*, 918
and status offenses, 954
and vandalism, 253
Juvenile delinquency, 863-864, 900-904
and Juvenile Justice and Delinquency Prevention, Office of, 905
and disorderly conduct, 86
and diversion, 616
and drug courts, 619
joyriding, 157
and *parens patriae*, 918
and shoplifting, 215
and television news, 236
and vandalism, 253
Juvenile justice, 27-28, 74-75, 905-908, 941
Juvenile Justice and Delinquency Prevention, Office of, 905
and capital punishment, 573, 576
courts, 908-909
and forestry camps, 757
and restitution, 692
and rules of evidence, 893
status offenses, 954
and suspects, 229
and vandalism, 253
youth authorities, 841-842

Juvenile justice system
and criminal justice system, 71
Juvenile probation, 811
Juvenile waivers to adult courts, 907-909
Juveniles, 870

K
K-9, 506
KGB, 452-453
Kansas
courts, 73
sex offense laws, 922
Kansas City Preventive Patrol Experiment, 68, 518
Kent State University massacre, 484
Kentucky
Stanford v. Kentucky, 602
Batson v. Kentucky, 569-570
Stanford v. Kentucky, 708-709
political corruption, 180
Kerner Commission, 493
Kickbacks, 178
Kidnapping, 122-123, 131-132, 136-139, 153, 308, 845
Brady v. United States, 572-573
and Federal Bureau of Investigation, U.S., 451-452
and Lindbergh law, 358
and *Miranda v. Arizona*, 372
United States v. Alvarez-Machain, 408
and bounty hunters, 850
and carjacking, 31
and child abduction, 32, 153
and federal law, 468
and motor vehicle theft, 157
as theft, 239
Klaas, Polly, 813
Kleptomania, 215
Knapp Commission, 474, 501-503
Knowledge, 309, 375
Ku Klux Klan, 119, 139-140, 257-258
and Hoover, J. Edgar, 122
and Secret Service, 528
and posses, 517
and vigilantism, 254

L
LGBTQ, 765
LGBTQ prisoners, 765
LSD (lysergic acid diethylamide), 445-446
Labor Department, U.S., 773, 951
Labor racial unrest
and National Guard, 483
Labor strikes, 482

Labor unions
and Hobbs Act, 121
Labor unrest
Boston police strike, 427
Larceny, 308
Las Vegas, 114
jaywalking in, 133
Latent evidence, 359, 910
fingerprints, 884, 911
Law Enforcement Assistance Administration, 168-169, 476, 479
Juvenile Justice and Delinquency Prevention, Office of, 905
Law Enforcement Code of Ethics, 507
Law Enforcement Education Program, 169
Law codes, 407, 835, 968-969
Law enforcement, 72, 475-478
and criminology, 81
and federal government, 72
Law enforcement organization, 448-449, 454, 462, 510, 514-515, 517-518, 891-892, 956
Law-enforcement officers, 370
Law-enforcement organization, 521
Laws, 59
Lawsuits, 498
Layering stage, 155
Layers of information, 894
League of Nations, 733
Learned responses, 376
Lease system, 748
Legal defenses
cultural, 314
Legal terms and principles, 455-456, 522, 541
Legislative branch, 71
Legislative intent, 709
Legislators, 59
Lesser-included offenses, 358
and Uniform Code of Military Justice, 368
Lethal injection, 574, 600, 624
"Letter from a Birmingham Jail" (King), 852
Liability
and proximate cause, 386
Lie detectors, 925
Life imprisonment, 698
Lindbergh kidnapping, 358
and Federal Bureau of Investigation, U.S., 452
Lineup, 509
LinkedIn, 952
Literacy tests, 355
Litigation, 458
Livor mortis, 914
Lobbying organizations

Subject Index

Mothers Against Drunk Driving (MADD), 155-156
Local law-enforcement, 477
Local prosecutors, 686
Locard's Exchange Principle, 889, 964
Logic bombs, 872
Loitering, 86, 140-141, 411
London Metropolitan Police Force, 476
Lone wolf, 911, 967
Los Angeles
    King beating case, 472-474
    forensic laboratory, 889
    police corruption, 502, 631
    police department, 457
    riots, 473, 484
    youth authorities, 841
    youth gangs, 971
Los Angles
    SWAT teams, 531
Loss prevention, 519
Lotteries, 113-115
    and cybercrime, 872
Louisiana
    Mardi Gras, 128
    political corruption, 180
    segregation, 355
Lynching, 141-142, 326
    of gamblers, 114
    and homicide, 161

M

MOVE bombing, 481-482
Machine guns
    and youth gangs, 902
Mafia, 143, 170-173
    and Federal Bureau of Investigation, U.S., 452
    and RICO, 191
    and extortion, 22
Magna Carta, 517, 721
Mail fraud, 192
Maine
    prisoner rights, 335
Majority-rule verdicts, 644
Mala in se, 60, 306, 359-360
    and murder, 160
Mala in se offenses, 299
Mala prohibita, 60, 306, 359-360
Malice, 361
    and civil disobedience, 852
    and common law, 299
    and crimes of passion, 64-65
    and murder, 161
Malpractice, 620
Mandamus, writ, 664
Mandatory sentencing, 8, 272, 444, 641-642, 650, 664-666, 692, 703
    three-strikes laws, 716-717

and alcohol abuse, 8
and clemency, 584
cruel and unusual punishment clause, 697-698
and mitigating circumstances, 374
and presentence investigations, 681
and prison overcrowding, 795
and violent criminals, 76
Manhattan Bail Project, 361-362
Manslaughter, 144-145, 161, 308
    and common law, 299
    and crimes of passion, 64-65, 299
    and premeditated murder, 65
    types, 300
Manufacturing of crime, 325
Marijuana, 171, 190, 445
    and Drug Enforcement Administration, U.S., 444
    decriminalization of, 93, 315
    detection of, 384
    and juvenile crime, 811, 832
    and victimless crime, 832
Marijuana sales, 377
Marion Penitentiary, 823
Market allocation, 274
Marriage
    bigamy and polygamy, 20-21
Marshals Service, U.S., 468, 470-471, 480-481
Martial law, 363
    and SWAT teams, 532
Martinson Report, 68
Maryland
    Agnew scandal, 179
    Barron v. Baltimore, 346
    Booth v. Maryland, 378
    Smith v. Maryland, 910
    boot camps, 747
    highway patrol, 459
    medical examiners, 865
Mass and serial murders, 145-149
Mass murderers, 145-149
    and animal abuse, 10
Massachusetts
    Boston police, 500
    Boston police strike, 427, 483
    National Guard, 483
    capital punishment, 574
    gun laws, 703
    lottery, 115
    prisons, 750, 786
    probation in, 807, 809
    prostitution laws, 38
McClesky v. Kemp, 714
Meat-eaters, 474
Media, 952-953
    Amber Alerts, 138
    and white-collar crime, 78

and computer crime, 856
and corporate scandals, 52-53
and criminals, 78
and false convictions, 629
and hate crime, 119
and insanity defense, 318
and kidnapping, 137
and missing persons, 153
and murder, 161
and polygraph testing, 926
role in defining crime, 62
and sports, 222
television news, 235-236
and victimology, 834
Media consumption, 235
Mediation courts, 594
Mediation, victim-offender, 827
Medicaid, 110, 131
Medical and health issues, 41, 737-739, 751, 761-762, 765-766, 770-772
Medical examiners, 165, 889, 913-914
    and coroners, 865, 913
    and autopsies, 19-20, 914
    and cold cases, 432
    and inquests, 648
Medical model of offender treatment, 766
Medicare, 110, 131
Medication-assisted treatments (MATs), 770
Mens rea, 60, 65, 198, 304-305, 309, 316, 366-367, 375, 403
    and regulatory crime, 201
    and sports violence, 224
Mental and physical illness, 766
Mental disorder, 929
Mental disorders, 27-28, 582-583, 737-739, 761-762, 766, 929-930
    and forensic psychology, 108
    and gun laws, 338
    and competency to stand trial, 585-586
    and cruel and unusual punishment, 575, 602
    and defendant self-representation, 605
    and diminished capacity, 319
    and insanity defense, 347-349
    kleptomania, 215
    pedophilia, 921-923
    and police, 514
    and probate courts, 594
    and rape, 198
    and solitary confinement, 151, 821, 823
    and stalking, 226
Mental illness, 583
Mental illness and crime, 150-152

Mental incapacitation, 586
Mentally incompetent, 586
Mercy killing, 657
Methadone, 771
Methamphetamines, 171, 444, 446
    Ecstasy, 445
Mexican Mafia, 819
Mexico
    and extradition, 408
    borders, 425-426
    counterfeiting in, 57-58
    and extradition, 333
    illegal immigrants from, 124-126
Michigan
    Detroit riots, 484
    Harmelin v. Michigan, 641-642
    National Guard, 484
    capital punishment, 574
    drug laws, 665
    rape laws, 198
Migrant smuggling, 123
Militarism, 532
Militarization, 544
Military
    martial law, 363
Military academies, 368
Military justice, 367-369, 923
    and war crimes, 259-261
Militia ideology, 203
Militias
    during Civil War, 242
    and National Guard, 482-484
    and hate crime, 119
    and right to bear arms, 202-204
    and slave patrols, 531
Minors, contributing to delinquency of, 863-864
Miranda Warnings, 370
Miranda rights, 229, 289, 369-371, 668-669
    and military justice, 369
Miranda warning, 702
Miscarriage of justice, 669
Misconduct, 464, 499
Misdemeanor
    kidnapping, 139
    theft, 238
Misdemeanors, 85, 306, 372-373
    blackmail, 24
    bribery, 26
    and violations, 373
    animal abuse, 11
    arson, 13
    bribery, 25
    computer crimes, 859
    defendants, 312
    definition of, 60
    disorderly conduct, 85-86

    extortion, 24
    indecent exposure, 128
    insurance fraud, 131
    and *nolo contendere* pleas, 671
    and statutes of limitations, 401
    and telephone fraud, 234
    and trespass, 248
    vandalism, 253
Misidentifications, 509
Missing persons, 152-154, 256, 466, 914
    and homicide, 164
    and police dogs, 506
Mississippi
    Brown v. Mississippi, 291-292
    Minnick v. Mississippi, 668-669
    discrimination in, 355
    political corruption, 180
    vigilantism is, 255
Missouri
    capital punishment, 576
Mistake of law, 307
Mistaken eyewitness, 627
Mistrials, 724
Mitigating circumstances, 374
    and presentence investigations, 681
M'Naghten rule, 307, 318
Mobile data computing, 862
Model Penal Code, 374
    and attempts to commit crimes, 18
    classification of crimes, 366
    and criminal intent, 304
    and duress, 331
    and pandering, 174
    and vagrancy, 411
Modus operandi, 390, 505, 938
Mollen Commission, 176, 494, 503
Monetary restitution, 693
Monetary settlements, 498
Money laundering, 154-155, 232, 466
    and Internet, 872-873
    and Interpol, 466
    and Patriot Act, 920-921
    and Secret Service, 528
    and Treasury Department, U.S., 245-246, 540
    and computers, 860
    and gambling, 114
    and organized crime, 171
    and political corruption, 179
Monopolies, 213-214, 274
Monopolization, 274
Monopoly, 274
Montana
    vigilantism in, 256
Mooching, 501
Moral compass, 508
Moral turpitude, 375

    and deportation, 608
Morality and public order, 41, 84-85, 208-209, 439, 454, 485-486, 522
Mothers Against Drunk Driving, 98, 834
Mothers Against Drunk Driving (MADD), 155-156
Motivation, 375
Motives, 375-376
    of serial killers, 146
Motor vehicle theft, 156-160
Multidisciplinary teams, 969
Multiple jurisdiction offenses, 376
Murder, 75, 160-166, 307
    and statutes of limitations, 432
    and common law, 299
    and consent, 317
    and death penalty, 573-578
    and federal, 468
    and motor vehicle theft, 157
    and poison, 963
    and reckless endangerment, 200
    spree killers, 149
    and statutes of limitations, 401
Murders, mass and serial, 145-149, 163
Muslims
    and Patriot Act, 921
    and hate crime, 119
Mutual pledge system, 65
M'Naughten Rule, 348

N

NSA (National Security Agency), 463
Naltrexone, 772
Narco-analysis, 702
Narcotics Anonymous, 618
Narcotics and Dangerous Drugs, Bureau of, 444, 446
Narcotics, Bureau of, 444-445
    establishment of, 446
National Academy of Corrections, 804
National Advisory Commission on Civil Disorders, 493
National Association for the Advancement of Colored People, 142, 601
    and Scottsboro cases, 699
National Association of Women Law Enforcement Executives, 547
National Border Patrol Strategy, 426
National Center for Missing and Exploited Children, 138, 153, 929
National Central Bureau, 466
National Child Abuse Registry, 845
National Commission on Correctional Health Care, 791
National Commission on Law Observance and Enforcement, 487

National Commission on the Causes and Prevention of Violence, 166-167
National Computer Crime Squad, 376
National Conference of Commissioners on Uniform State Laws, 966
National Crime Information Center, 424, 451, 470, 535, 862, 914-915
    and kidnapping, 137-138
National Crime Prevention Week, 104
National Crime Victimization Survey, 17, 80, 754, 767-768, 851
    and carjacking, 31
    and vandalism, 252-253
National Crime Victimization Survey (NCVS), 753, 837
National Do Not Call Registry, 234
National Drug Control Policy, Office of, 167
National Drug Enforcement Policy Board, 167
National Gay and Lesbian Task Force, 120
National Guard, 482-484
    and martial law, 363
National Hardcore Drunk Driver Project, 99
National Highway Traffic Safety Administration, 98, 158, 219, 458
National Hockey League, 223-224
National Incident-Based Reporting System, 22, 251, 862, 914
    and bribery, 26
National Institute for Standards and Technology, 858
National Institute of Corrections, 804
National Institute of Justice, 915
    DNA studies, 628
    boot camps study, 747
    and police brutality, 495
National Institute on Drug Abuse, 41
National Labor Relations Board, 595
National Law Enforcement and Corrections Technology Center (NLECTC), 861
National Organization for Victim Assistance, 768-769, 825
National Organization for Victim Assistance (NOVA), 836
National Organization of Black Law Enforcement Executives, 478
National Rifle Association, 204, 420
National Security Agency, 453, 858, 881
National Sex Offender Registry, 845
National Sheriffs Association, 478, 530
National Sheriff's Institute, 530
Native American casinos, 40, 115

Native Americans, 694
Nazi Low Riders, 819
Nebraska, 839
    political corruption, 180
Necessity, 316
Negligence, 375, 385, 499
Negligent acts, 411
Negligently, 304
Neighborhood watch programs, 297, 484-485, 973
Nevada
    capital punishment, 623
    gambling in, 114
    organized crime, 114
    prostitution in, 189
New Hampshire
    lottery, 115
New Jersey
    Megan's law, 397
    gambling in, 115
    lottery, 115
    rape laws, 195
New Mexico
    border patrols, 426
    political corruption, 180
    polygraph testing, 925
New Religious Movements (NRMs), 938
New York
    prisons, 784, 786
New York City
    Manhattan Bail Project, 361-362
    Tammany Hall, 258
    gangsters, 143
    geographic information system, 863
    police, 67, 72, 227, 434, 474, 500, 546-547
    police corruption, 501, 503
    political corruption, 178
    youth authorities, 841
    youth gangs, 971
New York City Police Department (NYPD), 402
New York Society for the Prevention of Cruelty to Children, 34
New York State
    Auburn prison system, 743-744
    Santobello v. New York, 698
    capital punishment, 623
    county police, 72
    drug laws, 665
    drunk driving laws, 98
    lottery, 115
    police, 487
    prisons, 74
New media
    and carjacking, 158
Newark Foot Patrol Experiment, 518

News media
    and carjacking, 31
    gag orders, 635
    "muckraking", 178
    and political corruption, 178
Nicaragua, 674
Night courts, 594, 670
Nine-Eleven attacks, 353, 882, 888, 946-948
    and criminology, 81
    and hate crime, 119
    and Homeland Security, U.S. Department of, 459-462
    and illegal aliens, 125
    and Internal Revenue Service, U.S., 465
    and Interpol, 467
    and Federal Bureau of Investigation, U.S., 451
    and Fourth Amendment, 394
    and Patriot Act, 920-921
    and police, 488
    and political crime, 76
    and psychological trauma, 514
    and racial profiling, 524
    and skyjacking, 217
    and state police, 459
Nixon, Richard M.
    and political corruption, 178
No bill, 637
Noble cause corruption, 485
No-knock warrants, 378
Nolle prosequi, 670
Nolo contendere, 670-671, 677-678
Nonviolent crimes, 838
Nonviolent resistance, 915-917
North Carolina, 840
North Dakota
    boot camps, 747
    political corruption, 180
Not guilty by reason of insanity (NGRI), 348
"Not-in-my-backyard", 769-770
Novel
    bleakHouse (Dickens), 505
Novels
    Clockwork Orange, A (Burgess), 691, 817
    Debt of Honor (Clancy), 882
    Dracula (Stoker), 146
    James Bond, 882
    Maggie: A Girl of the Streets (Crane), 144
    Patriot Games (Clancy), 882
    Shame of the Cities, The (Steffens), 144
    Silence of the Lambs (Harris), 470
    Sister Carrie (Dreiser), 144

The Criminal Justice System

Subject Index

Thirty-nine Steps, The (Buchan), 882
Nuestra Familia, 819
Numbers games, 114-115
Nuremberg Principles, 260
Nuremberg Trials, 351
Nuremberg tribunal, 351

O
Objections, 313, 671
    and court reporters, 593
Objective circumstances, 395
Objective reasonableness, 442
Obscene language, 85
Obscenity, 181-185, 192, 362
    and Comstock law, 43-44
    and commercialized vice, 39
Observational probable cause, 384
Obsessive-compulsive behavior, 215
Obstruction of justice, 671-672
    and RICO, 192
    and preventive detention, 382
Occupational Safety and Health Administration, 201
Occupational crime, 263
Offender websites, 397
Office of Strategic Services, 881
Ohio
    Kent State University massacre, 484
    Mapp v. Ohio, 362
    Terry v. Ohio, 404
Oklahoma
    boot camps, 747
Oklahoma City bombing, 912
Olfactory skills, 507
Olweus Bullying Prevention program, 28
Operation Continued Action, 112
Opinions, 555, 672
    and appellate process, 555
    and case law, 578-579
Opioid treatment breakthroughs, 770
Opioids, 41
Opium, 169-170
Opportunity reduction, 485
Oregon
    political corruption, 180
    and suicide, 228
Organized Crime Drug Enforcement Task Force, 446
Organized crime, 68, 76, 122-123, 170-173, 819, 891-892
    and Anti-Racketeering Act of 1934, 12
    and Federal Bureau of Investigation, 446, 470
    and gambling, 12, 122, 143, 173, 192
    and Internet, 871, 873
    J. Edgar Hoover and, 122
    Mafia, 143
    and Omnibus Crime Control and Safe Streets Act, 169
    and Prohibition, 186
    and RICO, 191-193
    and Wickersham Commission, 546
    and criminology, 81
    defined, 173
    drug trade, 446
    and electronic surveillance, 970
    and extortion, 22
    and gambling, 114
    and insurance fraud, 131
    and juries, 663
    and money laundering, 154-155
    and motor vehicle theft, 158
    and murder, 161
    and political corruption, 177-178, 180
    and political machines, 258
    and Prohibition, 178
    and white-collar crime, 262
    and youth gangs, 971
Original jurisdiction, 593
Outward Bound, 907
Overcriminalized, 832
Overcrowding, 803
Overreporting, 236
Overt behavior, 923
Own recognizance, 425
Oz (TV), 800

P
PCP (phencyclidine), 445-446
POST, 487, 490
Pacifism, 916
Palmer Raids, 450
Palmer raids, 773
Pandering, 38, 174
Paradigms, 208
Paramilitary, 492, 531
Pardons, 46, 673-675
    and amnesty, 554
    and clemency, 584
Pardons and parole, 777-778
Parens patriae, 899, 906-907, 918
Parents
    and Internet, 873, 928
    and vicarious liability, 306
    and child abduction, 32, 153
    and contributing to delinquency of minors, 863-864
    and corporal punishment, 590
    and criminal liability, 309, 339
    and deportation, 609
    and juvenile delinquency, 902
    and juvenile probation, 810
    and kidnapping, 138, 153
    and misbehaving children, 906, 954
    and *parens patriae*, 899, 906-907, 918
    and paternity testing, 877
    and reckless endangerment, 199
    and runaways, 154
    and vicarious liability, 411
Paris terrorist attacks (2015), 918
Parole, 74, 749, 773-777, 812
    Parole Commission, U.S., 779-780
    and criminal records, 869
    and federal law, 665
    and good time, 758
    and incapacitation, 764
    and indeterminate sentencing, 646
    origins of, 68
    and prison boards, 784
    and psychopathy, 188
    and recidivism, 813-815
    and rehabilitation, 816
    revocation of, 807
    and suspended sentences, 715
    and victim-offender mediation, 827
Parole, 132
Parole Commission, U.S., 779-780
Parole boards, 777
Parole officers, 780, 807-808, 814, 827
    and privacy rights, 935
Passion, crimes of, 64-65
Pat down, 402
Pat-downs, 380
Paternity testing, 877
Pathways perspective, 105
Patriot Act of 2001
    and Fourth Amendment, 394
Patrol Observation, 505
Patrollers, 530
Peace Officer Standards and Training, 487-488, 490
Peacemaking criminology, 174-175
Pedophilia, 514, 921-923, 926-929
    and Internet, 861, 872
    and commercialized vice, 38
    and sex offender registries, 396-398
Peer pressure, 440
Pelican Bay State Prison, 823
Pen registers, 880, 970
Penal Code, 279
Penal reform, 781
Penitentiaries, 783
Pennsylvania
    Crime Commission,, 970
    MOVE bombing, 481-482
    Walnut Street Jail, 838
    Whiskey Rebellion, 242
    capital punishment, 65, 575
    courts, 73

1097

Subject Index

drunk driving laws, 98
homicide in, 308
prisons, 743, 784, 816
state police, 534, 547
Pennsylvania system, 760
Pennsylvania system of corrections, 781
Penological methods, 817
People, 507
Per se offenses, 38, 274, 406
Peremptory challenges, 569-570, 603, 661
Performance enhancing drugs (PEDs), 84
Perjury, 176, 559
and attorney ethics, 559
and federal law, 334
and police corruption, 501
Permanent Court of International Justice, 733
Personal jurisdiction, 656
Personnel, 520
Peru
counterfeiting in, 58
Pervasive organized corruption, 502
Pervasive unorganized corruption, 502
Petit juries, 660
Peyote, 445
Philadelphia
MOVE bombing, 481-482
Walnut Street Jail, 838
voting fraud, 259
Philadelphia Experiment, 518
Phishing, 896
Photographic lineup, 509
Photographs, 257, 952
and assault, 17
and booking, 229, 281, 424
and child abuse, 36
and crime scene investigation, 165, 438-439, 889
and fingerprints, 911
and identification of suspects, 324, 627
and lynchings, 142
and rape, 197
and suspect identification, 230, 509
Physical force, 297
Physical punishments, 589
Physician-patient privilege, 383
Pickpocketing, 177, 207, 240
and robbery, 240
Pinterest, 952
Piracy, 334
Piracy at sea, 350
Placement stage, 155
Plain touch doctrine, 380
Plain view doctrine, 340, 363-364, 379-380

and search warrants, 394
Plea bargaining, 70, 312, 557-558, 572, 676-677, 698, 704
and convictions, 596
Supreme Court on, 572-573, 698
and Unabomber, 250
and adversary system, 616
and attorneys, 608
binding nature of, 698
and concurrent sentences, 587
and district attorneys, 615
and false convictions, 631
and lesser-included offenses, 358
origins of, 67
and prosecutors, 687-688
and public defenders, 685
Pleas, 677-678
nolo contendere, 670-671, 677-678
"Plowshares eight", 916
Police, 370, 475-478, 488-490
and bribery, 474
and computer information systems, 861-863
and counterfeiting, 58
and criminology, 81
and deadly force, 441-442
detectives, 504-506
ethics, 507-509
and hate crime, 118
high-speed chases, 386, 457-458
and murder, 163
and neighborhood watch programs, 484-485
origins of, 66
power to stop and frisk, 289, 401-402
and privacy rights, 934-936
and Prohibition, 68
psychological testing of, 514
standards and training, 487-488
strikes, 427
and suicide, 227
and traffic law, 719
and vandalism, 253
Police Corps program, 489
Police Executive Research Forum, 478
Police academies, 478, 489, 491-493, 535-536
and hate crime, 118
international, 488
Police accountability, 422
Police brutality, 473, 493-497, 541
and King beating case, 472-474
and civilian review boards, 431
and hate crime, 493
and police corruption, 501
and women officers, 489
Police brutality., 500

Police chiefs, 477, 498
and sheriffs, 498
Police civil liability, 487, 497-499
and police corruption, 502
Police corruption, 22, 434, 436, 464, 474, 500-504
Los Angeles, 631
and civilian review boards, 431
and ethics, 507-509
history, 68
and perjury, 176
and police brutality, 501
and traffic fines, 719
and white-collar crime, 263
Police courts, 594
Police custody, 370
Police departments
internal affairs, 463-464
sex offender registries, 397
Police detectives
and homicide, 163
Police dogs, 506-507, 544
Police lineups, 230, 509-510
Police militarization, 510
Police misconduct, 474
and false convictions, 631
and internal affairs, 463-464
Police powers, 72, 285, 344-345, 427-428, 439, 448-449, 454, 510-515, 518, 541, 942-943
and common law, 538
and deadly force, 495-496, 538-539
reasonable force, 526-527
Police psychologists, 514
Police subculture, 514
Political corruption, 68, 177-181
and Federal Bureau of Investigation, 470
and voting fraud, 258-259
and white-collar crime, 263
Political crime, 76
and terrorism, 76
and criminology, 81
Political issues, 439, 510, 811-812, 957-962
Political machines, 258
Political patronage, 476
Poll taxes, 356
Polygamy, 20-21
Polygraph technology, 925
Polygraph testing, 230, 924-926
and employment, 520
Ponzi schemes, 50
Pornography, 38-39, 181-185, 835
and Comstock law, 43-44
and Internet, 856, 858, 871-872
and children, 33, 325, 353, 856-858, 922, 926-929

and commercialized vice, 39
and prostitution, 833
and sex offenses, 197
and victimless crime, 832
Pornography, child, 836, 926
Ports
security, 460
Posse Comitatus Act of 1878, 517
Posse comitatus, 65, 516-517
Post-traumatic stress disorder, 929
Post-traumatic stress disorder (PTSD), 829
Postal Inspection Service, U.S., 898, 929
Postmodernism, 63
Post-trial proceedings, 313
Precedent, 679-680, 709
Predictive policing, 437, 517, 956
Preemptory pleas, 557
Preliminary hearings, 69, 229, 311-312, 680, 715
Preponderance, 293
Preponderance of the evidence, 387, 708
Presentence investigations, 681
Presentments, 638
President, U.S.
and Treasury Department, U.S., 246, 540
and amnesties, 554
appointment of judges, 654
and assassination, 161
and attorney general, U.S., 469
and deportation, 608
and military law, 367
pardon power, 554, 674
and treason cases, 242
President's Commission on Law Enforcement and Administration of Justice, 68, 168, 487, 931, 970
President's Commission on Organized Crime, 970
Pressure cooker bombs, 849
Presumed innocent, 278
Presumption of innocence, 278, 380-381, 566, 660
and preventive detention, 381
Pretrial disclosures, 613
Pretrial proceedings, 311
Pretrial release, 229, 361-362, 840
and drug testing, 95-96
and privacy rights, 935
and work-release programs, 840
Preventive detention, 300, 381-382, 564-565
Supreme Court on, 944
Preventive opportunities, 411
Preventive patrol, 518

Price discrimination, 274
Price-fixing, 213, 274
price gouging, 50
Principals (criminal), 185-186, 271, 306
Print media, 931-934
and police detectives, 505
Prison and jail systems, 783-787
Prison camps, 786-787
Prison code, 794
Prison escapes, 787-788
Prison gang, 819
Prison guards, 789
and solitary confinement, 821
and suicide, 228
Prison health care, 790-791
Prison industries, 792-793
Prison inmate subculture, 793
Prison overcrowding, 794-797
and Auburn system, 743
and sex offenders, 397
and "war on drugs", 92
and work camps, 838-839
Prison rape, 798
Prison violence, 800-802
and overcrowding, 796
Prison/prisoner classification systems, 797
Prisoner escapes, 748
Prisoner rights, 784, 801-802
and indeterminate sentencing, 646
Prisoners
and alcohol abuse, 8
and religion, 816, 821, 838
rights, 935
rights of, 68
and suicide, 228
Prisonization, 793
Prisons, 590, 741-742, 751, 759-760, 765, 781-787, 793, 797-799, 802-803, 805, 811-815, 819-820
Auburn system, 743-744, 784-785
Elmira system, 775
and boot camps, 746-747
congregate system, 784
and drug testing, 96
elderly inmates, 755-756
history, 67
security, 787-788
solitary confinement, 820-821
suicide in, 228
supermax prisons, 822-824
and women, 546, 548
Prisons, Bureau of, 804
and supermax prisons, 822-824
Prisons, Federal Bureau of, 74, 468, 471, 729, 786-787, 804-805
forestry camps, 757

military prisoners, 779
and "war on drugs", 92
Privacy, 966-967
and DNA testing, 877
and Fourth Amendment, 362
Supreme Court on, 377
and abortion, 3
and electronic surveillance, 909-910
and exclusionary rule, 409
and search and seizure, 391-393, 413-414
and search warrants, 394
and surveillance cameras, 954-955
and trespass, 246-249
Privacy rights, 917-918, 934-936
Privacy rights and criminal justice, 936
Private detectives, 505
and attorneys, 607
and citizen's arrests, 297
and wiretaps, 970
and women, 549
Private police, 297, 519-520, 534
and women, 546, 549
Private police and guards, 519
Private-sector business, 792
Privately retained experts, 626
Privatization, 805
Privatization of institutional and community corrections, including faith-based programs, 805
Privileged communications, 382-383
Pro bono, 636, 685
Probable cause, 278, 283, 285, 288, 296, 343, 347, 383-385, 387, 391, 393, 513, 557-558, 680
and reasonable suspicion, 371, 384, 402
and *habeas corpus*, 640
and police powers, 513
and reasonable suspicion, 387-388
and sobriety testing, 219-220
probation, juvenile, 811
Probate courts, 594
Probation, 74
and just deserts, 808
adult, 806-808
and drug courts, 618
and drug testing, 96
and execution of judgment, 625
intensive, 96, 808
juvenile, 253, 809-811, 841, 906
origins of, 68
and presentence investigations, 681
and rehabilitation, 816
and restitution, 693
Probation and pretrial release, 956
Probation officers, 549, 808
and privacy rights, 935

Subject Index

Probation, adult, 806-808
Probation, juvenile, 809-810
Problem-oriented policing, 521
Procedural due process, 322
Procedural justice, 522
Product liability suits, 386
Profession, 487
Professional standards, 485-486, 510, 522, 681-682, 805, 836-837
Professionalization, 431, 476
Profiling, 511, 514
    of serial killers, 149
Progressive Era, 778
Prohibition, 6, 186-187
    and Alcohol, Tobacco, Firearms and Explosives, U.S. Bureau of, 419
    and Olmstead, Roy, 917
    and Wickersham Commission, 545-546
    and *ex post facto laws*, 328
    and federal prisons, 804
    and organized crime, 178
    and police, 68
Proof beyond a reasonable doubt, 293
Propaganda of the deed, 958
Property bond, 566
Property, defense of, 396
Prosecution, 637, 681-682, 818, 835, 845
    of mass murderers, 148
    of serial killers, 147, 149
    and statutes of limitations, 401
Prosecution, immunity from, 644
Prosecutor, 347
Prosecutorial abuse, 681
Prosecutorial discretion, 443, 598
Prosecutors, 558, 677
    and adversary system, 688
    and *voir dire*, 727
    and arson, 14
    and bribery, 292-293
    and defense attorneys, 612-613
    and drug courts, 618
    ethics of, 558
    and false convictions, 631
    and *nolle prosequi*, 670
    origins of, 66-67
    and political corruption, 180
    and strict liability offenses, 403
    and trials, 721-724
Prosecutors, public, 686-688
Prospective jurors, 727
Prostitution, 38, 835
    and Mann Act, 143-144
    and gambling, 114
    male, 38
    pandering, 174
    and victimless crime, 832

Protective responsibilities, 528
Prowling, 411
Proximate cause, 385-386
    and traffic law, 406
Psychiatric evaluation, 586
Psychiatric symptoms, 929
Psychological analysis, 816
Psychological problems of prisoners' families, 752
Psychological profiles, 514
Psychological profiling, 936-938
Psychological testing, 514
Psychologists, 627
Psychology
    forensic, 107-109
    and police work, 514
    and polygraph testing, 924-926
Psychopathy, 187-189
Psychopathy Checklist-Revised (PCL-R), 188
Psychosis, 188
Public Integrity Section, 179
Public Safety Exception, 371
Public defenders, 683-685
    and drug courts, 618
Public disgust, 178
Public duty and self-defense, 316
Public notification, 397
Public opinion
    on crime, 412
    and demonstrations, 917
    and lynching, 142
    and police strikes, 534
    and surveillance cameras, 955
Public-order offenses, 189-190, 833
Public prosecutors, 686-688
    and grand juries, 687
Public schools, 440
Public spaces, 954
Puerto Rico
    courts, 595
Punishment, 208-209, 611, 648-649, 688-692, 741-742, 759-760, 777-778, 781-782, 802-803, 811-812, 826, 845
    in Colonial America, 66
    and deterrence, 703
    and Supreme Court, U.S., 714
    community service, 750-751
    and deterrence, 611
    and sentencing, 703-705
Punitive damages, 386-387
Puritans
    and gambling, 113
Purpose, 375
Pyramid schemes, 50, 52

Q
Quakers, 574, 784, 915
Qualified immunity, 499
Quid pro quo, 211

R
R.A.V. v. City of St. Paul, 118, 190-191, 257
Racial profiling, 326, 402, 525, 676
    and *Whren v. United States*, 414-415
Racial profiling and criminal justice, 523-525
Racial segregation, 354
Racism, 473
Racketeer Influenced Corrupt Organizations Act, 55
Racketeering Influenced and Corrupt Organizations Act
    and witness protection program, 728
Radical Islam, 923
Radio
    and trials, 720
Ransom
    and extortion, 22
Rap sheets, 867-868
Rape, 34, 193-199, 308, 753
    and abortion, 3
    and animal abuse, 10
    and assault, 16-17
    and capital punishment, 585
    and common law, 300
    and false convictions, 630
    and motor vehicle theft, 157
    in prisons, 801
    and psychological profiling, 938
    and psychopathy, 188
    in schools, 946
    statutory, 300
    and victimization, 80
Rape trauma syndrome, 197, 825
Rape trauma syndrome., 198
Realignment (PSR) policy, 811
Reasonable and proportionate force, 395
Reasonable belief, 378
Reasonable doubt, 313, 387, 596, 607, 708
    and asset forfeiture, 284
    and burden of proof, 292
    and circumstantial evidence, 295-296
    and convictions, 588
    and defense attorneys, 608
    and duress, 324
    and harmless error, 642
    and presumption of innocence, 380
    and regulatory crime, 201

Reasonable force, 507, 526-527
Reasonable person, 395
Reasonable suspicion, 345-346, 364, 377, 384, 387-388, 513
   and stop and frisk, 229
   and probable cause, 371, 384, 402
   and suspects, 229
   and vehicle checkpoints, 543
Recidivism, 81, 305, 694, 813-815
   and Auburn system, 744
   and alcohol abuse, 8
   and boot camps, 746-747
   and community service, 751
   and psychopathy, 187-189
   and rehabilitation, 816-817
   and restitution, 693
   and restorative justice, 694
   and sex offenders, 396-397
   and supermax prisons, 822-824
   and suspended sentences, 715
   and three-strikes laws, 716-717, 813
   and white-collar crime, 262
   and work camps, 839-840
Reciprocal-disclosure, 613
Reckless endangerment, 199-200
   and HIV, 740
Reckless indifference, 718
Recklessness, 304, 309, 375
Reconstruction
   and Posse Comitatus Act, 517
Reconstruction era, 531
Records management systems, 862
Recovery, 826
Recreational and medical marijuana movements, 200
Recruits, 491
Recuse, 651
"Red Scare", 773
Reddit, 952
Reefer Madness, 201
Refuge, houses of, 906, 918
Registered sex offenders, 649
Regulatory crime, 201-202, 264
Rehabilitate, 773
Rehabilitation, 562-563, 690, 737-739, 751, 759-760, 770-772, 777-778, 781-782, 805, 811-812, 815-817
   and community-based corrections, 74
   and boot camps, 746
   and forestry camps, 756-757
   and retribution, 816
   of sex offenders, 396
   and work camps, 838-839
   and work-release programs, 840
   and youth authorities, 841-842
Rehabilitation programs, 814
Rehabilitative penology, 766

Reintegrated into society, 778
Reintegrative Shaming Experiments study (RISE), 563
Reintegrative shaming, 562
Relationship counseling, 816
Relativity of crime, 201
Release on recognizance (ROR), 566
Religion
   and Interpol, 466
   and corporal punishment, 589
   and hate crime, 117-120, 948
   and homicide, 161
   and nonviolent resistance, 915-916
   and plural marriage, 21
   and prisoners, 816, 821, 838
Religious sects and cults, 938
Reprieves, 46, 584
Reproductive rights, 3-5
Requisition warrants, 333
Res judicata, 710
Residency restrictions, 649
Residential programs, 810
Resisting arrest, 396, 527
Respondeat superior, 411
Restitution, 102, 692-693
   fines, 632-633
   and juvenile offenders, 905
   and presentence investigations, 681
   and work-release programs, 840
Restitution programs, 693
Restorative conferencing, 563
Restorative justice, 174, 448-449, 562-563, 692-695, 752-753, 827
   and community service, 750-751
Restorative justice (RJ), 562
Restraining orders, 695
Retribution
   and capital punishment, 576
   and just deserts, 663-664
   and probation, 809
   and punishment, 691, 827
   and rehabilitation, 816
   and restorative justice, 693
   and sentencing, 703
Retributive justice system, 827
Retributivism, 691
"Reverse sting" operations, 448
Reversible error, 695-696
"Revolving door" justice, 619, 758, 813-815
Rhode Island
   and capital punishment, 575
   political corruption, 180
   prosecutors, 686
   state police, 535
   treason law, 242
Right of allocution, 704
Right to bear arms, 202-204

Right to counsel
   and Sixth Amendment, 303
Rights of the Child, 591
Rigor mortis, 913
Rioting, 666-667
   in prisons, 796, 801
Riots
   and National Commission on the Causes and Prevention of Violence, 166-167
   and National Guard, 484
   and Omnibus Crime Control and Safe Streets Act, 169
Risk assessment, 583
Robbery, 100-102, 204-207, 308
   carjacking, 31
   and extortion, 22
   larceny, 177
   pickpocketing, 177, 240
   and theft, 238
Rohypnol, 887
Roman Catholics
   and abortion, 3
   and Ku Klux Klan, 140
Rotten apples, 502
Rotten pockets, 502
Roving wiretaps, 967
Royal Canadian Mounted Police, 254
Ruby Ridge, federal raid on, 420
Runaway children, 153, 841
Russia
   counterfeiting in, 57-58
Russian Revolution, 773
Rwanda, 352, 493-497

S
SWT, 924
Safe retreat, 396
St. Clair Commission, 494
Saint-Denis area of Paris, 919
Salami slicing, 856
San Bernardino terrorist attack (2015), 942
San Francisco
   and Alcatraz, 822
   computer crime, 873
   gambling in, 113
   vigilantism in, 255-256
"Sanctuary laws", 125
Satisfaction, 826
Savings and loan association scandal, 264
Scandinavia's prison experience, 818
Scanning, Analysis, Response, and Evaluation (SARA) Problem-Solving Model, 521
Schall v. Martin, 944
Schizophrenia, 150

Subject Index

School law
    and searches, 377
School violence, 944-945
    and Secret Service, 528
Schools
    and privacy, 377, 935
    and vandalism, 253
Schools of criminology, 208
Schools of thought, 208
Science and Technology directorate, 460
Scotland Yard, 505
Scottsboro cases, 678-679, 699-701
Search and seizure, 294-295, 363-366, 391-393, 404, 409, 413-414, 455-456, 966-967
    and damages, 290-291
    and diplomatic immunity, 320
    and "good-faith" exception, 343-344
    knock-and-announce principle, 415
    and "plain view" rule, 340
    and privacy rights, 934-936
    and probable cause, 383-385
    schools and, 377
    and vehicle checkpoints, 542-544
Search and seizure activities, 934
Search warrant, 343
Search warrants, 293-294, 343, 363-364, 393-395, 532
    and Patriot Act, 920
    and bounty hunters, 850
    and plain view doctrine, 379-380
    "sneak and peek", 920
Searches
    warrantless, 285-287, 475
Searches of houses, 380
Second Amendment, 202
Second-strike enhancement, 716
Secret Service, U.S., 527-529
    and Homeland Security, U.S. Department of, 461
    and identity theft, 898
    and Pinkerton, Allan J., 505
    and Treasury Department, U.S., 244, 539
    founding of, 56
Securities and Exchange Commission (SEC), 53, 111, 155, 201, 266
    and insider trading, 128
Securities theft, 239
Security threat groups (STGs)/prison gangs, 819
Security videotape footage., 849
Seditious libel, 210-211
Segregation
    and Civil Rights movement, 916
    jim crow laws, 354-356
    and sit-ins, 141

Seize assets, 481
Selective Incorporation, 48
Self-defense, 202, 307, 316
Self-esteem, 440
Self-incrimination, 370, 701
Self-reported data, 768
Self-victimization, 761
Self-defense, 395-396
Self-incrimination
    and Fifth Amendment, 303
Self-incrimination, privilege against, 289, 701-702
Sensational criminal cases, 720
Sensational stories, 235
Sentence, 677
Sentences
    concurrent, 587-588
Sentencing, 648-650, 703-705, 811-812, 825-826
    and Supreme Court, U.S., 714
    three-strikes laws, 716-717
    and aggravating circumstances, 271-272
    blended sentences, 571-572
    and drug testing, 95
    execution of judgment, 624-625
    and *habeas corpus*, 640
    indeterminate, 646-647, 664-665, 690, 703, 749, 775, 784, 906
    and juvenile justice, 908
    mandatory, 8, 272, 374, 444, 584, 650, 664-666, 681, 703
    and mitigating circumstances, 374
    and parole, 773-777
    and presentence investigations, 681
    and prison overcrowding, 795
    of serial killers, 149
Sentencing Guidelines, U.S., 103, 692, 817
Sentencing commission, 301
Sentencing decisions, 826
Sentencing guidelines, U.S., 705-706
Sentencing ranges, 272
Separate-but-equal principle, 355, 710
September 11, 2001, 967
Sequential lineups, 509
Serial killers, 145-149
    and Violent Criminal Apprehension Program, 256-257
    and animal abuse, 10
    and psychological profiling, 938
Serial offenders, 938
Serious crimes, 335
Serious injury, 378
Serpico (film), 474
Seventh Amendment, 659
Sex discrimination, 948-951
    and Alcohol, Tobacco, Firearms and

The Criminal Justice System

    Explosives, U.S. Bureau of, 420
    and law enforcement, 546-549
Sex offender registration, 845
Sex offender registries, 396-398, 922
    and indecent exposure, 128
Sex offenses, 122-123, 131-132, 193-199, 398-399, 648-649, 798-799, 835, 845, 968-969
    adultery, 5-6
    and capital punishment, 585
    and children, 33-38
    pedophilia, 921-923
    prostitution, 143-144
    and punishment, 690
    and rules of evidence, 389
Sex trafficking, 835
Sexting, 927
Sexual Assault Victims' Bill of Rights, 754
Sexual abuse
    and children, 33
Sexual assault, 17, 799
    definitions of, 193
    and police, 489
Sexual harassment, 213, 411
    in corrections work, 548
    in law enforcement, 548
    in police academies, 492
    in prisons, 801
    and youth authorities, 842
Sexual harassment and criminal justice, 211-212
Sexual offenses
    and kidnapping, 139
Sexual orientation
    and hate crime, 118, 267, 833
    and pedophilia, 922
Sexual predators, 927
Shakedowns, 501
Shaken-baby syndrome, 33
Shawshank Redemption, The, 800
Sheriffs, 72, 500, 529-530
    and police chiefs, 498
    and posses, 517
Shield laws, 194
Shire reeve, 529
Shire rieve, 65
Shock incarceration, 746-747
Shock incarceration., 907
Shock probation, 810
Shoe prints, 888, 952, 965
Shoplifting, 76, 214-216, 240, 297, 373
    and three-strikes laws, 717
    and trespass, 248
    and youth gangs, 972
Showups, 509
Silence of the Lambs (Harris), 470
Silver platter doctrine, 414

Sing Sing prison, 690
Singapore, 590
Single-issue terror, 960
Sit-ins, 916
    and civil disobedience, 141, 852-853
Situation analysis, 518
Sixth Amendment, 523, 604, 620
Skimming, 896
Skinheads, 119
Skip tracers, 566
Skyjacking, 217-219, 350, 353
    and U.S. Marshals, 480
    and terrorist attacks, 946-948
Slave patrols, 530-531
Slave trade, 350
Slavery, 122
    and assault, 16
    and case law, 578
    and corporal punishment, 589
"Smash-and-grab" theft, 157
Smell detection, 506
Smishing, 896
Smoking, 863
    criminalization of, 60
Snapchat, 952
SoA(SWT), 924
Sobriety testing, 219-220, 543
Social contract, 486
Social justice, 136
Social media, 952
Society for Krishna Consciousness (Hare Krishna) (ISKCON), 939
Society for the Prevention of Cruelty to Animals, 9
Society for the Prevention of Cruelty to Children, 34
Sociology
    definitions of crime, 59-63
    and victimology, 833
Sociopathy, 187
Solicitation, 836
Solicitation to commit a crime, 307
Solicitor general of the United States, 469
Solicitor general, U.S.
    and attorney general, 559
Solitary confinement, 741, 765, 820-821, 838
    and Auburn system, 743
    and mental disorders, 151, 823
    and supermax prisons, 822-824
South Carolina, 530
South Dakota
    boot camps, 747
    political corruption, 180
Spam, 856
Spatial patterns, 894
Special Response Teams, 420

Special prosecutors, 469
Special weapons and tactics (SWAT), 531-532, 544
Specific selection terms, 967
Spectrography, 890
Speeding, 366, 405, 459, 718
Speeding detection, 405, 459
Speedy and public trial, 47
Speedy trial right, 568-569, 707
Speedy trials, 289
Spoofing, 872
Sport Illustrated, 56
Sport cultures, 223
Sports, 221-224
    and Title IX, 950
    and bribery, 26
    and disorderly conduct, 86
    and moral turpitude, 375
Spousal rape, 195-196
Spree killers, 149
Stakeouts, 533
Stalking, 225-226, 871
    online, 856
    and trespass, 247-248
Stand Your Ground laws, 676
Standard Oil Company, 213
Standard model of policing, 521
Standard of proof, 384
Standards, 487
Standards of proof, 707-708
    and child abuse, 36
Stanford University swimmer, 754
Stare decisis, 239, 273, 299, 378, 556, 709-710
    and appellate process, 556
    and case law, 578-579
    and opinions, 672
State Bureau of Investigation, 438
State Criminal Alien Assistance Program, 125
State courts, 593
State of Emergency, 919
State police, 477, 534-536
    and National Guard, 482-484
    and homicide, 164
State prison, 336
Status offenses, 954
    and Juvenile Justice and Delinquency Prevention Act, 904
    and diversion, 907
Statute, 680
Statute of Winchester of 1285, 455
Statutes, 400-401
Statutes of limitation
    and homicide, 163
Statutes of limitations, 401
    and cold cases, 432-433

    and dismissals, 613
    and extradition, 333
    and murder, 432
Statutory rape, 193, 198, 300, 308, 403
    and consent, 317
    and strict liability offenses, 403
Sting operations, 325, 447, 536-537
Stock market
    crash, 52
    fraud, 886
    insider trading, 128-129
    regulation of, 52
Stop and detain, 388
Stop and frisk, 289, 384, 392, 401-402, 404
    and reasonable suspicion, 229, 387-388
Strategic policing, 537-538
Street art, 252
Street smarts, 802
Strict liability, 309
Strict liability offenses, 403
Subject-matter jurisdiction, 656
Subpoenas, 710-711
    and contempt of court, 587
    and coroners, 865
    and legislative hearings, 643
    and summonses, 710-711
    and witnesses, 732
Substance abuse, 41, 84, 200, 737-739, 770-772, 929-930
    and child abuse, 35
    and recidivism, 815
Substance misuse, 737
Substance-use disorder, 8, 737
Substantial capacity test, 348
Suicide, 164, 226-228, 299
    and coroners, 865
    and document analysis, 878
    and euthanasia, 228
    evidence for, 848
    and medical examiners, 913
    and mental illness, 150-151
    and terrorism, 218
    and toxicology, 963
    and traffic fatalities, 914
Summonses, 581, 711
    and booking, 425
    vs. subpoenas, 710
Supermax prisons, 787, 814, 820, 822-824
    and solitary confinement, 820
Supervised savings accounts, 840
Supreme Court, U.S., 73, 655, 711-714
    and capital punishment, 713-714
    and Fourth Amendment, 288
    and Scottsboro cases, 700
    and sentencing, 714

Subject Index

and appellate process, 556
and attorney general, U.S., 469
and capital punishment, 68, 574
and *certiorari*, 556, 579-580
and cruel and unusual punishment, 575
and hate crime, 118
and incorporation doctrine, 346-347
jurisdiction of, 656
and juvenile justice, 906
and military courts, 367
and police brutality, 495
and police powers, 511
and privacy rights, 934-936
published opinions, 672
and right to bear arms, 204
and sex discrimination, 950
and sexual harassment, 211
and three-strikes laws, 717
Supreme Court, U.S., and criminal rights, 711-713
Supreme courts, state, 654
Supreme, U.S.
 and state supreme courts, 654
Surety bond, 566
Surveillance, 934
 and privacy rights, 934-936
 and stakeouts, 533
Surveillance cameras, 954-955
 and robbery, 207
"Survivalist" mindset, 532
Suspects, 229-230
Suspects in custody, 370
Suspended sentences, 714-715
 and discretion, 444
 and probation, 809
Symbionese Liberation Army, 453, 531
Synthetic drugs, 84

T

TSA (Transportation Security Administration), 463
Tammany Hall, 178, 258
Tax evasion, 230-232, 244-245, 539-540
 and Capone, Al, 465
 and Agnew, Spiro, 179
 corporate, 263
 and organized crime, 171
Tax law
 and Justice Department, U.S., 470
 and Treasury Department, U.S., 244-246, 539-541
Teamsters Union, 121, 179
Teapot Dome scandal, 450
Tear gas, 337, 482
Technology, 436-437, 490, 493, 894, 952-953, 956

Technology's transformative effect, 956
Telecommunications identity theft, 895
Telemarketing, 51
Telemarketing fraud, 111, 233-234, 452, 895
Telephone fraud, 233-235
Telephones
 arrestee right to use, 282
 call records, 763
 and privacy, 910
 wiretapping of, 879-880, 909, 917
 and wiretaps, 970-971
Television
 and Rodney King case, 472
 and courtroom testimony, 364
 crime dramas, 78
 and emergency planning, 461
 and sports, 223
 and surveillance cameras, 954-955
 violence on, 167
Television news, 235-236
 and carjacking, 158
Television ratings, 235
Television shows
 Oz, 800
 CSI: Crime Scene Investigation, 866
 and crime labs, 866
Temperance movement
 and alcohol abuse, 6
1033 program, 510
Tennessee
 Payne v. Tennessee, 378-379
 attorneys general, 561
 capital punishment, 574
Terms of probation, 692
Terrorism, 350, 462, 466, 510, 848-849, 891-892, 918-919, 923, 942-943, 957-962, 966-967
 and conspiracy, 45, 921
 and Federal Bureau of Investigation, 470
 and Homeland Security, U.S. Department of, 459-462
 and Ku Klux Klan, 139-140
 and Patriot Act, 920-921
 and SWAT teams, 532
 and Secret Service, 528
 and computer forensics, 860, 871, 873-874
 and criminology, 81
 and drive-by shootings, 91
 and extortion, 23
 and hate crime, 119
 and international law, 353, 466-467
 Nine-Eleven attacks, 946-948
 and police work, 488
 and political crime, 76
 and wiretaps, 970

Terrorist attacks, 912
Testimony, 626, 715-716
 and appellate process, 653
 cross-examination, 598-599
 hearsay, 340-341
 and rules of evidence, 388-390
 and witnesses, 730-733
Testimony, eyewitness, 626-628
Tetrahydrocannabinol (THC), 200
Texas
 boot camps, 747
 border patrols, 426
 and capital punishment, 577
 drug laws, 597
 illegal aliens, 125
 prisons, 74, 824
Texas Mafia, 819
Texas, University of, 146
The Sentencing Project, 689
Theft, 238-241, 501
 and embezzlement, 238
 and robbery, 238
 and capital punishment, 239
 and identity fraud, 239
 identity theft, 895-898
 and robbery, 205
Theory, 208
Theory of atavism, 209
Theory of deterrence, 208
Therapy, 514
Thermal imagers, 475
Threat of force, 205
Three-strikes laws, 412, 444, 651, 666, 716-717, 765, 776, 785, 813
 and incapacitation, 690
"Throwaway" children, 154
Tire-tracks, 888, 952
Tithings, 65
Title 42 of the United States Code, Section 1983, 499
Tobacco, 419-421
Tool marks, 888
Torah, 239
Torts
 and punitive damages, 386-387
Torture, 353, 575, 589, 821
 police use of, 545
 and punishment, 689
Total institutions, 793
Totality of circumstances, 384
"Totality of the circumstances", 343
Totality of the circumstances, 303
Toxic waste, 103, 265
Toxicology, 20, 197, 865, 963-964
 and drug testing, 95
Trace evidence, 165, 875, 888, 964-965
 and DNA testing, 875-877
 and assault, 17

1104

bloodstains, 848
and crime labs, 866
and crime scene investigation, 438-439
fingerprints, 884-885
metal identification, 866
and police dogs, 507
preservation of, 580
shoe prints, 888
Tracking, 506
Traffic control, 534
Traffic courts, 653, 718-719
Traffic fines, 719-720
Traffic law, 404-407
and hit-and-run accidents, 120-121
and alcohol abuse, 7
and drunk driving, 97-100
fines, 632, 719-720
jaywalking, 133-134
and joyriding, 157
and police, 719
and search and seizure, 414-415
Traffic schools
and drunk driving, 100
Traffic tickets, 405, 711, 718-719
Training, 487, 519
Training academies, 491
Training programs, 509
Training, law-enforcement, 169
Transparency, 495
Transparency International, 180
Transportation Security Administration, 218, 460
Trap-and-trace, 880, 935
Trauma, 929
Treason, 241-244, 334
and capital punishment, 574
and death penalty, 573
Treasury Department, U.S., 244-246, 539-541
Secret Service, 527-529
and counterfeiting, 56
establishment of, 465
and narcotics, 245, 445-446, 540
Treatment, 771
Trespass, 246-249
in Colonial America, 66
and computer crime, 856
and computers, 858
and robbery, 204, 238-239
and shoplifting, 240
and sports, 222
Trespassing
and burglary, 358
and civil disobedience, 853
and cybercrime, 874
and stalking, 225
Trial by jury, 46, 598

Trial consultants
forensic psychologists, 108
Trial courts, 555, 593, 653
Trial procedures, 681-682
Trial publicity, 720-721
Trials, 715, 721-724
cross-examination, 598-599
and depositions, 610-611
and gag orders, 635
objections, 671
right to speedy, 707
testimony, 715-716
verdicts, 726-727
witnesses, 730-733
True bill, 637
Trust, 464
Truth serum, 702
Twitter, 952
tying arrangement, 274

U
U.S. Attorneys, 469
U.S. Code, 376
U.S. Constitution, 46, 656
U.S. Customs and Border Protection, 425
U.S. Department of Justice, 891
U.S. Marshals Service, 470
U.S. Supreme Court, 46
USA FREEDOM Act (2015), 966
Undercover police, 447
and entrapment, 318
and sting operations, 447, 536-537
Unidentified Persons System (NamUs), 152
Unification Church, 939
Uniform Code of Military Justice, 243, 367-369
Uniform Crime Report (UCR), 753
Uniform Crime Reports, 64, 251, 768, 851, 862
and arson, 14
and assault, 15
and carjacking, 31
and computer crime, 857
and criminology, 80
and extortion, 22-23
and fraud, 110
and kidnapping, 139
and rape, 196
and robbery, 205
and vandalism, 252
Uniform Crime Reports (UCR), 68
Uniform Juvenile Court Act of 1968, 965-966
Uniform laws, 965-966
Uniformed, 488
United Church of Christ Commission

for Racism and Justice, 770
United Nations, 351, 444, 481
and war crimes, 261
World Court, 733-734
and terrorism, 353
and war crimes, 260
United States Code
and counterfeiting, 56, 58
and telephone fraud, 233
United States Code Annotated, 408
United States Criminal Code
and child pornography, 927
United States Reports, 672
United States Sentencing Commission, 725
and identity theft, 898
United States Statutes at Large, 407-408
United States Steel Corporation, 214
Unlawful deadly force, 395
"Unlawful enemy combatants", 962
Unqualified counsel, 620
Unreasonable searches and seizures, 46
Unreasonable suspicion, 388
Unreported crimes, 768
Unwelcome sexual advances, 211
Urban crime, 206
Use of force, 493, 541
Use-of-force, 423
Use-of-force continuum, 541
Utah
and gambling, 113-115
Utilitarianism, 689-691

V
Vagrancy, 140-141
Vagrancy laws, 410-411
Vandalism, 252-253, 427-428, 693, 810
and burglary, 29-30
and cybercrime, 872
and graffiti, 116-117
and hate crime, 118
and vehicles, 286
Vehicle checkpoints, 459, 542-544
Venue
and personal jurisdiction, 656
Vera Institute, 361-362
Verdicts, 675, 724, 726-727
and reversible error, 695-696
Vermont
political corruption, 180
prisoner rights, 335
Vicarious liability, 306, 309, 411-412
and sexual harassment, 212
Vice
commercialized, 38-41
Victim assistance programs, 824-825
Victim blaming, 830

Subject Index

Victim-impact evidence, 378-379, 731
Victim impact statements, 768, 825
Victim-offender mediation, 694, 827
Victim recovery stages, 827
Victim-blaming, 225
Victimization, 28, 761
    and alcohol abuse, 7
    and battered wife syndrome, 745
    and consumer fraud, 49
    and rape, 80
Victimization surveys, 830
Victimization theories, 829
Victimless crime, 85, 135, 832-833
    commercialized vice, 38-41
    decriminalization of, 40, 832
    drug use, 94
    moral turpitude, 375
    and political corruption, 177
    and polygamy, 21
    public order offenses, 190
    status offenses, 954
Victimless crimes, 200
Victimology, 80, 753, 833-834
Victims, 27-28, 104-106, 131-132, 648-649, 752-753, 761-762, 825-826, 835-837, 845, 929-930, 942-943, 968-969
    National Crime Victimization Survey, 767-768
    National Organization for Victim Assistance, 768-769
    consent of, 317
    and presentence investigations, 681
    and print media, 932
    and punitive damages, 386-387
    and restorative justice, 693-695
    and sports violence, 224
Victims' Assistance Legal Organization, 825
Victims of Trafficking Act of 2015, 835
Victims services, 836
Victims' bills of rights, 768
Victims' right movements, 836
Victims' rights, 768
Vienna Convention on Diplomatic Relations, 320
Vietnam War
    and National Guard, 484
    amnesty of war resisters, 554
    opposition to, 484, 554, 851, 916
    veterans of, 314
Vigilante groups, 254
Vigilantism, 66-67, 254-256, 500, 503, 517
    lynching, 141-142
    and sex offenders, 398
Violations
    and misdemeanors, 373

Violence, 761
    and battered child syndrome, 745
    and battered wife syndrome, 745
Violent Crime Control and Law Enforcement Act of 1994, 489
Violent Criminal Apprehension Program, 256-257
Violent crime, 205, 510, 845, 848-849, 918-919, 929-930, 942-943, 957-962
    and alcohol abuse, 8
    in prisons, 800-802
    in schools, 944-945
Virginia
    sentencing in, 412
    treason law, 242
    vigilantism in, 255
Visas, 375
Visible police presence, 518
Vocational training, 816
Voice examination, 888
Void-for-vagueness doctrine, 323
Voir dire, 312, 603, 661, 722, 727
Voting fraud, 178, 258-259
Voting rights, 354-356

W

Walnut Street Jail, 67, 838
War crimes, 259-261, 350
"War on drugs", 69, 167-168, 283, 448, 685, 795
    and legalization, 92-94
    and prison populations, 92, 784
"War on terror", 511
Warrant arrest, 279
Warrantless arrest, 279, 283
Warrantless arrests, 312
Warrantless automobile searches, 286
Warrantless searches, 285-287, 289, 475
    and Patriot Act, 920
    and probation and parole officers, 935
Warrants
    and summonses, 711
Warrior versus guardian mentality, 544
Washington
    three-strikes laws, 716
Washington State
    juvenile justice, 908
    mandatory sentencing, 665
    rape laws, 195
    three-strikes laws, 412
Washington, D.C.
    foreign embassies, 528
    riots, 167
Watchmen, 431
Watergate scandal, 179, 674

    and Federal Bureau of Investigation, U.S., 451
    grand jury in, 638
Watts riot, 531
    and National Guard, 484
Weapon of mass destruction, 849
Web technology, 956
Web-jacking, 872
What works, 449
Whiskey Rebellion, 242, 554
Whistleblowing, 264, 266
White-collar crime, 51-55, 59-60, 76, 100-102, 110-113, 261-266, 886-887
    and bribery, 26
    and computer crime, 858
    and conspiracy, 45
    and criminology, 81
    and extortion, 22
    and Federal Bureau of Investigation, 470
    and fines, 633
    and forensic accounting, 886
    and identity theft, 898
    and organized crime, 262
    and political corruption, 180
    and prisons, 786
    and the media, 78
    investigation of, 506
    regulatory crime, 201-202
    statistics on, 80
    telephone fraud, 233-235
Whitechapel murders, 936
White primaries, 356
Wickersham Commission, 68, 178, 187, 487, 545-546
Wilderness programs, 810, 907
Willful, 305
Winchester, Statutes of, 296
Wire transfers, 155
Wiretaps, 879-880, 947
    and Patriot Act, 920
Wiretaps and criminal justice, 970-971
Wisconsin
    political corruption, 180
Witness protection program
    federal, 728
Witness protection programs, 728-730
    and Organized Crime Control Act, 173
    and Victim and Witness Protection Act, 824
    federal, 470
Witness security, 480
Witnesses, 730-733
    confrontation of, 290, 364-365
    cross-examination, 598-599
    and depositions, 610-611

and evidence, 389
and gag orders, 635
and grand juries, 637
and hearings, 643
and immunity, 469
juvenile, 37, 364-365
and rules of evidence, 388-390
and summonses, 711
Witnesses, expert, 625-626
Women
and equal protection under the law, 326
and juries, 661
in law enforcement and corrections, 489, 546-549
as serial killers, 146
and sexual harassment, 211-213
and stalkers, 226
Women's issues, 104-106, 122-123, 752-753
Work camps, 838-839
Work-release programs, 749-750, 840
Working conditions, 793
World Court, 733-734
World Trade Center, 510
1993 bombing, 860
2001 attack, 882, 888
World War I
and treason, 243
World War II
counterfeiting during, 56
cryptology, 881
espionage during, 451
and treason, 243
and war crimes, 260
World Wide Web, 111, 856
WorldCom, 54
Worms, 871
Wrongful arrest, 669
Wrongful-death, 499
Wyoming
highway patrol, 535

X
Xanax, 85

Y
Youth authorities, 841-842
Youth gangs, 162, 902, 971-973
and graffiti, 252
and youth authorities, 841
Youthful offenders, 253

Z
Zealously advocate, 620
Zimbabwe, 493-497

Grey House Publishing

2017 Title List

Visit www.GreyHouse.com for Product Information, Table of Contents, and Sample Pages.

General Reference
An African Biographical Dictionary
America's College Museums
American Environmental Leaders: From Colonial Times to the Present
Encyclopedia of African-American Writing
Encyclopedia of Constitutional Amendments
An Encyclopedia of Human Rights in the United States
Encyclopedia of Invasions & Conquests
Encyclopedia of Prisoners of War & Internment
Encyclopedia of Religion & Law in America
Encyclopedia of Rural America
Encyclopedia of the Continental Congress
Encyclopedia of the United States Cabinet, 1789-2010
Encyclopedia of War Journalism
Encyclopedia of Warrior Peoples & Fighting Groups
The Environmental Debate: A Documentary History
The Evolution Wars: A Guide to the Debates
From Suffrage to the Senate: America's Political Women
Gun Debate: An Encyclopedia of Gun Control & Gun Rights
Political Corruption in America
Privacy Rights in the Digital Era
The Religious Right: A Reference Handbook
Speakers of the House of Representatives, 1789-2009
This is Who We Were: 1880-1900
This is Who We Were: A Companion to the 1940 Census
This is Who We Were: In the 1900s
This is Who We Were: In the 1910s
This is Who We Were: In the 1920s
This is Who We Were: In the 1940s
This is Who We Were: In the 1950s
This is Who We Were: In the 1960s
This is Who We Were: In the 1970s
This is Who We Were: In the 1980s
This is Who We Were: In the 1990s
U.S. Land & Natural Resource Policy
The Value of a Dollar 1600-1865: Colonial Era to the Civil War
The Value of a Dollar: 1860-2014
Working Americans 1770-1869 Vol. IX: Revolutionary War to the Civil War
Working Americans 1880-1999 Vol. I: The Working Class
Working Americans 1880-1999 Vol. II: The Middle Class
Working Americans 1880-1999 Vol. III: The Upper Class
Working Americans 1880-1999 Vol. IV: Their Children
Working Americans 1880-2015 Vol. V: Americans At War
Working Americans 1880-2005 Vol. VI: Women at Work
Working Americans 1880-2006 Vol. VII: Social Movements
Working Americans 1880-2007 Vol. VIII: Immigrants
Working Americans 1880-2009 Vol. X: Sports & Recreation
Working Americans 1880-2010 Vol. XI: Inventors & Entrepreneurs
Working Americans 1880-2011 Vol. XII: Our History through Music
Working Americans 1880-2012 Vol. XIII: Education & Educators
Working Americans 1880-2016 Vol. XIV: Industry Through the Ages
World Cultural Leaders of the 20th & 21st Centuries

Education Information
Charter School Movement
Comparative Guide to American Elementary & Secondary Schools
Complete Learning Disabilities Directory
Educators Resource Directory
Special Education: Policy and Curriculum Development

Health Information
Comparative Guide to American Hospitals
Complete Directory for Pediatric Disorders
Complete Directory for People with Chronic Illness
Complete Directory for People with Disabilities
Complete Mental Health Directory
Diabetes in America: Analysis of an Epidemic
Directory of Health Care Group Purchasing Organizations
HMO/PPO Directory
Medical Device Market Place
Older Americans Information Directory

Business Information
Complete Television, Radio & Cable Industry Directory
Directory of Business Information Resources
Directory of Mail Order Catalogs
Directory of Venture Capital & Private Equity Firms
Environmental Resource Handbook
Food & Beverage Market Place
Grey House Homeland Security Directory
Grey House Performing Arts Directory
Grey House Safety & Security Directory
Hudson's Washington News Media Contacts Directory
New York State Directory
Sports Market Place Directory

Statistics & Demographics
American Tally
America's Top-Rated Cities
America's Top-Rated Smaller Cities
Ancestry & Ethnicity in America
The Asian Databook
Comparative Guide to American Suburbs
The Hispanic Databook
Profiles of America
"Profiles of" Series – State Handbooks
Weather America

Financial Ratings Series
TheStreet Ratings' Guide to Bond & Money Market Mutual Funds
TheStreet Ratings' Guide to Common Stocks
TheStreet Ratings' Guide to Exchange-Traded Funds
TheStreet Ratings' Guide to Stock Mutual Funds
TheStreet Ratings' Ultimate Guided Tour of Stock Investing
Weiss Ratings' Consumer Guides
Weiss Ratings' Financial Literary Basic Guides
Weiss Ratings' Guide to Banks
Weiss Ratings' Guide to Credit Unions
Weiss Ratings' Guide to Health Insurers
Weiss Ratings' Guide to Life & Annuity Insurers
Weiss Ratings' Guide to Property & Casualty Insurers

Bowker's Books In Print® Titles
American Book Publishing Record® Annual
American Book Publishing Record® Monthly
Books In Print®
Books In Print® Supplement
Books Out Loud™
Bowker's Complete Video Directory™
Children's Books In Print®
El-Hi Textbooks & Serials In Print®
Forthcoming Books®
Law Books & Serials In Print™
Medical & Health Care Books In Print™
Publishers, Distributors & Wholesalers of the US™
Subject Guide to Books In Print®
Subject Guide to Children's Books In Print®

Canadian General Reference
Associations Canada
Canadian Almanac & Directory
Canadian Environmental Resource Guide
Canadian Parliamentary Guide
Canadian Venture Capital & Private Equity Firms
Financial Post Directory of Directors
Financial Services Canada
Governments Canada
Health Guide Canada
The History of Canada
Libraries Canada
Major Canadian Cities

Grey House Publishing | Salem Press | H.W. Wilson | 4919 Route, 22 PO Box 56, Amenia NY 12501-0056

SALEM PRESS

SALEM PRESS

2017 Title List

Visit www.SalemPress.com for Product Information, Table of Contents, and Sample Pages.

Science, Careers & Mathematics
- Ancient Creatures
- Applied Science
- Applied Science: Engineering & Mathematics
- Applied Science: Science & Medicine
- Applied Science: Technology
- Biomes and Ecosystems
- Careers in The Arts: Fine, Performing & Visual
- Careers in Building Construction
- Careers in Business
- Careers in Chemistry
- Careers in Communications & Media
- Careers in Environment & Conservation
- Careers in Financial Services
- Careers in Healthcare
- Careers in Hospitality & Tourism
- Careers in Human Services
- Careers in Law, Criminal Justice & Emergency Services
- Careers in Manufacturing
- Careers in Overseas Jobs
- Careers in Physics
- Careers in Sales, Insurance & Real Estate
- Careers in Science & Engineering
- Careers in Sports & Fitness
- Careers in Technology Services & Repair
- Computer Technology Innovators
- Contemporary Biographies in Business
- Contemporary Biographies in Chemistry
- Contemporary Biographies in Communications & Media
- Contemporary Biographies in Environment & Conservation
- Contemporary Biographies in Healthcare
- Contemporary Biographies in Hospitality & Tourism
- Contemporary Biographies in Law & Criminal Justice
- Contemporary Biographies in Physics
- Earth Science
- Earth Science: Earth Materials & Resources
- Earth Science: Earth's Surface and History
- Earth Science: Physics & Chemistry of the Earth
- Earth Science: Weather, Water & Atmosphere
- Encyclopedia of Energy
- Encyclopedia of Environmental Issues
- Encyclopedia of Environmental Issues: Atmosphere and Air Pollution
- Encyclopedia of Environmental Issues: Ecology and Ecosystems
- Encyclopedia of Environmental Issues: Energy and Energy Use
- Encyclopedia of Environmental Issues: Policy and Activism
- Encyclopedia of Environmental Issues: Preservation/Wilderness Issues
- Encyclopedia of Environmental Issues: Water and Water Pollution
- Encyclopedia of Global Resources
- Encyclopedia of Global Warming
- Encyclopedia of Mathematics & Society
- Encyclopedia of Mathematics & Society: Engineering, Tech, Medicine
- Encyclopedia of Mathematics & Society: Great Mathematicians
- Encyclopedia of Mathematics & Society: Math & Social Sciences
- Encyclopedia of Mathematics & Society: Math Development/Concepts
- Encyclopedia of Mathematics & Society: Math in Culture & Society
- Encyclopedia of Mathematics & Society: Space, Science, Environment
- Encyclopedia of the Ancient World
- Forensic Science
- Geography Basics
- Internet Innovators
- Inventions and Inventors
- Magill's Encyclopedia of Science: Animal Life
- Magill's Encyclopedia of Science: Plant life
- Notable Natural Disasters
- Principles of Astronomy
- Principles of Biology
- Principles of Chemistry
- Principles of Physical Science
- Principles of Physics
- Principles of Research Methods
- Principles of Sustainability
- Science and Scientists
- Solar System
- Solar System: Great Astronomers
- Solar System: Study of the Universe
- Solar System: The Inner Planets
- Solar System: The Moon and Other Small Bodies
- Solar System: The Outer Planets
- Solar System: The Sun and Other Stars
- World Geography

Literature
- American Ethnic Writers
- Classics of Science Fiction & Fantasy Literature
- Critical Approaches: Feminist
- Critical Approaches: Multicultural
- Critical Approaches: Moral
- Critical Approaches: Psychological
- Critical Insights: Authors
- Critical Insights: Film
- Critical Insights: Literary Collection Bundles
- Critical Insights: Themes
- Critical Insights: Works
- Critical Survey of Drama
- Critical Survey of Graphic Novels: Heroes & Super Heroes
- Critical Survey of Graphic Novels: History, Theme & Technique
- Critical Survey of Graphic Novels: Independents/Underground Classics
- Critical Survey of Graphic Novels: Manga
- Critical Survey of Long Fiction
- Critical Survey of Mystery & Detective Fiction
- Critical Survey of Mythology and Folklore: Heroes and Heroines
- Critical Survey of Mythology and Folklore: Love, Sexuality & Desire
- Critical Survey of Mythology and Folklore: World Mythology
- Critical Survey of Poetry
- Critical Survey of Poetry: American Poets
- Critical Survey of Poetry: British, Irish & Commonwealth Poets
- Critical Survey of Poetry: Cumulative Index
- Critical Survey of Poetry: European Poets
- Critical Survey of Poetry: Topical Essays
- Critical Survey of Poetry: World Poets
- Critical Survey of Science Fiction & Fantasy
- Critical Survey of Shakespeare's Plays
- Critical Survey of Shakespeare's Sonnets
- Critical Survey of Short Fiction
- Critical Survey of Short Fiction: American Writers
- Critical Survey of Short Fiction: British, Irish, Commonwealth Writers
- Critical Survey of Short Fiction: Cumulative Index
- Critical Survey of Short Fiction: European Writers
- Critical Survey of Short Fiction: Topical Essays
- Critical Survey of Short Fiction: World Writers
- Critical Survey of World Literature
- Critical Survey of Young Adult Literature
- Cyclopedia of Literary Characters
- Cyclopedia of Literary Places
- Holocaust Literature
- Introduction to Literary Context: American Poetry of the 20th Century
- Introduction to Literary Context: American Post-Modernist Novels
- Introduction to Literary Context: American Short Fiction
- Introduction to Literary Context: English Literature
- Introduction to Literary Context: Plays
- Introduction to Literary Context: World Literature
- Magill's Literary Annual 2015
- Magill's Survey of American Literature
- Magill's Survey of World Literature
- Masterplots
- Masterplots II: African American Literature
- Masterplots II: American Fiction Series
- Masterplots II: British & Commonwealth Fiction Series
- Masterplots II: Christian Literature
- Masterplots II: Drama Series
- Masterplots II: Juvenile & Young Adult Literature, Supplement
- Masterplots II: Nonfiction Series
- Masterplots II: Poetry Series
- Masterplots II: Short Story Series
- Masterplots II: Women's Literature Series
- Notable African American Writers
- Notable American Novelists
- Notable Playwrights
- Notable Poets
- Recommended Reading: 600 Classics Reviewed
- Short Story Writers

Grey House Publishing | Salem Press | H.W. Wilson | 4919 Route, 22 PO Box 56, Amenia NY 12501-0056

SALEM PRESS

2017 Title List

Visit www.SalemPress.com for Product Information, Table of Contents, and Sample Pages.

History and Social Science
- The 2000s in America
- 50 States
- African American History
- Agriculture in History
- American First Ladies
- American Heroes
- American Indian Culture
- American Indian History
- American Indian Tribes
- American Presidents
- American Villains
- America's Historic Sites
- Ancient Greece
- The Bill of Rights
- The Civil Rights Movement
- The Cold War
- Countries, Peoples & Cultures
- Countries, Peoples & Cultures: Central & South America
- Countries, Peoples & Cultures: Central, South & Southeast Asia
- Countries, Peoples & Cultures: East & South Africa
- Countries, Peoples & Cultures: East Asia & the Pacific
- Countries, Peoples & Cultures: Eastern Europe
- Countries, Peoples & Cultures: Middle East & North Africa
- Countries, Peoples & Cultures: North America & the Caribbean
- Countries, Peoples & Cultures: West & Central Africa
- Countries, Peoples & Cultures: Western Europe
- Defining Documents: American Revolution
- Defining Documents: American West
- Defining Documents: Ancient World
- Defining Documents: Civil Rights
- Defining Documents: Civil War
- Defining Documents: Court Cases
- Defining Documents: Dissent & Protest
- Defining Documents: Emergence of Modern America
- Defining Documents: Exploration & Colonial America
- Defining Documents: Immigration & Immigrant Communities
- Defining Documents: Manifest Destiny
- Defining Documents: Middle Ages
- Defining Documents: Nationalism & Populism
- Defining Documents: Native Americans
- Defining Documents: Postwar 1940s
- Defining Documents: Reconstruction
- Defining Documents: Renaissance & Early Modern Era
- Defining Documents: 1920s
- Defining Documents: 1930s
- Defining Documents: 1950s
- Defining Documents: 1960s
- Defining Documents: 1970s
- Defining Documents: The 17th Century
- Defining Documents: The 18th Century
- Defining Documents: Vietnam War
- Defining Documents: Women
- Defining Documents: World War I
- Defining Documents: World War II
- The Eighties in America
- Encyclopedia of American Immigration
- Encyclopedia of Flight
- Encyclopedia of the Ancient World
- Fashion Innovators
- The Fifties in America
- The Forties in America
- Great Athletes
- Great Athletes: Baseball
- Great Athletes: Basketball
- Great Athletes: Boxing & Soccer
- Great Athletes: Cumulative Index
- Great Athletes: Football
- Great Athletes: Golf & Tennis
- Great Athletes: Olympics
- Great Athletes: Racing & Individual Sports
- Great Events from History: 17th Century
- Great Events from History: 18th Century
- Great Events from History: 19th Century
- Great Events from History: 20th Century (1901-1940)
- Great Events from History: 20th Century (1941-1970)
- Great Events from History: 20th Century (1971-2000)
- Great Events from History: 21st Century (2000-2016)
- Great Events from History: African American History
- Great Events from History: Cumulative Indexes
- Great Events from History: LGBTG
- Great Events from History: Middle Ages
- Great Events from History: Modern Scandals
- Great Events from History: Renaissance & Early Modern Era
- Great Lives from History: 17th Century
- Great Lives from History: 18th Century
- Great Lives from History: 19th Century
- Great Lives from History: 20th Century
- Great Lives from History: 21st Century (2000-2016)
- Great Lives from History: American Women
- Great Lives from History: Ancient World
- Great Lives from History: Asian & Pacific Islander Americans
- Great Lives from History: Cumulative Indexes
- Great Lives from History: Incredibly Wealthy
- Great Lives from History: Inventors & Inventions
- Great Lives from History: Jewish Americans
- Great Lives from History: Latinos
- Great Lives from History: Notorious Lives
- Great Lives from History: Renaissance & Early Modern Era
- Great Lives from History: Scientists & Science
- Historical Encyclopedia of American Business
- Issues in U.S. Immigration
- Magill's Guide to Military History
- Milestone Documents in African American History
- Milestone Documents in American History
- Milestone Documents in World History
- Milestone Documents of American Leaders
- Milestone Documents of World Religions
- Music Innovators
- Musicians & Composers 20th Century
- The Nineties in America
- The Seventies in America
- The Sixties in America
- Survey of American Industry and Careers
- The Thirties in America
- The Twenties in America
- United States at War
- U.S. Court Cases
- U.S. Government Leaders
- U.S. Laws, Acts, and Treaties
- U.S. Legal System
- U.S. Supreme Court
- Weapons and Warfare
- World Conflicts: Asia and the Middle East

Health
- Addictions & Substance Abuse
- Adolescent Health & Wellness
- Cancer
- Complementary & Alternative Medicine
- Community & Family Health
- Genetics & Inherited Conditions
- Health Issues
- Infectious Diseases & Conditions
- Magill's Medical Guide
- Nutrition
- Nursing
- Psychology & Behavioral Health
- Psychology Basics

Grey House Publishing | Salem Press | H.W. Wilson | 4919 Route, 22 PO Box 56, Amenia NY 12501-0056

2017 Title List

Visit www.HWWilsonInPrint.com for Product Information, Table of Contents and Sample Pages

Current Biography
Current Biography Cumulative Index 1946-2013
Current Biography Monthly Magazine
Current Biography Yearbook: 2003
Current Biography Yearbook: 2004
Current Biography Yearbook: 2005
Current Biography Yearbook: 2006
Current Biography Yearbook: 2007
Current Biography Yearbook: 2008
Current Biography Yearbook: 2009
Current Biography Yearbook: 2010
Current Biography Yearbook: 2011
Current Biography Yearbook: 2012
Current Biography Yearbook: 2013
Current Biography Yearbook: 2014
Current Biography Yearbook: 2015
Current Biography Yearbook: 2016

Core Collections
Children's Core Collection
Fiction Core Collection
Graphic Novels Core Collection
Middle & Junior High School Core
Public Library Core Collection: Nonfiction
Senior High Core Collection
Young Adult Fiction Core Collection

The Reference Shelf
Aging in America
American Military Presence Overseas
The Arab Spring
The Brain
The Business of Food
Campaign Trends & Election Law
Conspiracy Theories
The Digital Age
Dinosaurs
Embracing New Paradigms in Education
Faith & Science
Families: Traditional and New Structures
The Future of U.S. Economic Relations: Mexico, Cuba, and Venezuela
Global Climate Change
Graphic Novels and Comic Books
Guns in America
Immigration
Immigration in the U.S.
Internet Abuses & Privacy Rights
Internet Safety
LGBTQ in the 21st Century
Marijuana Reform
The News and its Future
The Paranormal
Politics of the Ocean
Prescription Drug Abuse
Racial Tension in a "Postracial" Age
Reality Television
Representative American Speeches: 2008-2009
Representative American Speeches: 2009-2010
Representative American Speeches: 2010-2011
Representative American Speeches: 2011-2012
Representative American Speeches: 2012-2013
Representative American Speeches: 2013-2014
Representative American Speeches: 2014-2015
Representative American Speeches: 2015-2016
Representative American Speeches: 2016-2017
Rethinking Work
Revisiting Gender
Robotics
Russia
Social Networking
Social Services for the Poor
Space Exploration & Development
Sports in America
The Supreme Court
The Transformation of American Cities
U.S. Infrastructure
U.S. National Debate Topic: Educational Reform
U.S. National Debate Topic: Surveillance
U.S. National Debate Topic: The Ocean
U.S. National Debate Topic: Transportation Infrastructure
Whistleblowers

Readers' Guide
Abridged Readers' Guide to Periodical Literature
Readers' Guide to Periodical Literature

Indexes
Index to Legal Periodicals & Books
Short Story Index
Book Review Digest

Sears List
Sears List of Subject Headings
Sears: Lista de Encabezamientos de Materia

Facts About Series
Facts About American Immigration
Facts About China
Facts About the 20th Century
Facts About the Presidents
Facts About the World's Languages

Nobel Prize Winners
Nobel Prize Winners: 1901-1986
Nobel Prize Winners: 1987-1991
Nobel Prize Winners: 1992-1996
Nobel Prize Winners: 1997-2001

World Authors
World Authors: 1995-2000
World Authors: 2000-2005

Famous First Facts
Famous First Facts
Famous First Facts About American Politics
Famous First Facts About Sports
Famous First Facts About the Environment
Famous First Facts: International Edition

American Book of Days
The American Book of Days
The International Book of Days

Monographs
American Reformers
The Barnhart Dictionary of Etymology
Celebrate the World
Guide to the Ancient World
Indexing from A to Z
The Poetry Break
Radical Change: Books for Youth in a Digital Age

Wilson Chronology
Wilson Chronology of Asia and the Pacific
Wilson Chronology of Human Rights
Wilson Chronology of Ideas
Wilson Chronology of the Arts
Wilson Chronology of the World's Religions
Wilson Chronology of Women's Achievements

Grey House Publishing | Salem Press | H.W. Wilson | 4919 Route, 22 PO Box 56, Amenia NY 12501-0056

LF
27V
B
SK
R